THE MOST TRUSTED NAME IN TRAVEL

Frommer's®

NEW ZEALAND

3rd Edition

By Kate Evans & Naomi Arnold

FrommerMedia LLC

Frommer's New Zealand, 3rd edition

Published by:

FrommerMedia LLC

ISBN 978-1-62887-669-7 (paper), 978-1-62887-670-3 (ebk)

Editorial Director: Pauline Frommer
Editor: Holly Hughes
Production Editor: Erin Geile
Compositor: Lissa Auciello Brogan
Cartographer: Andy Dolan
Photo Editor: Meghan Lamb
Indexer: Kelly Henthorne
Cover Designer: Dave Riedy

Front cover photo: Mount Cook standing high above the blue waters of Lake Pukaki in New Zealand's South Island. © Avant Visual / Shutterstock

Back cover photo: Hot sulphur springs in North Island of New Zealand. © Donvictorio / Shutterstock

For information on our other products or services, see www.frommers.com.

FrommerMedia LLC also publishes its books in a variety of electronic formats. Some content that appears in print may not be available in electronic formats.

Manufactured in Malaysia

5 4 3 2 1

HOW TO CONTACT US

In researching this book, we discovered many wonderful places—hotels, restaurants, shops, and more. We're sure you'll find others. Please tell us about them, so we can share the information with your fellow travelers in upcoming editions. If you were disappointed with a recommendation, we'd love to know that, too. Please write to: Support@FrommerMedia.com

FROMMER'S HEART RATINGS SYSTEM

Every hotel, restaurant, and attraction listed in this guide has been ranked for quality and value. Here's what the hearts mean:

Recommended
Highly Recommended
A must! Don't miss!

AN IMPORTANT NOTE

The world is a dynamic place. Hotels change ownership, restaurants hike their prices, museums alter their opening hours, and busses and trains change their routings. And all of this can occur in the several months after our authors have visited, inspected, and written about, these hotels, restaurants, museums and transportation services. Though we have made valiant efforts to keep all our information fresh and up-to-date, some few changes can inevitably occur in the periods before a revised edition of this guidebook is published. So please bear with us if a tiny number of the details in this book have changed. Please also note that we have no responsibility or liability for any inaccuracy or errors or omissions, or for inconvenience, loss, damage, or expenses suffered by anyone as a result of assertions in this guide.

CONTENTS

LIST OF MAPS v

1 THE BEST OF NEW ZEALAND 1

2 NEW ZEALAND IN CONTEXT 16

Looking Back: New Zealand History 16

New Zealand Today 22

Art & Architecture 22

Books & Films 24

Eating & Drinking 25

Lay of the Land 30

When to Visit 33

New Zealand Calendar of Events 36

Speaking Enzed 37

3 SUGGESTED NEW ZEALAND ITINERARIES 42

New Zealand in 1 Week 42

New Zealand in 2 Weeks 45

New Zealand for Families 50

7-Day South Island Motorhome Tour 54

A Cultural & Historical Tour of the North Island 57

The Regions in Brief 60

4 AUCKLAND 68

Essentials 68

Neighborhoods in Brief 71

Fast Facts: Auckland 73

Exploring Auckland 74

Outdoor Activities 89

Spectator Sports 92

Where to Stay in Auckland 92

Where to Eat in Auckland 103

Auckland Shopping 114

Auckland After Dark 116

A Side Trip to Waiheke Island 119

A Side Trip to Aotea/Great Barrier Island 126

5 NORTHLAND 133

Whangārei 134

The Bay of Islands 143

The Far North & the Kauri Coast 156

6 WAIKATO, THE BAY OF PLENTY & THE COROMANDEL 165

Hamilton & the Waikato 165

The Coromandel 179

Tauranga & the Bay of Plenty 190

7 ROTORUA, TAUPŌ & THE RUAPEHU REGION 207

Rotorua 207

Taupō 229

The Ruapehu Region 246

8 TAIRĀWHITI GISBORNE & HAWKE'S BAY 265

Tairāwhiti Gisborne & the East Coast 265

Hawke's Bay 277

9 TARANAKI & WHANGANUI 294

New Plymouth & the Taranaki Region 294

Whanganui 307

10 WELLINGTON & THE WAIRARAPA 315

Wellington 315

Neighborhoods in Brief 319

The Wairarapa 344

11 MARLBOROUGH & NELSON 357

Picton 357

Blenheim 365

Nelson & Tasman 372

Abel Tasman National Park & Golden Bay 383

12 WEST COAST & THE GLACIERS 390

Westport 394

Karamea 397

Punakaiki 400

Greymouth 403

Hokitika 407

Franz Josef & Fox Glaciers 411

13 CHRISTCHURCH & ENVIRONS 418

Essentials 418

Exploring Christchurch 421

Side Trips from Christchurch 440

14 QUEENSTOWN, WĀNAKA & FIORDLAND 450

Queenstown 450

Wānaka 476

Te Anau & Fiordland 484

15 AORAKI/MOUNT COOK, MACKENZIE & WAITAKI 495

Lake Tekapō 495

Aoraki/Mt. Cook Village 501

Twizel 507

Waitaki District 510

Ōamaru 511

16 DUNEDIN, SOUTHLAND & STEWART ISLAND 518

Dunedin 518

The Catlins 538

Gore 543

Invercargill 544

Bluff 549

Rakiura/Stewart Island 550

17 PLANNING YOUR TRIP TO NEW ZEALAND 558

Entry Requirements 558

Getting There 559

Getting Around 560

Tips on Accommodations 566

Responsible Tourism 568

Fast Facts: New Zealand 570

INDEX 574

LIST OF MAPS

New Zealand in 1 Week 43

New Zealand in 2 Weeks & New Zealand for Families 47

Other Suggested New Zealand Itineraries 55

The North Island at a Glance 61

The South Island at a Glance 65

Central Auckland 76

Northland 135

Waikato, the Bay of Plenty & the Coromandel 167

Rotorua & Environs 209

Taupō & the Ruapehu Region 231

East Coast & Hawke's Bay 267

Taranaki to Wellington 295

Wellington City 316

The Kāpiti Coast & the Wairarapa 347

Marlborough, Nelson & Beyond 358

West Coast 391

Christchurch 423

Central Queenstown 451

Te Anau & Fiordland 485

The MacKenzie Country 497

Dunedin 519

Southland 539

ABOUT THE AUTHORS

Kate Evans is a Kiwi journalist and the author of *Feijoa: A Story of Obsession and Belonging,* which traces the globetrotting story of New Zealand's favorite fruit (which is actually from South America). After 12 years traveling the world, she's now happily putting down roots in Raglan with her family—while deepening her relationship with the wider North Island for Frommer's. Her work has appeared in *The New York Times, The Guardian, The Washington Post,* and *Scientific American,* and she is a regular contributor to *New Zealand Geographic.* Read more at kateevans.org.

Naomi Arnold is a journalist and author living in Nelson, at the top of New Zealand's South Island. A lifetime lover of print, she has written feature stories for most New Zealand magazines and newspapers and international publications including *The Guardian, The Washington Post, Gastro Obscura, Lonely Planet,* and *BBC Travel.* Her six books cover topics including New Zealand conservation and astronomy, and her latest, *Northbound,* is a memoir of walking the length of New Zealand on Te Araroa in 2024. Read her work at naomiarnold.net.

ABOUT THE FROMMER TRAVEL GUIDES

For most of the past 65 years, Frommer's has been the leading series of travel guides in North America, accounting for as many as 24% of all guidebooks sold. I think I know why.

Though we hope our books are entertaining, we nevertheless deal with travel in a serious fashion. Our guidebooks have never looked on such journeys as a mere recreation, but as a far more important human function, a time of learning and introspection, an essential part of a civilized life. We stress the culture, lifestyle, history, and beliefs of the destinations we cover, and urge our readers to seek out people and new ideas as the chief rewards of travel.

We have never shied from controversy. We have, from the beginning, encouraged our authors to be intensely judgmental, critical—both pro and con—in their comments, and wholly independent. Our only clients are our readers, and we have triggered the ire of countless prominent sorts, from a tourist newspaper we called "practically worthless" (it unsuccessfully sued us) to the many rip-offs we've condemned.

And because we believe that travel should be available to everyone regardless of their incomes, we have always been cost-conscious at every level of expenditure. Though we have broadened our recommendations beyond the budget category, we insist that every lodging we include be sensibly priced. We use every form of media to assist our readers and are particularly proud of our feisty daily website, the award-winning Frommers.com.

I have high hopes for the future of Frommer's. May these guidebooks, in all the years ahead, continue to reflect the joy of travel and the freedom that travel represents. May they always pursue a cost-conscious path, so that people of all incomes can enjoy the rewards of travel. And may they create, for both the traveler and the persons among whom we travel, a community of friends, where all human beings live in harmony and peace.

Arthur Frommer
(1929–2024)

1

THE BEST OF NEW ZEALAND

"Last, loneliest, loveliest, exquisite, apart," wrote English novelist Rudyard Kipling when describing Auckland after a visit to New Zealand/Aotearoa in 1891. His observation has been echoed by many who have visited the country in the years since. About the size of the United Kingdom, but with a population of just over 5 million as compared with nearly 70 million in the UK, it's a country that punches above its own weight.

New Zealand is like a cleverly wrapped gift that continually reveals surprises. Adventure seekers will find heart-stopping thrills. Ecotourists can explore national parks, penguin colonies, marine parks (whales, dolphins, sea lions) and forest walkways, enlivened by birds found nowhere else on Earth. From one day to the next you may find yourself surrounded by snowcapped mountain peaks and glaciers; rafting in a subterranean cave system; lost in a lush rainforest; boutique shopping in a buzzy city; or making your way across a stark volcanic valley. New Zealanders are also proud of their origin story, and increasingly celebrate Māori history precolonization, including that of the seafaring Polynesian explorers who first landed on Aotearoa approximately 800 years ago.

But while the places you visit, the hotels you sleep in, and the adventures you have will shape your experience of Aotearoa (the Māori word for New Zealand, roughly meaning "the land of the long white cloud"), what you will remember most is the warm and genuine welcome of the people. There's a Māori proverb that captures this sentiment well: *He aha te mea nui o te ao? Māku e kii atu: He tāngata, he tāngata, he tāngata.* "What is the most important thing in the world? Well, let me tell you: It is people, it is people, it is people."

THE most authentic NEW ZEALAND EXPERIENCES

- **Try a Kiwi-invented sport:** New Zealanders are a creative bunch who have invented a range of unusual and incredibly fun and adrenaline-pumping activities. You can thank Kiwis for jetboating, Zorbing, blocarting, and riverbugging. Take your pick of weird and wonderful activities in Rotorua (chapter 7) or Queenstown, the country's adventure capital (chapter 14).

- **Visit a Māori marae:** Experience the *hongi* (the formal nose-to-nose Māori greeting), see deeply moving *kapa haka* (song-and-dance) performances, and eat from a traditional underground *hāngī* (oven). Do this in the Bay of Plenty (chapter 6) or Rotorua (chapter 7) as part of an organized tour experience, or seek permission to visit one of the dozens of *marae* (village commons) in the East Cape (chapter 8).
- **See a city rise again:** There are few places in the world where you can see in one city block the devastation of an earthquake and the beauty of a city rebuilt. A renewed Christchurch is taking shape after its near-destruction in 2011, and the results are impressive. See chapter 13.
- **Take a farm tour:** The only thing more impressive than seeing farmers shear sheep is watching their whip-smart cattle dogs in action rounding up the flocks. Farmstays across the country offer tours of their massive properties, including at Ruapehu's remote **Blue Duck Station** (p. 262).

Jetboating through the Shotover River Canyons near Queenstown with Nomad Safaris.

THE best NEW ZEALAND NATURE EXPERIENCES

- **Look for glowworms:** Waitomo's caves (p. 173) are lit up by the ethereal blue-green phosphorescence of these cool little critters. But you can actually find them in groves, forests, and caves across the country, including on a twilight kayak tour with Riverside Adventures outside Cambridge (p. 171).
- **See endemic NZ wildlife flourishing:** Invasive stoats and rats have devastated the country's native plants, insects, and animals, but efforts to save this unique ecosystem are underway in NZ's incredible predator-free wildlife sanctuaries, such as the Waikato's **Sanctuary Mountain Maungatautari** (p. 171), Wellington's **Zealandia** (p. 328), or Dunedin's **Orokonui Ecosanctuary** (p. 526). You can find foraging **kiwi** on Rakiura/Stewart Island (p. 555) or visit the only mainland breed colony of **royal albatrosses** in the world in Dunedin (p. 528). Penguins are found in many coastal crannies, including in Ōamaru, where **kororā/little penguins** put on a nightly show as they rush up from the sea to their nesting places (p. 514). And last but not least, wave off thousands of **godwits and gannets** at Farewell Spit (p. 388).

The Waitomo Glowworm Caves are an otherworldly sight, their walls lit up by tiny phosphorescent creatures.

- **Soak in waters heated by geothermal activity:** New Zealand is renowned for its volcanic activity, resulting in hidden hot pools across the North Island. While much of this activity is centered in Taupō and Rotorua, you can dig your own hot pool in the sand on **Hot Water Beach** (p. 184) in the Coromandel, or just outside the fishing village of **Kāwhia** in the Waikato (p. 173).
- **Stargaze in the darkest skies:** Stars, galaxies, and planets look close enough to touch when a knowledgeable guide is on hand to identify and point them out in the clear night skies of International Dark Sky Reserves. See Tekapo and Aoraki/Mount Cook in the Mackenzie Country in chapter 15.
- **Learn what it means to "tramp":** For such a small country, NZ boasts an enormous amount of backcountry—and Kiwis absolutely love getting out for a "tramp" (Kiwi for "hike"). Wherever you are, there's a hike or bike ride worth doing (see "Outdoor Pursuits" in each regional chapter), offering views and experiences you won't get from the window of a car. NZ categorizes its best hikes as "Great Walks," while the best bike rides are "Great Rides."

NEW ZEALAND'S best ARCHITECTURAL LANDMARKS

North Island

- **St. Mary's Church** (Tikitiki, East Cape): This ornate Māori church was built in 1924 to honor the soldiers of Ngāti Porou who died in World War I. The interior, carved by a local *iwi* (tribe) is a masterpiece of intricate Māori design. See p. 271.
- **Hundertwasser Art Centre & Wairau Art Gallery** (Whangārei, Northland): Thirty years in the making, this museum sheds light on the life and legacy of Austrian-Kiwi artist Friedensreich Hundertwasser. He believed the straight line was "godless," so this building is a lopsided blur of color, with not a godless line to be found. See p. 138.
- **Hamilton Gardens** (Waikato): A marvel of landscape architecture, this 54-hectare (133-acre) botanic garden offers up fantasy environments such as a Surrealist Garden that will make you feel like you've fallen down a rabbit hole, and an Italian Renaissance section that looks like it was airlifted from Tuscany. See p. 168.
- **Napier's Art Deco Downtown** (Hawke's Bay): This seaside city was forced to reinvent itself in 1931 after an earthquake razed the city, killing 256 people. It rose again, with 140 new buildings constructed in the Art Deco and Spanish Mission styles in vogue at the time. Today this collection of buildings is considered one of the world's best preserved, most handsome Art Deco neighborhoods. See p. 279.

South Island

- **The Christchurch Transitional Cathedral** (234 Hereford St., Christchurch): When the original Christ Church Cathedral was badly damaged by earthquake in February 2011, the Anglican diocese found a temporary solution: the Transitional Cathedral. Designed by Japanese architect Shigeru Ibu, it is constructed largely of cardboard and light timbers, most visible in the exterior walls of huge cardboard "tubes." The interior of the cathedral is bathed in the natural light streaming between the tubes. See p. 424.

- **The Arts Centre** (30 Worcester Blvd., Christchurch): Designed by architects Benjamin Mountford and Samuel Hurst Seager and built in 1876 as an education facility, this pleasing collection of neo-Gothic buildings is clustered around a lovely quadrangle. In 1973 it became the Christchurch Arts Centre, housing artist studios, theaters, a dance school, galleries, shops, cafes, and restaurants. Badly damaged in the 2011 earthquake, it has recently reopened after a NZ$200-million restoration. See p. 421.
- **Ōamaru's Victorian Precinct** (Harbour/Tyne sts., Ōamaru): This cluster of 19th- and early-20th-century streets, ornate limestone buildings, and warehouses has been expertly restored as a vibrant area for gallery-hopping, shopping, nightlife, and dining. A short walk away, the 1907 Ōamaru Opera House has a dizzyingly beautiful interior with elaborate plastering, gilding galore, and an Edwardian proscenium arch. See p. 511.
- **Dunedin Railway Station** (Anzac Ave., Dunedin): Opened in 1906, this impressive decorative building was described by its architect as "Flemish Renaissance." We're a long way from Belgium, but you have to love such a flamboyant face for a port cargo railway station. See p. 521.

Christchurch's Transitional Cathedral, also known as the Cardboard Cathedral, is a dazzling and innovative piece of architecture.

THE best PLACES TO STAY IN NEW ZEALAND

Countrywide

- **Canopy camping:** This collection of privately owned, wonderfully comfortable cabins, glamping tents, and holiday homes are what many Kiwis choose for their own holidays. The vast majority are set on farmland and feature somewhere to cook (although that can range from a full kitchen to just a camp stove or BBQ area) and such niceties as outdoor bathtubs or wood-fired hot tubs. Some of their more unusual offerings include a hobbit house in the Waikato (p. 176), a hotel tucked into a boat in Whanganui (p. 313), and the opportunity to glamp inside Auckland's Eden rugby stadium (p. 99).

North Island

- **Treetops Lodge & Estate** (Horohoro): For privacy and posh, this luxury lodge is hard to beat. Its vast grounds include an 800-year-old forest, trout streams, and lakes. Go horseback riding, fish for trout, or dine on Michelin-starred meals. See p. 225.
- **Huka Lodge** (near Taupō): Built in 1924 as a rustic fishing camp on the trout-rich Waikato River, this place has been stunningly upgraded into a luxury country retreat where every guest need is catered to. The fly-fishing is still superb, of course. See p. 238.
- **Ahu Ahu Beach Villas** (Ōakura): This lovely beach accommodation of four units and three family villas was crafted from all manner of recycled and

There's a cozy, country-cottage vibe to the Ahu Ahu Beach Villas in Ōakura.

repurposed bits and pieces—100-year-old French clay tiles, power poles, driftwood. They're as amazing as their location, overlooking the Tasman Sea. See p. 305.

- **Wharekauhau Country Estate** (Featherston): The current Prince and Princess of Wales (William and Kate) stayed at this 2,000-hectare (5,000-acre) working sheep station, with views out over Palliser Bay. This award-winning estate offers royals and non-royals alike loads of luxury and comfort. See p. 354.
- **Lake Taupō Holiday Resort** (Taupō): The best accommodation deals in NZ come courtesy of campgrounds, known here as "holiday resorts" or "holiday parks." Not just a place to park your RV or pitch your tent, they typically also have self-contained accommodation, including cabins and motel rooms, and countless facilities geared to families. The Lake Taupō Holiday Resort is a shining example, with its heated outdoor pool (complete with swim-up bar and grotto); volleyball, basketball, and tennis courts; and all sorts of wheeled toys for rentals. See p. 240.

South Island

- **14th Lane Urban Hotel** (Blenheim): Formerly a pub, this building was originally earmarked to become a hostel. Instead, it's been transformed into a boutique hotel in the heart of Blenheim with eight spacious, bright, and airy rooms that provide the ideal reprieve after a day at Marlborough's wineries. See p. 369.

With glass walls and ceilings, the accommodations at SkyScape (see p. 8) immerse guests in the rural landscape, starry nights, and wide horizons of Mackenzie country.

- **Maruia River Retreat** (Murchison): Run by two yoga teachers, this wellness retreat's seven private villas are set within a 500-acre nature sanctuary, the perfect setting for a literal interpretation of forest bathing. See p. 394.
- **Observatory Hotel** (Christchurch): You'll think you're staying in Harry Potter's Hogwarts in this boutique property located within the historic Arts Centre buildings. See p. 431.
- **The Theatre Royal Hotel** (Kumara): Enjoying a stylish resurgence, the Theatre Royal Hotel was rescued from dishevelment and restored to its Victorian glory days, with deliciously cozy en suite rooms, a busy bar, and a good restaurant. See p. 405.
- **SkyScape** (Mackenzie): On this family-owned high-country beef and cattle station, you'll be able to lay back and look at the stars in your all-glass abode. See p. 508.

THE best RESTAURANTS IN NEW ZEALAND

North Island

- **The French Café** (Auckland): The accolades and awards keep coming for this eatery, where exquisitely prepared food meets impeccable service in a smartly designed modern-farmhouse setting. See p. 111.
- **The Duke of Marlborough Hotel** (Russell): "Refreshing rascals and reprobates since 1827," goes the slogan, but this beautiful heritage hotel has made *Cuisine* magazine's top restaurant list for good reason. Sample Bay of Islands oysters or meltingly tender pork while you consider how far this settler town has come from its 19th-century moniker "the hellhole of the Pacific." See p. 152.
- **Blue Duck Station's Chef's Table Experience** (Whakahoro, Ruapehu): Whakahoro (pop. 8) has become a go-to culinary pilgrimage destination thanks to its Chef's Table Experience, which begins with a 2-hour ATV safari to look for blue ducks (*whio*) in the waterfalls, followed by a 10-course degustation overlooking Tongariro and Whanganui National Parks. See p. 262.
- **Craggy Range** (Havelock North, Hawke's Bay): This winery restaurant showcases the region's best ingredients, including local fish, lamb and venison, with most of its produce grown on-site. See p. 292.
- **Wallingford Homestead** (Central Hawke's Bay): Headed by chef Chris Stockdale (who was named "one to watch" in the 2022 NZ Cuisine Awards), this spot serves up classic and beautifully plated slow food in a historic country setting. Plan your visit for when the property's 1,700 truffle trees are being harvested. See p. 289.
- **Logan Brown** (Wellington): One of New Zealand's best-known restaurants for good reason, this constantly evolving institution in funky Cuba Street has been delighting fine-diners since 1996 with its focus on sustainably-grown

A sophisticated Wellington crowd gathers for sustainably produced gourmet food at Logan Brown.

Many of New Zealand's best restaurants can be found at countryside wineries, like Tussock Hill Vineyard near Christchurch.

produce and responsible seafood. Corinthian pillars and chandeliers set off an artisan gourmet experience. See p. 335.

South Island

- **Arbour** (Blenheim): We love it for its culinary finesse, use of seasonal ingredients, and wine-matching flair. See p. 371.
- **Grizzly Baked Goods** (Christchurch): Melt-in-your mouth bear claws and filling bagel sandwiches are served at this hole-in-the-wall takeout spot, which always sells out early. See p. 438.
- **Hokitika Sandwich Company** (Hokitika): The magic formula here is fresh everything: freshly baked bread (once they run out, they stop making sandwiches for the day); local meats, cheeses and greens; and condiments made in-house daily. See p. 410.
- **Tussock Hill Vineyard** (Cashmere, Christchurch): High in the Port Hills, this restaurant's food and wine is as good as its view, offering unique twists on Kiwi classics. See p. 436.

THE best CULTURAL EXPERIENCES & GUIDED TOURS

North Island

- **Footprints Waipoua** (Hokianga, Northland): A twilight tour with this Māori-owned tour operator through the Waipoua Forest—home to 2,000-year-old giant kauri trees—is an evening spent immersed in myth and culture. See p. 160.

- **The Legendary Black Water Rafting Company** (Waitomo): This underground tubing adventure will see you jumping off waterfalls backwards in the dark and floating on your back along an underground river lit only by glowworms. See p. 174.
- **Mount Tarawera** (Rotorua): In 1886, this volcano erupted, engulfing the beautiful Pink and White Terraces, the birthplace of NZ's tourism industry. Today, you can climb inside its rainbow-hued crater, which has to be seen to be believed. Tour operator Kaitiaki Adventures will take you there and make sure you get home safely. See p. 211.

South Island

- **Dark Sky Project** (Tekapo): New Zealand has some of the clearest night skies in the world, and this Māori-led dark sky preservation and admiration project will take you on a fascinating tour of the universe as seen from the southern hemisphere. It's so moving it'll make you want to tackle light pollution in your hometown. See p. 500.
- **Tales from Darkest Dunedin** (Dunedin): Yes, you'll wander through a cemetery, but this isn't a ghost tour. Instead, guide Gregor Campbell is a historian who takes visitors to where the city's most famous founders are buried, recounting their sad and sometimes scandalous life stories. See p. 529.
- **The Pelorus Mail Boat Cruise** (Marlborough): Spend a day cruising the waters of the Pelorus Sounds and helping to deliver mail and supplies to the locals—and their friendly dogs—in boat-in-only locations. See p. 361.

Pelorus Mail Boat tours give a unique glimpse of rural life around the Marlborough Sounds.

- **Waka Abel Tasman** (Kaiteriteri, Nelson): Board a traditional double-hulled *waka* (canoe) and spend half a day exploring the coastline near Split Apple Rock while learning more about Māori culture. See p. 385.
- **Watch This Space** (Christchurch): Thanks to this charitable trust, an art historian and street artist will guide you around Christchurch's streets, explaining the city's heritage and plans for the future. See p. 428.

THE best CYCLE TRAILS IN NEW ZEALAND

- **Timber Trail** (85 km, 2 days): Following old logging trails through a reclaimed forest of ancient rimu and tōtara, this delightfully remote route runs from Pureora to Ongarue in the heart of the North Island. Features include eight suspension bridges and the world's only bikeable railway spiral. See p. 253.
- **Alps to Ocean** (310km, 6 days): View sweeping landscapes from behind the handlebars on this trail, which runs from the Tasman Valley in Aoraki Mount Cook National Park to Ōamaru's Victorian Harbor Precinct. The mountains are gigantic and jagged, the lakes huge and about 50 shades of blue, and you'll pedal past cliffs of clay, hydro dams, and ancient drawings in limestone caves. Accommodation includes former schoolhouses, country cottages, restored railway sheds, and farm lodges. See p. 507.
- **Otago Central Rail Trail** (150km, 1–5 days): This visually striking ride follows an old train track bed through the glorious Central Otago countryside. It's like being in a landscape painting, though rail bridges and a tunnel or two add a touch of drama. At the end of each day, you're rewarded with a restaurant or pub and a charming place to lay down your head (and bicycle). See p. 530.
- **Lake Dunstan Trail** (55km, 1 day): One of New Zealand's newest trails is also one of its best, running from historic Clyde to just-as-historic Cromwell, skirting around the edges of the overwhelmingly blue Lake Dunstan. See p. 462.

Where trains once chugged, cyclists now zoom, taking in some of the most dramatic vistas of the South Island on the Otago Central Rail Trail.

THE best MUSEUMS IN NEW ZEALAND

North Island

- **Tāmaki Paenga Hira Auckland War Memorial Museum** (Auckland): This monumental museum, perched on the rim of an ancient volcano enveloped in parks and gardens, holds the world's largest collection of Māori and Polynesian artifacts, plus an interactive volcano gallery and a lovely sculpture walk. See p. 80.
- **New Zealand Maritime Museum** (Auckland): Located right on the harbor, this museum contains working displays and exhibitions documenting 1,000 years of New Zealand maritime history. Watch traditional boat craftsmen, learn about America's Cup history, and take a breezy harbor ride on a heritage sailing ship. See p. 83.
- **Tawhiti Museum** (Hāwera): Former art teacher Nigel Ogle created cunning life-size exhibits and scale models that encapsulate the history of Taranaki. Take a ride around the museum environs on the **Tawhiti Bush Railway,** a little logging train. See p. 299.
- **Museum of New Zealand Te Papa Tongarewa** (Wellington): New Zealand's national museum has been the capital's top attraction since it opened in 1998. It brings fun into the museum experience with interactive technology and world-class exhibitions that eloquently tell the story of Aotearoa—its art, culture, history, and environment. See p. 321.

Engaging exhibits, like this larger-than-life figure of World War I hero Spencer Westmacott, make the Museum of New Zealand Te Papa Tongarewa one of Wellington's most popular attractions.

South Island

- **Omaka Aviation Heritage Centre** (near Blenheim): This is a must-visit for anyone with an interest in aviation, World War I, or history in general. Who knew those early flyboys had so many aircraft at their disposal, or that so many clever chaps could manufacture these planes, let alone fly them? Fascinating, funny, and inspirational. See p. 366.
- **Dunedin Museum of Natural Mystery** (Dunedin): At once creepy and fascinating, this is a weird and wonderful private collection of bones, cultural objects, and ethnological art curated by artist Bruce Mahalski. See p. 522.
- **The Lost Gypsy** (the Catlins): Artist and inventor Blair Somerville showcases his whimsical automatons here, including large-scale kinetic sculptures like a bicycle-powered television. See p. 540.
- **Toitū Otago Settlers Museum** (Dunedin): This museum not only focuses on how our great-grannies lived and worked, but it pays attention to 20th-century details as well. Vintage washing machine anyone? Or a Buick? Plan on a couple of hours, maybe more, as every corner of this museum has interesting objects and exhibitions. See p. 525.
- **Bill Richardson Transport World** (Invercargill): Who knew old trucks could hold so much interest for so many people? Transport World displays vehicles sourced not only from local Invercargill sheds, but incredible treasures discovered in the U.S. as well, including Henry Ford's first cars right up to the Model T. See p. 546.

THE best BEACHES IN NEW ZEALAND

North Island

- **Waiheke Island's Onetangi Bay:** A half-hour's drive from downtown Auckland, stand on the bay's wide stretch of golden sand and you can see for miles. On a clear day, lay out a towel and gaze at the steep pinnacles of Aotea/Great Barrier Island and Little Barrier, off in the hazy distance. There might even be a few glimpses of the Coromandel in between deliciously warm swims. See p. 122.
- **Karikari Peninsula's Beaches** (Northland): This is the Far North at its subtropical best, where endless sweeps of sparkling white sand are lapped by crystal-clear, azure-blue waters. And from Tokerau Beach to Rangiputa to Matai Bay, you may have miles of it to yourself for beachcombing, sunbathing, and swimming (with care). See p. 161.

South Island

- **Tāhunanui** (Nelson): The sea is shallow and warm here, with gentle waves and a good-for-families beach with a plethora of activities: bumper cars, paddleboarding, kart racing, and a skating rink. See p. 376.

Horseback riding on dramatic Wharariki Beach.

- **Mārahau to Tōtaranui** (Abel Tasman National Park): The sand here is golden, unlike that of the South Island's east coast, where it is universally beige. The beaches are tucked between rocky (often limestone) outcrops and bush that reaches almost to the tide mark. These sands are hard to beat for sheer romanticism. See p. 383.
- **Wharariki** (Golden Bay): This is a walking beach, not a beach for swimming. Wild seas pound it, giant sandhills are shaped by the strong winds off the Tasman Seas, and all is drama. It is a wilderness place with dramatic caves and quiet rock pools. See p. 388.

NEW ZEALAND IN CONTEXT

2

Kia ora! Welcome to New Zealand/Aotearoa. Get used to this greeting because you will hear it—and likely use it—plenty during your New Zealand experience. It means "hello" as a greeting, or "go well" as a farewell. This chapter is designed to help you understand more about New Zealand's fascinating culture, language, history, and people.

LOOKING BACK: NEW ZEALAND HISTORY

Polynesian Explorers & Māori Settlers

As a visitor to New Zealand, you'll hear widely varying (and not always linear) oral traditions about the arrival of the first Polynesian explorers. No one version is authoritative, but one of the most common centers around **Kupe**—according to some tribal stories, the first Polynesian to arrive, sailing from Hawaiki, the traditional place of Māori origin. (The exact location of Hawaiki also isn't necessarily clear. It could be a real place, or simply a spiritual location.) Other legends discuss a fleet of seven canoes that arrived during "the great migration" to key locations across **Aotearoa** (the Māori name for New Zealand, which translates to "land of the long white cloud").

From an archaeological perspective, evidence indicates that Aotearoa's first permanent settlers came here no later than 1300, likely travelling from East Polynesia (specifically the Society Islands, the southern Cook Islands, and the Austral Islands in French Polynesia). At least 40 legendary *wakas* (double-hulled sailing canoes) are documented in oral histories, which may have arrived over a period of decades or even, potentially, centuries. This was no small feat; the Polynesians relied on ancient navigational aids—such as the stars, birds, and clouds—to travel thousands of miles to their new home.

It wasn't until the mid-14th century that **Māori** arrived in great numbers, with dogs and rats also making the voyage. These settlers found abundant seafood and wildlife in their new land (including the moa, an ostrich-like, flightless bird that was hunted to extinction within a few centuries), which they supplemented with tropical plants like taro, yams, and *kūmara* (sweet potato) they'd brought

The Honor Code of the Māori

The term *Māori* didn't come into use until the arrival of Europeans. It's important to note that Māori did not identify as a collective group, or see themselves as living within a unified "nation." They were different *iwi* (peoples or tribes), and relations between them were governed by the concepts of *mana* (status) and *utu* (reciprocity). Conflict would break out when tribes competed for resources or land, or when an individual or tribe wanted to increase their *mana*. *Utu* (payback) was also a part of the ethos surrounding conflicts and compromises. The importance of these cultural values systems is critical to understanding the first interactions between the Europeans and the Māori.

from home. The cultivation of these imported vegetables and animals gradually led to an agricultural society in which Māori lived in permanent villages based on a central *marae* (village common or courtyard) and *whare rūnanga* (meeting house). This is where the distinctive Māori art forms of woodcarving and tattooing evolved.

Europeans "Discover" New Zealand

The first recorded sighting of New Zealand by Europeans occurred in December 1642. **Abel Tasman** (1602–1659) was scouting territory for the Dutch East India Company and spied the west coast of the South Island. He entered Mohua, later called Golden Bay (now the site of beautiful **Abel Tasman National Park,** p. 384), and met the Māori before even reaching land. As his two ships anchored, two *waka* paddled out to inspect the ships and challenged the intruders with trumpet blasts, possibly to frighten away what they perceived as dangerous spirits. In response, the Dutch fired a cannon, provoking an angry response. The next day, Māori attacked and killed four sailors. (For many years to come, Golden Bay would be known as Murderers' Bay thanks to this incident.) Tasman retreated and, failing to find a suitable landing spot, sailed on to Tonga and Fiji.

A statue of Captain James Cook stands in Victoria Square in Christchurch.

When **Captain James Cook** (1728–1779) left England in 1768 on the *Endeavour,* he carried orders from King George III to sail south in search of the "continent" reported by Abel Tasman. If he found it uninhabited, he was to plant the English flag and claim it for the king; if not, he was to take possession of "convenient situations," but only with the consent of the Indigenous people. On October 6, 1769, Nicholas Young, 12-year-old son of the ship's surgeon, spotted New Zealand's North Island from his perch in the mast. Naming the headland Young Nick's Head, Cook sailed into the bay and anchored. With the help of a young Tahitian priest, Tupaia (who had sailed with the crew as a guide and interpreter), Cook tried to make contact with Māori, but to disastrous result. Like the Indigenous people in Golden Bay over 125 years earlier, the local *iwi* (tribe), Ngāti Oneone, were confused by the strange vessel, believing it might be a giant bird or a floating island. When the Europeans approached, they were greeted by Māori in what experts say was a "ceremonial challenge." Having never seen a *haka* (a ceremonial war dance) before, the Europeans thought they were under attack. They shot and killed Te Maro, a Ngāti Oneone leader. In the ensuing days, several more conflicts and skirmishes broke out, resulting in the death of at least nine more Māori, including the chief, Te Rakau. After less than a week in the area, Cook departed, unable to secure food and water for his men. He named the bay Poverty Bay because, as he noted in his journal, "it afforded us not one thing we wanted." Today, the bay has been renamed Tūranganui-a-Kiwa, and Cook's landing is commemorated with the **Puhi Kai Iti Cook Landing Site** in Gisborne (p. 268)

Disappointed, Cook nevertheless claimed the country for King George, conveniently dispensing with the proviso about the Indigenous people's consent. Sailing north, he rounded the tip of the North Island and went on to circumnavigate both islands. During the next 6 months, he accurately charted the country, though he missed one of its most beautiful areas, **Milford Sound** (p. 488), since its entrance is virtually invisible from the open sea.

European Colonizing & Upheaval

In the latter half of the 18th century, sealers and whalers discovered rich hunting grounds around New Zealand. Traders and merchants moved in next, attracted by New Zealand's flax, its abundance of trees for shipbuilding, and the lucrative trading of muskets and other European goods with the Māori. In their wake, great forests were felled and bushlands disappeared. Contact between Europeans and Māori became more frequent, and most, if not all, encounters were peaceful. In the early 1830s, **missionaries** arrived, and began putting the Māori language in writing (largely for the purpose of translating and printing the Bible), establishing mission schools, and upgrading agricultural methods using plows and windmills.

Back in Britain, the newly formed **New Zealand Company** began sending ships to buy land from the Māori and establish permanent settlements. Between 1839 and 1843, the New Zealand Company sent out 57 ships carrying 19,000 settlers, the nucleus of the permanent British population. The influx of so many immigrants had a devastating impact on Māori culture, leading to the erosion of many traditional practices. Diseases were introduced, against which the Māori had no immunity, and alcohol became a destructive new influence. The sale of weapons to the Māori intensified intertribal warfare; they resulted in the **Musket Wars** (1818–1840), a series of thousands of battles in which an estimated 20,000 people died. In 1769, the Māori population is estimated to have been about 100,000; by 1896, it had plunged to just 42,000.

Racial tensions intensified, as did intertribal warfare, and "immoral" behavior escalated among the new European arrivals. Kororāreka (modern-day **Russell** in the Bay of Islands, see p. 148) was known as the "hellhole of the Pacific" for its brothels and violence. The British government came under pressure to intervene. In 1833, it placed New Zealand under the jurisdiction of New South Wales in Australia, with British Resident **James Busby** to keep law and order. Unfortunately, with little support and no means of enforcing his authority, Busby was completely ineffective. The acquisition and trading of land across cultures led to more violence and conflict, and British humanitarians expressed concerns about the effects of colonization on the Indigenous people.

The Treaty of Waitangi

To control the new settlers, regulate land transactions, and to protect Māori, the British government made the decision to annex New Zealand, and in 1839, the government sent **Captain William Hobson** to sort out these concerns. Hobson arranged for an assembly of 40 chiefs at the Busby residence in the Bay of Islands. There, on February 6, 1840, the Treaty of Waitangi between Māori and the Crown was signed after lengthy debate. (A visit to the **Waitangi Treaty Grounds**, p. 146, is key to understanding this turning point in New Zealand history.) Another 500 chiefs added their names when the treaty was circulated around the country.

Māori chiefs were gathered by British Consul William Hobson to sign the controversial Treaty of Waitangi in 1840.

Unfortunately, there were two versions of the Treaty—one in English and one in te reo Māori (the Māori language)—and they weren't exact translations. In the English version, the treaty guaranteed Māori "all the rights and privileges of British subjects" in exchange for their acknowledgment of British "sovereignty," while granting the Crown exclusive rights to buy land from the Māori. In the te reo Māori version, Māori were guaranteed self-governance—two promises that don't necessarily align.

So instead of easing tensions, the Treaty of Waitangi ushered in one of the bloodiest periods in New Zealand's history, with many of the conflicts centered around the forced sale of Māori land. Over the next 20 years, thousands—mainly Māori—would lose their lives and land in fierce battles. The British finally emerged the "victors," but the seizure of Māori land continues to be the subject of debate today.

From Waitangi to Independence

In the 1860s, gold was discovered on the South Island's West Coast. The ensuing **gold rush** opened up huge tracts of Central Otago, and Cobb & Co, a stagecoach company, began to link the major towns from Christchurch south, eventually adding coach service across Arthur's Pass to the gold fields of Westland. By the end of the 1860s, gold-rich **Dunedin** (p. 518) was by far the largest city in the country. Advances in rail transport flourished during this period, and New Zealand entered a period of lively economic activity that was to see it through the 1870s and 1880s. **Whaling** brought an influx of international whalers along with traders, more missionaries, the development of onshore whaling stations, and new housing settlements. Many whalers left their ships to marry into Māori families—the fact that there are many Māori families today with Scandinavian names is part of that legacy. In 1892, the first refrigerated shipment of lamb to England heralded a new era in beef and lamb exports.

History was made a year later when New Zealand became **the first country in the world to allow women to vote.**

In 1914, 100,000 New Zealanders joined the Australia–New Zealand Army Corps to fight in World War I; tragically, New Zealand lost more soldiers per

RECOMMENDED reading & listening

Want to know more about the events that shaped NZ's culture and value systems? ***The Penguin History of New Zealand*** has been a best-seller since its original 2004 publication for good reason. Written by award-winning Kiwi historian Michael King in a balanced and incredibly readable format, it covers everything from the country's geological formation up until the early 21st century, while also dispelling common historical myths.

Looking for a way to make your flight time pass faster? Radio New Zealand's podcast ***The Aotearoa History Show*** delivers the goods in bite-size episodes of 25 minutes or less. It's available on Apple Podcasts, Spotify, or wherever you listen to podcasts: rnz.co.nz/programmes/the-aotearoa-history-show.

A 21st-Century Challenge: the COVID Pandemic

In March 2020, when COVID-19 was declared a pandemic, the New Zealand government responded with one of the world's strictest lockdowns. Borders were closed—and would remain so for more than 2 years—with returning citizens and residents required to complete a mandatory 2-week hotel quarantine. The strategy proved effective, and the country recorded one of the world's lowest rates of COVID-19 mortalities. Though many industries were hit hard—particularly tourism and hospitality—the economy was relatively protected and recovered rapidly, with low rates of unemployment documented throughout the pandemic.

capita than any other nation. The Depression of the 1930s brought unemployment, work camps, and riots to New Zealand, much as it did around the planet. As the country was climbing out of that tragedy, World War II struck, and Kiwi soldiers returned to battle in 1939. After the war, however, in 1947 the Statute of Westminster granted New Zealand full **independence from Britain.**

Meeting 20th-Century Challenges

For many, the 1950s were a golden era. The economy had long since settled, men were back from war, and, for the first time, New Zealand's population hit 2 million. Achievements began piling up: New Zealander **Edmund Hillary** (1919–2008) and Sherpa Tenzing Norgay became the first men to summit Mount Everest, the newly crowned Queen Elizabeth II was the first royal visitor, and the **Auckland Harbour Bridge** (p. 83) heralded a new age of modernity when it opened in 1959.

But by some measures, New Zealand was not as developed as many other Western nations. Case in point: It wasn't until 1960 that the first television transmission took place! In addition, the country's dependence on protected wool, dairy, and meat exports to Britain ended when the UK entered the European Common Market in the 1970s. New Zealand was forced to diversify and do business with many other countries, but it cleared that hurdle. By the mid-1980s, meat, wool, and dairy products accounted for just under 50% of export income.

The mid-1980s also saw the complete deregulation of the domestic economy. It took a decade of struggle for many industries to come to terms with the changes. (NZ's sheep numbers dropped from 70 million in 1982 to the present low of around 23 million.) The stern belt-tightening ultimately bore fruit, however, and by 1993, the economy was flourishing. In the late '80s, a shift to skills-based immigration resulted in increased multi-culturalism, with more immigrants arriving from the wider Pacific (including Samoa and Tonga), Korea, Thailand, India, and China.

In 1987, a tribunal was set up to address Māori issues dating from the settlement years (1839–43). A balance of that land was returned to Māori ownership, and many tribes have since established lucrative business and corporate entities in the seafood, forestry, farming, and tourism industries. After nearly becoming extinct, te reo Māori was named an official language in New Zealand (along with New Zealand sign language) in 1987.

NEW ZEALAND TODAY

New Zealand is a young nation, growing and changing rapidly, with multiculturalism playing a major role in the way Kiwis live. Acknowledgement of the effects of colonization on Māori has continued since the 1987 tribunal. On June 24, 2022, Matariki (the Māori New Year) was named an official public holiday.

The economy has been transformed by the shift to skills-based immigration: While forestry, fishing, and agriculture exports still play a major role in the country's GDP, the nation's top industries are now professional scientific and technical services; manufacturing; healthcare; construction; tourism; and education and training. New Zealand today welcomes immigrants from all corners of the globe and they enrich the nation—be it in education, music, hospitality, or agriculture. Their cultural hearts beat strongly, adding vibrancy to daily life. New Zealand artists, writers, musicians, actors, and filmmakers have developed an enthusiastic international audience.

ART & ARCHITECTURE

Visual Arts

New Zealand's artistic roots are a mix of European tradition and Pacific, especially Māori, influences. In some ways the two are quite different. The early Europeans favored landscapes and figurative art, often painting subjects from literature; the Māori traditions of carving and tattooing were a means of creating records of genealogy, chronicling historical events, and sharing knowledge.

Intricate Māori woodcarvings cover the walls of Te Whare Rūnanga, the meetinghouse at Waitangi.

Among the most famous older Kiwi works (you may encounter them on your travels) are late-19th-century paintings of prominent Māori chiefs, warriors, and women by **Gottfried Lindauer** (1839–1926) and landscape art by **Augustus Earle** (1793–1838). Historic Māori flax weaving and carving, the latter done in wood, bone, and greenstone, are prized today, and considered masterworks in their own rights. In New Zealand, art isn't confined to galleries and museums—it can be found spraypainted on the side of buildings and down alleyways, in *maraes* (Māori village commons or courtyards), and on the faces and bodies of Māori, with *tā moko* (Māori tattoos) currently experiencing a resurgence.

In the 20th century, New Zealand became a haven for artists and makers, with many setting up shop in enclaves within the Nelson/Tasman, Coromandel, Northland, and Whanganui regions. Transplanted Austrian visual artist **Friedensreich Hundertwasser** (1928–2000) is celebrated in a new **art gallery** in Whangārei (p. 138) and his **public toilets** in Kawakawa (p. 138); esteemed potter **Barry Brickell** (1935–2016) left a quite different legacy with **Driving Creek Railway** in the Coromandel (p. 182).

Architecture

When the first settlers arrived, the only structures were the Māori-built *raupo* (reed) *whare* (houses). The British quickly felled trees and began building very English cottages (and later bigger houses and mansions). As wealth in the colony increased, so did the stature and durability of the buildings. New Zealand's first substantial buildings were erected by missionaries in the Bay of Islands around 1814. You can still visit **Kemp House** and the **Stone Store** in Kerikeri (p. 149), both constructed in a Georgian style that set the tone for much that was to come.

Today in the wealthier suburbs of Auckland (Remuera, Parnell, Mount Eden, Devonport); Wellington (Thorndon, Mount Victoria); Christchurch (Fendalton, Merivale); and Dunedin (Māori Hill) you'll still find many fine, large Georgian-style and Victorian homes. **Christchurch** (p. 418) and **Dunedin** (p. 518) are known for their Victorian Gothic architecture, while central **Napier** (p. 279) was rebuilt almost entirely in Art Deco style after a massive 1931 earthquake obliterated the city. And in **Ōamaru** (p. 511) in the South Island, you'll find an impressive collection of classical and Renaissance-style buildings complete with Corinthian pillars.

Central Hawke's Bay and the South Island still have huge homesteads from the Victorian era. If you're lucky, you may get to stay in some that have been converted into lodges or upmarket bed-and-breakfast accommodations, such as Canterbury's **Otahuna Lodge** (p. 432). One of the finest examples of Queen Anne architecture in Australasia, it's been beautifully restored and converted into luxury accommodation.

Throughout the country, from tiny towns to large cities, there are also hundreds of examples of excellent ecclesiastical architecture worth visiting. In the more remote areas of Northland and East Cape, you'll find exquisite little Māori churches, including **St. Faith's Church** in Ōhinemutu, Rotorua (p. 220), and **St. Mary's** at Tikitiki on East Cape (p. 271). Both feature intricate carving and tukutuku paneling that you won't see anywhere else in the world.

Contemporary architecture—both domestic and commercial—is increasingly finding "a New Zealand voice." Buildings are being constructed to reflect the landscape, with stunning examples found across the country.

Pitched roofs, locally sourced or laminated timber, folded forms, and an emphasis on sustainability dictate much of the country's current architectural trends. Geographic isolation has also resulted in making use of what's at hand, which is why you'll see plenty of homes, offices, and even storefronts built out of shipping containers. Wineries, too, are at the leading edge of New Zealand contemporary architecture. Fine examples include **Cable Bay** (Waiheke Island; see p. 124), **Craggy Range** (Hawke's Bay, see p. 292), and **Elephant Hill** (Hawke's Bay; see p. 283).

> **Christchurch: Architectural Work in Progress**
>
> Canterbury's 2010 and 2011 earthquakes were an opportunity for the city of **Christchurch** to reinvent itself. While you'll still see evidence of the disaster in vacant buildings and empty lots, you'll also find stunning new earthquake-proof buildings, such as the **Tūranga public library** (p. 424), and innovative structures like the **Transitional Cathedral** (p. 424).

BOOKS & FILMS

Literature & Fiction

Katherine Mansfield (1888–1923) put New Zealand on the literary map with her still-admired short stories set in New Zealand, although she spent most of her adult life in Europe; you can visit her girlhood home in Wellington (p. 325). Among contemporary fiction writers, **Keri Hulme** won the prestigious Booker McConnell Prize for *the bone people* in 1985; the late **Janet Frame** became famous for *Owls Do Cry*, *An Angel at My Table*, and several others; **Owen Marshall** is perhaps our finest living short-story writer; and the late **Barry Crump** is a legend of a completely unique, raw, backcountry style, with titles including *A Good Keen Man* and *Hang On a Minute Mate*. The prolific **Catherine Chidgey** has released a slew of bestselling, critically-acclaimed literary fiction in the last decade such as the elegant psychological thriller *Pet* (Te Herenga Waka University Press, 2023).

Top Māori writers include **Becky Manawatu, Tina Makereti, Witi Ihimaera, Patricia Grace,** and **Alan Duff.** In addition, **Maurice Gee, Maurice Shadbolt, Fiona Kidman,** and **Lauris Edmond** all warrant attention. Some newer books we'd recommend include Manawatu's *Auē* and *Kataraina* (Mākaro Press, 2022 and 2024); and **Eleanor Catton**'s 2013 Booker-winning *The Luminaries* or 2023 novel *Birnam Wood* (Te Herenga Waka University Press).

Film

Director Peter Jackson—whose 1994 film *Heavenly Creatures* won the Silver Lion at the Venice Film Festival—grabbed headlines in 1997 when he secured Hollywood funding for the ***Lord of the Rings*** trilogy. The *Lord of the Rings* went on to win a cluster of Oscars and cement NZ as Middle-earth forever. Jackson has since added to his success with *The Hobbit* and the 2022 *The*

Sets from the *Lord of the Rings* films can be visited at Hobbiton, a tourist attraction on the North Island.

Rings of Power series. Jackson's special effects company, **Wētā Workshop,** is open to visitors in Wellington (p. 323), with another tourist attraction in Auckland (p. 81), while sets from the Hobbit movies have been turned into tourist attractions near Cambridge in the Waikato (see p. 170).

Filmmaker and actor Taika Waititi, who wrote and directed the TV series *Flight of the Conchords,* has earned international acclaim with *Jojo Rabbit, Boy, Thor: Ragnarok,* and ***Hunt for the Wilderpeople*** (2016), which is set in NZ.

Two of Māori author Alan Duff's novels have also been made into successful films; ***Once Were Warriors*** and ***What Becomes of the Broken Hearted?*** shocked audiences with their true-to-life violent portrayal of Māori gang society. Niki Caro's ***Whale Rider*** in 2002 (based on the Witi Ihimaera book) won international acclaim. And in 2020, Eleanor Catton's ***The Luminaries*** was turned into a miniseries.

In 2022, filmmaker Jane Campion won an Academy Award for Best Director for her 2021 film ***The Power of the Dog***. It wasn't the first time she's been recognized for her work; in 1993, her film ***The Piano*** was nominated for nine Academy Awards. (Star **Anna Paquin,** of Wellington, won one for Best Supporting Actress.)

International filmmakers are also attracted to the country's diverse landscapes. New Zealand has played backdrop to *Wolverine*, 2018's *A Wrinkle in Time*, Disney's live-action *Mulan*, and *The Lovely Bones*. Much of *The Chronicles of Narnia: The Lion, the Witch and the Wardrobe* was filmed in the South Island, while Tom Cruise filmed *The Last Samurai* in the North Island's Taranaki district.

EATING & DRINKING

New Zealand's strong culinary scene may come as a surprise. The island nation's relative isolation has resulted in a food industry that emphasized the hyper-local long before it was ever a fad. NZ produces some of the world's finest seafood, produce, and award-winning wine, beer, and spirits—not to mention training internationally recognized chefs. That's not to say it's all fine dining: Nothing beats getting takeaway fish and chips from a beachside food truck or mom-and-pop corner store, a Kiwi classic.

New Zealand hasn't had a long tradition of premier service in restaurants, however—for many young people, being a server is a reluctantly sought holiday job to earn money for university studies, and it sometimes shows. However, many polytechnics now offer proper training, presenting hospitality as a career option, not just a seasonal ordeal. Service glitches can also be attributed to a post-pandemic labor shortage. In rural areas, young people tend to move away to the cities rather than take service jobs, and major tourist centers have a very transient population of restaurant employees.

New Zealand restaurants are either licensed to serve alcohol or BYO (bring your own); some are both. BYO of course is cheaper, as you don't have to pay the restaurant's surcharge on the wine, though some BYO establishments charge a corkage fee (usually NZ$3–NZ$8) for opening the wine bottle. ***Note:*** BYO means wine only, not beer or any other alcoholic beverages.

Tipping is not customary. When you look at menu prices, keep in mind that tax and gratuities are factored into the total cost of your meal. Servers in NZ are paid at least minimum wage (a decent NZ$23.50 an hour), rather than being dependent on tips as they are in the U.S. With that being said, if you'd like to show appreciation for good service, particularly at a fine dining establishment, gratuities are appreciated.

Cafe Culture

Cafes in NZ typically serve cabinet food (premade sandwiches, salads, pastries, and quiches), alongside hot breakfasts and lunches. If you're working remotely while you travel, be aware that the culture of treating cafes like coworking spaces generally doesn't exist. That's not to say laptops are off-limits; it just means that if you sit at a table for a long time without ordering food, you're likely overstaying your welcome.

Dining hours vary from one establishment to another. You can expect cafes to open between 6am and 9am and close as early as 2pm. (You may have a hard time getting a good coffee after 3pm.) Except for the major cities, you may have difficulty finding a meal between the hours of 3pm and 5pm, when kitchens are generally closed. Finally, most restaurants outside of major cities have **reduced hours during the winter months.** We've done our best in this guide to indicate accurate hours for each business, but it pays to double-check opening times before arrival. For business hours, Facebook and Instagram pages tend to be a more reliable source of info than websites, which are updated less often.

Food

New Zealand is a land of edible bounty: Canterbury lamb; Central Otago pinot noir; Bluff and Nelson oysters; Kaikōura crayfish; West Coast whitebait; South Island venison; Marlborough green-lipped mussels; Akaroa salmon; Stewart Island blue cod; Central Otago cherries and apricots—and you shouldn't miss any of it. With so much fresh produce, seafood, and meat grown and farmed here, the emphasis tends to be on locally sourced and in-season ingredients. The listings in this guidebook generally include examples of dishes restaurants might serve, but often menus change seasonally. **Dietary**

Share plates are a popular trend at New Zealand restaurants, such as these at Apachè in Wellington.

needs (including vegetarian, vegan, and gluten-free foods) are generally well catered for, although you may find this is less the case in rural settings, particularly in the South Island.

You're more likely to eat at independently owned restaurants rather than chains, particularly outside of the major urban centers. The trend is toward upscale food in relaxed, contemporary settings, with **share plates** a popular dining trend. In the country's main cities, you'll also have access to Indian, Thai, Vietnamese, Japanese, Chinese, Korean, Middle Eastern, and Italian cuisines, to name a few. The one category New Zealand seems to struggle with? Mexican. (You'll find it, but it's always a gamble.)

A Note on Prices

Throughout this book, we organize restaurants by price categories. Here's what they mean:

Inexpensive (up to NZ$150)
Moderate (NZ$151–NZ$300)
Expensive (NZ$301 and more)

On top of the usual restaurant and cafe experiences, you'd be doing yourself a disservice if you miss trying a few iconic Kiwi meals, including **fish and chips.** Many still offer the meal—deep-fried battered fish and fat potato fries—wrapped in newspaper. The individually sized **meat pie** is another Kiwi favorite, although its name is a bit of a misnomer—increasingly, you'll find veggie versions of this dish. Every convenience store, service station, and bakery in the country has a pie warmer.

Long evenings tend to lend themselves to eating outdoors, making the **barbecue** a summer favorite. It invariably includes sausages (not hot dogs) and

THE TASTE OF māori COOKING

The traditional **Māori *hāngī*,** where food is cooked underground, is a must-do experience. Traditionally, it involves lighting a fire and putting large stones in the embers to heat. Simultaneously, a large pit is dug. The heated rocks are then transferred into the pit and covered with wet sacking and/or wet newspapers. Prepared lamb, chicken, pork, fish, shellfish, and vegetables (most commonly sweet potato, pumpkin, and cabbage) are wrapped in leaves, placed in flax baskets (now made of wire or mesh), and lowered into the cooking pit, covered with more newspaper and earth, and left to steam. The moist, tender, melt-in-your-mouth food is lifted a few hours later.

With its distinctive smoky flavors, hāngī food is not to everyone's taste. If you'd like to give it a try, ask at visitor centers for tour operators who include a hāngī. You'll find this readily in **Rotorua** (see p. 207), where hāngī meals are commonly offered as part of a cultural performance package.

But Māori food isn't limited to hāngī. Across the country, chefs are embracing and reinterpreting native ingredients and traditional cooking techniques, including in a fine dining context. (Try Mount Maunganui's **Izakai** [p. 205], which serves Japanese food with a Māori twist.) Recipes may include *tītī* (muttonbird), *horopito* (a pepper tree), *pikopiko* (fern shoots), *kawakawa, kūmara* (sweet potato), *pāua* (abalone), or *kina* (sea urchin). Whitebait (a collective name for the juveniles of six native fish species, considered to be the caviar of NZ) is another popular ingredient, but since four out of five whitebait species are endangered, we don't encourage visitors to order it.

steak, accompanied by salads. It may also include barbecued fish, chicken, vegetables, scallops, and crayfish straight from the ocean.

Drink

In 2000, New Zealand's **wine** exports totaled around NZ$100 million; by 2024, they were NZ$2.1 billion. That's rapid growth by anyone's standards, and as you drive around New Zealand you'll probably wonder if there'll be any farmland left in another 10 years, such is the coverage of flourishing vines.

It was a very different story 30 to 40 years ago when the nation's vineyards and wineries were restricted to a few long-standing operations in West Auckland and Hawke's Bay. That all changed in the 1990s when a British wine critic tagged New Zealand sauvignon blanc as "arguably the best in the world." Since then, the growth in the wine industry has been stratospheric. There are now 10 major winegrowing regions spanning latitudes 36 to 45 and the entire length of the country. That makes for some diverse growing conditions and some very distinct wine styles. Turns out they can just about grow anything here, although it is pinot noir and sauvignon blancs that have made the country famous internationally. There is also growing recognition of NZ's chardonnay, méthode traditionelle sparkling wines, rieslings, cabernet sauvignon, and merlot. Major wineries in all the wine regions have been highlighted throughout the guide and can be found along the **Classic New**

Tasting the pinot noir at Cable Bay Vineyards, on Waiheke Island near Auckland.

Zealand Wine Trail (classicwinetrail.co.nz).

To say that New Zealand is a nation of **beer** drinkers is an understatement. Beer arrived with the European settlers, but despite its long history, for years the beer scene was dominated by mass-produced, thin ales and just a few major breweries (Lion and DB, for example). In the last 20 years, however, microbreweries have proliferated all over the country. You can travel from one end of the country to the other—heck, from one end of the supermarket beer chiller to the other—and never drink the same beer twice. To name just a few top brewers, there's **Hallertau** in Auckland (p. 113), **McCashin's** in Nelson (where the hop-growing industry thrives; p. 382), and **Canyon Brewing** in Queenstown (p. 471). Craft beer tours (self-guided and guided) are particularly popular in Wellington.

The spirits industry is also seeing massive growth with an influx of new micro distilleries. Fifteen years ago, there were perhaps a dozen; today there are upwards of 130. **Gin** is, by far, the most popular spirit being produced, often with native botanicals. The good news? That also means that a booming whiskey industry isn't far off. (Many distillers make gin to maintain profitability while they wait for their whiskeys to age.)

In the non-alcoholic category, one must-try is the ever-popular soda **Lemon & Paeroa,** aka L&P. Ever since therapeutic spring water was discovered in the little Thames Valley town of Paeroa in the 19th century, it's been a huge hit. Now we have many new players (too many to list) bringing us a whole range of new **soft drink** and **kombucha** flavors, such as feijoa.

Coffee is the other revolution. New Zealanders have become a nation of high-quality caffeine addicts, with countless roasting companies in most cities

HONEST eats

Across New Zealand, it's not uncommon to see honesty boxes located at farm gates. Selling everything from avocados, kiwis, and feijoas to fresh bread and bouquets of flowers, these roadside stalls are usually unattended and operate on the honor system. Drop your cash in a lockbox and help yourself to whatever you please. It always pays to have some gold coins on hand for a quick road-trip treat.

and cafes serving excellent espresso on every corner, even in the smallest towns. If New Zealanders frequent a franchise, they tend to be loyal to a New Zealand–based operation—Starbucks has struggled here. Brands to look for are **Allpress, Coffee Supreme, Atomic, Ozone, L'affare,** and **Rocket.** Organic and fair-trade coffee is readily available.

LAY OF THE LAND

New Zealand is part of a fiery rim of volcanoes that encircle the Pacific Ocean. The last large eruption occurred in 2019, when Whakaari (White Island) exploded without warning, tragically killing 22 people and seriously injuring 25.

Today, New Zealand bears all the hallmarks of a tumultuous geologic history. It may have a reputation for being "very green," but most visitors are astonished to discover a small country of incredible geographic diversity. There are 500-million-year-old marble outcrops on the top of Tākaka Hill in Tasman, and volcanic ash and pumice have created a barren, desert-like landscape in the central North Island. Franz Josef is one of the fastest-moving glaciers in the world, and the Marlborough Sounds are a labyrinth of islands and waterways. Parched tussock country and strange rocky outcrops cover Central Otago, and the wide spread of the Canterbury Plains is evidence of pre-human glacial erosion.

Despite all this earthly fury, the land has an endless coastline of stunning beaches—white or golden sand on the east coasts, black or gray on the west coasts. Craters have filled to create jewel-like lakes, and rivers and streams are the endless arteries and veins that feed lush flora.

Flora & Fauna

WILDLIFE

For 70 million years, New Zealand has been completely separate from all other landmasses. It's been left with a few unusual creatures as a result: four flightless birds (the **kiwi, weka, kākāpō,** and **takahē**), the world's only alpine parrot (the **kea**), giant flightless crickets (**wētā**), and an ancient reptile (the **tuatara**). The **kiwi** has been embraced as a national symbol, so much so that many New Zealanders are quite happy to be called Kiwis themselves. And the **tuatara**—which possesses a third eye on the top of its head—is being encouraged to breed in captivity to ensure it will be around for future generations to marvel at.

Apart from that, there's a not a lot in terms of endemic wildlife. The only native mammals are the endangered **long-** and **short-tailed bats**, not much bigger than your thumb. Any other wild mammals you sight—including goats, rabbits, possums, deer, hedgehogs, boars and wallabies—are invasive species. So are the peacocks and turkeys you'll see across the North Island. In fact, there are dozens of introduced mammals, birds, fish, insects, and even a lizard and frog or two.

Most damaging, however, are the 30 million Australian possums (not to be confused with opossums) that are eating native forests at a rate of 21,000

A tuatara.

tonnes (23,100 tons) of vegetation every night, devastating native plant and birdlife. The problem is only compounded by stoats and rats, which eat both bird eggs and chicks. In an effort to protect vulnerable bird species, there are now more than 80 eco-sanctuaries, including predator-free islands and fenced wildlife sanctuaries across the country. The government has also set the ambitious target to eradicate all predators by 2050. As a result, trapping programs are common—and don't be surprised if you see a Kiwi speed up to hit a possum crossing the road.

The good news is there's nothing dangerous. The only one that comes close is the poisonous **katipo spider,** which you're unlikely to even see, unless you're on the western beaches of the North Island (it's a small black spider with a bright red stripe on its abdomen). There are sometimes **sharks** in the waters, though, so be sure to ask the locals about this, even though shark attacks are rare. **Mosquitoes** do not carry any diseases, but they and the small black **sand flies** are prolific biters, particularly near water. They're found throughout the country but are most likely to be a nuisance on the South Island's West Coast or in Fiordland.

BIRD-WATCHING NZ's bird life is abundant, and its native birds (around 250 species) in particular are a rich lot, attracting birdwatchers from all over the world. Because of New Zealand's isolation and the evolutionary patterns that have developed here as a result, many species are found nowhere else in the world. The green-feathered **bellbird** is the songster supreme. The handsome inky **tūī,** with his white-tufted neck, comes a close second. The flightless **weka** is rowdy rather than tuneful—you'll see him in the bush or poking his nose into campsites (he will definitely run off with your food bag if you're not careful). The green-and-orange **kea** is a cheeky alpine parrot with a reputation for mischief on the ski fields and in high-country camps. Make sure you don't leave any belongings about, as keas love to steal whatever is not locked away, especially anything shiny—they are notorious for damaging mirrors, aerials, and other car attachments; and their large, strong beaks will give you a nasty bite, so don't feed them.

Seabirds abound and you'll be delighted by nesting **albatross** and **gannets, white herons, penguins,** and many more. The **Miranda Seabird Coast near Thames** on the Coromandel Peninsula is home to 8,500 hectares (21,000 acres) of tidal flats that attract millions of migratory species every year.

Farewell Spit northwest of Nelson is another major migratory path, and **South Brighton Spit** in Christchurch attracts millions of godwits every year on their return from Siberia. You can enjoy seabird tours at **Kaikōura** (p. 449). **Otago Peninsula** is home to both albatross and penguin colonies, which you can visit. Another not-to-be-missed bird-watching location is Ōkārito on the West Coast, home to the white heron nesting colonies. Keep in mind that the only access to these protected areas is via guided tours, which I've listed in the appropriate chapters. **Stewart Island** is another destination for birdwatchers. Not only does it have a wealth of pelagic species which you can arrange to see by boat; it also has easy access to **Ulva Island,** a protected bird sanctuary that is home to several unique species. One of the delights here is the tiny native robins that are surprisingly tame and fearless. If you scratch the ground gently, they will hop right up to your feet, providing you with unforgettable photo opportunities.

Stewart Island (p. 550) and **Kāpiti Island** (p. 345) are two of the few places in New Zealand where you can join nighttime kiwi-spotting tours that take you out into the wild to see this native icon. Another option is to visit one of the country's fenced predator-free sanctuaries (I've listed these in their respective regions), which often also feature nighttime tours. You'll be very lucky to see or hear a kiwi in the wild on your own, as they tend to forage deep in the bush at night, or on remote, often inaccessible beaches.

PLANT LIFE

New Zealand's diverse vegetation ranges from coastal grasses and moss-covered **rainforests** to dense **primeval forests** of ancient podocarp trees. Palms, lush ferns, orchids, Norfolk pines, bougainvillea, flame trees, and hibiscus flourish. In the far north, the Waipoua Forest is home to giant **kauri trees** (p. 160), one of the oldest species in the world. Tāne Mahuta, the largest of the kauri trees, is said to be over 2,000 years old. In the central North Island and throughout the mountainous regions of the South, there are fields of tussocks, beech forests, and gigantic tree ferns.

A pōhutukawa tree.

Because of that same geographic isolation that shaped its bird life, 84% of New Zealand's flowering plants are found nowhere else in the world. For example, the iconic **harakeke** (New Zealand flax) only grows naturally here and on Norfolk Island. **Cabbage trees**—characterized by their spiky sword-like leaves—are endemic. Likewise, the flowering **pōhutukawa** trees, known as the New Zealand Christmas tree for their bright-red flowers in December, grow mostly in coastal forest on the North Island. Conversely, Radiata pine and Douglas fir, which grow in massive forests on both islands, were planted for forestry and are not native.

> **Only in NZ: Places Can Be Persons**
>
> In 2014, New Zealand passed a groundbreaking law granting **Te Urewera** (once a national park) legal personhood status. Since then, the **Whanganui River** and **Mount Taranaki** have also been recognized as legal persons. The result? If there is any kind of abuse or threat to these places—such as pollution—they are able to sue, as a company can.

New Zealand is a highly productive agricultural country, and during early settlement, much of the land was developed at the expense of native forests. Lush pastoral lowlands were coaxed out of swampland, and many high-country farmlands are littered with the rotting tree stumps of once-thriving forests. Before the arrival of people, it's estimated 80% of the country was covered in native forest; today, that number is closer to 33%. In recent decades, there's been a proactive stance toward what remains, including through the careful management of 13 national parks.

The best way to get a feel for New Zealand as it once was is by exploring some of these conservation areas. But, as will be mentioned many times throughout this guide, the New Zealand wilderness should not be underestimated. It should be treated with great respect and preparation, as many thousands of people have been lost in the bush, some never to be found again. Don't take the warnings lightly.

WHEN TO VISIT

New Zealand is in the Southern Hemisphere; therefore, all seasons are the opposite of those in North America, Europe, and other Northern Hemisphere locations.

There really isn't a bad time to travel to New Zealand, with some important caveats. First, most Kiwis take their annual holidays between Christmas and February 1, putting pressure on accommodations and attractions across the country. This is also true for other school holiday periods throughout the year. (See "Holidays," below, for dates.) Not only do you have to book well in advance, dynamic pricing (pricing that fluctuates based on demand) can put a big dent in your wallet during busy periods. Conversely, in the dead of winter (July–Aug), many tourism and hospitality owners take their own vacations, meaning they may have reduced hours or may be shut altogether. Other activities—such as the country's Great Walks—may also be inaccessible in winter weather.

So, when is the best time to journey to NZ? Unless your intention is a ski holiday, I'd recommend October through December, when prices are generally lower and crowds are thinner. (Just be aware that those months are springtime, which often comes with a deluge of rain.) Alternately, in February through April, the weather tends to be more stable, making it an ideal time to visit.

Weather

New Zealand's climate, especially by Northern Hemisphere standards, is pretty mellow for much of the year. You'll find a far greater seasonal difference in the South Island than in the subtropical North, and don't believe anyone who says it never gets cold here or that there are no extremes. (North Americans will feel this especially in New Zealand homes and even some hotels, which tend not to be well-insulated. Central heating is incredibly rare, with most buildings instead heated by electric space units or wood fireplaces.) In Central Otago, winter temperatures are often 14°F (–10°C) and sometimes as low as –4°F (–20°C), with summers up to 100°F to 104°F (38°C–40°C). By comparison, the northern part of the North Island is subtropical.

What isn't mild, however, is the wind. Partially located on the Roaring Forties, the country doesn't have any other landmasses for protection, so New Zealand is very exposed, with highly changeable weather conditions.

Add mountains to the mix and you get the bonus of a lot of rain. The west coast of the South Island can get up to 100 inches or more of rain annually, while just over the Southern Alps to the east, rainfall is a moderate 20 to 30 inches annually. Rain is also heavier on the west coast of the North Island, averaging 40 to 70 inches annually. Milford Sound, though, beats the lot; it's the wettest place in the country, with a phenomenal 365 inches of rain a year.

THE SEASONS

The country experiences a full four seasons, but don't be surprised if you hear locals and tour operators speaking only in terms of "winter" and "summer" in regard to seasonal changes in hours or prices. Summer is generally regarded as November to March, while winter is April to October.

SPRING (SEPT, OCT, NOV) The countryside is flush with new green grass, baby lambs, and blooming trees. Christchurch in the spring means blossoms, bluebells, and daffodils in abundance; Dunedin is a splurge of rhododendron color. The weather can still be very changeable right up to November, so come prepared with rain gear. In the South Island, it's not unusual to get a late snowfall.

SUMMER (DEC, JAN, FEB) From Christmas to the end of January, New Zealand goes on holiday and visitor hotspots fill up, with prices also increasing. Planning and booking ahead is the way to go. Foodies take note: This is stone fruit season, with cherries, apricots, peaches, and nectarines at their ripest. In Otago, the wildflowers are blooming and vineyards are heavy with fruit.

AUTUMN (MAR, APR, MAY) The best months to visit are February, March, and April. Temperatures are pleasant—in April you'll still be wearing summer clothes in the upper North Island. The most spectacular autumn colors are found in Queenstown, Central Otago, and Christchurch. Late April sees the grape harvest coming in.

WINTER (JUNE, JULY, AUG) Ski season! Ski areas in Queenstown, mid-Canterbury, and the Central Plateau in the North Island should be open for business. Resort towns around ski areas will be bustling. Elsewhere, some businesses may be closed as owners go on their own holidays.

Average Seasonal Temperature & Rainfall

Temperatures reflected are daily average (°C/°F). Rainfall reflects the daily average in millimeters/inches (mm/in.) and is accurate within 1 millimeter.

	SUMMER	FALL	WINTER	SPRING
BAY OF ISLANDS				
MAX. TEMP	25/77	21/70	16/61	19/66
MIN. TEMP	14/57	11/52	7/45	9/48
RAINFALL	7/0.28	1/0.44	16/0.64	11/0.44
AUCKLAND				
MAX. TEMP	24/75	20/68	15/59	18/65
MIN. TEMP	12/54	13/55	9/48	11/52
RAINFALL	8/0.32	11/0.44	15/0.6	12/0.48
ROTORUA				
MAX. TEMP	24/75	18/65	13/55	17/63
MIN. TEMP12/54	9/48	4/39	7/45	
RAINFALL 9/0.36	9/0.36	13/0.52	11/0.44	
WELLINGTON				
MAX. TEMP	20/68	17/63	12/54	15/59
MIN. TEMP	13/55	11/52	6/43	9/48
RAINFALL	7/0.28	10/0.4	13/0.52	11/0.44
NELSON				
MAX. TEMP	22/72	18/65	13/55	17/63
MIN. TEMP	13/55	8/46	3/37	7/45
RAINFALL	6/0.24	8/0.32	10/0.4	10/0.4

	SUMMER	FALL	WINTER	SPRING
WESTPORT				
MAX. TEMP	22/72	17/63	13/55	15/59
MIN. TEMP	12/54	10/50	5/41	8/46
RAINFALL	12/0.48	14/0.56	15/0.6	16/0.64
CHRISTCHURCH				
MAX. TEMP	22/72	18/65	12/54	17/63
MIN. TEMP	12/54	8/46	3/37	7/45
RAINFALL	7/0.28	7/0.28	7/0.28	7/0.28
MOUNT COOK				
MAX. TEMP	20/68	14/57	8/46	14/57
MIN. TEMP	9/48	4/39	-1/30	4/39
RAINFALL	12/0.48	13/0.52	13/0.52	14/0.56
QUEENSTOWN				
MAX. TEMP	22/72	16/61	10/50	16/61
MIN. TEMP	10/50	6/43	1/34	5/41
RAINFALL	8/0.32	8/0.32	7/0.28	9/0.36
INVERCARGILL				
MAX. TEMP	18/65	15/59	11/52	15/59
MIN. TEMP	9/48	6/43	1/34	5/41
RAINFALL	13/0.52	14/0.56	12/0.48	13/0.52

Holidays

National public holidays include New Year's Day (Jan 1), New Year's Holiday (Jan 2), Waitangi Day (Feb 6), Good Friday (varies), Easter Monday (varies), ANZAC Day (Apr 25), Queen's Birthday (first Mon in June), Matariki (varies, but usually a Friday in late May to early July), Labour Day (last Mon in Oct), Christmas Day (Dec 25), and Boxing Day (Dec 26).

Regional anniversary holiday days include Wellington (Jan 22), Auckland (Jan 29), Nelson (Feb 1), Otago (Mar 23), Southland (Mar 23), Taranaki (Mar 31), Hawke's Bay (Nov 1), Marlborough (Nov 1), Westland (Dec 1), and Canterbury (Dec 16). Regional holidays are always observed on a Monday. If the date lands on a Friday or weekend, the holiday is observed on the following Monday. If it falls earlier in the week, it is observed on the preceding Monday.

School holidays consist of three midterm breaks—in April, July, and October—that last for 2 weeks each, plus 6 weeks for the end of the school year, which starts around Christmas and last until around the end of January. Kiwi families do much of their traveling during these periods, so book early.

New Zealand Calendar of Events

More information can be found in the regional chapters that follow and by going to the Tourism New Zealand website at **newzealand.com**.

JANUARY

Auckland Anniversary Day Regatta, Auckland. "The City of Sails" hosts this colorful annual sailing event, attracting both local and international competitors and spectators. Check regatta.org.nz or call ✆ **0800/734-2882** in NZ. Last Monday in January.

World Buskers Festival, Christchurch. A week of zany street entertainment is provided by leading entertainers. Visit worldbuskers festival.co.nz or call ✆ **03/366-6366.** Mid- to late January.

Wellington Cup Race Meeting, Wellington. This leading horse-racing event (galloping) is held in conjunction with the National Yearling Sales. Go to jointheaction.co.nz or call ✆ **04/528-9611.** or go to Late January.

FEBRUARY

Coast to Coast Race, South Island. This major multisport endurance race from Kumara on the West Coast to Sumner, Christchurch, features a 33km (20-mile) mountain run followed by a 67km (42-mile) kayak race and a 142km (88-mile) cycle dash. Visit coasttocoast.co.nz or call ✆ **03/450-1955.** Early–mid-February.

Waitangi Day Celebrations, Waitangi Treaty Grounds, Bay of Islands. New Zealand's national day celebrating the signing of the Treaty of Waitangi. Call ✆ **09/402-7437.** February 6.

Art Deco Festival, Napier. A fun celebration of the city's Art Deco heritage includes dancing, jazz, vintage cars, walks, and tours. Most participants dress in 1920s and 1930s fashions. Check artdecofestival.co.nz or call ✆ **06/835-0022.** Mid-February.

Aotearoa New Zealand International Festival of Arts, Wellington. The largest and most prestigious event on the New Zealand arts calendar draws top overseas and national artists and entertainers, creating a vibrant mix of all art forms, from contemporary dance to fine music and theater. Visit festival.nz or call ✆ **04/473-0149.** Late February to March.

MARCH

Auckland Arts Festival. Held annually, this is an extravaganza of national and international dance, music, theater, and visual arts. Check aucklandfestival.co.nz or call ✆ **09/309-0989.** March.

Celebrate Pasifika Festival, Auckland. Auckland's Pacific Island communities celebrate the largest cultural festival in the South Pacific. Not to be missed. Go to aucklandnz.com/pasifika. Second week of March.

Hokitika Wildfoods Festival, Hokitika. A culinary adventure for the brave and curious, this 1-day event explores the full range of New Zealand's wild foods, including wild pig, possum pâté, goat, various bugs and insects, honey, fish, and venison. Check wildfoods.co.nz or call ✆ **027/204-1139.** Mid-March.

APRIL

Warbirds Over Wānaka, Wānaka. One of the best air shows in the world, it combines classic vintage and veteran aircraft, machinery, fire engines, and tractors with dynamic Air Force displays and aerobatic teams in the natural amphitheater of the Upper Clutha Basin. Visit warbirdsoverwanaka.com or call ✆ **03/443-8619.** Easter weekend (in even-numbered years only; in odd years the planes thrill punters at Omaka near Blenheim, classicfighters.co.nz).

Arrowtown Autumn Festival, Arrowtown. A week of market days, music, and street entertainment celebrates the gold-mining era. Visit arrowtownautumnfestival.org.nz or call ✆ **028/429-8339.** Mid- to late April.

MAY

Matariki Festival. The rising of the cluster of stars also known as Pleiades marks the start of the Māori new year. Officially named a public holiday in 2022, it's celebrated across the country. Visit matarikifestival.org.nz. In late May, June, or July.

JUNE

Steampunk Festival, Oamaru. Celebrating the sub-genre of science fiction, this unusual weekend festival sees people riding penny-farthings and showing off futuristic Victorian clothing. Go to steampunk.org.nz for details. Early June.

National Agricultural Fieldays, Hamilton. One of the largest agricultural shows in the world, this event exhibits the best of New Zealand agriculture, horticulture, floriculture, and forestry products. Visit fieldays.co.nz or call ✆ **07/843-4497.** Mid-June.

JULY

Wairarapa Festival of Christmas, Greytown. A taste of the Northern Hemisphere Christmas season in New Zealand, this month-long winter celebration brings revelers out-of-doors to enjoy spectacular lighting, food, night markets. and workshops. Visit greytownvillage.com/festival-of-christmas. July.

AUGUST

Bay of Islands Jazz and Blues Festival, Bay of Islands. More than 50 jazz bands from New Zealand and overseas provide live entertainment at various places around Paihia and Russell. Visit boimusicfestivals.com. Early to mid-August.

SEPTEMBER

WOW (World of Wearable Art), Wellington. This creative extravaganza in Wellington should not be missed. Visit worldofwearableart.com. Late September to early October.

Alexandra Blossom Festival, Alexandra. An annual parade of floats and entertainment celebrates the onset of spring. Visit blossom.co.nz. Late September to early October.

Rotorua Marathon, Rotorua. A full marathon around Lake Rotorua attracts over 500 serious competitors. Call ✆ **09/477-0210** or check rotoruamarathon.co.nz. Mid-September.

OCTOBER

Nelson Arts Festival, Nelson. Twelve days of music, dance, theater, and street performances runs throughout the city. Check nelsonartsfestival.co.nz. Mid-October.

NOVEMBER

Toast Martinborough, Martinborough. An annual wine-and-food festival. Go to toastmartinborough.co.nz. Mid- to late November.

NZ Cider Festival, Nelson. Taste more than 100 varieties of cider while enjoying leafy, convivial Founders Park, with all-day music, food trucks, and a dedicated kids' zone. Visit nzciderfestival.com. Mid-November.

The Royal A&P Show of New Zealand, Christchurch. The country's largest agricultural and pastoral event includes thoroughbred and standard-bred racing and the New Zealand Cup. Go to theshow.co.nz or call ✆ **03/343-3033.** Second week of November.

SPEAKING ENZED

The common language might be English, but here in NZ conversation is peppered with quintessentially Kiwi words, phrases, and colloquialisms. While you're bound to encounter lots of strange words on your trip through New Zealand, here are some everyday ones and what they mean.

Bach A vacation house
Bench Countertop
Bludge Borrow
Bonnet Hood of car
Boot Trunk of car
Bush Forest
Carpark Parking lot or parking space
CBD Central Business District or downtown core
Chilly bin Cooler (U.S.), esky (Aus.)

Choice Something that is awesome or cool
Chur Thank you
Cocky A farmer
College High school
Cot Crib (place where a baby or toddler sleeps)
Crib Term for holiday house in Otago or Southland
Cuppa Cup of tea
Dairy Convenience store
DOC Department of Conservation
Duvet Comforter or quilt
Fanny Female genitalia; you'll shock Kiwis if you call the thing you wear around your waist a "fanny pack"
Fortnight A 2-week period
Footpath Sidewalk
Get stuck in Get started
Gumboots Rubber boots or wellies
Grizzle Complain
Grog Alcoholic drinks, as in "Where's the grog?"
Hire Rent
Hooker Front-row rugby player
Hotties Hot-water bottles used to heat beds when there is no electricity or electric blankets
Inner-city An area located in or close to the city's center. This term does not denote socio-economic status and often an inner-city location is desirable.
Jandals Flip-flops
Judder bars Speed bumps
Jug Electric kettle or a pitcher
Kiwi Both a New Zealander and the bird
Kiwifruit A kiwi fruit
Lay-by A roadside rest area
Loo Toilet
Long drop Outhouse
Lounge Living or sitting room
Mate Friend
Mozzie Mosquito
Nappy Diaper
Pushbike Bicycle
Queue Line, to wait in line
Serviette Napkin
Servo Service station
Shingle A gravel road; may also be called a metal road
Shout Treat someone (usually refers to a meal or a drink), buy a round
Single bed Twin bed
Singlet Tank top

Slip A landslide
Smoko Morning or afternoon break
Spa Hot tub
Stubbies Shorts
Ta Thank you
Tiki tour The scenic route
Torch Flashlight
To call To visit or to contact by telephone
Togs Swimsuit
To ring To phone
Track Trail for hiking
Tramping Hiking
Ute Truck
Varsity University, college
Wop wops The middle of nowhere

Food Terms

Afghans Popular Kiwi cookies made with cornflakes and cocoa
ANZAC biscuits Cookies popular during World War II but not actually posted overseas as often believed. They were made with golden syrup rather than sugar to get around sugar rationing.
Bangers Sausages
Biscuits/bikkies Cookies
Beetroot Beets
Blue vein Blue cheese
Capsicum Red or green pepper
Cellar door A winery with a tasting room
Chips French fries, though often thicker
Chocolate fish A chocolate-covered marshmallow
Chook Chicken
Entrée Appetizer or first course. The second course in NZ is the "main."
Fizzy drink Soda or soft drink
Hogget A lamb that is more than 1 year old
Ice block A popsicle
Jelly Gelatin dessert
Lemonade Sprite or 7Up
Lolly/lollies Candy
Macca's McDonald's
Marmite A popular yeast-based breakfast spread
Pāua Albalone or edible sea snail
Pavlova Popular dessert named after ballerina Anna Pavlova; consists of layered meringue, cream and topped with fruit or chocolate
Pie A savory or meat-filled pastry, often individually sized (*Pie* is very rarely used to describe a sweet American-style pie.)

TE REO māori

Te reo Māori ("the Māori language") is one of New Zealand's official languages. A Polynesian dialect, it was first given a written form in the early 19th century by missionaries and British linguists. Today, many te reo Māori terms and words are in common use. Throughout your trip to New Zealand, you will hear te reo ("the language") words used daily by both Māori and Pākehā (non-Māori), so it pays to learn more than a few of them. (Case in point: It's not unusual to see restrooms for *wahine* and *tāne* rather than *women* and *men*.) Here are some of the words you're most likely to encounter:

Aotearoa New Zealand
Aroha Love
Haka Dance (war, funeral, and so on)
Hāngī Oven made by filling a hole with heated stones, and the feast roasted in it
Haere mai Welcome
Hapū Subtribe; also pregnant
Hongi The traditional greeting that involves a pressing together of noses
Iwi Māori tribe
Kai Food
Ka pai Good work or well done
Karakia Prayer
Kia ora Hello, Go well
Koha Donation or offering
Marae Courtyard, village common
Mana Prestige, authority, status; a supernatural force or energy in a person
Pā Stockade or fortified place
Pākehā Caucasian person; primarily used to refer to those of European descent
Poi A ball—traditionally made with flax—with string attached, twirled in action song
Pounamu Greenstone or jade
Tangi Funeral with mourning and lamentation
Taonga Treasure
Tapu Taboo; a religious or superstitious restriction
Tuna Eel
Tiki Human image, sometimes carved of greenstone
Waiata Song
Whare House
Whānau Family
Whakapapa Genealogy or ancestry
Whenua Land, also placenta

Many place names can also be explained by their prefixes and suffixes. For example

Ao Cloud
Ika Fish
Nui Big, or abundant
Roto Lake
Rua Cave, or hollow, or two (Rotorua's two lakes)
Tahi One, single
Te The
Wai Water
Whanga Bay, harbor, inlet, or stretch of water

For more resources and information, visit reomaori.co.nz and maoridictionary.co.nz.

Pikelets Small pancakes served with a cup of tea; often topped with jam and cream
Pipis Shellfish similar to cockles
Plonk Cheap wine
Pudding Dessert
Rocket Arugula
Saveloy or sav A cooked smoked sausage
Scone A biscuit served with morning or afternoon tea

Silver beet Swiss chard
Snarlers Sausages
Takeaway Takeout or to-go food
Tamarillo Tree tomato
Tomato sauce Ketchup
Water biscuit Cracker
Weet-Bix A breakfast cereal similar to shredded wheat packed flat to a brick shape
Whitebait Tiny juvenile fish, with a delicate taste; may be served floured and fried or mixed in a batter as a patty
White tea Tea with milk added

SUGGESTED NEW ZEALAND ITINERARIES

3

We hear it all the time: "This is such a small country; we never realized there would be so much to see!" We're talking white-sand beaches, verdant vineyards, sprawling glaciers, geysers, and jagged peaks. On the cultural side, you have moving Māori performances, heritage architecture, and smart and quirky museums. Country comes to city in restaurants big and small, where farm-to-table menus draw from a bounty of produce, seafood, and wines. Make the most of your New Zealand trip—and your time—with the following suggested itineraries.

We also take a look at the regions, to help those who'd prefer to plan their own itineraries. For a small country, New Zealand's challenging geography (mountains, rivers, sea crossings) means many miles must be traveled to reach the best attractions. Fortunately, the travel links are easy: National airline Air New Zealand is backed up by smaller regional airlines, the InterCity coach system connects business centers with practically every visitor attraction, and in-between are busy shuttle buses and scenic train lines transporting visitors to popular destinations.

NEW ZEALAND IN 1 WEEK

Many visitors make the mistake of thinking they can knock off a big portion of the country in just 1 week. But for such a "small" country, 1 or even 2 weeks is not nearly enough time. (Biggest rookie mistake: trying to cram Australia and New Zealand into one vacation.) Sure, it's possible to see parts of the country in a week, but you'll only get a very small taste of what it has to offer, and it will require early starts and long days.

For the sake of time, you'll need to ditch the car and fly instead. Regional airports are well-serviced, which will help you save time. But domestic flights come at a high environmental cost, so ultimately, we beg you to reconsider the length of your holiday—or scale back what you want to see. (It is possible, for example, to do

New Zealand in 1 Week

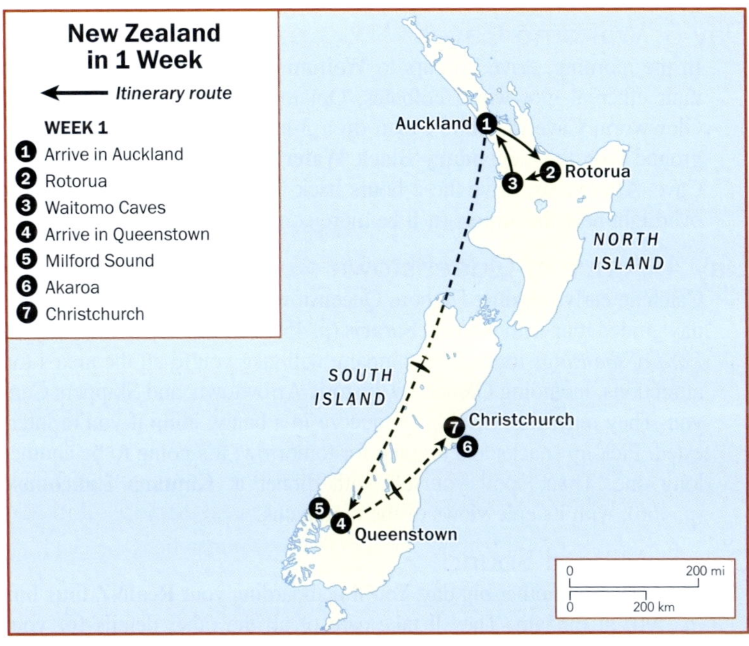

a fair chunk of just the North Island in 1 week—although again, with early starts and long days.)

Day 1: Arrive in Auckland

Try to arrive early and focus your attention on the hospitality and yachting hub of the **Viaduct** (p. 82), a great introduction to New Zealand's passion for boats. Go for a 2-hour morning sail on one of the **America's Cup Boats** (p. 89) moored here, and keep an eye out for dolphins in the Hauraki Gulf. Spend your afternoon at **Tāmaki Paenga Hira Auckland War Memorial Museum** (p. 80) before catching a cab to the hip neighborhood of Ponsonby for boutique shopping and dinner.

Day 2: Rotorua

Pick up a rental car in Auckland and spend the morning driving the 2½ hours to Rotorua. Once there, head to **Te Puia** (p. 213) to see its geothermal wonders, including bubbling mud and massive geysers. This will take the better part of your day, but leave time in the late afternoon for a walk in the awe-inspiring **Whakarewarewa Redwoods Forest** (p. 211). While you're there, pick up some takeaway food from **Eastwood Cafe** (p. 227) for tomorrow's lunch, as eating options in Waitomo are limited.

That evening, catch a shuttle from your hotel to a nighttime Māori cultural performance and dinner at **Te Pā Tū** (p. 219).

Day 3: Waitomo Caves

In the morning, drive 2 hours to **Waitomo Caves** (p. 173), known for their ethereal glowworm colonies. Opt to explore the main Waitomo Glowworm Cave (45 min.), then do a 3-hour rafting adventure underground with the **Legendary Black Water Rafting Co.** in the Ruakuri Cave. Afterwards, drive the 2 hours back to Auckland. If you can, stay overnight near the airport (it'll be more convenient).

Day 4: Arrive in Queenstown

Catch an early morning flight to Queenstown to arrive in time for a full-day guided tour with **Nomad Safaris** (p. 459). While they're marketed as *Lord of the Rings* tours, this company will take you to all the area's top attractions, including Glenorchy, historic Arrowtown, and Skippers Canyon. They may even be able to squeeze in a bungy jump if you're interested. Pick up snacks and a lunch for tomorrow; it's going to be another long one. Then, spoil yourself with dinner at **Kāmana Lakehouse** (p. 466), with its epic views of the mountains.

Day 5: Milford Sound

Get ready for another big day. You'll be boarding your **RealNZ tour bus** (p. 490) at 6:55am. They'll take care of all the other details for your 12-hour trip to Fiordland—including a scenic cruise on **Milford Sound,**

A boat glides through the spectacular Milford Sound.

known for its jaw-droppingly beautiful peaks and massive waterfalls that crash straight into the sea. Overnight in Queenstown; try the hip **Sherwood** (p. 468).

Day 6: Christchurch/Akaroa

Catch the 8:50am flight from Queenstown to Christchurch, which takes about 70 minutes. Take a cab or bus into the city for a walking tour with **Watch This Space** (p, 428), then see more sights with **Christchurch Attractions** (p. 428); options includes a tram tour, gondola ride, or punting on the Avon. Or rent a car to explore the picturesque harborside French village of **Akaroa** (p. 441). In the evening, have dinner at one of the restaurants in **Riverside Market** (p. 437), then go for a nighttime wander past the **Transitional Cathedral** (p. 424) and through the **Arts Centre** (p. 421), which showcases the Victorian architecture Christchurch was known for prior to the 2011 earthquakes.

Day 7: Christchurch

Return to the airport to catch your international flight home. If you have time before the flight, visit the nearby **Willowbank Wildlife Reserve** (p. 427), where you're sure to see a kiwi. If you decide you were silly to try to cram it all into a week, see the next itinerary.

NEW ZEALAND IN 2 WEEKS

Two weeks in New Zealand gives you more opportunities to drive between destinations and take in the color of the provinces. Still, don't underestimate the time your journey will take. New Zealand has good roads, but even national highways are mostly single-lane, and often narrow, steep, and winding. As a visitor, you will be driving considerably slower than locals, who are used to the twisty roads (and Google Maps' estimates are based on their driving times, not yours), plus you'll want to stop for photos along the way. This itinerary gives you a taste of both main islands, sticking to areas with the greatest concentration of activities.

Day 1: Arrive in Auckland

Arrive in Auckland ready to sightsee until you drop. You'll be getting around via the double-decker **Auckland Explorer Bus** (p. 72)—the cheapest and easiest way to see as much as possible in 1 day. The bus drives through the leafy **Botanic Gardens** (p. 88) and through Parnell village. You'll set eyes on **Mission Bay**'s pretty beach promenade, and hop off to get a taste of Māori culture at the **Tāmaki Paenga Hira Auckland War Memorial Museum** (p. 80). Spend the afternoon witnessing movie magic at **Wētā Workshop Unleashed** (p. 81), an attraction created by the film studio behind Peter Jackson's *Lord of the Rings* films. That night, head for dinner and a stroll at the **Viaduct** (p. 82), the city's buzzing waterside hospitality complex, with people-watching aplenty.

Up, up, up into the canopy! Visitors at Whakarewarewa Redwoods Forest tackle the Redwoods Altitude challenge course, which includes narrow rope bridges.

Day 2: Hobbiton & Rotorua

Pick up a rental car in the city and spend your morning driving to **Hobbiton** (p. 170), an impressive film set where part of the *Lord of the Rings* and *The Hobbit* movies were made. After your tour at Hobbiton, drive to Rotorua, where you'll spend the night. From your hotel, take a shuttle to **Te Pā Tū** (p. 219). In addition to dinner, here you'll experience a Māori cultural show.

Day 3: Rotorua

Spend your morning exploring the thermal sights of **Te Puia** (p. 213), before heading to **Whakarewarewa Redwoods Forest** (p. 211) and late lunch at nearby **Eastwood Cafe** (p. 227). While you're there, pick up some takeaway sandwiches to have for dinner, as eating options in Waitomo are limited. Then, drive the 2 hours to Waitomo, where you'll stay overnight.

Day 4: Waitomo Caves & Taupō

You'll spend the morning with glowworms at **Waitomo Caves** (p. 173). If you're game, consider adding a whitewater rafting experience underground (see **DAY 4** of the 1-week itinerary). Afterwards, drive the 2 hours to Taupō. For dinner, board **Sail Barbary**'s electric yacht (p. 233). Pizza and drinks will be served on the evening tour as you cruise across Lake Taupō to the **Māori rock carvings.** Overnight in Taupō.

New Zealand in 2 Weeks & New Zealand for Families

Day 5: Tongariro National Park & Wellington

A morning's drive will take you along the shore of **Lake Taupō** (p. 229), making plenty of stops for photos, to the stark beauty of **Tongariro National Park** (p. 247). Budget enough time for a quick walk in the park, perhaps the **Mounds Walk** (p. 251), which will take you just 20 minutes. For lunch, stop in the mountain town of **Ohakune,** at the park's southern end. From here, it's onward through the heartland's farming area. If it's summer and the days are long, you can follow SH2 to stop off for dinner in **Greytown** (p. 350) before tackling the winding and steep Remutaka Range to Wellington. (In winter, it's best to skip Greytown and head straight to Wellington before it gets dark.) Or, you can take the less-taxing (but somewhat less scenic) route on SH1 along the **Kāpiti Coast** (p. 344). Either way, you'll end up in **Wellington.** We recommend staying at a hotel in the city center, close to attractions and the ferry docks.

Day 6: Wellington

In the morning, head straight to **Museum of New Zealand Te Papa Tongarewa** (p. 321), which eloquently tells the story of Aotearoa and is a must-visit. After lunch along the wharf, spend the afternoon at **Zealandia** (p. 328) to see endemic birds and reptiles within a massive fenced predator-free sanctuary. That night, grab dinner on hopping **Cuba Street** (p. 338), where you'll find plenty of different cuisines for a range of budgets.

Day 7: Wellington to Picton

Catch an early ferry to Picton. The 3½-hour ferry ride is one of the most scenic in the world, carrying you through the Marlborough Sounds to the South Island. Keep an eye out for dolphins and whales. Drive to **Blenheim** and freshen up at your hotel. Afterwards, you'll have enough time to check out a nearby winery or two before dinner at **Arbour** or **Frank's Oyster Bar** (p. 371) and a good night's rest.

Two of the Victorian Gothic buildings at Christchurch's beloved Arts Centre.

Day 8: Christchurch

From Blenheim, it will take you 4 or 5 hours to drive south to Christchurch. Stop for lunch in **Kaikōura** and to see the seals at play along the **Kaikōura Peninsula Walkway** (p. 449). You should arrive in **Christchurch** (p. 418) by mid-afternoon. Check into your hotel, then explore the

Touring the wine country near Queenstown with Altitude Tours.

compact city center, including the remarkable **Transitional Cathedral, Arts Centre, Botanic Gardens,** and **Riverside Market,** where you can grab dinner. If you've still got energy left, get an ice cream on **New Regent Street** or a drink at **The Last Word** (p. 439).

Day 9: Mackenzie Country

Your next city destination, **Queenstown,** is a 6- to 7-hour drive from Christchurch. It may be tempting to skip the drive and fly, but then you'd miss out on the turquoise-blue waters of **Lake Tekapō** and **Lake Pukaki,** as well as seeing the sky-high peak of **Aoraki/Mount Cook.** To split up the drive, spend the night at **Tekapō** (p. 499). Visit the **Dark Sky Project** (p. 500) and take a nighttime stargazing tour to the **Mt. John Observatory** (p. 500).

Day 10: Queenstown

In the morning, drive the remaining 3 hours to **Queenstown.** Your time here will be limited, so shortlist the kind of adventure you'd like. Jetboating? Bungy jumping? Ziplining? Whitewater rafting? Queenstown is known for its adrenaline-thrill activities. For something more relaxed, take an afternoon cruise across Lake Wakatipu on the vintage steamship **TSS *Earnslaw*** to Walter Peak (p. 454) or book a half-day wine tour with **Altitude Tours** (p. 458). For dinner, head to historic **Arrowtown** (p. 474), a charming 1860s-era mining town with an impressive line-up of fine restaurants.

Day 11: Central Otago

Your **Trail Journeys** shuttle will pick you up early and take you to historic **Cromwell.** Spend half a day on e-bikes cycling along the **Lake Dunstan Trail** (p. 462) to cute little historic **Clyde,** where you can enjoy lunch at a cafe before perusing the shops and art galleries. After catching your transfer back to Queenstown, book a relaxing soak at the **Onsen Hot Pools** (p. 455).

Day 12: Te Anau

In the morning, drive to **Te Anau** (p. 484), the gateway to **Milford Sound.** Lunch in town at the **Sandfly Café** before climbing aboard a jetboat for a tour of Lake Manapouri with **Fiordland Jet.** Along with lots of fun spins in the boat, you'll also get a brief walk along the legendary **Kepler Track** for a taste of a Great Walk. Afterward, stop by **Fiordland Cinema** for a cocktail with some truffle fries or baked brie before a screening of the 30-minute **Ata Whenua** film, which will give you a greater understanding of Fiordland National Park. Dinner at the **Redcliff Café** or **The Fat Duck Gastropub** will power you for the day ahead.

Day 13: Milford Sound

It's possible to self-drive to Milford Sound, but we prefer booking with a tour operator, who can help you avoid hitting scenic stops at the same time as the big tour buses. (It also frees you to enjoy the scenery instead of having to navigate what's considered one of NZ's most perilous roads.) **Trips & Tramps** (p. 489) will take you to Milford and back, with several short hikes along the way. It'll also arrange your boat cruise (or kayak, upon request) in Milford Sound and provide lunch. You'll arrive back to Te Anau at 5pm. If it's summer, enjoy the long daylight and drive back to Queenstown; in winter you may want to spend another night in Te Anau, rather than driving the winding road back to Queenstown in the frosty dark.

Day 14: Queenstown & Christchurch

Enjoy a leisurely morning in Queenstown, including a visit to the **Kiwi Park** (p. 456), where you're guaranteed to see the country's most famous bird. Then, fly to Christchurch to connect with your international flight.

NEW ZEALAND FOR FAMILIES

Kids love New Zealand. There are enough weird, wonderful, curious, funny, and interesting things on these islands to amuse the most inquiring child's mind. This itinerary runs a little over 2 weeks and hits the kid-friendly highlights of both North Island and South Island.

Day 1: Arrive in Auckland

Start with an easy day, checking out combo deals and family passes at the visitor center at the **Viaduct** (p. 70), where the kids can investigate the boats at the **New Zealand Maritime Museum** (p. 83); a museum visit includes a cruise on the historic scow *Ted Ashby*. Book an afternoon session at **Wētā Workshop Unleashed** (p. 81), where kids will witness absolute movie magic. Afterwards, give them a bird's-eye view of the city from the **Sky Tower** (p. 79), zooming into the sky in its exterior glass lift, with an exciting walk over the glass floor. Dine in the revolving restaurant at the top.

Day 2: Auckland Sights

At **Kelly Tarlton's Sea Life Aquarium** (p. 86), you'll stay dry beneath an acrylic dome in Underwater World while sharks and stingrays swim overhead. Spend the afternoon at **Tāmaki Paenga Hira Auckland War Memorial Museum** (p. 80), especially its superb **Weird & Wonderful Discovery Centre,** where youngsters can open drawers and touch exhibits.

Day 3: More of Auckland

Arrive early at **Auckland Zoo** (p. 75), which has heaps of great stuff for kids. Check out the daily animal encounters and view sea lions through underwater viewing windows. Drive to **Butterfly Creek** (p. 86) to flirt with winged beauties and see animals at Buttermilk Farm.

Day 4: Drive to Rotorua

Rent a car from the city and start the 3-hour drive to Rotorua early. Stop in **Hamilton** (p. 165) along the way and spend an hour wandering

The Surreal Garden at Hamilton Gardens play tricks with perspective.

through the **Hamilton Gardens.** (Kids will love the Surreal Garden, which makes them feel like Alice in Wonderland.) Just north of Rotorua in Ngongotahā, visit the **National Kiwi Hatchery** (p. 214) to see baby kiwi chicks, then spend the rest of the afternoon at the adjacent **Agrodome** (p. 214), which has a hive of kids' activities.

Day 5: Rotorua

The kids will be screwing up their noses at the smell of sulfur in the air, so show them what it's all about. Drive to **Waimangu Volcanic Valley** and **Wai-O-Tapu** (p. 217) to see geysers, giant steaming hot pools, and bubbling mud. Allow half a day for both or, if you have to choose, 2 hours for Waimangu Volcanic Valley. Back in town, feed the kids from one of the takeaway stands at the lakefront and then let them loose at **Skyline Skyrides** (p. 214), where they can plummet downhill on a luge, or better still, have an adventure in the giant inflatable **Zorb** (p. 221).

Day 6: Māori Cultural

Spend the morning investigating the wonders of **Te Puia** (p. 213), which includes the **Whakarewarewa Thermal Reserve** and the **New Zealand Māori Arts & Crafts Institute.** Stay and watch Pōhutu Geyser blow its top. In the afternoon, head to **Whakarewarewa Redwoods Forest** (p. 211) and explore the treewalk. Set the evening aside for dinner and a Māori cultural show at **Te Pā Tū** (p. 219).

Day 7: Drive to Wellington

The drive south normally takes about 5 hours, but allow a day. Stop en route at **Lake Taupō** (p. 229) and visit **Huka Falls** (p. 231), just off the main highway north of Taupō. Let the kids blow off some steam at **The Landing** (p. 234), with its indoor trampoline park and mini-golf. Have a picnic at one of the little beaches around the lake, then drive on south into **Tongariro National Park** (p. 247) for beautiful mountain landscapes. Maybe there'll be time to squeeze in a snack stop at **Greytown** (p. 355) before you wind your way across the Remutaka Range and down into Wellington, where you'll be staying for the next 2 nights.

Day 8: Wellington

Spend your morning hours exploring the **Museum of New Zealand Te Papa Tongarewa** (p. 321), the country's national museum. Among kids' favorite exhibits here are the earthquake room and the giant squid. Let the kids run free along the waterfront after that—there'll be boats and action aplenty. Ride the **Cable Car** (p. 321) to the top, where it's just a short walk to the **Botanic Garden** (p. 326) and the **Space Place** planetarium in the Carter Observatory (p. 326). Hopefully you can also squeeze in a visit to **Zealandia,** the world's first urban wildlife sanctuary, where you can spot rare native species (p. 328). Wander down **Cuba Mall** (p. 341) for an early dinner and let the kids get splashed by the iconic Bucket Fountain.

Day 9: Wellington to Nelson

Leave Wellington on the 9am ferry and have an early lunch or late breakfast on board (the ferry has movies and play areas for children) as you sail across the straits to the South Island. Arrive in Picton and drive west to Nelson, where you'll be staying the next 3 nights. Twenty minutes before you reach the city, you'll hit **Cable Bay Adventure Park** (p. 376), which has 4WD bike adventures and the irresistible Skywire, a sort of flying fox meets ski chairlift. For dinner, the **Boat Shed Cafe** (p. 382) is an iconic Nelson restaurant; try the All-Day Menu if the dinner menu looks too grownup.

Day 10: Nelson

After a big couple of travel days, opt for an easy day out at **Tāhunanui Beach** (p. 376). If the kids tire of water play, they can have a blast on the rides at **Nelson Fun Park** (p. 376) or thrill to close encounters with wallabies, meerkats, and monkeys at the **Natureland Zoo** (p. 376)—both at Tāhunanui.

Day 11: Abel Tasman National Park

Drive up the coast of Tasman Bay to **Kaiteriteri** and its lovely, gentle golden-sand beaches. Book a tour of **Abel Tasman National Park** with **Waka Abel Tasman** (p. 385), which combines paddling with Māori culture. At the end of the day, return to Nelson.

Paddling along the shoreline of Abel Tasman National Park on a cultural tour with Waka Abel Tasman.

Day 12: The West Coast

From Nelson, take the SH6 through the Buller Gorge to **Westport**—it's a 4-hour drive but will likely take you longer, as it's twisty, mountainous, and has a lot of worthy pit stops (stop for lunch in **Murchison,** p. 392). From Westport, head down the West Coast, stopping to do a short coastal walk at Punakaiki's **Pancake Rocks** (p. 400). Stay overnight in **Hokitika** (p. 407), where you can walk to the glowworm dell after dark.

Day 13: Hokitika & West Coast Wildlife Centre

Let the kids search for greenstone along Hokitika's beach. Older kids will love carving their discoveries into wearable jewelry at **Bonz 'n' Stonz Carving Studio** (p. 409). Grab lunch at the **Hokitika Sandwich Company** (p. 410) and then drive to **Franz Josef,** where you can spend the afternoon touring the indoor hatching home for Rowi kiwi at the **West Coast Wildlife Centre** (p. 413). The smaller township of **Fox Glacier** is another 30 minutes' drive.

Day 14: The Glaciers

As soon as you arrive in Franz Josef, confirm your **heli-hike glacier adventure** (p. 412). Weather can change abruptly, so take the first available flight. If flights are a no-go, take the gentle half-hour walk to a view of the glacier. In the afternoon, return up the coast 2 hours to **Kumara,** where you can spend the night at the historic **Theatre Royal Hotel** (p. 405). (If your little ones are afraid of ghosts, stay in one of the hotel's brand-new cottages, just in case.)

Day 15: Christchurch

This is a long day's drive to Christchurch, so make plenty of stops. Continue along SH 73 via Otira and **Arthur's Pass** (p. 445) to Christchurch. Schedule a stop at the **Otira Stagecoach Hotel** (p. 446) for a meal or to simply gawk at the array of sometimes-macabre collectibles. At **Castle Hill/Kura Tawhiti** (p. 446), kids can clamber over the unusual limestone formations. Spend the night at a Christchurch airport hotel before flying out the next day.

7-DAY SOUTH ISLAND MOTORHOME TOUR

The point of traveling by motorhome is to set your own route and timetable—not to mention save money thanks to your rolling kitchen and lowered lodging costs. This itinerary is based on motorhome pickup in Christchurch and drop-off in Queenstown. Check that your proposed motorhome provider has a depot in Queenstown, if it incurs a drop-off fee and how much, and if there is a free transfer to/from the drop-off point to the Queenstown airport and/or the town center. For motorhome driving tips and freedom camping laws, see chapter 17.

Other Suggested New Zealand Itineraries

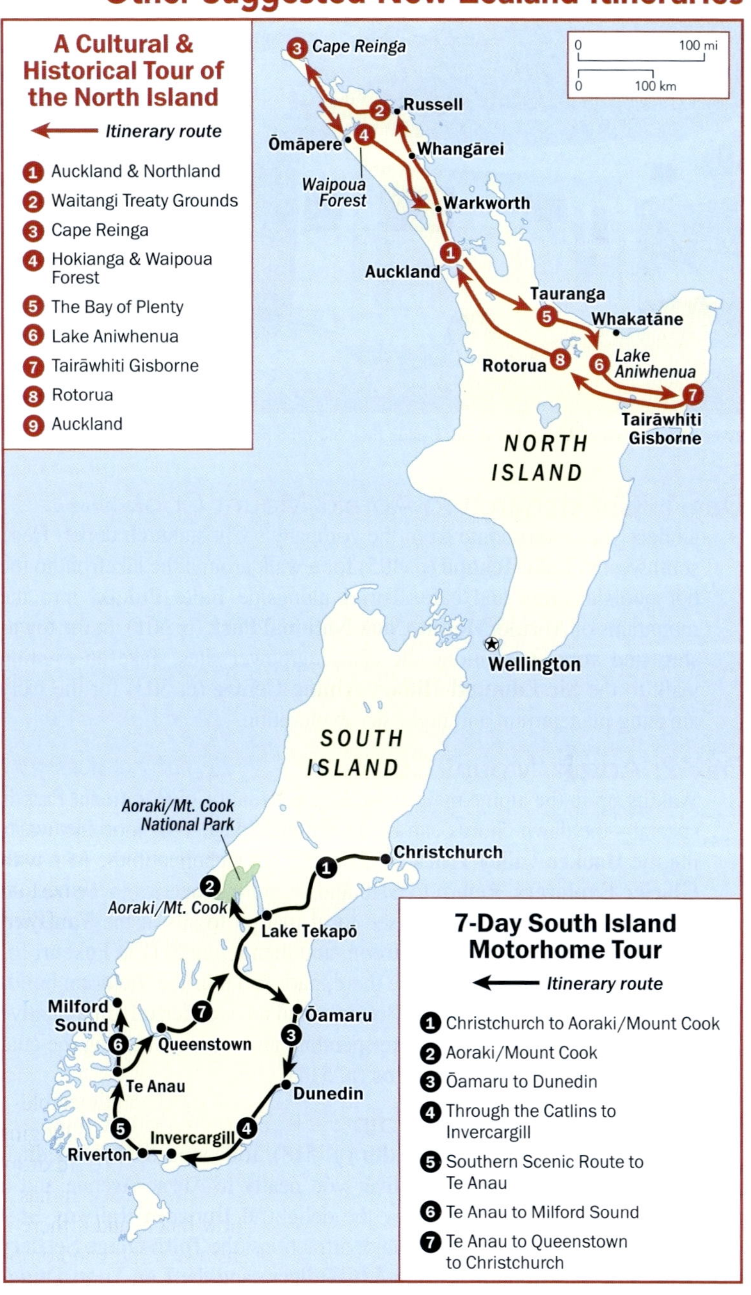

RVers enjoy a view of Aoraki from right beside their motorhome.

Day 1: Christchurch to Aoraki/Mount Cook

Collect your motorhome from the company's Christchurch depot. Head southwest to **Lake Tekapō** (p. 495) for a walk around the lakefront to the hot pools/ice rink and cafe. Travel alongside **Lake Pukaki** into the mountains of **Aoraki/Mount Cook National Park** (p. 501). In the township find your spot among the camping/power sites. Take an evening walk to the **Sir Edmund Hillary Alpine Centre** (p. 503) for the truly amazing planetarium and night sky exploration.

Day 2: Aoraki/Mount Cook

Waking up in the alpine majesty of Aoraki/Mount Cook National Park is special—the dawn chorus can be deafening. Spend your morning walking the **Hooker Valley Track** or checking out icebergs on the lake with **Glacier Explorers.** Return to SH8 and shop for groceries in **Twizel.** At Ōmarama take SH83. Stop to see local marine fossils at the **Vanished World Centre** (p. 511) in Duntroon, and then rejoin SH1 at Pukeuri for the short drive to Ōamaru. Once there, park and tour the Victorian buildings of the **Ōamaru Heritage Precinct** and the wonderfully imaginative **Steampunk HQ** (p. 514), before spending an evening watching the cute little locals of **Ōamaru Penguins** (p. 514).

Day 3: Ōamaru to Dunedin

Leave Ōamaru early for **Dunedin** (p. 518), following SH1. Dunedin's one-way street system will deliver you neatly to Anzac Avenue and a carpark for your motorhome by the delightful **Dunedin Railway Station,** a short walk to the city's major attractions: the **Toitū Otago Settlers Museum;** the **Dunedin Public Art Gallery;** and the **Lan Yuan Dunedin Chinese Garden.** Spend your afternoon exploring the **Orokonui Ecosanctuary** (p. 526) or the **Albatross Colony** (p. 528) on the Otago

Peninsula. Spend the night out in Portobello (there are sites at the Portobello Village Tourist Park) to avoid driving back in the dark.

Day 4: Through the Catlins to Invercargill

Follow SH1 to the Ōwaka turnoff (SH82) and take the Southern Scenic Route via the **Catlins** (p. 538), stopping at some of its magnificent natural features (**Pūrākaunui Falls, Tautuku Beach, Lake Wilkie, Cathedral Caves, Curio Bay**). Surprisingly, the Catlins also has a quirky side, including Blair Somerville's whimsical creations at the **Lost Gypsy Gallery** (p. 540) at Papatōwai. It's only a 2-hour drive without stops, but if you're enjoying the attractions it will take you the full day to reach **Invercargill** (p. 544). where you can park for the night.

Day 5: Southern Scenic Route to Te Anau

Continue your journey on the Southern Scenic Route, this time via Riverton, Tuatapere, and Manapouri to Te Anau. **Riverton** is a fishing and holiday destination nestled into the rocky coastline with sweeping views of the ocean, while Manapouri is the gateway to the Sounds of Fiordland (tours to **Doubtful Sound,** p. 491, start here). In about 15 minutes from Manapouri you will be in **Te Anau** (p. 484).

Day 6: Te Anau to Milford Sound

No driving today. Sign up for a small group tour to **Milford Sound** (p. 488). It's not that distant, but the road is tricky, the scenery can distract, and it's better viewed than driven, especially in a motorhome. Choose a day tour (such as **Trips & Tramps,** p. 489) that includes transfers, lunch photo opportunities, short walks, and a boat cruise on Milford Sound (seeing seals, dolphins, and waterfalls). Back in Te Anau, catch an evening screening of the film *Ata Whenua* at **Fiordland Cinema** (p. 487).

Day 7: Te Anau to Queenstown to Christchurch

On your last day in the ruggedly beautiful south, you'll drive to Queenstown via the rural villages of Mossburn and Athol, where you'll find coffee, snacks, and souvenirs. From Kingston on, the road north follows the shoreline of **Lake Wakatipu,** one of the most stunning drives in the country. Stop carefully for photographs—the road is narrow! Drop off your motorhome at the depot, then find a transfer into town to enjoy **Queenstown** (p. 450) and a night in a hotel for a change!

A CULTURAL & HISTORICAL TOUR OF THE NORTH ISLAND

With its authentic Māori tourism experiences, Aotearoa offers an opportunity to immerse yourself in an entirely new culture. This itinerary introduces you to Māori traditions, as well as to the early European settlers who also shaped today's New Zealand.

Day 1: Auckland & Northland

Pick up a rental car from the airport, and begin your drive to Northland, which retains a strong Māori influence. In **Whangārei,** stop for lunch and a tour at the **Hundertwasser Art Centre** (p. 138). which is also home to the **Wairau Māori Art Gallery.** After lunch, continue your drive to Paihia, the gateway to the **Bay of Islands.** Some of the earliest archaeological records of Polynesian explorers have been found here. Take the car ferry to romantic **Russell** (p. 148), the country's first European settlement and capital. Have dinner on the waterfront and spend the night.

Day 2: Waitangi Treaty Grounds

After a relaxing breakfast, catch the ferry back to Paihia and head to the **Waitangi Treaty Grounds** (p. 146), the country's most important historic site, where the signing of the first accord between the British Crown and the Māori people took place. You'll want to budget at least 3 hours to visit this huge site and take in a cultural performance. In the afternoon, enjoy a boat cruise among the islands with **Explore Group** (p. 148).

Day 3: Cape Reinga

From Paihia, it's a 2½-hour drive to sacred cultural site **Cape Reinga** (p. 158). One of the northernmost points in the country, it's where Māori spirits travel after death and enter the underworld, via an ancient pōhutukawa tree. It's also incredibly pretty, with the Tasman Sea and the Pacific Ocean colliding beneath a lighthouse in a spectacular swirl of currents. You'll need a full day to hit up other sites along the way, including the **Te Paki Sand Dunes** (p. 158) and **Ninety Mile Beach** (p. 158).

Demonstrating the use of traditional Polynesian *waka* (boats) at the Waitangi Treaty Grounds.

Return south, but this time via Northland's West Coast. Overnight in Ōmāpere on the **Kauri Coast.**

Day 4: Hokianga & Waipoua Forest

Spend your morning watching a cultural presentation at **Manea Footprints of Kupe** (p. 159), a 75-minute show and museum that tells the story of Aotearoa's first explorer. That afternoon, travel back through the **Waipoua Forest,** where **Tāne Mahuta** (p. 160), the country's biggest kauri tree, lives. Ask the interpreters on-site to tell you the story of Tāne Mahuta's role in the creation of the world. Hit the road by late afternoon, heading south toward Auckland. Instead of the city, we recommend staying overnight in the **Matakana** area (p. 131).

Day 5: The Bay of Plenty

From Matakana, it will take you just over 3 hours to get to the **Bay of Plenty,** but start your morning slowly, to avoid rush-hour congestion when skirting Auckland. Arriving in Tauranga in the early afternoon, cross the bridge to **Mount Maunganui** (p. 205) to grab lunch, then join the Māori-owned **Mauao Adventures** (p. 194) for a guided walk around the iconic peak of Mount Maunganui, including its ancient burial sites and birthing springs. That night, eat at **Izakai** (p. 205), which is renowned for its casual Japanese-Māori fusion pub food.

Day 6: Lake Aniwhenua

Drive 90 minutes inland to Lake Āniwhenua, where you'll find Māori-owned **Kohutapu Lodge** (p. 196). The family behind this regenerative accommodation business is renowned for giving back to the surrounding community. They'll also take you a tour of the **Whirinaki Te Pua-a-Tāne Conservation Park** (p. 196), where guides share traditional medicinal cures, stories, and history about the ancient forest. Overnight at the lodge and enjoy a *hāngī* meal.

Getting up close to stingrays with Dive Tatapouri (see p. 60).

Day 7: Tairāwhiti Gisborne

It's over 3 hours to Tairāwhiti Gisborne, on the east coast. Once there, download the **Te Papa app** and start a self-guided walking tour of Captain Cook's original landing site in the country—the same spot where Polynesian seafaring voyagers landed hundreds of years earlier. You can visit many *marae* by appointment, including **Te Poho-o-Rawiri Marae** (p. 270), one of the largest Māori *whare runanga* (meeting houses) in NZ. Overnight at **Tatapouri Bay Oceanside Accommodation** (p. 275).

Day 8: Tairāwhiti Gisborne & Rotorua

In the morning, see the area's wild stingrays with **Dive Tatapouri** (p. 273) and reflect on how the North Island is said to be a stingray that was fished up by the god Māui. Spend 4 hours driving to **Rotorua** (p. 207). That night, take in a cultural show and modern interpretation of Māori food at **Te Pā Tū** (p. 219).

Day 9: Auckland

Return to Auckland, where the exhibits at **Tāmaki Paenga Hira Auckland War Memorial Museum** (p. 80) will now hold so much more meaning, significance, and context.

THE REGIONS IN BRIEF

The North Island

AUCKLAND Auckland is, without a doubt, the most cosmopolitan of New Zealand's cities, with hundreds of restaurants, great shopping, first-rate tourist attractions, and a beautiful waterfront to explore. What you think of Auckland (and how much time you'll actually want to spend here) ultimately depends on how much you like cities. Some people think 2 nights isn't nearly enough; others are annoyed at themselves for spending that much time here. Using it as a base, however, you can head out from Waitematā Harbour for some of the world's finest sailing, marine wildlife watching, and fishing, or strike out on day trips to some of the North Island's best attractions, including the beautiful vineyards of Waiheke Island, the West Coast surf beaches, and the bush tracks of the Waitākere Ranges.

NORTHLAND **Te Tai Tokerau/Northland** deserves at least 2 to 3 nights to hit up its most important cultural, historical, and natural attractions, including the **Bay of Islands** (and the Waitangi Treaty Grounds), the **Waipoua Forest** (home to massive 2,000-year-old kauri trees), and **Cape Reinga.** While the Bay of Islands gets its fair share of tourism, head into the **Far North** and all the people suddenly fade from view. I'd argue that this area, of any in New Zealand, feels like an entirely different country, both in terms of its ecology and its culture, which is heavily influenced by both Māoridom and its remote location. Of course, if you're just looking to soak it all in, there's plenty of fishing, boating, camping and beaches to enjoy.

WAIKATO, THE BAY OF PLENTY & THE COROMANDEL With their population of glowworms, the **Waitomo Caves** have traditionally been Waikato's biggest attraction, although more recently Matamata's **Hobbiton** is coming a close second. In the region's largest city, Hamilton, **Hamilton Gardens** is the top such attraction in New Zealand. Also in Waikato is the hippie and surfer mecca of **Raglan** on the West Coast.

North Island at a Glance

The pastoral landscapes of the Waikato have been rebranded as Lord of the Rings territory at Hobbiton, near Matamata.

The sun-drenched paradise of the Bay of Plenty is increasingly popular with North American snowbirds and young surfers, thanks to its growing culinary scene, paired with beachy and outdoor offerings. The fast-growing port city of **Tauranga** and its beach suburb, **Mount Maunganui,** are thriving hubs; head inland towards the misty mountains of **Te Urewera** or farther south to **Whakatāne** and you'll find immersive rural Māori cultural experiences, alongside geothermal activity.

The **Coromandel Peninsula,** to the east of Auckland, is more rugged, with a craggy coastline and white sand beaches on the eastern side. Accommodation is mainly privately owned *baches* (cabins) and there are few restaurants, but its most famous attractions (**Cathedral Cove** and **Hot Water Beach**) don't necessarily require an overnight stay.

ROTORUA, TAUPŌ & RUAPEHU **Rotorua** (technically within the Bay of Plenty) is on almost every visitor's hit list, and some would say that makes the area objectionably touristy. I can't disagree. But! But! Rotorua is also objectively one of the country's top draws, both for its unusual geothermal landscape (impressive geysers, the largest hot springs in the world, bubbling pools of mud, and more) and outstanding Māori cultural shows. In terms of adventure tourism, Rotorua also gives Queenstown serious competition, with ziplining, mountain biking, Zorbing, and countless other wacky activities. All these pastimes can also be accessed from both **Tauranga** and **Taupō,** which are less tourist-crammed than Rotorua. The latter sits on the edges of Lake Taupō, the country's largest lake, a destination with plenty of family-friendly holiday activities.

South of Taupō in the **Ruapehu** region, the stunning volcanic landscape of **Tongariro National Park** is a paradise for outdoor adventurers, especially skiers. The region also holds **Whanganui National Park,** where lush native bush envelops one of the country's most beautiful rivers. Personally, I love Ruapehu, but it best suits travelers who aren't hung up on staying in the nicest hotel or eating the best meals.

TAIRĀWHITI GISBORNE & HAWKE'S BAY **Tairāwhiti Gisborne** and the **East Cape** are both largely untouched destinations rich in authentic Māori cultural experiences, with great surf beaches and lots of vineyards. You'll need a good chunk of time to visit one or both. My recommendation? If you have 2 weeks or less to spend in NZ, skip Gisborne and head straight to **Hawke's Bay.** A foodie fantasy made real, it's home to some of the country's best wineries, restaurants, cideries, breweries, distillers, and accommodations. It's also one of the top spots on the planet for Art Deco architecture.

TARANAKI & WHANGANUI If you want the best of small-town, provincial New Zealand, this is it. You can't help but feel that, stuck out here on its own western peninsula, it couldn't care less about the rest of the country. **New Plymouth** has a surprisingly vibrant cultural scene, **Mount Taranaki** and the sea are big attractions for trampers and surfers, and the region's gardens are stunning. Set on the edges of the Whanganui River, **Whanganui** has a thriving arts community with some very cool galleries.

WELLINGTON New Zealand's capital has a well-deserved reputation as one of the coolest little cities in the world. Whereas Auckland is what I'd call

Cathedral Cove Kayak Tours explores the white-sand beaches and wave-sculpted rocks of the Coromandel's east coast.

The Wellington Cable Car affords spectacular views on its steep climb to the top part of the city.

an "every city," the very walkable (and very windy) Wellington has a vibe all its own. Its young and entrepreneurial population has birthed top restaurants, vintage shops, performing arts venues, and a thriving craft beer scene. It's also home to the **Museum of New Zealand Te Papa Tongarewa,** the country's splendid national museum.

The South Island

MARLBOROUGH & NELSON If you travel via ferry from the North Island to **Picton,** you'll pass through the **Marlborough Sounds.** More than just a port stop, it's a destination in itself with bush-rimmed bays and inlets offering sailing, kayaking, hiking, biking, and wildlife watching. Nearby **Blenheim** is a sea of vineyards, producing globally recognized sauvignon blancs. Characterized by three national parks and good swimming beaches with golden sand, the **Nelson/Tasman** area on the shores of Tasman Bay is a top region to visit for the arts, crafts, wines, gourmet restaurants, and alternative off-grid living. Outdoor pursuits run the gamut from wet and wild (canyoning) to calm and sunny (kayaking in **Abel Tasman National Park**).

WEST COAST & THE GLACIERS It takes a special type of person to make it out here on the wet and wild West Coast, so characters abound, especially from **Greymouth** northbound to remote **Karamea.** South of Greymouth is where most of the tourists head, first to the cool little coastal town of **Hokitika,** then onwards to the **Franz Josef** and **Fox Glaciers.** This is raw beauty at its best, where you'll find glaciers reaching nearly to the coast, massive mountains, and lush West Coast rainforest.

CHRISTCHURCH & CANTERBURY Christchurch is the starting point for many people heading out on their South Island explorations. Two massive earthquakes in 2010 and 2011 caused much damage, but a new Christchurch

South Island at a Glance

The resident sheep herd at Wilderness Lodge, set amid the spectacular mountain peaks of Arthur's Pass.

has risen from the rebuild. Beyond the city, the surrounding Canterbury region offers cycling, hiking, climbing, and surfing; the city is an excellent base for exploring the seaside town of **Akaroa,** the mountain peaks of **Arthur's Pass,** whale watching at **Kaikōura,** the vineyards of the **Waipara Valley,** or the hot springs of **Methven** or **Hanmer Springs.**

QUEENSTOWN & FIORDLAND Although **Queenstown** is known as the "adventure capital," it's got something to suit everyone, including heaps of family-friendly activities, fascinating historical sites, and even its own wine region, the **Gibbston Valley.** It should go without saying it's not a hidden secret; year-round, its streets are packed with international visitors and Kiwis celebrating bachelor or bachelorette parties. Nearby **Wānaka** will appeal to those looking for a little more space, with its wide-open lake and distant mountains. Fiordland's **Milford Sound** (which is best accessed after overnighting in **Te Anau**—not Queenstown), also lives up to its reputation—and more. This is what people come to New Zealand for, with dramatic peaks and countless waterfalls flowing directly into the sea (countless visitors, too, unfortunately).

A Glacier Explorers tour visits the iceberg-fed Tasman Lake in Aoraki/Mount Cook National Park.

THE MACKENZIE COUNTRY, AORAKI/MOUNT COOK & WAITAKI DISTRICT This is the region of superlatives: postcard-perfect vistas of the country's highest mountain (**Aoraki/Mount Cook**), the bluest lakes (**Tekapo** and **Pukaki**), and the brightest milky way (within the **Dark Sky Reserve**). You don't have to be outdoorsy to love it, but if you're a hiker, mountaineer, cyclist, or birdwatcher, you'll get that much more out of it. Yet, despite being one of NZ's most trafficked tourist destinations, there are considerably fewer restaurants and accommodations at both Lake Tekapō and Aoraki/Mount Cook Village than you might expect. The Waitaki District has a string of picture-perfect lakes and, in **Ōamaru,** a splendidly preserved Victorian town that has become ground zero for the retro-futuristic steampunk aesthetic.

The hoiho/yellow-eyed penguin, the rarest penguin on the planet, is most easily spotted on the Otago Peninsula outside of Dunedin.

DUNEDIN, SOUTHLAND & STEWART ISLAND **Dunedin** is gorgeous and gothic, with grand buildings and rich Scottish heritage. And **Southland**? This quiet achiever has so many outstanding natural features that authorities have designated its coastal circuit the "Southern Scenic Route," which includes **the Catlins** area. Large and barely populated, **Rakiura/Stewart Island** is one of the best places to see a kiwi, but even more than that, its awesome skies and landscapes make it simply one of New Zealand's most special places.

AUCKLAND

This is it: our biggish, brashest, and most cosmopolitan center, the City of Sails, where you can almost always see the Sky Tower, even when you're wandering in the rugged bush of the Waitākere Ranges or sipping a pinot gris on Waiheke Island. Visitors will love exploring the area around the Viaduct Harbor and Britomart, with its shopping and restaurants, and the city's galleries, museums, and other urban delights are world class. But even here, just as in the rest of New Zealand, nature takes center stage—Auckland is a city of volcanoes, islands, forest, and beaches.

ESSENTIALS

Arriving

BY PLANE **Auckland Airport** (aucklandairport.co.nz; ✆ **09/275-0789**) is 21km (14 miles) south of the city beside the Manukau Harbour. It's about 30 minutes from the central city when traffic is flowing normally. The **International Terminal** has a shopping area with around 30 retail outlets, including a duty-free shop. The **Domestic Terminal** is a 10-minute walk from the International Terminal (follow the signs); there's also a free inter-terminal bus, departing every 15 minutes between 5am and 10:30pm.

If you have time to kill in the airport, you can store your bags in the International Terminal (by door 3 of the ground floor) with **Secure Travel** (secure-travel.co.nz; ✆ **09/255-5659**), starting from NZ$12. In the domestic terminal, you'll find self-service storage lockers on the ground floor of carpark R, which can be paid for with a card. Luggage carts are free of charge and available throughout both terminals. Free unlimited Wi-Fi is also available in both terminals, although you have to provide an email address to use it. For currency exchange, **Travelex** (travelex.co.nz; ✆ **0800/666-391** in NZ) booths are located both before and after security in the international terminal, but you'll get a better exchange rate at one of the airport's **ATMs,** which can be found in both terminals.

Depending on the size of your group, **Super Shuttle** (supershuttle.co.nz; ✆ **09/522-5100**) may be the most affordable option for getting downtown. It offers door-to-door shared transport, starting from NZ$35 per person. It may be booked in advance, or upon arrival at the airport.

At the international terminal, a taxi stand is located near door 8 (and near door 4 at the domestic terminal). You can expect to pay a flat rate of between NZ$62 and NZ$99 into the city. Try **Auckland Co-op Taxis** (cooptaxi.co.nz; ✆ **09/300-3000**) or **Corporate Cabs** (corporatecabs.co.nz; ✆ **09/377-0773**).

Ride-share services are also available. These include **Uber** (uber.com), **Bolt** (bolt.eu/en-nz), and local company **Zoomy** (zoomy.co.nz), which pays drivers a fair wage and is often the most affordable. Both operate from the airport and may be pre-booked via their respective apps. The designated ride-share pickup areas are well-signed and can be found outside door 11 at the international terminal, and behind the multi-story parking lot at the domestic terminal. Ride-share fares vary dependent on demand and time of day, but you can generally expect to pay about NZ$50 to NZ$60 to get to the heart of Auckland from the airport.

BY TRAIN & COACH (BUS) The **Britomart Transport Centre,** operated by **Auckland Transport** (at.govt.nz; ✆ **09/366-4467**), is the city's major transportation hub, located at the bottom of Queen Street in the central city by the ferry terminals. It's where intercity and commuter rail, buses, taxis, and ferry services connect. The building is open Monday to Thursday 5am to 11pm, Friday 5:30am to 1am, Saturday 6:30am to 12:30am, and Sunday 6:30am to 11pm. There you'll find food outlets, convenience stores, toilets, ticketing agents, and a transport information booth. Electronic lockers for storing small to medium-sized luggage can be found at the downtown ferry terminal. They may be paid for with a credit card.

Auckland's Settlement

The te reo Māori name for Auckland is *Tāmaki Makaurau,* which roughly translates as "desired by many." It's not because Aucklanders have loose morals: In pre-European times, the area was coveted by many *iwi* (tribes) for its fertile, volcanic soils and its handy locations between two resource-rich coasts. Over the centuries, it was claimed by at least 18 tribes. The Hauraki Gulf was first settled by Māori about 700 years ago, with some of the earliest settlements dating back to the 12th century. At the peak of their prosperity in 1750, the Tāmaki tribes' population numbered in the tens of thousands. Then, in 1840, William Hobson chose the Auckland isthmus as the site for the country's first capital (once again, thanks to its abundant resources) naming it after his patron, Lord Auckland.

As you drive across Auckland, you'll see dozens of hills scattered across the city, including Mount Eden and One Tree Hill. In fact, these are actually the 53 cones of the Auckland volcanic field, which is not extinct but dormant. These Tūpuna Maunga (ancestral mountains) are at the heart of the spiritual, ancestral, and cultural identity of the 13 *iwi* and *hapū* (Māori tribes and subtribes) of Auckland—and to this day many of the peaks display the horizontal terracing that signifies a *pā* site (a fortification built on a hill) was once there. Most of them double as urban parks, with only pedestrian access to their summits, and the spectacular view they give you over the city's suburbs and harbors is well worth the short climb.

Geared towards international visitors, **Great Journeys of New Zealand** (greatjourneysnz.com; ✆ **04/495-0775**) runs a **Northern Explorer train** route that stops in Hamilton, Otorohanga (for Waitomo Caves), Taumarunui, Waimarino (Tongariro National Park), Ohakune, Palmerstone North, and Wellington. It's primarily intended as a scenic train (rather than a commuter route), so it doesn't run every day, but it does the trick if your timing is flexible, with journeys from NZ$249. **InterCity** (intercity.co.nz; ✆ **09/623-1503**) buses arrive and depart from the SkyCity bus terminal, 102 Hobson St.

BY CAR Many major rental agencies can be found at the Auckland airport, but be aware that the counters for some (including Enterprise and Alamo) are located off-site in the Park-and-Ride lot. It's a 10-minute ride from the terminal in a free shuttle bus, which runs every 10 minutes 24/7 from a clearly marked pickup/drop-off point in front of both terminals.

State Highway 1 (SH1) goes through Auckland and out the other side: You'll be arriving in the city from the south if you come from the airport.

Visitor Information

The official visitor website for the region is **aucklandnz.com**. The Department of Conservation's (DOC's) website (doc.govt.nz) has information about national parks, marine reserves, walks, and DOC campgrounds.

The **Tāmaki Makaurau Auckland isite–Visitor Information Centre** (✆ **09/365-9918**) is located across the road from the main ferry terminal, at 188 Quay St. It's open 9am to 5pm on weekdays and until 4pm on weekends.

Special Events

The annual **Auckland Anniversary Day Regatta** ♥♥♥ (regatta.org.nz; ✆ **0800/734-2882** in NZ), held on the last Monday in January, is a brilliant spectacle on the water. The annual **Auckland Arts Festival** ♥ (aaf.co.nz; ✆ **09/309-0989**) finishes off the summer in March with an eclectic mix of the best local and international arts and cultural events. Also in March, the city's status as the largest Polynesian city in the world is celebrated with the **Pasifika Festival** (facebook.com/PasifikaFestivalAKL), showcasing food, performing arts, and Pacific culture. In midwinter (June–July) the **Matariki Festival** (matarikifestival.org.nz) brings in the Māori new year with a variety of star-themed and cultural events. And in November, the **Auckland Marathon** (aucklandmarathon.co.nz) is pretty much your only chance to head over the iconic Harbour Bridge on foot. There are five race distances, all offering spectacular scenery as you puff your way around the coastline of this watery city.

For more events, visit **aucklandnz.com** or **aucklandlive.co.nz**.

City Layout

Greater Auckland is really five regions—cosmopolitan Auckland, multicultural Manukau, beachy North Shore, the beautiful rainforest of the western Waitākere Ranges, and out East, where city meets country—plus the two most popular islands: Waiheke and Great Barrier Island/Aotea. You can pick up a city map from the visitor center.

Aucklanders work and play along the city's extensive waterfront, with two protected harbors.

MAIN ARTERIES & STREETS Auckland's main drag is **Queen Street,** which ends at **Customs Street,** 1 block from waterfront **Quay Street.** At the other end of Queen Street is **Karangahape Road** (known simply as "K Road").

Neighborhoods in Brief

Waitematā Harbor Along the waterfront you'll find, from west to east: the **Wynyard Quarter** (a newer waterfront development), **Viaduct Harbor** (packed with restaurants and shops), and **Queens Wharf** (home to the ferry terminal), flanked by upscale shopping and entertainment districts **Commercial Bay** and **Britomart.** Major big-box hotels and chain stores are in the surrounding area.

Ponsonby/Herne Bay Bohemian (Ponsonby) meets rich (Herne Bay): These two stylish suburbs are possibly Auckland's hippest place to stay, full of trendy restaurants, TV stars, and wannabes. The lovely old wooden buildings also house some gorgeous specialty shops and delightful B&Bs.

Mount Eden/Epsom In these leafy suburbs, rich folk live in enormous wooden mansions, next door to students in rather more rundown shared villas. The villages are pretty and filled with good eateries and shops, not to mention B&Bs if you want somewhere quiet to base yourself. One Tree Hill and Cornwall Park are close by.

Parnell/Newmarket Two more well-heeled suburbs, Parnell Village has great restaurants and cafes and is handy to the museum and the lovely Auckland Domain, while Newmarket is great for shopping, including Westfield, the country's largest mall.

Mission Bay/St. Heliers Did you bring your rollerblades? This is where you can show off your prowess on a sunny day when all you have to worry about is which restaurant-with-a-million-dollar-view to eat at later.

Devonport/Takapuna Across the bay, Devonport is an "old money" suburb, Takapuna a bit more nouveau riche. "Devo" has some terrific B&Bs and pretty shops. Don't tackle the Harbour Bridge at rush hour; take a ferry instead, like the locals do.

Titirangi The gateway to the Waitākere Ranges, this western suburb is where you can find Airbnbs and holiday rentals immersed in native bush, along with cafes, art galleries, and a more laid-back Auckland experience.

Getting Around

BY TOUR BUS The **Auckland Explorer Bus** (explorerbus.co.nz; ✆ **0800/439-756** in NZ) is a very convenient method of getting to and from the city's top attractions. This sightseeing double-decker bus leaves every 30 minutes from all stops, with the first bus of the day departing at 9am from 23 Customs Street East. The last tour terminates at 5pm. It stops at nine major attractions, including SkyCity, the Auckland Museum, and SEA LIFE Kelly Tarlton's Aquarium. You can purchase 24- or 48-hour bus passes, starting from NZ$70 adults, NZ$35 children, and NZ$190 for families. Combo passes, which cover entry to the major sites as well as the bus fare, are a smart purchase.

BY PUBLIC TRANSIT **Auckland Transport** (**AT;** at.govt.nz; ✆ **0800/10-30-80** in NZ) operates the city's buses, trains, and ferries. You can plan trips and see timetables on its website.

Cash is not accepted on buses. On all public transit, you can now pay with contactless debit and credit cards or Apple Pay. That costs the same as using an **AT HOP card** (at.govt.nz/bus-train-ferry/at-hop-card), so for a short stay I wouldn't bother getting a card unless you're travelling with children (you can only get these reduced fares using an AT HOP card). Fares start at just NZ$0.85 and work their way up to NZ$10—but there's also a daily cap, so you'll never pay more than NZ$20 in a day.

AT HOP cards cost NZ$5 and can be pre-loaded with any amount you choose. They can be purchased at most convenience stores (see AT's website for a full list of retailers), the isite, train stations, and from a vending machine at the airport, just outside door 4 at the domestic terminal. There is also an AT HOP app available for download on the app store, which allows you to check your card's balance, plan trips, and receive notifications when it's time to get on and off. Paying for your trip with this app is not yet possible.

By Bus The **CityLink Bus** (red) does a circuit from the Wynyard Quarter, along Queen Street, along K Road and back again every 7 to 8 minutes from 6am to midnight. The **InnerLink Bus** (green) makes a slightly bigger circle, from Britomart to Parnell, Newmarket, along K Road and Ponsonby Road, and back to Britomart via SkyCity. It runs every 10 or 15 minutes from 6:10am to midnight. The **OuterLink Bus** (orange) leaves from Wellesley Street to inner-city suburbs Parnell, Newmarket, Epsom, Balmoral, Mount Eden, St. Lukes, Mount Albert, Point Chevalier, Westmere, and Herne Bay. It runs every 15 minutes from 6am to midnight.

By Train The suburban train system runs from Britomart in Auckland on four lines: the Eastern (to Manukau, which in the future will run all the way to the airport), the Western (to Swanson, on the eastern edges of the Waitākere ranges), the Southern to Papakura, and the Onehunga (to Onehunga).

By Ferry Ferries to Devonport, Waiheke Island, and other Hauraki Gulf destinations depart from Queen's Wharf roughly every 30 to 40 minutes. Most ferries are part of the AT network and can be paid for with an AT HOP or contactless card. The ferry to Waiheke, however, is operated by Fullers, and must be paid for separately. If you want to take a car to Waiheke, the car ferry leaves from a completely different location, out east in Half Moon Bay. (See "A Side Trip to Waiheke Island," p. 119, for details.)

BY SCOOTER There are a number of shared scooter operators in Auckland, notably **Lime** (li.me) and **Flamingo** (flamingoscooters.com/city/auckland). Users must download the app to use and pay for the scooters, from NZ$1 to unlock and NZ$0.45/minute. Helmets are not compulsory but are recommended and often supplied with the scooters. Scooters may be ridden on the sidewalk or the road.

BY TAXI Typical rates for taxis start at about NZ$5 and charge NZ$2.50–NZ$3 per kilometer (0.62 mile). You can flag one down, phone for one, or go to the main taxi stand on the corner of Customs Street West and Queen Street. **Auckland Co-Op Taxis** (cooptaxi.co.nz; ✆ **09/300-3000**) and **Corporate Cabs** (corporatecabs.co.nz; ✆ **09/377-0773**) are both reliable. Ride-share services include **Uber** (uber.com), **Bolt** (bolt.eu/en-nz), and NZ-based **Zoomy** (zoomy.co.nz). All three use surge pricing, so while they're typically cheaper than cabs, they can be more expensive in periods of high demand.

BY CAR Traffic congestion is a real problem in Auckland, especially during morning and evening rush hours. Parking is also quite expensive in the downtown city core, with most hotels charging NZ$50 a night for valet parking. Paid parking lots (open 24/7 and found throughout the central city) will also cost you around NZ$30 to NZ$50 per day. For cost savings, it's best to avoid picking up a rental car until you're ready to leave the city. Car rentals from downtown locations also tend to be more affordable than those at airport locations.

[FastFACTS] AUCKLAND

Currency Exchange Most banks, both in the city and in the suburbs, can exchange money. They are generally open Monday to Friday 9am to 5pm. You'll find several **Travelex NZ** branches at Auckland International Airport and the Domestic Airport, but frankly, using an **ATM** will get you a better exchange rate.

Dentists There are usually emergency dentists in the **White Cross accident and urgent medical centers,** which are all over Auckland. Go to whitecross.co.nz to find the nearest one. These have different opening hours, usually closing between 8pm and 10pm, though some are open 24 hours a day.

Doctors The **CityMed Medical Centre,** 8 Albert St. (citymed.co.nz; ✆ **09/377-5525**), is centrally located, or try one of the **White Cross clinics** (whitecross.co.nz).

Embassies & Consulates Embassies are in Wellington (see chapter 17). Auckland has consulates of the **United States,** Level 3, 23 Customs St. E (✆ **09/303-2724**); **Canada,** Level 9, 48 Emily Place (✆ **09/309-3690**); **Ireland,** Level 3, 205 Queen St. (✆ **09/977-2252**); and the **United Kingdom,** IAG House, 151 Queen St. (✆ **09/303-2973**).

Emergencies Dial ✆ **111** to call the police, fire, or ambulance services. For non-urgent police matters, call the **Central Police Station** (✆ **09/302-6400**).

Hospitals **Auckland City Hospital,** 2 Park Rd.,

Grafton (✆ **09/367-0000**), is the city's main trauma and accident hospital.

Lost Property Call the Central Police Station (✆ **09/302-6400**) or any local police station.

Luggage Storage & Lockers You could ask at the isite, but a better bet is checking sites like **Stasher** (stasher.com) or **Bounce** (bounce.com) which both have lockers in various locations around the city; prices start from NZ$3.50.

Newspapers & Magazines The *New Zealand Herald* is the daily Auckland paper.

Post Office For *poste restante* (held mail) pickup, go to Victoria Street Box Lobby at 151 Victoria Street W. For other branches, visit nzpost.co.nz.

EXPLORING AUCKLAND

The Top Attractions

All Blacks Experience ♥♥ ATTRACTION Even if you don't watch rugby, you probably know the All Blacks; the sports team is responsible for introducing Māori culture to the world with their famed pre-game *haka* performances. Opened in 2020, the immersive All Blacks Experience covers the history of rugby in NZ and its role in shaping the country's national identity. Frankly, how you'll rate this attraction heavily depends on your level of interest in the sport. The 45-minute guided tour includes learning about the team's dressing room rituals, interactive team games that require zero athletic ability, and a simulation of what it's like to walk out onto the field to a cheering crowd and face the All Blacks as they perform the ceremonial haka. The highlight, though—and the thing you'll want to budget extra time for—is the kid-pleasing **Step Up** section, where you can test your own skills, including agility, kicking, and passing. Regardless of whether you're a superfan or just learning about rugby, you'll learn something new.

88 Federal St., Level 4, Sky City Precinct. experienceallblacks.com. ✆ **0800/2665-2239.** NZ$69 adults, NZ$35 children 5–11, NZ$173 family of four. Daily 9:30am–5pm. Last tour departs 4pm.

The All Blacks rugby team intimidating the competition by performing a traditional *haka*.

A young couple in an old masters gallery at Auckland Art Gallery Toi o Tāmaki.

Auckland Art Gallery Toi o Tāmaki ♥♥ ART MUSEUM New Zealand's most important art space, this is the best place to see people stroking their little beards and opining intelligently about what they see in front of them. And what they see is a really pretty impressive collection of more than 15,000 artworks set on four floors: historic, modern, and contemporary New Zealand art, plus international paintings, sculptures, and prints from the 11th century to today, all enclosed in a complex that melds an early French Renaissance–style building from 1887 with a rather expensive extension completed in 2011. It won the World Architecture Festival's World Building of the Year award in 2013, so enjoy the extraordinary space as well as the artwork. As for the art, it runs the gamut from works by Old Masters to groundbreaking Māori and Pacific pieces you simply won't see anywhere else. Exhibitions change regularly. We highly recommend the gallery tours, but they must be booked in advance. Budget an hour for your visit.

Corner of Wellesley & Kitchener sts. aucklandartgallery.com. ✆ **09/379-1349.** Free admission; fees for some special exhibitions. Daily 10am–5pm.

Auckland Zoo ♥♥ ZOO Even people who don't like zoos should enjoy this one. Set among the trees next to Western Springs Park, conservation and natural environments drive everything at this not-for-profit outfit, where admission fees help support conservation projects here and overseas. The zoo is organized by continent; there's an African Safari Track (including cheetahs, giraffes, lions, rhinos), a South East Asia Track (orangutans, tigers, otters, and a new climate-controlled humid wetland forest), Australian and South American sections featuring kangaroos and monkeys, and Te Wao Nui, showcasing

Central Auckland

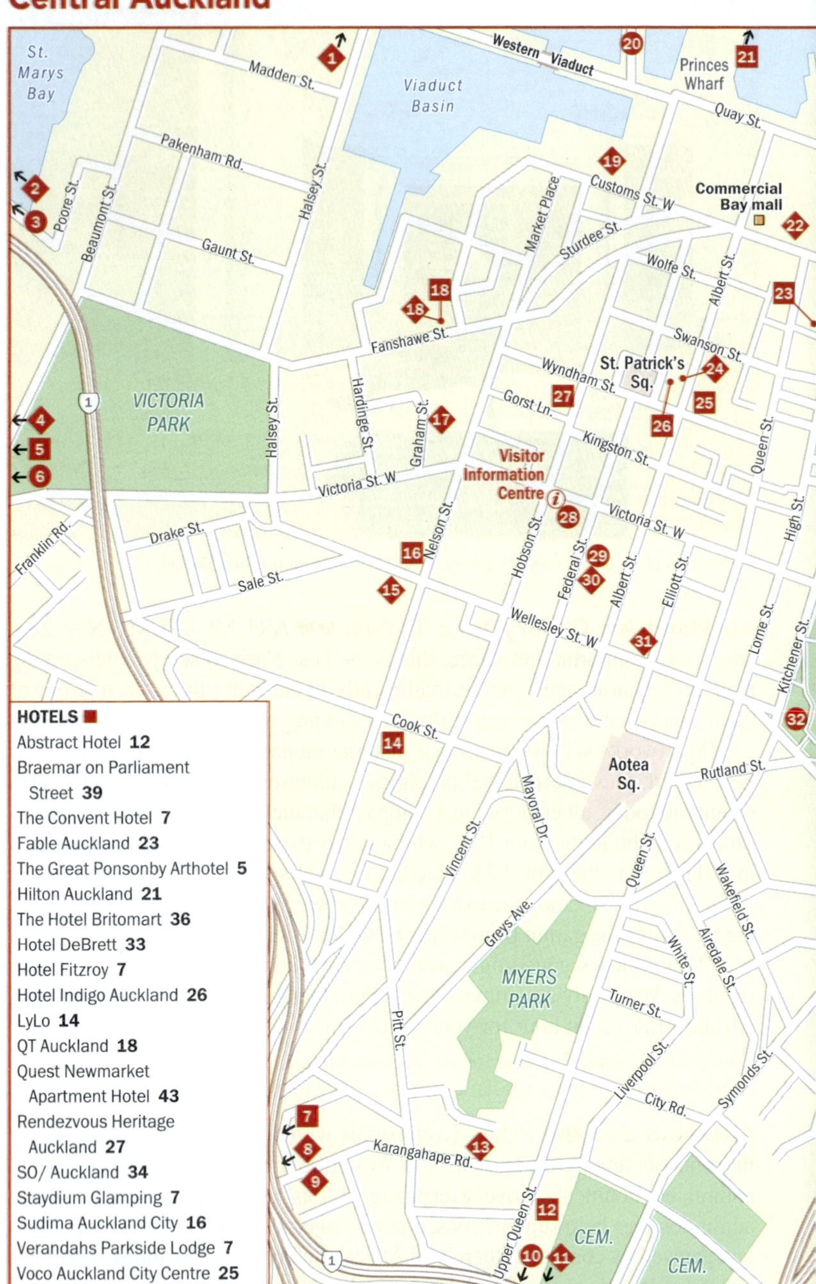

ATTRACTIONS
All Blacks Experience 29
Auckland Art Gallery Toi o Tāmaki 32
Auckland Bridge Climb and Bungy 3
Auckland Zoo 6
Eden Park Tours 10
Museum of Transport and Technology 6
New Zealand Maritime Museum 20
Sky Tower 28
Tāmaki Paenga Hira Auckland War Memorial Museum 44
Wētā Workshop Unleashed 29
RESTAURANTS
Amano 38
Auckland Fish Market 1
Baduzzi 1
Bistro Saine 24
Blue Rose Catering 11
Bodega Deli and Eatery 8
Café Hanoi 35
Cazador 11
Cibo 40
Cocoro 8
Dizengoff 4
Elliott Stables 31
The Engine Room 2
Esther 18
Federal St. at SkyCity 30
Forest 11
The French Café 11
Gemmayze Street 13
Harbour Eats 22
Just Like Martha 11
Kingi 37
Non Solo Pizza 41
Odette's 15
Origine 22
Ponsonby Central 8
Prego 4
Sails 2
San Ray 8
Scratch Bakers 17
Soul Bar & Bistro 19
Sri Penang 9
Tasca 42
Queens Wharf
Captain Cook Wharf
Marsden Wharf
Tyler St.
Quay St.
Britomart mall
Galway St.
Commerce St.
Customs St. E
Britomart Pl.
Gore St.
Fort St.
Beach Rd.
Shortland St.
Emily Place
Chancery St.
Eden Crescent
Anzac Ave.
Kitchener St.
Bowen Ave.
Waterloo Quadrant
Parliament St.
Ronayne St.
ALBERT PARK
Princes St.
Symonds St.
Alten Rd.
Churchill St.
Parnell Rise
Wynyard St.
Wellesley St. E
Grafton Rd.
CARLAW PARK
Cheshire St.
Falcon St.
Ruskin St.
Parnell Rd.
Scarborough Terr.
Stanley St.
Gibraltar Cres.
AUCKLAND DOMAIN
16
NORTH ISLAND
Auckland
SOUTH ISLAND
Wellington
Christchurch
Dunedin
Grafton Rd.
0 0.25 mi
0 0.25 km

Auckland Food Tours

With its wealth of incredibly fresh foods and delicious produce—think seafood, top-quality beef and lamb, world-renowned wine—New Zealand is a very attractive foodie destination. Food tours of Auckland play on that interest, allowing visitors to meet artisan producers and sample their wares. **The Big Foody ♥♥** (thebigfoody.com; ✆ **0800/366-386**) offers three tempting options daily, including the Auckland in the Afternoon walking tour (NZ$205), which focuses on chocolate, ice cream, and locally crafted beers and wine; or the morning Tastebud Tour (NZ$265), which goes by minibus to the farmer's market on the weekends, a coffee roaster on weekdays, and many places in between.

In the hills, you'll find **Nourishing Nature ♥♥♥** (velskov.com), a unique—if not cheap—travel experience that, as it says on the tin, is nourishing in all possible senses. **Velskov**—the name means "well forest" in host Mamakan's native Danish—is a 10-acre native forest farm high in the Waitākere Ranges, 45 minutes from central Auckland. Over 4 hours, you'll learn about the New Zealand bush; forage edible leaves, berries, and fungi; and help to prepare these traditional delicacies alongside artisanal cheeses, meats, and bread in a spectacular open-air glasshouse inspired by the *pīwakawaka* (native fantail)—which you're likely to see flitting about as you forage. You'll end by planting a native tree. Book direct or via the Hotel Britomart, which will add transport from your accommodation for an extra fee. It's available on Wednesdays, 9am to 2:30pm (also on other days for groups of 6 or more) and costs NZ$399 per person.

Baking artisanal bread in the glasshouse on a Nourishing Nature food tour.

Farther afield, **Matakana Tours ♥♥** (matakanatours.co.nz; ✆ **09/422-2500**) offers day trips to the northern Matakana region, where you'll taste the region's finest and meet the makers, including winemakers, chocolatiers, and oyster farmers. On an all-day taste tour (with pickups from your accommodation in Auckland), you'll typically visit two wineries and three producers. Prices run NZ$325 and up.

indigenous species like little blue penguins, fur seals, and kiwi. Every day there are many excellent free, interactive talks given by the keepers all over the zoo—I especially recommend the Hidden New Zealand one at 1pm in Te Wao Nui (don't be late, since they shut the doors) where you can get a close-up look at giant wētā, tuatara, and various native birds.

Motions Rd., Western Springs. aucklandzoo.co.nz. ✆ **09/360-3805.** Admission varies according to demand, NZ$29–NZ$35 adults, NZ$17–NZ$20 children 4–14. Open daily 9:30am–5:30pm; last admission 4:35pm. Parking NZ$8.

Eden Park Tours ♥ TOUR Originally a natural amphitheater formed by a nearby volcano, the hallowed ground of Eden Park stadium is home to the All Blacks, NZ's national rugby team, and is the largest sports stadium in the country. On this backstage tour, you'll have the opportunity to go sit in the coach's hot seat, visit the players' changing rooms, walk out onto the field and see the stadium's best-kept secrets (like its legendary "rock room"). Not just for sports fans, this 90-minute tour also examines the stadium's historic and cultural role, as well as its architecture and engineering. For adrenaline junkies, there's the **Rooftop Walk** ♥—a stroll 110 feet over the field, which offers unparalleled views of Mount Eden, One Tree Hill, and the Waitākere Ranges. You'll be rewarded for your bravery with a photo of you hanging out over the turf.

Reimers Ave., Kingsland. edenpark.co.nz. ✆ **09/815-5551.** Stadium tours NZ$50 adults, NZ$20 children 6–15, families NZ$100; rooftop tours NZ$89 adults. Thurs–Sun 2pm. Tour times subject to availability. Rooftop tours offered upon request.

Museum of Transport and Technology (MOTAT) ♥ MUSEUM Victorian brass-helmeted firemen pedaling around on ancient bikes with hoses attached, bewhiskered gentlemen working at a forge, ladies in period costume doing pioneer things—these are all sights you might see at MOTAT, along with a plethora of planes, trains, and automobiles. MOTAT is the biggest museum of its type in the country, covering 16 hectares (40 acres) in beautiful Western Springs park, 5km (3 miles) from the city center. It has permanent exhibitions, such as the innovative, interactive **Te Puawānanga Science and Technology Centre,** as well as changing displays. A vintage tram carries visitors to the Aviation Hall, located in a separate building. Skip the overpriced cafe and have a picnic at Western Springs—look out for the black swans.

805 Great North Rd., Western Springs. motat.org.nz. ✆ **0800/668-2869** in NZ, or 09/815-5800. NZ$19 adults, NZ$10 children 5–15, NZ$45 families. Daily 10am–4pm.

Sky Tower ♥ ATTRACTION At 328m (1,076 ft.), the Sky Tower is the tallest manmade structure in the Southern Hemisphere, affording views over the sprawling mass of Auckland and its islands and harbors. It has two observation decks, including a glass lift and glass floor panels. Access to the observation decks is by three glass-fronted elevators, which can whiz up the building in 40 seconds. The Sky Deck is the highest public viewing area, with 360-degree views through seamless glass. How you'll feel about this attraction really depends on how deep your pockets are. Personally, I think it's a steep fee to pay, given the number of high-rise hotels that have opened in recent years with rooftop bars offering beautiful vistas of the city and beyond. (A cocktail costs less.) But hey—to each their own.

What might be more worth the outlay are the thrill rides attached to the structure. Visitors can get outside the glass observation deck on AJ Hackett's **SkyWalk** ♥♥ (NZ$215), a platform on the tower's exterior. They're strapped in, but there are no guardrails. Next level up on the scary scale: **SkyJump** ♥♥

(NZ$330), which is kind of like a foot-first bungy, plunging down 53 stories at 85 km/hour (53 miles/hour).

SkyCity, Victoria & Federal sts. skytower.co.nz. ✆ **0800/759-2489** in NZ, or 09/363-6000. NZ$47 adults, NZ$32 ages 10–14, NZ$25 children 3-9, NZ$125 families. Book in advance online for discounts. Daily 8:30am–late.

A brave soul does the SkyJump from the Sky Tower.

Tāmaki Paenga Hira Auckland War Memorial Museum ♥♥♥

MUSEUM This first-rate museum experience gives a marvelous introduction to New Zealand history and culture. Its collection of Māori and Polynesian artifacts is the world's largest, but that's just the beginning of the attractions here, part of which is the architecture of the building itself. Crafted from Portland stone, it was designed as a war memorial to the heroic valor of the New Zealand soldier and the "classical" tragedy of battles such as Gallipoli; its colonnades are said to be almost a replica of the Parthenon's in Greece. The museum stands alone in the Auckland Domain, on the rim of an ancient volcano surrounded by parks and gardens. Of the two entrances, the original harbor entrance has stunning views; the newer rear dome entrance in the Atrium shows off contemporary New Zealand architecture.

Get a shaky start at **Volcanoes,** a gallery that introduces you to the turbulent natural history of Auckland, one of the only cities in the world built on an active (but dormant) volcano field. The interactive movie room, simulating the birth of a new volcano, will have you thinking we're slightly crazy for living here at all.

Key attractions in the extensive **He Taonga Māori (Māori Treasures) Gallery** include an impressive 25m (80-ft.) war canoe chiseled from one enormous *tōtara* trunk and covered with intricate carvings. That same artistry is reflected in the 26m (85-ft.) *wharenui* (meetinghouse), with its carved and painted walls and rafters. Also on display are greenstone weapons, tools, and feather cloaks. Twice a day—at 11am and 1:30pm—*kapa haka* performances by members of the local Ngāti Whātua Māori *iwi* (tribe) bring the culture to life. It's well worth the additional cost of NZ$35 adults, NZ$18 ages 5 to 13, and NZ$94 families. (In 2025, asbestos was discovered in the building's roof, requiring extensive repairs; the Māori gallery may still be closed when you visit, but the performances still happen, and the artifacts can be seen in other areas of the museum.)

The other thing that's worth the cost? The guided tour, which will point out objects you might otherwise miss and provide important context typically not

Kapa haka cultural performances at the Tāmaki Paenga Hira Auckland War Memorial Museum.

included on tiny placards. If you've just arrived in NZ, these two add-ons are an excellent introduction and starting point for things you might experience elsewhere in the country, particularly where Māori history and culture is concerned. The **Gallery Highlights Tour ♥♥**, held daily at 10:45am and 2:15pm, costs NZ$20 adults, NZ$10 for ages 5 to 15.

The museum is easy to negotiate. Just remember that the first floor is about the people, the second is about the land, and the third is the war memorial. The moody **Pacific Pathways** houses a world-renowned collection of Pacific artifacts; *New Zealand at War: Scars on the Heart* tells an emotional story of New Zealand in conflict, from the Land Wars of the 1840s to its present-day peacekeeping operations. The first-floor **Natural History Galleries** showcase everything from dinosaur skeletons to live seaside rock pools.

To get the most of your visit, allow 3 hours minimum. An on-site cafe is open during museum hours (although the service can be patchy, and the coffee isn't always the best). There are two very good shops worth a visit. Be sure to take a stroll around the magnificent **Auckland Domain sculpture walk** featuring eight works by New Zealand artists. A map can be found online at edmistontrust.org.nz/major-projects/domain-sculpture-walk.

Auckland Domain. aucklandmuseum.com. ✆ **09/309-0443.** NZ$28 adults, NZ$14 children 5–15. Mon–Fri 10am–5pm (Tues until 8:30pm), Sat–Sun 9am–5pm.

Wētā Workshop Unleashed ♥♥♥ ATTRACTION From secret doorways, to a mini house of horrors, to getting miniaturized in *Honey, I Shrunk the Kids* fashion, Wētā Workshop's attraction is 90-minutes of non-stop interactive fun. The special effects company, best known for the Lord of the Rings franchise, also has an attraction in Wellington (see p. 323); choosing between the two ultimately depends on your interests and group. The Auckland site is more of a Universal Studios–style attraction, which I'd argue is better value for money, more fun for kids (although there are some bits that may scare smaller children; these can be bypassed upon request), and way more

Iconic Rangitoto

Rising up from the Hauraki Gulf, the symmetrical cone of Rangitoto Island is one of Auckland's most visible icons. Of the 48 dormant volcanoes scattered across the Auckland region, it is the largest and the youngest. The island is accessible by ferry during the day, and visitors can walk up a scoria path from the wharf right to the crater rim. It's a wonderful day out, just a 25-minute cruise from downtown Auckland. You can also get to Rangitoto with **Auckland Sea Kayaks ♥♥** (aucklandseakayaks.co.nz; ✆ **09/213-4545**), which offers a guided 7-hour sunset tour to the island and its summit. It costs from NZ$195 and includes a Kiwi-style barbecue dinner cooked on the beach.

interactive. Visitors learn the secrets of movie-making through the lens of fictional horror, sci-fi, and fantasy films, as though they were really in production. (Once you hear the storylines, you'll be disappointed that they're not real movies!) There are virtual makeup mirrors, stations where you can practice your own costume and character-making skills, and more.

88 Federal St., Level 5, Sky City Precinct. wetaworkshop.com/tours. ✆ **04/909-4035.** NZ$69 adults, NZ$35 children 6–14, NZ$125 families. Book online for discounts. Daily 10am–6:30pm. First tour at 10:10am, last tour 4:10pm (occasional evening tours available).

Waitematā Harbour & Viaduct Basin

Auckland's Viaduct Basin on the Waitematā Harbour, more commonly called "the Viaduct," is a glitzy waterside precinct created in 2000 to support America's Cup–related syndicates, corporations, superyachts, and the public together in one venue. It's composed of apartment blocks, hotels, restaurants, cafes, bars, shops, markets, and every facility an earnest yachtie could want. In 2000, 2003, and 2021, the village was the place to soak up the excitement of the America's Cup challenge, with millions of visitors crammed in along with thousands of competitors, team personnel, and international press. In addition to the America's Cup action, the village played host to up to 80 luxury **superyachts** on each occasion, the largest gatherings in the Southern Hemisphere, turning Auckland into a Pacific Monte Carlo.

Visitors today can experience grand-prix sailing on an authentic America's Cup yacht, *NZL41,* built for the 1995 San Diego Challenge, or *NZL68,* with **Explore Group** (exploregroup.co.nz; ✆ **0800/397-567** in NZ, or 09/359-5987). Over the 2-hour tour, you can be as involved as you want in the crewing action, no experience necessary. Tours depart at 11am and 2pm daily and cost NZ$210 adults, NZ$150 ages 10 to 15. (Children 9 and under are not permitted to sail.)

The Viaduct Harbour development—along with its waterside neighbors Wynyard Quarter, Queen's Wharf, Britomart, and just across the street, Commercial Bay—has changed the face of Auckland forever, providing a fistful of fabulous restaurants, clubs, and bars that have endured. It is a marvelous place to explore, and given that some of Auckland's best eateries are here, you'll

Sail around Waitematā Harbour on an America's Cup yacht with Explore Group.

likely visit it at some point during your stay.

Auckland Bridge Climb and Bungy ♥♥ ATTRACTION Bring on the nerves of steel for **Auckland Bridge Climb.** Based on the successful Sydney activity, walkers are guided underneath and over the top of Auckland Harbour Bridge. The 2-hour adventure, operated by heights experts AJ Hackett, begins with a full briefing by a professional guide at the base complex. Guests are then fitted with overgarments, radio headsets, and safety harnesses. The climb is achievable for people of almost all ages and all fitness levels, but you must be older than 8 and preferably not have a fear of heights. Not adrenaline-pumping enough? You can add-on a **bungy jump** from the bridge if you're feeling particularly brave (and don't mind getting your hair wet, as there's a good chance you'll touch the ocean below). There's limited parking on site, but you can walk from city hotels or catch the complimentary shuttle bus (which can be booked when you purchase tickets).

105 Curran St., Westhaven Reserve, Herne Bay. bungy.co.nz. ✆ **09/360-7748.** Bridge climb NZ$165 adults, NZ$125 ages 8–14. Bungy jump NZ$260 adult, NZ$220 children ages 10 and up only. Daily 9am–4pm.

The New Zealand Maritime Museum.

New Zealand Maritime Museum ♥♥♥ MUSEUM The National Maritime Museum is a superlative museum of the sea. Inside are 14 galleries, holding fascinating exhibitions documenting 1,000 years of New Zealand maritime history, as well as exploring the place of boats in modern NZ culture. These range from a look at the America's Cup, to exhibits on Polynesian boating, to a 1950s beach shop and *bach* (holiday house) display, which sums up the quintessential Kiwi seaside holiday experience. Visitors also get the chance to hit the high seas aboard the historic scow *Ted Ashby*, which takes to the water for a 60-minute ride every day except Monday (sailings 11:30am and 1:30pm for an extra cost).

Hobson Wharf, Viaduct Harbour. maritimemuseum.co.nz. ✆ **09/373-0800.** NZ$24 adults, NZ$12 ages 5–14, free for children 4 and under, NZ$58 families. Museum Combo (museum entry plus *Ted Ashby* harbor cruise) NZ$63 adults, NZ$30 children 5–14. Daily 10am–5pm.

Devonport

Catching the ferry to Devonport is one of the nicest day outings you can have in Auckland. Ferries are part of the AT public transit network, with departures every 40 minutes or so; the trip takes about 12 minutes (fares are NZ$7.40 adults, NZ$4.44 children with an AT HOP card, or a cash fare of NZ$11.50 adults, NZ$6.50 for kids.)

The two historic backbones of the village are Victoria and Church streets, now the main business area, where many of the buildings date to the first European settlement. You can download a free self-guided walking map at devonportmuseum.org.nz/projects, or take a 1-hour minibus tour with **Devonport Explorer Tours** ♥ (devonporttours.co.nz; ✆ **09/357-6366**), which visits both Mount Victoria and North Head beaches (allow 2 hr. if you include the ferry trip from Auckland). The cost is NZ$40 per adult and NZ$30 for children; booking ahead is essential. Tours run daily with multiple departure times in the morning and afternoon.

At the colorful **Art by the Sea,** King Edward Parade and Church Street (artbythesea.co.nz; ✆ **09/445-6665**), you'll find top-quality work by New Zealand artists. It's right next door to cafes and across the road from the sea; hours

From many parts of Devonport, you get wonderful views of Auckland and the Hauraki Gulf.

are Monday through Saturday 10am to 5pm and Sunday 11am to 4pm. **Peter Raos Glass Gallery ♥♥**, Shop 5, 2 Queens Parade (peter-raos.com; ✆ **09/445-4278**), is also worth checking out for handmade art glass and jewelry by local resident and master glass artist Peter Raos. It's open by appointment. At **Devonport Chocolates ♥**, 17 Wynyard St. (devonportchocolates.co.nz; ✆ **09/445-6001;** open daily 9:30am–5pm), you can see chocolate being made.

The town has two museums worth visiting: **Devonport Museum ♥**, 31A Vauxhall Rd. (devonportmuseum.org.nz; ✆ **09/445-2661**), open Tuesday to Thursday from 10am to noon and weekends from 2pm to 4pm with free admission; and the **Devonport Naval Museum ♥**, 64 King Edward Parade, Torpedo Bay (navymuseum.co.nz; ✆ **09/445-5186**), open daily from 10am to 5pm, with free admission. The former tells the story of Devonport through historical artifacts and natural-history displays. The latter, housed in a 19th-century submarine mining station, showcases the story of the New Zealand Navy.

The peninsula is dotted with two small volcanic cones, both of which sport excellent harbor and city views. From the village center you can walk straight up **Takarunga/Mount Victoria.** A longer walk away, at the peninsula's tip, **Maungauika/North Head** was once a significant defense spot for both Māori and the Europeans. The volcanic hill was developed during the war and is honeycombed with underground tunnels, chambers, and gun emplacements—a very fun and free adventure for the kids, while you take in the enormous views.

There are also three excellent white-sand beaches in close range—**Devonport,** a good swimming spot with a playground; **Cheltenham,** a safe tidal beach; and **Narrow Neck Beach,** with safe swimming and a playground.

Historic Houses

All three of these historic houses are managed by Heritage New Zealand; more information on all of them is available at visitheritage.co.nz/visit/auckland.

Alberton ♥♥ (100 Mount Albert Rd., ✆ **09/846-7367**) is perhaps the finest of all of Auckland's historic homes that are open to the public. This once-simple farmhouse built in 1863 grew into the fairy-tale mansion that stands today, providing an intimate glimpse into Victorian life. It's open Wednesday through Sunday 10:30am to 4pm; admission is NZ$10 adults and free for those under 18.

Ewelme Cottage ♥ (14 Ayr St., Parnell; ✆ **09/524-5729**) was built for the Rev. Vicesimus Lush from 1863 to 1864 and named for Ewelme Village in England. The roomy kauri cottage is authentically preserved, right down to its 19th-century wallpaper. It contains an important collection of more than 800 books. Admission is NZ$10 adults, free for under-18s. It's open Sunday only, 10:30am to 4:30pm.

Highwic ♥ (40 Gillies Ave., Epsom; ✆ **09/524-5729**), is one of New Zealand's finest Gothic Revival houses. Built in 1862, it gained additions modeled from an American pattern book in 1873. Its distinctive architecture and gardens offer insight into the lives of the wealthy Victorian family who retained possession of it until 1978. Admission is NZ$10 adults, free for accompanied children. It's open Wednesday through Sunday 10:30am to 4:30pm.

Especially for Kids

In addition to **Auckland Zoo,** the **Sky Tower, MOTAT,** and the **Auckland Museum's Weird and Wonderful Discovery Centre** (all above), there's New Zealand's biggest amusement park, **Rainbow's End** ♥, on the corner of Manukau Station Road and Great South Road, Manukau City (rainbowsend.co.nz; ✆ **0800/438-672** in NZ, or 09/262-2030). This is one attraction you really need to have a couple of rug rats in tow to get the most out of. Get ready for the Stratosfear, the Fear Fall, the Power Surge, and the double-loop Corkscrew Coaster. It's not Disneyland, but these thrill rides, combined with more gentle activities like the Enchanted Forest Log Flume, Gold Rush, and the newly rebuilt big swingin' Pasifica Pirate Ship, should keep youngsters happy. For the very wee ones, there's magical fun to be had in the Kidz Kingdom. Super Passes (which include unlimited all-day rides) are NZ$80 adults, NZ$72 ages 2 to 13, with automatic discounts for more family members. It's open weekdays from 10am to 4pm and until 5pm weekends.

Butterfly Creek ♥ WILDLIFE CENTER This is a fun thing to do if you've time to kill before taking a flight—it's just a few minutes' drive from Auckland International Airport. Despite the name, this attraction goes well beyond fluttering insects (although there are more than 20 species in the Butterfly House). Most come to see the saltwater crocodiles, the giant wētā (like grasshoppers on steroids), a pretty freaky range of reptiles, some cotton-top tamarin monkeys, kiwi in the nocturnal house, cute fluffy critters at Buttermilk Farm, and the tropical aquarium.

10 Tom Pearce Dr., Manukau. butterflycreek.co.nz. ✆ **0800/132-101** in NZ, or 09/275-8880. NZ$32 adults, NZ$16 ages 3–16, NZ$85 families. Wed–Fri 9:30am–4pm; Sat–Sun 9:30am–5pm.

Kelly Tarlton's Sea Life Aquarium ♥ AQUARIUM Kiwi diver Kelly Tarlton (who died in 1985) had a big dream. He envisaged an **Underwater World** where the whole family could make like divers without getting wet—moving along a conveyor belt beneath an acrylic dome while sharks, stingrays, eels, and numerous other species swam overhead. And that's what you can do here, as well as watching rays clamber up their keepers during feeding time in **Stingray Bay,** meeting king and gentoo penguins in a **Penguin Passport tour,** freaking yourself out in a **Shark Dive,** or seeing Antarctica penguins up-close in the **Antarctic Ice Adventure.** The aquarium's newest addition, the $1.4-million **Sea Cave Adventure,** opened in 2022 courtesy of a partnership with the DOC (Department of Conservation). It consists of four themed chambers where visitors encounter local species like native octopus, eel, and crayfish. Kids will love the opportunity to handle starfish and other sea creatures.

23 Tamaki Dr., Orakei. kellytarltons.co.nz. ✆ **0800/805-050** in NZ, or 09/531-5065. NZ$45 adults, NZ$32 ages 3–14, free for children 2 and under, families NZ$154. Book online to save up to 25%. Shark Cage Adventure from NZ$109; Penguin Passport from NZ$175. Daily 9:30am–5pm (last entry 4pm).

Hanging out with gentoo penguins at Kelly Tarlton's Sea Life Aquarium.

Parks & Gardens

The Auckland area has 22 regional parks, covering 37,038 hectares (91,484 acres) and more than 500km (310 miles) of walking tracks. The **Auckland Domain ♥♥**, the city's oldest park, is an imposing crown of green just minutes from the city center. Within it, the **Wintergarden,** the steamy **Tropical House,** and **Fernz Fernery** are botanical showcases for indigenous and exotic plant specimens. Admission is free. The Wintergarden is open daily from 9am to 4:30pm in winter and until 5:30pm in summer. There are also extensive formal gardens, sweeping lawns, statuary, duck ponds, sports grounds, and dozens of picnic spots. Free and ticketed concerts are regularly held in the Domain. The Domain has several well-signposted entrances; two of the busiest are on Stanley Street and Parnell Road. There are also entrances on Grafton Road and Park Road.

Epsom's **Cornwall Park ♥♥** (Auckland's largest) is like the countryside in the middle of the city: It has sheep, stone walls, and lovely walks—especially in spring when there are lambs and daffodils. In the middle of it is One Tree Hill, which should be called None Tree Hill, after a protesting Māori activist chopped down its namesake tree with an axe in 2000 (negotiations over a replacement tree are nearing an end). The **Cornwall Park Visitor Center** (cornwallpark.co.nz; ✆ **09/630-8485**) has maps and information on walks. Access is via Greenlane Road, Manukau Road, or Campbell Road.

The **Parnell Rose Garden ♥** and **Dove-Myer Robinson Park ♥** (named after a popular former city mayor) are off Gladstone and Judges Bay roads in Parnell. One of the city's first churches, little St. Stephen's Chapel, is also here.

A bucolic country landscape in sprawling Cornwall Park (see p. 87).

The **Auckland Botanic Gardens** ♥, 102 Hill Rd., Manurewa (aucklandbotanicgardens.co.nz; ✆ **09/267-1457**), cover 64 hectares (158 acres) and are home to more than 10,000 plants. The gardens are open daily from 8am to 8pm in summer and 8am to 6pm in winter. Guided tours by mini-train cost NZ$4 adults and NZ$2 ages 3 to 13. Tickets can be purchased from the visitor center, with tours lasting 25 minutes.

Also worth a look is **Eden Gardens** ♥, 24 Omana Ave., Mt. Eden (edengarden.co.nz; ✆ **09/638-8395**), a former quarry that's now a showplace for an amazing collection of rhododendrons, camellias, azaleas, hibiscus, bromeliads, palms, and many other subtropical species. The gardens are open daily 9am to 4pm; the on-site cafe is open to 3pm. Admission is NZ$12 adults, free for children under 12.

Organized Tours & Cruises

You can book several half- and full-day tours of Auckland and its environs at the visitor center. Half-day tours cover city highlights, while all-day tours usually include something of the east or west suburbs, the zoo, or the vineyards.

IN THE CITY

The hilariously named **Aucky Walky** (auckywalky.co.nz; ✆ **021/378-267**) offers a range of guided walks from

Ice cream cones make a perfect end to a Taste Auckland Walk with Aucky Walky.

NZ$89, including an Art Walk where you'll learn the stories behind the city's murals, sculptures, and landmarks, and a Taste Auckland walk (N$189, including food) where you can sample eateries selected for their "great tastes, cool vibes and hard-to-find locations."

BUSH & BEACH

Bush and Beach ♥♥ (bushandbeach.co.nz; ✆ **09/837-4130**) will take you out to the wild west coast to experience the elemental side of Auckland. Half- or full-day tours may include visits to a gannet colony, a winery, or a virgin rainforest (NZ$105–NZ$400 per person). Their Best of Both Worlds Tour City and Nature Tour (NZ$295) provides a good overview of Auckland's diversity, taking in the city in the morning and the bush and beaches of West Auckland in the afternoon. Wear comfortable walking shoes.

ON THE WATER

Auckland won't deprive you of an opportunity to get out on the waves. In addition to the opportunity to sail on America's Cup racing yachts (see "Waitematā Harbour & Viaduct Basin," p. 82), **Explore Group ♥♥** (exploregroup.co.nz/auckland; ✆ **800/397-567** in NZ) operates a 2½-hour dinner cruise aboard a sailboat (departs at 6pm, NZ$150 adults, NZ$150 ages 5–15) and a 6-hour dolphin watching excursion (departing daily in summer, Wed–Sun in winter; NZ$170 adults, NZ$85 ages 5–15, families NZ$425). Both depart from the Viaduct. For a shorter marine mammal-watching experience **Auckland Whale and Dolphin Safari ♥** (awads.co.nz; ✆ **09/357-6032**) offers a daily 4½-hour eco-cruise on the Hauraki Gulf, departing at 10:30am (NZ$219 adults, NZ$145 ages 14 and under, NZ$639 for two adults and two kids).

IN THE AIR

Island Aviation (islandaviation.co.nz/tours; ✆ **022/643-7440**), based on Waiheke Island, offers scenic flights over Auckland's harbors and islands in a Havilland Beaver Float Plane, which seats up to eight passengers. It operates 7 days a week during daylight hours, with tours starting from NZ$199—if you're lucky you'll spot whales or even manta rays. They'll also fly you to Aotea/Great Barrier or other remote island spots. Island Aviation is the first certified carbon-zero air operator in Australasia, and it is involved in reforestation and removing pests from the Gulf's islands.

OUTDOOR ACTIVITIES

CYCLING Based at the Park Hyatt downtown, **Power to the Pedal** (powertothepedal.com; ✆ **021/082-94218**) offers a range of e-bike tours, from a 90-minute "night lights" trip (NZ$115) to a 3½-hour jaunt around the city's iconic sights (NZ$180). Pre-booking is essential, minimum age 14.

For mountain and touring bike rentals, hit up **Adventure Cycles,** 9 Premier Ave., Western Springs (adventurecycles.co.nz; ✆ **021/245-3868**). Rates start at NZ$30 per day or NZ$120 per week, panniers are also available, and free with every bike is a helmet, lock, tool kit, and water bottle, plus maps and tips.

Go West, Young Traveler: The Waitākere Ranges & Muriwai

Driving the 25 minutes west into the **Waitākere Ranges ♥♥♥** is one of the best day trips you can make from Auckland. This mountainous region is draped in lush rainforest and stunning waterfalls, and the west coast beaches are pure, wild, black-sand drama—nothing like the calm golden coves of the Gulf.

You can choose from half a dozen spectacular beaches, all highly recommended—from south to north, they're Whatipu, Karekare, Piha, Anawhata, Te Henga/Bethell's Beach, and Muriwai. And you do have to choose—these cliffs are so rugged, no road runs along the coast, and the separate roads out to each beach are winding and narrow; take your time or spend the night at one of the many Airbnbs nestled in the bush. The only real town is **Piha ♥♥**, a surfer's mecca of beachfront baches/cottages (including many you can rent) and the stunning **Lions Rock** lookout. Just outside of Piha you'll also find **Kitekite Falls ♥♥**, one of the region's most scenic spots. The track to the falls starts from the end of Glen Esk Road and takes about 60 minutes, mainly along boardwalks. (There are some steep portions, but these can be avoided.) Bring your swimsuit; there are refreshing spots to swim at the top of the falls. Clean your boots and stay on the track to protect trees from kauri dieback disease.

Another highly recommended half-day walk, the **Omanawanui Track ♥♥♥** (2–3 hr.) starts at **Whatipu** and offers stunning views of bush, hills, and the mouth of the Manukau Harbour down the coast.

Muriwai, the northernmost of the beaches, has a large campground (muriwaibeachcampground.co.nz) with cabins starting from NZ$100. Near it is the impressive **Muriwai Gannet Colony ♥♥♥**, where 1,200 pairs of gannets nest between August and March. Just off Waitea Road is a viewing platform where you can watch these majestic large birds court and raise their young. This is also doable as a day trip; Muriwai is only a 45-minute drive northwest of Auckland's city center.

For more information on the area, visit the **Arataki Visitor Centre** (the gateway to the Waitākere Ranges Regional Park), 300 Scenic Dr., Nihotupu (✆ **09/892-4777**). RVers can park at the center overnight for a small fee, and there are glowworms found near it. It's open daily from 9am to 5pm.

GOLF You'll find more than 40 golf courses in the Auckland region, including the new-in-2023 **Te Arai Links ♥♥♥** (tearai.com; ✆ **09/883-4600**). It features two courses, including one designed by Tom Doak, located on the spectacular coastline. The **Auckland Golf Association** (aucklandgolf.nz; ✆ **09/218-6323**) is an excellent resource for researching other courses, as it lists par values and current greens fees.

JETBOATING **Auckland Adventure Jet ♥** (aucklandadventurejet.co.nz; ✆ **0800/255-538** in NZ) will whisk you out onto Waitematā Harbour for a thrilling 35-minute high-speed ride for NZ$109 adults, NZ$69 kids under 14. Jetboats depart hourly from Pier 3A at the ferry Terminal at 99 Quay Street, at the bottom of Queen Street. Remember, though, that jetboats can be found throughout NZ—it might be best to save this activity for a braided river on the South Island.

KAYAKING Ian Ferguson was one of New Zealand's top athletes; he competed in five Olympic games, won four gold medals and one silver, and in 1996 was named New Zealand Olympian of the century. He is also the man behind **Fergs Kayaks ♥♥** (fergskayaks.co.nz; ✆ **09/529-2230**), located at **Ian Ferguson Marine Sports Centre,** 12 Tamaki Dr., east of the harbor in Okahu Bay. It has several kayaking options, such as a 7-hour Rangitoto day trip (NZ$215, departing daily at 8:30am) which involves a 75-minute paddle out to the island and a 45-minute hike to its summit over the lava fields and regenerating bush (Rangitoto—see box p. 82—only erupted out of the sea 600 years ago). **Auckland Sea Kayaks ♥♥** (aucklandseakayaks.co.nz; ✆ **0800/999-089** or 09/2134-545) hosts a similar trip but at night, offering a spectacular night view of Auckland from the island's peak. It leaves at 4pm in summer, 2pm in winter, takes 6 to 7 hours, and costs around NZ$195, including a barbecue dinner. Both outfits will also take you paddling across to Motukorea/Browns Island (a shorter trip), and the latter also offers a 2½-hour nighttime City Lights tour around the inner harbor with great sunset views of the skyline and Harbour Bridge.

Auckland Sea Kayaks' popular City Lights tour.

And for something truly special, head out in a kayak at night with **Social Nature Movement** (socialnaturemovement.nz) to float in the eerie blue glow of ocean bioluminescence (NZ$110, book online for discounts, transport from the CBD costs an extra NZ$50).

SAILING You'll find numerous brochures about sailing charters at the Auckland visitor center. See also "Organized Tours & Cruises," above.

SURFING If you've never taken to the board or want to improve your skills, **Piha Surf School** (pihasurfschool.com; ✆ **09/812-8123**), on the west coast at Piha Beach (see box p. 90), offers lessons by internationally qualified instructors (1½ hr.; $150 for one-on-one instruction and $80 group lesson).

SWIMMING Accessible from Tamaki Drive (where there's frequent bus service from Britomart), the beaches at Judges Bay, Okahu Bay, Mission Bay, Kohimarama, and St. Heliers Bay are popular inner-harbor swimming spots. But my pick is Devonport's pōhutukawa-fringed Cheltenham Beach (see p. 85)—at mid- or high tide in summer, I reckon it's one of the world's best city beaches.

WALKING Aside from the many excellent walks out west in the Waitākeres, the city offers options, too: the promenade of **Tamaki Drive ♥♥** is an easy, enjoyable stroll from the central city around to the pleasant seaside suburbs of Mission Bay and Kohimarama. Climbing to the top of **One Tree Hill, Mount Eden,** or any of the other suburban volcanoes also offers a bit of pleasant physical exertion with a side of views.

For something more strenuous, an excellent self-guided trek is the **Coast to Coast Walk ♥♥♥**, a 4- to 6-hour walk through the inner city and suburbs. A comprehensive map, available from the visitor center or online at auckland-council.govt.nz, shows the 15km (10-mile) route.

SPECTATOR SPORTS

For information on current events, check out the events listings at aucklandnz.com.

HORSE RACING There are races all year round at Ellerslie Racecourse, 100 Ascot Ave., Remuera (aucklandracing.co.nz; ✆ **09/524-4069**), but the annual highlight Is **Champion's Day,** which usually takes place in late February or early March. It's the biggest day in New Zealand thoroughbred racing, with over 30,000 spectators.

Alexandra Park Raceway, at Greenlane West Road, Epsom (alexandra park.co.nz; ✆ **09/631-1163**), is the largest harness racing course on the North Island, with 35 race nights a year. Regular **Night Trotting** meets are on Friday nights.

RUGBY Check **Eden Park**'s website (edenpark.co.nz) for current schedules of **All Blacks** (men's) and the **Black Ferns** (women's) and fiercely fought provincial rugby games nationwide. The rugby season runs from April to September. For rugby match information, contact **New Zealand Rugby Football Union** (nzrugby.co.nz; ✆ **04/499-4995**).

WHERE TO STAY IN AUCKLAND

In recent years Auckland really has grown into the city it has always wanted to be, complete with a terrific range of accommodations. At certain times of year (especially over the summer months, or when a big international musician is visiting) there can be high demand for beds at every level, so it pays to book ahead, especially since dynamic pricing is the standard. Apartment and room rentals, through such sites as Airbnb and Vrbo, are an affordable alternative to hotels and are plentiful, especially in Auckland's surrounding suburbs.

Due to high **parking** costs, we don't recommend keeping a rental car if you're staying downtown, but if you must, know that hotels only offer valet parking, which costs NZ$50 to NZ$60. There are many public parking lots throughout the city's core, with discounted overnight rates if you self-park. However, self-park pricing can be confusing, and add up to as much or more than hotel valet parking.

Downtown/Central City

EXPENSIVE

Fable Auckland ♥♥ Formerly known as the Hotel Grand Windsor, this 10-story hotel is housed in one of the city's oldest skyscrapers. Over the last decade, the heritage building has been beautifully restored throughout, with rooms decorated in a regal manner, reminiscent of styles popular at the turn of the century and through to the 1920s: lots of jewel-toned fabrics, jewel tiling, and gilded wallpaper. It's a mature and elegant space for discerning travelers who want a touch of luxury in a central location.

58–60 Queen St. fablehotelsandresorts.com. ✆ **09/309-9979.** 79 units. NZ$304–NZ$500. **Amenities:** Restaurant; bar; gym; sauna; concierge; free Wi-Fi.

Hilton Auckland ♥♥ There's no other Hilton in the world quite like this property, located right in the heart of Viaduct Harbour. It's almost completely surrounded by water, perched on the end of Princes Wharf like the giant ship that inspired it and like the cruising behemoths that dock alongside it. Rooms are modern, and surprisingly stylish—not overly large in some cases, but with excellent beds, blue rugs in an abstract wave pattern, fabulous bathrooms, and stellar sea views. For even better views, opt for one of the 12 deluxe corner rooms that feature two whole walls of glass. The suites are shaped like the bow of a ship and boast vast decks. And you could do far worse if you choose to eat in-house at **Fish**—head chef Shane Yardley's exciting menu is well worth staying in for.

Princes Wharf, 137–147 Quay St. hilton.com. ✆ **0800/448-002** in NZ, or 09/978-2000. NZ$323–NZ$1,100. 165 units. Valet parking NZ$60. **Amenities:** Restaurant; bar; babysitting; concierge; gym; outdoor pool suspended from 4th-floor bridge; room service; free Wi-Fi.

The Hotel Britomart ♥♥♥ This gorgeous hotel is fully deserving of its many awards. It's the accommodation centerpiece of Auckland's most upscale entertainment and shopping precinct, and when you book a room, "you get a key to the neighborhood," as hotel staff will tell you. Top restaurants, atmospheric bars, and shops featuring local designers are just a few steps away. Even better is the genuine commitment to sustainability at NZ's first "5 Green Star" hotel. The structure was built with as many recycled materials as possible, the NZ-made coconut-husk slippers are compostable, the rooms are put to sleep when not in use, and pillows are stuffed with recycled plastic bottles (though I didn't personally find them the comfiest). The blackout blinds are next-level—ideal for sleeping off jet lag—as are the beautifully decorated minibars stuffed with boutique Kiwi products. As a guest, you can also access The Libraries—a series of smart, relaxing rooms showcasing local history, art, and design, where you can enjoy a cocktail or meal or taste wine served on a slab of 40,000-year-old swamp kauri wood. They've even developed a "regenerative tour" with the forest farm Velskov (see box p. 78), offering a special

Groovy mid-century modern design adds hipster cred to a stay at Hotel DeBrett.

mid-week package for two including a night's accommodation, the tour, and breakfast at hotel restaurant Kingi for NZ$1,238.

29 Galway St. thehotelbritomart.com. ✆ **09/300-9595.** 104 units. Doubles NZ$287–NZ$819, suites NZ$425–NZ$900. Valet parking NZ$60. **Amenities:** Restaurant; bar; concierge; spa; free Wi-Fi.

Hotel DeBrett ♥♥♥ Out the door is hip High Street, inside the chic oasis that is the Hotel DeBrett. This boutique labor of love started life as the Commercial Hotel in 1841. Today, its interiors are a hymn to mid-century modern design: 25 stylish and surprising rooms and suites with groovy multicolored striped rugs, chairs that look like set pieces from the TV series *Mad Men,* and luxe bathrooms with deep soaking tubs, rainfall showers, radiant heating in the floors, and de-misting mirrors. The restaurant is terrific, the bar atmospheric, and there's a drawing room filled with art, books, movies, and music. ***Warning:*** You just might be inclined to purchase the hotel's acid-green velvet bathrobes.

2 High St. hoteldebrett.com. ✆ **09/925-9000.** 25 units. Doubles NZ$320–NZ$570. Rates include continental breakfast. Valet parking. **Amenities:** Restaurant; bar; babysitting; concierge; nearby gym; massage; free Wi-Fi.

QT Auckland ♥♥ It's hard not to love the design-forward QT chain of hotels—in a same-same hotel landscape where Art Deco reigns supreme, QT is offbeat, with modern artwork by local artists, rooms that are thoughtfully designed with rainfall showers and luxe soaker tubs, and dining options that showcase local ingredients. The chain's Auckland outpost is no exception. Its restaurant **Esther ♥♥♥** is so good that it deserves its own listing (so I gave it one; see p. 104); the rooftop bar—with Nitro espresso martinis on tap—buzzes with the local after-work crowd. If you just want to enjoy a quiet glass of wine in the hotel lobby, you've come to the wrong place, but if you want a hotel that adds to the city's vibrant energy, rather than being siloed from it, QT won't disappoint.

4 Viaduct Harbour Ave. qthotels.com/auckland. ✆ **09/379-9123.** 150 units. NZ$404–NZ$818. Valet parking NZ$45. **Amenities:** Restaurant; bar; gym; room service; free Wi-Fi.

SO/ Auckland ♥ SO/ is part of a trend of designer art hotels popping up across NZ, this one in a building that was once the Reserve Bank and stashed gold bars in its vault (now the underground spa). Depending on your taste, you'll either love it or hate it. My sister and I felt like someone had typed "avant-garde hotel" into an AI generator—something about it doesn't feel quite human—but it deserves credit for paying homage to the city's history and geology. The interior, inspired by Auckland's volcanic heritage, features a mega chandelier and seats made from upended couches in a cave-like black lobby, while its "liquid"-themed rooms are meant to create the illusion of being surrounded by molten lava, with their fiery artwork and textiles. Each room features a freestanding soaker bathtub (but oddly there's no door on the ensuite toilet). The rooftop bar is worth it for the cityscape and harbor views, if not the food.

Corner of Customs St. E. & Gore St. so-auckland.com. ✆ **09/379-1860.** 130 units. NZ$270–NZ$700. Valet parking NZ$50. **Amenities:** Restaurant; bar; patisserie; club lounge; spa; gym; swimming pool; sauna; room service; free Wi-Fi.

Voco Auckland City Centre ♥♥ In the same high-rise tower as the **Holiday Inn Express Auckland City Centre,** the Voco made big waves when it opened in 2022, mostly owing to the 38th-floor **Bar Albert,** the city's highest rooftop bar, with its impressive views of the neighboring Sky Tower and the harbor. It's still popular with the after-work crowd, and it doesn't take bookings—you'll want to get there promptly for 5pm. (Cocktails are priced for the vantage point, at NZ$18–NZ$26.) The good news is that if you're a hotel guest, it's much cheaper to just enjoy the scenic vistas from the floor-to-ceiling windows in your room. There, you'll also find an incredibly comfortable bed, rain showerheads, Chromecast-enabled TVs, and blackout blinds. The hotel is also working towards sustainability, with water bottle refill stations built into the hallways.

13 Wyndham St. ihg.com/voco/hotels. ✆ **09/883-2999.** 201 units. NZ$228–NZ$800. Valet parking NZ$55. **Amenities:** Restaurant; lobby bar; gym; laundry room; free Wi-Fi.

MODERATE

Abstract Hotel ♥♥ If you think you might partake of a night out on the city's hopping K Road, this glam bolthole is a fun, affordable choice. It's a stone's throw from the restaurants and clubs—as well as many of the city's daytime attractions—and its dark-hued, stylish rooms stay dark in the morning, too, thanks to decent blackout blinds. We like the one- and two-bedroom metro units, which have a separate lounge and kitchenette space as well as an en-suite bathroom.

8 Upper Queen St. abstracthotel.co.nz. ✆ **09/320-1671.** 273 rooms. NZ$140–NZ$310. **Amenities:** Restaurant; bar; spa; library; free Wi-Fi.

Braemar on Parliament Street ♥♥ History and character are at the heart of this three-story Edwardian gentleman's townhouse (ca. 1901); you feel it as soon as you walk in. Hosts Sue and John Sweetman have an astonishing collection of historic Auckland photographs, and their welcoming manner makes this place a home away from home. The four rooms in this delightful B&B—two with en suite bathrooms, two with shared bathroom—are packed with charm (think Persian rugs and Victorian antiques). The Batten Suite (once home to legendary pilot Jean Batten's father) is the best and biggest. It's the only upmarket B&B in the central business district, and it's just a short walk from trendy High Street, downtown activities, and transport systems. Warning to allergy sufferers: There's a resident toy poodle and two cats on-site.

7 Parliament St. aucklandbedandbreakfast.com. ✆ **0800/155-463** in NZ, or 09/377-5463. 4 units. NZ$280–NZ$450. Rates include breakfast. Free parking. **Amenities:** Pool; free Wi-Fi.

Hotel Indigo Auckland ♥♥ There's something intimate and relaxing about the Hotel Indigo, even though it's actually a large hotel just 2 blocks from the Sky Tower. Perhaps it's the location on a quiet pedestrian square—west-facing rooms look vertiginously down onto St. Patrick's Cathedral and out across the Harbour Bridge to the Waitākeres—or maybe it's the restful green, gold, and brown tones of the small, delightful lobby, where light streams in through a huge window, illuminating wooden floors, leather couches, textiles and ceramics, and piles of art and travel books for browsing. Completed in 2025 as part of IHG's international brand of boutique Indigo hotels, this Auckland outpost features some lovely local touches—stepping out of the elevator on your floor you'll see photos and stories about a certain part of the city, like One Tree Hill or Queen Street. The carpet is printed with old Auckland street maps, and rooms are supplied with top-quality Kokako

Sunset views from a corner room at the Hotel Indigo Auckland.

pour-over drip coffee and a selection of Zealong teas in cute jars. Rooms are simple, with the panorama outside taking center stage (ask for one with a corner view, with windows on two sides). Breakfast is in the hotel's excellent **Bistro Saine** ♥♥♥ (see p. 103).

53 St. Patrick's Sq. ihg.com/hotelindigo. ✆ **09/610-8400.** 225 units. Doubles NZ$229–NZ$375. Valet parking NZ$60. **Amenities:** Restaurant; gym; free Wi-Fi.

Rendezvous Heritage Auckland ♥ The Heritage has size, location, and friendly service on its side. Just a short walk from main shopping and entertainment areas, the hotel has two distinct parts: the "hotel" wing in a restored landmark Art Deco building (a former department store); and the purpose-built "tower" wing. The Heritage is starting to show its age, but its amenities—including an all-weather outdoor tennis court and a rooftop swimming pool with harbor views—make up for it. Note for drivers: A Wilson carpark next door may have lower rates than the Heritage valet service, depending on length of stay (but only if you're parking less than 12 hours, and use the Parkmate app—otherwise you're better off with the valet rate).

Hotel Wing, 35 Hobson St.; Tower Wing, 22–24 Nelson St. heritagehotels.co.nz. ✆ **0800/368-888** in NZ, or 09/302-1277. 274 units. Doubles NZ$180–NZ$350. Valet parking NZ$45. **Amenities:** 2 restaurants; bar; concierge; hair salon; 2 gyms; hot tub; rooftop pool; indoor lap pool; room service; sauna; lit tennis court; free Wi-Fi.

Sudima Auckland City ♥♥ A stone's throw from SkyCity, this relatively new hotel (it opened in 2021) has some of the city's best views of both the Sky Tower and the nearby harbor. Its location is central, but because it's on the outskirts of the central city, and not so close to surrounding buildings, it doesn't get too much street noise. If you want a vibrant night scene, you'll find it in the downstairs restaurant **East** ♥♥, which has become a destination for locals with its all-veggie, Asian-inspired menu. (Trust me when I say you won't even notice the meat is missing.) Or head upstairs to the rooftop **Sunset** ♥♥ bar, named for its end-of-day views over the harbor. Rooms are comfortable and decorated in a contemporary fashion with neutral colors (mercifully, Sudima seems to have escaped the neo–Art Deco design trend cursing many of the city's newer hotels). At the end of the day, it's a hotel chain—but at least it's an NZ-grown one.

63–67 Nelson St. sudimahotels.com. ✆ **09/399-2360.** 194 units. NZ$269–NZ$512 double. Valet parking NZ$55. **Amenities:** Restaurant; 2 bars; gym nearby; room service; free Wi-Fi.

INEXPENSIVE

Backpackers and digital nomads alike will love **LyLo** ♥♥, 54 Cook St. (lylo.com/auckland; ✆ **09/379-6633**), a pod-style flashpacker hostel that opened in 2022. Owned by the same folks behind the QT hotels brand, its single pods are private units within a shared room separated by privacy screens, each with its own USB charging port, dedicated storage locker, and personal fan. They start from NZ$56. Private rooms from NZ$109, but if you want your own private bathroom, too, you'll need to spend at least NZ$116.

In Ponsonby/Grey Lynn

EXPENSIVE

The Great Ponsonby Arthotel ♥♥ This restored villa, owned by hosts Sally James and Gerard Hill, enjoys a quiet location within walking distance of the best of Ponsonby. It's now slightly dated, but it's a great place for kicking back, with a sunlit lounge bulging with books, lots of New Zealand art and magazines, verandas for unwinding, and both cooked and continental breakfast. Rooms are comfy and reflect a colorful Pacific mood with bright shades of turquoise and yellow, along with Pasifika woven artwork. Three suites have both bathtubs and showers. The lovely Dunedin Room has its own deck, while the upstairs penthouse has a sitting room and balcony. The Palm Garden studios offer extra space, and some come with a kitchenette and minibar.

30 Ponsonby Terrace. greatpons.co.nz. ✆ **0800/766-792** in NZ, or 09/376-5989. 11 units. NZ$330–NZ$450. **Amenities:** Free off-street parking, free use of bikes; free Wi-Fi.

Hotel Fitzroy ♥♥ Boutique in both its name and size, this 10-room inn has all the character of a bed-and-breakfast, while offering the privacy and services of a hotel. Housed in an early-20th-century villa, the Luxury Rooms, which are named for notable figures in Auckland's history, aren't large—nor is the tiny library where canapes and drinks are served every evening—but they're well-appointed, with Chromecast-equipped TVs, under-floor heating, and complimentary minibars. The Superior Rooms, in a separate new build out back, are slightly larger in size, but if you're here to explore the neighborhood, we doubt you'll notice the difference (other than in price). The best feature is the breakfast—much like a bed-and-breakfast, it's a huge hot and

Startlingly colorful walls and a family-home vibe are some of the hallmarks of the Great Ponsonby Art Hotel.

cold spread—except instead of having to make awkward conversation with other guests, it's delivered every morning to the privacy of your room.

43 Richmond Rd., Grey Lynn. fablehotelsandresorts.com/hotels/hotel-fitzroy. ✆ **09/558-1955.** 10 units. NZ$459–NZ$549. Rates include breakfast and complimentary evening drinks. Free street parking overnight. **Amenities:** 24-hr. room service; free Wi-Fi.

MODERATE

The Convent Hotel ♥♥ Originally built in 1922 as the St. Joseph's Convent, this Spanish Mission–style building fell into disrepair when it became a boarding house in the '90s. (I heavily discourage you from Googling "before" pictures.) Now it's been restored to its original glory by the same property developer behind the Ponsonby Central retail complex. On the hotel's walls, religious iconography sits next to Andy Warhol prints and dried floral arrangements, creating an effect that's more "Like a Prayer" Madonna than "Mary, mother of Jesus" Madonna. There is just the right number of avant-garde touches to make it interesting without being too edgy. (Most are tasteful, but if you have coulrophobia—a fear of clowns—consider this fair warning: There are clown paintings in the reception area.) There are eight styles of rooms, most of which are compact, owing to the building's original purpose; those wanting a bit more room to spread out can book into the Chapel (located in the former chapel, naturally), which includes a balcony and kitchenette, or the two-bedroom Mother Superior Suite, which has a full kitchen. Meanwhile, the boutique hotel's on-site restaurant, **Ada ♥♥♥**—which serves up homemade Italian fare—will have you saying, "Praise be."

454 Great North Rd. theconventhotel.co.nz. ✆ **09/266-8368.** 22 units. NZ$179–NZ$399. Free off-street parking. **Amenities:** Restaurant; bar; free Wi-Fi.

INEXPENSIVE

Verandahs Parkside Lodge ♥♥ A cheap and cheerful option, Verandahs comprises two substantial Victorian dwellings just off Ponsonby Road. It's been renovated for use as a hostel, but rooms retain some of these structures' former life, including ornate tiled fireplaces. Both buildings back onto Western Park, which can serve as a shortcut into the city. The Lodge has two good-size lounges and a huge kitchen full of every pot or utensil you'll ever need. It's very popular with young international travelers, but the size and variety of rooms available—singles, doubles, dorms, and a family room—make the Lodge suitable for all age groups and budgets.

4–6 Hopetoun St. verandahs.co.nz. ✆ **09/360-4180.** 17 units. NZ$45–NZ$150. **Amenities:** Kitchen; lounge; travel desk; free Wi-Fi.

In Mount Eden & Newmarket

EXPENSIVE

Staydium Glamping ♥♥♥ This might just be one of the most weirdly wonderful stays in NZ: two luxury glamping domes set among the stands at Eden Park, home to the All Blacks Rugby team. I'll be honest: There's something eerie and disconcerting about sleeping in a sporting stadium alone overnight. But these glamping domes are surprisingly cozy and, dare I say it, even a bit romantic. Each overlooks the iconic Eden Park sign and faces the setting sun, and has luxurious details like custom artwork, a Dyson hair dryer, wireless pods for charging phones, Le Creuset crockery, and honey made by Eden Park's very own bees. Each dome has its own bathroom (complete with a towel warmer) and a microwave and fridge within. You're only about 2m away from the neighboring dome, but it feels incredibly private with heavy curtains. The only catch? This is a working stadium, so maintenance staff may be walking around in the morning, particularly before events. Want to stay on a game day? There's a waiting list, so now is the time to get on it.

Reimers Ave., Mount Eden. edenpark.co.nz/experience/staydium-glamping. ✆ **09/815-5551.** 2 domes. NZ$350 double; inquire for game day pricing. Rates include a stadium tour. Free off-street parking. **Amenities:** Free Wi-Fi.

MODERATE

Quest Newmarket Apartment Hotel ♥ If you like to cook up a storm while you're traveling, then these serviced apartments are ideal in more than one way: Not only do they come equipped with excellent kitchens, but there's a good supermarket within walking distance. If that idea doesn't appeal, you'll be pleased to know you're close to any number of cafes and restaurants, plus some of Auckland's best boutique shopping. All the studios and apartments (some with two or even three bedrooms) get a lot of light, though the decor is typical chain hotel (so not much sense of place here). The Quest is also a 20-minute walk up the street to Parnell Village.

31–39 Davis Crescent, Newmarket. questapartments.co.nz. ✆ **09/520-3000.** 49 apts. NZ$230–NZ$480. Parking NZ$20. **Amenities:** Gym; free Wi-Fi.

In Takapuna & Devonport

MODERATE

Admirals Landing Bed and Breakfast ♥♥ This waterfront home owned by well-traveled Howard and Joy Mace is typical of all that's good about staying in Devonport. It's just a short walk to a range of restaurants and cafes, village shops, a golf course, and some of Auckland's best beaches. The two rooms (Waterfront and Paua) are light and bright with everything you'll need for a comfortable stay; the Waterfront Room, which boasts 11 windows, offers excellent views in almost every direction. The highlight here, though, is the hosts, who offer tons of helpful advice for getting the most out of your visit. Joy's knowledge of NZ and the area is unparalleled. If you're keen to know more about this attractive seaside suburb, book yourself on one of Joy's guided heritage walks up Mount Victoria and around the village.

11 Queens Parade, Devonport. admiralslanding.co.nz. ✆ **09/445-4394.** 2 units. NZ$210–NZ$255. 2-night stay min. Rates include breakfast. Children accepted by special arrangement. **Amenities:** Free Wi-Fi.

Emerald Inn ♥♥ For those who want to be practically on the beach, the self-catering options available here are many and varied. Although parts of the exterior look a little dated, the resort-style rooms (decorated with palm tree pillows and pineapple sculptures) are fresh and clean and have all the amenities

Friendly hosts and a seaside location make the Admiral's Landing a nice choice for lodgings.

you'd expect from good quality holiday accommodation. Best of all, it's only a few steps to one of Takapuna's most popular cafes (the **Takapuna Beach Café ♥♥**, which has the country's best salted caramel gelato), where you can watch all the comings and goings on land and water. If sand is not your thing, you can lounge by the Inn's pool. And if you want to spread out a bit more, there are also villas (for a minimum of 5 nights) and cottages (a minimum of 3 nights) available.

16 The Promenade, Takapuna. emerald-inn.co.nz. ✆ **09/488-3500.** Studios NZ$175–NZ$305. Free parking. **Amenities:** BBQ; guest laundry; swimming pool; free Wi-Fi.

Out West/Waitākere Ranges

For pure rainforest magic, the area around Piha Beach has dozens of stunning Airbnb properties sheltered in the bush, including guesthouses, tiny houses, and glamping. Otherwise, beach and wilderness lovers should consider **Bethells Beach Cottages ♥♥**, 267 Bethells Rd., Bethells Beach, Waitākere (bethellsbeach.com; ✆ **09/810-9581**), where two wooden cottages and a self-contained apartment are set in lush private gardens, overlooking the wild western seas and the sunset, for NZ$345 to NZ$395. They're decorated with lovely bohemian touches—lots of brick, wood, shells, and curves—and you'll have access to a woodfired barbecue and a Scandinavian-style hot tub (shared with visitors in the other cottages)—the ultimate Kiwi getaway.

Or you can spend your nights in a rainforest retreat at **Waitākere Resort and Spa ♥♥**, 573 Scenic Dr., Waiatarua (waitakereestate.co.nz; ✆ **09/814-9622**), which offers hotel rooms, villas, and apartment accommodation. A favorite wedding venue for Aucklanders, this resort-style complex has good water views, a swimming pool, a day spa, and a fine-dining restaurant. Rates run from NZ$210 to NZ$499. Book direct for combo packages, which include breakfast and dinner.

If you can snap it up, though, my pick is **Dusk and Dawn Domes ♥♥♥** (canopycamping.co.nz/dusk-and-dawn), set in the kauri forest above Titirangi. You'll get exclusive access to a pair of clear geodesic domes—one for cooking and lounging, the other for sleeping, or gazing at the stars from your bed—joined by a deck overlooking bush, city, harbor, and islands. The owners live in a dwelling behind, so it's not completely secluded, but you'll feel like it is when you soak in the spa pool watching the sunrise—or sunset, since, as the name suggests, both are stunning here.

Near the Airport

The **Novotel Auckland Airport ♥**, Ray Emery Drive (novotel.com; ✆ **09/365-0000**), is almost attached to the international terminal. It has 263 formulaic but comfortable rooms and suites from NZ$275 and good online specials. Less expensive **ibis Budget ♥**, 2 Leonard Isitt Dr. (accorhotels.com; ✆ **09/255-5152**), has 125 rooms that are cramped, but serviceable for a short layover. Expect to pay at least NZ$175, although rates can exceed NZ$200 if not booked in advance. Parking is free, and the hotel is walking distance from the terminal and also on the route of the **Yellow Bus** (yellowbus.co.nz; ✆ **09/917-5175;** NZ$8.50).

MODERATE

Naumi Hotel Auckland Airport ♥♥ Who says airport hotels have to be sterile and boring? Not Naumi. A 5-minute drive from the airport, this affordable, art-driven hotel has rooms and suites in four bold themes: the all-pink Blush rooms (no rose-colored glasses necessary), the Oasis rooms (calming modern spaces with Art Deco accents), the Ziggy suite (a technicolor dream inspired by fashion designer Missoni), and the Dotty suite (paying homage to Japanese artist Yayoi Kusama with its infinite dots). Freestanding soaker tubs, free parking, free Yellow Bus ticket to the airport, and ample amenities (including an outdoor pool and 3-hole golf course, perfect for long layovers) round out the experience. Book direct in advance at least 14 days for considerable discounts.

153 Kirkbride Rd., Mangere. naumihotels.com/aucklandairport. ✆ **09/912-3333.** 193 units. NZ$155–NZ$770 double. Free parking. **Amenities:** Bar; restaurant; gym; pool; yoga garden; golf course; free Wi-Fi.

Outdoor pool at the arty Naumi Hotel Auckland Airport.

WHERE TO EAT IN AUCKLAND

A mecca for NZ's best chefs and culinary stars, Auckland is home to some of the country's best restaurants serving "New Zealand Modern"—a style defined by an emphasis on local and seasonal ingredients often combined with Asian, French, or British cooking techniques. Of course, you'll find all types of cultural cuisines in the city's many corners, with some of the best restaurants located along Viaduct Basin and the Wynyard Quarter, in Britomart and Commercial Bay, and on Ponsonby Road. If you venture farther out into the suburbs, there are hundreds more restaurants, cafes, and delis to choose from—basically anywhere you can squeeze in a couple of chairs and a few tables.

Most of the cheap eats in and around the city tend to be Asian eateries. You'll also have good luck finding inexpensive restaurants along K Road and farther out in the suburbs.

Like most New Zealanders, Aucklanders dine early, so when a restaurant is listed as being open until "late," that generally means around 9pm. You'll be lucky to find any kitchens open past 11pm.

Downtown & Along the Harbor

EXPENSIVE

Amano ♥♥♥ ITALIAN Amano is a Britomart institution. Line up with the city workers for takeaways—great coffee, New Zealand's best almond croissant, creme brûlée donuts, a wide range of fancy filled buns and sandwiches—or sit down in the rustic-industrial interior, strung with thousands of dried flowers. There's a choice of breakfast cocktails (fancy a passionfruit martini or a rhubarb cosmo?) and the lunch and dinner offerings focus on Italian-inspired dairy, seafood, pasta, and meat—burrata, Hawkes Bay lamb, Fiordland venison, Southland smoked fish.

68 Tyler St. savor.co.nz/amano. ✆ **09/394-1416.** Main courses NZ$28–NZ$49. Daily 7am–late.

Baduzzi ♥♥ ITALIAN Okay, so the name translates to "meatballs," but you're going to get a whole lot more than your mom's go-to dinner when you rock up here. For starters, Baduzzi is in a very cool location, right near the water and close to a bunch of other eateries, and while many of the dishes have an Italian bent, it also serves some excellent steak and seafood. And I actually thought I'd died and gone to heaven when I first tasted the crayfish meatballs. In the unlikely event that you need further convincing, it's run by two of the most experienced and well-respected chefs in town. Trust me—it's good.

10–26 Jellicoe St., Wynyard Quarter. baduzzi.co.nz. ✆ **09/309-9339.** Main courses NZ$32–NZ$48. Reservations required. Daily 11:30am–late.

Bistro Saine ♥♥♥ FRENCH Open "from breakfast to bonsoir," this new-in-2025 offering in the Hotel Indigo draws inspiration from New York's French bistros. Vegetarians won't find many options here, but the local seafood, organic chicken, braised pork, and sausages are all excellent. The wine list is extensive—featuring NZ, Australian, and European wines—and the sommelier Pierre Bernardeau has Michelin-star experience. It's small, so it pays to reserve if you're with a group and you want to eat between 6 and 8pm. Thanks to the soft lighting and dark wood it has a lovely cozy feel—and the acoustics are great, so a table for two feels quite private.

51 Albert St. bistrosaine.co.nz. ✆ **09/610-8404.** Main courses from NZ$34. Dinner reservations recommended. Open daily 6:30–10:30am, noon–3pm, and 5–10pm.

French flair elevates the menu at Bistro Saine.

Esther ♥♥♥ MEDITERRANEAN Celebrated Australian chef Sean Connolly is behind the Mediterranean-inspired menu and the design of the open, country-style kitchen (complete with a gold-plated pizza oven). Heavy on the local—such as daily caught seafood—it's intentionally simple food without many frills, allowing the flavor of the ingredients to shine through. The menu changes monthly, but you can expect dishes like baked saganaki cheese with honey and chili; fresh pasta with Te Anau saffron; Pacific rock oysters; and slow-roasted merino lamb shoulder with anchovies. Save room for dessert; staff confess they can't get enough of the burnt Basque cheesecake.

4 Viaduct Harbour. estherrestaurant.com. ✆ **09/379-9123.** Mains NZ$25–NZ$49. Mon–Tues 6:30am–10:30am and 5:30pm–late; Wed–Fri 6:30am–10:30am, noon–4pm, and 5:30pm–late; Sat–Sun 7am–11am and 5:30pm–late.

Kingi ♥♥ SEAFOOD/BREAKFAST Like the Hotel Britomart next door, Kingi celebrates sustainability, and its seafood is sourced accordingly, with oysters from Waiheke Island, *kahawai* (a type of fish found in the waters of NZ and Australia) from Little Barrier Island, and blue cod from the Chatham Islands. The menu will even tell you the name of the fisher who caught it. More than that, it's my pick for a fish-free breakfast spot—its take on huevos rancheros (a kūmara tortilla with fried eggs and mole) really hits the spot. Of course, you can also start your morning with some smoked fish (accompanied by eggs and rosti) if you prefer. It's a cozy spot for chilly mornings, set in the historic Masonic House with exposed brick walls and a massive fireplace.

29 Galway St. kingibritomart.com. ✆ **09/300-9596.** NZ$38–NZ$49. Dinner reservations recommended. Daily 7am–late.

Origine ♥♥♥ FRENCH It can be a little tricky to find the entrance to Origine—up several escalators in the Commercial Bay mall—but it's absolutely worth the scavenger hunt. Affable chef Ben Bayly, who now has his own national TV show, serves French cuisine with a Kiwi twist in a calm, high-ceilinged glass-fronted space with a view of the harbor and the ferries coming and going. Expect slow-cooked beef-cheek bourguignon, lobster, and all the

The chic harborview dining room at Origine.

French classics like escargot, French onion soup, profiteroles, and soufflé.

Level 2A of Commercial Bay. origine.nz. ✆ **027/674-4463.** Main courses NZ$39–NZ$99. Mon–Fri 8am–late, Sat 11am–late, Sun noon–late.

Sails ♥ SEAFOOD Bart Littlejohn's family established this Auckland icon set smack in the middle of Auckland's biggest marina many years ago. For a long time it was the go-to place for special occasions, but a recent revamp has seen it take on a more casual ambience. It's still the perfect spot to enjoy an array of seafood while looking out over the marina and deciding on which yacht you'd like to sail away. Always on the menu: a range of fresh oysters and an expertly cooked catch of the day.

103–113 Westhaven Dr., Westhaven Marina. sailsrestaurant.co.nz. ✆ **09/378-9890.** Main courses from NZ$40. Reservations required. Wed 6:30pm–late, Thurs–Sun noon–late.

Soul Bar and Bistro ♥♥ SEAFOOD Excellent international food served in a prime Viaduct Harbor location with fabulous people-watching: Those are the strong reasons those in the know continue to choose this Auckland institution. On any given day you're likely to spot the odd famous face (well, famous in New Zealand) along with the business crowd and high-flyers in general. The meat- and seafood-heavy menu isn't great for those with dietary restrictions, but vegetarians will find a few pastas and salads to choose from.

Hobson and Customs St. W. soulbar.co.nz. ✆ **09/356-7249.** Main courses NZ$23–NZ$50. Reservations recommended. Daily 11am–late.

When the weather's nice, be sure to ask to sit on Soul Bar and Bistro's view-rich patio.

skycity & FABULOUS FEDERAL ST.

Also known as **Federal St. at SkyCity,** this formerly nondescript downtown side-street is now a premium dining destination, with the beautiful, five-star SkyCity Grand Hotel—and several of its flagship restaurants—at its center. **MASU by Nic Watt** ♥♥ (an acclaimed chef), which features the traditional Japanese robata style of cooking over an open charcoal grill, won Best New Restaurant in *Cuisine* NZ's Good Food Awards. Not only is the food fabulous, but watching the incredible range of activity in the open kitchen is positively addictive. Leading Aotearoa chef Michael Meredith is in charge at nearby **Metita,** named after his mother, who once ran a food stall in Samoa's Apia market. Dining here is a unique experience—the tagline is "Pacific cuisine, reimagined." Don't skip dessert, and even the mocktails are mind-blowing; I highly recommend the navy-blue Mist of Ana Ahu. The menu helpfully contains a glossary of unfamiliar Samoan words. For more casual dining, pop across the road to Kiwi celebrity chef Al Brown's **Depot Eatery** ♥ (depot eatery.co.nz) for oysters and everything meat or—right next door—his **Federal Delicatessen** ♥ (thefed.co.nz), with its menu and decor inspired by classic Jewish NYC diners. Book for all the above at skycityauckland.co.nz/restaurants.

MODERATE

Café Hanoi ♥♥ MODERN VIETNAMESE Café Hanoi uses heaps of fresh herbs, delicious seafood, and free-range chicken and pork in its takes on Hanoi street food and the cuisines of Northern Vietnam. Can't decide what to get? Along with its a la carte menu (designed for sharing) Café Hanoi now offers a four-course offering for NZ$65. (There's also a special menu for plant-based eaters.) Get here early—it's often closed by 9pm.

27 Galway St. cafehanoi.co.nz. ✆ **09/302-3478.** Main courses NZ$15–NZ$34. Reservations required. Mon–Fri noon–3pm and 5pm–late, Sat–Sun 5pm–late.

Odettes ♥♥ NEW ZEALAND/FUSION A seriously good casual eating experience for breakfast and lunch, Odettes emphasizes Mediterranean and North African sharing plates, but not just *any* sharing plates—expect some very interesting flavor and texture combos, especially with the accompaniments. The food changes seasonally: A recent menu included burnt eggplant with goat feta, zucchini fritters with haloumi, market fish carpaccio with pickled fennel, and fried brussels sprouts with miso maple syrup. There are loads of vegetarian and gluten-free options.

Shed 5, City Works Depot, 90 Wellesley St. W. odettes.co.nz. ✆ **09/309-0304.** NZ$19–NZ$35. Mon–Fri 7am–3pm, Sat–Sun 8am–3pm.

INEXPENSIVE

Your best bet for cheap eats may be to head to one of the city's food halls, where you can often get a tasty, filling meal for as little as NZ$15. Not to be confused with middle-America mall food courts, these collections of eateries are filled with independent food vendors in kiosks, sometimes with their own individually decorated seating areas. Commercial Bay's **Harbour Eats** ♥♥

Café Hanoi evokes the shabby chic allure of its namesake city.

dining hub, 21 Queen St., Level 2, is a glowing example; it seats 650 spread across two hallways and hosts a diverse range of vendors serving up Thai, Middle Eastern, Korean, Indian, Mexican, South American, Greek, and Vietnamese food. There are also a handful of dine-in restaurants and pubs here. **Elliott Stables ♥**, 39 Elliot St. (elliottstables.co.nz) in the CBD, is even more boutique. It has 10 on-site eateries, serving up bao buns, fresh juices, Malay street food, pizzas, and tacos from **Taco Amaiz ♥♥**, which has quickly won fans for its fresh Kiwi ingredients and authentic Mexican flavors. The food court is open daily from noon to 9pm.

Finally, if seafood is your thing, the **Auckland Fish Market ♥♥**, 22 Jellicoe St. (afm.co.nz), has its own food hall, where you can sample catches straight from the sea. Individual vendors have individual hours, but it's generally open from 8am to 5pm.

Scratch Bakers ♥♥ CAFE You'll want to eavesdrop for the latest news in this alleyway cafe; located right across from the *New Zealand Herald* office, it's where all the "journos" (journalists) come to get their caffeine fix. It produces some of the most beautiful pastries in Auckland (its baked goods,

ice cream, YOU SCREAM . . .

Giapo Grazioli's amazing ice cream creations have thrilled customers ever since he first opened **Giapo ♥♥**, 12 Gore St. (giapo.com), in 2008. Every single ingredient (and I mean *everything*) is made on the (entirely gluten-free) premises, so it's little wonder that this haute ice cream establishment just keeps on cleaning up all the relevant awards. They're artworks in their own right. (Case in point: The cones are shaped like realistic giant squids, or comical helicopters.) Go. Just as soon as you can.

Fish 'n' Chips—A Kiwi Ritual

If you're lucky enough to visit Auckland over the summer months and you fancy doing the "when in Rome" thing, head to one of the following establishments and invest in a fragrant package of piping-hot golden chips (aka French fries) and fish coated in a delicious crisp batter, all wrapped in newspaper. The combo will cost you a very affordable NZ$10 to NZ$15. **FishSmith** (200 Jervois Rd., Herne Bay; daily noon–9pm) or **Greenwoods Fresh Catch** (1 Pah Rd., Epsom; daily 11:30am–2pm and 4:30–8pm) are the best choices. And where should you go to eat it? I highly recommend a beach or maybe a park. Anywhere outdoors on a fine evening is good—just watch out for the seagulls.

including scones, brioche, and pies, are served at cafes and restaurants across the city). Of course, there's also a full menu if you're looking for something more substantial, but I'm here for everything that involves butter.

5 Graham St. scratchbakers.co.nz. ✆ **09/307-2323.** NZ$10–NZ$25. Mon–Fri 6:30am–3pm.

Karangahape Road

K Road might be colorful and gritty, but it also has some excellent dining options. Down at the end of St. Kevin's Arcade, by the huge windows looking out to Myers Park and the Sky Tower, is Lebanese restaurant **Gemmayze Street** ♥♥♥, 183 Karangahape Rd. (gemmayzestreet.co.nz). Chef Samir Allen's Lebanese ancestors arrived in New Zealand 130 years ago, but he's still deeply connected to the culture—and the food. Here, as in Lebanon, you can simply say "jeeb" (bring) and a parade of delicious mezze—hummus, haloumi, scampi, and *shish barak* (dumplings)—will arrive at your table (from NZ$65 per person). It's open Tuesday to Saturday from 6pm until late. If you visit in the morning instead, the same light-drenched courtyard tables are used by **Bestie Cafe** ♥♥ (bestiecafe.co.nz), a top brunch spot with all the usual classics, but elevated by its innovative sides, like haloumi bites with hot honey and herb whipped ricotta, or beetroot cured salmon with burnt orange cream cheese. It's open daily until 2:30pm.

Sri Pinang ♥ MALAYSIAN This popular K Road restaurant never disappoints—but it can get awfully busy, so phone ahead or get there early. In 2022, it made Condé Nast *Traveler* Magazine's list of restaurants around the world "worth travelling for." Angie's roti curry at NZ$14 is, in my book, the best value around, but Sri Pinang is also justly famous for its beef rendang. As we went to press, it was only open for lunch, but call ahead to check, as it may open for evenings again in the future.

356 Karangahape Rd. ✆ **09/358-3886.** NZ$15–NZ$20. Mon–Fri 11:30am–2:30pm.

Ponsonby

Despite the recent closure of a number of top fine-dining options, this suburb still has excellent eateries of all types, with many spots evolving from daytime cafe to nighttime wine-bar. Standing the test of time, *la grande signora* **Prego ♥♥**, 226 Ponsonby Rd. (prego.co.nz; ✆ **09/376-3095;** mains NZ$26–NZ$58), has been here since the 1980s—a long time in Auckland restaurant history—and is as good as it ever was. Serving Italian, with a dedicated vegan menu and gluten-free options, it's open daily from noon until late. Another mainstay of the strip, **Dizengoff ♥**, 256 Ponsonby Rd. (✆ **09/360-0108**), is a top spot for breakfast fare, with its balsamic mushrooms on ciabatta being a favorite. It's open daily from 6:30am to 3pm.

Come to **Bodega Deli and Eatery ♥**, 86 Ponsonby Rd. (bodegadeli.co.nz) at lunchtime for superlative (if expensive) sandwiches (11am–2:30pm)—think cold cuts and provolone, chicken cutlets in vodka sauce, wagyu beef, or Cajun prawns on soft yet crispy housemade bread (NZ$18–NZ$20). Mornings it's the home of sfogliatelle and other pastries, and in the evenings (Thurs–Sat from 4pm) it's a great place for a wine or chocolate negroni and some people-watching, though the food runs more to drinking snacks than a proper dinner.

The ground floor food hall at **Ponsonby Central ♥♥**, 136 Ponsonby Rd. (ponsonbycentral.co.nz), offers 20 eateries alongside boutique shopping. There's something here for every budget and taste preference (try **Burger Burger ♥** or **Ola's Arepas ♥**); it's open daily 9am to 9pm. Up on the second floor, the **Ponsonby International Foodcourt ♥♥**, 106 Ponsonby Rd. (ponsonbyfoodcourt.co.nz), feels more like an authentic Asian hawker-center; it's open daily 11am to 10pm. In the same complex, the **Blue Breeze Inn ♥**, 146 Ponsonby Rd. (thebluebreezeinn.co.nz; ✆ **09/360-0303**), will have your taste buds thinking they are in China (main dishes designed for sharing are NZ$18–NZ$42), and the rest of your senses reveling in the Pacific Island atmosphere, complete with cocktails that complement the experience. It's open daily for lunch and dinner.

The Blue Breeze Inn.

Cocoro ♥♥♥ JAPANESE Serious Auckland foodies rate this as the city's best Japanese restaurant, and having experienced chef Makoto Tokuyama's magic touch, I'm inclined to agree. The freshest of seafood is front and center (and the chef's specialty), but a sprinkling of meaty dishes includes grilled Wagyu filet and charcoal-finished duck leg confit. Although a la carte dining is an option, I highly recommend one of the three degustation menus, which can be paired with either sake or wine.

56a Brown St. cocoro.co.nz. ✆ **09/360-0927.** Degustation menu from NZ$150. Reservations essential. Tues–Thurs 5:30–late, Fri–Sat noon–2pm and 5:30–late.

San Ray ♥♥ MODERN NEW ZEALAND Owned by the team at **Cazador** ♥♥ on Dominion Road (see p. 111), this airy new place serves bistro classics with a Mexican and Southern Californian flavor, cooked over coals and woodfire—steaks, venison, Tajín fries, mimosas, and micheladas. Try the woodfired chicken, which has been prepped for 3 days before it arrives, perfectly done, on your plate. The patio garden is lovely place for a breakfast of jalapeño cornbread or buckwheat churros with espresso chocolate sauce.

Cooking over the woodfire at San Ray.

118 Ponsonby Rd. sanray.nz. ✆ **09/360-0486.** Main courses NZ$30–NZ$55. Mon 8am–3pm, Tues–Fri 8am–9:30pm, Sat 9am–9:30pm, Sun 9am–4pm.

Mount Eden & Surrounds

Blue Rose Catering ♥♥ CAFE This quirky cafe is a worthwhile stop if you want to try some authentic, casual, and affordable Māori and Pasifika cuisine. Eating at Blue Rose is kind of like hanging out in your Polynesian nana's lounge room—in fact chef Lenny Stevens' Gisborne grandma had exactly this blue-rose wallpaper when Stevens was a kid in the '80s. He has

Meat pies play a starring role on the menu at the quirky, homey Blue Rose Catering.

both Māori and Cook Island ancestry, and both sides are on display in the cafe's award-winning pies: try the Māori stone-cooked hangi with pork belly, kūmara, and gravy; or the Pasifika palusami, with corned-beef, taro leaves, and coconut cream. The pies are large and fairly heavy, so you'll want to walk them off out West or up nearby Mount Albert or Mount Eden.

414 Sandringham Rd. bluerosecatering.co.nz. ✆ **09/846-1579.** Pies $11, all-day breakfast and lunch NZ$12–NZ$30. Mon–Fri 7am–3pm, Sat–Sun 8am–4pm.

Cazador ♥♥ GRILL/FUSION Carnivores are well catered to at this family-owned Dominion Road mainstay, where the meat is wild and sourced directly from hunters—think coal-grilled venison, kingfish crudo, or fried duck hearts—and the chefs make their own charcuterie, which you can also buy from the on-site delicatessen. For the full experience, go for the Feast sharing menu (NZ$99), with optional matching drinks.

854 Dominion Rd. cazador.co.nz. ✆ **09/620-8730.** Main courses NZ$42. Reservations advised. Wed–Sun 5pm–late.

Forest ♥♥♥ VEGETARIAN Named Restaurant of the Year in Auckland's 2024 Metro Best Restaurant Awards, this cozy, colorful space gives you a choice of sitting in the dining room or at the bar, watching chef Plabita Florence in action. Her creations are experimental and umami-laden—like smoked squash with Marmite cream and peas, or halloumi with eggplant and sour plum. If you happen to visit during the autumn *feijoa* (pineapple guava) season, don't miss Florence's famous deep-fried feijoa with Earl Grey custard—you could not wish for a more nostalgic, classically Kiwi dessert. There are only 17 tables, so book well ahead.

243 Dominion Rd. forestrestaurant.co.nz. ✆ **0210/901-3352.** Sharing plates NZ$28–NZ$37. Wed–Sun 5–10pm.

The French Café ♥♥♥ FRENCH/KIWI One of the most celebrated independent restaurants in Auckland for more than 20 years, now under the leadership of executive chef Sid Sahrawat and his partner Chand, the French Café continues to rack up the accolades (the latest being three hats as awarded by the Cuisine NZ Good Food Awards, the country's highest culinary honor). Suffice to say that dining here is an unforgettable experience, combining exquisite food (a recent summer menu featured white asparagus, smoked eel, and finger lime; and Hawke's Bay lamb with agria potato, vindaloo, and fenugreek) with impeccable service and a wonderful ambience. The attention to detail at every level really has to be experienced to be believed. Come on a Sunday evening to enjoy a three-course fixed menu for just NZ$75.

210 Symonds St. thefrenchcafe.co.nz. ✆ **09/377-1911.** Main courses NZ$48, 6-course tasting menu NZ$185. Reservations required. Tues–Fri 5:30pm–late, Sat noon–3:30pm and 5:30pm–late; Sun 5:30pm–late.

Just Like Martha ♥♥ CAFE A true local secret, this is the kind of place Aucklanders drive to for brunch and don't want to tell their friends about, lest they accidentally generate lines. The baked goods—often decorated with

Exquisitely plated tasting menu courses at The French Café (p. 111).

fresh, edible flowers—are beautiful enough to bring to your in-laws for dinner (if you don't eat the treats before you get there). The cooked menu, with lots of vegan options, are just as good; I'm particularly partial to the green chile scrambled eggs, and the creamy mushrooms. It probably won't surprise you to learn that the "Martha" in question is the queen of all things delicious—and slightly pretentious—Martha Stewart.

985 Mt. Eden Rd. justlikemartha.com. ✆ **09/974-4273.** Main courses NZ$12–NZ$22. Daily 7am–4pm.

Parnell/Newmarket

In Parnell, **Cibo** ♥, 91 St. Georges Bay Rd. (cibo.co.nz; ✆ **09/303-9660**), has for years been a favorite among the expense-account crowd. We recommend it because the quality and range of dishes (an Asian/Kiwi fusion) adds up to much more than the bill at the end. In Newmarket, **Tasca** ♥, 25 Nuffield St. (tasca.co.nz; ✆ **09/522-4443**), serves Spanish tapas with lots of vegan and vegetarian options.

Non Solo Pizza ♥♥ ITALIAN BRASSERIE This is the perfect place for a lazy afternoon in a sunny courtyard (or inside), sipping on the best wines and working your way through a feast of Italian favorites. We're talking pizzas, pastas, small plates to share, or a genuine big-table meal with friends or family. Top dishes are the homemade chicken-and-spinach ravioli tossed in thyme, sage, basil, and vine-ripened mushrooms; and tiger prawns pan-fried in garlic. Luscious desserts are the ultimate finish for a terrific, relaxed dining experience.

259 Parnell Rd. nonsolopizza.co.nz. ✆ **09/379-5358.** Main courses NZ$20–NZ$40. Reservations recommended. Daily noon–late

WEST meets EAST

If you're searching for a good range of different international cuisines, look no further than storied **Dominion Road,** a major arterial road that runs north-south across most of the central isthmus for more than 7km (4½ miles), cutting through the middle of Mt. Eden and running to Mt. Roskill in the south. It's so beloved by locals, an extremely catchy song was written about it by The Mutton Birds in 1992 (look it up—it's a classic). It was recently estimated that over 80 different cultural groups are represented up and down this colorful route across the city. Wherever possible, make a reservation, especially on weekends, but a number of the most cheap and cheerful don't take bookings—you'll have to take your chances. Some restaurants are not much more than hole-in-the-wall dumpling and noodle houses where the number of people crammed in at any time testifies to the good, cheap food. But there are also several top fine-dining options worth making a pilgrimage to, including **Forest** ♥♥♥ (p. 111) and **Cazador** ♥♥ (p. 111).

North Shore & Riverhead

The Engine Room ♥♥, 115 Queen St., Northcote Point (engineroom.net.nz; ✆ **09/480-9502**), is still among the best the North Shore has to offer. Its fabulous cookbook makes a very worthy souvenir. Mains from NZ$43 to NZ$51.

Hallertau Brewery ♥♥ BREWPUB Hallertau's brewery has become a weekend destination for many Aucklanders. The main draw is the beer—including the genre-defying #9, also known as "the beer of Auckland." But there's also an extensive wine list, superb thin-crust wood-fired pizzas, a huge outdoor beer garden, and a play structure for kids. Add in homemade sauces and bread, eggs laid by free-roaming chickens, and even kombucha on tap, and you've got a good day ahead of you. ***Note:*** Indoor seating is limited, and Hallertau is about a 25-minute drive from the city, so save this for a sunny day when you're tired of being a tourist. Reservations on weekends are advised. A secondary location also now exists southeast of the city in similarly rural Clevedon.

1171 Coatesville Riverhead Hwy., Riverhead. hallertau.co.nz. ✆ **09/412-5555.** Main courses NZ$18–NZ$36. Tues–Sat noon–10pm; Sun noon–9pm.

Near the Airport

My absolute favorite place to go during a layover is the always accommodating **Kawau Kitchen** ♥♥, 6 Leonard Dr. (kawaukitchen.co.nz; ✆ **09/255-5515**). It punches well above its weight for an airport restaurant, possibly because it's the go-to spot for all the flight attendants in training at the airline school across the street. The light and airy space serves tasty cabinet food, perfect cups of coffee, and all-day breakfast and lunch. (My go-to is the chile scrambled eggs with marinated feta and kimchi.) It's totally worth walking the 15 minutes from the airport terminal.

AUCKLAND SHOPPING

Auckland's shops are generally open daily 9am to 5pm; many stay open later on Thursday and Friday. ***Tip:*** Some shops will post your purchases home, thereby avoiding the 15% Goods and Services Tax you pay on most items in this country.

Central City

In the heart of the central business district, **Britomart** ♥♥♥ (britomart.org) is a whole lot more than the headquarters of Auckland's public transport system at the bottom of Queen Street—it's the precinct where you'll find some of New Zealand's hippest designers and coolest eateries. Top Kiwi designers **Karen Walker, Trelise Cooper, World, Zambesi, Juliette Hogan, Allbirds,** and **Sylvester** all have stores here. A full list of retailers is at britomart.org.

We also like the **High Street–Vulcan Lane–O'Connell Street** area ♥♥♥ (heartofthecity.co.nz) for Kiwi fashion houses, accessories, and art, not to mention primo coffee and food. Also here is the excellent bookstore **Unity** ♥♥♥, 19 High St. (unitybooks.co.nz; ✆ **09/307-0731**), where you can find the works of most contemporary Kiwi authors. The **Vault** ♥, 13 High St. (thevaultnz.com; ✆ **09/377-7665**), is the place for reasonably priced New Zealand and international design items—everything from jewelry to stationery to small gifts.

Chancery Square, 34 Courthouse Lane (chancerysq.co.nz), is packed with international brand stores, exclusive fashion names, cafes, and restaurants.

All manner of chain stores line **Queen Street** from top to bottom, but I think you find much better shops down the little side streets running off it. Among the excellent specialty shops, **Fingers** ♥♥, 2 Kitchener St. (fingers.co.nz; ✆ **09/373-3974**), is Auckland's most established New Zealand jewelry collective. **Kura Gallery** ♥♥, 95A Customs St. W (kuragallery.co.nz; ✆ **09/302-1151**), has a range of original New Zealand art and crafts.

The central city's newest shopping complex, **Commercial Bay** ♥, 7 Queen St. (commercialbay.co.nz), houses mainly chain stores, but these include made-in-NZ brands like **Aotea** (aoteamade.co.nz), a skincare brand similar to Australia's Aesop; **Edmund Hillary** (buckinghams.co.nz/collections/edmund-hillary-collection), an outdoors-themed lifestyle label; and NZ women's-wear label **Twenty-Seven Names** (twentysevennames.co.nz).

Antiques Hunting

The most popular concentrations of antiques stores are around the Epsom area and in Parnell, Remuera, and the inner city. In Epsom, check out **John Stephens Antiques,** 15 Shore Rd. (✆ **09/529-1660**); and **Country Antiques,** 489 Manukau Rd. (✆ **09/630-5252**). In Remuera, look for **Abbey Antiques,** 87 Great South Rd. (✆ **09/520-2045**), and several others on the same stretch of Great South Road.

GOING TO market

For a definitively Pacific experience, visit the **Otara Market ♥♥♥**, Newbury St., Otara (✆ **09/274-0830**), on Saturday from 6am to noon. It's the largest Polynesian market in the world, with larger-than-life personalities, exotic foods and smells, wonderful *tapa* cloth, flax mats, and baskets, and bone carvings.

There's a strong Polynesian and Asian influence at the extensive **Avondale Market,** Avondale Racecourse, Ash Street (avondalesundaymarkets.co.nz; ✆ **09/818-4931**), held on Sunday from 5am to noon. It features a mass of fruit, vegetables, new and used clothes, and bric-a-brac, but no fast-food or drink stalls.

An excellent **City Farmers' Market** runs every Saturday morning from 8am to noon in the large courtyards behind the Britomart Transport Centre on Gore Street.

In Parnell, the **Parnell Market** (parnellmarkets.co.nz; ✆ **022/551-4444**) is hosted by Italian-style delicatessen Buono every Saturday from 8am to 1pm on Saint Georges Bay Road.

Enjoy a great day in the country at the acclaimed **Matakana Village Farmer's Market ♥♥♥** (visitmatakana.co.nz), which showcases artisan foodstuffs, gourmet delicacies, wine, and produce. It's within an hour's striking distance of Auckland by car—and you can make a day of it by visiting the gorgeous white-sand beaches of **Omaha ♥♥** or **Tāwharanui Regional Park ♥♥♥**.

Ponsonby & Herne Bay

The suburb of Ponsonby is best known for its bars and eateries, but you could spend all day browsing in its gorgeous design and fashion stores. Some of New Zealand's best designers have branches here, including **World, Andrea Moore, Cybèle, Karen Walker,** and **Ruby.** You'll find local art and design treasures at **Bijoux Gallery ♥♥**, 8 Ponsonby Rd. (www.bijoux.co.nz); and **the Poi Room ♥♥**, 130 Ponsonby Rd. (thepoiroom.co.nz). My all-time favorite New Zealand lingerie brand **Ohen ♥♥♥**, 58 Brown St. (ohenunderwear.com), has its fit room here—book ahead for a fitting—as does lovely Waiheke "eco-luxe" organic yoga wear outfit **WE-AR ♥♥**, 22 Ponsonby Rd. (we-ar.com).

Parnell/Newmarket

Shopping Parnell is a special experience, albeit an expensive one. You'll find all sorts of exclusive gifts in a rabbit's warren of little historic buildings, restored to picturesque splendor, that stretch along a mile of **Parnell Road** (parnell.net.nz). **Newmarket** (newmarket.co.nz) has more than 40 designer fashion stores and New Zealand's largest concentration of shoe stores—20 of them!—with the hot spots being **Nuffield** and **Teed streets ♥♥♥**, where you'll find high-end stores of iconic international and Kiwi fashion brands like **Karen Walker, Trelise Cooper, Sylvester,** and **Zambesi.** There are a number of excellent cafes and restaurants here, too.

AUCKLAND AFTER DARK

Auckland has something for everyone—the adventurous, the sophisticated, the young, and the young at heart. From 24-hour casinos and live theater to cinema, clubs, pubs, bars, and dance spots, you can party all the way to breakfast time.

For tickets to events, plus info on what's on here and around New Zealand, peruse the sites of **Ticketek** (ticketek.co.nz; ✆ **09/307-5000**) or **Ticketmaster** (ticketmaster.co.nz; ✆ **09/970-9700**).

The Performing Arts

Auckland Live ♥♥♥, 50 Mayoral Dr. (aucklandlive.co.nz; ✆ **09/309-2677**), is the cultural core of Auckland, located in the central area bordered by Mayoral Drive and Albert, Wellesley, and Queen streets. It includes the **Aotea Centre** (✆ **09/307-5060**), opened in 1990 by Dame Kiri Te Kanawa, which features theater, ballet, dance, opera, major stage productions, art exhibitions, and lots of local drama; and the **Auckland Town Hall,** with its Great Hall (modeled after the Gewandhaus Concert Hall in Leipzig, Germany, bombed during World War II), regarded as one of the finest acoustically tuned concert halls in the world; it schedules regular performances by the Auckland Philharmonia and the New Zealand Symphony Orchestra.

More experimental and edgy theatre including comedy, dance, drag, and cabaret can be seen at **Q Theatre,** 305 Queen St. (qtheatre.co.nz), and the neighboring **Basement Theatre,** Lower Greys Ave. (basementtheatre.co.nz), where you'll find a young, diverse late-night crowd spilling outside on warm nights. I highly recommend its regular Friday night improv show, starting at 10pm (choose what you pay from NZ$12.)

Kiwis hanging out at the Aotea Centre.

PLACE YOUR bets: A NIGHT AT THE CASINO

Located below the SkyTower, **SkyCity Auckland Casino,** Victoria and Federal streets (skycityauckland.co.nz; ✆ **0800/759-2489** in NZ, or 09/363-6000), is the largest casino in New Zealand, hosting some 12,000 gamblers per day. Thanks to a vast expanse of gaming tables (blackjack, roulette, craps, Caribbean stud poker, baccarat, tai sai, pai gow, and money wheel), an 80-seat keno lounge, and more than 1,200 slot machines, it never feels too crowded. Note that hats or caps are not permitted (except for religious or cultural reason or within the Poker Zone), nor is torn or dirty clothing. The casino is open 24/7.

The **SkyCity Theatre** ♥ is a 700-seat theater featuring state-of-the-art technology and major local and international performers in dance, theater, rock, pop, jazz, and cabaret. For details on events, call ✆ **0800/759-2489** or visit skycity.co.nz.

The Live Music Scene

Check out heartofthecity.co.nz or undertheradar.co.nz for the latest on the music scene. You'll find jazz and rhythm-and-blues gigs at bars, restaurants, and hotels around the city. For punk or rock, head to the funky underground **Whammy Bar,** St. Kevin's Arcade, 183 Karangahape Rd. (undertheradar.co.nz).

For a thumping good night, try **Studio The Venue,** 340 Karangahape Rd. (studiovenue.co.nz; ✆ **09/3580-994**), not far from the central city, which has a great lineup of local and international artists of rap, hip hop, hard rock, pop rock, and more. The large **Spark Arena,** 42–80 Mahuhu Crescent, Parnell (sparkarena.co.nz; bookings at ticketmaster.co.nz or ✆ **0800/111-999**), is where you can catch a star-studded concert or top international artist. The venue holds 12,000 people, but it is a little soulless and cavernous. Catch a bus from the city or walk (about 20 min.).

If Irish music is your thing, you'll find it at **Danny Doolan's** ♥, Viaduct Harbour (goodspiritshospitality.co.nz/danny-doolans; ✆ **09/358-2554**), offering food and live entertainment 7 nights a week. The **Powerstation** ♥♥♥, 33 Mount Eden Rd., Eden Terrace (powerstation.net.nz), has been the iconic starting point for many well-known New Zealand groups including internationally recognized Shihad. It features local talent as well as high-profile international names.

The Club & Bar Scene

If you want a night with the work-hard, play-hard business crowd, head to the **Parnell** neighborhood; older, richer, devil-may-care types flock to **Viaduct Harbour** and its many night-time haunts. A younger, funkier set hangs out in **High St./Vulcan Lane** or at **Britomart** in the inner city; most of the all-night clubs, drag clubs, and gay bars are along **Karangahape Road;** and **Ponsonby** is a favored upmarket place for drinks, dinner, and a general wind-up before hitting the club scene. The hottest spots in town change regularly; my advice is to ask a local who dresses like you where they like to go.

DOWNTOWN **The Churchill** ♥ claims to be the highest rooftop bar in Auckland city, with sparkling nighttime views down the length of Queen Street and across to the Sky Tower. Come here if you love gin—and if you're overwhelmed by the many options on the menu, flip to the 10-10-10 page, where you pick a gin, a mixer, and a botanical from a more manageable list. If you're a group of chatty, exuberant women, though, beware—on our visit we got told off by the bartender for laughing too loudly. It's at the top of the Four Points by Sheraton Hotel (396 Queen St.; thechurchillauckland.co.nz; ✆ **09/393-8240**). All the new rooftop hotel bars (including at the **Rooftop at QT** ♥♥, Voco's **Bar Albert** ♥♥, SO/'s **HI-SO** ♥, and the Sudima's **Sunset Bar** ♥♥) are super popular with locals and visitors alike, so expect lines to get in. See the hotel section for our write ups. For something lower-key, **Sweat Shop Brew Kitchen** ♥♥, 7 Sale St., Freemans Bay (sweatshopbrew.co.nz; ✆ **09/307-8148**), has a restaurant, live music stages, a microbrewery, private bars, and a huge outdoor deck. If you like an activity while you down a beer, I recommend teeing-up at **Holey Moley** ♥♥, in Viaduct Harbour at 204 Quay St. (holeymoley.co.nz; ✆ **09/887-4205**), a super-fun bar with a 27-hole mini-golf course spread over two levels.

In **Britomart,** classy new bars seem to spring up by the minute. **The Caretaker** ♥♥♥, hidden downstairs on Roukai Lane (caretaker.net.nz), bills itself as a New York–style cocktail lounge, inspired by the golden age of bartending, and drinking here is certainly a fun time. There's no menu; instead, one of the hosts will interview you about your preferences, and a suspender-clad bartender will surprise you (if you don't like it, you can send it back, and you can always order a classic). The underground speakeasy vibes are impeccable, and there's live jazz on Sundays, Mondays, and Tuesdays at 9pm. The **Chamberlain** ♥♥,

A glamorous, sky-high cocktail bar, the Churchill draws locals as well as hotel guests.

The tiny Lime Bar.

48 Tyler St. (thechamberlain.co.nz; ✆ **09/300-5279**), is an industrial-style bar with a strong focus on craft beers; there are around 15 on tap.

PONSONBY **Lime** ♥, 167 Ponsonby Rd. (limebar.co.nz; ✆ **09/360-7167**), is the smallest bar of all, and everyone, just everyone, is determined to be first or second here—after that, there's often a queue to get in. **The Whiskey** ♥, 210 Ponsonby Rd. (thewhiskey.co.nz; ✆ **09/361-2666**), has a chic interior and a great late-night rock music scene on Friday and Saturday. The atmosphere at **Chapel Bar and Bistro,** 147 Ponsonby Rd. (chapel.co.nz; ✆ **09/360-4528**), is stylish and relaxed, a bit like a neighborhood local. At groovy **Bedford Soda and Liquor** ♥♥, 4 Brown St. (bedfordsodaliquor.co.nz; ✆ **09/3787-5362**), inspired by Brooklyn backstreet dive bars, you can imbibe handmade sodas, innovative alcoholic and non-alcoholic cocktails, and tasty meatballs. The very popular **Malt Public House** ♥, 442 Richmond Rd., Grey Lynn (maltpublichouse.co.nz; ✆ **09/360-9537**), feels like a local corner pub, but with more warmth and style.

LGBTQI+ Friendly Clubs

As with the rest of New Zealand, queer travelers will find their welcome in any venue. But Auckland also has great gay nightlife, with some reliable favorites. K Road is the home of most venues: **Eagle Bar** ♥♥, 259 Karangahape Rd. (✆ **09/309-4979**), is a down-to-earth mixed-crowd kind of bar (open 7 days until late), while **Family Bar** ♥, 270 Karangahape Rd. (✆ **09/309-0213**), is Auckland's most popular drag/DJ bar/club (also open 7 days until late). One other in this colorful area is the super fun **Caluzzi Bar and Cabaret** ♥♥♥, 461 Karangahape Rd. (caluzzi.co.nz; ✆ **09/357-0778**), which offers drag cabaret shows with dinner.

Another destination is Ponsonby Road, which plays host to the Auckland Pride Parade each February (aucklandpride.org.nz). Here you'll also find one of the world's only lesbian history museums, the **Charlotte Museum Te Whare Takatāpui-Wāhine o Aotearoa** ♥, just off K Road at 1A Howe Street (charlottemuseum.co.nz; ✆ **022/850-1013;** free admission; Wed–Fri 10am–4pm, Sat 11am–4pm).

A SIDE TRIP TO WAIHEKE ISLAND

This divine little paradise is just 35 minutes from downtown Auckland by ferry. Of its permanent population of about 9,000, nearly 1,500 commute to the city each day to work; in summer, the island's population swells to over 40,000 as visitors come to holiday in the enchanting mix of white-sand beaches, lush native bush, green farmland, top wineries and vineyards, and swish little cafes and restaurants. I strongly recommend a stay of at least 1 or 2 nights, although it's also possible to get a good taste on a day trip from Auckland.

Essentials

ARRIVING **Fullers Ferries** (fullers.co.nz; ✆ **09/367-9111**) operates from downtown Auckland to Waiheke Island, with departures nearly every half hour. Ferries depart from Pier 2, Quay Street, in Central City. Most sailings are met by buses, shuttles, tour buses, and taxis at Matiatia, near the main township of Oneroa. The Fullers trip takes 35 minutes and costs NZ$62 round-trip for adults, NZ$28 children 5 to 15—check online for off-peak deals.

The **SeaLink Travel Group** (sealink.co.nz; ✆ **0800/732-546** in NZ, or 09/300-5900) runs a passenger/car ferry from Half Moon Bay, Pakuranga, arriving at the Kennedy Point Wharf, which is east of Matiatia. Ferries run every hour daily between 6am and 6pm. The fare is around NZ$160 to NZ$180 round-trip for a car and driver. Additional travelers or passengers without cars pay NZ$29.50 adults and NZ$14 children 5 to 15. Reservations are essential.

GETTING AROUND For information on Waiheke Island bus services, visit **Auckland Transport** (at.govt.nz). Buses can be paid for using an **AT HOP card** (see p. 72 for details). You can also hire a car at **Waiheke Auto**

Waiheke has some of the loveliest beaches in all of New Zealand.

Rentals, Matiatia Wharf (waihekerentals.co.nz; ✆ **09/372-8998**), which has good hourly rates and offers pickup and key drop-off service; expect to pay premium prices for fuel, however. Four-wheel-drive vehicles, scooters, motorbikes, and mountain bikes are also available. For bicycle, e-bike, e-moped, and scooter rental—imagine tripping around the island on a red Italian Vespa!—contact **Bikes and Beyond,** Matiatia Wharf carpark (see-nz.com/waiheke-island; ✆ **09/205-02233**). Rates begin at NZ$85 per day.

VISITOR INFORMATION The visitor website for the island is **tourismwaiheke.co.nz**.

ORIENTATION Waiheke Island is approximately 19km (12 miles) long and has 90km (56 miles) of coastline, 40km (25 miles) of which is white-sand beaches. **Oneroa,** the largest shopping village on Waiheke, is a 15- to 20-minute uphill walk from Matiatia Wharf, where the passenger ferries dock. It's a 10-minute drive from the Kennedy Point Wharf, where the car ferry docks. This western end of the island has the most settlement around **Sandy** and **Enclosure bays** and **Palm Beach. Ostend** and **Surfdale** also have shops and cafes, including a substantial supermarket in Ostend. Oneroa has an excellent grocery store as well, but the best supermarket is in Surfdale.

SPECIAL EVENTS The **Waiheke Island Jazz & Blues Festival ♥♥** (waihekejazzfestival.co.nz; ✆ **027/498-4658**), at Easter, attracts musicians and visitors from around the country. **Sculpture on the Gulf ♥♥♥** (sculptureonthegulf.co.nz; ✆ **09/372-9907**) is an unforgettable outdoor exhibition of large-scale contemporary sculpture along Waiheke Island's coastal walkway. It is held every other year; the 2027 show will run from February 26 through March 29.

Exploring Waiheke Island

In Oneroa, a top stop is the **Waiheke Community Art Gallery ♥♥**, 2 Korora Rd. (waiheke artgallery.org.nz; ✆ **09/372-9907**), which exhibits the works of resident artists and craftspeople on the island. It's open daily from 10am to 4pm. In the same complex you'll find the **Waiheke Musical Museum ♥** (musicalmuseum.org.nz), which has a collection of beautiful old instruments and hosts monthly free concerts. It's open 10:30am to 1:30pm Friday to Sunday.

The **Waiheke Island Historic Village and Museum ♥**, 165 Onetangi Rd. (✆ **09/372-2970**), is overlooked by a fortified Māori settlement site first inhabited some 700 years ago. Inside old cottages are collections of furniture, books, documents, and photographs. It's open Wednesdays and weekends year-round from 11am to 3pm; entry is by donation. Catch the Onetangi Bus no. 1 to get there.

If you're here on a Saturday, get up early for the **Ostend Market ♥**, Ostend Hall, on the corner of Ostend Road and Belgium Street (facebook.com/waihekeostendmarket; ✆ **0210/686-603**). A colorful assemblage of local pottery, island-made goods, fruit and vegetables, herbal remedies, massage, plants, herbs, and more; it's held from 8am to 1pm.

GUIDED TOURS

Fullers' Waiheke Hop-on Hop-off Explorer Tour ♥♥ (fullers.co.nz; ✆ **09/367-9111**) meets visitors at the ferry and drops them off at key spots—wineries, art galleries, beaches, nature walks, and restaurants—supplying commentary along the way. With 15 stops, the entire loop takes 80 minutes to complete, with buses picking up from stops every 30 minutes (allow a full day for the entire mission, though). It operates Thursday through Sunday and costs NZ$99 adults, NZ$51 for children or NZ$209—but is a particularly good value as it includes the cost of your ferry ticket.

An excellent way to get a feel for Waiheke is to go with **Ananda Tours ♥♥** (ananda.co.nz; ✆ **09/372-7530** or 027/233-4565). It offers private and group art studio, gourmet food and wine, and eco-walking tours with knowledgeable guides; prices begin at NZ$185 per person. For a wine tour of several vineyards, contact **Waiheke Island Wine Tours ♥♥** (waihekeislandwinetours.co.nz; ✆ **09/372-2140**). Wayne Eagleton will pick you up from the 10am ferry at 10:35am, and your tour will be finished in time for the 4pm ferry. A shared tour is NZ$165 per person (over 18).

For an entirely different take on the island, the wellness-focused **Terra and Tide ♥♥** (terraandtide.co.nz; ✆ **021/669-722**) offers customized walking tours of the island's bushes, beaches, bays, art galleries, and yes, even wineries. Inquire for pricing.

OUTDOOR PURSUITS

We highly recommend driving out to glorious **Onetangi Bay ♥♥♥**—to my mind, one of the best beaches in New Zealand. Here you can swim and surf

Ziplining over Waiheke's native forest with EcoZip Adventures.

in crystal-clear water with views as far as the eye can see. If you want to feel the true spirit of freedom, take it all off at the western end of **Palm Beach,** a small bay used for nude swimming.

Guided kayaking tours are available from **Kayak Waiheke ♥♥**, Matiatia Bay (kayakwaiheke.co.nz; ✆ **09/372-5550**), from NZ$125. It's located right by the ferry terminal, and you can also rent kayaks, SUPs and electric bikes here too.

Freedom can also be found flying (fully clothed) over grapevines and native forest. **EcoZip Adventures ♥♥**, 150 Trig Hill Rd. (ecozipadventures.co.nz; ✆ **09/372-5646**), will pick you up from the ferry terminal and take you on a 3-hour ziplining adventure. You'll do just three ziplines, but they're up to 200m (656 feet) long, and each one is a double—two lines side-by-side—meaning you can fly alongside or even race a friend. The views are outstanding. You must be between 30kg (66 lb.) and 125kg (275 lb.) to zip. Adults NZ$149, children NZ$89, families NZ$387.

Visiting Vineyards

More than 40 vineyards operate on Waiheke Island, where the Mediterranean-style climate is perfect for growing grapes (and olives). Some of the country's best reds come from the island. Pick up the free **Waiheke Winegrowers' Map** or check out the **Waiheke Winegrowers' Association website** (waihekewine.co.nz). Plan your visits around mealtimes, because several growers have excellent restaurants. Our favorites for both the wine and the restaurants include:

- **Stonyridge ♥♥♥**, 80 Onetangi Rd. (stonyridge.com; ✆ **09/372-8822**). In 1987, Stonyridge produced the first Larose vintage, immediately judged one of the world's top reds by the *London World Guide to Cabernet.* Tours of the cellar, vineyard, and olive grove (with two wine tastings) begin at 11:30am on Saturday and Sunday; admission is NZ$15 per person (complimentary with wine purchase). You'll also get incredibly picturesque vineyard views from its restaurant, which also happens to be one of the nicest places on the island to dine. Reopening after renovations in early 2026, this is a lunch only venue (daily in summer; Sat–Sun in winter) and serves a set menu for NZ$79 per person—add a guided wine-tasting for NZ$30 per person.

A vineyard lunch at Stonyridge.

The Good Oil

Waiheke is fast becoming known for its premium extra-virgin olive oils, with some 20,000 olive trees growing on the island. Harvest season is April through May or June, and there is no better place to sample than **Allpress Olive Grove ♥**, 1 Gordons Rd., Rocky Bay (allpressolivegroves.co.nz; ✆ **09/372-6214**). It's open daily 10am to 4pm, and 15-minute guided tastings cost NZ$10—book ahead online. If money's no object, you can stay the night among the olives in a range of luxurious holiday homes (from NZ$1,950 per night!)—and an informal bistro will be open too by the time you read this.

- **Mudbrick Vineyard and Restaurant ♥♥**, 126 Church Bay Rd., Oneroa (mudbrick.co.nz; ✆ **09/372-9050**), is another magical setting for a meal. There are actually two restaurants here—the main Mudbrick fine-dining restaurant and the more casual Archive Bistro. Both open daily from 11:30am to 9:30pm and have sweeping views over rolling farmland to the sparkling waters of the Hauraki Gulf. The accommodations here are beautiful, too, with a range of luxury cottages from NZ$350 to NZ$1,500 per night.
- **Cable Bay Vineyards ♥♥♥**, 12 Nick Johnstone Dr., Oneroa (cablebay.nz; ✆ **09/372-5889**), is an architecturally arresting complex that includes the winery, tasting room, restaurant, bar, and an art gallery—and boasts dramatic views across vines, bush, fields, and Motukaha Island just off the coast. Its tasting room is open daily from 11am to 5pm. Lunch at its restaurant The Verandah is available Thursday to Monday, with dinner also served on Fridays and Saturdays.
- **Kennedy Point Wines and Olive Oil ♥**, 44 Donald Bruce Rd., Kennedy Point (kennedypointvineyard.com; ✆ **09/372-5600**), has a winery and tasting room in a lovely setting. A tasting of three wines plus an olive oil tasting costs NZ$20 (Thurs–Sun 11am–4pm or by appointment).
- **Passage Rock Wines ♥♥**, 438 Orapiu Rd. (passagerock.co.nz; ✆ **09/372-7257**), is the most awarded winery on the island, and its wines have grabbed international attention. Not quite as famous, but just as good, are the wood-fired pizzas at the cafe bistro here. The vineyard is open Wednesday to Sunday 11am to 5:30pm.

Where to Stay on Waiheke Island

This is an island of holiday homes, bed-and-breakfasts, and private cottages (including those directly on vineyards)—not hotels or motels. Check Airbnb.com or Bookabach.com for the best deals and the most options.

The Boatshed Hotel ♥♥ There's a real feel of New Zealand about this gorgeous spot above the beach, overlooking little Oneroa. To call it "relaxed

Beachy luxury at Waiheke's The Boatshed Hotel.

luxury" is a little vague; suffice it to say there's a clean-cut elegance to the marine-themed suites. The Boatshed offers terrific sea views from private balconies and every comfort, right down to heated bathroom floors. For something special, splurge on the three-story Lighthouse Suite, which has a private top-floor lounge and a first-floor bedroom with commanding views and a balcony. Ground-floor rooms are more spacious.

Tawa and Huia sts., Oneroa. boatshed.co.nz. ✆ **09/372-3242.** 7 units. NZ$920–NZ$1,550. Rates include breakfast and airport & ferry transport. Children 11 and under not accepted. **Amenities:** Dining room; bar; bikes; concierge; room service; watersports equipment rentals; free Wi-Fi.

Where to Eat on Waiheke Island

In addition to the vineyard restaurants outlined above (see "Visiting Vineyards," p. 123), there are a number of good spots to grab a meal. In Oneroa village, **Vino Vino ♥**, behind Green Hills Wines and Spirits (vinovino.co.nz; ✆ **09/372-9888**), is a local favorite for big Mediterranean platters and a la carte dining on a huge deck with stunning views (open daily 9am–late). If you're after a tasty pizza or a curry dish, **The Middle Waiheke Restaurant ♥**, located in Surfdale Village at 18 Hamilton Rd. (✆ **09/372-5309**), has takeaways and a delivery service.

In Oneroa you'll find some of the country's best ice cream at **Island Gelato ♥♥♥**, 106b Ocean View Rd., Oneroa (islandgelato.co.nz). It's won a swag of awards and features both classic Italian flavors and more unusual Kiwi ones like tamarillo, feijoa coconut swirl, and Pic's peanut butter caramel (it also has outlets at a few other city locations, including the downtown ferry terminal).

Casita Miro ♥♥♥ SPANISH Recently voted Auckland's best destination restaurant, Casita Miro is like a little slice of Spain in the middle of a very Kiwi paradise. Though it's located at a winery, here the food comes first, and it is excellent—tapas and *raciones* featuring veggies from the glorious on-site garden, and olive oil, olives, citrus, and oysters all grown on the island. There's a mosaic sculpture inspired by Antoni Gaudi's Parque Güell in Barcelona, and views for days. (It's about a 15- to 20-min. walk uphill from Onetangi Beach.)

3 Brown Rd. Onetangi. casitamiro.co.nz. ✆ **09/372-7854.** 3-course menu NZ$85, wine matches NZ$49; tapas and raciones NZ$12–NZ$38. Daily Sun–Fri 11am–2:30pm, Sat 11am–2:30pm and 5–7pm (check ahead for winter hours).

MORE wineries AROUND AUCKLAND

Waiheke Island may be Auckland's prettiest wine region, but it's far from the only place in Auckland where grapes are grown. In fact, there are 85 vineyards throughout the region—and you don't even have to board a ferry to taste the good drop.

Henderson Valley is the country's oldest grape-growing area, settled by Croatian and other Northern Hemisphere immigrants in the early 1900s. Today, this tradition continues in the northwestern suburbs at **Kumeu** (about 30 min. from the central city) and north in **Matakana** (about 45 min. north, and a lovely destination in its own right—see p. 131). Cabernet sauvignon is the most commonly planted grape; chardonnay and sauvignon blanc are the main white varieties. Following are some notable vineyards to visit:

- **Babich Wines ♥♥**, 10 Babich Rd., Henderson (babichwines.co.nz; ✆ **09/833-7859**): One of the region's most picturesque wineries, Babich has a pleasant picnic area near its shop and vintages going back to 1990. Only 20 minutes from Central City, it's open Monday to Friday,10am to 4pm (tastings not available).
- **Brick Bay ♥♥♥**, 17 Arabella Lane, Snells Beach (brickbay.co.nz; ✆ **09/425-4690**): Yes, this vineyard produces very nice wines, but the best reason to head here is for its **Glass House Restaurant ♥♥** (serving brunch, lunch, and grazing meals), a stunning spot cantilevered over a glistening pond. It also has an on-site sculpture trail (which takes about 1 hr. to walk) with ever-changing installations by some of NZ's best contemporary artists. Restaurant reservations are highly recommended; none needed for wine tastings. It's open daily 10am to 4pm (until 9pm Saturdays).
- **Sculptureum ♥♥♥**, 40 Omaha Flats Rd., Matakana (sculptureum.nz; ✆ **09/422-7375**): This vineyard not only has a sculpture garden and fine dining restaurant, **Rothko ♥♥♥** (✆ **022/883-0932**), but also features six

A SIDE TRIP TO AOTEA/GREAT BARRIER ISLAND

Imagine pristine white-sand beaches empty of people, lush mountains, and a vast network of walking tracks. Add rare birds and plant life, a sea full of dolphins, a permanent population of around 1,200, and a seductive, laid-back lifestyle, and you have New Zealand's sixth-largest island, Aotea, also known as Great Barrier Island. DOC administers about 60% of the island—locals like to say there are more conservationists per square inch here than anywhere else in New Zealand.

This seductive paradise is *the* place if you're looking for a unique New Zealand wilderness experience. It's New Zealand as it used to be—all 285 square km (111 sq. miles) of it. It's isolated, yet it's only a 30-minute plane ride north from the country's biggest city. It's a place the locals call "the Barrier" and I call "heaven." Get yourself there and you'll remember it forever.

modern art galleries (including a glass room with massive Chihuly chandeliers and a portrait of Marlon Brando made from chewing gum), gardens studded with strange technicolor sculptures, aviaries, and "Rabbiton" (inhabited by different breeds of purebred rabbits). You'll need to budget 2 hours to explore the site, more if you plan a wine tasting (weekends 11am–3pm, NZ$10). The gardens and gallery are open daily 10am to 4pm and cost NZ$42 adults, NZ$19 ages 6 to 14. Reservations are required for Rothko (opening hours vary seasonally) but there's also a casual walk-in restaurant called Freddie's, which serves many of Sculptureum's wines.

- **Soljans Estate ♥**, 366 St. Hwy. 16, Kumeu (soljans.co.nz; ✆ **09/412-5858**): Soljans produces internationally competitive wines. It has cellar sales and tastings, and a nice bistro. The winery is open daily 10am to 5pm.
- **West Brook Winery ♥♥**, 215 Ararimu Valley Rd., Waimauku (westbrook.co.nz; ✆ **09/411-9924**): With lovely parklike grounds, pétanque, and giant chess in the garden, this is a pleasant place for a picnic; snacks are available for purchase, but there's also an on-site pizza restaurant. It's open daily 11am to 5pm; bookings on weekends are essential.

Several companies offer organized wine tours. **Auckland Wine Tours** (aucklandwinetours.kiwi; ✆ **027/ 800-0298**), has a mix of scenic half- and full-day tours to Kumeu and Waiheke from NZ$177. **Bush and Beach ♥♥** (bushandbeach.co.nz; **09/837-4130**) has a daily afternoon wine tour to Kumeu (including a visit to spectacular Muriwai Beach) for NZ$310, and private full-day tours to Matakana for NZ$2,050 for two people. **Fine Wine Tours ♥♥** (finewinetours.co.nz; ✆ **0800/023-111** in NZ, or 021/626-529) has an appealing selection of private food and wine tours (NZ$398–NZ$698).

However, if you do choose to visit this island, know that it doesn't come cheap—and you definitely need more than 1 night to soak it all in. Plan your visit around the weather forecast, too, so you can stargaze under one of the clearest night skies in the world.

Essentials

ARRIVING **Barrier Air** (barrierair.kiwi; ✆ **0800/900-600** in NZ, or 09/275-9120) runs daily 30-minute flights to the island from Auckland International Airport, North Shore Aerodrome, and Kaitaia, Kerikeri, Tauranga, and Whitianga. You can only take 20kg (44 lb.) of baggage (although you can pay more for extra) and flights cost NZ$89 to NZ$295 one-way. **Island Aviation** (islandaviation.co.nz; ✆ **09/390-1122** or 022/643-7440) also flies daily to Great Barrier island from the North Shore and Waiheke Island; one-way flights start at NZ$179. Most flights land at **Claris Airfield** in the center of the island. They're all in tiny planes and are incredibly scenic—sit by the window if you can.

Flying is generally quicker and cheaper, and it's easy to pick up a rental car at the Claris Airfield (see below). There is, however, car ferry service from Auckland, landing at Tryphena, at the southern end of the island. **SeaLink,** 45 Jellicoe St., Auckland Viaduct (sealink.co.nz; ✆ **0800/732-546** in NZ, or 09/300-5900), runs 4½- to 5-hour trips to the island multiple times a week, with daily departures in the summer (timetables vary). The *Eco Islander* has a cafe and two theaters showing movies and documentaries. The long trip can be grueling when the sea is rough. Round-trip fares are around NZ$1,000 for a car and driver, NZ$200 per additional adult, and NZ$150 children ages 5 to 15.

Arguably the best option is to purchase a package from the wonderful **Currach Irish Pub** in Tryphena (currachirishpub.co.nz; ✆ **09/429-0211** or phone the inimitable Orla on **021/174-1537;** see p. 131) which gets you two return flights from Auckland, 2 nights' accommodation for two people, plus 2 days' car hire for NZ$1,200 (inquire for extensions and modifications).

ORIENTATION Great Barrier Island is approximately 15km (9⅓ miles) wide and 45km (19 miles) long, with Mount Hobson (621m/2,037 ft.) rising in the center. The island landscape is rugged, and much of it is inaccessible by road. The west coast has steep forested ranges running down to the sea; the east coast offers sweeping, white-sand beaches and rolling hills. The main areas of settlement are **Port Fitzroy** in the north; **Claris, Whangaparapara,** and **Okupu** in the center; and **Tryphena** in the south. Good roads connect them all. Claris and Tryphena are the main villages, though neither is much more than a few shops, cafes, a pub, and a post office. Port Fitzroy boasts one store and a dive station. There are no banks or ATMs on the island (although many businesses accept credit cards). Be prepared to pay more for basic supplies than you would on the mainland.

GETTING AROUND **By Car** Reasonably priced rental options include **Claris Rental Cars** ♥♥ (clarisrentalcars.com; ✆ **021/174-1537**) or **Medlands Car Rentals** ♥ (bookitnz.campermate.com/medlands-rentals; ✆ **09/4290-861**). All operators offer free delivery to Claris Airfield and Tryphena Wharf. Prices start at around NZ$75 per day. **Aotea Rentals** (aoteacarrentals.co.nz; ✆ **0800/426-832** in NZ) offers a similar service and prices from around NZ$90 per day for a 4WD. Don't expect anything too flash or even clean; vehicles on Aotea are meant to be functional. Be forewarned that roads are often narrow and unpaved, and there are no streetlights. Notify your rental car provider of where you intend on driving, as a 4WD may be necessary (even if you're just heading to your accommodation). Expect to pay premium for fuel, with gas costing over NZ$4 per liter.

By Bus & Shuttle You'll find limited scheduled public transport on the island, but regular bus services meet boats and planes. **Great Barrier Travel** (greatbarriertravel.co.nz; ✆ **0800/426-832** in NZ, or 09/429-0474) has daily service to walking tracks, beaches, and Port Fitzroy, and offers shuttle rides to/from the airport.

By Scooter **Motu Bikes,** across from the airport at 67 Hector Sanderson Rd. (motubikes.co.nz; ✆**022/344-0645**), rents out Kiwi-designed electric

2-wheel-drive motorbikes for NZ$75 per day. For the adventurous, this may be your best option in fine weather; you'll definitely save on fuel. Included in the price is a helmet, first-aid kit, tiedowns for your luggage, and rain gear and a drybag.

VISITOR INFORMATION Maps and leaflets are available at the unstaffed **Great Barrier Island Information Centre,** Main Road outside Claris Airfield (greatbarrier.co.nz; ✆ **09/429-0767**). Check the website for island information.

SPECIAL EVENTS In January, the **Rarohara Kūtai & Kai Festival**—an annual celebration of mussels in Port Fitzroy (✆ **09/429-0072**)—provides stalls, entertainment, and as many succulent mussels as you can eat.

Exploring Aotea/Great Barrier Island

Great Barrier has a rich history. Māori have inhabited the island for over 700 years, and Europeans created a thriving timber industry, milling the huge stands of native kauri trees for the shipbuilding industry. The island was a whaling station until the 1960s, and the relics of old stamping batteries attest to a rich gold- and silver-mining history. The remains of the **Oreville Stamping Battery** are beside the road from Claris on the way to Whangaparapara. Also in this area is the popular **Kaitoke Hot Springs Track,** which leads to natural hot springs in a creek. The springs are 45 minutes in along a pretty wetland track. Use the roadside toilet—it's the last one you'll see for a while. Don't put your head under the water surface (harmful bacteria thrive in such conditions), and don't forget insect repellent.

Farther north, at Port Fitzroy, **Glenfern Sanctuary ♥♥♥**, Glenfern Road (glenfern.org.nz; ✆ **09/429-0091**), is one of the most pristine, fascinating

Forest meets the sea in Aotea.

Star Light, Star Bright

In 2017, Aotea was named an **International Dark Sky Sanctuary**—a special designation reserved for particularly remote locations with zero light pollution. It is one of only about sixteen in the world. Without any light pollution, it's ideal for amateur astronomers—particularly in the winter, when night skies are clearer and stars are more visible. You could rely on a solid app, or you could cozy up on the beach in a "moon chair" with **Good Heavens ♥♥** (goodheavens.co.nz; ✆ **09/429-0876**). Co-owner Deborah Kilgallon describes herself as a "professional stargazer" rather than an astronomer, but her scientific understanding of the stars will make you believe otherwise. Over a 2-hour period (NZ$130 adults; NZ$65 children), Kilgallon will walk you through the Greek and Māori constellations that make up the southern hemisphere sky and point her telescope at the brightest and the most intriguing objects in the night sky.

native wildlife sanctuaries anywhere, founded in 1992 by the late Tony Bouzaid. Well over 8,000 trees have been planted as part of an ongoing reforestation project; timber boardwalks make the hiking easy. The sanctuary also now offers accommodations (p. 131).

Even farther north, you'll find the **SS *Wairarapa* Walkway** at the very beautiful (and deserted) **Whangapoua Beach.** The steamer wrecked on cliffs near Miners Head on October 29, 1894, with the loss of around 130 lives. A little gravesite at the northern end of the beach serves as a reminder of one of New Zealand's worst shipping disasters.

Near the airport in Claris, the community-run **Aotea Arts & History Village ♥**, 80 Hector Sanderson Rd. (aoteaahv.nz; ✆ **09/429-0580**), is a museum, art gallery, archives, workshop space, and yoga studio all at once. The gallery carries everything from paintings, prints, and weaving by local artists to tie-dye shirts (for when you're really feeling the island vibes). Open daily 10am to 4pm in summer; reduced hours in winter. More local works can be seen at the carefully curated **Elephant Gallery ♥**, in Puriri Bay (✆ **027/961-4315;** summer months Mon–Fri 10am–4pm, call for winter hours).

OUTDOOR PURSUITS

A range of tracks crisscross **Mount Hobson,** a focal point for keen hikers. There are stunning views from the top on a clear day, and at 672m (2,220 ft.), the summit is the main nesting ground for the rare black petrel. It's at least a 3-hour round-trip walk, which can be extended into the **Aotea Track,** a 2- or 3-day walk staying in Department of Conservation huts.

You'll find some of the least crowded surf in the country here on Aotea's west coast—although given the frequent presence of sharks (and dolphins), you might not want to paddle out entirely alone. Surfboards, SUPs, and wetsuits can be hired from the **Salty Bushman ♥♥** at 67 Hector Sanderson Rd., Medlands Beach (✆ **027/255-3773** or 027/203-7475). Soft tops go for NZ$40 per day, shortboards NZ$50, wetsuits NZ$20.

Where to Stay & Eat on Great Barrier Island

If you plan on visiting Great Barrier Island in summer, book accommodations well in advance. Dining options on the island are few and far between, so I'd recommend booking a self-catering accommodation and bringing groceries with you. During the pandemic, many of the larger (that is, four rooms or more) lodges shut their doors, and many of the remaining providers are pretty off-grid. Many don't have websites; check Airbnb or Vrbo for up-to-date options.

Accommodations (mainly cottages) are spread across the island, but most visitors end up in Tryphena, where you'll find a general store, sheltered beaches, and the lively, welcoming **Currach Irish Pub ♥♥♥**, 78 Blackwell Dr. (currachirishpub.co.nz; ✆ **09/429-0211**). It's the social heart of the island, pretty much its sole remaining dinnertime restaurant, and according to its force-of-nature owner Orla Cumisky, the only entirely solar-powered Irish pub in the world. The food is hearty and beautifully presented—think gnocchi with goat cheese, truffle oil, and dates; or Malaysian curry-braised lamb with roasted capsicum hummus; plus a range of woodfired pizzas—with five chefs serving up to 300 people a night in summer (mains NZ$32–NZ$40). It's open weekdays from 4pm and weekends from 2pm. There are regular musical, comedy, and cultural evenings—Thursday is open-mic night, and a great place to mingle with the locals. I also highly recommend staying here; the six rooms are light-filled, comfortable, right by the water, and cost NZ$200 to NZ$250 per night.

Another option is **Glenfern Sanctuary ♥♥♥**, 20 Glenfern Rd., Port Fitzroy (glenfern.org.nz; ✆ **09/4290-091**), which offers a lovingly restored workers' cottage from 1916 (NZ$200–NZ$250 per night) or one of the island's oldest homesteads (sleeps up to 10 people; NZ$800 per night), built in 1901. The real highlight is the location: Both the cottage and the homestead are located within a 240-hectare (nearly 600-acre) fenced predator-free wildlife sanctuary (p. 129), alive with native birdsong and laced with walking trails. All of the proceeds from the accommodation go back to supporting the sanctuary and its inhabitants. A 2-night minimum stay is required.

In Claris, **My Fat Puku ♥** (myfatpuku.co.nz; ✆ **04/290-811**) offers cabinet food, a brunch menu, decent coffee, and real-fruit ice creams daily from 9am to 2pm, plus wood-fired pizzas on Friday and Sunday from 5pm to 7pm. Call ahead to confirm seasonal hours.

En Route to Northland: Matakana & Surrounds

Located 88km (42 miles) north of Auckland, **Matakana** is a worthwhile stop on the way to Northland, and a great day-trip destination in its own right. The village has great shopping and restaurants, a Saturday market, lots of accommodation options, and the quirkiest wee cinema you ever did see (the ceiling of the Paradiso theater will take your breath away). There are nearby wineries and sculpture parks (see box p. 126), plus **Tāwharanui Regional Park ♥♥♥**, a predator-free sanctuary with sparkling white-sand surf beaches and bushwalks alive with birdsong. A short drive up the coast near tiny, picturesque **Leigh,** go snorkeling or hire a glass-bottomed kayak at the **Cape Rodney-Okakari Point Marine Reserve (Goat Island)** ♥♥♥, the southern hemisphere's oldest marine protected area. A short walk up the hill from the beach, kids will love the touch tank and interactive displays at the **Goat Island Marine Discovery Centre** ♥♥ (goatislandmarine.co.nz; ✆ **09/923-3645**), open 10am to 4pm daily during summer and weekends in winter (adults NZ$10, kids 5–15 NZ$6, family NZ$25). For great coffee, fish and chips, and burgers, stop in at **Leigh Eats** ♥♥ 18 Cumberland St., Leigh (leigheats.co.nz; ✆ **09/4226-035;** closed Mon).

En Route to the Coromandel Peninsula: The Pacific Coast Highway

From Auckland, the Pacific Coast Highway (not exactly a highway in the American sense of the word) leads down the west coast of the Firth of Thames and west again to Thames and the Coromandel Peninsula. It moves along the **Seabird Coast** ♥, where **Kaiaua Fisheries,** 939 E. Coast Rd., Kaiaua (✆ **09/232-2776**), serves some of the best fish and chips in the country; it's open daily 9am to 9pm. Make time to stop at the **Pūkorokoro Miranda Shorebird Centre** ♥, East Coast Rd. (shorebirds.org.nz; ✆ **09/232-2781**). Its 8,500 hectares (21,000 acres) of tidal flats are the summer feeding grounds for millions of migratory birds—including bar-tailed godwits, which make a record-breaking trip each spring, flying some 13,000km (8,000 miles) non-stop from Alaska to this estuary (and a handful of others around NZ) in just over a week.

NORTHLAND

Although the Bay of Islands—a sun-soaked paradise of 144 islands scattered across turquoise-hued waters—is what most people know of Te Tai Tokerau Northland, this subtropical peninsula is also rich in history and story. Here, you can stand awestruck beneath the gigantic kauri tree named for Tāne Mahuta, the Māori god who separated his parents to create the world of light. Nearby, at Manea Footprints of Kupe in the Hokianga, you'll learn about the Polynesian navigator Kupe's arrival on these islands 700 to 1,000 years ago, and the great ocean-crossing migration his tales of discovery prompted. Here also lies Waitangi, the "birthplace of the nation," where the nation's founding document, the Treaty of Waitangi, was signed between Māori and representatives of the British Crown in 1840. And it's the location of Aotearoa's most significant spiritual site: Te Rerenga Wairua Cape Reinga on the North Island's northern tip is where Māori spirits depart the country after death, returning to the land of their ancestors—Hawaiki—after casting a last look back.

The region is made up of two contrasting shorelines. On the east—where most of the population lives—white beaches curve around sheltered coves, giving endless summer vibes. (It's often called "the winterless north," and does tend to be slightly warmer than other regions, though it's also prone to occasional storms and cyclones.) On the west are kauri forests, giant harbors, and long stretches of wild, dune-backed beaches pounded by the Tasman Sea. Northland's remoteness and size is not to be underestimated; making the pilgrimage to the northern tip of Cape Reinga from Auckland takes 6 hours at minimum. To do the region any justice, you'll need at least 3 days, although you could easily spend more than a week here.

Northland has four main areas: Whangārei and surrounds, the Bay of Islands, the Far North, and the Kauri Coast and Hokianga region. The population is sparse—just under 200,000 for an area slightly smaller than Connecticut (13,789 sq. km/5,324 sq. miles). You'll have large patches all to yourself, so start exploring.

WHANGĀREI

169km (105 miles) NE of Auckland; 62km (38 miles) S of Paihia; 58km (36 miles) E of Dargaville

On the east coast, Whangārei (pop. 54,000) is the first major Northland municipality you'll encounter after leaving Auckland. It used to be a place that most visitors passed through on their way to sexier destinations farther north, but with a redeveloped waterfront area, it's now a top spot to linger on a Northland odyssey. The Town Basin hums with activity as locals and visitors enjoy galleries (including the country's first dedicated public Māori art gallery), artist studios, cafes, and a marina full of yachts. There are beaches here too, of course; around 40 are located within a 30-minute drive of the town.

Whangārei is a gateway to the wonderful but largely unsung Whangārei Heads and the Tūtūkākā Coast. The Poor Knights Islands Marine Reserve is widely regarded as having some of the best diving in the world, and big-game fishing (outside the marine reserve, of course) is another drawcard.

Essentials

ARRIVING & GETTING AROUND It's possible to get to Whangārei by plane or bus, but accessing other areas of Northland, even by guided trip, is difficult from Whangārei, unless you have ample time to spare. **BusLink** (buslink.co.nz; ✆ **09/438-7142**) connects Whangārei to regional centers throughout the entirety of Northland. To maximize your time, it's best to either hire a car in Auckland or rent one upon arrival in Whangārei.

Whangārei's lively marina, viewed from the porch of a heritage building on the quayside.

Northland

Cape Reinga
Lighthouse
North Cape
Te Paki
Te Paki Rec. Res.
Great Exhibition Bay
PACIFIC OCEAN
Ninety Mile Beach
Pukenui
Cape Karikari
Tokerau Beach
Doubtless Bay
Mangōnui
Taipa
Taupo Bay
Cavalli Is.
Awanui
Coopers Beach
Whangaroa
Kaitaia
Kaeo
Ahipara
Cape Wiwiki
Herekino Forest
Raetea Forest
Waipapa
Kerikeri
Bay of Islands
Cape Brett
Northland Cons. Park
Broadwood
Waitangi
Russell
Warawara Forest
Paihia
Ōhaeawai
Moerewa
Hokianga Harbour
Kaikohe
Russell Forest
Oakura
Poor Knights Is.
Opononi
Taheke
Ōmāpere
Kaiikanui Forest
Whananaki
Waimamaku
Matararua Forest
Waipoua Forest
Hikurangi
Matapouri
Marlborough Forest
Tutukaka
Aranga
Kamo
Parakao
Whangārei
Kaihu
Mungatapere
Whangārei Harbour
Avoca
Mata
Bream Head
Dargaville
Ruakākā
Baylys Beach
Tangihua Forest
Bream Bay
Waipu
Hen & Chickens Is.
Paparoa
Ruawai
Matakohe
Kaiwaka
TASMAN SEA
Tinopai
Wellsford
Pakiri
Pouto
Matakana
North Head
Lighthouse
Kaipara Harbour
Warkworth
South Head
South Head
NORTH ISLAND
Auckland
Area of detail
SOUTH ISLAND
Wellington
Christchurch
Dunedin
Orewa
Silverdale
Kaukapakapa
Helensville
Whangaparāoa
Riverhead
Takapuna
Waitākere
AUCKLAND
0
25 mi
25 km

By Car Whangārei is a 2-hour drive from Auckland. Major car rental companies have offices at both the Auckland and Whangārei airports.

By Plane Whangārei is a 35-minute flight from Auckland with **Air New Zealand** (airnewzealand.co.nz; ✆ **0800/737-000** in NZ), which offers several flights a day. **Sunair** (sunair.co.nz; ✆ **07/575-7799**) flies from other North Island regional hubs (such as Gisborne and Hamilton) into Whangārei multiple times a week. **Whangārei Passenger Services** (whangareibus.co.nz; ✆ **09/438-6005**) will take you from the airport into Whangārei, but must be pre-booked.

By Coach (Bus) **InterCity** (intercity.co.nz; ✆ **09/623-1503**) passes through Whangārei on its morning and afternoon routes.

VISITOR INFORMATION Northland's visitor website is northlandnz.com/visit. The **Whangārei isite Visitor Centre,** 92 Otaika Rd., Whangārei (whangareinz.com; ✆ **09/438-107**), is open from 9am to 4:30pm weekdays, with extended hours over summer.

En Route to Whangārei

As a straight shot, the drive from Auckland to Whangārei takes just over 2 hours. But if you're more about journeys than destinations, there are countless spots to stop along the way. Here are three of the best.

With beaches come surf, including at **Waipu Cove Beach** ♥♥, where there's plenty of parking and the busy oceanfront cafe **The Cove Waipu** ♥♥ (thecovecafe.co.nz; ✆ **09/432-0234**), open daily from 9am until 9pm. During the summer, this is also where you can find **Learn 2 Surf Waipu's kiosk** ♥♥ (learn2surf.co.nz; ✆ **021/719-773**), set up daily. Owners Grae and Ellen Snelling have over 15 years of teaching experience, and their approach makes it easy for even the uncoordinated to get up on their first go. Lessons are often available on the day-of, but it's best to make a booking in advance. Ninety-minute group lessons for kids are NZ$50, NZ$70 for adults 16 and up. Private lessons start at NZ$100. If you're after a bit more of an adventure, drive 30 minutes inland on a gravel road to the **Waipu Caves Scenic Reserve.** The caves are free to enter and feature stalactites, stalagmites, and glowworms, but they're also undeveloped—you might find yourself walking along a slippery track and through high water or tight squeezes, so come equipped with a flashlight and proper footwear, and take care not to touch the cave walls. For a lower risk factor, **Waipu Caves Farm Park,** 5 minutes down the road, offers educational guided experiences of its private Milky Way Glow Worm Caves for NZ$45 adults and NZ$30 for ages 5 to 15.

Closer to the coast, a short detour off the main highway from Auckland to Whangārei, is **Bennett's of Mangawhai** ♥♥, 52 Moir St., Mangawhai (bennettschocolate.co.nz; ✆ **09/431-5500**). When you enter its courtyard, you might think you've missed your turn and somehow wound up in the south of France. Creeping vines cover the atrium's walls, and people linger over coffee around a fountain. There's even a vendor selling fresh flowers. The main attraction, though, is the *chocolat*—handmade on-site by the Bennett family from raw Belgian chocolate. On weekdays, you can watch chocolatiers in action, producing massive chocolate fish (an iconic Kiwi treat containing raspberry-flavored marshmallow), feijoa caramel chocolates with vodka, vegan truffles, and even chocolate sheep, all beautifully presented in gift-worthy boxes. It's open daily from 9am to 4:30pm; the excellent on-site cafe runs from 8am to 3pm.

It's worth making the 25-minute detour to **The Kauri Museum ♥♥** (5 Church Road Matakohe (kaurimuseum.com; ✆ **09/431-7417**). (It could also be the start of a recommended clockwise loop of Northland, up the west coast and down the east.) Says director Jason Smith, "It's the perfect place to enter the region and get context for everything else you're going to see." Until a few hundred years ago, this part of NZ was cloaked in a vast forest of kauri—among the largest and longest-lived trees in the world, which also happen to produce exceptional timber. Kauri logging was a mainstay of the NZ economy for more than a century, until it ended in 1985. The 60+-year-old attraction is currently pivoting from a traditional settler museum to a much more ambitious (and interesting) natural history museum, aiming ultimately to tell the full story of kauri from its botany to its wholesale extraction and the settler lifestyles it fueled. It's jam-packed with moving engines driving cogs and saws, life-size historical dioramas, polished glowing orbs of kauri gum, and kauri furniture and carvings; instead of a dinosaur or whale skeleton, a 60-foot slab of a 700-year-old kauri tree takes pride of place in the main hall. It's open daily 9am to 5pm (NZ$25 adults, NZ$8 ages 5–15, NZ$55 families), and the **Gumdiggers Café** across the road serves a wide range of cabinet food, brunch staples, and burgers, with nice views of the (now kauri-less) countryside.

Exploring Whangārei

The **Town Basin** by the harbor is the place to go for a wander. There, you'll find the **Burning Issues Gallery ♥**, 8 Quayside (burningissuesgallery.co.nz; ✆ **09/438-3108;** open daily 10am–4pm), where you can watch master glass-blower Keith Grinter (keithgrinter.com) at work. If you're fine with a gentle reminder that your time on holiday is slowly ticking away, there's the **Claphams National Clock Museum ♥** (claphamsclocks.com; ✆ **09/438-3993;** daily 9am–5pm; admission NZ$10 adults, NZ$5 kids), which displays the personal collection of Archibald Clapham, who came to NZ in 1903 and amassed 400 clocks and music boxes. Outside, the **Rolling Ball Clock** will fascinate kids and adults alike, especially on the hour—it's both kinetic sculpture and accurate timepiece, the result of 14 years of experimentation by a group of local community members. The Town Basin is also home to the **Whangārei Art Museum** (whangareiartmuseum.co.nz; ✆ **09/430-4240;** daily 10am–4pm; entry by donation) and the area's main attraction, the new **Hundertwasser Art Centre and Wairau Māori Art Gallery** (see below).

Just 3 minutes west of the town, **Kiwi North ♥**, 500 State Hwy. 14 (kiwinorth.co.nz; ✆ **09/438-9630;** daily 10am–4pm; admission NZ$20, NZ$5 for kids 5 and over) encompasses the Whangārei Museum, Kiwi House, and

Heritage Park, all situated on a 25-hectare (62-acre) historic farm. The museum showcases natural history, historic Māori, and early-settler collections, while the Kiwi House is home to a number of these iconic birds, as well as *tuatara,* an endemic reptile that has been around since dinosaurs roamed the earth. All in, it's a good introduction to the region's history, with the bonus opportunity to see a kiwi. A pass for two adults and three kids is NZ$65.

Located next door to Kiwi North is the **Whangārei Native Bird Recovery Centre** ♥ (nbr.org.nz; ✆ **09/438-1457;** Mon–Thurs 9am–4pm, Fri 10am–4pm). Visitors are welcome to peer into the aviaries, which contain native birds in different stages of recovery; you're not guaranteed to see any particular species, but they may include moreporks (owls), kiwi, and white herons. *Koha* (donations) are welcome.

Just off State Highway 1, **Whangārei Quarry Gardens** ♥, 37A Russell Rd. (whangareigardens.org.nz; ✆ **09/437-7210;** visitor center daily 9am–5pm), is an old quarry that's been converted by volunteers into a lush subtropical paradise. On-site are numerous walking trails and a very good cafe; entry is by *koha* (donation), or you can pay for a guided tour, either on foot or by golf cart (book at least 48 hours in advance).

Surrounded by lush native bush, the picturesque **Otuihau/Whangārei Falls** ♥ (5km/3 miles north from the town center on the Tūtūkākā Rd.) cascade for 36m (85 ft.) over basalt cliffs, making for a lovely picnic place. (***Note:*** If it's a dry summer, there may not be much water flowing.) There are plenty of walking trails nearby, including some that go past ancient kauri trees. Just don't leave valuables in your car in the carpark—it's a bit of a hotspot for break-ins.

Hundertwasser Art Centre and Wairau Māori Art Gallery ♥♥♥

ART MUSEUM In 2022, after 20 years in the making, this extraordinary museum opened. The last authentic building ever designed by world-renowned visual artist and architect Friedensreich Hundertwasser—one of only 30 worldwide—it's arguably a bigger attraction than the art it houses. In characteristic Hundertwasser fashion, it's a lopsided blur of color, with not a straight line to be found. ("The straight line is godless," wrote the artist, who said it reminded him of soldiers lining up during his years as a Jewish boy in Nazi-occupied Germany.) Even the floors and pavement surrounding the building are uneven, so leave your heels at home. Exhibits shed light on the life and legacy of the man, with galleries showcasing Hundertwasser's illustrations, architectural models, textiles (including, morbidly, the very carpet he died on in 2000), and some of his inventions (such as the composting toilet the artist said turned "shit" to "gold"). The roof, which you can walk around on, is covered in native plants—part of Hundertwasser's commitment to leaving space for nature to flourish.

Hundertwasser highly respected Indigenous and Māori artwork, so it's only fitting that the museum is also home to the **Wairau Art Gallery,** the largest contemporary Māori art gallery on the planet. Its importance can't be understated, but it's surprisingly small; during my last visit, there was only enough

Opened in 2022, the one-of-a-kind Hundertwasser Art Centre was designed by iconoclastic Austrian artist Friedensreich Hundertwasser.

room for five pieces of artwork to be displayed. Exhibits change every 3 months.

It takes about an hour to work your way through both galleries (more if you stop for a drink at the art center's popular **Aqua Restaurant**), but a guided tour is a must to truly appreciate the building's design. Local guides also lend a personal touch to their tours with their stories; many were friends with the man himself, others were instrumental in helping see the project come to fruition. Tours cost NZ$20 and are held Thursday through Sunday at 11am.

81 Dent St. Whangārei. hundertwasserartcentre.co.nz. ✆ **09/430-4221.** NZ$25 adults, NZ$15 kids up to 16, families NZ$65. Open daily 10am–4pm.

OUTDOOR PURSUITS

Keen hikers should consider the **Te Whara Track ♥♥♥**, one of the country's best day hikes. A challenging 7.5km (4.7-mile) climb through the coastal forest along an ancient Māori route, it rewards those who attempt it with spectacular 360-degree panoramic views of Te Whara Bream Head and its surroundings. It can be accessed via Ocean Beach parking lot on Ranui Road and takes about 5 to 6 hours—but you'll need to organize transportation back to your car, as it's one-way. (Ask at the isite if there's a transportation provider or local lodging currently offering shuttle service.)

ESPECIALLY FOR KIDS

Tu Tika Tours' ♥♥♥ 1-hour waterfront walk (tutikatours.co.nz; ✆ **021/507-826**) will show you Whangārei through the eyes of a local Māori family (NZ$95). Run by the Hardings (Mervyn, Rangimarie, and their five kids), the tour explains the cultural, spiritual, and historical context behind popular roadside attractions such as Otuihau/Whangārei Falls and Mount Parihaka. Mervyn used to be a performer at the Auckland Museum, so his presentation skills are top notch. Expect to be asked to sing along (in te reo Māori, of course) and to laugh—a lot—on this family-friendly tour.

Adrenalin ♥, 27 Hukerenui Rd., Ruatangata West (adrenalinadventurepark.co.nz; ✆ **021/231-0890;** open only during summer), is the go-to for water-based sports, including wakeboarding and NZ's largest waterpark and inflatable obstacle course.

A day hike on the Te Whara Track (p. 139) climbs through coastal forest along a traditional Māori footpath.

Where to Stay in Whangārei

If you're travelling by motorhome, Whangārei District Council has a progressive view on freedom camping and even allows overnight parking for non-self-contained vehicles in some locations—check its website (wdc.govt.nz) for which ones. There are several waterfront spots along the shoreline leading towards Whangārei Heads, but they fill up early.

Paid holiday parks, motels, and hotels are also easy to find, with **Distinction Whangārei Hotel and Conference Centre,** 9 Riverside Dr. (distinctionhotelswhangarei.co.nz; ✆ **09/430-4080**), being one reliable if generic option, with rooms starting from NZ$189.

If you're willing to stay outside the city in private or glamping-style accommodation, you'll have an even better selection. At the end of a peninsula near Tūtūkākā, the **Pacific Rendezvous Resort Motel,** 73 Motel Rd. (pacificrendezvous.co.nz; ✆ **0800/999-800** in NZ), has 30 one-, two-, and three-bedroom apartments and is on a headland with direct access to two beaches, with loads of activities for families. Apartments start from NZ$279. It fills up months in advance for the summer season (Dec–Feb), so make your booking early.

Kauri Villas ♥♥ A half-hour drive from the city out toward Whangārei Heads is this lovely place, set in 10 acres of gardens, where you have the choice of three 1- or 2-bedroom cottages, typically with polished wooden floors and restful blue-toned decor. From the heated pool there are sweeping views over Parua Bay. The Kohinui and Camellia cottages both have full kitchens, while the smallest Kingfisher cottage just has a kitchenette.

73 Owhiwa Rd. kaurivillas.co.nz. ✆ **09/436-1797.** Villas NZ$200–NZ$250 double, extra guests NZ$40. **Amenities:** Heated pool; hot tub; games room; free Wi-Fi.

Lodge 9 ♥♥ Directly in Tūtūkākā, Lodge 9 is a contemporary boutique hotel with six generous rooms located right at the dive center and across from the marina. Featuring artwork by celebrated Ngāpuhi artist Emily Karaka, it has a genuine commitment to sustainability, and it offers countless ways to warm up after a day of diving, including a heated saltwater pool, sauna, and fireplace. Included in the rate is a massive breakfast spread, which straddles the line somewhere between a "continental breakfast" and a "hot breakfast" with fresh bread made daily. A common area is also available for preparing small meals.

9 Rona Place, Tūtūkākā. lodge9.co.nz. ✆ **09/434-3867.** From NZ$195, 2-night min. 6 rooms. **Amenities:** Pool; sauna; free Wi-Fi.

Lupton Lodge ♥♥ The outskirts of Whangarei are characterized by mature trees and dry stone walls encircling contented cows, much like the

DIVE, DIVE, dive!

Established in 1981, **Poor Knights Islands Marine Reserve ♥♥♥** is a unique ecosystem where the clear waters near the edge of the Continental Shelf meet subtropical currents. The result is what's widely considered one of the world's best subtropical diving locations, with good year-round visibility, 125 species of fish, and a wide variety of underwater cliffs, rock stacks, and sea caves (including one that's believed to be the largest in the world). It lies a 1-hour boat ride offshore. **Tūtūkākā** (a 30-min. drive from Whangārei) is the closest access point.

There are several boat operators in Tūtūkākā, including family-owned **Dive! Tutukaka ♥♥** (diving.co.nz; ✆ **0800/288-882** in NZ, or 09/434-3867). You'll have no trouble finding it—just look for the World's Largest Scuba Tank across from the marina. Some of Dive! Tutukaka's fully qualified dive masters are award-winning underwater photographers, so if you have an underwater camera, this is the place to use it. Dives are from NZ$329 with hired gear; snorkeling is NZ$245. Tours run year-round but advance booking is advised for December or January. There's also **Dive Now ♥** (41 Clyde St.; facebook.com/DiveNowWhangarei; ✆ **021/090-**9069), another great operator offering similar trips costing NZ$359 for diving with hired gear or NZ$239 for snorkeling.

If you don't snorkel or dive but still want to experience the Poor Knights, **Dive! Tutukaka** also runs "Perfect Day" cruises during the summer months (aperfectday.co.nz), including sightseeing, kayaking, stand up paddleboarding, sea cave exploration, optional snorkeling, swimming, and lunch. The trip costs NZ$255 adults, NZ$149 for children under 15. A family pass for two adults and two children is NZ$659 but must be booked directly.

A diver explores the Poor Knights Marine Reserve.

setting for this lovely B&B. It's a bit like being in Thomas Hardy's Wessex, except the lodge is a beautiful, sparkling-white villa built in 1896 instead of a crumbling farmhouse. Guests stay in spacious king rooms, studios, and apartments all set within the house and a converted two-story barn. Breakfast is a highlight.

555 Ngunguru Rd. luptonlodge.co.nz. ✆ **09/437-2989.** 6 units. From NZ$185 room, from NZ$350 apt. **Amenities:** Laundry service; game room; free Wi-Fi.

Where to Eat in Whangarei

A cluster of restaurants sits in the Town Basin beside the marina, serving breakfast, lunch, and dinner. Vegans and coeliacs are well taken care of at **Quay Kitchen** ♥, 31 Quayside (thequaykitchen.co.nz; ✆ **09/430-2628**), which has half a dozen plant-based and/or gluten free Mexican, Japanese and Middle Eastern dishes on its menu, in addition to meaty Kiwi faves like pork belly and beef brisket. The top reason to choose it? Its view-rich location right on the water. **TopSail** ♥♥♥, 206 Beach Rd., Onerahi (www.topsail.co.nz; ✆ **09/436-2955;** mains NZ$50–NZ$54; Wed–Sat from 6pm), is the special occasion pick in these parts. Impeccable service, views of Whangārei Harbour, and such signatures dishes as venison with blueberries and pork belly with crispy crackling make this the place to visit when you're in a celebratory mood. Also in the pricey bracket is newcomer **Acropolis** ♥♥, 325 Port Rd., Port Whangārei (acropolis.co.nz; ✆ **09/430-0279;** open 5–8pm Tues–Sat and for lunch Wed–Sat 11:30am–2pm), but the waterfront setting is spectacular. A cheaper Greek-cuisine option in town is Local Talent Taverna—it lacks the views, but has a fun vibe regardless, is an easy walk from the town basin, and the simple menu is packed with fresh flavor (localtalenttav.com; 99 Cameron St.; ✆ **022/199-4190;** Tues–Wed 5–9pm, Thurs–Sat noon–10pm).

Awanui oysters, served briny and fresh, at the waterside restaurant TopSail.

If you make it out to Tūtūkākā, try the justifiably popular and tasty **Schnappa Rock ♥♥**, Marina Road, Tūtūkākā (schnapparock.co.nz; ✆ **09/434-3774;** Tues–Sat 8am–late, Sun 8am–5pm). Fully renovated in 2022, this humming beach spot serves superlative seafood sided (often) with greens from the kitchen's garden. Just across the road at the marina, **Marina Woodfired Dining ♥♥** (www.marinawoodfireddining.co.nz; ✆ **09/434-3166**) is open every day for coffee and sandwiches from 7am to 9pm, with their signature pizzas available from 3pm. Each one is handmade in a Napoli style with fresh homemade sauce, resulting in soft, chewy crusts. Waterside dining available in summer.

THE BAY OF ISLANDS

Bay of Islands: 237km (147 miles) N of Auckland; Cape Reinga: 431km (267 miles) N of Auckland

Within the **Te Pēwhairangi Bay of Islands'** natural harbor, there are around 144 islands between Cape Brett and the Purerua Peninsula. The most touristy spot in Northland, the subtropical shores here are basically just one big swimming pool. If it's summer, you'll want to spend much of your time in the warm blue waters diving, fishing, dolphin-watching, sailing, or lying on a gorgeous beach just about anywhere in the region. However, that's not all there is to see here: This is also where you can visit the **Waitangi Treaty Grounds,** a historic site that every visitor wanting to understand modern NZ should experience.

Essentials

ARRIVING

Air New Zealand (airnewzealand.co.nz; ✆ **0800/737-000** in NZ) flies daily from Auckland to **Kerikeri (Bay of Islands Airport),** with a shuttle bus to Paihia. **InterCity** (intercity.co.nz; ✆ **09/583-5780**) provides bus service to Paihia and Kerikeri. From Auckland to Paihia takes about 3 hours by car.

GETTING AROUND

It's possible to arrive in Paihia by plane or bus, then hop on day tours farther north, including to Cape Reinga. Several companies operate 15-minute passenger ferries connecting Paihia to Russell, including the Blue Ferry, and the Happy Ferry, and **Northland Ferries** (northlandferries.co.nz; ✆ **0800/222-979** in NZ only). They run roughly half-hourly, but the timetables change all the time, so check with the isite for the latest schedule. Round-trip fares—also in flux—are around NZ$18 for adults, NZ$9 for children 5 to 14; bring cash in case the Eftpos machines aren't working. Although Russell can be accessed without the ferry via Waikare Road or Russell Road, both routes are winding, narrow and take longer. The car ferry, which leaves from Opua, is the most relaxed option. It runs roughly every 15 minutes, with fares for cars and motorhomes ranging from NZ$18 to NZ$27, dependent on size. The ferry lands at Okiato, a 10-minute drive from Russell. **Bay of Islands Water Taxi**

(✆ **09/402-5454**) offers 24-hour charters; fares depend on the time of day and number of passengers.

ORIENTATION

Paihia is the hub of the region's visitor action. Virtually all tours and cruises for the Bay of Islands start here, and the town is just a short (1.5km/1-mile) walk to **Waitangi,** where the historic Treaty Grounds are located. Paihia's main street is Marsden Road, which runs along the waterfront. Williams Road is a one-way street perpendicular to the coast; many of the shops are here. The historic village of **Russell** is across the water, and its main street, The Strand, runs along the waterfront. **Kerikeri** is a 20-minute drive north of Paihia off SH10. Less touristy than Paihia, it offers more services, including larger grocery stores.

Once you leave Kerikeri, the population noticeably thins out. Most settlements around **Doubtless Bay** are small fishing villages with holiday homes, including **Mangōnui, Coopers Beach, Cable Bay, Taipa,** and **Tokerau Beach.** From here, the big bay extends in a sandy arc along the eastern side of the **Karikari Peninsula.**

VISITOR INFORMATION

Northland's visitor website is **northlandnz.com**. The **Bay of Islands isite Visitor Information Centre** is at the Wharf, Marsden Road, Paihia (✆ **09/402-7345**), and is open daily 8:30am to 5pm in winter and 8am to 6pm in summer.

SPECIAL EVENTS

Cruising past the famous Hole in the Rock, a natural tunnel in Motu Kōkako Island, is a highlight of Fuller's Bay of Islands boat tours.

The most important event in the region—and arguably the country—is NZ's national holiday of **Waitangi Day,** which celebrates the birth of the nation. It's observed annually on February 6, with events held at the Waitangi Treaty Grounds. Visit www.waitangi.org.nz for events schedules.

Exploring the Bay of Islands

PAIHIA/WAITANGI/KAWAKAWA

Maybe this is obvious, but I'm going to spell it out in case it isn't: Visiting the Bay of Islands (BOI) isn't just about exploring what's on the land, but rather what's on and in the water. The most popular boat tours go to the famed Hole in the Rock (a massive archway island boats can drive through, except in big swells), stop to snorkel among the islands' many hidden coves and bays, and cruise through the bay to see the resident pod of bottlenose dolphins. (As of 2021, swimming with dolphins in the BOI is no longer permitted, and boats can't approach closer than 300m, but that doesn't stop you watching them at play from a respectful distance.)

Day trips with Carino Wildlife Island combine sailing around the Bay of Islands with a stop-off at an island for snorkeling and/or a nature hike.

As the area's epicenter, Paihia is the best place to base yourself for organized tours. You don't need to prebook activities unless you're visiting during the peak summer months (from mid-Dec until the end of Jan), particularly if going with larger operators, such as Fullers Bay of Islands—they also run some trips during the winter when many other outfits don't.

If I only had time for one boat tour in the BOI, it would be with **Carino Wildlife Cruises ♥♥♥** (wildlifecruises.co.nz; ✆ **09/402-8040**) aboard its 50-foot sailing catamaran. Sure, you might miss out on the Hole in the Rock, but it's got all the best elements of the perfect day out: snorkeling near a remote island beach, a barbecue lunch on the yacht, and a captain who is so well-acquainted with all the resident dolphins that she knows each of them by name. (Carino is the only yacht licensed to view marine mammals here.) A family-owned business, Carino gives more personalized experience than some of the larger operators do. ***Big bonus:*** A portion of your ticket goes toward supporting local marine conservation efforts. The 6-hour tour departs daily from September through April at 8:40am and returns at 3:15. It costs NZ$206 adults or NZ$141 kids 4 to 14. Lunch is an extra NZ$14.

You can also get your dolphin fix on a cruise with **Explore's Dolphin Eco Cruise ♥** (exploregroup.co.nz; ✆ **0800/397-567** in NZ, or 09/359-5987), which also has a license. In addition to a cruise on the water, the 5½-hour tour includes snorkeling and a visit to Urupukapuka Island's conservation area to spot birdlife, hire a kayak, and eat lunch at the licensed cafe. The trip operates from October to April, with pickup from Russell or Paihia wharves, and costs NZ$165 for adults, NZ$83 for children ages 5 to 15. If you're keen on visiting the Hole in the Rock (a natural rock arch that boats can pass through), jump on **Explore's Discover the Bay** 4½-hour trip, which runs daily all year round, or in summer, its 1½-hour **Ocean Adventure** ♥ super-fast speedboat instead.

Kawakawa, 16km/10 miles south of Paihia, was mildly famous for being the only town in the country to have a railway line running through the middle of it. (Gabriel, the vintage steam train, still trundles through town on Fri, Sat, and Sun; visit www.bayofislandsvintagerailway.org.nz for tickets and timetables.) That all changed in 1999 with the addition of an unlikely attraction—**a public restroom on the main street** ♥♥♥. Designed by late Austrian artist Frederick Hundertwasser (whose legacy also lives on at Hundertwasser Art Centre in Whangārei; see p. 138), the stalls are a kaleidoscopic riot of mosaic tiles, wonky walls, bottle windows, and glowing ceramic pillars—and there's a tree growing out of the middle of it. The loo was so popular that in 2020, Kawakawa unveiled **Te Hononga Hundertwasser Memorial Park** ♥, a town-center-like complex, inspired by Hundertwasser. Located right off the main street, it's a dreamy camping spot, with free RV parking places overlooking a creek, free Wi-Fi, clean showers, and public restrooms that rival the original with rainbow-tiled floors.

Nearby, you'll find the **Kawiti Caves/Waiomio Caves,** just south of Kawakawa at 49 Waiomio Rd. (kawiticaves.co.nz; ✆ **09/404-0583**), which are replete with glowworms, stalactites, and Māori history. Daytime admission is NZ$50 for adults; NZ$30 for children ages 5 to 15, or you can book a longer, bespoke twilight tour for NZ$200 adults, NZ$150 kids.

Waitangi Treaty Grounds ♥♥♥ HISTORICAL SITE This isn't just a historical site—it's *the* historical site. And it's a damn good one. The 18.5-hectare (46-acre) Waitangi Treaty Grounds tell the story of modern New Zealand: The flagstaff that stands tall in these grounds marks the spot where Māori chiefs signed a treaty with the British Government on February 6, 1840. It granted Māori the rights of British subjects in exchange for ceding "all rights and powers of sovereignty" to the Crown, a confusing agreement if there ever was one. Understanding the Treaty of Waitangi (and its mistranslation and later breaches by the British and their descendants) is key to understanding the political constitution of the country and modern-day Māori-Pākehā relations (*Pākehā* being the word for New Zealanders of European descent; Tauiwi is often used to describe more recent migrants from all over).

In addition to entry to two interactive museums (including the new 28th Māori Battalion Museum, which tells that World War II story), visits are centered around a 50-minute guided tour (offered every 30 min. during the summer) that's far from a dry recitation of facts. Instead, the superb tour guides relate the site to their own ancestors and history, making the Treaty's

The Waitangi Treaty Grounds are home to one of the most magnificent *whare runanga* (meeting-houses) in the country. It contains elaborately carved panels from Māori tribes all around New Zealand.

modern-day connection clear. Headsets are distributed so that even in a large group, everyone can hear the guide clearly. The fee also includes a rousing half-hour cultural performance in a *whare rūnanga* (House of Assembly), which is a short but sweet version of what you may see elsewhere in the country, except at a lower cost. You can pay extra for an immersive 2½-hour cultural performance and hāngi buffet dinner, which is worth the cost if you don't plan to partake in this type of experience elsewhere (such as in Rotorua, which is legendary for these experiences; see chapter 7).

Among the Treaty Grounds' dazzling treasures are a 37.5m-long (115-ft.) war *waka* (canoe), Ngā Toki Matawhaorua, carved from three kauri trees. It's still a living and seaworthy vessel, paddled around the bay by about 150 men and boys each Waitangi Day (Feb 6). There's also the dainty 19th-century house where the treaty was signed (visitors learn about British Resident James Busby, who lived there with his family 1830–40); and a copy of the treaty in te reo Māori (the Māori language) set in the room where it was drawn up. Even if you're not into history, 2 hours here will fly by quickly. If you are, budget for at least 4 hours—there's a decent on-site cafe if you need sustenance.

Note: Every year on Waitangi Day (Feb 6), the grounds host a celebration commemorating the signing of the treaty. While it's free and open to visitors—with a dawn service, food stalls, and performances—the museum's buildings are closed on this date.

Waitangi Treaty Grounds, Tau Henare Dr., Waitangi. waitangi.org.nz. ✆ **0800/9248-2644** in NZ, or 09/402-7437. Admission (valid for 2 consecutive days) NZ$74 non-resident adults, NZ$37 youth 13–17, free for children 12 and under. Dec 26–Feb 28 9am–6pm; Mar 1–Dec 24 9am–5pm; closed Christmas Day. Hāngi and Concert Evening (available several times a week Oct–Apr), which includes free shuttle service, NZ$150 adults, NZ$75 children 5–12.

RUSSELL

"Romantic Russell" earns its nickname. It's a town designed for date nights, with restaurants overlooking the harbor, rows of historic wooden buildings, regular live music on the promenade, and wineries nearby—and its main strip was recently named the prettiest in New Zealand by international travel website WorldAtlas. Hike up Flagstaff Hill for jaw-dropping views of the Bay of Islands and you'll see the eponymous flagstaff that was hacked down by Ngāpuhi chief Hōne Heke four times between 1844 and 1845.

At the **Russell Museum ♥**, 2 York St. (russellmuseum.org.nz; ✆ **09/403-7701;** daily 10am–4pm; NZ$12 adults, free for children up to 14), there are all sorts of bits and bobs from Māori and European early days, including a one-fifth replica of Captain Cook's *Endeavour,* moa bones you can touch, artifacts from the whaling era, and some souvenirs from American author Zane Grey's swordfishing years, when he dubbed the Bay of Islands "the angler's Eldorado." New Zealand's oldest wooden church, the **Anglican Christ Church,** established in 1836, is behind the museum. You can still make out the holes made by musket balls during the sacking of Russell by the Māori chief Hōne Heke in 1845. It's open every day from 9am to 5pm.

At the south end of The Strand, you'll find **Pompallier Mission ♥** (pompallier.co.nz; ✆ **04/472-4341;** NZ$10 adults, free for children; daily 10am–4:30pm Nov–Apr, 10am–3:30pm May–Oct), built in 1841 by the eponymous French bishop who hoped to convert Māori to the Roman Catholic faith. He and the Marist brothers spent 7 years (1842–49) printing and binding bibles in Māori, and this beautiful French Lyonnaise mission house (New Zealand's oldest surviving Catholic building) housed the printing works and

island IN THE SUN

The Bay of Islands contains some 144 islands, but its biggest, most famous, and one of the most accessible is **Urupukapuka.** Its pest-free status has made it an important breeding ground and habitat for rare native birds, including North Island robins (*toutouwai*), North Island saddlebacks (*tīeke*) and whitehead (*pōpokotea*). It's also the only island in the bay where you can camp overnight, with some 23 beaches for snorkeling and swimming, including **Otehei Bay.** The island has a fully licensed cafe year-round; paddleboard and kayak rentals during the summer months, courtesy of **Bay of Islands Kayaking** (bayofislandskayaking.co.nz; ✆ **021/272-3353**); and walks ranging in length from 30 minutes to 5 hours. **Explore Group** (exploregroup.co.nz; ✆ **0800/397-567** in NZ, or 09/359-5987; NZ$65 adults, NZ$35 children ages 5–15) offers a year-round ferry service to Otehei Bay, departing from Paihia and Russell. It only takes about 40 minutes to reach Urupukapuka, making this a doable half-day or full-day excursion. But if you want to stay a while, campsites may be booked through the Department of Conservation (DOC; doc.govt.nz).

Hell Hole No More

Russell was NZ's biggest town (and original capital) before 1840 and was dubbed "the hell hole of the Pacific" thanks to the uncouth behavior of its whalers, traders, and sailors. In those days, Russell was called Kororāreka, which translates to "sweet penguin." Legend says that a Māori chief who was hurt in battle asked for penguin broth while he was convalescing. "How sweet is the penguin," he is reputed to have said.

tannery. Guided tours (NZ$20) explain the complex printing and tanning processes and are worth the outlay.

KERIKERI

A bustling town surrounded by orchards and vineyards, Kerikeri is the commercial center of the Bay of Islands, but it also has some important historical sites. Established in 1819 and situated in a picturesque location beside the Kerikeri River, the **Kerikeri Mission Station** ♥, 246 Kerikeri Rd. (visit heritage.co.nz), was one of the first places in the country where Māori invited visitors to live among them.

The **Kerikeri River Track,** a lovely 5.3-mile walking path out to Rainbow Falls, begins at two of New Zealand's oldest buildings. Completed in 1822 to house the Anglican Church Missionary Society, the Georgian-style **Kemp House** is said to be the oldest building in New Zealand. Next door is the **Stone Store,** the country's oldest stone building, which has been operating as a store since 1835. On the ground floor, a period gift shop is stocked with modern interpretations of what it might have once sold (think yarn, candle snuffers, seeds, and toy soldiers), while upstairs is a museum. Tours of the two buildings are held multiple times daily for NZ$20—inquire at the Stone Store to confirm staff availability. Both are open daily from 10am to 4pm.

Just up the hill, a 10-minute walk, is the **Kororipo Pā** site, the fortress that was home to Mission's Māori protector, Hongi Hika. It was the stronghold of the Ngāpuhi *iwi* (tribe) but little remains of the fort itself because Māori constructed all their pre-European buildings out of wood, and none have survived. You will, however, see remains of the ingenious trenches. (Māori are credited with inventing trench warfare.) Just across the river at **Te Ahurea** (teahurea.co.nz; ✆ **09/407-6454**), there's a reconstruction of a *kainga* (a fortified pre-European Māori village). The small attraction is open 10am to 4pm daily from November to March and Tuesday to Sunday April to November. Self-guided tours are only NZ$10 (children NZ$5), but the 40-minute guided tours don't cost much more (NZ$20 adults, NZ$10 children, free for kids 5 and under) and really help make the site come alive. Tours are held at 11am and 2pm.

If you like your greenery, check out **Wharepuke,** 190 Kerikeri Rd. (wharepuke.co.nz; ✆ **09/407-8933;** NZ$10 adults, NZ$5 children, free for kids under 5; daily 9am–5pm), a subtropical "Garden of National Significance" lovingly tended by gardener Robin Booth. Within the garden's 5 acres, you'll find more than 40 contemporary sculptures on display. Wander around by yourself or let Booth guide you for an extra fee (advance bookings required). Be sure to have a look at the art gallery and really quite revolutionary non-toxic printmaking studio, run by Booth's son-in-law Mark Graver.

If you're around on the weekend, markets are a great way to meet the locals. The indoor/outdoor **Old Packhouse Market ♥♥**, 505 Kerikeri Rd. (theoldpackhouse.co.nz; Sat 8am–1:30pm, Sun 9am–1pm)—dubbed the "beating heart of Kerikeri"—hosts 60 to 100 vendors, selling ready-to-eat meals as well as local produce and artisanal goods. Saturday is the main event here. On Sunday, try the **Kerikeri Farmers' Market ♥♥**, 10 Hobson Ave. (bayofislandsfarmersmarket.co.nz; Sun 8:30am–midday), where you'll find the freshest local seasonal produce, cheese, preserves, free-range eggs, artisan food, and locally grown and roasted coffee. (From Oct–Apr, it sets up shop in Paihia's Village Green on Thursday mornings, too.)

Outdoor Pursuits

BIKING The community-run **Waitangi Mountain Bike Park ♥♥**, 33 Bayly Rd. (ridewaitangi.nz; ✆ **6421/187-8192**) is giving Rotorua a ride (get it?) for its money as one of the best bike parks in NZ. Its 50km (31 miles) of trails range from grade two to five, and there's also a pump track. Visitors can rent bikes (including mountain e-bikes) from Paihia Mountain Bike's on-site kiosk, though booking in advance online is recommended (paihiamountainbikes.co.nz). Adult rentals start at NZ$79 for a half day; e-bikes cost extra. Kids' rentals start at NZ$40 for a half day. Check if the shuttle is operating—it was on hiatus in 2025—if it is, it drops cyclists at the top of the runs so they can get in more rides without having to slog uphill.

FISHING The Paihia visitor center has a list of light-line fishing charters, most of which supply rods and bait and range for about NZ$100 per person

Relax Like a Warrior

For a relaxing, unique, and highly recommended excursion, head 25 minutes southwest of Kerikeri to **Ngawha Springs ♥♥♥**, 303 Ngawha Springs Rd., Kaikohe (ngawha.nz; ✆ **09/405-2245**). Māori have soaked in these healing geothermal waters for 400 years: According to local tradition, after one battle, warring warriors from both sides repaired to the springs to recover peacefully side by side. Something of that vibe remains. Colors and temperatures vary naturally from day to day, so hop in and out of the 16 pools until you find your perfect spot. Like us, you might find yourself trading riddles with strangers while soaking in a sulfurous, inky black pool. Owned by the local hapū, the complex has recently been renovated and features lovely storytelling and signage, but the pools themselves remain pleasingly rustic—only timber frames separate you from the natural springs. For health reasons, don't put your head under, and for cultural reasons, you're asked not to soak while menstruating. Ngāwhā is open for five 2-hour sessions per day, Wednesday to Sunday—booking online in advance strongly recommended. Adults cost NZ$40, kids NZ$20, families NZ$110.

LET'S go SAILING

What could be lovelier than exploring the Bay of Islands by yacht? A trip on the tall ship ***R Tucker Thompson*** ♥♥, Maritime Building, Paihia (tucker.co.nz; ✆ **0800/882-537** in NZ, or 09/402-8430), is the ultimate in romantic sailing—and it's a not-for-profit, so your trip also supports young locals to participate in these voyages. The 19th-century replica schooner operates from November to April; a day out costs NZ$179 for adults and NZ$89 for children over 5. Morning tea, lunch, and an island swim are included. For almost half the price, there are also shorter sundowner sailings starting at 4pm.

Or, for a down-to-earth day out December through May, try highly rated **Barefoot Sailing Adventures** (barefootsailing.co.nz; ✆ **027/478-4234**). Six-hour small-group catamaran trips cost NZ$210 for adults and NZ$189 for kids, including lunch—and you can even help sail the boat if you like. Evening cruises feature a warm swim and a cold beer, and cost NZ$90—but book ahead, since sailings require a minimum number of passengers to proceed.

for a 4-hour snapper excursion. For game fishing, try **Earl Grey Fishing Charters,** Paihia and Russell Wharf (earlgreyfishing.co.nz; ✆ **09/407-7165**), which will customize a trip to your requirements.

GOLF Tee off in paradise at the **Waitangi Golf Club** (waitangigolf.co.nz; ✆ **09/402-8105;** greens fees NZ$70 for 18 holes). Clubs, shoes, and cart rentals are available. At the Rosewood Kauri Cliffs lodge near Matauri Bay (see p. 152), **Kauri Cliffs'** ♥♥♥ award-winning par-72 David Harman–designed golf course (ranked as one of the best in the world) is open to the public, with green fees for international visitors starting at NZ$425 for 9 holes during the winter (the price doubles during the summer months). In addition to carts, you can also hire a caddie for the day.

Where to Stay in the Bay of Islands

During the summer holiday period of December and January, the population in the Bay of Islands balloons from about 2,000 to more than 30,000—so book well in advance during these times. In addition to the options listed below, there are hundreds of listings for holiday homes and apartments in the region on airbnb.co.nz or bookabach.co.nz.

Which town to stay in? Paihia might be cheaper, but it's a Las Vegas showgirl to Russell's Met Opera star. Paihia lacks the charm of Russell and is dominated by family-friendly motels and bigger chain hotels. On the other hand, it's more convenient to stay here if you're taking tours, and it has more places to eat—so you don't need to gulp down your dessert for fear of missing the last ferry back to Russell. The more commercial Kerikeri is also a great non-waterfront option, although you'll have to drive to Paihia for most water-based excursions.

PAIHIA/OPUA

The **Scenic Hotel Bay of Islands** ♥ (scenichotelgroup.co.nz; ✆ **03/357-1919;** NZ$173–NZ$385 double) is an affordable chain-hotel option within easy walking distance of the beach and eateries. The comfortable family rooms have high wooden ceilings and stained-glass doors, there are dedicated accessible rooms, and the grounds abound with subtropical palms and a pool—but the staff weren't especially friendly on our visit. The **Tarlton's Lodge** ♥♥♥, 11 Sullivans Rd. (tarltonslodge.com; ✆ **09/402-6711;** NZ$385–NZ$695 double), overlooks Paihia, which means splendid views. It's a 15-minute trek into town (uphill on the return), but that distance also means absolute peace and quiet (this is an adults-only B&B, which also helps) and room for such niceties as outdoor spa tubs on each of the private terraces. Plus, the service here couldn't be warmer. A top pick.

If you want a romantic getaway, **The Sanctuary at the Bay of Islands** ♥♥, SH11, Port Opua (sanctuarybayofislands.co.nz; ✆ **09/402-6075;** NZ$485 winter, NZ$655 summer, including breakfast), is the place for it. Though it's only 5 minutes from Paihia, there are just four units, so it will just be you, a handful of other lucky folks, and the native birds. Views over the bush to the sea are to die for, the beds are high quality, and gracious host/owner Glenys is an excellent cook.

RUSSELL

Five minutes' drive out of town, **Russell Orongo Bay Holiday Park,** 5960 Russell-Whakapara Rd. (russellaccommodation.co.nz; ✆ **09/403-7704**) has won tourism and sustainability awards for its predator control work. As visitors, you reap the rewards—it's highly likely you'll see or hear a kiwi while staying here (walk along the Kiwi Trail between 9–10pm for the best chance). There are a wide range of camping sites, rooms, studios, cabins, and bungalows available, starting from NZ$55 for a powered site and NZ$85 for the simplest cabins. The **Top 10 Holiday Park,** 1 James St. (russelltop10.co.nz; ✆ **0800/148-671** in NZ, or 09/403-7826), has the views, and the town location, but is pricier. Glamping tents (summer only), cabins, and rooms cost NZ$120 to NZ$365, and powered sites start at NZ$88.

The Duke of Marlborough ♥♥♥ New Zealand's first licensed hotel claims that it's been "refreshing rascals and reprobates since 1827," but these days it serves a more discerning crowd. Little wonder, as the historic building has been chicly refurbished with nods to the past (chandeliers, Victorian-style bathroom fixtures, caveman-style faux-animal-pelt throws on the beds) and a prime harbor-front location. Get a sea-facing room and you can sit on your balcony with a drink and watch old salties rowing their dinghies home as the sun sets over the water, before falling asleep below the Duke of Marlborough crest painted above your bed.

35 The Strand, Russell. theduke.co.nz. ✆ **09/403-7869.** 38 units. NZ$165–NZ$350. **Amenities:** Restaurant; free Wi-Fi.

KERIKERI

Rosewood Kauri Cliffs ♥♥ Of the three NZ luxury lodges owned by American billionaire Julian Robertson, Kauri Cliffs, about 25 minutes from Kerikeri, is rumored to be his favorite. Evidence of his favoritism can be found in the three new Residences: four-bedroom villas with private pools built for each of his sons but open to the public when the gents are not in residence. Of the three Rosewood properties, it's also where golf is most central to the experience. The pro shop is set right in the main lodge; from the veranda, as you enjoy inclusive multi-course meals, you can watch golfers tee-off on the award-winning par-72 David Harman-designed golf course. Even if golf isn't your thing, there's plenty to do, with 2,630 hectares (6,500 acres) to explore: collecting rose-hued shells at Pink Beach; sea kayaking, land-based fishing or swimming at the sheltered turquoise blue Waiaua Bay; or surfing at the white-sand Little Takou beach.

139 Tepene Tablelands Rd., Mātauri Bay. kauricliffs.com. ✆ **09/407-0010.** 22 suites, one 2-bedroom cottage, three 4-bedroom villas. Suites NZ$3,150–NZ$3,795. Rates include breakfast, a la carte dinner, use of all facilities except golf and spa treatments. **Amenities:** Restaurant; bar; babysitting; mountain bikes; concierge; golf course; gym; Jacuzzi; outdoor pool, indoor lap pool; room service; sauna; spa; 2 tennis/pickleball courts; free Wi-Fi.

Wharepuke ♥♥ The local botanical gardens (p. 149) are really, er, branching out: You can eat at the award-winning **Māha Restaurant** ♥♥ (p. 156); check out the art gallery, greenery, and printmaking studio; and stay in one of five quirky self-contained eco-cottages hidden in the verdant grounds. The Booth family has owned this land since 1938, and patriarch

On an overnight stay at the Wharepuke botanical gardens in Kerikeri, guests wake up to lush subtropical beauty right outside their cottage doors.

Robin has been lovingly planting subtropicals since 1993. The sustainably built cottages—which are walking distance to Kerikeri—are simply furnished but spotlessly clean, and have everything you might need to cook a simple meal. The biggest perk, of course, is living inside this amazingly lush garden.

190 Kerikeri Rd., Kerikeri. wharepuke.co.nz. ✆ **09/407-89333.** 5 units. NZ$200–NZ$220 double; NZ$20 per extra person. **Amenities:** Restaurant; airport shuttle; tour desk; free Wi-Fi.

Where to Eat in the Bay of Islands

PAIHIA/WAITANGI

Cheap and cheerful is the order of the day in Paihia, where the restaurants lining the main streets and hidden along the laneways cater to hangry tourists looking for a quick bite. If you like Asian or seafood in particular, you'll have your pick.

Hidden down an alleyway, **Third Wheel Coffee Co.** ♥♥, 78–94 Marsden Rd. (facebook.com/thirdwheelcoffeeco; ✆ **027/844-7333**), is where locals go to get their caffeine fix. There is no a la carte menu, so you'll want to get here early for the cabinet food, including cinnamon buns, the moistest of cakes and scones, savory muffins, and veggie moussaka. It's all made fresh daily and sells out fast, for good reason.

Also down an alley, **Tipsy Oyster Tapas and Bar** ♥♥, 24 Kings Rd., Paihia (tipsyoyster.com; ✆ **09/945-8395;** daily 1pm–late), specializes in, you guessed it, cocktails and shellfish. In fact there are eight different fresh oyster options, from Korean-style with kimchi to tempura fried, for NZ$4.50 each. A selection of tapas and burgers rounds out the menu, and all is served in a brightly painted bar with indoor and outdoor seating, often to the accompaniment of live music.

For waterfront dining, **Charlotte's Kitchen** ♥♥, 69 Marsden Rd. (charlotteskitchen.co.nz; ✆ **09/402-8296;** daily 11:30am–late), is run by the owners of Russell's famed Duke of Marlborough Hotel (p. 152) and focuses on seasonal produce (lots of good options for vegans) and local seafood, like Waikare Inlet oysters. Mains are expensive (NZ$26–NZ$45), due to Charlotte's prime location right at the end of the wharf, but they are designed to be shared Don't want to break the bank? Charlotte's has wood-fired pizzas as well, starting at NZ$20. Book ahead, even on a winter weeknight, if you want to be sure of a table after returning from a tour!

Terra Restaurant ♥♥♥ MODERN NEW ZEALAND Terra is Paihia's top dining option, thanks to a wonderfully imaginative chef who whips up unusual but tasty treats like grilled pork neck with persimmon puree, duck with mandarin and poached fig, and Italian biscuits with coffee and Frangelico jelly. The presentations are Instagram-worthy, servers are gracious, and each course is better than the last—a complete package recognized with a prestigious hat in the 2024 Cuisine Good Food Awards. Needless to say, reservations are recommended.

Grilled octopus comes with crisp chardonnay and sweeping vineyard views at Sage Restaurant.

76 Marsden Rd. terrarestaurant.co.nz. ✆ **09/945-8376.** Mains NZ$36–NZ$55. Wed–Sun, set seatings 5:30–6pm and 8pm.

RUSSELL

The Duke of Marlborough ♥♥ MODERN NEW ZEALAND The Duke has gone from serving pretty good pub-style food with pretty so-so service to making Kiwi gourmet food mag *Cuisine*'s list of top restaurants. Heavy on seafood and local meats, specialties here include Bay of Islands oysters, Houhora pork, and Northland free-range chicken—with just a few vegetarian options (like roasted celeriac with mushrooms, or stone fruit and beetroot salad). The desserts are great, too. Make a reservation for a waterfront table on the patio.

The Strand, Russell. theduke.co.nz. ✆ **09/403-7869.** Reservations required for dinner in summer. Main courses NZ$25–NZ$36. Daily 11:30am–9pm.

Sage Restaurant ♥♥♥ MODERN NEW ZEALAND A short drive out of Russell, you'll find Sage at Paroa Bay Winery. One of the region's top dining options, its seasonal menu features high-end Northland meats and fish, most of which come from down the road, like lamb loin with kūmara puree, or salt-brined kingfish crudo with pickled grapes. A farther-afield exception worth sampling is the risotto with Fiordland crayfish (where the fishery is in much better shape than the one in the north).

46 Otamarua Rd., Russell. thelindisgroup.com/sagerestaurant. ✆ **09/403-8270.** Mains NZ$45–NZ$65. Wed–Sun noon–9pm.

KERIKERI

You may not be eating oceanside in Kerikeri, but there's no lack of stunning settings. Case in point: the **Plough and Feather** ♥, 215 Kerikeri Rd. (ploughandfeather.co.nz; ✆ **09/407-8479;** daily noon–9pm, from 10am Sun), which overlooks the Kerikeri River and sits directly beside the Stone Store, NZ's oldest surviving stone building. It's an English-style gastro pub with live music on Friday nights. The food is good (mains NZ$28–NZ$50), but what is really stellar is the location. **Marsden Estate Winery ♥♥**, 56 Wiroa Rd. (marsdenestate.co.nz; ✆ **09/407-9398;** mains NZ$20–NZ$38; daily 10am–3:30pm), is another looker, with meals served in a grape-bedecked courtyard a short 5-minute drive from Kerikeri. A producer of wines you're unlikely to find anywhere else (such as chambourcin, a French red hybrid, and a sparkling rosé), the winery serves food that complements the excellent vino—locally caught fish, grass-fed beef, and a refreshing ceviche salad, along with vegetarian and gluten-free options.

Also in a destination-worthy setting, **Māha Restaurant at Wharepuke ♥♥**, 190 Kerikeri Rd. (maharestaurant.co.nz; ✆ **09/945-6551;** mains NZ$38–NZ$45; Tues and Wed 5pm–late, Thurs–Sat noon–3pm and 5pm–late, though hours may vary seasonally), sits among the subtropical gardens and sculpture park at Wharepuke (p. 149). People travel from far and wide to try the chef's unusual Asian-fusion dishes.

THE FAR NORTH & THE KAURI COAST

Visiting the remote **Far North** region requires a time investment, but those who make the journey will be rewarded with kauri forests, immersive Māori cultural experiences, and some of the most jaw-dropping vistas Northland has to offer. Here you can explore **Te Oneroa a Tōhe 90-Mile Beach** (one of the longest stretches of sand in NZ); slide down the massive **Te Paki Sand Dunes;** and visit **Te Rerenga Wairua Cape Reinga,** the point at which Māori spirits access the underworld. Finally, **Hokianga** on the Kauri Coast is where you'll find the ancient giant kauri trees including **Tāne Mahuta** or "God of the Forest." It's also home to a new interactive museum celebrating Kupe, the Polynesian explorer who discovered NZ.

Essentials

ARRIVING

Kaitaia Airport offers a time-saving gateway to Cape Reinga and the Far North, though it is somewhat lacking in services and amenities. **Great Barrier Airlines** (barrierair.kiwi; ✆ **0800/900-600** in NZ, or 09/275-9120) flies from Auckland to Kaitaia and also provides a charter service. **InterCity** (intercity.co.nz; ✆ **09/583-5780**) provides bus service to Kaitaia. To get to the Kauri Coast, you'll need to hire a car in Auckland or in Paihia. From Auckland to Kaitaia via the east coast takes about 5 hours.

GETTING AROUND

Rental companies have become leery of visitors driving on 90-Mile Beach (which is actually more like 90 kilometers), so if you hanker to cruise along the vast sands, it's best to take a coach tour (see below). With countless

The lighthouse at Cape Reinga, the northeastern tip of New Zealand, is a top destination for a Fullers Bay of Islands bus tour of the Far North.

campgrounds and camping spots people can use free of charge, Northland is also an ideal spot to travel by motorhome or camper van. **BusLink** (buslink.co.nz; ✆ **09/438-7142**), a public transit service, connects to smaller regional areas throughout the entirety of Northland, including Hokianga and the Far North.

ORIENTATION

Kaitaia is the biggest town in the Far North. The unbroken sandy sweep of 90-Mile Beach (actually only 55 miles) runs from Cape Reinga in the north to **Ahipara** in the south. On the west coast, **Opononi** and **Ōmāpere** sit at the mouth of **Hokianga Harbour,** 89km (55 miles) south of Kaitaia. This is the main access for the Waipoua Forest's kauri trees, about a 25-minute drive south along the coast.

VISITOR INFORMATION

Northland's visitor website is **northlandnz.com**. The **Far North isite Visitor Information Centre** is at the Te Ahu Civic and Community Centre, on the corner of Matthews Avenue and South Road in Kaitaia (teahu.org.nz; ✆ **09/408-9450;** daily 8:30am–5pm).

Exploring the Far North

KAITAIA TO CAPE REINGA

The **Te Ahu Museum** (teahumuseum.nz; ✆ **09/408-9457**), in the Te Ahu Centre at the corner of Matthews Avenue and South Road in Kaitaia, tells the overlapping story of early Māori settlement and the new immigrants, many from Dalmatia. The latter played a large part in the region's kauri gum industry.

A 10-minute drive north up State Highway 1 in Awanui, **Kā Uri,** 229 SH1 (ka-uri.com; ✆ **09/406-7172**), is an intriguing enterprise owned and operated by Ngāti Kurī (the local iwi). Kauri logs dating back as far as 45,000 years ago have been pulled from local swamps and transformed into smooth golden works of art, including cutting boards, bowls, and even a massive staircase *inside* a tree trunk. It's open daily and free to enter, there's a good cafe on site, and you can often watch the artisans at work.

A short drive west from Awanui on State Highway 10, the town of Taipa on Doubtless Bay is home to **Taipa Salt Pig,** 384 State Highway 10 (thetaipa saltpig.com; ✆ **021/995-961**), a company making both fancy salt and bottled water from local seawater. For NZ$15 you can watch how they do it (call to arrange), and they have a shop too.

Continue up State Highway 1 to Waiharara, where you can see the remnants of ancient buried kauri forests, over 42,000 years old, at **Gumdiggers Buried Forest Park ♥**, Heath Road (gumdiggerspark.co.nz; ✆ **09/406-7166;** open daily). "Gumdigger" was a nickname for Northland's early European settlers, who dug here for the amber-like resinous lumps of kauri gum—a valuable commodity back in the 1800s, primarily for its use in varnishes. A preserved gumfield, this attraction offers tremendous insight into the tough lives of the early gum-digging pioneers.

CAPE REINGA

At the northernmost tip of New Zealand, **Te Rerenga Wairua Cape Reinga ♥♥♥** is where the Tasman Sea and the Pacific Ocean meet. It's also part of Te Ara Wairua or the "spirits' pathway." Māori believe that this is where their souls travel after death, before climbing down the roots of an 800-year-old pōhutukawa tree into the underworld, resurfacing at Manawatāwhi Three Kings Islands (which you can see from the cape on a clear day) to take one last look at Aotearoa before rejoining their ancestors in Hawaiki. You can see this tree just beyond the cape's lighthouse, which is an easy 15-minute walk downhill on a wide paved pathway. Since this is a site of spiritual significance, the consumption of food and drink isn't permitted here. (If you feel hunger coming on, take the turnoff just before Cape Reinga to **Tapotupotu Bay,** an ideal picnic spot with a good swimming beach.) The road to Cape Reinga is fully paved, and there's a large parking lot with toilets.

The cape is perched at the top of the Aupōuri Peninsula, with **Te Oneroa a Tōhe 90-Mile Beach ♥♥** (actually only 55 miles long) running all the way down its west coast. Kiwis love to drive on 90-Mile Beach, but your rental car agency won't allow it, because people frequently get stuck in the sand.

The giant, golden **Te Paki Sand Dunes ♥♥** are located at the end of Te Paki Stream Road. And we mean giant! They're 150m (nearly 500 ft.) high and stretch for miles. It's hard work climbing the dunes—massive kudos if you slide down them more than four times—but incredibly fun. In summer, you'll find a truck on site renting sandboards for NZ$15 (bring cash). Don't take any electronics or car keys up to the top of the dune with you; you're bound to lose them. Do bring sunscreen and water, and consider packing goggles on a windy day and socks on a hot one.

A visitor prepares to sandboard down one of the mountainous Te Paki Sand Dunes.

You can self-drive to all of these locations, but it's a long day that will take 8 or more hours round-trip, depending on your starting point. A more relaxing option is to take a bus tour. There are a few smaller operators, but the main game in town is now **Fullers Bay of Islands** (dolphincruises.co.nz; ✆ **0800/653-339** in NZ, or 09/402-7421), which does an 11-hour Cape Reinga tour from Paihia—they'll pick you up from your hotel there in the morning, or from stops at Mangōnui, Taipa, or Awanui farther north. The trip also includes basic lunch (think fish and chips or a pie and salad), a morning tea stop at Kā Uri, driving on 90-Mile Beach, and sandboarding either there or at the giant Te Paki sand dunes (2023's Cyclone Gabrielle shifted sand and blocked the access, and as of 2025 the company was still negotiating access to the site). The best thing about the tour, though, is the *whakawhanaungatanga*—the practice of creating and relationships and cohesion through shared experiences—fostered by the storytelling driver-guides during the day-long trip. For a single traveler it arguably costs less than you'd spend on fuel driving up there and back yourself: NZ$175 for adults and NZ$88 for children ages 5 to 15.

Exploring the Kauri Coast

Located along the Kauri Coast (or Northland's west side), the **Hokianga Harbor** is an estuary that extends inland for 30km (19 miles) from the Tasman Sea. Its main settlements, with tourist-facing services, are **Ōmāpere, Opononi,** and **Rawene.** If you arrive after driving through the Waipoua Forest (see "Northland's Ancient Giants," p. 160), be sure to take the lefthand turn-off to the "Scenic Lookout." At the road's end is the **Arai Te Uru Recreational Reserve,** where a 20-minute walk along the **Signal Station Track** provides spectacular views on the harbor and its headlands.

Manea Footprints of Kupe ♥♥ ATTRACTION Northland isn't just the birthplace of modern NZ—it's also the cradle of Māori nationhood. According to local tradition, Hokianga Harbor is where the Polynesian explorer Kupe landed after discovering New Zealand many hundreds of years ago, and where he left from to return home at the end of his life. This facility, which opened at the end of 2020, is more than just a museum dedicated to his story—it's a multisensory, interactive space, where the region's culture; history, and stories are passed on. After a traditional *pōwhiri* (welcome ceremony), you'll be invited into the theater for a 20-minute presentation on Kupe's arrival in Aotearoa. Presented in 4D, the performance—which is aided by live actors—is delivered with humility and humor and is appropriate for all ages (although there's a chance small children may find the fight scene with the monster octopus Te Wheke-a-Muturangi a bit scary). For a deeper dive, the interactive gallery delivers short videos focusing on the region's history and culture. The highlight, though, is meeting the young staff who work

NORTHLAND'S ancient GIANTS

In **Waipoua Forest ♥♥♥** and the smaller **Trounson Kauri Park,** experience the awesome—in the proper sense of the word—power of kauri, which are among the largest and oldest trees in the world. Massive in both stature and presence, photos don't do these giants justice. In Waipoua, **Tāne Mahuta (God of the Forest)** is the largest and estimated to be around 1,500 years old. **Te Matua Ngahere (Father of the Forest)** is shorter, but even older, possibly exceeding 2,500 years. Te Matua is an easy 45-minute roundtrip walk from the parking lot, while Tāne Mahuta is located nearly roadside. A DOC interpreter or Te Roroa ambassador is typically on site daily at Tāne Mahuta to share stories and act as *kaitiaki* (guardians). The trees need it; kauri dieback disease is threatening their future, as it kills nearly every tree that it infects—and it's spread by soil contact. Several walks in the area are now closed due to this disease, which isn't well understood and for which there is no cure. Always clean and disinfect footwear—even if it's been in storage for years—at the provided cleaning stations and stick to the trails. To learn more, visit kauridieback.co.nz.

Both massive trees can be freely accessed from well-signed areas along SH12, but for a truly awe-inspiring experience, take a twilight tour with **Footprints Waipoua ♥♥♥** (footprintswaipoua.co.nz; ✆ **09/405-8207;** NZ$115 adults, NZ$55 children). Visiting the giants as dusk falls in the company of a talented Māori guide—who shares both botanical and cultural context, and sings and chants to these ancient beings in Te Reo Māori as you approach them—is a magical moment that will send shivers up your spine.

Learn more about kauri trees and their importance to this region at the Kauri Museum in Matakohe (see p. 137).

here—all are descendants of Kupe, who are carrying his legend on. The full experience takes 75 minutes.

41 Hokianga Harbour Dr., Opononi. maneafootprints.co.nz. ✆ **0800/9248-2644.** NZ$75 adults, NZ$12 kids 13–16, NZ$6 kids 5–12, NZ$150 family of 4. Daily 9am–5pm.

Outdoor Pursuits

BEACHES Good swimming beaches dominate the whole northeast coast, from Auckland up. The farther north you go, the better and more deserted the beaches get. Those along Doubtless Bay and the **Karikari Peninsula,** including **Tokerau Beach ♥♥**, are favorites. **Rangiputa Beach ♥♥**, in particular, is great for kids; there's lots of shade and it's calm and shallow. Beaches on the east coast are calmer than those on the west, so don't expect to swim at 90-Mile Beach; it has lot of riptides and strong currents.

WALKING The famed **Te Araroa Trail**—which stretches the length of NZ—starts at Cape Reinga. Needless to say, there's some solid hiking to be had in this neck of the woods, with over 100 DOC tracks in the area. The 16.5km track to the historic **Cape Brett ♥♥** lighthouse is one of my favorite tracks in the country for its scenery, solitude, and spiritual significance (Rākaumangamanga was one of the original landing points for early seafaring Polynesians), but it isn't for the faint of heart. Look at an elevation map before you commit to it, as even the fittest will find it takes 8 hours one-way. The reward is a night spent in the former lighthouse keeper's house (now a DOC hut) at the other end. A 3-hour (one-way) version exists as well, if combined with a water taxi (boiwatertaxi.co.nz) to Deep Water Cove.

Where to Stay in the Far North & Kauri Coast

THE FAR NORTH

If you're travelling by campervan or motorhome, you're in luck in the Far North. There are plenty of free camping spots and affordable holiday parks (campgrounds), alongside the usual offering of motels, hotels, and Airbnbs.

Cable Bay Stays ♥♥ Here you can have a classic Kiwi "bach" experience—owners Brian and Rosemary want to give you the beach holidays they remember having here as kids, and their comfortable holiday apartments are accordingly decorated in full '60s glory, with fun colors and matching crockery. But they've got the best bits of the 2020s, too—fully equipped kitchens and modern bathrooms with great showers. They're also absolute beachfront, right on the lovely golden sands of Cable Bay, with a playground next door, and the excellent Cable Bay Store a short walk away for morning coffee, ice creams, and gourmet pies. They even supply body boards and cricket gear for the kids to borrow.

333 State Highway 10, Cable Bay. cablebaystays.co.nz. ✆ **021-557504.** 12 apts. NZ$149–NZ$299. **Amenities:** BBQ; free Wi-Fi.

The Old Oak ♥♥ Crisp, fresh decor has brought this Mangōnui landmark back to life. The inn, founded in 1861, had its heyday in the 19th century, then fell on hard times as a grotty backpacker lodge. It's finally been

The beachfront "baches" at Cable Bay Stays (p. 161) were designed to re-create the carefree summer holidays the owners remember from their childhoods.

restored to a place worthy of spending the night, with each room showcasing a little piece of history among the handsomely minimalist contemporary furnishings: One features a cross over the bed made from the fussy Victorian curlicues once on the front veranda, another has a headboard made from the old kauri mantle that used to surround the cooking fireplace. Play a game of pétanque in the garden, which features organic herbs, veggies, and a formal rose bed, before heading straight out your door to walk along the waterfront. (No children allowed.)

66 Waterfront Rd., Mangōnui. theoldoak.co.nz. ✆ **09/406-1250.** 7 rooms and suites. NZ$250–NZ$395 double. **Amenities:** BBQ; pétanque court; free Wi-Fi.

Riverside Escapes ♥♥♥ Riverside Escapes had me at "outdoor bathtub," but the deal was sealed when I discovered that said bathtub was in the middle of an olive grove overlooking a river, right beside a hammock. Yes, please! The property features two glamping units, each situated in private locations within the olive grove: the Green Rabbit, a self-contained little cabin, and the River Bothy, which has more space to sprawl out, though much of it—including the kitchen—is outdoors. Built to be entirely self-sustaining and off-grid, this property isn't for everyone. Toilets are composting, there's no Wi-Fi, and cellphone reception is patchy—but that's exactly the point. Why look at your phone when you can watch the mist rise off the river from the comfort of your bed? And should you get bored (you won't), there are plenty of surrounding beaches and coves nearby to explore. The ideal couples or solo retreat; both can be booked through Canopy Camping.

Leccino Valley Rd., Mangōnui. riversideescapes.co.nz. ✆ **021/210-6691.** 2 units. NZ$295–NZ$325 double. 2-night min. stay. **Amenities:** BBQ; kitchenette; no Wi-Fi.

THE KAURI COAST

With a vantage point high over the hills, **Rawene Holiday Park ♥♥** (1 Marmon St. West; raweneholidaypark.co.nz; ✆ **09/405-7720**) is the best spot to watch the day's end over the Hokianga Harbour, because the tiny village of Rawene is one of the few places where you can watch the sun both rise and set over water. Sure, the shared kitchen could use some love, but the clean communal bathrooms and outdoor pool more than make up for it. Also, that view! This is also one of the most affordable campgrounds in the area at only NZ$25 per person for a powered site, or NZ$65 for the smallest cabins with access to a communal kitchenette and bathroom.

The Sands Hotel Hokianga ♥♥ After a full makeover in 2025, the insides of the Sands Hotel's 43 villas, hotel rooms, and apartments look as good as the views outside. Stay in one of the beachfront options and there's nothing between you and the glorious Hokianga Harbor. It's a short drive from here to both the Waipoua Forest and Manea Footprints of Kupe. There's a pool and a gym, bikes and kayaks are available for hire, and in the on-site Bryers Restaurant, acclaimed Fijian-Indian chef Priya Darshani serves up Asia-Pacific specialties as well as burgers and fries.

334 Hokianga Harbour Drive, Ōmāpere. thesandshotel.co.nz. ✆ **09/405-8737.** Rooms NZ$159–NZ$325 in winter, NZ$230–NZ$425 in summer. Free parking. **Amenities:** Restaurant; pool; gym; laundry; free Wi-Fi.

Where to Eat in the Far North & Kauri Coast

THE FAR NORTH

The "world-famous" **Mangōnui Fish Shop ♥**, Waterfront Drive (mangonuifishshop.com; ✆ **09/406-0478;** daily 10am–7pm), has a rival. Sure, the fish practically leap out of the water onto your plate here, and yes, they are delicious, but all the tour buses stop here and so does every other tourist coming to this little fishing village in Doubtless Bay. Locals get their fix instead from **Fresh and Tasty Takeaways ♥**, Waterfront Drive (facebook.com/mangofreshtas; ✆ **09/406-0082**). It's significantly cheaper, quicker, and still serves up a decent feed of the Kiwi classics.

A few bays along, the **Cable Bay Store ♥♥**, State Highway 10, Cable Bay (facebook.com/cablebaystore), is famous for its ice creams but also serves up breakfasts and a wide range of tasty cabinet food, from pies to wraps, bagels, sandwiches, and hearty salads.

Food options thin out considerably north of Kaitaia, so if you're headed up to Cape Reinga for the day, it's the place to stop and fill up. Especially because the town is home to **Peekaboo Backyard Eatery ♥**, hidden just off the main strip at 5 Bank St. (facebook.com/peekaboo.backyard.eatery.kaitaia; ✆ **09/408-4320;** Tues–Sun 8am–8pm). A pleasant surprise after a long drive, the contemporary space boasts a backyard beer garden, complete with kids' playset. Breakfast is served until 11:30am, at which point the menu switches to share plates and sourdough pizzas fired in a Neapolitan oven. It's so good it won the top honors at the 2025 Lion Hospitality New Zealand Business Awards, including being crowned Best Café in the country.

The rough-and-ready Boatshed Cafe in Rawene, a local favorite for breakfast and lunch.

Just a short detour down the road, you'll find Ahipara's **North Drift Cafe** ♥, 250 Ahipara Rd. (facebook.com/northdriftcafe; ✆ **09/409-4093;** daily 8am–2pm). Everyone, including kids, is catered to with an affordable menu (mains NZ$10–NZ$22) that includes everything from breakfast items to burgers, pasta, and nachos.

THE KAURI COAST

When you're in an area this remote, eating options are fairly limited. Unless you're a fan of bland pub food and warm white wine, you'd be well advised to stock up on supplies and cook for yourself (or picnic) if you plan on staying for any period of time. There are some exceptions to this rule, though: The revamped restaurant at the Sands Hotel in Ōmāpere (see above) looks promising, and the **Boatshed Cafe** ♥♥ in Rawene, 8 Clendon Esplanade (facebook.com/boatshedcaferawene; ✆ **09/405-7728;** mains NZ$25 on average; daily 7:30am–4:30pm), is one of the region's best breakfast and lunch options. Up on poles, the shed sticks right out over the mud, tide, and mangroves, and you can sit on the deck and watch the ferry ply the harbor while eating bagels, focaccia, brie-stuffed brioches, or leek-and-mussel pot pie. Dishing up Thai food and breakfast goodies, **The Landing Cafe,** located beside the isite in Opononi, is open Tuesday to Sunday 8am to 2pm, Wednesday to Saturday 5 to 7pm.

WAIKATO, THE BAY OF PLENTY & THE COROMANDEL

6

Ask a Kiwi to describe the following: The Bay of Plenty? Sun. The Coromandel? Beaches. Waikato? Cows. But one word isn't nearly enough to accurately describe any region, and Waikato is no exception. If you're tempted to detour around the Waikato and its mighty river (New Zealand's longest), please reconsider. This energetic and ever-changing region is home to some of the country's best attractions, including Hobbiton, the bohemian surfing town of Raglan, the Waitomo Glowworm Caves, and, yes, a few (million) cows.

Northeast of Waikato, the **Coromandel Peninsula** is a much-loved playground for North Islanders, with a rich gold-mining history and contrasting coasts: the jagged but sheltered west coast running alongside the Firth of Thames, and the beautiful sandy oceanside bays of the east coast. Following the Pacific Coast Highway from Auckland will take you through the Coromandel's small seaside villages, around endless beaches and bays, and over rugged hill country into the heart of an area made famous by logging, gum digging, and bohemian artists. A holiday favorite of Aucklanders, it gets very crowded in peak summer.

South of Coromandel on the east coast, the aptly named **Bay of Plenty** is another region awash with beach communities, but inland BOP (as it's abbreviated) has its charms, too: misty mountains, one of the last prehistoric rainforests in the world, and some of the best spots in the country to experience authentic Māori culture.

HAMILTON & THE WAIKATO

127km (79 miles) S of Auckland; 107km (66 miles) NE of Rotorua; 107km (66 miles) E of Tauranga

A quick 90-minute drive south of Auckland, Hamilton is New Zealand's largest inland city, with a population of around 192,000, but it doesn't have all that much to interest visitors (except its spectacular botanical gardens). The surrounding Waikato region, however, has more than a few treasures. Not far from Hamilton is the Hobbiton set from the *Lord of the Rings* movies, and the Waitomo Caves, renowned for their otherworldly glowworms. If you have time, I also suggest stopping in the pretty town of Cambridge, soaking in the hot pools at Te Aroha, or catching a wave or browsing some art in the laid-back surf town of Raglan.

Essentials

ARRIVING

BY PLANE **Air New Zealand** (✆ **0800/737-000** in NZ) has daily flights to Hamilton from the main centers. The airport is about 15 minutes' drive south of the city. **Super Shuttle** (supershuttle.co.nz; ✆ **0800/748-885**) will transport you there from the airport.

BY TRAIN While primarily intended as a scenic train, KiwiRail's **Northern Explorer** route (greatjourneysnz.com; ✆ **0800/872-467** or 04/495-0775) also does the trick of getting tourists from Auckland or Wellington to Hamilton. Fares start at NZ$98. The new **Te Huia** commuter train (tehuiatrain.co.nz; ✆ **0800/205-305**) runs several daily roundtrip services from Auckland to Hamilton. The trip takes 2½ hours and costs NZ$40 one way (or buy a Bee Card for NZ$5 onboard the train and your ticket will cost just NZ$24). It works out both cheaper and more comfortable than most bus trips.

BY COACH (BUS) **InterCity** (intercity.co.nz; ✆ **09/583-5780**) links Hamilton to other major centers. **Luxury Airport Shuttles** (luxuryairportshuttles.co.nz; ✆ **07/547-4444**) offers a shared shuttled service between Auckland, Hamilton, Rotorua, Tauranga, and surrounding areas.

GETTING AROUND

A car is probably the best way to explore the area; Hertz and Avis have locations both in town and at the Hamilton airport, or try **Waikato Car Rentals,** 2F Brooklyn Rd. (waikatocarrentals.co.nz; ✆ **0800/154-444** in NZ, or 07/855-0094). **Hamilton Taxis** (hamiltontaxis.co.nz; ✆ **0800/477-477** in NZ, or 07/847-7477) is a 24-hour service with a rank at the Hamilton airport. Uber is available.

You can also get transfers to the Waikato's most popular destinations from Hamilton. For a list of current transfer services to **Hobbiton,** visit hobbitontours.com/en/plan-visit/transfers. **Real New Zealand Adventures** (realnewzealandadventures.com; ✆ **07/878-7580**) offers a transfer service to the Waitomo Caves with customized tours. **BUSIT's 23 Raglan** service (busit.co.nz/regional-services/raglan; ✆ **0800/205-305** in NZ only) runs daily from Hamilton to Raglan and includes surfboard and luggage racks. For more local and regional buses, shuttles and taxis, visit the **Hamilton Transport Centre,** 373 Anglesea St. (✆ **0800/205-305**), open weekdays 8am to 4:30pm.

VISITOR INFORMATION

The Waikato's tourism website is **waikatonz.com**. The **Hamilton isite Visitor Centre,** 120 Victoria St. (visithamilton.co.nz; ✆ **07/958-5960**), is open

Waikato, the Bay of Plenty & the Coromandel

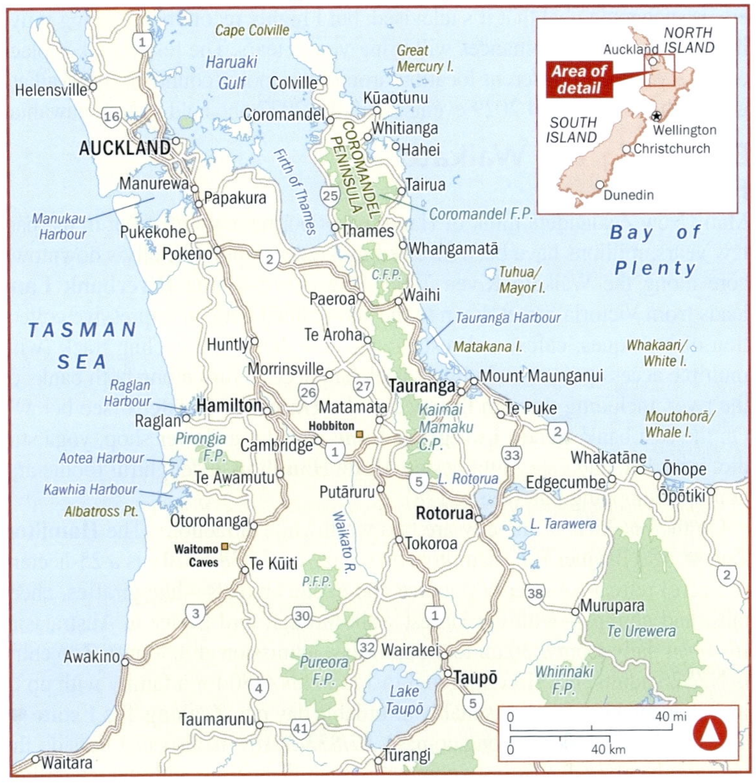

daily from 10am to 5pm. The **Cambridge isite,** corner of Queen and Victoria streets (cambridge.co.nz; ✆ **07/823-3456**), is open weekdays from 10am to 4pm and weekends from 10am to 2pm. The **Waitomo Caves Discovery Centre and isite,** 21 Waitomo Caves Rd. (waitomocaves.com; ✆ **07/878-7640**), is open Monday to Thursday 9am to 11am, Friday to Sunday 9am to 3pm. Fashioned to look like a Hobbit house, the **Matamata isite,** 45 Broadway (matamatanz.co.nz; ✆ **07/888-7260**), is open daily 9am to 3pm.

SPECIAL EVENTS

From tractor pulls to food vendors and dog shows, **Fieldays** (fieldays.co.nz; ✆ **07/843-4499**)—the biggest agricultural show in the Southern Hemisphere, held in Hamilton in late November—is entertaining even for urbanites. Hamilton also plays host to March's **Balloons Over Waikato** (balloonsover waikato.co.nz; ✆ **07/856-7215**), a massive free-to-attend hot air balloon festival. ***Top tip:*** If you want to attend the sought-after ZURU Nightglow event—an opening ceremony combining live music, choreographed hot air balloons, and fireworks —you'll have to sign up online for the ballot.

In February, the **Te Matatini Kapa Haka Aotearoa Festival ♥♥♥** (tematatini.co.nz), a competition of the country's best Māori cultural performers, is such a big deal that it's televised, but I highly recommend seeing it live if you can—the performances will bring you to tears. The festival takes place every 2 years at a different location around the motu (country); the Waikato gets both the 2027 and 2029 events, with the 2027 one held at Ngāruawahia.

Exploring the Waikato

HAMILTON

Many New Zealanders think of Hamilton as boring and gritty, but in the past few years, millions have been invested into redeveloping the city's downtown core along the Waikato River. Today, the award-wining **Riverbank Lane** leads from Victoria Street down to the shore, lined with an impressive collection of boutiques, cafes, and restaurants. A walking and cycling track (with multiple access points, including wheelchair access) runs along both banks of the river, including through the spectacular **Hamilton Gardens** (see below). On the east bank, trendy **Lovegrove Lane** includes a flower shop, yoga studio, juice bar, and cafe, right beside **Made Hamilton,** a delightful foodie and boutique shopping hub (see p. 178).

On the outskirts of the city are two worthwhile attractions. The **Hamilton Zoo ♥**, 183 Brymer Rd. (hamiltonzoo.co.nz; ✆ **07/838-6720**), is a 25-hectare (62-acre) retreat for over 600 native and exotic animals—like giraffes, cheetahs, and chimps—with the largest walk-through bird aviary in Australasia. It's open daily from 9:30am to 4:30pm (last admission at 3:30pm). Zoo entry is NZ$26 adults, NZ$13 children 3 to 15, and NZ$80 for a family with up to four kids, making for a reasonably affordable day out. **Zealong Tea Estate ♥**, 495 Gordonton Rd. (zealong.com; ✆ **07/853-3018**), is also just outside the city. It's New Zealand's only commercial tea plantation, with over 1 million tea plants in cultivation. Zealong's tea house serves high tea (complete with tea-infused patisserie treats) Thursday to Monday from 10am to 5pm.

Oddest Hamilton landmark? That would be the statue of the *Rocky Horror Picture Show's* **Riff-Raff.** The film's writer Richard O'Brien lived in Hamilton and worked next door to where the statue now stands on the south end of Victoria Street.

Hamilton Gardens ♥♥♥ GARDENS Said to be the most-visited attraction in Waikato, Hamilton Gardens is the city's one truly don't-miss experience. The site includes 18 themed, enclosed gardens set on 54 hectares (133 acres) beside the Waikato River, and each is transporting in its own way. The Surrealist Garden seems to bend the laws of nature, as strange biomorphic topiary move above you, thanks to carefully designed hydraulics. The Italian Renaissance Garden is a mix of geometric patterns and fine sculptures that seems lifted from Tuscany, while the Mansfield Garden is a time portal back to a 1922 garden party, complete with a live band and finger food. (Sadly, you can't eat it, but there is an on-site cafe.) Budget at least 90 minutes for the

The Mansfield Garden section of Hamilton Gardens pays tribute to NZ author Katherine Mansfield, best known for her short story "The Garden Party."

enclosed gardens, plus more time if you want to stage mini photoshoots (and trust us, you will).

Hungerford Crescent, Hamilton East. hamiltongardens.co.nz. ✆ **07/838-6782.** Outer gardens free; enclosed gardens NZ$20 adults, ages 15 and under free. Enclosed gardens daily 10am–6pm. Audio guides NZ$5.

Te Whare Taonga o Waikato Museum and Gallery ♥ MUSEUM
As is usually the case with regional museums, local history and culture are center stage in the Waikato Museum's 13 galleries. The collections hold more than 38,000 objects and include impressive Māori art, weaving, and carving from the area's Tainui people, including a 200-year-old carved *waka* (war canoe). **Exscite** is a lovely kid-friendly hands-on science gallery. Next door, but still part of the museum, in the old post office building is **ArtsPost,** with three galleries specializing in work by emerging artists and a shop that stocks New Zealand art and design pieces.

1 Grantham St. waikatomuseum.co.nz. ✆ **07/838-6606.** Free (Exscite NZ$5 adults, NZ$10 ages 3–15, NZ$29 family passes). Daily 10am–5pm.

CAMBRIDGE

Sprawling oak trees, antiques shops, historic churches, a cute main square—it's easy to understand why Cambridge has won both "most beautiful large town in New Zealand" and "New Zealand's most beautiful street." As the center of the Australasian thoroughbred horse industry, it's also a serious equestrian center; keep an eye out for sleek, expensive racehorses in paddocks on the outskirts of town. If you'd like to see some of the region's equine athletes in action, time your visit to coincide with a night when there's harness racing at the **Cambridge Raceway,** Taylor St. (cambridgeraceway.co.nz; ✆ **07/827-5506**). There are about 30 to 70 race dates a year.

THERE BE hobbits!

"Home is now behind you, the world is ahead!" Set deep in the rolling hills on the Waikato, you'll find the green pastures of the Shire, home to Frodo, Bilbo Baggins, and some 10,000 sheep. No epic journey is necessary; all you have to do to get to Middle-earth is hop on a tour bus at the **Hobbiton Movie Set ♥♥♥**, 501 Buckland Rd., Matamata (hobbitontours.com; ✆ **07/888-1505**). But be warned—you'll need to book well in advance, even weeks ahead during peak seasons. The 4.8-hectare (12-acre) site was the actual set used in Peter Jackson's *Lord of the Rings* films, and a tour of it allows you to walk inside enchantingly appointed hobbit holes (you can even lie on the beds or jump in the copper bath) and have a drink at the Green Dragon Inn. Evening tours include a banquet feast fit to feed a Hobbit, and on select weekends you can enjoy "second breakfast" at the Millhouse. The 2-hour basic tours depart daily roughly every 10 minutes (with the last tour departing at 4:10pm) and cost NZ$130 adults, NZ$65 children 11 to 17 (under 11 free), and NZ$332 for a family pass. Breakfast and banquets cost extra. Arrive at the Shire's Rest 15 minutes before your tour to pick up your ticket and board your bus.

Hobbiton may have the trademark, but it doesn't have a monopoly on Tolkien film locations. On the small and low-key tours offered by **Hairy Feet Waitomo ♥♥**, 1411 Mangaotaki Rd., Piopio, near Waitomo (hairyfeetwaitomo.co.nz; ✆ **07/877-8003**), you can visit a private farm with spectacular limestone cliffs and see locations where key scenes from *The Hobbit: An Unexpected Journey* were filmed. These include the spot where Gandalf gives Bilbo the sword known as "Sting." The 90-minute tours run several times a week and cost NZ$70 adults and NZ$40 children up to 14.

The sets from the Lord of the Rings movies are now explorable tourist attractions.

The region is also home to one of the most transcendent (and I don't use that word lightly) experiences in NZ. On a sunset tour with **Riverside Adventures' Twilight Glow Worm Kayak ♥♥♥** (riversideadventures.co.nz; ✆ **0800/287-448** in NZ, or 0277/287-448), you'll paddle over the submerged Horahora power station, before heading through a river gorge and past "glow-worm city" (a spot on the riverbanks where the creatures congregate)—the latter taking place in complete darkness and silence. The 4-hour tour costs NZ$149 adults, NZ$99 children 8 to 16, with a family pass available for NZ$480. This family-owned business also offers bike rentals and tours along the **Waikato River Trails** (waikatorivertrails.co.nz), a 65-mile path that winds along beside the river. The grade 2 and 3 trail follows old bush tramways from logging days and includes eight large suspension bridges. They're 15 minutes south of Cambridge in Piarere, at 362 Horohoro Rd.

About a half-hour's drive south in Pukeatua, **Sanctuary Mountain Maungatautari ♥♥** (sanctuarymountain.co.nz; ✆ **07/870-5180**) is a fully fenced predator-free wildlife preserve. It's one of dozens of such sanctuaries around the country, which protect endangered and endemic wildlife from stoats, possums, and rats. Although it isn't the glossiest, it is one of the most accessible—and one the largest of its kind in the world. Its 3,400 hectares (8,400 acres) are home to native species including the only mainland population of kākāpō, kiwi, tuatara (an ancient reptile), and giant wētā (a type of flightless cricket the size of a mouse). Visitor passes cost NZ$32, but the volunteer-led tours (starting at NZ$48) improve your chances of seeing the native birds and lizards. (For kiwi, book the private night tour for up to four people, which costs NZ$352 in total—book at least 48 hours ahead.) The visitor center is open from 9am to 4pm daily.

RAGLAN

Raglan is one of those surfing towns that act as a vortex—people intend to just stay a night and somehow are still there years, or even decades, later. (Consider this fair warning.) It's an undeniably pleasant place with a number of surf schools, boutique clothing shops, alternative cafes, and a genuine commitment to sustainability—bring your reusable cup! If your itinerary is too tight for a lifetime stay (or even just an overnight one), the seaside town can be visited as a day trip from Hamilton or Cambridge, though I'd recommend allowing longer. It's a 45-minute drive from Hamilton on SH23, but budget an extra hour for a side trip to the spectacular, 180-foot **Wairēinga/Bridal Veil Falls ♥♥**. Turn left at the signed turnoff at Te Mata Road, which later turns into Kawhia Road, and follow it for 4km (2½ miles) to the carpark. There's a wheelchair accessible viewing platform at the top, but the viewing platforms at the bottom offer the best views.

Once you reach Raglan, it's borderline mandatory to take a surf lesson or at least rent a board. A handful of companies offer both—we like the family-friendly **Raglan Surf School ♥♥** (raglansurfschool.co.nz; ✆ **07/825-7327** or 021/174-6329), which offers group (NZ$95) and private (from NZ$169) lessons at **Ngarunui Beach ♥♥♥**, the town's busy main beach off Wainui Road.

Surfers try their skill on one of Raglan's renowned left-hand point breaks.

That's also where you'll find the surf school's trailer, where you can rent wetsuits, surfboards, and bodyboards by the hour. (A board and wetsuit will run you NZ$40 for 3 hr.) Follow the coast road farther south along a narrow gravel road to the viewpoint at **Te Toto Gorge ♥♥**, which will reward you with a moment of genuine awe (not for those with vertigo). This is also the starting point for the challenging but highly recommended 6-hour roundtrip hike up bushclad **Mount Karioi ♥♥♥**, with views as far as Mount Ruapehu and Mount Taranaki in clear weather. (Be prepared to haul yourself up some very steep sections with the help of a rope.)

For the adventurous, **Raglan Rock ♥♥** 248 Wainui Rd., Riria Kereopa Memorial Dr. (raglanrock.com; ✆ **027/645-3547**), offers canyoning, caving, and other trips on and around Mount Karioi—try their nighttime abseiling trip down a waterfall, the way illuminated by glowworms (NZ$149 adults, NZ$95 kids). You can also hire kayaks by the jetty at the bottom of Bow Street—paddle over to the magical limestone formations on the far side of the harbor.

For a more sedate day out, take yourself on a DIY walking art tour. Start at the wharf, where potter **Tony Sly** (tonyslypottery.com) makes elegant, minimalist tableware, and **Soul Shoes** (soulshoes.co.nz) leatherworker Rob Galloway sells handmade bags, shoes, and accessories. Back towards town along Wallis Street, stop in **Bing Ceramics** (bingceramics.co.nz) to check out Sarah Bing's totally different ceramic style: colorful, quirky, and playful. You can even try your hand at painting your own pot, whenever the studio is open (10am–4pm Wed–Sun). On the main street, pop into **Jet Collective** (19a Bow St.), which features the work of six local makers. During the **Raglan Arts Weekend** (raglanartsweekend.nz) annually in late October, dozens of the town's artists open up their studios for exhibitions and demonstrations—check the website for maps and schedules.

Finally, the Raglan area is home to two new utterly delightful sauna spots, both costing around NZ$30 for a drop-in session. If you prefer rural vibes, native bush, a pristine stream, and cooling off via giant forest swing, head to **Pumula** ♥♥♥ 397 Ruapuke Rd. (pumularaglan.nz; ✆ **021/028-55243**)—I recommend the yoga+sauna combo. Or, if you'd prefer expansive coastal views of surf and horizon while you steam and soak in a range of cold and warm pools, try **Solspring** ♥♥♥ 611 Wainui Rd. (solspring.co.nz; ✆ **021/352-570**). There's yoga here too.

WAITOMO

A little dot on the map, Waitomo is famous for just one thing: its vast network of ancient limestone caves, many of which are inhabited by glowworms. Endemic to New Zealand and parts of Australia, glowworms are the larvae of a fungus gnat, which produces a blue-green bioluminescence to attract tasty flies and mosquitoes. Trust me when I say it's a phenomenon you don't want to miss. You can learn more about it at the small museum within the **Waitomo Caves Discovery Centre and isite Visitor Info Centre.**

Waitomo has three main "tourist caves": the **Waitomo Glowworm Caves, Aranui Cave,** and **Ruakuri Cave.** All charge an entrance fee, but several much smaller glowworm caves exist at designated DOC sites nearby that you can access for free, including along the 30-minute **Ruakuri Walk** ♥. Waitomo also isn't your only chance to see glowworms in NZ; they can be found in caves and along riverbanks and canyons throughout the entire country, although usually in smaller numbers.

Waikato Springs to Discover

About an hour south of Raglan (on a very remote, windy gravel road) is one of New Zealand's best-kept secrets: **Kāwhia Hot Water Beach** ♥♥♥. It offers a similar experience to Coromandel's famed Hot Water Beach (p. 184), but with black sand and without the crowds. If you arrive 2 hours on either side of low tide, the hot waters of the Te Puia Hot Springs bubble up to the surface, allowing you to dig your own sandy hot tub. Most bring their own spade or borrow one from a local campground, but I've found that using my hands is sufficient; you don't need to dig very deep. Head to the end of Ocean Beach Rd., where there's a parking lot and set of toilets. But there's not much else in Kāwhia—bring snacks.

An indoor experience worth stopping for can be found east in the Waikato, at the **Te Aroha Mineral Spas** ♥, Te Aroha Domain (tearohamineralspas.co.nz; ✆ **07/884-8717**). Situated in a restored Edwardian bathhouse, the spa offers private mineral hot tubs (from NZ$22 per adult and NZ$11 per child for 30 min.) and massage and beauty treatments (from NZ$60). Kids will prefer **Swimzone Te Aroha** (swimzonepools.co.nz; ✆ **07/884-4498**) next door—the bush-backed outdoor pools are full of fun play equipment, and parents can supervise from the hot tub.

Finally, for some of the clearest water you'll ever see, walk the **Blue Spring/Te Waihou Walkway,** which reopened in 2025, off SH5 just southeast of Tirau. It's 5km/3 miles one way, and while you can swim at the Whites Road end of the stream, don't be tempted to take a dip in the Blue Spring itself—help keep this magical spot pristine.

With that being said, if you're looking for the wow factor, shell out for a **Discover Waitomo** tour at the **Waitomo Glowworm Caves ♥♥**, 39 Waitomo Village Rd. (waitomo.com; ✆ **07/878-8228**). Of the three main caves, it's the star of the show. It's touristy, no doubt, but it's also undeniably impressive: A guided tour takes you through 250m (820 ft.) of spectacular underground scenery like the **Cathedral,** a cavern with such good acoustics that NZ's own opera star Dame Kiri Te Kanawa and the Vienna Boys' Choir have sung here. The tour includes a very short boat trip through the twinkly Glowworm Grotto (perfect for the 10-year-old in your party). One-hour tours depart around every 10 minutes starting at 8:30am, with the last tour at 6pm. Pre-booking is essential; tickets cost NZ$81 for adults, NZ$37 for children 4 to 14, and NZ$206 for a family pass. (Discounts are sometimes available on weekday tours; check the website for discount codes.)

Discover Waitomo also operates tours to **Aranui Cave** (which doesn't have glowworms due to the absence of water, but does have spectacular natural formations) and the **Ruakuri Cave** (where you can see glowworms up close). The latter was first discovered by Māori almost 500 years ago, and today you can do NZ's longest guided underground walking tour, which includes descending down a massive, impressively engineered spiral staircase.

That's a lot of options, so here's my advice: Combine a visit to the main Waitomo Glowworm Cave with a rafting adventure in the Ruakuri Cave. Best for those who want a rush of adrenaline, are physically agile, and don't mind getting wet, the **Legendary Black Water Rafting Company's Black Labyrinth tour ♥♥♥** (bookable with Discover Waitomo, see above) is a memorable 3-hour caving and tubing adventure. Visitors jump off waterfalls backwards in the dark and float on their backs along an underground river lit only by glowworms. Both morning and afternoon departures are available. It's NZ$193 adults, NZ$149 for youth (the tour is for those ages 12 and older), and NZ$571 for a family. Weekday and shoulder season promo codes are often available on Discover Waitomo's website.

On a Waitomo Adventures outing, adventurers can explore the Lost World cave system, which has its own glowworms and rugged caverns to navigate.

Visiting more than one cave is the best bang for your buck; when you choose a combo package for two or more caves, you'll save 33% off the ticket prices.

But wait! There are more caves, and ones most visitors don't know about. **Waitomo Adventures ♥♥**, 1227 Waitomo Valley Rd. (waitomo.co.nz; ✆ **07/878-7788**), offers three maximum adrenaline outings for the "fit and keen" into the Lost World cave system, including an all-day epic adventure involving a 100m abseil, spectacular glowworms, swimming, climbing, and jumping (NZ$925 including lunch and dinner.) Alternatively, opt for mental gymnastics instead and try their underground escape room (NZ$180 for up to eight people)

A more mellow and meditative option is the **Spellbound Glowworm and Cave Tour ♥♥**, 334 Boddies Rd. (glowworm.co.nz; ✆ **0800/773-552** in NZ, or 07/878-7622), which boasts such an unbelievable display by glowworms that renowned British naturalist Sir David Attenborough decided to feature them in two BBC documentaries. This tour is less touristy and more personalized (with smaller groups) than the main Waitomo glowworm caves. The shorter 1½-hour option, visiting one cave, costs NZ$79 for adults and NZ$25 for kids 14 and under; if you have 2½ hours you can visit two caves for NZ$99 adults, NZ$34 kids.

Where to Stay in the Waikato

IN & AROUND HAMILTON

If you're only in the Waikato to hit up Hobbiton and Waitomo, you'll be better off overnighting in Cambridge or the surrounding countryside, where there are plenty of cute Airbnb and private rentals to be found. But if you do want to stay in the city, the **Novotel Hamilton Tainui ♥**, 7 Alma St. (all.accor.com; ✆ **07/838-1366**), is one of the more reliable options. It unveiled a new wing with 40 executive rooms a couple of years ago, bringing its total to 217. Located right in the revitalized downtown core, it has all the amenities you'd expect from a chain (restaurant/bar/gym/spa). Rates are from NZ$300.

Fifteen minutes out of town, the **Hakarimata Hideaway Retreat ♥♥**, 161G Hakarimata Rd. (airbnb.co.nz/rooms/39011830), is a tiny house with big perks: The property has its own waterfall and glowworm dell. Owners

Underhill Valley (p. 176) is a one-of-a-kind off-grid earth house with a distinctly Lord of the Rings look.

Mark and June will happily take you for a short nighttime tour, but otherwise it's incredibly private and a steal at around NZ$160—just note no kids allowed.

If romance is what you're after and you've got a bigger budget, book a night at **Underhill Valley** ♥♥♥ (canopycamping.co.nz/underhill-valley) near Whatawhata. It's just 10 minutes from Hamilton, but feels a million miles away. Built into the hillside over several decades by owner Jess and her adventuresome father, the unique earth house has a grassy roof, rough-hewn wooden furniture, cozy furnishings, and a selection of drinking goblets that would make a hobbit jealous. It's completely off-grid, with a (very clean) composting toilet and no electricity, so you'll cook on the outdoor barbecue or indoor wood fire, soak in the outdoor bath, and light the night with dozens of provided candles, a truly magical experience that will make you feel transported to another time—or yes, Middle-earth. Nightly rates start from NZ$405 (this also isn't one for kids.)

CAMBRIDGE AREA

In the center of Cambridge, you'll find the delightful **Clements Hotel** ♥♥ 68 Duke St. (clements.co.nz; ✆ **07-974/9050**). There's been a hotel here since 1866, and this newly renovated 29-room boutique leans into the history. There are multiple places to gather—a cafe/wine bar, a restaurant with a sunny terrace and formal garden, and a basement speakeasy serving a bespoke Cambridge Distillery gin based on a rediscovered 1860s Irish recipe (a nod to Irish-born Archibald Clements, who built the original hotel 150 years ago). Rooms are elegant and luxurious, and the bathroom floors are tiled in striking Italian marble. Room rates are from NZ$450 per night.

Arriving on a stormy day, as I did, at the **housewithnonails** ♥♥♥ (yes, that's how they spell it), Waghorn Road, Wardville (housewithnonails.co.nz; ✆ **021/032-0176**), you might think you've come to Elrond's Last Homely House at the foot of the Misty Mountains. In this unique B&B, hosts Jen and Dewi welcome you into the hand-hewn dwelling Dewi built in 1992 out of macrocarpa timber felled by Cyclone Bola and salvaged from nearby farms. The kitchen is well-stocked and comforting, and the four upstairs bedrooms are a cottage-core dream with low lintels, linen sheets, a choice of pillows, and the kind of beds that make you sigh with happiness when you slide between the covers. The views stretch across cows and fields to the Wairere Falls pouring off the Kaimai Ranges—the North Island's highest waterfall, and a spectacular half-day hike. (Walk a little way up the track, Jen advises, for a free glowworm experience.) Rooms come with a substantial breakfast, and Dewi will roast tomahawk steaks upon request. Hobbiton is a 25-minute drive away. A night's stay will set you back NZ$333.

RAGLAN

There are many holiday rentals in and around Raglan—check Airbnb and Bookabach for old-school coastal holiday homes and cute rural tiny-houses. For a dreamy romantic stay, book one of the three private off-grid options

12km (7½ miles) out of town on the side of Mount Karioi at **Tiny House Escapes ♥♥** (tinyhouseescapes.co.nz; ✆ **021/225-4052**). I especially recommend The Treehouse, built into a pine forest with giant views of ocean and sky (NZ$205 low season, NZ$295 high season.)

If you'd rather be in the middle of things, **Bow Street Studios ♥♥** (bowstreet.co.nz; no phone) has seven lovely 2-story one-bedroom apartments surrounded by greenery, just a few steps from the harbor and the main street (NZ$269–NZ$350). And the **Raglan Backpackers ♥** 6 Wi Neera St. (raglan backpackers.co.nz; ✆ **07/825-0515**), centrally located right by the water, has small but spotless dorms NZ$42, private rooms from NZ$92, and surfboards, SUPs, kayaks, and wetsuits available for hire (guests get a discount).

WAITOMO

Waitomo isn't so much a town as it is a small cluster of motels and tourist attractions. It's more of a day-trip destination, unless you're intent on visiting some of the area's free glowworm caves at nighttime. If that's the case, then **Waitomo's Top 10 Holiday Park ♥** (waitomopark.co.nz; ✆ **05/0849-8666**) is as central as they come—it's right across the street from the info center. In addition to campsites (powered sites NZ$64), it has motel rooms (starting at NZ$217) and cabins (starting at NZ$138). If you're traveling with children, **Woodlyn Park,** 1177 Waitomo Valley Rd. (www.woodlynpark.co.nz; ✆ **078/786-666;** from NZ$180 per night), is the place to stay for novelty factor alone: Guests sleep in a "hobbit motel," boat, train, or plane. The interiors of the quirky rooms are formulaic compared to their exteriors and are showing their age. But kids will love it (adults without children should look elsewhere).

Where to Eat in the Waikato

HAMILTON

Most of the city's best restaurants, cafes, and bars can be found around the south end of Victoria Street. **Gothenburg ♥♥**, 17 Grantham St. (gothenburg.co.nz; ✆ **07/834-3562;** Mon–Fri 9am–10pm, Sat 11:30am–10pm), right next to the museum, is a stunning light-filled space, with high glass walls and river views. Its tapas menu is designed for sharing and has loads of vegetarian options like beetroot arancini and buffalo mozzarella curd with slow-roasted tomatoes, as well as meat and seafood sourced from local farms and fishers.

For coffee or bunch on the main drag, visit the extremely friendly **Kopi ♥♥**, 298 Victoria St. (instagram.com/cafe_kopi), which has a small but tasty range of breakfast staples on offer,

Hand-built out of salvaged timber, the welcoming housewithnonails has a cozy cottage charm.

plus an excellent Sri Lankan dahl. If you're lucky, your flat white will come with cute latte art and a joke. The cafe's sky-high ceilings and location on charming Riverbank Lane, right next to the city's best second-hand bookshop, make this a great place to linger. At the end of the laneway you'll find **Mr. Pickles Bar & Eatery ♥♥** (mrpickles.co.nz; ✆ **07/839-7989;** Tues–Sat noon–late), where dapper, talented bartenders serve up creative cocktails and share plates—chargrilled skewers, veal carpaccio, brussels sprouts with truffle miso. If you're in a group of four or more, you can pay NZ$65 per person and say "feed me," and they'll bring out their best and brightest.

Across the bridge in Hamilton East, **Made ♥♥♥** 401 Grey St. (madehamilton.co.nz; Mon–Fri 7am–6pm, Sat 7am–5pm, Sun 7am–4pm), is a gorgeous new urban precinct stuffed full of great eateries and artisan shopping. Two picks, though they're far from the only gems: Try the city's best croissants at the **Butter Boom Croissanterie,** and do a coffee tasting and watch the java artisans at work at **Grey Roasting Co.** For dessert, duck across the road to **Duck Island Ice Cream ♥♥**, 300a Grey St. (duckislandicecream.co.nz; daily 11am–10pm), the biggest thing that's come out of Hamilton in the last decade. There are now Duck Island shops across the North Island, but this is the original. Their signature scoop is "fairy bread" ice cream, named for a popular Kiwi kiddie treat involving sprinkles and white bread, but I prefer their white chocolate pomegranate macadamia—and in store you'll find even more unusual flavors.

CAMBRIDGE

Cambridge has a surprising number of accomplished eateries for its size. In a prime location overlooking the town clock, **Alpha Street ♥♥**, 47 Alpha St. (alphast.co.nz; ✆ **07/827-5596;** entrees NZ$18–NZ$34; Tues–Sun noon–late), is delightful whether you sit outside or in—the large patio faces the sun as it sets, but the interior, inside the historic National Hotel, is handsome, too. The seasonal menus emphasize small share dishes, including oysters and cheese plates, but larger plates for mains have a nice number of different elements to them, like pork belly with kūmara puree, winter greens, and yuzu citrus caramel. **Alpino Cucina e Vino ♥♥**, 43 Victoria St. (alpino.co.nz; ✆ **07/827-5595;** daily noon–late), serves authentic Italian food, including fresh-made pasta. **Onyx ♥**, 70 Alpha St. (onyxcambridge.co.nz; ✆ **07/827-7740;** Mon–Fri 11am–9pm, Sat–Sun 9am–9pm), does breakfast and tasty wood-fired pizzas and can accommodate a range of dietary needs.

RAGLAN

Raglan Roast Coffee ♥, hidden down Volcom Lane (raglanroast.co.nz; ✆ **07/282-1108**), is known around the country, but it's not the only java in town. My spot of choice, named after a local surf break, is bohemian **Indi's ♥♥**, 5 Bow St. (instagram.com/indi_raglan), which brews up organic, fair-trade, locally roasted Morning Glory beans. It's open daily 7:30am to 3pm, and it also serves pastries. Raglan's zero-waste ethos is taken seriously here: You can't get a takeaway cup, but they'll lend you an "ugly mug" to walk around town

Delectable tapas are meant for sharing at Gothenburg (p. 177), one of Hamilton's top restaurants.

with. **The Shack** ♥♥, 19 Bow St. (theshackraglan.com; ✆ **07/825-0027;** daily 8am–3pm), is impossible to miss thanks to its prime location on the corner of the main drag. Serving breakfast and lunch, it's fast and friendly, with plenty of vegan and gluten-free options.

New Raglan institution **ULO's Kitchen** ♥♥♥, 6 Wallis St. (✆ **07/595-0097** or 027/266-4442), is unbeatable for dinner; opened in 2020 by a creative Japanese family fleeing Fukushima, it features unique, colorful decor by artist Kyoko, great tunes played on vinyl by her husband Cian, and fresh flower–decorated Japanese dishes made by sister Eriko and dad Yoshi—like grilled Aburi scallops, sriracha salmon, or crispy chicken. Brother Takahiro serves up cocktails, and matriarch Yuko greets you at the door. Text to make a booking, or turn up early—this place is deservedly packed year-round. It's open Thursday to Sunday 5pm to 10pm.

WAITOMO

Eating options are limited in tiny Waitomo: Expect basic cafe and pub food that will fill your belly and that's about it—and even less if you arrive in the winter. If you plan on staying the night. **Huhu Café,** 10 Waitomo Caves Rd. (huhucafe.co.nz; ✆ **07/878-6674**), is your best dinner option. (It doesn't actually serve huhu grubs—beetle larvae, a chewy Māori delicacy with mercifully little flavor.) Instead, expect a menu heavy on meat, such as lamb curry or braised beef short rib. It's open daily in summer from noon until late, although winter hours may vary.

THE COROMANDEL

119km (74 miles) E of Auckland

In the 19th century, at the height of the gold rush, the towns of the Coromandel heaved with glinty-eyed gold prospectors. These hard-edged characters thronged to Thames, at the base of the peninsula, and drank away their cares at the 100-plus pubs that filled the town by 1868. Of these, just four remain today, but there's still plenty of colorful history to discover here.

From **Thames,** you can access the 70-mile-long peninsula's waters on the western side, including limitless opportunities for swimming and boating. North of Thames on the Hauraki Gulf, you'll find the somewhat bohemian village of **Coromandel Town** (sometimes it's just called "Coromandel," so take care not to get confused between the town and the greater region). In between the two is a stretch of baches (cottages), many owned by keen fishermen, some of which are available as holiday rentals.

The peninsula's eastern ocean-facing side is known for its white-sand beaches fringed by pōhutukawa trees, which flower red in the summer months, as well as **Hahei** (home to the famed Cathedral Cove and Hot Water Beach), **Whitianga,** and surfing paradise **Whangamatā.** All told, it's easy to see why this destination is beloved.

Yes, you could whiz around the Coromandel's entire coastline in a day (it only takes about 3 hours, driving from Thames to Coromandel Town, then through Whitianga toward Whangamatā), but this is truly a place to settle in and savor, preferably with a cold drink in one hand and your toes in the balmy waters.

Essentials

ARRIVING

Thames is about a 1½-hour drive from Auckland. Note that if you're departing for the Coromandel from Auckland during the holiday season (especially around Christmas and New Year's), be prepared for delays on the roads as Aucklanders make a mass exodus from the city for finer shores. **InterCity** (intercity.co.nz; ✆ **09/583-5780**) runs regular coach services between Auckland, Thames, Whitianga, and Coromandel. **Explore Group** (exploregroup.co.nz; ✆ **0800/360-3472** in NZ, or 09/367-9111) runs passenger ferries between Auckland and Coromandel Town during the summer, leaving the city on Friday afternoons and weekend mornings (9:30am), returning around lunch time. The 4-hour round-trip is NZ$135 for adults (return does not have to be the same day), NZ$68 children 5 to 15, families NZ$338. You can add on a return bus trip to Whitianga for an additional NZ$50 adults, NZ$25 kids.

GETTING AROUND

Driving is, by far, the best option for exploring the Coromandel, with some important caveats. If you're driving to the top of the peninsula, be warned that the road just north of Colville is unpaved. It's a gorgeous trip, but the road is steep and narrow with precipitous drops straight down to the sea—so you'll need to keep your wits about you. In that same vein, the 309 Road between Coromandel and Whitianga should only be tackled if you're a confident (left-side) driver. Don't be misled by the few miles of pavement at either end; the majority is a narrow gravel road and not suitable for motorhomes. The Tapu-Coroglen Road is also mostly gravel. However, you can easily circumnavigate the entire peninsula without getting on any of these roads. SH25 (the main road that loops around the Coromandel) is paved and offers better views.

VISITOR INFORMATION

The Coromandel's main tourism website is **thecoromandel.nz**. The **Coromandel Town Info Centre,** Samuel James Reserve (coromandeltown.nz; ✆ **07/866-8598**), is open daily from 10am to 3pm. The **Whitianga isite Visitor Centre,** 66 Albert St. (✆ **07/866-5555**), is open Monday to Friday 8:30am to 4pm, Saturday 8:30am to 2pm, and Sunday 8:30am to noon.

SPECIAL EVENTS

In March, the **Whangamatā Beach Hop** (beachhop.co.nz) takes over the streets for 5 days, celebrating '50s hot rods, classic cars, and a whole lotta rock 'n' roll.

Exploring the Coromandel

Besides the two outstanding natural attractions in Hahei, Cathedral Cove and Hot Water Beach (see p. 184), relaxing seaside is the main reason to visit the Coromandel Peninsula. But even if you arrive in the off-season, there's plenty to see and do. If you're travelling through the Coromandel in a clockwise direction starting from Thames, here's what you can expect to encounter.

Kiwi Christmas Trees

If you visit the Coromandel in December or January, you'll be in one of the best places to see the vivid red pōhutukawas in bloom. Nicknamed the "Kiwi Christmas tree," the endemic giants cling to the coast or spread out across the sands, then drop their stamens in crimson mounds. For New Zealanders, these iconic trees signify summer and good times.

Recalling Thames' 19th-century heyday as a goldrush boom town, the **Goldmine Experience** ♥, on SH25 in Thames (goldmine-experience.co.nz; ✆ **07/868-8514**), offers a 40-minute guided tour through a 19th-century gold stamper battery (an operation that would crush rocks to separate them from the gold they held). It's open daily from 10am to 4pm in summer and weekends, 10am to 1pm in the winter. Admission is NZ$25 adults, NZ$5 children ages 5 to 12. The nearby **Thames Historical Museum,** 503 Cochrane St. (thameshistoricalmuseum.weebly.com; ✆ **07/868-8509**), provides a window into the world of pioneer NZ, with over 30 handcrafted models of goldrush-era buildings. It's a small community

Sea views are framed by sweeping natural arches at Cathedral Cove.

The narrow-gauge Driving Creek Railway climbs upward through a regenerating kauri forest to spectacular views of the Coromandel.

museum, but it might be worth a gander if you have time, particularly for the low price of NZ$5 adults (kids go free). It's open daily 10am to 1pm.

A half-hour's drive north of Thames, just past Tapu, take the Tapu-Coroglen Road to **Rapaura Watergardens** ♥ (rapaurawatergardens.co.nz; ✆ **07/868-4821**), a New Zealand Garden of Distinction. It's 26 hectares (64 acres) of peaceful beauty, with lots of waterlilies. It's open daily from 9am to 5pm; admission is NZ$15 for adults, NZ$5 for children ages 5 to 15.

About 2.5km (1½ miles) east of Rapaura Gardens on the same road, a short track takes you to the most famous tree in these parts—the **Square Kauri.** This beauty, one of the largest on the peninsula, is about 1,200 years old and has a trunk that's completely square. ***Note:*** You'll have to climb 187 steps to get to it.

Just north of Coromandel, the **Driving Creek Railway** ♥♥♥, 380 Driving Creek Rd. (drivingcreek.nz; ✆ **0800/327-245** in NZ, or 07/866-8703), was a labor of love of Barry Brickell. A potter with a heart of gold, he arrived in the Coromandel in the 1970s and decided to leave his mark by spending the next 27 years replanting an entire forest *and* building New Zealand's only narrow-gauge mountain railway. Brickell passed away in 2016, but his legacy lives on with nearly hourly train rides starting at 9am. The railway is open from 9am daily until 5pm; rides for adults cost NZ$57, children NZ$32, families NZ$155. Adding to the experience is Driving Creek's new **Corozip** ♥, a zipline adventure over the regenerating kauri forest. It includes a short train ride and eight ziplines—including one that's 200m across—but is light on commentary (NZ$147 adults, NZ$107 children, NZ$419 family pass). There are also daily 1½-hour pottery classes for NZ$67, plus NZ$20 if you want to fire and glaze your pieces.

Along the 309 Road, a winding gravel road crossing the peninsula southeast from Coromandel Town to Whitianga, **The Waterworks** ♥♥, 471 The 309

Rd., Coromandel (thewaterworks.co.nz; ✆ **022/369-3907**), bills itself as a theme park, but its low-tech, tongue-in-cheek approach to getting kids (and big kids) to have fun with the physics and mechanics of water makes this a standout. Waterworks has more than 70 interactive sculptures to keep everyone happy firing water cannons, riding bikes to power fountains, and firing up giant barrel-and-kitchen-knife music boxes for hours. It's open daily 10am to 4pm. Admission costs NZ$28 adults and NZ$23 children ages 4 to 15, families NZ$85, with 10% off if you purchase online in advance. A short drive south of there, you can see one of the peninsula's best and most easily accessible stands of Kauri trees if you do the 5-minute **Waiau Falls** walk, 11km (7 miles) east of Coromandel town on the 309 Road.

Interactive sculptures at family-friendly Waterworks explain the physics of water power in an entertaining way.

Over on the east coast in Whitianga, the **Mercury Bay Museum** ♥, opposite the wharf (mercurybaymuseum.co.nz; ✆ **07/866-0730;** open daily 10am–3pm), is another small community museum (good for a rainy day). It covers the area's history, starting from the arrival of the Polynesian navigator Kupe (NZ$12.50 adults, free for children 14 and under).

For an appealing hike with views, take the **Whitianga Ferry** (whitiangaferry.co.nz; ✆ **07/866-5140**) passenger boat across to Ferry Landing, which has the oldest hand-hewn stone wharf in Australasia, built in 1837. The ferry operates daily from 7:30am to 9:25pm (roundtrip NZ$7 adults, NZ$5 children). It's just a few minutes from there to Front Beach/Maramaratotara Bay for a swim, or walk on to the **Shakespeare Cliff Lookout,** a 3km (1-mile) loop track to an impressive memorial to Captain Cook's visit to these parts. In between lies lovely **Flaxmill Bay.**

Also in Whitianga, **The Lost Spring** ♥, 121A Cook Dr. (thelostspring.co.nz; ✆ **07/866-0456**), is a Polynesian-themed geothermal hot pool and spa complex surrounded by lush tropical bush. It's kitschy but fun (imagine hot springs set in *The Flintstones*). You'll lay NZ$70 for a 120-minute pool entry, but be prepared to budget more—with poolside service, it's almost impossible to refuse a cocktail. Your tab will rack up quickly, but you can cut costs with a package. The "signature experience," for example, includes a meal, cocktail, and massage for NZ$210. The Lost Springs is open daily from 9:30am until 7pm (until 9pm Fri and Sat). Bookings are essential.

Around the headlands from Whitianga, **Hahei's Mautohe Cathedral Cove** ♥♥♥—famed for its dramatic natural stone archways that frame perfect white sands and aquamarine waters—is arguably the Coromandel's most

A PEEK AT paeroa

Paeroa, at the southern end of the Coromandel, may be best known for its giant "L&P" bottle (Lemon & Paeroa is a popular Kiwi soft drink) and its antiques (it's the antiques capital of NZ). But less than 10 minutes farther down SH2 from the town is one of the region's top natural and historic wonders: **Karangahake Gorge ♥♥**, a canyon full of waterfalls and walks through decommissioned gold mining tunnels. A favorite is the **Windows Walk,** an easy 30-minute trail that winds deep into pitch-black disused gold mines; bring a flashlight and wear waterproof shoes to hike it safely and comfortably.

The gorge is also the highlight of the **Hauraki Rail Trail ♥♥** (haurakirailtrail.co.nz), which bills itself as the easiest multi-day bike trail in the country. I'd add it's one of the most satisfying: 4 to 5 days and 197km (47 miles) of varied riding from the Thames coast into the Waikato through the historic gold-mining town of Waihī and ending in Matamata. Operators along the way, such as **Hauraki Bike Hire,** 6 Wharf St., Paeroa (haurakibikehire.co.nz), provide shuttle and luggage transfer and bike rental (comfort mountain bikes NZ$55 per day; e-bikes NZ$110 per day) and can arrange lodging.

If you just want to cycle a portion of the trail or explore one of the area's walks, the family-owned **Falls Retreat ♥♥**, 25 Waitawheta Rd., Waihī (fallsretreat.co.nz; ✆ **07/863-8770**), is a woodland oasis of pine trees near the top of the falls. While its three self-contained cottages (NZ$250–NZ$350 per night, including continental breakfast) are cozy and well-equipped, it's the on-site restaurant that makes this property a stand-out. Award-winning chef Brad King uses ingredients from the kitchen gardens to create complex dishes with earthy flavors and Asian influence, such as lamb rump served with black garlic agria, panko-crumbed miso eggplant, charred broccoli in almond, and Clevedon buffalo curd. Mains are NZ$32 to NZ$40, and reservations during the summer months are recommended. (Restaurant hours vary seasonally, but it's generally open Fri–Sun noon–late.)

popular site. The 5km (3.1 miles) roundtrip walking track to the cove has been restored after being closed for repairs for 2 years following Cyclone Gabrielle in 2023 (thanks to funding from the international visitor levy you pay on arrival). The trail itself isn't particularly exciting, but the end result is worth it. You can also get to the beach by kayak (see p. 186) or glass-bottom boat (p. 185). There is now no parking at the start of the walk; it's a half-hour walk up Grange Rd., but my advice is to park at the **Hahei Visitor Car Park** and take the frequent shuttle bus (cathedralcoveparkandride.co.nz). It costs NZ$8 roundtrip, kids 14 and under free, parking free). ***Warning:*** The rock falls and landslides that destroyed the previous track are an ongoing hazard; visit at low tide when there's more space on the beach away from the cliffs.

The second biggest draw in this region is **Hot Water Beach ♥♥** in Hahei, where you can dig a bathtub-sized hole in the sand and wallow around in natural thermally heated water—up to 147°F (64°C)—for 2 hours on either side of low tide. Sadly, the beach is a classic case of over-tourism; it can get so crowded during holiday periods that your neighbors might flick sand in your eyes as they dig. So, here's a secret: For a similar, but much more remote

Vacationers can dig out their own hot tubs in the sand at Hahei's Hot Water Beach.

black-sand experience, head to Kawhia's **Hot Water Beach** ♥♥♥ (about an hour's winding drive from Raglan in Waikato; see p. 173).

Organized Tours

Departing daily from Whitianga Wharf, **Cathedral Cove Scenic Cruises** ♥ (cathedralcovecruises.co.nz; ✆ **0800/888-688** in NZ, or 027/5555-152) head to the famous Cathedral Cove, exploring sea caves and islands along the way. The 2-hour Coves, Caves, and Coastline cruise costs NZ$135 adults, NZ$80 kids 4 to 15. **Sea Cave Adventures** ♥♥ (seacaveadventures.co.nz; ✆ **0800/806-060** in NZ) do much the same thing for NZ$135 adults and NZ$75 children 3 to 14. Also sailing out of Whitianga, the **Glass Bottom Boat** ♥♥ (glassbottomboatwhitianga.co.nz; ✆ **07/867-1962**) gives passengers a better look at the sea life of the area, which is a designated marine reserve—it doubled in size in 2025. The 2-hour tour to Cathedral Cove (snorkeling included) is NZ$140 adults, NZ$85 children ages 3 to 15, with family passes available.

For more wide-ranging tours of the area, John and Rose from **Kiwi Dundee Adventures** ♥♥♥, McBeth Road, Hikuai (kiwidundee.co.nz; ✆ **07/865-8809**), two of the country's top guides, will show you Coromandel (or the whole of New Zealand if you wish), hiking or touring, in 1 to 16 days. Day tours of the entire peninsula are from NZ$695 per adults and NZ$325 for kids 12 and under.

Outdoor Pursuits

BEACHES Beaches are found up and down both sides of the peninsula, but the clearest water and finest white sand is on the east coast. (The Hauraki Gulf, on the west side, is more of a fishing destination.) **Cathedral Cove, Hot Water Beach,** and **Whangamatā** are three of the most popular stretches of sand, but my picks include **New Chums Beach** (about a 30-min. scrambly walk from Whangapoua), which regularly tops lists of the world's best beaches. **Opoutere,** north of Whangamatā, is more accessible than New Chums, but still feels a world away. **Wyuna Bay,** a 10-minute drive northwest of Coromandel Town, is a family-friendly spot with a diving dock. There's also a fair number of freshwater swimming holes to be found, like **Hoffman's Pool** in Kauaeranga Valley (about 20 min. east of Thames in Coromandel Forest Park; drive just over a mile past the visitor center, and you'll see the signed parking lot). It's a local favorite for cliff jumping.

CANYONING Much of the Coromandel's rugged and wild interior is inaccessible—except on a tour with **Canyonz** (canyonz.co.nz;

✆ **0800/422-696** in NZ only). Its most popular excursion is to **Sleeping God Canyon ♥♥♥**. On this full-day tour, you'll rappel down nearly 1,000 feet, abseiling off 100-foot waterfalls and sliding down natural waterslides into deep dark pools. No canyoning experience is needed, but you'll need to be moderately fit, because the experience includes a demanding walk to the top. It costs NZ$450 per person, including lunch.

FISHING A number of charter operators work from Whitianga, Whangamatā, and Waihī. Tairua Beach is great for surfcasting, while Coromandel's northern islands are good for snapper. Try **Epic Adventures** (epicadventures.co.nz; ✆ **0800/374-269**) for half- and full-day excursions out of Whitianga (prices on application), and you could end up on their website holding an enormous fish and wearing a big grin.

GOLF The **Lakes Resort Pauanui,** 100 Augusta Dr., Pauanui (lakesresort.com; ✆ **07/864-9999**), is a championship 18-hole course, with accommodation and a restaurant. The **Dunes Golf Resort,** Matarangi (thedunes.co.nz; ✆ **07/866-5394**), is another top course with food and lodgings, as is the 18-hole **Mercury Bay Golf & Country Club,** Golf Road, Whitianga (mercurybaygolf.co.nz; ✆ **07/866-5479**). Green fees for all of the above range between NZ$40 and NZ$65 for 9 holes and NZ$55 and NZ$95 for 18 holes. For a deal, visit The **Thames Golf Club,** SH26, Thames (thamesgolf.co.nz; ✆ **07/868-9062**). The 18-hole course costs jus NZ$25 for 9 holes and NZ$50 for 18.

KAYAKING A lovely way to view the sheltered bays of the east coast is by kayak or stand-up paddleboard (SUP). **Cathedral Cove Kayak Tours ♥♥♥**

SUCH great HEIGHTS

In a country of towering peaks, summitting **The Pinnacles ♥♥** (759m/2,450 ft.) may not seem like much to brag about, until you've actually done this challenging walk, which follows a historic packhorse route. Even though we're in hobbit country, the track seems to be designed for Gandalf with its huge steps. The final hour from the hut to the summit climbs nearly 500 vertical feet, with hikers propelling themselves using metal rungs fastened into the side of rock. It's a rewarding, hugely popular trek to the Coromandel's highest point, with awe-inspiring views.

The ambitious and fit can complete the full **Kauaeranga Kauri Trail (Pinnacles Walk)** in a day (it takes about 8 hr. round-trip), but it's best done in two, with the final summit from the hut traditionally being done at sunrise (it's lovely at sunset, too—just bring a torch for the way down). Although the serviced hut has 80 bunks—making it the largest in the southern hemisphere—you must book online in advance with the Department of Conservation (DOC; doc.govt.nz; NZ$25 adults, NZ$12.50 children, NZ$10 extra Fri and Sat). The kitchen has gas cookers and pots and pans, but you'll need to bring your own plates, cutlery, pillows, and sleeping bags. Depending on the season, be prepared for a chilly night—the fireplace is in a separate room to the bunk rooms. A staffed DOC welcome center is located 8km from the trailhead, convenient for a final bathroom break, free maps, and to stock up on basic supplies before you head out.

(kayaktours.co.nz; ✆ **0800/529-258** in NZ, or 07/866-3877) does half-day tours from Hahei, costing from NZ$175 adult and NZ$105 kids 17 and under. An hour farther south in Whangamatā, **Surfsup** ♥♥ (surfsup.nz; ✆ **021/217-1201**) offers tours to the wildlife sanctuary of Whenuakura (Donut Island), which includes paddling into a secluded turquoise cave lagoon (but not landing on the island—it is *tapu* [sacred] and a wildlife sanctuary). A 2-hour tour costs NZ$105 (NZ$60 children 4–14), with a portion of the proceeds going to the island's conservation. Rentals for self-guided tours are also available. ***Tip:*** Book your trip for early morning to get the calmest sea conditions.

SNORKELING & SCUBA DIVING **Cathedral Cove Dive & Snorkel,** 48 Hahei Beach Rd., Hahei (cathedralcovedive.co.nz; ✆ **09/866-3955**), operates snorkeling trips for NZ$145 adults, NZ$100 kids 13 and under, dive trips from NZ$230, and PADI courses from NZ$340. **Dive Zone Whitianga,** 7 Blacksmith Lane (divezone.co.nz/whitianga; ✆ **07/867-1580**), operates similar diving trips to the Mercury Islands and Te Whanganui A Hei Marine Reserve and PADI courses—call or email for pricing.

SURFING Whangamatā is one of the region's best surf spots, with lessons for first-timers on offer. **Surf N Stay** ♥♥, 227 Beverley Terr. (surfnstaynewzealand.com; ✆ **022/102-2649**), offers small group surfing lessons starting from NZ$80, along with yoga retreats and beach accommodation.

WALKING The **Coromandel Forest Park** (see "Such Great Heights," p. 186) is the region's premier hiking destination. Go to the DOC visitor center near Thames, Kauaeranga Valley Road (doc.govt.nz; ✆ **07/867-9080**), for details. North of the park, you'll find the 34km/21mi **Pahi Coastal Walk** ♥♥ (pahicoastalwalk.co.nz; ✆ **021/816-228**), a fully catered 3-day hike over a large private farm with spectacular coastal views. It starts from NZ$850 for adults and NZ$750 for children.

Where to Stay Around the Coromandel

The Coromandel is a popular holiday spot for Aucklanders, which means you'll have to book well ahead if you're visiting between December and February. At any other time of year, however, there are lots of holiday homes (baches) for rent—check airbnb.co.nz and bookabach.co.nz. ***Top tip:*** **Canopy Camping** (canopycamping.co.nz) has a dozen exceptional cabins scattered around the peninsula, all overlooking wild bush or remote beaches.

The area's holiday parks are a more affordable option; besides campsites, most also offer self-contained cabins and motel rooms. If you're in a motorhome, there's some primo freedom camping up and down the coast, but you'll need to arrive early to score a waterfront spot. Otherwise, sites in the DOC campsites are available on a first-come, first-served basis, with fees typically ranging from NZ$10 per adult and NZ$5 per child. Go to doc.govt.nz for details.

THAMES

Just north of Thames, **Coastal Motor Lodge** ♥♥, 608 Tararu Rd. (coastalmotorlodge.co.nz; ✆) **07/868-6843;** NZ$160–NZ$240 double), is a seaview collection of A-frame chalets, motel units, and cottages framed by bush, with beautifully kept gardens. Get an upstairs unit and, with the sloping ceilings, you'll think you're sleeping in a cathedral.

COROMANDEL TOWN

The best choice for families in this area is **Tasman Holiday Park Coromandel ♥♥**, 636 Rings Rd. (tasmanholidayparks.com/nz; ✆ **07/866-8830**), which has a heated pool, go-karts, and other kiddie activities, set on 1.5 hectares (3½ acres) of grounds. It's also quite centrally located. Rates are from NZ$20 (for an unpowered site), cabins NZ$99 to NZ$169. Or sleep surrounded by native bush overlooking Coromandel Harbour at **Anchor Lodge ♥** (anchorlodgecoromandel.co.nz; ✆ **07/866-7992;** NZ$180–NZ$235 double) in one of 25 tidy and comfortable, if dull-looking, units.

WHITIANGA

Sovereign Pier on the Waterways ♥♥♥ The holiday resort of choice of the beautiful people (including a famed American country singer, just one of its celebrity guests), Sovereign Pier features private marina berths, a tennis court, and swell water views. Each of the spacious, self-contained units is privately owned and thus individually decorated (so you never know quite what the ambience will be like) but all have a good amount of space, lofty ceilings, private outdoor patios, and garages. Final perk: The resort lends shovels for use at nearby Hot Water Beach. ***Psst:*** Rumor has it that if you chat up some of the boat owners at the outdoor pool, you're likely to get invited for a sail.

73 S. Hwy. whitiangaholidays.co.nz. ✆ **07/867-1236.** 48 1- to 3-bedroom units. NZ$349–NZ$509, discounts for multi-night stays. **Amenities:** Laundry; outdoor pool; kayaks for hire; marina berths; boat launch; tennis court; fitness room; free Wi-Fi.

PAUANUI/TAIRUA

Grand Mercure Puka Park Resort ♥♥ This upmarket accommodation has always been the posh place to stay in Pauanui (unless you're on very good terms with some of the super-rich boaties who have holiday homes in the nearby Waterways subdivision). Rooms have the look of luxury "treehouses" thanks to their positioning up in the canopy (the kindly staff will lug your luggage to your lodging). Standard chalets have a shower-only bathroom; superiors are larger and have a bath and shower. Executive chalets have separate lounge/dining areas, and the Royal Puka Apartment is a freestanding two-story three-bedroom chalet.

Mount Ave., Pauanui Beach. pukapark.co.nz. ✆ **07/864-8088.** 50 units. NZ$308–NZ$358 standard chalet. **Amenities:** Restaurant; bar; babysitting; bikes; concierge; gym; Jacuzzi; outdoor pool; pétanque, room service; sauna; day spa; tennis court; watersports equipment rentals; free Wi-Fi.

WHANGAMATĀ

The rooms and hillside location are heavenly at **Brenton Lodge ♥♥♥**, 2 Brenton Place, Whangamatā (brentonlodge.co.nz; ✆ **07/865-8400**; NZ$320–NZ$355), with guest accommodations in two private lodges set in very pretty gardens, alongside a shared outdoor pool. Highlight of the stay: expertly cooked, elaborate breakfasts served in your room, or on the shared verandah.

Where to Eat Around the Coromandel

THAMES

Thames has traditionally been a town you pass through on your way somewhere else, but its historic buildings house a few treasures, foremost among them **Café Melbourne ♥♥**, 715 Pollen St. (facebook.com/CafeMelbourne GrahamsTown; ✆ **07/868-3159;** weekdays 8am–4pm, weekends 9am–4pm). Owner Kim is from Melbourne; her husband Russell, the chef, is from Thames, and they've started a nice little operation, serving creative takes on comfort food like coconut and sago porridge with stewed seasonal fruit, and smoked brisket quesadillas. Behind the cafe is a collection of specialty food shops selling the makings for a nice picnic—as well as **Awildian Gin** (awildian.com), open 11am to 3pm weekdays and until 2pm weekends, offering free tastings of their locally made and internationally award-winning gins.

COROMANDEL TOWN

Seafood is quite the thing around here, and available for takeaway so you can create your own picnic. First choice among the purveyors is the **Coromandel Smoking Co. ♥♥♥**, SH25, Tiki Rd. (corosmoke.co.nz; ✆ **07/866-8793;** daily 9am–5pm, reduced winter hours), which smokes fish, mussels, salmon, and roe above manuka wood. Second choice: the **Coromandel Oyster Company ♥♥**, SH25, 1611 Manaia Rd. (✆ **07/866-8028**), which also sells mussels, *pāua* (abalone), crayfish, and other seafood at wholesale prices. There's nothing glamorous about the joint; everything comes in takeaway form. But it's fresh, and there's outdoor seaside seating (including aboard retired oyster fishing vessels).

Pepper Tree Restaurant and Bar ♥, 31 Kapanga Rd. (peppertreerestaurant.co.nz; ✆ **07/866-8211;** daily 10am–9pm), is a different kettle of organically smoked fish altogether: It's a sit-down restaurant on the main street of Coromandel Town in an early-20th-century homestead with wraparound verandas—great if you want to watch the passing parade as you chow down on your market-fresh seafood dish.

WHITIANGA/HAHEI

Near Whitianga, at **Lukes Kitchen ♥♥**, 20 Black Jack Rd., Kuaotunu (lukes kitchen.co.nz; ✆ **07/866-4480**), people line up many nights of the week for the innovative wood-fired pizzas, including one topped with coconut chicken, pickles, and dukkah. In nearby Hahei, **The Pour House ♥**, 7 Grange Rd. (thepourhouse.co.nz; ✆ **021/035-1338;** Mon–Thurs 5pm–8pm, Fri–Sat noon–8:30pm), also serves pizza and a handful of other mains, but the real lure here is its wide range of craft beers on tap. **KaiZen at Go Vino ♥♥♥**, 19 Captain Cook Rd., Cook's Beach (govino.co.nz; ✆ **07/867-1215;** Thurs–Mon 5:30–9:30pm), is the place to go to celebrate a special occasion (or just to celebrate that you're on vacation!). The well-curated wines here are a highlight, with food that complements the vino, often in surprising ways (an appetizer of lightly seared ostrich, perhaps, or sashimi with an avocado sorbet). For brunch, **Eggsentric ♥♥**, 1049 Purangi Rd., Flaxmill Bay (theeggsentric.co.nz; ✆ **07/866-0307;** daily 7:30am–2pm), serves a range of epic breakfasts, plus primo fish dishes from 11:30am to 2:30pm. The cafe's hippie vibe, with oddball works of art inside and around the garden tables, is part of its charm.

PAUANUI/TAIRUA

Dining options are limited in Pauanui, but the **Miha** at the **Grand Mercure Puka Park Resort** ♥ (p. 188) serves both lunch and dinner. Mains are around NZ$39; the atmosphere is pleasant and the food solidly tasty. Better yet, drive to Tairua and eat at **Tairua Beach Club** ♥♥♥, 128 Paku Dr. (tairuabeach club.co.nz; ✆ **07/280-0185**), a labor of love for owner/chef Graeme Riki, who developed his chops cooking at some of Auckland's finest restaurants. Riki seasons his European-style creations with herbs and microgreens grown on site, and serves them in a room brightened by dozens of cut-glass hanging lanterns, enveloped in the fronds of hanging plants (it's a groovy look). Mains cost around NZ$45.

WHANGAMATĀ

For an extremely memorable (if expensive) meal, head to **Camina** ♥♥♥, 708 Port Rd. (camina.co.nz; ✆ **07/280-4522;** Wed–Sat 5:15pm–late). Started by a pair of friends who met in the surf, the vibe is inspired by the ancient connection between humans and fire; all meals are flame cooked, adding a delicious smoky flavor to sharing plates of harissa chicken, pork skewers, or market fish. ***Tip:*** Sit at the bar to watch the chefs cook on the open fire. For a cheaper option, try **Chilli Cove Indian Eatery** ♥♥, 608 Port Rd. (chillicove.co.nz; ✆ **07/865-6860;** Mon–Wed 4–10pm, Thurs–Sun 11am–2pm and 4–10pm). Its butter chicken and honey chili cauliflower fritters are legendary in these parts.

A sizzling meal straight off the grill at Camina, in Whangamatā.

TAURANGA & THE BAY OF PLENTY

208km (129 miles) SE of Auckland; 86km (53 miles) NW of Rotorua

They don't call it the Bay of Plenty for nothing: This region, from **Waihī Beach** in the north to Ōhope in the south and stretching inland towards toward Taupō, is a paradise of sun-drenched orchards, geothermal attractions, and 125km (78 miles) of white-sand beaches. The kiwifruit capital of NZ, it's also home to countless hiking trails and hot pools, and an evolving culinary and craft beer scene. These are just a handful of the reasons the BOP is popular with expats as a place to put down roots.

A sweeping view over the Bay of Plenty from the summit of Mauao/Mount Maunganui.

Tauranga, the fifth-largest city in NZ (and the fastest-growing), has a population of around 160,000. With the country's largest port, it's a cruise ship dock, as well as home to two marinas full of boats. The waterfront downtown has received some love in recent years and has become a lovely place to stroll. Still, most visitors will find themselves gravitating to the white-sand beaches, boutiques, and eateries of nearby **Mount Maunganui** (technically, it's a suburb of Tauranga, but longtime locals will insist it's its own municipality).

The BOP is also home to Whakaari/White Island near **Whakatāne**, a marine volcano that was the region's main attraction until its tragic eruption in December 2019. Tours to the island are no longer permitted, but there are other worthwhile attractions in the area, including a hot water beach and the chance to see kiwi (the birds) in the wild.

Although "Bay" of Plenty implies this region is all next to the water, farther inland you'll find raw and unscripted Māori experiences deep in the mountainous and misty **Te Urewera,** a former national park that gained legal personhood status in 2014 (see p. 196 for what that designation means) or nearby **Whirinaki Te Pua-a-Tāne Conservation Park.**

Essentials

ARRIVING

Air New Zealand (airnewzealand.co.nz; ✆ **0800/767-767** in NZ) offers daily direct flights from Tauranga to Auckland, Wellington, and Christchurch. The airport is in Mount Maunganui, 5km (about 3 miles) from Tauranga city. Taxis are available at the airport. **InterCity** (intercity.co.nz; ✆ **09/583-5780**) has daily coach services to/from Auckland, Napier, Rotorua, Taupō, Tauranga, Thames, and Wellington. By **car,** it takes about 2½ hours to drive from Auckland to Tauranga, about 1½ hours from the Coromandel and Hamilton, and 1 hour from Rotorua.

GETTING AROUND

If you just intend to stay in the Tauranga or Mount Manganui vicinity, it's easy to explore the BOP by public transit and day tours. The council-subsidized public transport system, **Bay Bus,** runs its Bayhopper network covering the Western Bay and Tauranga urban area, as well as runs between Tauranga and Whakatāne. Phone the call center (baybus.co.nz; ✆ **0800/422-928** in NZ) for information. It's open Monday to Friday from 7am to 6pm.

VISITOR INFORMATION

The Bay of Plenty's official visitor website is **bayofplentynz.com**. The **Tauranga isite Visitor Information Centre,** 1 Devonport Rd. (✆ **07/578-8103**), is open Monday to Saturday 9am to 5pm (it's set to move in 2027, however). There's a Mount Maunganui satellite isite at Te Papa O Ngā Manu Porotakataka, 137 Maunganui Rd. (hours vary). The **Whakatāne Visitor Centre,** 144 The Strand (whakatane.com; ✆ **07/308-6058**), is open Monday to Friday from 9am to 3:30pm and Saturday 9:30am to 2pm.

SPECIAL EVENTS

In January, Katikati hosts its **Avocado Food & Wine Festival** (katikatiavofest.co.nz), which features cooking demonstrations, live music, and street vendors. Also in January is the **One Love Festival** (onelovefestival.co.nz), a 2-day music festival of reggae and rock and in Mount Maunganui. Every Easter, Tauranga plays host to the **National Jazz Festival** (jazz.org.nz), which runs for a week with free and ticketed performances. In late April, the **Flavours of Plenty Festival** (flavoursofplentyfestival.com) celebrates food and the autumn harvest with events around the BOP, featuring kūmara, truffles, avocado, kiwifruit, and other locally grown delicacies. And in mid-May, the **Ōhiwa Oyster Festival** (ohiwaoysterfest.com) takes place in Ōhope—a day of live local music, coastal vibes, and of course fresh oysters.

Exploring the Bay of Plenty Coast

TAURANGA

In the city center, walk south along the eastern waterfront starting at Dive Crescent. Just past Hamilton Street, you'll see a huge, spectacular kids' playground, and near it a bronze sculpture depicting the cats and dogs of beloved children's books *Hairy Maclary*, written by local Lynley Dodd. Older kids and teenagers might like to join local youths and "pop a manu" (a v-shaped dive bomb invented by Māori and Pasifika communities, now the subject of nationwide competitions) from adjacent Coronation Pier. A sign helpfully demonstrates the various options for making as big a splash as possible.

One block inland from here, the **Tauranga Art Gallery ♥♥**, 108 Willow St. (artgallery.org.nz; ✆ **07/578-7933**), presents historical and contemporary art, with more of an emphasis on the latter, which is appropriate given the modernity of the building. Along with touring exhibitions from other institutions, it exhibits artist projects that speak about this locality. The gallery is open daily from 10am to 4pm; entry is NZ$7, free for children under 12.

There are always new paintings to see at the Art Gallery in Tauranga.

The Elms Te Papa Tauranga, 15 Mission St. (theelms.org.nz; ✆ **07/577-9772**), is the oldest European heritage site in the BOP. Built in 1847, it also happens to be one of the finest examples of colonial architecture of its time, with the clean, simple lines of the earliest settler buildings. The mission station was established in 1838 by Archdeacon Alfred Brown, who built his freestanding library the following year (before he built the main homestead, so important were his books to him). You can visit daily from 10am to 4pm. Entry is NZ$20 adults, including a tour of the house. Children go free.

The Historic Village ♥♥, at the south end of 17th Avenue West (historicvillage.co.nz; ✆ **07/571-3700**), is anything but trapped in the past. This precinct is home to communication organizations, boutique shopping, cafes, art galleries, creative arts hubs, and a tattoo gallery, all housed in a collection of original and replica buildings from early Tauranga. It's adjacent to parkland with walking trails running alongside the Kopurererua Stream, making it a lovely place to go for a coffee, lunch, and a wander. It also plays host to regular free events, including markets.

Just a 10-minute drive southwest from central Tauranga, **McLaren Falls Park ♥**, McLaren Falls Rd. (✆ **07/577-7000**), is a 190-hectare (470-acre) park that's home to a very pretty lake and walking trails. If you stay till it gets dark, you'll pass a glowworm dell along the Waterfall Track, a short loop walk that takes about 20 minutes. It also has one of the best tree collections on the North Island. It's open from 7:30am to 7:30pm in summer and until 5:30pm in winter. A 5-minute drive up SH29 from McLaren Falls, I highly recommend a quick stop or picnic lunch at the **Poripori Water Holes ♥♥♥** (10 Poripori Rd., Tauriko), a series of natural pools in the Wairoa river. There are shallow pools suitable for little kids and lovely jumping rocks for bigger ones. It's just off the highway and access is free. ***A warning:*** Before you hop in, check manawaenergy.co.nz/wairoa because dams upstream are occasionally opened, causing flash flooding.

Tauranga's past is brought to life in its well-preserved historic section (see p. 193).

MOUNT MAUNGANUI

Linked to Tauranga by highway bridges, Mount Maunganui is a hotspot in summer for surfers, golfers, and snowbirds. Looming over the long expanse of beach is an extinct volcano known as **Mauao ♥♥**. There's an array of intersecting walking tracks around and over it. The 3.4km (2 mile) walk around its base is one of NZ's most popular, taking around 45 minutes. Several routes of varying steepness and length climb to Mauao's 232m (761-ft.) summit, which affords 360-degree views of the bay and Matakana Island to the north. The tracks are well-signed, or you can download a map from bayofplentynz.com. There are no toilets on the track, so use the facilities before you depart.

For a more culturally significant experience, contact Māori-owned **Mauao Adventures** (mauaoadventures.co.nz; ✆ **022/882-2979**) for a guided tour of the mountain's ancient burial and birthing springs. They also offer fun group *waka ama* (outrigger canoe) paddling lessons, starting from NZ$75 for one hour.

Situated at the base of Mauao, the **Mount Hot Pools,** 9 Adams Ave. (mounthotpools.co.nz; ✆ **07/577-8551**), are a nice place to warm up and chill out. These are saltwater pools, not mineral springs, with temps up to 39°C (102°F); the active and children's pools are 32°C (90°F). There is a large public pool, two outdoor Jacuzzis, three private Jacuzzis and a toddlers' pool with a slide. General admission is NZ$28.20 for adults and NZ$16.20 for kids 3 to 15. Private pools are NZ$70.50 for two adults or NZ$87.10 for a family (but only kids 11+ are allowed, and you can't bathe alone for safety reasons). It's open Monday to Saturday from 7am to 10pm.

From the Mount you can take a scenic spin on the water with **Kewpie Cruises ♥**, Pilot Bay Wharf (kewpiecruises.co.nz; ✆ **021/605-965**). The good ship *Kewpie* is a beautifully restored 14m (46-ft.) solid kauri ferryboat that used to ply the waves farther north on the Bay of Islands Cream Trip run.

Nowadays, it does several pleasure cruises around the Bay of Plenty, including a 1-hour inner harbor cruise, stopping off at Matakana Island, where you can hop off and catch the boat when it comes around again. It's good value (NZ$40 adults, NZ$20 children 12–16, and free for under-12s), with multiple departures daily.

NORTH FROM TAURANGA

Heading north from Tauranga on SH2, the town of **Katikati** is considered the country's avocado capital; what makes it worth a stopover for visitors are the more than 40 murals spread along its streets.

A magnificent 9km (5½-mile) swath of white sand at the northern end of the Bay of Plenty, **Waihī Beach** is popular with Kiwi holidaymakers, who come here in droves during the summer to swim, fish, and surf; Waihī Beach has one of the safest surf breaks in the country. **Waihī Beach Surf School,** Brighton Recreational Reserve (beachsurfschool.co.nz; ✆ **027/245-8593**), will rent you a board starting from NZ$40 to NZ$70. SUPs and lessons are also available.

SOUTH FROM TAURANGA

A 20-minute drive southeast from Tauranga on SH2, the little town of **Te Puke** all but sustains the kiwifruit industry in NZ (see "A Fruit by Any Other Name," below). While it once had visitor attractions themed around the multimillion-dollar export (you'll still see signs for these along the highway), none are presently in operation, but head along SH2 about 5km south of town and you can still get a great photo op beside a giant plastic slice of the fruit.

Quieter than Tauranga but just as perfectly situated, **Whakatāne** is the sunniest place in the North Island, with great beaches. It's provincial New Zealand at its finest: relaxed, friendly, and offering so many ways to make your holiday perfect. It's also the Kiwi Capital of the World™, where the birds have been known to wander into people's backyards. Keep an eye out for them—or for one of their 10 bronze facsimiles throughout the area. On Fridays in April, May, or June—kiwi calling season—the **Whakatāne Kiwi**

A Fruit by Any Other Name

While we commonly associate kiwifruit with NZ, they're not native to the country. In fact, they haven't even always been called kiwis. In 1906, they were first brought to NZ from China, and were then known as Chinese gooseberries. (To complicate matters further, they're not even related to the Grossulariaceae family, to which gooseberries belong.) The crop took off and in the 1950s, NZ began exporting the fruit to the U.S.—but at the height of the Cold War, a rebrand was in order. Prominent produce company Turners and Growers proposed calling them "melonettes," but the idea was shot down, as melons were subject to high import tariffs. It wasn't until 1959 that they were given their new name: kiwifruit. Today, Te Puke calls itself the "Kiwifruit Capital of the World," even though China is actually the world's largest exporter. That's why the fruit has acquired yet another name: "Zespri," a brand that differentiates NZ's kiwifruit from that grown in other countries.

A LAND OF one's own

Isolated, immense, and starkly beautiful, the misty mountains of **Te Urewera** are the largest protected area on the North Island. Home to nearly every species of native bird, this national park gained legal personhood status in 2014—the first of its kind in the world to do so (see p. 33 for more on that). Now, as ever, the fiercely independent Ngāi Tūhoe people, or the "Children of the Mist," act as the *kaitiaki* (guardians) of Te Urewera. They're currently developing innovative land management solutions, including a "green" highway made of natural materials leading to **Lake Waikaremoana,** one of NZ's 10 Great Walks. Like all Great Walks, the 46km (28.5-mile) trek may be booked through DOC's online booking system (doc.govt.nz).

This isn't an area that you can tick off the list in a day, but you can get a taste with tours run by **Manawa Honey** ♥♥♥ in Ruatāhuna (manawahoney.co.nz/tours; ✆ **07/366-3166**), an award-winning, Tūhoe-owned sustainable honey business. As well as the sweet stuff, they offer 2-day eco-cultural trips including marae accommodation, traditional welcome, forest and honey tours—or you could opt for river fishing on horseback (contact for pricing; costs range from NZ$900–NZ$1,200 per person).

Adjacent to Te Urewera, **Whirinaki Te-Pua-a-Tāne Conservation Park** boasts spectacular waterfalls, rich biodiversity, and ancient podocarp (Southern Hemisphere conifers) and beech forests. A spiritually significant site, it's best accessed on a guided cultural tour with **Whirinaki Forest Footsteps** ♥♥ (whirinakiforestfootsteps.co.nz; ✆ **07/366-4777**). The full-day tour—which includes an introduction to traditional Māori medicine—costs NZ$295 for adults and NZ$195 for children, with pickups available from Rotorua. Many guests add a stay at the tour company's **Kohutapu Lodge** (kohutapulodge.co.nz; ✆ **021/804-012**) on the edges of Lake Aniwhenua, which offers accommodations ranging from basic cabins and cottages (from NZ$120–NZ$220 per night) to a luxury self-contained home (NZ$1,500). Both the tour company and the lodge are run by the Toe Toe family, who are lauded throughout Oceania as innovators in the regenerative tourism space. Every year, these tourism ventures allow them to support their local community, including providing meals and school uniforms to children in need.

Lake Waikaremoana in Te Urewera National Park.

Trust (whakatanekiwi.org.nz) offers very popular guided night walks for NZ$20 (NZ$10 for kids under 16).

The **Whakatāne Library and Exhibition Centre/Te Kōputu a Te Whanga a Toi,** 46 Kakahoroa Dr. (whakatanemuseum.org.nz; ✆ **07/306-0509**), houses the **Whakatāne District Museum,** telling the stories of the district, with three gallery spaces that offer local and touring exhibitions. It's open Monday to Friday 9am to 5pm and weekends 10am to 2pm.

A little farther down the coast, **Ōhope** is home to what continues to be voted NZ's "best-loved beach." Sweeping for 11km (6¾ miles) along the Pacific Coast, it's usually crowded with families. If you take a short walk over the hill at its north end, you'll come to an absolute gem: **Otarawairere ♥**, a secluded beach that can only be accessed by foot or kayak. Farther west, near Kutarere, **Ōhiwa Harbour ♥** is another lovely place to explore on foot or by water. It's safe for swimming and kayaking and is also a haven for birdlife: Godwits migrate from Alaska every year to nest on its shores.

Organized Tours

Because Tauranga is a cruise-ship port, a lot of day tours have sprung up in the area. We recommend the tours led by local Les Millard, whose company **Travel Ed ♥♥** (traveled.co.nz; ✆ **022/049-4465**), focuses on the interconnected history of *iwi* across the North and South Island (his own Māori ancestry lies within the *iwi*/tribes from Tauranga to Whakatāne, as well as the Waikato and King Country). A former teacher in international schools, Les tailors tours to his audiences (from kids to adults), including visits to the Pāpāmoa Hills, where you can see NZ's best concentration of traditional *pā* sites (fortresses). After a tour, you can choose to add on a visit to **Izakai ♥♥♥** (see p. 205), an award-winning Japanese-Māori fusion restaurant owned by Les's son, Liam. Tours start from a 3-hour walk up Mauao (NZ$70 adults (NZ$45 children under 12) to a 6-hour journey from Tauranga to Rotorua (NZ$230 adults, NZ$180 kids).

WHAKAARI/WHITE ISLAND today

For decades, **Whakaari/White Island**—which sits 29 miles out to sea—has been one of the BOP's most fascinating attractions. The only active marine volcano in NZ, it has steaming geothermal vents, bubbling mud pools, and the remains of a doomed sulfur-mining enterprise. However, after the volcano erupted in December 2019, killing 22 and injuring 26, all visits to the island have ceased. The only way to see it now is by scenic flight, including those offered by **White Island Flights,** 224 Aerodrome Rd., Whakatāne Airport (whiteislandflights.co.nz; ✆ **07/308-7760**). There's no doubt that flying over a steaming volcano is a surreal experience, but it's also a pricey one at NZ$349 for a 1-hour flight.

You can also get a look at the volcano's steam plumes from afar from neighboring Moutohorā (Whale Island), which you can visit on a guided tour with **Diveworks Charters ♥♥**, 31 Quay St., Whakatāne (diveworks-charters.com; ✆ **027/244-4964**). Home to saddlebacks, kakariki, tuatara, and fur seals, Whale Island has its own geothermal activity, and offers panoramic views of the region from its summit, including White Island on a clear day. Tours cost $140 adults, NZ$70 children, and last from 9am to 2pm—call or email for departure dates. The company also runs a 4-hour dolphin and seal encounter, including snorkeling off Moutohorā, for NZ$200.

Taste of Plenty ♥ (tasteofplenty.co.nz; ✆ **07/571-2453**), based in Mount Maunganui, offers a range of guided food tours in a minibus, with scenic stops and a minimum of five tastings, starting from NZ$70 per person.

Farther down the coast, the Māori-owned oyster farm and takeaway shop **Tio Ōhiwa,** 111 Wainui Road, Ōhope (ohiwaoysters.com/oyster-tours; ✆ **07/312-4565**), runs cruises on the peaceful Ōhiwa Harbour, featuring beautiful islands, history and culture, and a tour of the oyster farm. A 1-hour boat trip costs NZ$80, but oyster-lovers should go for the 2-hour version, which includes a look at the oyster processing plant, an oyster-shucking lesson, and a generous tasting. Tours leave from the Port Ōhope Wharf at 342 Harbour Rd. Note that fresh oysters may not be available offseason, December to March.

Outdoor Pursuits

DOLPHIN SWIMMING **Dolphin Seafaris** ♥♥, 101 Te Awanui Dr., Mt. Maunganui (nzdolphin.com; ✆ **07/577-0105**), boasts a 95% chance of seeing wild dolphins, with the possibility of swimming with them on a purpose-built boat. (There are times that the tour operator may not allow swimmers to enter the water for ethical reasons, such as if the dolphins are at rest.) You may also see whales, seals, turtles, and little blue penguins on this 6-hour tour, departing daily at 9am November to April (upon request in winter months). It's NZ$165 for adults; NZ$125 for kids 5 to 16; and NZ$550 for a family of four. If you don't see dolphins, you can return another day for free. **Bay Explorer** ♥♥, Wharf St. & The Strand, Tauranga (bayexplorer.co.nz; ✆ **021/605-968**) offers half-day dolphin and marine wildlife tours (no swimming) for NZ$175 adults, NZ$75 kids 6 to 12, families NZ$399; book direct online for discounts.

FISHING **Blue Ocean Charters,** Tauranga Bridge Marina, Tauranga (blueocean.co.nz; ✆ **07/544-3072**), offers full-day, twilight, and overnight trips in the abundant waters around Mayor Island. Half-day reef fishing trips are NZ$1,750. Twelve-hour game-fishing trips are NZ$3,500 (max. four people).

KAYAKING **Waimarino Kayak Tours** ♥♥ (glowwormkayaking.com), based out of the Waimarino Adventure Park at 36 Taniwha Place, Tauranga (waimarino.com; ✆ **07/576-4233**), offers a 3-hour evening tour of Lake McLaren, where there's a canyon with thousands of glowworms. It departs daily before sunset, costs NZ$265, and is suitable for ages 8 and up. The Big Kanu trip heads to the same location in, yes, a big canoe (NZ$175). Kayak and paddleboard hire is also available. In the Whakatāne area, **KG Kayaks** ♥♥, 93 Kutarere Wharf Rd., near Ōhope (kgkayaks.co.nz; ✆ **07/315-4005**), offers rentals and guided tours around the Ōhope Beach area, Ōhiwa Harbour, and out to Moutohorā/Whale Island off the Whakatāne coast. Rentals are from NZ$35 per hour, and guided tours start from NZ$125 for 2 hours.

SUPING Porina McLeod of **Mauao Adventures** ♥♥, 169 Maunganui Rd., Mt. Maungaui (mauaoadventures.co.nz; ✆ **022/648-7313**), is as passionate about the land that she comes from as she is about the sea that she paddles on. Her team offers SUP hire (NZ$30 per hour), express on-shore SUP lessons (NZ$40), 1-hour intro lessons on water (NZ$75), a 2-hour SUP Adventure

Riverbugging the Rapids

Want to experience the thrill of whitewater, without actually picking up a paddle? Riverbugging, yet another Kiwi invention, involves lightweight inflatable rafts that are incredible easy to maneuver—they're akin to floating down a river in a super comfortable recliner chair, where your legs dangle in the water, although you can ride them like a boogie board if you prefer. Don Allardice, an experienced whitewater paddler and the co-owner of **Riverbug.nz ♥♥♥** (riverbug.nz; ✆ **022/344-5002**), is their number one ambassador, offering superfun, accessible, and safe half-day trips coasting over rapids on the Wairoa and Tarawera River near Tauranga. My pick is the Action Bug excursion on the Rangitaiki River, which floats past high canyon walls and waterfalls and over Class II rapids. You're going to get wet—very wet—but even during the winter months, the high-quality wetsuits, booties, and gloves keep you warm. Tours start from NZ$149 adults, NZ$125 kids.

(NZ$125), and even SUP Surf lessons (inquire for pricing for those with a bit more experience). In Ōhope, paddle the beautiful Ōhiwa lagoon on a SUP from **Takutai Adventures ♥♥**, 340 Harbour Rd. (takutaiadventure.co.nz; ✆ **021/149-1972**), for NZ$30 per hour. They also offer e-bike hire, surf lessons, and even SUP yoga (NZ$45 for an hour).

SURFING Guy and Rebecca of **Hibiscus Surf School ♥♥**, Main Beach, Mt. Maunganui (surfschool.co.nz; ✆ **07/575-3792**), are expert surfing teachers. In addition to the basics, they give pupils the lowdown on local surf and ocean conditions. Beginner group lessons from NZ$79 for 2 hours. In Ōhope, contact **Takutai Adventures** (see SUPing, above).

WALKING Midway between Tauranga and Te Puke, at **Pāpāmoa Hills Cultural Heritage Regional Park,** a 45-minute walk will take you to the 224m (735-ft.) summit, where you'll be rewarded with sweeping 360-degree views, including of the site's seven historic *pā* (Māori fortress) sites. The park's entrance is at the end of Poplar Lane. From the north end of Waihī Beach, there's an easy 45-minute walk to pōhutukawa-fringed **Orokawa Bay,** or you could continue another 45 minutes' walk to **Homunga Bay.** You can either return the same way or arrange a pickup at Ngatitangata Road.

WATERSPORTS The family-owned **Aqua360 ♥♥**, Pilot Bay, Mt. Maunganui (aqua360.co.nz; ✆ **021/2782-360**), offers jet skis, wakeboards, water skis, and tubes that you can tow behind them. Jet-ski rentals include equipment and fuel, starting from NZ$230 for an hour. Fishing gear hire is also available. Or you can take a morning or afternoon 2-hour guided tour of the area, starting with breakfast or lunch and then cruising along the island-studded coast by jet ski. Call for pricing.

Where to Stay Around the Bay of Plenty

Like much of New Zealand, beaches in this region heave with tourists over the summer months, so if you're planning to visit between December and

Stand-up paddleboarding (aka SUPing) off the coast of Whakatāne.

February, it's a good idea to book in advance. There are few conventional hotels in the Tauranga or Mount Maunganui area—most visitors stay in self-contained apartments in managed buildings designed for long getaways. In Pāpāmoa Beach, Waihī Beach, and farther afield, you will find private baches (holiday cottages) and holiday homes for rent, as well as holiday parks (campgrounds). Book the former on Airbnb, Vrbo, and other sites.

TAURANGA

With a location just steps from the water, and two owners who make every guest feel like a VIP, one of the top picks in Tauranga is the **Harbour View Motel & Apartments ♥♥**, 7 Fifth Ave. E (harbourviewmotel.co.nz; from NZ$195). Yes, it's a refurbished 1970s-era motel, but it has been elevated by pretty colors and nice furnishings used throughout, and a carefully tended garden. Plus, how many lodgings offer free kayak and bike rental? Another spot that is worth the rave reviews is the **Clarence Hotel ♥♥**, 51 Willow St. (clarencetauranga.co.nz; ✆ **07/574-8200**), a 10-room boutique hotel in Tauranga's historic post office (ca. 1906). The rooms aren't massive, but they're elegant and quiet with nice lighting and black marble bathrooms. (Fun detail: In one of the rooms, the former post office safe is now a shower.) Rooms range from NZ$200 to NZ$380—there are three sizes and price points—and you'll want to budget extra for a meal at its celebrated restaurant (see p. 204). Just down the street, the **Hotel Armitage and Conference Centre ♥**, 28 Brown St. (hotelarmitage.co.nz; ✆ **07/578-9119**), is one of the city's only large hotels, with more than 80 rooms. They are spacious and well-appointed, but the decor's generic, the balconies look over the carpark, and it's very much a business rather than a holiday vibe.

We should also mention the **Trinity Wharf Tauranga ♥** (trinitywharf.co.nz; ✆ **07/577-8700**), which became Insta-famous for its harborfront rooms hanging over the water. Unfortunately, all that hype has taken its toll, and the rooms are starting to show signs of wear and tear. But you can't beat the location, or the infinity pool, which seems designed for social media stars. Rooms start from NZ$280, but you'll pay more for sea views, which start at around NZ$350.

Wanderlust Hostel ♥♥ Once upon a time, this historic building directly on Tauranga's waterfront was a five-star hotel. Now, thanks to owners Sarah Meadows and Matt Young (the couple met as backpackers) it's been transformed into a five-star hostel. Light and airy, with high ceilings and a design that retains many of the building's original details (like slots used to dispose of razors in the bathrooms and rimu wood doors) the hostel is fully equipped for modern travelers. Bunk rooms feature air-conditioning, thick mattresses, plenty of room for luggage, and USB outlets, and the kitchen has gas stoves. The private rooms are just as comfortable, though they can be loud (this is an old building, so sound travels). The hostel's focal point is its rooftop terrace, which boasts sunrise views over the ocean.

105 The Strand. wanderlustnz.co.nz. ✆ **07/262-0027.** 30 units. NZ$40–NZ$60 dorms; NZ$160–NZ$166 private room. **Amenities:** Kitchens; laundry; free Wi-Fi.

Watercliff ♥♥♥ After retiring from dancing at age 30, principal ballerina Delia Harris returned home to the Bay of Plenty with her British engineer husband, Josh, to start a family. She wanted to create a space she could share with visitors, while also uplifting the surrounding community. New in late 2022, Watercliff reflects the couple's combined creativity, practical know-how, and grace. Its four cabins are located at the bottom of a valley, facing a small river backed by a lush cliffside of green native bush. There's a little riverside beach for swimming or kayaking, and rooms come equipped with a picnic set, a perfect companion on one of the hiking trails (complete with glowworms) that run through the property's 18 hectares (44 acres). That is, if you even want to leave your room. Off-grid without sacrificing luxury, Watercliff's cabins are decorated in natural hues with a few unexpected pops of color (like rose-colored basins); they feature kitchenettes, radiant heating in the floors, and some have two-person outdoor bathtubs on expansive

Soak in an outdoor tub on the deck of a modern cabin at Watercliff, with its river beach, hiking trails, and lush stand of native bush.

verandas. The only downsides (an upside for some) is that there's no Wi-Fi here, and cellphone service is patchy.

80 Lawry Lane, Omanawa (20 min. drive from downtown Tauranga). watercliffstay.com (book via canopycamping.co.nz). ✆ **027/229-7833.** 4 units. Cabins NZ$500 (discounts for longer stays). **Amenities:** Kitchenette; BBQ.

NEAR MT. MAUNGANUI

Mount Maunganui Beachside Holiday Park ♥, 1 Adams Ave. (mountbeachside.co.nz; ✆ **07/575-4471**), is a very popular campground located right next to the Main Beach, with cabins starting from NZ$105—or, for a classic Kiwi experience, stay in a retro caravan for NZ$85 to NZ$117. **The Beaumont Apartments ♥**, 12 Maunganui Rd. (beaumontapartments.co.nz; ✆ **0800/423-286** in NZ, or 07/575-0688; doubles NZ$250, two-bedroom apartments NZ$300–NZ$400), have an excellent location at the foot of Mauao and walking distance from the main beach, the Pilot Bay Harbor, and the hot pools. Apartments are privately owned and thus individually decorated with different configurations and sizes. A swimming pool, private covered parking, gym, and barbecue are all on site. ***Tip:*** It's worth splashing out the extra cash for a room with a view.

Tasman Holiday Parks Pāpāmoa ♥♥ There'll be no complaints about the views if you stay here: This holiday park in the ocean suburb of Pāpāmoa couldn't be closer to the long, white-sand beach that stretches for miles in either direction. The villas and units are light, bright, modern, and spacious, and the newly developed pool has a positively resort-like feel. If you can afford it, grab a beachfront room; you'll love sitting on your deck and watching the sun set over the water.

535 Pāpāmoa Beach Rd., Pāpāmoa. tasmanholidayparks.com/nz. ✆ **0800/232-243.** 38 units. Powered sites NZ$69–NZ$99, cabins NZ$250–NZ$350, villas NZ$400–NZ$690. **Amenities:** BBQ area; bikes for hire; kids' playground; holiday kids' club; Jacuzzi; mini-tennis court; pétanque; free Wi-Fi in villas.

WAIHĪ BEACH

Bowentown Beach Holiday Park ♥♥ A short drive from the shops of Waihī Beach, this family-run holiday park sits at the end of headland, nestled between the sea and the bush. It has direct access to both the oceanside surf beach and sheltered Anzac Bay, which is popular for kayaking, fishing, and swimming. Not camping? Not a problem. It offers self-contained cabins, motel rooms, and its unique Kombi cabins, which are custom-built to look like Volkswagen vans. Painted in bright splashes of color, the Kombis have lots of homey touches, such as retro tea canisters and mugs, colorful bunting, and seashell mirrors. They're situated right beside the well-equipped and clean toilet and kitchen block, which also includes a games room, an adults-only TV room, and a barbecue area. An on-site cafe serving fresh coffee rounds out the experience.

510 Seaforth Rd., Waihī Beach. bowentown.co.nz. ✆ **07/863-5381.** 170 sites and units. Campsites NZ$62–NZ$70 for 2 people; cabins, rooms, and villas NZ$139–NZ$289; Kombis NZ$149–NZ$169. **Amenities:** Coffee shop; TV lounge; games room; kids' playground; private spa pool; laundry; bike, surfboard and pedal kart hire; free Wi-Fi.

WHAKATĀNE/ŌHOPE

Formerly known as the White Island Rendezvous, **Awa Motel ♥♥**, 15 The Strand E., Whakatāne (awamotel.co.nz; ✆ **07/308-9500;** NZ$185–NZ$257), is tucked between the Whakatāne River and a pōhutukawa-topped cliff. The only accommodation of its type in town, the Awa has numerous options, including studios, apartments, and villas. Soundproofing between rooms could be better, but otherwise this is a smart budget choice.

The **Ōhope Beach Top 10 Holiday Park ♥♥**, 367 Harbour Rd., Ōhope Beach (ohopebeach.co.nz; ✆ **0800/264-673** in NZ, or 07/312-4460), has cabin, motel, and apartment accommodations right on the beach. A top pick for families, the property has a playground and a pool with hydro slides. Rates are from NZ$150 for a standard cabin to NZ$350 for a two-bedroom apartment. Powered camp sites are from NZ$35. **Ōhope Beachpoint Apartments ♥♥**, 5 West End Rd., Ōhope (beachpoint.co.nz; ✆ 07/312-6100), has a home-away-from-home vibe with 1- and 2-bedroom units along with a gym, library, and heated pool. (Some people even live in these apartments year-round.) Top draw: the beach on your doorstep. Rates from NZ$250 to NZ$365, prices rise in summer holidays.

Wainui Seaside Glamping ♥♥♥ About a 10-minute drive from Ōhope, Aleisha Wyllie and Tony Bland's sprawling property is right on the shores of Ōhiwa Harbour. Here, at the bottom of a hill, you'll find Seaside Escape, an expansive glamping tent situated right in the sweet spot of it all. It has a self-contained kitchen and a separate bathroom with shower and a composting toilet, but the layout isn't great for those with accessibility issues. (Tony and Aleisha will meet you at the top to bring your belongings to the bottom.) Guests also have use of kayaks and an outdoor tub that faces the ocean. Don't be surprised if Aleisha leaves some extra sweet treats in your fridge—she's a published cookbook author who specializes in vegan and whole foods. Guests can also choose to stay in the property's settler-style

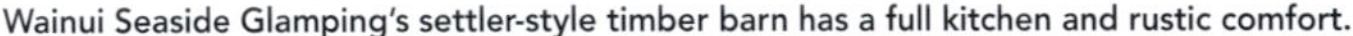

Wainui Seaside Glamping's settler-style timber barn has a full kitchen and rustic comfort.

timber barn, Barnie, which exudes warmth and comfort with its full-sized kitchen, fireplace, and secluded outdoor tub.

34 Burke Rd., Wainui. seasideglamping.nz (book via canopycamping.co.nz). 2 units. NZ$395. Rates include breakfast. **Amenities:** Outdoor bathtub; kayaks; kitchen.

Where to Eat Around the Bay of Plenty

TAURANGA

For brunch, head to local favorite **Benny & Brew ♥♥** (facebook.com/bennyandbrew; ✆ **027/350-6315;** daily 8am–2:30pm). It's hidden in the suburbs at 100 Grange Rd., Otūmoetai, but well worth the trip for dishes like eggs benedict with chipotle hollandaise served over cheesy potato waffles. For excellent contemporary Asian cuisine, try **Macau ♥♥**, 59 The Strand (dinemacau.co.nz; ✆ **07/578-8717;** Tues–Sat noon–late), where the presentation is as beautiful as the food. Meanwhile, if you're after Italian, **Sugo ♥♥**, 19 Wharf St. (sugosugo.co.nz; ✆ **07/571-4138;** weekdays 4:30–9:30pm, Sat noon–9:30pm, Sun noon–8:30pm), has made its name with fresh-made pasta, seafood, and Neapolitan-inspired pizzas. The prices reflect the provenance of the ingredients, with mains costing NZ$36 to NZ$54. On the city center waterfront, head to **Bobby's Fresh Fish Market ♥♥**, 1 Dive Crescent (✆ **07/578-1789**), for cheap and basic but extremely fresh fish & chips—you can eat it just feet from the fishing boats (don't feed the hopeful seagulls). Check out some of the more unusual "seafood" they offer—when I was there it included whole smoked muttonbird, a native seabird harvested from remote islands by Māori with special ancestral rights. For drinks and a pubby dinner, **The Cider Factorie ♥**, 50 Oikimoke Rd., Te Puna (theciderfactorie.co.nz; ✆ **07/552-4558;** main courses NZ$15–NZ$22; Wed–Sun 11am–5pm), is a fun stop on the edge of town. In addition to classic apple and pear ciders, they craft one from a South American fruit called the *feijoa* (or pineapple guava) which Kiwis are obsessed with—for good reason. They're delicious.

Clarence Tauranga Restaurant ♥♥♥ MODERN NEW ZEALAND Set in the city's historic post office, with elegant green leather banquettes indoors and a lovely leafy patio out, this is a place to see and be seen. And eat very well. Guests have a choice of a la carte dining and degustation menus for both lunch or dinner, all featuring upmarket pan-Mediterranean cuisine and fresh local ingredients—burrata with caviar, octopus pizza, or market fish with elderflower and macadamia.

51 Willow St. clarencetauranga.co.nz. ✆ **07/574-8200.** Main courses NZ$31–NZ$49. Mon–Fri 7am–10pm, Sat noon–10pm, Sun noon–9pm.

Somerset Cottage ♥♥ MODERN NEW ZEALAND They take their food pretty seriously at Somerset Cottage, which is a fine-dining restaurant, a cooking school (four series a year), and an online food store all wrapped into one yummy package. The restaurant part of the enterprise has been pleasing locals and visitors since 1986; the cooking school was established the following year. Chef Rick Lowe says he's not allowed to take certain favorite dishes off the menu, including Momofuku-style steamed pork buns with pork belly, twice-baked cheese soufflé with oven-roasted paprika pears, and duck with vanilla and coconut-scented kūmara mash and orange sauce—we suggest you see why.

30 Bethlehem Rd., Bethlehem. somersetcottage.co.nz. ✆ **07/576-6889.** Main courses NZ$45–NZ$52. Wed–Sat 5:30pm–late.

NEAR MOUNT MAUNGANUI

You'll find a handful of food trucks lined up along the Main Beach, but for something more substantial, Maunganui Road will likely be your main go-to, with plenty of cheap and cheerful options. For pizza, head to **Rustica** ♥, 10 Adams Ave. (bopple.app/rustica/menu; ✆ **07/572-0396**), for authentic Italian sourdough, or **Rita's** ♥♥ 103 Maunganui Rd. (ritas.nz), for Detroit-style square deep-dish pizzas and amazing cocktails and local beer. Open daily from noon.

My personal favorite spot to stop for gelato is **Sea People** ♥♥, 107a Maunganui Rd. (seapeople.co.nz), where every scoop is gluten-, dairy-, and soy-free—but certainly not lacking in flavor. Or try **Mount Made Ice Cream** ♥♥, 262 Maunganui Rd. (mountmade.co.nz; ✆ **07/572-0992**), which serves ice cream made with local ingredients, including dairy-free alternatives. Farther east along the long stretch of white sand, by the Omanu Beach surf club, is the beachfront caravan **Mount Delice** ♥ (✆ **027/382-7685**), where Sylvain Degraux serves homemade gelato (try the acai) as well as pastries, coffee, and brisket sandwiches under beautiful umbrellas painstakingly crocheted by his mother-in-law.

There are loads of good brunch options in the central Mount area, but in the beachy suburbs on the way to Pāpāmoa, **Special Mention Café** ♥♥♥, 399 Ocean Beach Rd. (instagram.com/specialmention_atk; ✆ **022/175-6536**), deserves, um, a special mention. This welcoming neighborhood place, frequented by families and digital nomads alike, has great coffee, cardamom buns, and scones—and an out-of-the-ordinary breakfast menu featuring treats like house-made crumpets with Biscoff and pecans or French omelet with kūmara, kimchi, and pecorino. It's open daily until 2pm. Once you get to Pāpāmoa, for the perfect grab-and-go meal before your walk on the beach, swing by **Gather Café** ♥♥, 552 Pāpāmoa Beach Rd. (instagram.com/gather.papamoa; daily 6:30am–2pm). Catering to a range of dietary needs, it serves plenty of raw food and vegan treats in the cabinet, along with its legendary smoothies.

Izakai ♥♥♥ MĀORI-JAPANESE As the demand for Indigenous cuisine grows, it's only natural to see restaurants doing twists on the traditional. But Izakai—a Japanese izakaya using Māori ingredients and cooking techniques—isn't just relying on a gimmick. Within months of opening, it became a favorite with locals, landing coverage in international publications and garnering several awards. Situated on the edge of a shopping complex in a pub-style space, it's known for foods that replicate the flavors of cooking in a traditional Māori earth oven, including hāngī-style pork belly or lamb shoulder ramen, yakitori prawn skewers with manuka honey glaze, and creamed pāua (abalone) dumplings—all made with local ingredients.

Bayfair Shopping Centre, Maunganui Rd. izakai.co.nz. ✆ **07/572-0484.** Main courses NZ$19–NZ$25. Daily 11:30am–late.

An array of vegetarian dishes at Izakai.

WAIHĪ BEACH

The award-winning **Surf Shack Eatery** ♥♥, 123 Emerton Rd. (surfshack.nz; ✆ **027/389-8781**), not only has some of the best burgers in town, it's also dog-friendly with plenty of pooches on the patio to pat. Kids are also well-catered for with pint-size meals for NZ$15. It's open Wednesday to Sunday, 9am to 2pm.

WHAKATĀNE/ŌHOPE

These beach towns are not overflowing with great eateries, but there are a few. Although hidden in a motel, Whakatāne's **Cafe Awa** ♥, 15 The Strand (awamotel.co.nz/cafe.html; ✆ **07/308-9500;** daily 7am–2pm), is fresh and bright inside, with some limited outdoor seating. Serving mainly breakfast and top-notch coffee, it also is a smart pick for grabbing packed lunches for any tours you're booked on.

For dinner, the popular **Cigol** ♥♥, 14 Richardson St. (cigol.co.nz; ✆ **020/471-5071**), serves beautifully presented Korean food with a Kiwi Pacific twist, share-plate style—think chargrilled bulgogi lamb rack, coconut kingfish, or garlic prawns with cashew cream. There are loads of vegetarian and gluten- and dairy-free options here too. It's open Tuesday to Saturday 5:30pm to late.

In Ōhope, **Fisherman's Wharf Café** ♥♥, 340 Harbour Rd. (facebook.com/pg/fishermanswharfcafe; ✆ **07/312-4017**), has a beachy vibe and a deck right next to the harbor. It serves—you guessed it—fresh fish and shellfish. Hours vary seasonally, but it is generally open daily from 5:30pm in the summer months; it does takeout food as well as sit-down meals. **Chez Louis'** ♥ food truck is usually at Maraetotara Reserve at Ōhope Beach Wednesday through Sunday (facebook.com/ChezLouisWoodfirePizzas; ✆ **021/054-9643**), serving wood-fired pizzas, including a country French version with sour cream, mushrooms, onion, bacon, garlic, cheese, and herbs. Check its Facebook page for hours and location. Oyster-lovers should head straight to **Tio Ōhiwa Oysters & Takeaways** ♥, 111 Wainui Rd. (ohiwaoysters.com), which also serves fish and chips, burgers, and smoked mussels, daily from 10am to 6pm. The family business also offers tours of the oyster farm and harbor (see p. 198).

ROTORUA, TAUPŌ & THE RUAPEHU REGION

7

Located in a collapsed volcano caldera, Rotorua sits on top of one of the most awesome and concentrated volcanic areas in the world. In every direction is tangible evidence of a riotous geological past extending back millions of years. The Te Arawa people settled the area in the mid-14th century; in the 19th century, their descendants began tourism here, guiding visitors to the famous Pink and White Terraces, once known as the Eighth Wonder of the Natural World. The 1886 eruption of Mount Tarawera destroyed the terraces, but the legendary Māori hospitality lives on in Rotorua's spas, cultural parks, and geothermal reserves.

Volcanic activity was also responsible for forming Lake Taupō. In A.D. 186, an enormous eruption—estimated to have been 100 times greater than that of Washington state's Mount St. Helens in 1980—tore a savage hole 30km (20 miles) wide, 40km (25 miles) across, and 180m (600 ft.) deep. Today, we're thankful for that. Where would New Zealand holidaymakers be without the cool blue waters that provide ideal conditions for fishing, water-skiing, swimming and boating?

Southwest of Taupō is the otherworldly volcanic region known as Ruapehu, which includes the volcanoes Mount Tongariro, Mount Ruapehu, and Mount Ngāuruhoe. Home to two Great Walks, two national cycle trails, three ski areas, and a dual UNESCO World Heritage Site, the region is a magnet for adventure and landscape junkies. The mystical Whanganui River also has its source in this region, deep in the national park that takes its name.

ROTORUA

221km (137 miles) SE of Auckland; 86km (53 miles) S of Tauranga

Welcome to "Rotovegas." Rotorua runs stiff competition with Queenstown for the title of the "Disneyland" of New Zealand—which is

Like Old Faithful in Yellowstone National Park in the United States, the Lady Knox geyser at Wai-O-Tapu erupts on a regular schedule.

little surprise, given that it's the birthplace of the country's thriving tourism sector. Since the 1800s, visitors have flocked to this strange town (current pop. 78,000) to see geothermal activity in action. More than 200 years later, that's still one of the area's main drawcards, with steam puffing out of street-side gutters, bubbling pools of mud found in public parks, and the curious smell of rotten eggs everywhere (thanks to the sulfur produced by the various geothermal features). The activities in Rotorua are just as peculiar. It's the birthplace of Zorbing: rolling down a hill in a giant inflatable ball filled with water. It's also where visitors can soak in geothermal-heated pools, zipline over waterfalls, and take in cultural shows by the country's very best *kapa haka* performers.

So Rotorua is a much-hyped destination for good reason: You shouldn't skip it. However, its rows of motels and many tourist attractions grate on some visitors, as does the ever-present smell of sulfur. If you're on a tight schedule, 2 to 3 days is more than enough time to budget here, and if you want quiet and fresh air, you can easily find it by booking accommodation in the outer-lying communities around Lake Rotorua.

Essentials

ARRIVING

Air New Zealand (airnewzealand.co.nz; ✆ **0800/767-767** in NZ) has daily services to and from the major centers. The regional airport is a 10-minute drive from the city; **Rotorua Taxis** (rotoruataxis.co.nz; ✆ **07/348-1111**) will get you there. **InterCity** (intercity.co.nz; ✆ **07/348-0388**) has daily coach service to and from the major cities, departing and arriving from the visitor center. **Ready2Roll Shuttles** (ready2roll.co.nz; ✆ **021/258-9887**) will transport you from Auckland or Hamilton, and provide transportation to nearby attractions through the Bay or Plenty and Waikato, including Waitomo and Hobbiton.

Rotorua & Environs

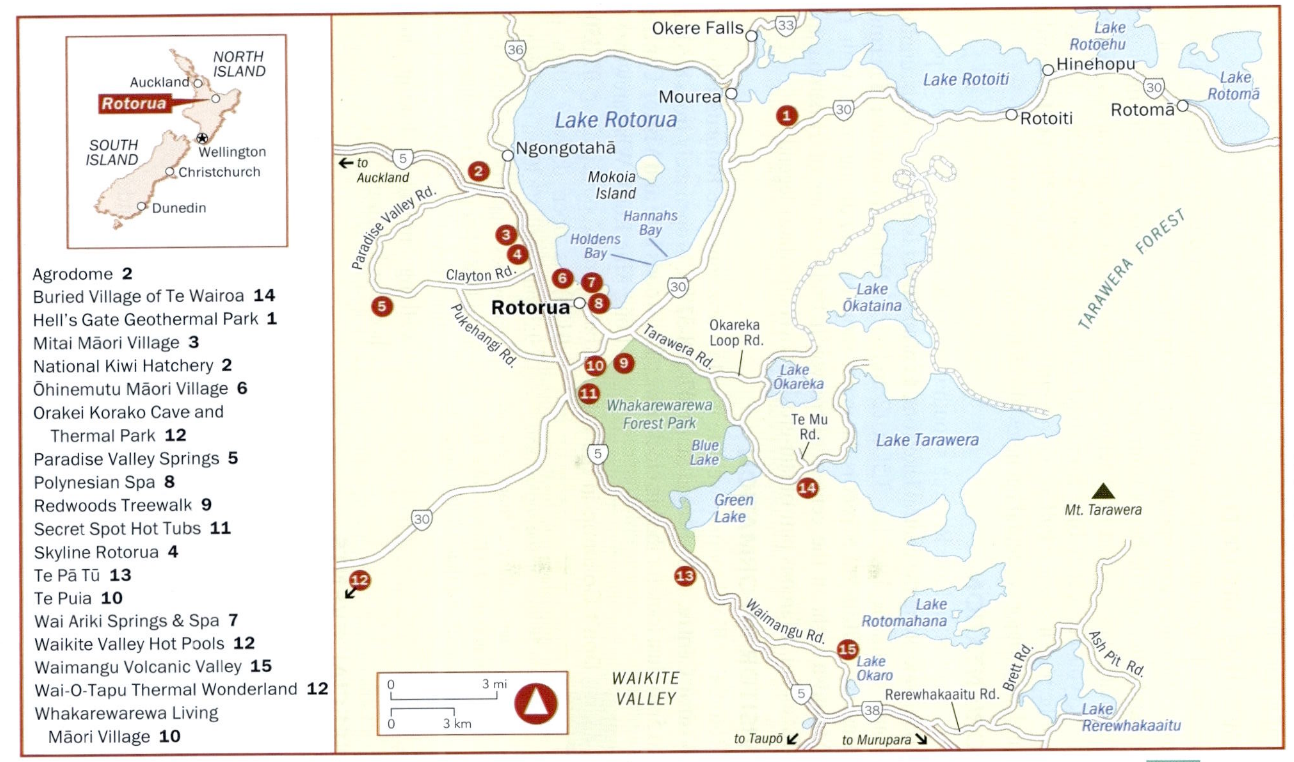

Rotorua is just an hour's drive from Taupō, Hamilton, and Tauranga, a 2½-hour drive from Auckland, and 5½ hours from Wellington. The roads are good, but watch out for logging trucks, which frequent the highways in this area.

GETTING AROUND

As one of NZ's most visited tourist areas, Rotorua is easily explored without a car. Most day tour operators offer pickup from your accommodation or the central isite. Shuttle buses from the visitor center head out to the main geothermal areas—ask staff for details and costs. To get around Rotorua on your own, you can catch **Bay Bus** (baybus.co.nz; ✆ **0800/422-928**), the city's public transit service; call a taxi (rotoruataxis.co.nz; ✆ **07/348-1111**); or order an Uber. Major car rental agencies also have outlets in Rotorua.

ORIENTATION

Rotorua lies on Lake Rotorua's southwestern shore, with a lovely new pedestrian zone along the central lakefront. **Fenton Street** is the main road, running south from the lake for 3.5km (2 miles) to **Whakarewarewa Thermal Reserve. Tūtānekai Street** is the major shopping and dining street, with **Te Manawa** right in the center, where you'll find carvings of Hinemoa and Tūtānekai, a famous pair of star-crossed lovers in Māori legend.

VISITOR INFORMATION

Rotorua's official tourism website is **rotoruanz.com**. The **Rotorua isite and Visitor Centre,** 1167 Fenton St. (✆ **07/348-5179**), is open daily from 8:30am to 5pm. Just look for the big clock tower. **Redwoods isite and Visitor Centre,** Long Mile Road, Whakarewarewa Forest (redwoods.co.nz; ✆ **07/350-0110**), is open daily 9:30am to 9:30pm, until 10:30pm in summer; it provides maps for the 5,600-hectare (13,838-acre) exotic-pine plantation forest, a popular spot for walking, mountain biking, and horseback riding.

> **Don't Go Jump in the Lake**
>
> There are 18 lakes in the region, and you can swim in many of them—except Lake Rotokākahi, the Green Lake. It's *tapu* (sacred) and thus off-limits even for a little dip.

SPECIAL EVENTS

Rotorua is well known for its cycling, running, and racing events, the most notable of which is the **Crankworx** (crankworx.com) mountain biking festival in March. In November, there's the **NZ Blues and BBQ Festival** (bluesandbbq.co.nz) featuring live music and slow-cooked food.

Exploring Rotorua

Most visitors come to Rotorua to see its geothermal wonders and Māori cultural shows, then to relax in a spa or pursue adventure sports like hiking, mountain biking, or ziplining. Visiting the geothermal reserves (**Te Puia, Wai-O-Tapu, Hell's Gate,** or **Waimangu**) is a must. Most tours combine learning about natural thermal processes with an introduction to Māori history and sometimes the opportunity to see a *kapa haka* cultural show. Of course, this all comes at a cost, but there are many geothermal attractions you can see for free. One example is **Kuirau Park** ♥, right in the center of town, which would be a typical city park if it weren't full of (fenced) steam vents and mud pools. For more on the area's geothermal attractions, see p. 215.

Mount Tarawera ♥♥♥, located 24km (15 miles) southeast of the city, shouldn't be overlooked as an attraction. In 1886 the mountain dramatically blew its stack, destroying Māori villages, killing around 120 people, and engulfing the beautiful Pink and White Terraces, the birthplace of NZ's tourism industry. But it's peaceful today, and you can explore its rainbow-colored crater on a guided hike with **Kaitiaki Adventures** ♥♥ (kaitiaki.co.nz; ✆ **07/357-2236**). It's an easy half-day adventure in the sense that you don't have to walk far (you'll drive most of the way up the mountain), but will challenge those with knee or balance issues, or a fear of heights. (There are times you'll need to use all fours to make your way along the crater's ridgelines. If you have hiking poles, bring them.) Operating twice daily, the trek costs NZ$205 for ages 7 and up. Alternately, you can book a 40-minute flightseeing tour with **Volcanic Air** (volcanicair.co.nz; ✆ **07/348-9984**) by helicopter, which includes a landing and guided walk for NZ$630 adults, NZ$473 ages 2 to 11. It departs from Lake Rotorua's lakefront.

Finally, make some time to stroll along the **Lakefront.** Fully redeveloped in 2024, it's now a gorgeous vehicle-free public park with boardwalks out over the lake, two excellent playgrounds, Māori sculptural artworks, and lots of aquatic birdlife.

Note: **Rotorua's Museum** has been closed since 2016 for earthquake strengthening. It's anticipated to reopen in 2027.

THE MAJOR SIGHTS

Buried Village of Te Wairoa ♥ ARCHAEOLOGICAL SITE The village of Te Wairoa once stood here, before it was covered in ash and pyroclastic flow during the eruption of Mt. Tarawera in 1886. Today, visitors can walk through its once-buried buildings, which have been excavated to floor level, including the remains of Māori *whare* (houses), the Rotomahana Hotel, and a flour mill. It's an easy 1km (half-mile) walk outdoors, which can be extended by visiting Wairere Falls. (There's a series of narrow, steep and slippery stairs to get there, but it's worth the trek.) The accompanying museum tells the tragic tale through artifacts recovered from the site. Unfortunately, the presentation and layout are dated; I'd give the Buried Village a miss if you're short on time. However, if you're a history or volcano buff, it's a compelling add-on when paired with a visit to the **Waimangu Volcanic Valley** (p. 217), where the terraces once stood, or inside the crater of **Mt. Tarawera** itself (see above).

1180 Tarawera Rd. buriedvillage.co.nz. ✆ **07/362-8287.** NZ$30 adults, NZ$10 ages 13–18, free for kids 12 and under, family NZ$60. Wed–Sun 10am–4pm.

Redwoods Treewalk ♥♥♥ PARK/ATTRACTION Rotorua's Whakarewarewa Forest—also called "The Redwoods"—is known for its massive stands of 75m-tall (250-ft.) California Coast Redwoods, first planted in

Climbing the circular stair up to the Redwood Canopy is just the beginning of the adventure at Redwoods Altitude.

Rotorua in 1901 as an experiment by the timber industry to see if they'd be commercially viable. Due to the climate and volcanic soil, these trees grew far faster than their ancestors did in California, achieving heights in just 100 years that would have taken several hundred in North America, but they weren't of high enough quality to harvest. This attraction is all that remains of the extensive plantings.

Visitors have several ways to enjoy the forest. The park is a mecca for mountain biking; cyclists zip between the trees on a vast network of trails, and hikers can do walks on the ground, free of charge. But the marquee activity is the **Redwoods Treewalk,** a 40-minute stroll along a series of 28 suspended swing bridges ranging in height from 9 to 20m (30–65 ft.), strung between these giants. At night, these walkways are illuminated by lanterns and artful light installations (a dazzling, otherworldly effect) and given the name **Redwoods Nightlights.** This is a very popular evening attraction, but for safety (and ambience), numbers are strictly limited.

General admission tickets (NZ$42 adult, NZ$26 kids 5–15, family passes available) can be used at any time of the day or night. However, if you want to go at dusk or early evening—which is especially magical, with tūī and other birds singing around you—or you are short on time, I recommend paying NZ$10 more for a Fast Pass online, which allows you to specify your entry time and skip the queue. On the other hand, if you're in no rush, there's often quite a festival vibe in the queue, with a popcorn truck and a movie showing on a big screen under the trees to entertain the kids.

A new-in-2025 attraction, **Redwoods Glowworms,** is a short spin through a simulated cave with 1,500 real glowworms (NZ$29 adults, NZ$15 kids, half price as an add-on to a Treewalk or Nightlights ticket). Skip this if you're planning to visit Waitomo or take a **Taiao Adventures** glowworm kayak in

Rotorua (p. 222), but if you don't think you'll see glowworms in the wild on your NZ trip, this is a quick, easy way to learn something about them and bask in their eerie turquoise light.

Finally, for daredevils, there's the **Redwoods Altitude** course (NZ$125), a combination of walkways, ziplines, and rope bridges that swing a terrifying 25m (82 ft.) above the ground. This more intensive experience is guided and takes 2 hours; participants must weigh between 30kg and 120kg (66–264 lb.). 1 Long Mile Rd./Tītokorangi Dr. treewalk.co.nz. ✆ **027/536-1010.** Treewalk daily 9am–sunset, Nightlights sunset–late (last entry 10:30pm). Altitude tours 10am & 1pm, bookings essential.

Te Puia ♥♥♥ GEYSER/CULTURAL EXPERIENCE Just 5 minutes from downtown, this is one of Rotorua's top attractions: It's a one-stop shop for Māori culture, nature, conservation, and a new, completely unique, immersive nighttime experience. Situated in the Whakarewarewa geothermal valley, the 60-hectare (148-acre) Te Puia complex is home to a kiwi house, more than 500 steaming, bubbling, seething geothermal features, and the **New Zealand Māori Arts and Crafts Institute.** Established in 1926, the latter has interactive galleries where flax weavers and carvers of stone, bone, and wood practice their craft. (A portion of the entry fee goes towards scholarships for Māori students to learn these traditional arts.) Over in the geothermal area, the **Pōhutu Geyser** (the largest in the southern hemisphere) erupts up once or twice an hour, up to heights of 30m (98 ft.).

Wood-carved masks at Te Puia's Māori Arts and Crafts Institute.

There are day and night experiences on offer, and both are excellent. During the day, **Te Rā** features a 90-minute guided tour of the geothermal area—you'll pay an extra NZ$35 for a traditional welcoming *pōwhiri,* songs, and *haka* (it's worth it—the *kapa haka* performers here are among the best in the country.) But this steaming, historic valley is arguably even more evocative at night. The **Te Pō** experience (2 hr. 45 min.) includes a cultural performance, a night viewing of the Pōhutu Geyser (accompanied by some excellent hot chocolate), and a *hāngī* buffet dinner. Book in advance, as it often sells out.

New in 2025, the nighttime **Te Mārama Geyser Light Trail** is a feast for the senses. Lasers play above the steaming sulfurous pools, hillsides are illuminated, and colored lights transform boiling mud and geysers into otherworldly scenes, all set to a soundtrack by Māori singer-songwriter Maisey

NGONGOTAHĀ: fun central FOR KIDS

Just up the lake shore 10 minutes' drive from Rotorua, Ngongotahā offers a number of attractions that will delight youngsters. Smaller kids will love meeting Kiwi farm animals at the **Agrodome** ♥, 141 Western Rd. (agrodome.co.nz; ✆ **07/357-1050**), where you can watch sheep shearing and sheepdogs in action. A tour of the farm and a show costs NZ$59 for adults and NZ$30 for kids ages 3 to 15. It's open daily from 9am to 5pm—but check the website for tour and show times. On the same site, you can get up close to NZ's famous native birds at the **National Kiwi Hatchery** ♥♥♥ (nationalkiwihatchery.org.nz; ✆ **0800/724-626** in NZ or 07/350-0440). One of the country's largest kiwi conservation projects, it hatches up to 120 eggs between September and March every year. Entry and a 1-hour guided tour is NZ$60 adults, NZ$30 ages 5 to 15, NZ$159 families. There's also a superb behind-the-scenes exclusive tour (suitable for kids aged 12 and up, NZ$1,250 for up to four people, NZ$299 per additional person) that takes visitors behind the glass to watch the kiwis being weighed and fed. Visitors interact directly with husbandry experts and take pictures with the chicks (although they are not allowed to touch them). Best of all: 100% of your entry fee goes to the National Kiwi Recovery Trust. Advance bookings are essential. It's open daily from 9:30am to 2:30pm.

For more wildlife action, head out west of town to **Paradise Valley Springs** ♥, 467 Paradise Valley Rd. (paradisevalleysprings.co.nz; ✆ **07/348-9667**), where you can see New Zealand birds (such as kea, the world's only mountain parrot), trout, eels, and assorted exotic wildlife, including—somewhat unexpectedly—lions. It's NZ$38 adults and NZ$19 kids 5 to 15; a family pass is NZ$105. It's open daily 8am until dark (last entry 5pm).

On the road back to Rotorua, stop off in Fairy Springs and take a gondola ride up to **Skyline Rotorua** ♥, 178 Fairy Springs Rd. (skyline.co.nz; ✆ **07/347-0027**), to marvel at the views—or to hurtle down the hill on a luge. Night luging is an option on weekends, with some of the tracks lit up by hundreds of colorful LED lights. The **Skyswing** is also a big deal here: Three people go up, then away like a crazy pendulum at speeds of up to 140kmph (90mph). And, of course, there's also a **zipline.** Admission varies based on what rides you want to experience but starts at NZ$45 for adults and NZ$29 for children ages 6 to 14, with

Rika. Allow at least an hour, but you can linger as long as you like. Check online for this experience's showtimes—they change with the seasons.

Hemo Rd., Te Whakarewarewa Valley. tepuia.com. ✆ **07/348-9047.** Te Rā NZ$100 adults, NZ$50 ages 5–15, NZ$270 family; with cultural performance NZ$135 adult, NZ$76 children, NZ$365 family. Te Pō NZ$195 adults, NZ$135 children. Te Mārama NZ$49 adults, NZ$25 children, NZ$132 family.

Whakarewarewa Living Māori Village ♥♥♥ CULTURAL EXPERIENCE The Tūhourangi-Ngāti Wāhiao have been hosting visitors since the early 1800s. This is a working, modern Māori village in the middle of a geothermal area where the locals still use the hot water for cooking and washing, as they have been doing for hundreds of years. Offerings include a guided village tour, a cultural performance (held daily at 12:30pm; bookings encouraged, as seating is limited); and access to the self-guided geothermal packages and family passes available. If your kids are old enough to go on the rides alone, you can take part in a decidedly more adult affair: wine tasting. At the top of the gondola is the tasting room for **Volcanic Hills Winery** ♥ (volcanichills.co.nz; ✆ **07/282-2018**), with panoramic views of the valley.

For other kid-friendly adventure activities, including uniquely New Zealand sports like Zorb, Swoop, and the Schweeb(??!!), see the "Outdoor Pursuits" section on p. 220.

Staff member showing visitors a kiwi chick at the National Kiwi Hatchery in Ngongotahā.

trails. There are a range of ticket combos to choose from based on what you want to see.

17 Tryon St. Whakarewarewa Village. whakarewarewa.com. ✆ **07/349-3463.** All-day passes NZ$119 adults; NZ$62 ages 5–15. Daily 8:30am–4pm.

GETTING INTO HOT WATER: SPAS

What goes together like banana and pancakes? Geothermal activity and hot pools. Some get down and dirty in the mud, others are all about relaxing in mineral-infused waters.

- **Free hot pools:** If au natural is your thing, **Kerosene Creek** ♥, located about 30 minutes south of Rotorua off SH5, is probably the area's most-hyped wild swimming spot. The heated stream is free to access, but you have to drive down the pothole-riddled Old Waiotapu Road for 2km (1¼ miles) to get there. Your second task will be to cover your eyes to avoid seeing garbage left by others. But if you can achieve both of these feats, you'll find yourself submerged in a deep heated creek surrounded by forest, complete with steaming waterfalls. (Be sure to lock your vehicle and carry valuables with you, as break-ins are frequently reported in this area.)

Just 10 minutes farther south, the **Hot and Cold Pools ♥♥** off Waiotapu Loop Road are not quite as photogenic (no waterfalls here) but they're cleaner and easier to access (and for these two reasons, a better bet for those with small children). You can find them right before Wai-O-Tapu Thermal Wonderland, but note that roadside parking at the site is limited. There are no bathrooms or changing rooms at either site.

- **Hot pools with an entrance fee:** Right on the lakefront, stunning **Wai Ariki Hot Springs & Spa ♥♥♥** (wai-ariki.co.nz; ✆ **07/349-7111**) weaves all the best aspects of Rotorua into one—geothermal waters, Māori culture, nature, and relaxation. Opened in 2023 by iwi Ngāti Whakaue, the building itself is an award-winning architectural marvel, and inside, its 2-hour signature restorative journey (daily 9am–10pm, NZ$175) tells the story of the great chief Ngātoroirangi while pampering you in an ever-changing series of hot-and-cold delights. It begins with a *karakia* (blessing). Then there are showers that mimic waterfalls, saunas and a "frigidarium," pools of varying temperatures (including one nourished with native plants), a very civilized geothermal mud experience, and a steam room designed to feel like the inside of the earth. You can also choose to just bathe in the five pools, which look out over bush and birds to the lake (1 hr., NZ$99). A wide range of Māori-accented spa treatments are also available, and there's a great gift shop and cafe out front. This is a quiet, peaceful, adults-only place (ages 16 and up). Book ahead for your preferred time slot.

Bathers relaxing in the pools at Wai Ariki Hot Springs & Spa.

A sought-after soak spot since 1972, **Polynesian Spa ♥♥** (polynesianspa.co.nz; ✆ **07/348-1328**) has been voted one of the top 10 natural spas in the world six times by *Condé Nast Traveler.* It has 26 pools in total, with areas set aside for families or adults-only. Admission starts at NZ$31, but pools with a lake view cost extra (from NZ$80), as do treatments at the on-site spa. It's also not exactly a hidden treasure; it attracts plenty of bathers during peak hours. If you're looking for a quiet and serene spot to soak, arrive early in the morning, or pony up for a private pool. Daily 9am to 11pm.

WHAT'S COOKING? geothermal gems

If you're new to geothermal activity, the whiff of sulfur and the sight of steam wafting can be a little unsettling. But humans have been living alongside this peculiarity of the Earth's crust for a long time now. There are lots of places you can see this energy force at work.

Waimangu Volcanic Valley ♥♥♥, 587 Waimangu Rd. (waimangu.co.nz; ✆ **07/366-6137**), a 20-minute drive south of Rotorua, calls itself "the world's youngest geothermal system." It appeared after the dust (and ash) had settled following the eruption of Mount Tarawera on June 10, 1886, making it the only hydrothermal system in the world formed in historic times as a result of a volcanic eruption. On the gentle downhill 1.5km (1-mile) walk through the valley, you'll pass **Frying Pan Lake** (the world's largest hot spring), and the extraordinary blue **Inferno Crater** lake (the intensity of its color varies based on its level, which rises and falls on a regular 38-day cycle). At the end of the path, a shuttle will carry you back to the top, but I recommend paying extra for the boat cruise on **Lake Rotomahana,** which passes over the site of the lost Pink and White Terraces. The whole experience takes 2 hours, or around 3 with the boat trip. It's relatively expensive, at NZ$75 (NZ$45 children 6–15, NZ$225 families) for a self-guided walk; or NZ$180 (NZ$90 children 6–15, NZ$530 families) with the boat cruise added, but you're paying for fascinating history, a convenient set-up, and helping to restore and protect this unique, ever-changing natural landscape. Waimangu is open daily from 8:30am to 5pm, with the last entry at 3:30pm.

Waimangu's colorful Frying Pan Lake.

Another 10 minutes down the road, **Wai-O-Tapu Thermal Wonderland** ♥♥♥ (waiotapu.co.nz; ✆ **07/366-6333**) might not have the dramatic history, but it is much cheaper, and more visually stunning. Allow up to 2 hours to wander around the park, although the most impressive bits are mostly in the shorter 40-minute walk. These include the **Artist's Palette,** a huge silica terrace of hot and cold pools and steaming fumaroles where minerals turn the ground everything from burnt orange and red to bright yellow, white, and purple; the ochre-fringed **Champagne Pool;** and the extraordinary chartreuse-green **Devil's Bath,** which is full of sulfur but looks like the makings of a really nasty cocktail. The famously reliable **Lady Knox Geyser,** a short drive away, is part of the ticket price; it performs daily at the civilized hour of 10:15am. Wai-O-Tapu is open daily 8:30am to 4:30pm (last entry 3pm). Admission is NZ$45 adults, NZ$15 kids 5 to 15, and NZ$105 families. If you want to see quite a large mud pool but don't want to pay, look out for the signpost just before the park.

On SH5, closer to Taupō than Rotorua, the unspoiled geothermal area of **Orakei Korako Cave and Thermal Park** ♥♥♥ (orakeikorako.co.nz; ✆ **07/378-3131**) involves a very short ferry ride across the Waikato River and an energetic walk around the reserve. It features one of only two geothermal caves in the world (you'll have to go to Italy to see the other one) as well as geysers, hot springs, and mud pools. Entry is NZ$51 adults, NZ$24 ages 6 to 16, and NZ$132 for a family. It's open from 8am; the last ferry leaves at 4pm.

Claiming to be Rotorua's most active geothermal field, **Hell's Gate Geothermal Park and Mud Spa** ♥ (hellsgate.co.nz; ✆ **07/345-3151**) lies 15km (9 miles) northeast of Rotorua on SH30. We have playwright George Bernard Shaw to thank for the name: When he visited in 1934, he reportedly said, "This could be the very gates of hell." The 20-hectare (50-acre) Māori-owned reserve is indeed a steaming moonscape of sulfur formations, gloopy mud, and the largest hot waterfall in the Southern Hemisphere. You can slather the stuff all over yourself, then have a soak in an ordinary hot mineral pool. However, don't expect massages or body treatments; the "spa" in Hell's Gate's name is simply the Kiwi term for "hot pool." It's not a luxury facility, and what you think of the experience really depends on what price you're willing to pay for the novelty of rolling around in warm mud with a bunch of strangers—some people love it and others hate it. For just the mud bath, you'll pay NZ$90 adults, NZ$45 children, and NZ$250 for a family; for the full experience, including walking trails, an opportunity to try carving, and the mud pools, it's NZ$115 adults; NZ$58 children; NZ$320 families. It's open daily from 10am to 8pm (or 6pm in winter).

A fun new offering is **Secret Spot Hot Tubs** ♥♥ in the mountain bike carpark off Waipa State Mill Road (secretspot.nz; ✆ **07/348-4442**). This quiet "forest bathing" spot away from the hum of downtown Rotorua became a favorite of locals when it opened right before the pandemic. Most were drawn in by the complimentary "shinny dipping" sessions: soaking your feet in mini-tubs while indulging in a craft beer. Full body soaks, in hot tubs filled with natural spring water (read: no smell!), can be individually booked for hour-long sessions. Set against a forest backdrop, they're not entirely private (you can see your neighbors), but you'll be won over by the service (just hit the call button to have drinks delivered to your tub) and the cheeky signage. The tubs cost NZ$43 per adult and NZ$15 for kids 5 to 14. (Kids under 5 not allowed.) It's open daily from 9am to 10pm.

My vote for best value, though, is **Waikite Valley Hot Pools** ♥♥♥, 648 Waikite Valley Rd. (hotpools.co.nz; ✆ **07/333-1861**), which is absolutely worth the half-hour drive from town, or as a stop-off on the way to Taupō (or better yet, stay overnight—it has a lovely, affordable campsite including powered RV sites). It offers half a dozen perfect-temperature pools fringed by tree ferns, overlooking stunning countryside and a steaming stream. The water is drawn daily from Te Manaroa, a nearby boiling spring (take a short walk through the bush to admire it) and the pools are drained each evening, ensuring they're always clean and fresh. There's also a cafe and private pools. Admission to the general pools is just NZ$27.50, NZ$14.20 for a child, and NZ$73.50 for a family (and is included free when you camp here). It's open daily 10:30am to 8pm.

MĀORI CULTURAL EXPERIENCES

While Rotorua is far from the only spot in the country where you can partake in Māori-led tourism experiences, if you're keen to see a full-scale Māori cultural show, this is the best place to do it. And if you're inclined to think these kinds of entertainments are cheesy or cringe, think again—the mostly young guides will introduce you to Te Ao Māori, the Māori world, with both gravitas and humor. Cultural shows typically include a *kapa haka* (traditional song and dance) performance and may also include a *hāngī* (earth oven banquet). The latter is a traditional Māori method of cooking, in which a large pit is dug in the ground and filled with a wood fire topped by stones. These are heated through, and then flax baskets of food (mostly meat and veg) are placed on top and covered with damp cloths. Earth is piled on top to create a natural oven. It generally takes about 3 hours to cook, and then dinner is served—everything tastes of earthy smoke. The flavor may be a bit of an acquired taste, but it's an experience you shouldn't miss.

Three major players specialize in these multifaceted cultural performances: **Te Pā Tū, Mitai Māori Village,** and **Te Puia.** All start their evening extravaganzas—which last 3 to 4 hours—around 6:30pm and include lodging pickup and drop-off. All also include a reconstructed village where you can see the daily activities and traditional rituals of the local tribes, and you can learn how Māori use indigenous plants for medicinal purposes.

- **For the best food:** Formerly known as Tamaki Māori Village, **Te Pā Tū ♥♥♥**, 1220 Hinemaru St. (te-pa-tu.com; ✆ **07/349-2999**), used the pandemic as an opportunity to reinvent its offerings. Its new experiences are incredibly interactive, with storytelling and theater woven throughout. From October to April, it's a summer harvest celebration; from May to September, a winter Matariki ceremony. Guests are ushered into the village in a traditional *pōwhiri* (welcome ceremony) by costumed hosts, where they enjoy canapes made with indigenous ingredients, learn to play stick games, perform with *poi,* and do a *haka.* Then, after a *kapa haka* performance, they sit down for a multi-course meal—not the *hāngī* buffet from tourism days of yore, but dishes shared family-style. The menu, designed

Storytellers arrive in a warrior canoe during a cultural performance at Mitai Māori Village.

by celebrated local chefs, changes based on what's in season and includes elevated plays on traditional *hāngī* and boil-ups. It's a LOT of food. Vegetarian and gluten-free meals are available. The entire experience costs NZ$270 adults, NZ$115 ages 5 to 15.

- **For a traditional hāngī experience: Mitai Māori Village ♥♥**, 196 Fairy Springs Rd. (mitai.co.nz; ✆ **07/343-9132**), is similar but presents food in a more traditional manner. You'll have a chance to see how *hāngī* is prepared, which is then served in a buffet. This location also has glowworms within its bush. It costs NZ$129 for adults, NZ$26 for ages 10 to 15, and NZ$26 for ages 5 to 9. Family passes are also available.
- **For geyser action with dessert: Te Pō** at **Te Puia ♥♥** (see p. 213) puts on an evening show and meal along the same lines, with the added bonus of visiting an erupting geyser while sipping hot chocolate. It costs NZ$195 for adults, NZ$135 for ages 5 to 15. Family passes are also available.

In addition to these specialists, some of the larger hotels put on their own cultural experiences and *hāngī.* They tend to be more affordable (if lacking in ambience), so ask when you book if this is an option.

Outsiders are also welcome to visit **Ōhinemutu Māori Village ♥** on the lakefront. Go to the end of Fenton Street and keep heading west until you see the historic Tama-te-Kapua meetinghouse, cemetery, and the lovely little **St. Faith's Anglican Church.** Admission to the church is a NZ$5 donation, and you must ask permission before entering: There's usually someone there who will show you around, but you're not allowed to take photographs inside. The church is beautifully decorated with *whakairo* (carvings) and woven *tukutuku* wall panels. A modern feature is the window that depicts Jesus wearing a Māori cloak—if you sit in the right place with the lake behind him, he appears to be walking on water. The village has lots of thermal activity: The local ladies even cook their Christmas hams over grates in a couple of places. Please be courteous and thoughtful—the village isn't a tourist attraction; it's where people live.

Outdoor Pursuits

Rotorua is an outdoor adventurer's playground, so this is far from an exhaustive list of all the activities offered. Ask at the visitor center if you have a special interest that isn't covered below, as you'll likely find somewhere to do it.

ADRENALINE ACTION **Velocity Valley ♥♥** (velocityvalley.co.nz; ✆ **07/357-4747**) is best known as the inventor of the insane activity called **Swoop.** Those who try it are strapped into a hang-gliding harness with two others and lifted 40m (131 ft.) in the air. After pulling a ripcord they experience the feeling of flying at 130kmph (81mph) with a G-force factor of 3. You must be at least 1m (3-ft. 3-in.) tall to swoop. For NZ$195 you can do four rides (or ride one four times) including the Swoop, the Agrojet (jetboating), the Freefall Xtreme (indoor sky diving), and the Shweeb (the only pedal-powered monorail track in the world). Velocity no longer offers bungy jumping, but for NZ$175 you can try **Vertigo**—a unique activity where you're dropped 43m (141 ft.) onto a safety net below, in what they promise will be "the longest 4 seconds of your life."

The Birthplace of Zorbing

While Kiwi inventions like bungy jumping and jetboats are synonymous with adventure, Zorbing belongs in a category all its own. Here's the drill: You crawl inside a giant inflatable ball—filled with just a splash of water to make things extra silly—then roll down the side of a hill. It's absolutely ridiculous, which is exactly the reason you should do it. **Zorb Rotorua ♥♥♥**, 525 Ngongotahā Rd., Fairy Springs (zorb.com; ✆ **0800/646-768** in NZ, or 07/343-7676), is where the sport (if you can call it that?) was invented, and it's also the only place in NZ that you can Zorb down a hill. There are four tracks, including the mega-fun Sidewinder. Hot tubs at either end of the tracks and a sauna keep you toasty warm in between runs. It's not cheap, at NZ$49 to NZ$69 for a single ride (NZ$155 for all four tracks) and chances are you'll want to purchase the hilarious photographs afterwards (you'll be equipped with a GoPro before your ride), which costs extra. But holidays are about having fun, and this is a guaranteed ticket to laughter. Kids can ride from 5 years old.

FISHING Lakes Rotorua, Tarawera, Ōkataina, and Rotoiti are jumping-off points for some of New Zealand's best wild trout fishing. The season runs from October through June. The greatest trout population is in Lake Rotorua, where rainbow trout average 1.5 to 2kg (3–4½ lb.) and brown trout 3kg (6½ lb.). Your fishing guide can sort out your license. **Cruise and Fish Rotorua** (cruiseandfish.co.nz; ✆ **021/951-959**) transports guests by 4WD or helicopter (and then in a boat, obviously) for fly- and spin-fishing around the central North Island. The marketplace site fishingbooker.com lists other companies along with helpful user reviews.

GOLF The Arikikapakapa course at the **Rotorua Golf Club ♥♥**, 399 Fenton St. (arikikapakapagolfrotorua.co.nz; ✆ **07/348-4051**), is a links-style 18-hole course that's unique because golfers tee off next to a boiling mud pool! Greens fees are NZ$65 and club hire is NZ$35.

HORSEBACK RIDING **Horse Trekking Lake Okareka ♥**, 51 Acacia Rd., Lake Ōkareka (treklakeokareka.co.nz; ✆ **021/292-2233**), canters through the lakes region of Rotorua on rides that range in length from 30 minutes to 2½ hours. A guide expert in helping "nervous beginners" is part of the package. Rides start from NZ$120, with treks departing daily at 10am and 1:30pm.

KAYAKING & WHITE-WATER RAFTING Rotorua is the gateway for the Tutea Falls on the Kaituna River, the highest commercially rafted falls in the world (it's a whopping 7m/23-ft. drop). Recommended operators for excursions on the river include **River Rats Raft and Kayak** (riverrats.co.nz; ✆ **07/345-6543**), **Kaitiaki Adventures** (kaitiaki.co.nz; ✆ **07/357-2236**), **Rotorua Rafting** (rotorua-rafting.co.nz; ✆ **021/0260-7441**), and **Kaituna Cascades Rafting** (kaitunacascades.co.nz; ✆ **07/345-4199**). All offer nearly identical products, although Rotorua Rafting is just a hair cheaper at NZ$125 (you'll pay around NZ$139 for the others). Only ages 13 and over can go over the falls. All three companies also offer rafting on other surrounding rivers in

Whitewater rafting on the Kaituna River, home to Tutea Falls.

the area, including the Rangitaiki, Tongariro, and Wairoa rivers, and some offer kayaking trips to the hot springs on the far side of Lake Rotoiti.

Alternatively, you can head down the Kaituna in a tandem kayak (you in the front, your guide in the back) with **New Zealand Whitewater Academy** (nzwhitewateracademy.com; ✆ **027/347-8080**). It costs NZ$297, plus an extra NZ$60 for the GoPro footage at the end. No experience is necessary.

For a more serene, if equally awe-inspiring excursion, head out with **Taiao Adventures** ♥♥♥ (taiaoadventures.com; ✆ **022/427-9136**) on a nighttime glowworm kayak. For NZ$189 (adults, kids are NZ$119) you'll paddle in a leisurely fashion across Lake Ōkareka, then into some beautiful glowworm caves, where you'll truly appreciate the critters' Māori name *titiwai,* meaning "lights reflecting on water." This friendly team also offers a private daytime kayaking trip on Lake Rotomahana to the steaming cliffs, starting from NZ$750.

MOUNTAIN BIKING Rotorua is the mountain biking mecca of NZ (and that's a big deal, given that people across the country love the sport). Its epicenter is the **Whakarewarewa Forest** ♥♥ (see p. 211), on Waipa State Mill Road. That's where you'll find **Mountain Bike Rotorua** (mtbrotorua.co.nz; ✆ **07/348-4295**), which rents bikes, helmets, and more. It's open daily from 9am to 5pm. Rentals start at NZ$45. If you prefer the thrill of downhill riding to the slog of going up, its shuttle buses will carry you to four hilltop spots within the park, with tickets starting from NZ$15. Or try **Planet Bike** ♥♥, 8 Waipa Bypass Rd. (planetbike.co.nz; ✆ **07/346-1717**), which does rentals starting from NZ$45 for 2 hours (e-bikes from NZ$110). Lessons for first-timers are also available (NZ$150).

Go to **riderotorua.com** for everything you need to know about Rotorua's other world-class trails, maps, shuttles and activities.

WALKING Rotorua has a number of delightful hikes, particularly around the region's picturesque lakes. One of the finest is the 25-minute **Motutara**

Walkway ♥♥, which meanders around the lakefront to Sulphur Bay, passing mud pools and sulfur vents along the way. Some 12km (7 miles) southeast of Rotorua, the lovely **Lake Ōkareka Walkway ♥** is a 2.5km (about 1.5-mile) stroll around the lake and back again. It takes about 1½ hours, and you'll see plenty of bird life. Farther afield, **Whakarewarewa Forest** (see p. 211) has a number of well-marked walking tracks for all ages and levels of fitness—but keep in mind it's not a native NZ bush environment, but rather a forest of Californian trees. Trail walks range from 30 minutes to 3½ hours. The most popular trail, the 2km (1.25-mile) **Redwood Memorial Grove Track ♥♥**, features giant 67m (219-ft.) California coastal redwoods that were planted in 1901; it takes 30 minutes if you leave from the visitor center.

ZIPLINING Rotorua is home to multiple experiences that will send you flying through the air—and through the beautiful native bush your admission ticket helps to protect. First, there's the award-winning **Rotorua Canopy Tours ♥♥♥**, 147 Fairy Springs Rd. (canopytours.co.nz; ✆ **07/343-1001**), voted NZ's number one activity on Tripadvisor several years in a row. Its tour takes place in a rare virgin forest studded with towering ancient rimu trees and is a ziplining trip for purists. On the Ultimate Canopy Tour—which is longer, faster, and higher than its Original Canopy Tour—participants spend 3½ hours flying over the forest, including on a 400m tandem zipline (NZ$259 adults, NZ$229 children 10–15; family pass available, as well as combo deals with Secret Spot Hot Tubs [p. 218]). If you're lucky, a friendly resident North Island robin will follow your group as you go. Alternatively, even locals are thrilled by the set-up at **Rotorua Ziplines ♥♥** (rotoruaziplines.nz; ✆ **021/026-07441**), which flies across Ōkere Falls. The 2-hour tour includes four epic zips, a swing bridge, and a network of elevated boardwalks with a side of Māori history. It's NZ$169 adults, NZ$119 kids 5 to 12. It can also be booked as a combo with Rotorua Rafting (see "Kayaking," above).

Where to Stay in Rotorua

Fenton Street is "motel mile," with many properties boasting private Jacuzzis in each room. However, not all of them are thermally heated mineral pools: Some are just ordinary old hot water. If you're visiting during the warm summer months, it's also worth noting that some motels may not have air-conditioning, due to the air's high sulfur content.

Arista of Rotorua ♥♥ The secret to standing out as a motel in a sea of motels? It all comes down to service and caring owners. Mike and Annemarie Gallagher bought what was a rundown motel in 2011 and have since transformed it into a truly family-friendly getaway, completed with an outdoor children's play area, covered barbecue area, and unusually spacious guestrooms. Each self-contained apartment-style unit even has its own individual "hot tub." OK, they're actually just giant outdoor circular baths, and you'll be able to hear your neighbors over the jets, but they're still a nice touch.

296 Fenton St. aristaofrotorua.co.nz. ✆ **0800/114-562** in NZ, or 07/349-0300. 16 units. NZ$224–NZ$449 double. **Amenities:** Playground; BBQ area; free Wi-Fi.

Aura ♥♥♥ Best value in town? That would be this friendly place, which is within easy walking distance of many of the city's attractions and restaurants—it's across the road from the brilliant **Wai Ariki Hot Springs & Spa** (p. 216)—and lends its guests free scooters in case they don't want to foot it. Rooms are fairly basic, but have good quality beds, kitchenettes, and private outdoor heated mineral pools. There's also a swimming pool, trampoline, and lawn games to keep the kids busy, and a geothermal steam box set in the ground for guests who want to try cooking the Indigenous way. But what we really love about the Aura is its commitment to sustainability: Its lights run on solar power whenever the sun is shining, water is heated by geothermal energy, food scraps are composted to fertilize the gardens, and a portion of the nightly rate is donated to local land trusts and social organizations. For a more boutique accommodation experience, check out **Ripple Rotorua,** run by the same people a little way out of town.

1078 Whakaue St. aurarotorua.co.nz. ✆ **07/348-0134.** NZ$170–NZ$275 double. 22 units. **Amenities:** Swimming pool; thermal pools; kitchenettes; laundry; BBQ area; bike storage; free Wi-Fi.

Black Swan Lakeside Boutique Hotel ♥♥♥ With just nine rooms, this upmarket little gem is packed with style and personality. It sits right down on the lake surrounded by beautifully tended formal gardens with a conservatory and lots of other lovely spots for relaxation (like a secret grotto). Inside, the classic decor got a full refresh from new owners in 2022. A fulltime chef bakes tasty treats for your room and also whips up delicious dinners on request. And because it's several miles from the geothermal sites, there's no sulfur smell here.

171 Kawaha Point Rd. www.blackswanhotel.co.nz. ✆ **07/346-3602.** 9 units. NZ$656–NZ$800 double. Rates include breakfast; dinner on request. **Amenities:** Croquet and pétanque lawns; Jacuzzi; pool; room service; free Wi-Fi.

On The Point – Lake Rotorua ♥♥♥ Though it's just a 10-minute drive from the center of town, this gated haven feels completely secluded, set at the tip of a peninsula with vast views over the lake and surrounding hills. Though it might be a five-star luxury lodge, it's not adults-only—kids will love the tennis court, fun two-story playhouse, and the sheep, ponies, and donkeys they can feed in the steep fields tumbling down to the lake. (Ask the staff for carrots.) The room decor is perhaps slightly dated, but the on-site restaurant offers fine, intimate candlelit dining, and the service at this women-run place is as exceptional as the location.

214 Kawaha Point Rd. onthepoint.co.nz. ✆ **0800/743-000** in NZ, or 07/350-3232. 7 suites, 2 cottages, 2 apartments. NZ$930–NZ$1,535. **Amenities:** Restaurant; tennis court; gym; library; private hot tubs or spa baths; private laundry facilities; free Wi-Fi.

Regal Palms ♥♥ Your children will never be bored at Regal Palms. With a greater variety of facilities than almost any other hotel in town, there's always a golf ball to putt into a hole here, or a jungle gym to climb. Adults also will be pleased, thanks to the on-site spa and sauna, in-room hot tubs, a well-equipped gym, and a welcoming bar. Add to all this generous apartment-style rooms and friendly service, and you have a real winner.

350 Fenton St. regalpalms.co.nz. ✆ **0800/743-000** in NZ, or 07/350-3232. 44 units. NZ$250–NZ$400 double. **Amenities:** Bar; outdoor pool; sauna; day spa; gym; tennis courts; minigolf; nearby golf course; kids' playgrounds; BBQ areas; free Wi-Fi.

Regent of Rotorua ♥♥ What was originally a run-of-the-mill 1960s motel complex is today one of the chicest lodgings in town, thanks to crisp and very contemporary black-and-white decor. Its small central pool area is an oasis on a hot summer's day, complete with beanbags, lounge chairs, and tables from which to sip cool wine. There's an on-site restaurant, but it's only a short walk to Eat Streat (see "Where to Eat," below). As for the rooms, they feature very good bedding, and come in a range of sizes, from the very compact "Cutie" rooms (best for solo visitors), to sprawling two-bedroom suites.

1191 Pukaki St. regentrotorua.co.nz. ✆ **0508/734-368** in NZ, or 07/348-4079. 35 units. NZ$250–NZ$542 double. **Amenities:** Restaurant; bar; concierge; mini-gym; outdoor pool; thermal indoor pool; free Wi-Fi.

Silver Fern Rotorua ♥♥ You'll get very friendly service and clean, spacious rooms at this quality motel on the main drag. Accommodation ranges from studios to two-bedroom suites. Every room comes with a spa bath or spa pool, and there's also a day spa on site, one that's way more affordable than many others in town.

326 Fenton St. silverfernrotorua.co.nz. ✆ **0800/118-808** in NZ, or 07/346-3849. 25 units. NZ$205–NZ$365 double. Breakfast on request. **Amenities:** Babysitting; bikes; laundry; room service; day spa; EV charging; free Wi-Fi.

Treetops Lodge and Estate ♥♥♥ Treetops has the feel of a large and very luxurious hunting lodge—which is what it is, but much more besides.

The imposing Great Room at the main lodge at Treetops Lodge and Estate.

The region's poshest accommodation, Treetops is also about preserving things: the native creatures that live on the 1,000-hectare (2,470-acre) property, which includes an 800-year-old forest surrounded by an additional 24,300 hectares (60,000 acres) of DOC land, seven trout streams, and four lakes. You don't need to crunch the numbers to realize that this is a pretty private place to stay, although it's just a 30-minute drive from Rotorua. Seeing it from the back of a horse with an experienced guide is a sublime experience, and it will make settling back in your large and stylishly appointed suite even more of a delight. The place is so spacious you drive a golf cart down to the main lodge for dinner cooked by Michelin-star chefs—a very fine experience indeed.

351 Kearoa Rd., RD1, Horohoro. treetops.co.nz. ✆ **07/333-2066.** 14 units. NZ$2,000–NZ$2,600. Rates include dinner & breakfast. Long-stay rates available. **Amenities:** Restaurant; bar/lounge; bike rentals; concierge; room service; watersports equipment rentals; games room; library, day spa; sauna; gym; free Wi-Fi.

Where to Eat in Rotorua

If you're a foodie, you'll find more to tickle your tastebuds in Taupō than in Rotorua—most options here are decent, but not superlative. The obvious go-to is **Eat Streat,** a pedestrian-only strip at the lake end of Tūtānekai Street offering all-weather alfresco dining. With some 12 restaurants and cafes, ranging from burger bars to Indian cuisine to a wine bar, it makes it a bit easier to find consensus on dinner, with plenty of vegetarian, vegan, and gluten-free options. One fave is **Atticus Finch** ♥♥ (atticusfinch.co.nz; ✆ **07/406-0400;** daily noon–2:30pm and 5–10pm), which serves small and large Mediterranean-themed share plates. It's big on cocktails made with fresh herbs and fruit, alongside a good selection of wines and craft beers. To satisfy your sweet tooth, head to **Lady Janes Ice Cream Parlour** ♥, at the far end of the street—though its offerings of classic Kiwi ice cream brands are basically the same as the scoops served at any country corner store, for higher prices.

A block farther down you'll find **The Fainting Goat** ♥♥ 1154 Tūtānekai St. (www.thefaintinggoat.co.nz; ✆ **07/348-8411;** daily noon–late, which in Rotorua means 9pm). It was meant to be a beer-focused bar when it opened after the pandemic, but its food is so good, people keep coming here for dinner instead. It serves up a decent array of gastro-pub share plates like venison carpaccio, pulled-lamb sliders, and salt-and-pepper squid. In summer, the cheer spills out onto the streetside tables, but there aren't many inside, so book ahead or come early.

The owners of the late great Terrace Kitchen have now opened **Parc** (1029 Tutanekai St.), a hole-in-the-wall spot that's a great place to grab a takeaway coffee or real-fruit ice cream before wandering along the lakefront.

If you're here on Thursday, mingle with the locals at the **Rotorua Night Markets** ♥ (facebook.com/rotoruanightmarket), open 4pm to 8pm in Kuirau Park near the thermal footbaths. (Check the Facebook page to make sure of the current location.) It offers a huge range of food truck options as well as locally made gifts and crafts, and live entertainment.

Getting away from the tourist drag (even if just by a few blocks) will reward you with some other solid options. **Urbano** ♥, 289 Fenton St. (urbanobistro.

co.nz; ✆ **07/349-3770;** Mon–Sat 9am–9pm, Sun 9am–3pm), is a modern bistro that does contemporary, unfussy breakfast, brunch, lunch, and dinner in the "motel mile" area of Rotorua.

Ciabatta Cafe and Bakery ♥♥ BAKERY It might be set in the middle of an industrial area, but this locals' secret is just 5 minutes' drive from both town and the Redwoods, and is a great place to stock up on lunch for a day of adventures—there are generously sized meat and salad sandwiches and rolls on the bakery's own bread, plus cronuts, pretzels, and very good quiches. It's also a nice place to eat in, with funky rustic decor and intimate booths. The wall covered in sticky notes from fans of all ages tells its own story!

38 White St., Fenton Park. ciabattabakery.co.nz. ✆ **07/348-3332.** Sandwiches NZ$14–NZ$19. Tues–Fri 8am–3pm, Sat 8am–2pm.

Capers Café + Store ♥♥ CAFE/DELI This award-winning place is a bit of an Aladdin's Cave. It takes its food and coffee very seriously, but it's also a purveyor of delicious local and imported goodies like sauces, chocolates, teas, balsamic vinegars, and dressings, many of which make good presents to take home. It transforms from a nice breakfast and lunch venue (eat in or takeaway) to a great spot for (early) dinner, serving dishes like bang bang prawn poke bowl, pork belly bao buns, and steak breakfast.

1181 Eruera St. capers.co.nz. ✆ **07/348-8818.** Main courses NZ$26–NZ$36. Dinner reservations recommended. Daily 7am–7pm.

Eastwood Cafe ♥♥ CAFE I was heartbroken to learn that Rotorua's Terrace Kitchen, which I considered one of the best spots to eat on the North Island, shuttered during the pandemic. The only thing that made the loss bearable was when I learned Terrace's owners were behind a new cafe located directly across from the Redwoods Forest (p. 211). Selling "pizza, beer, and other stuff," it's the perfect place for a midday refuel after conquering your fear of heights at the Redwoods Treewalk. It's located in the Scion Innovation Hub, giving it borderline corporate vibes, but you can ward those off by sitting outdoors.

End of Titokorangi Dr. eastwood.cafe. ✆ **07/345-5444.** Main courses NZ$18–NZ$32. Daily 8am–3pm (Fri until 8pm).

Fat Dog Café and Bar ♥ CAFE This cafe has been here so long that the original fat dog must have gone to the great kennel in the sky years ago. It's a crazy, colorful, chaotic gathering place for every man and his (fat) dog, and nobody stands on ceremony. Service is very quick, and portions are generous. It serves tasty, fresh, original takes on breakfast standards—like corned beef hash with paprika hollandaise or a Greek-style eggs with halloumi—as well as burgers, pastas, and buddha bowls. The cabinet food is great too—chunky sweet slices and the biggest cheese scones I've ever seen.

1161 Arawa St. www.fatdogcafe.co.nz. ✆ **07/347-7586.** Main courses NZ$29–NZ$33. Daily 7am–3pm-ish.

Poco Tapas and Wine Bar ♥♥ SHARE PLATES This intimate 40-seat wine and tapas bar is hidden on the second floor looking out above Rotorua's main shopping street. Bring some friends, because it's all share plates with a menu that changes seasonally. Dishes tend to incorporate endemic ingredients with Middle Eastern dishes, such as the crispy potatoes and kawakawa oil, roasted *kūmara* (sweet potato) hummus, or harissa prawns. The service, food, and wine list are all impeccable—so much that you might find yourself ordering one more glass of wine than you intended. Take a taxi and you'll thank me later.

1183 Arawa St. poco.nz. ✆ **07/262-6119.** Share plates NZ$12–NZ$28. Tues–Sat 4pm–late.

Regent Room Restaurant and Wine Bar ♥♥ MODERN NEW ZEALAND In keeping with everything else about the boutique **Regent of Rotorua** hotel (see p. 225), the restaurant, which is open to the public, is stylish and sumptuous. That goes for the food as well. Regent Room serves all things fresh and seasonal; the meat courses are particularly good (including smoked duck breast and a trio of lamb), but there are also several inventive plant-based menu options.

1191 Pukaki St. regentrotorua.co.nz. ✆ **07/348-4079.** Main courses NZ$34–NZ$38. Dinner reservations recommended. Daily 6:30am–late.

Sabroso ♥♥♥ LATIN AMERICAN Originally from Venezuela, Sarah Little (alongside her husband and co-owner, John Loeffler) serve up all good things from the South American continent—tacos, chimichanga, chili con carne, Brazilian *moqueca* (a shrimp stew)—and people just can't get enough. One happy customer even told me she runs the Rotorua Marathon each year just so she can eat here! It's got great friendly service, wonderful authentic food, and loads of atmosphere, with vegan options. And yes, you can get sangria, margaritas, and mojitos. Book in advance; it's small and very popular.

1184 Haupapa St. sabroso.co.nz. ✆ **07/349-0591.** Main courses NZ$28–NZ$30. Dinner reservations recommended. Wed–Sat 5–9pm.

Shopping

One of the best places to find traditional Māori arts and crafts is at **Te Puia ♥♥** (tepuia.com; ✆ **07/348-9047**), which has stone, bone, and wood carvings for sale, all made on site. At **Mountain Jade ♥**, 1288 Fenton St. (mountainjade.co.nz; ✆ **07/349-3968**), you can watch master carvers working with greenstone (or *pounamu,* as Māori call it). It's fairly open about the fact that some of their stone has been imported, and the piece you've got your eye on might in fact have been carved in China from Chinese jade, not New Zealand greenstone. Just ask. It's open daily from 9am to 5pm.

En Route to Taupō

It's only 84km (52 miles) to Taupō via SH5 on very good roads. You'll pass one of the three main geothermal reserves—**Orakei Korako Geothermal Park and Cave**—although it's closer to Taupō than Rotorua (see "Geothermal Gems," p. 217). Eight kilometers (5 miles) before you reach Taupō, you'll see the **Wairakei Geothermal Power Station,** which performs the neat trick of turning underground energy into electric power.

TAUPŌ ♥

287km (178 miles) SE of Auckland; 84km (52 miles) S of Rotorua; 155km (96 miles) NW of Napier

Over the last decade, Taupō has become one of the most desirable places on the North Island for Kiwis to live and go on holiday, so it's in growth mode. Although it's not yet a resort-style destination, it's on its way there. In preparation for hosting the Iron Man world championships in 2024, the town's waterfront underwent a massive redevelopment to enhance its biggest asset: great Lake Taupō, the country's largest lake, at the heart of the North Island.

At 46km (28.5 miles) at its longest point, Lake Taupō is impressive not just for its size, but for what lies beneath: A magma chamber is located between 6 and 8km (3¾–5 miles) under its surface. In fact, the lake is actually the caldera of a super volcano, responsible for the most violent volcanic explosion the world has seen in the last 5,000 years. (It's estimated that it spewed ash as high as 50km/31 miles into the atmosphere.) Although it last erupted 1,800 years ago, the volcano remains active today, with volcanic unrest being detected as recently as late 2022. Despite its explosive history, the water is on the frigid side—even in summer, it can sit around 15°C (59°F), except at a few magic spots where thermal streams run into the lake.

It is, however, crystal clear, and kids love swimming in it. You'll also find plenty of other activities catering specifically to young families. And while Rotorua might get most of the attention for being a geothermal wonderland, Taupō has its own geysers, hot springs, and silica terraces to explore. As a result, Taupō's small urban population of 26,000 can double in the summer months, so expect it to be a little crowded during these times and book in advance.

Alternately, look to Lake Taupō's southern shores, where you'll find Tūrangi. Sitting on the banks of the Tongariro River, the little town is famous for its rainbow trout fishing, but it's also a popular base from which to start the Tongariro Alpine Crossing, go skiing on Mount Ruapehu (which is visible across the lake), try out whitewater rafting or horse riding, or base yourself for adventures in the surrounding regions.

Essentials

ARRIVING

Air New Zealand (airnewzealand.co.nz; ✆ **0800/737-000**) flies to Taupō from Auckland, with connections to other destinations. **Great Lake Taxis** (greatlaketaxis.co.nz; ✆ **07/377-8990**) provides a shuttle service, as well as service in and around Taupō.

SH1 and SH5 pass through Taupō. It's 1 hour to Rotorua, 2 hours to Napier, Waitomo, Hamilton, and Tauranga, 3½ hours to Auckland, and about 5½ hours to Wellington. **InterCity** (intercity.co.nz; ✆ **09/583-5780**) buses from all over the North Island arrive and depart daily from the Taupō Visitor Information Center.

GETTING AROUND

Like much of NZ, this is a destination best suited to those self-driving. Roads in the area are very good, but this part of the world gets pretty cold in winter, so beware of ice. Also watch out for logging trucks.

VISITOR INFORMATION

Go to lovetaupo.com, the website for **Destination Great Lake Taupō,** the district's tourism organization. There is no local isite, but the **Taupō Visitor Information Centre** at 30 Tongariro St. (✆ **07/376-0027**) is open weekdays from 9am to 4:30pm and on weekends from 10am to 1pm. The **Tūrangi Visitor Information Centre** at Ngawaka Place (✆ **07/386-8999**) is open weekdays from 10am to 4pm and Saturday from 10am to 1pm.

SPECIAL EVENTS

Taupō is known for its athletic events, including **Ironman New Zealand** and **IronMāori.** But if you're just a regularman or regularwoman (rather than one made of metal) you might be more interested in the **Taupō Winter Festival** (taupowinterfestival.co.nz) in July, featuring music and theater performances, roller discos and ice rinks (a novelty on this side of the world)—or, in the last weekend of October, the **Graffiato Festival** (taupostreetart.com), New Zealand's longest running street-art festival, which has transformed the town's laneways with 100-plus giant, vibrant works of art.

Exploring Taupō

Taupō sits at the northeastern tip of the lake, where the Waikato River, New Zealand's longest, flows out of the lake's Tapuaeharuru Bay. **Tongariro Street** is the main drag. Perpendicular to that are **Te Heuheu** and **Horomātangi streets,** two of several that form the main shopping area. Tongariro Street runs into **Lake Terrace,** which runs around the lake and where most of the motels are situated.

Most visitors come to Taupō for outdoor adventures on and around the lake, but there are a few cultural attractions in town. The **Taupō Museum** ♥, 4 Story Place (taupodc.govt.nz; ✆ **07/376-0414**), blends the story of settlement here with the things that make this place what it is: namely, volcanic activity and the lake, which are intertwined, given that one was formed by the other. Add in fishing, logging, and Kiwis on holiday and you've got yourself a museum. One unique museum feature is a permanent exhibit of the **Ora Garden of Wellbeing,** a New Zealand garden based on Māori spiritual beliefs that

Some of the beautiful pieces at Lava Glass.

Taupō & the Ruapehu Region

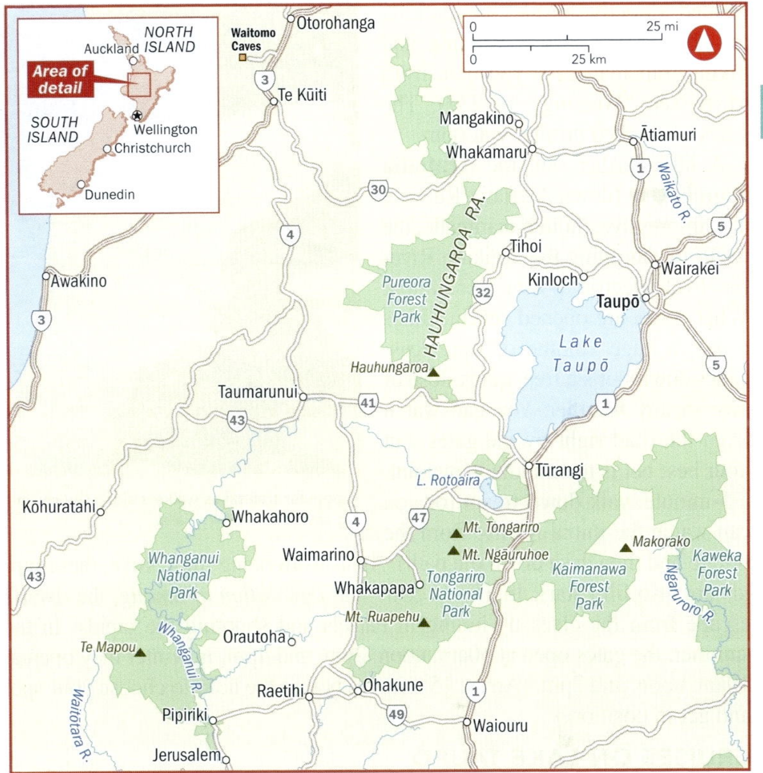

once won a gold medal at the Chelsea Flower Show in the U.K. Museum admission is NZ$6 (free for ages 17 and under); it's open daily 10am to 4:30pm.

Yet another New Zealand Garden of Distinction is located a short drive north of town at **Lava Glass ♥**, 165 SH5 (lavaglass.com; ✆ **07/374-8400**), the world's first (and potentially only) carbon-neutral glassblowing studio. Just beyond the gallery, you'll find award-winning glassblower Lynden Over at work on designs that mimic the colors of local landscapes, including Huka Falls and the Tongariro Alpine Crossing. Around 600 of his large-scale creations can also be found in the **Sculpture Garden,** including a water feature, giant tulips, and a rainbow. To see both the garden and Lynden's studio costs NZ$20, or NZ$70 for a family.

At the top of the hill about 1.6km (1 mile) north of Taupō, **Huka Falls ♥♥** is an impressive sight, with 22,000 liters (nearly 9,000 gal.) of water squeezing through a narrow chasm before crashing 20m (65 ft.) into a super-turbo washing machine of churning mayhem. (*Huka* is the Māori word for "foam.") It's not a huge drop—it's more of a horizontal waterfall than a vertical one—but the power is incredible. You don't have to walk far—the falls are located directly beside the parking lot—but there's also a walking and biking trail that leads you here from town (see "Walking," p. 237). The gates are locked promptly at 6pm.

A popular trail takes walkers along the churning cascades of Huka Falls.

A little farther out, the **Aratiatia Rapids ♥♥** (down Aratiatia Rd.) are also impressive, though manmade, the result of damming the Waikato River for hydroelectric power generation. When gates are opened several times a day, a huge volume of water cascades down—it's a free, quick dose of awe in any weather. You can watch from the road right by the gates, but your best bet is the middle viewpoint, a 5-minute walk downstream (or you can watch the initial release from the bridge and then dash down the path). Apart from being impressive, these rapids are also film stars. In *The Hobbit: The Desolation of Smaug*, the dwarfs escape from the elves by hiding in barrels and shooting the rapids. In the summer, the gates open at 10am, noon, 2pm, and 4pm; in winter they open at 10am, noon, and 2pm. (Arrive 15 minutes before the hour to choose your spot and get in position.)

CRUISES ON LAKE TAUPŌ

Taupō is New Zealand's biggest lake by a large margin: It's about the size of Chicago. If you want to have a closer look, a number of operators will get you out on the water. All operators offer a similar experience, including a visit to the **Māori rock carvings ♥♥**. Accessible only by boat, these were carved in the late 1970s by Matahi Brightwell (who is also credited with revitalizing the sport of *waka ama,* or outrigger canoe racing), but even though they're not ancient, they are impressive. (See if you can spot the numerous small carvings, including one that is reputedly a naked depiction of one of the artist's girlfriends.) Ultimately, your choice of operator depends on how much time you have and how you want to travel—yacht, motorboat, or vintage steamboat. All the following trips leave from **Taupō Marina,** typically with morning, afternoon, and evening departures available. They may be booked at the visitor center or harbor office.

Chris Jolly Outdoors (chrisjolly.co.nz; ✆ **07/378-0623**) and **Ernest Kemp Cruises** (ernestkemp.co.nz; ✆ **07/378-9222**) both offer 90-minute express trips if you're pressed for time; Chris Jolly runs five trips per day on a standard motor launch costing NZ$59 for adults, NZ$20 for ages 5 to 18; Ernest Kemp's take place on a replica steamboat at 12:30pm for NZ$50 per adult and

NZ$15 kids—though for NZ$5 more you can do a 2-hour trip (10:30am or 2:30pm). In summer Kemp also runs an evening cocktail cruise at 4:30pm for the same price (though you'll have to purchase your own cocktails from the onboard bar).

> **Moon Walk**
>
> The **Craters of the Moon,** off SH1 north of Taupō (cratersofthemoon.co.nz), is a geothermal area run by a local trust, which means it's super affordable (NZ$10 adults, NZ$5 children; daily 9:30am–5pm). The 45-minute walk will take you along boardwalks through a strange and constantly changing landscape that only appeared in the 1950s following the opening of a geothermal power station.

If you want to feel the wind in your hair, hop aboard a beautiful old yacht (sail-powered but with an electric engine) with **Sail Barbary** ♥ (sailbarbary.com; ✆ **07/378-5879**). These tours last 2½ hours and cost NZ$59 adults, NZ$29 infant to age 15; evening tours cost slightly more but include pizza and a drink. Swimming is encouraged! **Taupō Sailing Adventures** (tauposailingadventures.co.nz; ✆ **022/189-1847**) offers similar trips on either a luxury catamaran or sloop.

GETTING INTO HOT WATER: SPAS

Like Rotorua, Taupō is a great place to steep your body in the natural mineral waters that flow out of the ground. **Taupō DeBretts Hot Springs** ♥♥, Napier/Taupō Road, SH5 (taupodebretts.co.nz; ✆ **07/378-8559**), in the native-bush-filled, tropical-feeling Onekeneke Thermal Valley, has been helping Kiwis (and others) to relax for more than 120 years. The water here is thought to have almost magical properties, providing therapeutic relief for muscular, bone, and skin ailments. The complex has three thermal outdoor pools, 12 private pools, a children's warm-water playground, and two tube waterslides, as well as a barbecue and picnic area and a day spa. Admission is NZ$24 for

Boat trips on huge Lake Taupō, from kayaks to steamboats, generally visit the intriguing rock carvings by Māori artist Matahi Brightwell.

adults, NZ$13 for children ages 4 to 12; NZ$7 for the waterslides. (***Top tip:*** If you visit during the day, they'll give you a ticket to return for free in the evening.) The complex is open daily from 8:30am to 8:30pm.

Little ones are not welcome in the pools at **Wairakei Terraces and Thermal Health Spa** ♥ (wairakeiterraces.co.nz; ✆ **07/378-0913**), which for locals and visitors alike tends to be a drawcard. The amenities are basic (one large changing room for both genders, one toilet stall, and one shower), but the three pools themselves (which range in temperature from 36°–40°C [97°–104°F]) are well-maintained and picturesque, with a hot waterfall. They're NZ$27 for ages 14 and up. Children, however, are welcome on Wairakei's Terrace Walk, which leads through native bush past a manmade silica terrace and geyser. It only costs NZ$15 adults and NZ$7.50 for kids, but if you're headed onwards to Rotorua, save your money for the real deal.

Just north of town, **Otumuheke Stream Spa Thermal Park** ♥♥♥ is a totally free public access area, where a small hot stream runs into the clear, cool waters of the Waikato River. Although the park received a significant upgrade a few years ago (including the addition of changing rooms, lockers, toilets, and a coffee kiosk—but sadly, still no showers), it's in an otherwise

KID magnets

Rainy day? **The Landing** ♥♥♥ (thelanding.co.nz; ✆ **07/378-5633**), on the southern outskirts of town at 650 Lake Terrace, has entertainment for everyone: a trampoline park, soft play areas for younger children, a ninja warrior course, arcade, bowling alley, virtual reality center, gastropub, cafe, garden bar, and a sweet shop selling boozy shakes and freak (loaded) fries. (There's even a laundromat on-site, so you can take care of the washing while your kids play.) The highlight, though, is an outdoor minigolf course built to resemble the Lake Taupō region, complete with visitor information signs.

As the world's only geothermally heated prawn-breeding park in the world, **Huka Prawn Park** ♥ (hukaprawnpark.co.nz; ✆ **07/374-8474**) may sound like an esoteric attraction, but kids love it, including the 30-minute guided tour through the hatchery, where they can hand-feed baby prawns. If crustaceans aren't your kids' thing, there are also stand-up paddleboards, aqua trikes, pedal boats (thankfully shaped like swans, not prawns), and water cannons to play on. All-day passes cost NZ$27.50 for adults, NZ$15 for kids 5 to 15; and NZ$75 for a family of up to seven, which includes the tour. It's open daily from 10am to 3pm. A major redevelopment was taking place as we went to press, so check the website or at the Visitor Information Center for the latest.

Last but not least is **Timberline Racing Huskies** ♥♥, 36 Kilkenny Way, northeast of town in Broadlands (timberlineracinghuskies.co.nz; ✆ **021/705-250**). Snow may not be plentiful in these parts, but owners Steve and Taniya Coxhead will demonstrate how they race their Siberian Huskies in NZ during a 2-hour and Q&A tour of their kennel (NZ$45 adults, NZ$35 children and students 5 and up, NZ$150 families). Cuddles and photos with the pups are par for the course, but Steve and Taniya are also eager to explain the more technical aspects of racing and rearing these dogs.

Along with thermal pools, Taupō DeBretts Hot Springs (p. 233) has added fun water features for kids, reflecting Taupō's growing popularity as a family holiday destination.

completely natural setting. Best of all, it's an easy 5-minute walk from the parking lot to the thermal spot. The downside to its easy accessibility is that it can get crowded, especially during the holiday season, so get here early in the morning or later in the evening. As with all natural mineral pools, don't put your head under—in rare cases, dangerous amoebae in unchlorinated thermal water can be picked up through the nose. There's also **a hot-water beach** on the edge of Lake Taupō, between Napier Road and Waipahīhī Terrace, where another hot stream trickles into the lake.

Outdoor Pursuits

BUNGY JUMPING You don't even have to jump to be impressed by the scenery that surrounds the 47m (154-ft.) bungy platform cantilevered out over the Waikato River at **AJ Hackett Taupō Bungy and Swing** ♥♥ (bungy.co.nz; ✆ **0800/888-408**). You'll pay from NZ$275 for adults and NZ$235 for kids ages 10 to 14 (they must weigh at least 35kg/77 lb.). On-site is also the North Island's only bungy swing (NZ$240 adults, NZ$200 ages 10–14). The company offers free pickup from your hotel. It's open daily 9am to 4pm.

CLIMBING Try something a bit different at **Rock n Ropes** ♥, Karetoto Road, Wairakei Park (rocknropes.co.nz; ✆ **0800/244-508** in NZ), where you can hone your skills at rope walking, trapezing, rock climbing, and assorted other airborne fun. Courtesy transport to the site is available. Adventures here are reasonably priced from NZ$50 to NZ$80. It's open daily; advance bookings are required.

FLIGHTSEEING If you want to go up in a chopper to see the Māori Rock Carvings, Huka Falls, or even Tongariro National Park, try **Chopperworx** ♥ (chopperworx.co.nz; ✆ **07/377-0139**). Flights start from NZ$160 per person.

GOLF Frequently voted NZ's number one course, **Wairakei Golf and Sanctuary** ♥♥♥, 527 Wairakei Dr. (wairakeigolfcourse.co.nz; ✆ **07/374-8152**), is

The Angler's Eldorado

If catching a trout floats your boat, Lake Taupō—and especially Tūrangi (known as the trout fishing capital of NZ)—is the place to be. The first baby trout were released into this lake more than 100 years ago. In the 1920s, U.S. author Zane Grey visited the Tongariro River (the most important spawning river in the region) and raved about it in his book *Tales of the Angler's Eldorado, New Zealand.* These days you need a Taupō-issued fishing license for the lake and all its tributaries, which is good for a day or a full season. The minimum legal size is 35cm (16 in.), and the daily limit is six fish. The best river fishing is during the winter spawning runs (June–Sept), but lake fishing is good all year. There are dozens of fishing guides and charter operators, with widely varying prices; inquire at the visitor center for recommendations.

a championship course inside its own predator-free wildlife sanctuary. Greens fees are NZ$375 for international affiliated members, and you'll need to book in advance. **The Kinloch Club ♥♥**, 261 Kinloch Rd. (thekinlochclub.com; ✆ **07/377-8482**), is another one of New Zealand's top courses, and greens fees are an even more staggering NZ$450 in the winter and NZ$850 in the summer. For something more affordable, visit the **Taupō Golf Club ♥**, 32 Centennial Dr. (taupogolf.co.nz; ✆ **07/378-6933**), one of the very few New Zealand clubs to have two 18-hole courses: Choose between the Centennial (NZ$110) or the Tauhara (NZ$80) courses.

HORSEBACK RIDING After years living in cities, Sammii and John Ellis of **Korohe Horse Treks ♥♥**, 29 Kepa Rd., RD2 Tūrangi (explorelaketaupo.com; ✆ **022/167-2112**), returned home to their ancestral lands to raise their young family and to share their love of horseback riding (John won his first rodeo at 3 years old.) This is not your typical trail ride. Instead, the tour is tailored to your riding experience and confidence, and your guide will attentively coach you throughout. Tours start at NZ$80 and are for all ages. If you choose the "forest and river" trip, you'll have the opportunity to do multiple river crossings in the beautiful, chilly Waimarino, even if you're not an experienced rider. Be sure to ask John how he tames and trains wild horses—on the 3-hour rides you may even spot some.

JETBOATING Jetboats operate in a couple of spots on the Waikato River. **Hukafalls Jet ♥♥♥**, Wairakei Tourist Park (hukafallsjet.co.nz; ✆ **07/374-8572**), streaks around the base of the Huka Falls, doing 360-degree spins. It's the only company working the falls. A 30-minute ride is NZ$149 for adults and NZ$99 for kids under 15. **Rapids Jet,** Nga Awa Purua Rd., off Rapids Rd. (rapidsjet.com; ✆ **0800/727-437** in NZ, or 07/374-8066), runs upstream in the Nga Awa Purua rapids (just down from the famed Aratiatia Rapids); 35 minutes is NZ$155 for adults and NZ$89 for kids 5 to 15. Both companies offer combo deals with other excursions.

KAYAKING **Canoe and Kayak ♥** (canoeandkayak.co.nz; ✆ **0800/529-256** in NZ, or 07/378-1003) will guide you more gently down the Waikato. Its

2-hour tour includes a swim in a hot spring (NZ$90 adults, NZ$54 children aged 4–12). It also offers a 3-hour Māori carvings tour on the lake for NZ$135 per person. **Taupō Kayaking Adventures ♥**, Acacia Bay Road (tka.co.nz; ✆ **027/480-1231**), has a slightly larger selection of tours, with trips on the river costing NZ$95 for adults, NZ$75 for ages 17 and under, and paddles out to the rock carvings costing NZ$145 adults, NZ$125 children. It even has motorized kayaks available, making this an accessible activity. Both also offer canoe and kayak rentals.

MOUNTAIN BIKING Just across from **Craters Mountain Bike Park** (which has 50km of mainly grade 2 and 3 trails), you'll find **FourB ♥♥**, 413 Huka Falls Rd. (fourb.nz; ✆ **07/374-8154**), a one-stop shop for everything cycling related, including freedom bike hire, guided tours, and shuttle services. Suitable for confident riders, their 3-hour **Huka River Trail Guided E-Bike Tour ♥** takes you on grade 2–3 gravel tracks past Huka Falls and to some local secret geothermal spots, with commentary on the area's history and geology along the way. It costs NZ$299. If you're new to riding or prefer concrete and few hills, go for the guided Coffee and Caldera tour (NZ$349). If there's a group of you, ask about the Brews and Views trip—for NZ$289 you'll ride 19km to panorama spots overlooking the lake, tour the Lakeman Brewery, then ride back to town for dinner and a beer-tasting paddle at the brewery's restaurant **Jimmy Coops** (see p. 243). For information on cycling trails, go to biketaupo.org.nz.

SKYDIVING Taupō is one of the handful of places in the country where you can throw yourself out of a plane. If you're into that sort of thing, contact **Taupō Tandem Skydiving ♥** (taupotandemskydiving.com; ✆ **07/377-0428**). The selling point of skydiving here, rather than elsewhere, is the stability of the weather. (At Franz Josef, for example, weather frequently shuts flights down.) It's the best-priced skydive in NZ, and you'll also get epic views of the lake and surrounding volcanic landscape. You can choose to jump from 9,000 ft. (NZ$279), 12,000 ft. (NZ$329), or 15,000 ft. (NZ$379).

WALKING There are countless walks in the area, but the most popular for visitors is the 3km (2-mile) **Huka Falls Walk** from Spa Park in Taupō north

Hole-in-One Bonanza

Here's something you can try if you've spent all your money on greens fees: Win dinner or your hotel accommodations at the **Lake Taupō Hole in One Challenge** (holein1.co.nz; ✆ **07/378-8117**), now owned by local iwi Ngāti Tūwharetoa and spruced up in 2025. Whack your golf ball 102m (335 ft.) over the water, get it into the tiny hole in the middle of a floating pontoon on the lake, and you'll win the top prize: NZ$10,000. Apparently, there's one winner every 2 weeks, scoring adventure packages, products, or that 10 grand. It costs NZ$3 per ball, NZ$25 for 15 balls, NZ$35 for 30 balls, or NZ$50 for 50 balls. It's open daily from 9am to 5pm, though in summer may open late into the evening; check the website for details.

along the riverbank to the waterfall. If you continue on to Aratiatia Rapids, it will take another 2 hours. Another lovely, and much quieter, option is the forested hiking trail that encircles gorgeous **Lake Rotopounamu.** The 5km (3-mile) loop takes about 2 hours to complete—but the start of the trail is an hour's drive from Taupō, much closer to Tūrangi.

WHITE-WATER RAFTING If you've been in NZ long enough, you've no doubt heard about the country's efforts to eradicate invasive species and predators, in an effort to save the country's indigenous birdlife. However, many traplines and areas are difficult to access, including those along the Tongariro River. That's why **Tongariro River Rafting ♥♥♥**, 95 Atirau Rd., Tūrangi (trr.co.nz; ✆ **0800/101-024** in NZ, or 07/386-6409), protects pairs of endangered *whio* (blue ducks) that breed along the river. Not just your average whitewater rafting journey, on the one-of-a-kind Blue Duck Experience, you'll not only hit grade 3 rapids, you'll also help check and set traplines. The tour departs in the morning, and costs NZ$219 for ages 11 and up. Afternoon departures are available on the company's standard White Water Rafting excursions (NZ$199 adults, NZ$174 kids 11–16).

Where to Stay Around Taupō

EXPENSIVE

Belle vue Boutique Lodge ♥♥ The owners of Belle vue come from a background in weddings—and it shows. No details have been forgotten, and everything seems geared to romance, even if it's subtle. The house is all French doors, crown moldings, and chandeliers, with views out onto Acacia Bay. Although this is a bed-and-breakfast by definition, it's run more like a boutique lodge—guests have their own private lounge area, as well as access to a game room complete with a pool table.

39 Mapara Rd., Acacia Bay. bellevueboutiquelodge.co.nz. ✆ **07/377-6259.** 4 units. NZ$385–NZ$440 double. Rates include continental breakfast. **Amenities:** Dinner available on request; game room; free Wi-Fi.

Hilton Lake Taupō ♥♥ Perched on a hill above the Onekeneke Thermal Valley, the resort-style Hilton started life in 1889 as the Terraces Hotel. Housed within a stunning historic building, it has older and newer sections, but rooms are all large with views of the lake or the geothermal area. The new suites and fully self-contained apartments, with kitchens, will be especially prized by those traveling with kids. They have private terraces or balconies, which are perfect for gazing out over the lake.

80–100 Napier Rd. hilton.com/laketaupo. ✆ **07/378-7080.** 113 units. NZ$287–NZ$1,330. Free parking. **Amenities:** Restaurant; bar; concierge; outdoor geothermally heated pool; children's pool; sauna; geothermally heated Jacuzzi, gym; tennis court; room service; free Wi-Fi.

Huka Lodge ♥♥♥ Reopened in 2025 after a year-long centenary refit, Huka Lodge has come a long way from its origins in 1924 as a rustic fishing camp on the Waikato River. Sure, you can still fish here, but now, instead of just soaking in thigh-high river waters, you'll be able to soak in the resplendent

Soothing neutrals, quality furnishings, and top-notch service make the junior suites at Huka Lodge tremendously popular. Book well in advance.

luxury of one of the most awarded resorts in New Zealand. Where canvas fishing tents once stood, junior lodge suites have plush beds, deep soaker tubs, and floor-to-ceiling windows overlooking the river. It also has two "cottages"—though they are more like mansions at over 3,500 square feet. The lodge is set on 7 hectares (17 acres) of immaculate private land and the staff are real hospitality experts: They remember your name and drink preferences, making sure that you'll also remember the exemplary service long after you've left.

271 Huka Falls Rd. hukalodge.co.nz. ✆ **07/378-5791.** 20 suites, 2 cottages. NZ$3,800–NZ$19,000. Rates include airport transfers, breakfast, pre-dinner drinks, and dinner. 2-night min. stay (3 nights peak season.) **Amenities:** Dining room; bar; babysitting; free bike use; concierge; library; massage; outdoor pool; room service; tennis court; pétanque; free Wi-Fi.

Poronui ♥♥♥ This is primarily a luxury hunting and fishing lodge, so best avoid if you're not keen on killing things (although it pays to remember that most creatures legally killed for sport in this country are introduced pests). It's a bit like Huka Lodge (see above) but more remote and on a smaller scale, with a timber-ceilinged lodge for main meals (which may include game or fish you've caught yourself) and a roaring fire to relax by. There's even a dedicated fly-tying bench for anglers. It's set on 6,475 hectares (16,000 acres) of wilderness. Hunting and fishing expeditions can be arranged, or you might choose to just go walking in the native bush or take a horse trek. You'll have three accommodations options at ascending price points: the lodge cabins, luxury riverside camping at Safari Camp, or the elegant Blake House. Rates are significantly cheaper outside the summer peak.

Taharua Rd. poronui.com. ✆ **07/374-2080.** 7 cabins; Blake House; 2 luxury tents. Lodge rooms NZ$1,400–NZ$3,000; Blake House NZ$3,895–NZ$11,215 double (w/ or w/o private chef); Safari Camp NZ$1,500 for 1–2 people, NZ$2,000 for 3–4. Lodge rates include all meals. **Amenities:** Dining room; bar; massage and spa treatments; library; room service; free Wi-Fi.

The Telephone Exchange ♥♥ On a working dairy farm 25 minutes north of Taupō, you'll find this lovingly restored 1950s telephone exchange building, set under a cluster of eucalyptus trees in a perfectly pastoral setting. It has a separate kitchen (no stove though; all cooking must be done on the outdoor gas burner or barbecue) and bathroom hut, as well as an outdoor bathtub for one. Unlike some of Canopy Camping's more glamorous properties, this one puts the "camp" back in "glamping," mainly owing to the fact that there's no electricity. But what's romance if it isn't relying on the stars and candles to light up the night?

1051 Tirohanga Rd., Tirohanga. canopycamping.co.nz. ✆ **021/605-702.** 1 unit. NZ$260–NZ$280. 2-night min. stay. **Amenities:** BBQ; outdoor bathtub.

MODERATE

Lake Taupō Holiday Resort ♥♥♥ As I've mentioned elsewhere in this guide, campgrounds (known here are holiday parks), are an option even for non-campers, as they typically offer private accommodation and even resort-like facilities. The family-run Lake Taupō Holiday Resort takes this concept up three notches. It's the first place in the country to have a swim-up bar, but its heated outdoor pool also has a swim-in cave area, complete with fiber-optic lighting and wētās made by Wētā Workshop. Many amenities aside, there's a range of appealing, comfy rooms for those not traveling by RV nor willing to tent. Needless to say, it can get packed during school holidays, when the resort's population can swell to 1,000. But the rest of the year? Your whole family will think it's heaven on earth.

41 Centennial Dr. laketauporesort.co.nz. ✆ **0800/332-121** in NZ or 07/378-6860. Powered sites NZ$90; self-contained studios, cabins and luxury villas NZ$445–NZ$1,378. **Amenities:** 2 pools; bar; BBQs; laundry; playground; mini-golf; tennis courts; basketball courts; volleyball court; kitchen; games room; free Wi-Fi.

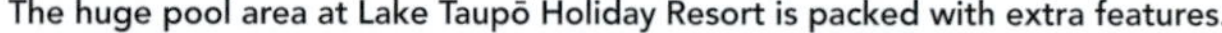
The huge pool area at Lake Taupō Holiday Resort is packed with extra features.

The Reef Resort ♥♥ One of the few properties located directly on the lake's edge (there's no road between the hotel and access to the lake, just a bike path), the Reef Resort has more going for it than just location. The staff are genuinely interested in ensuring you enjoy your stay, the pool area (which includes a geothermally heated hot pool) is pristine, and the rooms have spa baths, balconies or patios, and well-equipped kitchen facilities.

219 Lake Terr. reefresort.co.nz. ✆ **0800/733-378** in NZ or 07/378-5115. NZ$214–NZ$475 double. **Amenities:** Outdoor pool; hot pool; cruiser bikes for hire; guest laundry; BBQs; free Wi-Fi.

The Suncourt Hotel and Conference Centre ♥ You'll find decent rooms with cool wallpaper here, if not the comfiest beds, and a choice of room size from studios to three-bedroom apartments. Where this conference hotel stands out, though, is its location—the views from (most) beds look out across the lake to the snow-capped peaks of Tongariro National Park; the town's Sunday market is a stone's throw away; and most importantly, the hotel's new restaurant, **Lionel's ♥♥♥**, is one of Taupō's best (see p. 244). My advice? Go there for dinner *and* breakfast (not included in the room rate).

14 Northcroft St. suncourt.nz. ✆ **07/378-8265.** NZ$232–NZ$500. 52 units **Amenities:** Restaurant; outdoor pool; hot pool; playground; guest laundry; free Wi-Fi.

INEXPENSIVE

It seems that Taupō is where motels go to breed. With dozens available, choosing the right one can be hard. We like waterfront **Le Chalet Suisse ♥♥**, 3 Titiraupenga St. (lechaletsuisse.co.nz; ✆ **0800/178-378** in NZ), which has clean, roomy one- and two-bedroom apartments and is very handy to the main cafe and restaurant strip. Rates are from NZ$192 per night. Also recommended: the family-owned and -operated **Acapulco Motor Inn ♥**, 19 Rifle Rd. (acapulcotaupo.co.nz; ✆ **07/378-7174**), which offers roughly the same with fully self-contained units. It's located within walking distance to the lakefront and the downtown area. Rates run from NZ$159.

On the hostel front, there are clean, friendly, and hot tub–equipped backpacker accommodations at **Haka Lodge Taupō ♥♥**, 56 Kaimanawa St. (hakalodges.com/taupo; ✆ **07/377-0068**). Dorms start at NZ$36 and private rooms at NZ$56. At **Finlay Jacks Backpackers ♥♥**, 20 Taniwha St. (finlayjacks.co.nz; ✆ **07/378-9292**), you'll find cute, cozy timber pods (handmade by the owner) from NZ$40, private rooms from NZ$110, and welcoming communal areas with weekly music, movie, or "beading" nights.

Where to Stay Around Tūrangi

As a fishing destination, Tūrangi is primarily known for its fishing lodges.

Creel Lodge ♥♥ It's clear to see why these very affordable, self-contained units are a favorite for returning anglers, year-after-year. Decorated in the style of fishing lodges, each of the cottages is named after a fishing lure. There's an area for barbecuing, a fish tackle rental shop next door, and an exceptional on-site cafe that is a local secret. Oh, and the river is right out back, meaning you don't even have to drive anywhere.

183 Taupahi Rd. creel.co.nz. ✆ **07/386-8081.** 19 units. NZ$160–NZ$200. **Amenities:** BBQs; free Wi-Fi.

Accommodations at The Quarters have a laid-back, beachy vibe.

The Quarters ♥♥♥ There are no fish in sight here, just extremely comfortable apartments and studios, beautifully furnished in restful beachy tones—a luxury feel at a surprisingly affordable price. The lighting is lovely, the full kitchen has everything you'd want, and if you've been on the road a while, this place is like landing at home.

15 Taupahi Rd. thequarters.nz. ✆ **021/0826-6306.** 6 studios, 3 apartments, 1 cottage, 1 lodge sleeping 8–10. Studios NZ$112–NZ$245, lodge from NZ$450. **Amenities:** Laundry; free Wi-Fi.

River Birches ♥♥♥ This wonderfully serene luxury lodge is tucked away on the banks of the Tongariro River in Tūrangi, at the southern end of Lake Taupō. The fly-fisher in your party will love being in Trout Fishing Central (there's a webcam that spies on the fish to find the best spots!), but it's a perfect haven even if you have no interest in standing up to your waist in cold water. There are three suites in the main lodge and a separate three-bedroom

The main lodge at River Birches opens onto the Tongariro River, a hotspot for trout fishing, though it has plenty of charms for non-anglers as well.

cottage, plus cedar hot tubs and beautiful gardens to wander about in. Breakfast is a feast. Shuttle service is available to the Tongariro Alpine Crossing.

19 Koura St. riverbirches.co.nz. ✆ **0800/102-025** in NZ, or 07/386-0445. 3 suites, 1 cottage. Suites NZ$810–NZ$1,100, cottage from NZ$1,310. Rates include breakfast. **Amenities:** Guest lounge; hot tub; gym; DVD library; free Wi-Fi.

Where to Eat Around Taupō

TAUPŌ

Taupō is a foodie capital, and you'll be spoilt for choice with the many incredible fine-dining options around here. But if you've come to the region hoping to eat some of its famed brown or rainbow trout, you'll be disappointed to learn that it's illegal to sell your catch. You can hook and eat it yourself, but it won't turn up on restaurant menus.

Fortify yourself for the day with a flavorsome breakfast at **Replete Café and Store ♥♥**, 45 Heuheu St. (replete.co.nz; ✆ **07/377-3011;** Tues–Thurs 8am–4pm). This much-loved local institution sells an eclectic collection of homewares, and its deli cabinets are full of tasty things to take home. Full breakfast and lunch menus are also available. Don't be intimidated if there's a line: It moves quickly.

The **Cozy Corner ♥**, Shop 15, 19 Tamamutu St. (thecozycornertaupo.com; ✆ **07/377-1233**), has won a swag of awards for its social impact and sustainability, and has an expansive menu (including 26 kinds of tea and every alternative milk imaginable) that caters to both the health-conscious and those looking for comfort food. Think dairy-free coconut porridge or gluten-free banana bread, but also big breakfasts complete with streaky bacon. It's open for breakfast and lunch.

For a burger and a brew, head to **Jimmy Coops ♥♥**, 10 Roberts St. (jimmy coops.co.nz; ✆ **07/5950-8534**). Both beef and beer come from the owners' nearby Lakeman Farms and Brewery—where the cows eat the grain by-products from the beer-making. For NZ$16, you can taste four different Lakeman craft beers while looking over the lake—and the burgers are great too.

Or you could while away an entire sunny afternoon at the **Two Mile Bay Sailing Club ♥**, 331 Lake Terrace (2miletaupo.com; ✆ **027/588-6588**). The menu is limited, with a couple of brunch options and good wood-fired pizza, but the location and vibes are top-notch. It sits right out over the lake, and has the feel of an Italian beach club, with Peroni on tap; kayaks, paddleboards, and tiny sailing boats are available for hire in summer; and there's live music every Thursday, Friday, and Sunday.

The Bistro ♥♥♥ MODERN NEW ZEALAND This restaurant is owned by a dynamic chef named Jude Messenger, who runs a tight ship and has six kids, so he knows a thing or two about hard work. It's all worth it: The Bistro is continually ranked as one of the top restaurants in Taupō and was awarded a prestigious two hats by Cuisine's Good Food Guide in 2025. Messenger uses a wealth of New Zealand ingredients like Waikanae crab, Hawke's Bay

Sweet as...

Thanks to all the honey production, mead is taking off in a big way in NZ. One of the foremost producers is apiarist Jay Bennett, who runs **Beehave Craft Meadery** ♥♥, 116 Spa Rd. (beehave.nz). It has its own tasting room, where you can sample his award-winning creations, including the best-selling hopped and lemon-and-ginger varieties. A non-alcoholic version is also on offer. Tastings are free, with plans underway for tours of the production facility. For even more mead tastings, **Huka Honey Hive** ♥ (hukahoneyhive.com; ✆ **07/374-8553**) has the country's largest variety. It also carries the widest range of artisan honey in New Zealand—predominantly from multi-generational beekeepers and family-owned businesses—alongside mānuka honey skin and healthcare products. There's a kid-focused play area, so they can stay occupied coloring or watching busy bees in a glass-fronted hive, while you sample the mead and honey beer.

fish, and Taupō sirloin to create wonderful, reasonably priced food in a relaxed setting.

17 Tamamutu St. thebistro.co.nz. ✆ **07/377-3111.** Main courses NZ$40–NZ$49. Reservations recommended. Thurs–Mon 5–9pm.

The Brantry Restaurant ♥♥♥ MODERN NEW ZEALAND This fine-dining favorite hides its charms behind the rather uninspiring facade of a 1950s two-story house. But fans return here again and again for its excellent food, which embraces the trend towards sustainable and indigenous ingredients. The menu changes seasonally, but you can expect dishes such as beef carpaccio with *kawakawa* (a local herb), lamb loin with feta cheese from Clevedon, and chocolate mousse with *harakeke* (native flax) crumb. As at Embra (below), diners have to eat a minimum of three courses (for a very reasonable NZ$85), though it's not a set menu—you'll have about four entrees, four mains, and four desserts to choose from. There's outdoor dining during the warm months and an indoor fireplace during the cooler ones.

45 Rifle Range Rd. brantryeatery.co.nz. ✆ **07/378-0484.** 3 courses NZ$85. Reservations recommended. Tues–Sun 5:30–8:30pm.

Embra ♥♥♥ MODERN NEW ZEALAND Also with two hats, and a "best regional restaurant in NZ" gong, this intimate place opened in 2022 when Phill and Nora Blackburne returned to Phill's hometown after running successful restaurants in Edinburgh (or "Embra"). The prix fixe menu changes frequently, but features locally grown food artistically prepared with French and British techniques—like smoked kingfish kedgeree, or NZ Alpine salmon tart. Even the bread is spectacular.

97A Kaimanawa St. embra.nz. ✆ **07/929-8633.** 3-course meal NZ$105, 5-course meal NZ$135. Reservations recommended. Tues–Sat 5:30–11pm.

Lionel's ♥♥♥ MEDITERRANEAN Whether you come for breakfast, lunch, or dinner, the food at this newly reinvented bar and bistro is divine.

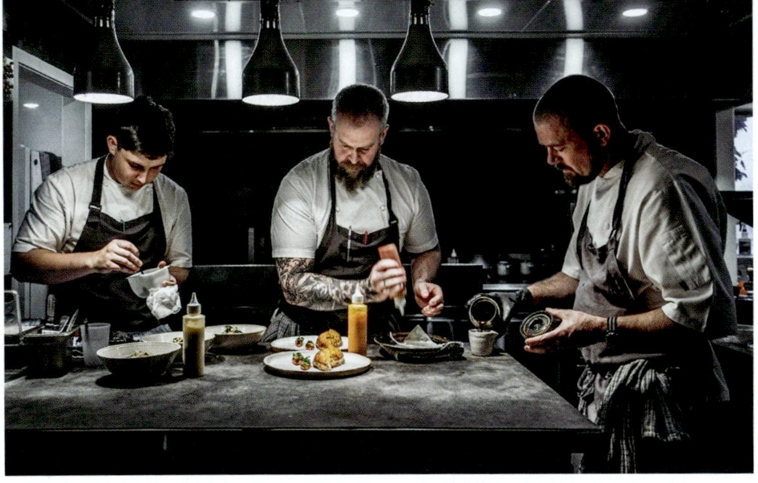

In Taupō, known for its many top-notch restaurants, the chefs at Embra have made their mark with artistic pix-fixe meals.

Rather surprisingly, since it's attached to a conference hotel, the ambience is excellent, too—lots of wood and leather and a lovely semi-outside area with olive trees in huge pots, and it's packed even on a mid-week evening. The handmade pasta is perfection, the kids' menu is just the right amount of interesting, and there are lots of one-of-a-kind cocktails and mocktails too—brown butter and sage sour, anyone?

14 Northcroft St. lionels.co.nz. ✆ **07/377-3111.** Main courses NZ$26–NZ$48. Reservations recommended. Daily 7am–10pm.

Plateau Bar + Eatery ♥♥ PACIFIC FUSION A long-lived locals' stalwart, Plateau features an array of sharing plates from the Pacific Ring of Fire—Aotearoa to Japan via Polynesia, the Philippines, and Peru. Think torched miso salmon, grilled sirloin with kūmara crisps, lamb rump with adobo sauce and goji berries, or *ika mata* (Polynesian raw fish in coconut milk).

64 Tūwharetoa St. plateautaupo.co.nz. ✆ **07/377-2425.** Reservations recommended. Main courses NZ$28–NZ$45. Tues–Fri 11:30am–late. Sat lunch 11:30am–3pm, dinner 4:30pm–late.

Deservedly popular Lionel's turns out excellent pasta and other Mediterranean-inspired dishes.

TŪRANGI

Hare and Copper Eatery ♥♥ SHARE PLATES This Tūrangi eatery might be hidden down a back road 5 minutes from the town center, but if you arrive on a Friday or Saturday night without a booking, you'll likely be turned away. A popular spot with locals, who swear by the truffle fries, sauteed prawns, and popcorn chicken, Hare and Copper is the creation of two former Wellington hospo experts, chef Andrew Wood and his partner Liliana Calva. The share plate menu changes regularly, but Wood's love of Asian cooking shines through, as do nods to Liliana's Mexican heritage, like *salsa macha* (a nutty salsa from Veracruz, Mexico) or ceviche. Housed in a former wine tasting room, there's limited indoor seating, but the lovely outdoor garden, complete with tiki torches, is very pleasant when the weather is nice.

134 Grace Rd. hareandcopper.co.nz. ✆ **07/386-0746.** Share plates NZ$12–NZ$29. Reservations recommended. Wed–Thurs 5pm–late; Fri–Sun noon–3pm and 5pm–late.

En Route to the Ruapehu Region

This is one of the most interesting bits of road in the North Island: The 101km (63-mile) drive to **Waimarino** hugs the eastern shore of Lake Taupō and down to Tūrangi at the southern end of the lake. A short detour off the road is the old-school but welcoming **Tokaanu Thermal Pools** (✆ **07/386-8575**). Even if you don't swim, it has a good free geothermal walk where you can see spluttering mud pools and steaming ponds, and the slightly warm river is full of trout.

South of Tūrangi, the **Tongariro National Trout Centre** ♥ (troutcentre.com; ✆ **07/386-8085**) is both a regional museum on fly-fishing and a small but well-kept aquarium with displays on endemic and introduced freshwater fish. Admission costs NZ$22 adults and NZ$12 for kids 5 to 16; it's open daily from 10am to 3pm. If you're not a fishing or fish enthusiast, you might want to skip it and just do the center's river walk, which takes about 30 to 45 minutes and is free. Tracing the path of the river, you'll see plenty of rainbow trout in their natural habitat and in fish hatching ponds—there's even an underwater observatory.

Leaving SH1, you'll take SH47, which will transport you into the other-worldly volcanic region; a high plateau of tussock, scoria plains, stunted forests, and awe-inspiring volcanoes. **Waimarino** (formerly National Park Village), at the junction of SH4 and SH47, is the entrance to the **Tongariro National Park**, but it's 15km (9 miles) from the Whakapapa ski field.

THE RUAPEHU REGION

101km (63 miles) SW of Taupō; 143km (89 miles) NE of Wanganui

Stretching from the volcanoes of Tongariro National Park to the banks of Whanganui River within the Whanganui National Park, the Ruapehu Region is a simply breathtaking part of New Zealand. Once known primarily for its winter skiing (where else can you glide down an active volcano?), it's shot to the top of many travelers' summertime itineraries thanks to the Tongariro Alpine Crossing and its mountain-biking opportunities. Regardless of the season you choose to visit, an experience around one of the three volcanic mountains and a trip down the river are both highly recommended, and very different, experiences.

On a clear day, **Tongariro National Park** ♥♥♥ never fails to fill me with awe. In my view, this is *the* most epic and spectacular landscape in a country heaving with beautiful places, and it's the first spot I tell friends to visit. It is the country's oldest national park (the fourth oldest in the world) and the world's first UNESCO dual World Heritage Area, recognized for both its outstanding natural and cultural features. The name refers to the smallest of the park's three sacred peaks: Mount Tongariro, Mount Ngāuruhoe, and Mount Ruapehu. In 1887, Te Heuheu Tūkino IV, Paramount Chief of the Tūwharetoa *iwi* (tribe), formed a joint partnership with the government in order to protect the mountains forever.

Today, the park covers an area of about 796 square km (495 sq. miles). **Mount Ruapehu,** at 2,797m (9,174 ft.), is the North Island's highest mountain and main skiing destination, including the Whakapapa, Tūroa, and Tukino ski areas. This volcano is by no means extinct: The last eruption, in 2007, was a small one that trapped a climber when a rock crashed through his tramping hut high on the mountain. He survived, although he lost a leg. An early-warning system is in place, however, so it's extremely unlikely you'll run into trouble.

Mount Ngāuruhoe (which *Lord of the Rings* fans will identify as "Mount Doom") is a perfect cone rising 2,290m (7,513 ft.). The *tapu* (sacred) peak is also active, but its last temper tantrum was in 1975, when it sent clouds of ash spewing into the atmosphere.

Mount Tongariro is the lowest and northernmost of the three, at 1,968m (6,455 ft.), although you can see from its shape that it must have been absolutely enormous once. (In truth, although Mount Ngāuruhoe is regarded as a separate volcano, it's actually Tongariro's youngest vent.) Its peaks form the end of a volcanic chain that extends to the islands of Tonga, 1,610km (1,000 miles) away. Tongariro had a burst of activity in 2012, the first since 1897.

Whakapapa Village and Waimarino are the two main (tiny) settlements closest to the Whakapapa ski area on the western side of Mount Ruapehu. **Whakapapa Village** sits at the highest elevation on the lower flanks of the mountain. Many lovely walks begin here, but there's only a handful of eating and sleeping options. Set a bit farther away, on the edge of the highway, **Waimarino**—previously, and confusingly, called National Park until its original Māori name was restored in 2024—has impressive views of all three mountains. Lodging and dining options have improved in recent years, and there's a small supermarket. The town of **Ohakune,** at the southern end of the park, has more of everything, and is the home base for the Tūroa ski field. (Tukino is a private club ski field.) Ohakune has a wide range of accommodations, cafes and restaurants, and a grocery store. It also has a 7.5m-tall (25-ft.) carrot, with a corresponding themed playground at the **Ohakune Carrotland** (an homage to the region's carrot-growing prowess), which is sure to win over little and big kids alike. If you're going to stay for any length of time, Ohakune is the best base for key activities in the region, including mountain biking, skiing, and hiking.

Cycling tourists in Tongariro National Park, New Zealand's oldest national park, with its namesake peak on the horizon.

At the end of the Forgotten World Highway, **Taumarunui** is Ruapehu's largest town, best known for its rail history and gardens. Finally, along the Whanganui River are two one-horse hamlets, **Pipiriki** and **Whakahoro,** so small they don't have fuel stations, grocery stores, or cellphone reception—but they are the starting point for some epic adventures.

Essentials

ARRIVING

Mount Ruapehu is about 4½ hours' drive from Auckland and Wellington. No airlines fly directly into the region; the closest airport is Taupō, though Palmerston North is not much farther and has more flights. Both are served by **Air New Zealand** (airnewzealand.co.nz; ✆ **0800/737-000**). Primarily a sightseeing train (with prices and departure dates that reflect this), **KiwiRail**'s Northern Explorer train (greatjourneysnz.com; ✆ **0800/872-467** in NZ) stops at Taumarunui, Waimarino, and Ohakune, leaving from Wellington and Auckland. You can expect to pay NZ$129 if you get off at one of these stops. **InterCity** (intercity.co.nz; ✆ **09/583-5780**) provides coach services from the major cities to the national park and surrounding alpine villages.

GETTING AROUND

A car is, by far, the best way to access this region, although you'll be able to do most major activities (such as the Tongariro Alpine Crossing) with the help of shuttle operators. If you're looking for a good ol' taxi after a good ol' night out in Ohakune, give **Chur Shuttles** (churshuttles.co.nz; ✆ **020/424-8777**) a call or text to make a booking.

VISITOR INFORMATION

The website for **Visit Ruapehu,** the region's tourism arm, is visitruapehu.com. The **Ohakune isite Visitor Centre,** 54 Clyde St., Ohakune (✆ **06/385-8427**), is open daily from 9am to 4pm. The **Tongariro National Park Visitor Centre,** Whakapapa village (doc.govt.nz; ✆ **07/892-3729**), is run by DOC and has an isite; it also has a fascinating display on the region's volcanoes and is a cozy place to thaw out if it's freezing outside. It's open daily 8am to 4:30pm and has the latest volcanic, weather, and track conditions. The **Taumarunui isite Visitor Centre,** 116 Hakiaha St., Taumarunui (✆ **07/895-7494**), is open daily from 9am to 4pm.

SPECIAL EVENTS

The ski season kicks off every first Saturday in June with the **Ohakune Carrot Festival** (facebook.com/ohakunecarrotcarnival), when the streets are taken over by stallholders, food trucks, and games. Countless hiking and cycling events are also on the agenda, including March's **Ring of Fire Festival** (rof.co.nz), with races ranging from 6 to 73km (3.7–45 miles).

Exploring the Mountains

ON THE SNOW

The Ruapehu region is lucky enough to be one of the few places in New Zealand where summer and winter are equally popular. Far from shutting down when it gets cold, the mountain and its tourism infrastructure are a hive of activity during the ski season, usually between June and October. A destination for international visitors and Kiwis alike, it attracts large numbers of locals on weekends—however, it can be very quiet mid-week compared to the South Island's ski fields.

Mount Ruapehu erupted spectacularly in 1995 and then again in 1996, shortly after scientists downgraded its danger rating after 8 months of relative inactivity. This led to the closure of the Whakapapa and Tūroa ski fields for 2 years. Nature has found its balance again: The mountain is quiet, and the skiing is good, provided enough snow falls in wintertime. If you want an

A snowboarder takes in the views, zooming down a slope of Mt. Ruapehu.

up-to-date picture of volcanic activity on the mountains, visit **geonet.org.nz** for the best scientific information. The two fields have more than 1,050 hectares (2,594 acres) of patrolled, skiable terrain and almost the same amount off-trail, with plenty of facilities and geographical variety to satisfy the most ardent powderhound. Following some financial drama, since 2025, Whakapapa and Tūroa have been operated separately, so you'll need separate ski passes for each one.

The **Whakapapa Ski Area** ♥♥ (whakapapa.com; ✆ **07/808-6151**), on the mountain's northwest side, is among NZ's largest ski areas. It has trails and runs to suit visitors of all abilities—from the Happy Valley beginners' slope to the black diamond runs out west. There's sledding for the kids, and the Sky Waka gondola offers spectacular sightseeing even for non-skiers—with views all the way to Mt. Taranaki on a clear day.

During the season—usually late July to October—the ski lifts operate daily from 9am to 4pm. Lift passes are cheaper during the week, and for the lower mountain only. They start from NZ$59 adults and NZ$39 kids, but you'll pay almost 3 times that for an all-mountain weekend pass. During the summer, sightseeing passes are also available. (See below for details on how to explore "on foot.")

Whakapapa has gear rental on-site (skis, snowboards, toboggans, pants, jackets and helmets), but expect to queue on weekends. Day rental of skis, boots, and poles is NZ$54 adults, NZ$49 kids 5 to 18, and free for the wee ones. A snowboard and boots costs NZ$54 adults and NZ$49 children. There are lots of other ski and snowboard rental companies dotted all over the region—I like to pick my gear up the evening before from **The Alpine Centre** ♥♥, 10 Carroll St. in Waimarino (thealpinecentre.co.nz), to avoid the queues (and pay a bit less).

The Whakapapa Ski area is among New Zealand's largest.

There are individual and group skiing and snowboarding lessons on the mountain as well; bookings are only necessary for private lessons. Private lessons range from NZ$279 for 2 hours to NZ$699 for 6 hours and run throughout the day. Two-hour group lessons are NZ$110 per person.

Tūroa Ski Area ♥♥ (pureturoa.nz) ✆ **06/928-7022**), which sits above Ohakune, is somewhat quieter than Whakapapa. It offers the longest vertical descent in Australasia (722m/2,369 ft.) and the highest ski lift in New Zealand, and it has great terrain for skiers and snowboarders of all abilities, from a beginners' area (the Alpine Meadow) right through to exciting backcountry trails and 25 black runs. The ski lifts operate daily from around 9am to 3:45pm. Tūroa has one gear rental outlet. Lift passes are NZ$99 on weekdays and NZ$159 on weekends, with discounts for kids and seniors.

Major accommodation providers run their own shuttle services to the ski hills. Otherwise, a full list of shuttle operators can be found on Ruapehu Tourism's website (visitruapehu.com/shuttles/mountain-shuttles), and you can expect to pay between NZ$25 and NZ$55 per person.

This is an alpine environment and needs to be treated with the greatest respect. The weather in the park is very changeable, and many park users have been caught out, even in the summer months. Always get the latest trail and weather details before entering the park, or you might find yourself enjoying an unscheduled helicopter ride. To get the latest snow conditions and ski information, check whakapapa.com/report or pureturoa.nz/snow-report.

ON FOOT

All three mountains have some truly fantastic walks—there aren't too many regions in the world where you can do short or multi-day routes in two national parks (Tongariro and nearby Whanganui National Park), traversing both thick bush and sparse volcanic lunarscapes. Walks range from a few minutes to a viewpoint to 3 days exploring the mountains—and the shorter, lower-elevation ones are manageable on a good day in all seasons.

For a really brief stroll, the **Mounds Walk** ♥♥ offers a photo-worthy vantage point of the three mountains, surrounding volcanic landscape, and sometimes even Mt. Taranaki to the west (see chapter 9). It has a series of short stairs, but it should only take you between 10 and 20 minutes to complete if you're crunched for time. It's accessed 5km (3 miles) below the Tongariro National Park Visitor Centre on SH48. Just north of Ohakune, the **Mangawhero Forest Walk** ♥ is a lovely 1-hour stroll through mossy alpine bush, with giant tree ferns and other tall trees.

The **Taranaki Falls Walk** ♥♥ is a 2-hour, 6km (4-mile) loop track that starts above Whakapapa village and goes through native bush and alpine tussock to Taranaki Falls, which drops 20m (66 ft.) over the edge of a large lava flow that was spat out of Mount Ruapehu some 15,000 years ago. The 7km (4.3-mile) **Silica Rapids Walk** ♥ takes 2 to 3 hours and also starts above Whakapapa Village. It covers the rapids' creamy-white terraces and then follows the cascading stream down through beech forest and subalpine vegetation to the mountain road a short way from where you started.

THE BEST 1-DAY walk IN THE WORLD?

The famed **Tongariro Alpine Crossing** ♥♥♥ (doc.govt.nz), at 20.2km (12.5 miles) long, arguably could be called the best day hike in the world. Most people start this 7- to 8-hour trek at the Mangatepopo Valley end. From there, you climb up Tongariro's Devil's Staircase and over a saddle between this mountain and its charmingly named "parasitic cone," Mount Ngāuruhoe, through stunning volcanic terrain to the Red Crater and the extraordinary Emerald Lakes and Blue Lake. However, there are also some downsides: After the initial "wow" at the highest point has worn off, most hikers find the last few hours to go downhill, both literally and figuratively. Then, there's the weather: In this fickle high-alpine environment, reasonably reliable forecasts are only available about 2 days out, so you'll need a somewhat flexible schedule, even in the summer, in case the walk is closed on the day you planned to hike. (Full refunds are offered by tour operators if the walk is cancelled due to bad weather.)

Supposing everything goes to plan, you can also do side trips, including the summit of Mount Tongariro, which takes another 90 minutes or so. (Mount Ngāuruhoe's peak, while accessible, is considered *tapu*/sacred, so avoid if you think you'll have trouble turning back just before the top.)

The hike involves an overall climb of 800m (2,600 ft.), with a couple of short, steep sections. Excluding total couch potatoes, most reasonably active folks can manage it. Being underprepared is far more of a hazard—be sure to bring plenty of warm layers, rain gear, and drinking water. Although it's open year-round, the walking season is usually November to May. If you go between the end of December and the first couple of weeks in January, it's a circus. If you choose to go in the winter, it's highly advisable you join a guided trip. And whenever you go, DOC prefers you book online—there's no charge, but knowing how many people walk the track helps them manage it better.

Many operators service this track: **Adrift Guided Outdoor Adventures** ♥, corner of SH4 and SH47, Waimarino

You'll need more time—and summertime, unless you're an avid mountaineer—for the **Tongariro Northern Circuit** ♥♥. It typically takes 3 to 4 days to get around the mountain, staying in backcountry huts along the way. If you aren't particularly well-equipped but want to do a multi-day expedition, several operators will rent you tramping boots, packs, and so on, including **Edge to Edge** (edgetoedge.co.nz; ✆ **07/892-3867**).

To explore Mt. Ruapehu itself, head to the Whakapapa ski hill (whakapapa.com; ✆ **07/808-6151**). Its latest addition is the **Sky Waka** ♥♥, NZ's highest and longest gondola ride up to the Knoll Ridge Chalet, from which—in summer—you can access the **Skyline Ridge** ♥♥♥. The 2-hour return walk is arguably the best short walk in the national park area; it peaks at 2,300m (7,545 ft.), from which you'll have breathtaking views of Mt. Ngāuruhoe and Lake Taupō. The Meads Wall (another *Lord of the Rings* fan favorite) and countless waterfalls are also accessible. The 1.8km (1-mile) ride—which costs NZ$39 for adults and NZ$19 for children 5 to 17, with a family pass for NZ$99—is worth it just for the surreal sensation of floating over volcanic (adriftnz.co.nz; ✆ **07/892-2751**), does summer and winter guided trips for NZ$195 per person. **Adventure Outdoors Tongariro NZ ♥**, 60 Carroll St., Waimarino (adventureoutdoors.co.nz; ✆ **0800/386-925** in NZ), is another good operator that does summer and winter guided trips; cost is NZ$345 per person.

But even if you're unguided, you'll need to book transport at either end. Yes, you can technically drive yourself to the parking lot, but parking is strictly limited to 4 hours, which isn't enough time to do the hike. **Tongariro Crossing Shuttles** (tongarirocrossingshuttles.co.nz) runs a return shuttle for NZ$70 adults and NZ$45 children. **Tongariro Track Transport,** 21 Carroll St., Waimarino (thetongarirocrossing.com; ✆ **021/351-103**), will also get you from A to B and back again for NZ$55 adults and NZ$45 for children under 15.

Many accommodations around the national park also provide shuttle service. But you don't need to stay in the Waimarino or Whakapapa villages to do this hike—you can also get transport from Ohakune, Ōwhango, Taumarunui, Tūrangi, or Taupō—though the last makes for a long day.

Passing the aptly named Emerald Lakes, one of many highlights on the Tongariro Alpine Crossing.

landscapes littered with flowing waterfalls. (If you're okay with heights, you can pay NZ$40 extra per cabin and get one with a terrifying glass floor!)

BY BIKE

The Ruapehu region has become a destination for cyclists of all skill levels, but especially mountain bikers. Two of the 22 rides on the New Zealand Cycle Trail originate or finish here, depending on which way you go. One is the highly rated **Timber Trail ♥♥♥**, which ends in Ōngarue, north of Taumarunui. If you want to do this one from the Ruapehu end, **Epic Cycle Adventures** (epiccycleadventures.com; ✆ **022/023-7958**) provides transport, bikes, and glamping. Shuttles are NZ$55 per person and bike hire is NZ$70 per day. **The Timber Trail Lodge** (timbertraillodge.co.nz; ✆ **021/562-001**) offers 20 rooms halfway along the trail, but most people book a full biking package, including accommodation, shuttles, and bike rental. They start from NZ$265.

The other trail is the awesome 231km (144-mile) **Mountains to Sea Trail ♥♥** (mountainstosea.co.nz), which is typically tackled from the Ohakune Old Coach Road on Mount Ruapehu. The 6-day ride starts with a thrilling 1,000m (about a half mile) descent from the Tūroa ski field—through both Tongariro and Whanganui national parks, along the Whanganui River Road, and finishing up in Whanganui, where the river meets the seas. Sections of the trail can be tackled individually, with the 15km (9-mile) **Ohakune Old Coach Road ♥♥** being the perfect introduction to the trail. It's grade 2 and takes about a half day to ride. Or you could try newly opened nearby sections **Te Ara Mangawhero** or **Te Hangāruru.** For bike rentals and shuttles, Ohakune has two excellent options—**TCB ♥♥**, 29 Ayr St. (tcb.nz; ✆ **06/385-8433**), which will rent you a mountain bike for half a day and drop you at the trail head for NZ$60; or **Kune Shuttles ♥♥**, 27 Goldfinch St. (kuneshuttles.co.nz; ✆ **022/583-1292**), which has the latest bikes and the most comfortable helmets I've ever worn from NZ$35 for a half day. Shuttles start at NZ$15 per person. Both companies also rent e-bikes.

The famous **42 Traverse** is one of the most popular 1-day mountain bike rides in the North Island, but the 46km (29-mile) route is not for the faint of heart. The Grade 3 trail follows old logging tracks through scenic native bush and streams from the Tongariro Forest near Waimarino to Ōwhango, with an overall descent of 570m (1,870 ft.) and some uphill bits as well.

Rainy Day Activities

Like all mountain regions, Tongariro can have fickle weather—which at times closes ski slopes (south-facing Tūroa cops the worst of it) and makes hiking ill-advised for inexperienced walkers. Luckily, there are a few options nearby to keep you occupied while you wait for the clouds to clear.

In the village of Raetihi, just west of Ohakune, **Dinosaur House ♥** 102 Seddon St. (dinosaurhouse.co.nz, ✆ **06/212-8978**), is one of those quirky micro-museums that are a window into someone's obsession—in this case, that of Ian and Sarah Moore, film buffs and dinosaur fans. The century-old county offices now bristle with replica fossils, animatronic dinosaurs, retro dino-themed arcade games, a documentary room, and *Jurassic Park* memorabilia, including one of Sam Neill's original costumes from the third movie in the franchise. (No, he hasn't visited, but his dino-loving grandson has.) It's kind of cheesy, sure, but it's a fun way to while away a few hours—my kids especially loved using paintbrushes to reveal replica skeletons in a sandpit in the garden. Open 10am to 4pm weekdays, 10am to 5pm on weekends, it costs just

Time for a Restful Soak

Ideal for resting sore bodies after a day out exploring, **Ohakune Hot Tubs ♥**, 27 Rimu St., Ohakune (ohakunehottubs.co.nz; ✆ **021/087-34724**), offers private hot tubs. The surrounds aren't the most picturesque (you'll be looking mainly at the privacy fencing, tree tops, or the stars above, if you go at night) and the amenities (including a bathroom and shower) are on the basic end of the spectrum, but the hot tubs themselves are brand-new stainless-steel wood-burning models, which create just the right amount of ambience. They cost from NZ$89 for an hour—$150 for four people—and BYO drinks are welcome. (Bring your own towel, too, or you can hire one there.)

Children love interacting with the alpacas at the Nevalea Alpacas ranch, near Taumarunui.

NZ$12 for adults, and NZ$10 for seniors and kids 3 to 15. While you're there, pop into the **Volcano Vibe Collective** ♥, 43 Seddon St. (✆ **027/422-2106**), a wee gallery showcasing local art, bespoke clothing, and natural skincare.

To learn about the region's volcanoes, you can't beat the free exhibits at the **Tongariro National Park Visitor Centre** ♥♥ in Whakapapa village (doc.govt.nz; ✆ **07/892-3729**), which take you through the natural, cultural, and explosive history of this wild and magical place via interesting displays, films, and a huge 3D model of the park.

Exploring Farther Afield

The mighty mountains are this region's biggest stars, but adventure can also be found on or around the Whanganui River. There's much to see and do along the narrow, winding **Whanganui River Road,** which runs 64km (40 miles) from the little settlement of Pipiriki to Whanganui (see p. 310 for details).

TAUMARUNUI

At the Taumarunui end of the Forgotten World Highway (see box p. 248), you may think you've been transported to France at **Lauren's Lavender Farm** ♥, 1381 River Rd. (laurenslavender.co.nz; ✆ **07/896-8705**), a particularly purple place when the lavender is in flower, from the end of December until early March. You can't walk between the rows (sorry, influencers) but you can relax in the gardens with a sandwich from the on-site cafe, or peruse beauty products at the shop. The farm is open from the end of October until the end of May; the cafe is open daily from 9am until late in summer and 10am to 3pm in winter.

Another worthwhile stop, up the highway north of Taumarunui, is **Nevalea Alpacas** ♥♥, 5446 SH4 (nevaleaalpacas.co.nz; ✆ **07/896-6333**), home to more than 1,000 alpacas. There are *cria* (baby alpacas) at Nevalea year-round, which you can meet during an Alpaca Encounter (if you book online, it's NZ$27.50 adults, NZ$20 children 2–15, NZ$69 family pass). For an extra fee,

ROAD TO nowhere

Running between Taumarunui in the Ruapehu region and Stratford in Taranaki, the **Forgotten World Highway (SH43)** ♥♥ is a remote and rural 155km (96-mile) stretch of road that was rarely used 2 decades ago. Now it's been recognized as a scenic gem, with steep, bush-covered gorges and passes, plunging rivers, and even a hand-hewn, single-lane road tunnel, known by locals as "the Hobbit's Hole." It follows ancient Māori trade routes and pioneers' farm tracks, through tiny settlements and fiercely independent **Whangamōmona.** This township declared itself a republic in 1989 after local boundaries were changed and the people found they were no longer Taranaki-ites but residents of the Manawatu-Wanganui region. To mark this spirited uprising, "Whanga" holds a Republic Day every January, and a new president is elected. (A goat, poodle, and turtle have all held office since.) You can even get your passport stamped here (although it's advisable not to, as it can invalidate them).

Forgotten World Adventures ♥♥♥, 9 Hakiaha St., Taumarunui (forgottenworldadventures.co.nz; ✆ **0800/724-522-78** in NZ, or 07/895-7181), offers an unusual way to explore this route—on decommissioned railway lines using golf carts that have been adapted to run along the rails. There are nine rail-cart and jetboat tours, ranging from a half-day tour (NZ$285 per person) to the 2-day ultimate tour (NZ$945 per person). Tours depart from Taumarunui, with combo packages available for jetboat and rail-cart packages.

Exploring an abandoned stretch of rural railway with Forgotten World Adventures.

you can cuddle a baby alpaca. Owners Leonie and Neville Walker will teach you how to walk the animal, hand-feed it, and explain the process of how its fiber is turned into the clothing that Leonie designs and knits herself.

THE WHANGANUI RIVER

Navigating the Whanganui River is, oddly enough, one of New Zealand's Great "Walks." No walking is necessary, though—you'll be traveling by canoe or kayak down a river with some 239 listed rapids, most being little riffles (Class I and II rapids), so even less-experienced folks can have a crack at it and come out smiling. The **Whanganui Journey** can be done in 3 or 5 days, depending on where you choose to start and end, staying at DOC huts or camping along the way. However, you can also opt to just do 1 night or even an afternoon on the river, which will give you a taste of the full journey on its most scenic portion between Whakahoro and Pipiriki. Most operators will only hire out canoes and kayaks during the Great Walks season

(Oct–Apr) for safety reasons. River levels also tend to drop later in the summer, so between October and December is the best time to get on the river.

You can do the journey independently, but I highly recommend taking a cultural guided trip with one of the Māori operators, like **Unique Whanganui River Experience ♥♥** (uniquewhanganuiriver.co.nz; ✆ **027/554-4426**). You'll learn about the Whanganui's personhood (it was granted legal status as a living being in 2017) and its significance as an ancestor of the local Māori people (whose lives were forever changed when European settlers destroyed their eel traps in the 1880s to allow steamboat access). Three-day all-inclusive trips start at about NZ$1,000 per person. **Owhango Adventures ♥** (canoewhanganuiriver.com; ✆ **07/895-4854**) has a similar offering, while **Canoe Safaris ♥**, in Ohakune (canoesafaris.co.nz; ✆ **06/385-9237**), is the pick for those hoping to refine their paddling skills. While owner Phil Collins's tours lack the cultural component (Collins is Australian), he'll teach you everything from the correct strokes to how to navigate a river and read rapids. His 3-day guided journeys are NZ$945 for adults, NZ$745 for children, all-inclusive.

Jetboat tours are also incredibly popular, with one of the most poignant destinations being to the **Bridge to Nowhere ♥♥**. Hidden in what now seems like the middle of, well, nowhere, it was built in 1935 north of Pipiriki at Mangapurua Gorge. Returning servicemen from World War I established a farming community here with their families, but life was tough, and by 1944 the valley was deserted. The bridge is one of the only remains of this settlement, and today it's only accessible by foot, boat, or bike. **Whanganui River Adventures ♥♥**, 2522 Pipiriki Raetihi Rd., Pipiriki (whanganuiriveradventures.co.nz; ✆ **0800/862-743** in NZ, or 06/385-3246), offers a half-day jetboat tour to the site departing daily at 10:30am. You'll need to pack your own lunch, and the 40-minute walk to the bridge can be slippery at times, but you won't regret the NZ$190 (for adults; NZ$95 children 5–15) it costs to get

Jetboating up the Whanganui River with Bridge to Nowhere Tours, which also runs the Bridge to Nowhere Lodge (see p. 262).

there. For NZ$220 (for adults; NZ$110 ages 5–15), you can opt to canoe the last 10km back (unguided and during summer only) to Pipiriki, which includes going over some rapids. Or, if you've got more time, try out the "Overnighter." After the jetboat tour, you'll canoe unguided down to a hut or campsite, where you'll spend the night before returning to base the next day.

Where to Stay Around Ruapehu

As usual, the key is to book ahead because of this region's year-round popularity, for the snow in winter and the tramping and mountain biking in the warmer months.

OHAKUNE

Because it's handy to the Tūroa ski area and only about an hour's drive to the Whakapapa slopes, Ohakune has plenty of lodging options, including hotels, motels, and many private holiday home rentals.

Before you choose a spot to stay, know that Ohakune has two distinct ends of town: the "day" end along SH49, where most of the shops and restaurants are, and the "night" end along Old Station Road near the railway station, known as such because it's the neighborhood for a solid après ski party. (The Junction, as it's also known, faded a bit during the pandemic years, but a revitalization project is currently underway.) You'll find accommodation spread throughout the 1½ miles in between the two points, so it all depends on whether you're more of a morning or a night person, so to speak.

The most well-known property on the "night" end is the family-owned **Powderhorn Chateau** ♥, 194 Mangawhero Terrace (powderhorn.co.nz; ✆ **06/385-8888**), which used to be the most upmarket place to stay in Ohakune. It has lost that distinction, but it's still the closest accommodation to the Tūroa field, located at the bottom of the mountain road. It's wall-to-wall pine inside and out—you'll swear you're in a ski chalet halfway up the Swiss Alps—and this large establishment provides a cozy, comfortable bulwark against bad weather. Its second-generation owners are in the process of upgrading rooms and bathrooms, but unfortunately its old bones mean sound does travel internally. It has two atmospheric restaurants and 30 rooms that start from NZ$350.

On the "day" end, you'll find the super centrally located **Snowman Lodge and Spa** ♥♥, 68 Clyde St. (snowmanlodge.nz; ✆ **06/385-8600**). While the reception area and on-site spa could do with some love, its new ensuite cabins are a deal for NZ$150. Located behind the main building, they feature kitchenettes, a private fenced outdoor seating area, and smart TVs. Even more affordable options include bunk rooms and rooms within the lodge with a shared bathroom.

The Peaks Motor Inn ♥, 128 Mangawhero Terrace (thepeaks.co.nz; ✆ **06/385-9144**), is a pleasant motel with warm, self-contained units (from NZ$169) and a sauna and Jacuzzi for chillier months. Five minutes outside of town, you'll find **The Ruapehu Country Lodge** ♥♥, 630 Raetihi–Ohakune Rd. (ruapehucountrylodge.co.nz; ✆ **06/880-0494**), a lovely bed-and-breakfast that backs onto the Waimarino Golf Course. Rates, which include breakfast, start from NZ$230.

Manuka Lodge ♥♥♥ This contemporary bed-and-breakfast (translation: there's not a doily in sight) is located in a residential neighborhood, but still has expansive views looking out towards Mt. Ruapehu. The rooms are spacious and bright, with luxurious touches (like honey-scented Koha Spa toiletries) throughout. While it's a traditional B&B in the sense that you're staying in someone's home and a cooked breakfast is provided, the owners Susie and Alan have their own private living area, while there's a private lounge for guests.

18 Manuka St. manukalodgenz.com. ✆ **06/385-8303.** 4 units. NZ$235–NZ$330 double. Rates include breakfast. **Amenities:** Guest lounge; outdoor hot tub; drying room for ski gear; free Wi-Fi.

Rocky Mountain Chalets ♥♥ These little stand-alone cottages are rather like *Doctor Who*'s Tardis: They're an awful lot bigger than they look on the outside, for a room rate that's a lot smaller than you'd expect. The cozy, stylish homes-away-from-home have two or three bedrooms; a couple of "executive" versions come with a fireplace and an outside Jacuzzi. Each is welcoming, luxurious, and fully self-contained, including a washing machine and dryer. Ride out a wet day watching the 50+ Sky channels or pop over to the gym and games room, which has a sauna and two more Jacuzzis attached.

20 Rangataua Rd. rockymountainchalets.com. ✆ **06/385-9545.** 42 chalets. Chalets NZ$250–NZ$390. **Amenities:** Guest lounge/games room; gym; Jacuzzis; sauna; free Wi-Fi.

Tongariro Suites ♥♥♥ Sophisticated, eco-friendly luxury comes to the country. This heavenly B&B is in Horopito, 7km (4⅓ miles) from Ohakune, and every unique, spacious suite frames Mount Ruapehu. The owners can't

Guests enjoy dinner on the porch of their spacious suite at Tongariro Suites, just outside the park in Horopito.

part the clouds, but they are available if you need anything. You probably won't: So much thought has gone into this beautifully landscaped property, especially its newest addition, the award-winning Nightsky Cottage, named for the stargazing skylights in the living room. Book direct for the best rates.

27 Hutiwai Rd., Horopito. tongarirosuites.co.nz. ✆ **022/088-7529.** 5 units. Suites NZ$310–NZ$669. Rates include breakfast. **Amenities:** Sauna; guest lounge; mountain bikes; laundry; free Wi-Fi.

WAIMARINO

In the last few years, more mid-range and boutique lodging options have opened here. This is certainly the most convenient place to stay if you're planning to tackle the Tongariro Alpine Crossing; it's also a good base for skiing and within a half-hour's drive of many walks and cycle trails. Most hotels offer shuttles to slopes or the start of the hike.

The Park Hotel Ruapehu ♥ At the heart of the village, the Park Hotel has good availability due to its size and recently refreshed rooms. But while the cosmetics have been improved, the bathrooms are small and the walls are thin. Given all the people waking up pre-dawn to conquer the Tongariro Alpine Crossing, don't count on sleeping in. But if you're among the early risers, this location will support you in your mission. The hotel offers a 2-night crossing package from October to April—if you're travelling as a couple or trio, it will cost you just NZ$249 for each.

Corner of SH4 and Millar St. the-park.co.nz. ✆ **0800/800-491** in NZ, or 07/892-2748. 80 units. NZ$155–NZ$190 double. **Amenities:** Restaurant; bar; outdoor hot tubs; limited free Wi-Fi.

Plateau Lodge ♥ Like other accommodations in the village, Plateau has a range of room options, from backpacker-style lodge rooms with shared bathroom all the way up to two-bedroom family suites with their own kitchen. What sets it apart is its new King studio pods, cabins that can fit up to three people (with one person sleeping on a pull-out couch). It's a tight fit, but you could probably even fit three into the massive outdoor soaker tub on the deck. Each pod also has its own fridge and microwave, but guests can also make use of the main lodge's communal kitchen and lounge. The downside? Although the cabins are free-standing, some are attached to the neighbor's decks, and sound does travel. Plateau Lodge also owns one of the area's largest shuttle companies (Tongariro Crossing Shuttles), so they can help you with transport to and from the hiking trails. Book direct for packages and mid-week deals.

17 Carroll St. plateaulodge.co.nz. ✆ **07/892-2993.** 24 units. NZ$85–NZ$250 double. **Amenities:** Kitchen; lounge; limited free Wi-Fi.

Tongariro Crossing Lodge ♥♥ While there are a variety of suites and units here, the new-in-2025 Garden Suites are especially desirable, beautifully designed with all mod-cons (great lighting, top shower, induction cooktop). They're spacious for a couple and doable, though a bit of a squeeze, for a family of four—the sofa bed easily converts to a second double bed. No hot tubs or communal spaces here, though. Like many places in Waimarino, the lodge offers a package for hikers doing the crossing, which includes a substantial in-room breakfast, a packed lunch, return transfers, and a 2-night stay starting from NZ$385 per person. Book direct for the best rates.

27 Carroll St. tongarirocrossinglodge.co.nz. ✆ **07/892-2688.** 12 units. NZ$195–NZ$340 double. **Amenities:** Free Wi-Fi.

WHAKAPAPA VILLAGE

The village at the base of Mount Ruapehu is a bit of a magnet for party-hearty ski bunnies in the winter, but there are some decent, affordable choices. Note that the famous Chateau Tongariro Hotel—the grand, Wes Anderson–esque building you see as you approach the mountain—was shuttered in 2023, its future uncertain due to high earthquake risk. In 2025, Ruapehu's mayor delivered a petition to parliament urging lawmakers to save the century-old, reputedly haunted icon—so watch this space.

The **Skotel Alpine Resort ♥**, 1 Ngāuruhoe Place (skotel.co.nz; ✆ **0800/756-835** in NZ, or 07/892-3719), is a big chalet-style place with rooms for every budget, from backpacker accommodation to superior rooms and self-contained cabins. It has its own restaurant and bar, sauna, and Jacuzzis, but walls are thin, so you likely will hear your neighbors. Rates range from NZ$95 to NZ$109 for backpacker rooms, and NZ$155 to NZ$340 for larger rooms and cabins. The resort offers ski and equipment rentals in winter and transport to walks.

Whakapapa Holiday Park ♥ (whakapapa.net.nz; ✆ **07/892-3897**) has cabins, a self-contained lodge that sleeps 32, RV and tent sites, and a fully stocked store. Prices start at NZ$79 per person for the lodge, NZ$27 per person for campsites, and NZ$85 to NZ$145 for cabins. It's the cheapest and closest accommodation to the ski area, with shuttles available to take you to the slopes and to the Tongariro Alpine Crossing.

TAUMARUNUI

Forgotten World Motel ♥, 9 Hakiaha St. (forgottenworldmotel.co.nz; ✆ **07/895-7181;** doubles from NZ$140), is owned by the people who run Forgotten World Adventures (see "Road to Nowhere," p. 256). This is a good, super-affordable base for those heading out on an early morning tour with the operator. Rooms are basic but clean. A short drive outside Taumarunui, **Omaka Lodge ♥♥♥**, 11 Omaka Rd. (omakalodge.nz; ✆ **07/974-8543;** NZ$255–NZ$1,350), is a handsome and welcoming B&B with six units, including a self-contained loft apartment, luxury cottage The Gardener's Folly, and campsites. Breakfast is made from produce grown on-site, but the highlight here is the 3½ acres of gardens, the setting for many weddings. There's a lovely outdoor pool as well.

If you're travelling with friends, **Oranleigh Lodge ♥♥♥**, 546 River Rd. (oranleighlodge.co.nz; on Airbnb; ✆ **027/494-1612**), makes an excellent

OUT OF THIS world: BLUE DUCK STATION

It's hard to believe that one of the country's most sought-after fine dining experiences *and* one of its most celebrated conservation projects are found together on a remote sheep and beef cattle farm deep in the Ruapehu. But that's exactly what you'll find at **Blue Duck Station ♥♥♥**, 4265 Oio Rd., Retaruke (blueduckstation.co.nz; ✆ **07/895-6276**). Owner Dan Steele named his 5,000-acre (2,023-hectare) property for the endangered *whio* (blue ducks) who live here, and for nearly 20 years, he's been committed to saving them, as well as the area's kiwis and bats. (Steele was part of the original group who started Predator Free 2050, a national initiative to eradicate invasive mammals from NZ.) Overnight guests at the station learn about his biodiversity efforts and regenerative farming practices on bush safaris, horse treks, mountain biking tours, kayaking trips, and jetboat rides, including the **Bridge to Nowhere** (p. 257). To guarantee availability, excursions should be booked up to a week in advance.

While Blue Duck Station once catered exclusively to hunters and backpackers in its rustic bush cabins and lodges, it recently leveled up with the addition of three new luxury cabins located "On the Top of the World" (as Steele calls this high-altitude spot on the property, 495m/1,624 ft. above sea level). The cabins are part of its much-lauded **Chef's Table Experience** (thechefstable.co.nz), which begins with a 2-hour ATV safari to look for blue ducks in the property's waterfalls, followed by a bacchanalian 10-course feast overlooking Tongariro and Whanganui National Parks The cost for a stay in the high country cabin is NZ$895 per person, including lodging, the property tour, dinner, and breakfast. But it's possible to experience this place much more cheaply by bunking at the Frontier Lodge, which isn't quite as swanky but is pretty darn comfortable.

Still too pricey? Inquire about volunteer opportunities to help plant trees and check traplines at this working ranch, which gets you a free stay, though you'll have to commit a good amount of time and sweat equity.

Note: The lodge is at the end of a long winding gravel road. Once you arrive, there's no cellphone reception and Wi-Fi is limited to the main dining area—which can be a good thing or a bad thing, depending on how you look at it.

home-away-from-home for a few days. The luxurious off-grid house is just 5 minutes from Taumarunui, 1 hour from the ski areas, and sleeps nine. The kitchen has everything you need to cook a feast. Floor-to-ceiling windows afford 360-degree views, including the snowcapped peaks of both Mt. Ruapehu and Mt. Taranaki. There's even a private walking track. Rates start at NZ$800 per night.

WHANGANUI RIVER

The **Bridge to Nowhere Lodge & Campground ♥♥**, Ramanui Landing (bridgetonowhere.co.nz; ✆ **0800/480-308** in NZ), is so remote you arrive by jetboat. It's NZ$130 self-catering per person in comfortable rooms with extraordinary views (NZ$25 to add breakfast), NZ$30 to NZ$50 for campsites.

Where to Eat Around Ruapehu

OHAKUNE

Eateries tend to come and go in little Ohakune, but a good feed at any time of day is never far away. Most of the food trucks and restaurants are on Clyde Street (the main drag through town) and along Goldfinch Street. For a sweet treat, grab a giant chocolate éclair filled with cream for NZ$4 from **Johnny Nation's Chocolate Éclair Shop ♥**, 78 Clyde St. (✆ **06/385-8152**). Across the road, **The Cyprus Tree ♥**, 77 Clyde St. (cyprustree.co.nz; ✆ **06/385-8857;** daily 5pm–9pm), is a welcoming spot where you can enjoy a mulled cider by the log burner or chill out with a craft beer in summer. (Owner Leah's great-great grandmother ran one of the first hospitality businesses in Ohakune, a sly-grog shop.) Joining the share plate trend, it serves Mediterranean-inspired small plates (calamari and octopus, spiced lamb roti, or beetroot and citrus salad). For a cold drink, head over to the tasting room at **Big Mountain Mead and Ruapehu Brewing Co. ♥**, 17 Goldfinch St. (bigmountainmead.com). While its beers (IPAs, stouts, and APAs) tend to be traditional, the mead is borderline experimental—it's super dry and incorporates local ingredients (like horopito and kawakawa), without a hint of sweetness.

It might be at the "night" end of town, but **Frank's Eatery & Bar ♥**, 2 Tyne St. (franksohakune.com; Wed–Sun 8am–4pm), is a good spot for brunch classics in an inviting setting—eggs every which way and burgers from noon on. Nearby, in the gorgeous old railway station, **Opus Fresh** (opusfresh.com; ✆ **022/3858-683;** daily 10am–5pm) will make you a latte laced with local Manunui honey—and while you drink it you can browse the stunning garments made by local fashion designers, or pat the two resident fluffy white dogs. The **Powderkeg ♥** at the Powderhorn Hotel (194 Mangawhero Terrace) has lively Swiss apres-ski vibes—with lots of dark wood and pool tables, it's a cozy place to spend a stormy afternoon. The food is fairly pricey, though, so if you're just after light meal, head next door to stalwart **La Pizzeria ♥** (6 Thames St.)—especially on Sundays, when you can get a large one for just NZ$15.

WAIMARINO

The village might have a reputation as a truck stop, but hidden in the old railway station is a gem of a wee restaurant, **The Station Cafe ♥♥** (station-cafe.co.nz; ✆ **027/232-4417;** Wed and Sun 8am–3pm, Thurs–Sat 8am–9pm). This friendly place serves up excellent, hearty food—orzo pasta with fried sage and roast pumpkin, gingery melt-in-the-mouth beef with greens—at very reasonable prices. Simple kids' meals are just NZ$10, and the NZ$11 desserts are top-notch. Trains are fairly few and far between on the main trunk line these days—hence the station's new gig as a cafe—but if you're in luck, a train might thunder past while you're eating.

You'll also get a lively dining experience at **Schnapps Bar ♥**, corner of SH4 and Findlay Street (schnappsbarruapehu.com; ✆ **07/892-2788;** daily

10am–late). You'll recognize it by the enormous driftwood kiwi sculpture and mini golf outside. Predictably for an outdoor-adventure type of region, the lamb shanks served on potato and *kūmara* (sweet potato) mash is the top seller.

Finally, grab a top-notch coffee from the friendly wāhine at **Tātahi/The Beach ♥**, a caravan right by the main road. It's open 7am to 3pm rain or shine.

WHAKAPAPA VILLAGE

There aren't many options in Whakapapa. If you're self-catering, the best place to shop for groceries is at the New World in Ohakune. (The Four Square in Waimarino is closer, but it has less choice and is more expensive.) Alternatively, you might find yourself sharing the **Terrace Restaurant and Bar** at the **Skotel** (see p. 261) with parties of hungry hikers or skiers. It does breakfast and dinner (no lunch) and is open daily.

En Route to Wellington

The quickest way is to get back onto SH1 (enjoy the atmospheric Desert Rd.) and follow it all the way down (or all the way up, if you're heading to Auckland and points north). For a leg stretch, the **National Army Museum ♥**, in Waiouru (armymuseum.co.nz; ✆ **06/387-6911**), may be of interest to military history buffs. Entry is NZ$15 for adults and NZ$5 for children. It's open daily from 9am to 4:30pm and has a cafe, a kids' area, and a gift shop.

TAIRĀWHITI GISBORNE & HAWKE'S BAY

8

Tairāwhiti Gisborne, once known as Eastland, is quintessential rural New Zealand: a wild and beautiful region where mass tourism is unheard of. Along the region's East Cape, Māori kids canter their horses bareback through tiny towns, and you can drive for miles along scenic coastal roads to deserted white-sand beaches but still find a restaurant that serves local wine and seafood. This is also where Captain Cook first landed, some 500 years after Polynesian voyagers settled these islands.

Travel south and you'll reach the Hawke's Bay region, where you'll find lush vineyards, upmarket bed and breakfasts, restaurants run by some of the country's best chefs, and all manner of ways to overindulge—this is the country's ultimate foodie destination. The region's long sunshine hours and fertile soil are put to good use growing 38 different grape varietals—the region was just crowned the newest Great Wine Capital of the world. But you'll also see rows of orchard fruit and vegetables, and fields full of fat, contented livestock.

Both regions were hit hard by 2023's Cyclone Gabrielle, but are now well and truly open for business again.

TAIRĀWHITI GISBORNE & THE EAST COAST

293km (182 miles) NE of Rotorua; 298km (185 miles) SE of Tauranga; 504km (312 miles) SE of Auckland

Gisborne (pop. 51,000) might be a small city, but it has a busy river port, an active commercial center, and standout town beaches. It's also New Zealand's third-largest grape-growing district, producing about 13% of the country's wine. The region is sometimes called the chardonnay capital—chardonnay accounts for more than half of all plantings—but this rather undersells it, since it also produces terrific gewürztraminer, viognier, pinot gris, merlot, and malbec. Gisborne is also arguably the birthplace of surfing in NZ, with multiple breaks and near-deserted beaches that stretch on forever. ***Fun fact:*** Every calendar day, it's the first city on the planet to greet sunrise. Fittingly, the Māori name for the region is Tairāwhiti: "the coast upon which the sun shines across the water."

Along the East Coast, biculturalism is a living, breathing way of life, not something put on for tourists. In some areas, more than 80% of the population is Māori—the highest proportion of Māori people anywhere in New Zealand—and te reo Māori is commonly heard and used in everyday life. While history fanatics once traveled here because it was Captain Cook's first landing site in 1769, there's increasing appreciation for the fact that hundreds of years earlier, it was also where some of the first *waka* (seafaring canoes) landed from Polynesia.

Essentials

ARRIVING

Air New Zealand (airnewzealand.co.nz; ✆ **0800/737-000** in NZ) has daily flights from major North Island cities to Gisborne's small regional airport (gisborneairport.nz), which is only 5km (3 miles) from the city center. There are no airport shuttles, but the arrivals hall has a number of rental car companies including **Hertz** (hertz.co.nz; ✆ **06/867-5204**) and **Avis** (avis.com; ✆ **06/868-9084**). Gisborne is about 6 to 7 hours' drive from both Auckland and Wellington. **InterCity** (intercity.co.nz; ✆ **09/623-1503**) has a daily bus service to Gisborne from Auckland, Wellington, and Rotorua.

GETTING AROUND

While there are some organized tours available, self-driving is by far the best way to get around Tairāwhiti Gisborne. From Ōpōtiki around the East Cape to Gisborne is a winding 334km (207-mile) route that will take about 6 hours at a reasonably brisk pace, but give yourself more time and stop overnight if you can. The more direct route between Ōpōtiki and Gisborne via SH2 takes about 2 hours. If you need a taxi in the town of Gisborne, try **Gisborne Taxis** (✆ **06/867-2222**).

VISITOR INFORMATION

The official tourism website for Tairāwhiti Gisborne is **tairawhitigisborne.co.nz**. The **Gisborne isite Visitor Information Centre,** 209 Grey St. (✆ **06/868-6139**), is open daily 9am to 5pm. The **Ōpōtiki isite Visitor Information Centre,** 70 Bridge St. (opotikinz.co.nz; ✆ **07/315-3031**), is open weekdays 9am to 4:30pm, weekends 9am to 1pm.

SPECIAL EVENTS

The Rhythm and Vines Music Festival (rhythmandvines.co.nz) is a 3-day music festival that runs from December 31 to January 1 (making it the largest gathering of people to see the first sunrise of the New Year in the world) and features top local and international artists.

Celebrated in May every year, the **Chardonnay Affair** (thechardonnayaffair.co.nz) is a weekend foodie event with tastings, historic steam train rides, and long table dinners in the vines.

East Coast & Hawke's Bay

Exploring Gisborne

The city of **Gisborne** (known fondly as "Gizzy"), the key population center of the region, lies at the northern end of Tūranganui-a-Kiwa/Poverty Bay. Two rivers, the Waimatā and the Taruheru, meet here to form the Tūranganui River, the country's shortest at just 1,200m (3,900 ft.). It's a small city, so the center is compact. As you walk along the harbor, keep an eye out for **Tairāwhiti Waka Hourua,** a 72-foot double-hulled sailing *waka,* one of only nine of its kind in the world. (It might be out voyaging.)

The free **Tupapa app** ♥♥ (tupapa.nz) is a video and audio tour of key sites along the waterfront. The app's walking tour will lead you across the river to the top of the **Titirangi Reserve** ♥ (also known as **Kaiti Hill**), where you'll get sweeping views of the surrounding area and much of Tūranganui-a-Kiwa/Poverty Bay. (You can also drive to the lookout.) At the foot of the hill on Kaiti Beach Road is Gisborne's most significant landmark, the **site of Captain James Cook's landing** in 1769. Compared to the standard monolith erected to celebrate Cook in 1969, the newer **Puhi Kai Iti Cook Landing Site** ♥ is rich in meaning and a beautiful piece of contemporary artwork. (The lighting at night is stunning.) It includes the largest *tukutuku* panels in the world, massive sculptures of gourds and nine metal-and-resin paddles commemorating the Māori warriors and chief killed by Cook's men in that first violent encounter. A pedestrian bridge shaped like a *waka* takes walkers from the site over the busy port road to Titirangi Reserve. Unfortunately, at the time of writing, interpretation panels for the site—which is complex in its symbology and meaning—weren't yet installed.

Alongside the monument commemorating Captain Cook's first landing in New Zealand, newer sculptures commemorate the early Polynesian explorers who also landed here.

The **Tairāwhiti Museum and Art Gallery** ♥♥, 10 Stout St. (tairawhiti museum.org.nz; ✆ **06/867-3832**), is an excellent regional museum with displays on the Māori and European settlement of the region, as well as geological and natural history. A maritime section includes the two-storied wheelhouse and captain's cabin of the *Star of Canada,* a cargo steamer that was blown onto the rocks on the Gisborne foreshore in 1912. The museum is open Monday to Saturday from 10am to 4pm and Sunday 1:30 to 4pm. Admission is NZ$5 for adults; free for children under 12.

For a magical night out, lounge on beanbags under stained-glass domes at the **Dome Cinema** ♥♥♥, 38 Childers Rd. (domecinema.co.nz; ✆ **027/590-2117**).

THE dual history OF POVERTY BAY

For decades, the history of Captain Cook's arrival in 1769 overshadowed that of the Polynesian voyaging explorers who charted the waters to New Zealand 500 years earlier, using only the movement of the sun, stars, clouds, ocean currents, whales, and birds to find their way here. Now, there's growing recognition that the exact spot where Cook landed is the same place where the Polynesian voyagers first arrived in their seafaring *waka*. This dual heritage is reflected with new sculptures and interpretative signs throughout the region, most importantly in Gisborne where the landing took place.

Cook called the area "Poverty Bay" after finding nothing he wanted here (which may have been because when he met Māori, he shot first and asked questions later). In 2013, students at Gisborne's Kāiti School were shocked to learn that Cook had given such a disparaging name to a beloved place that already had one. They collected a petition, held a march, met with local councilors, and in 2019 the bay was officially changed to Tūranganui-a-Kiwa/Poverty Bay—the original name honoring Kiwa, an early ancestor who arrived on the Horouta *waka*.

The velvet curtains, leather couches, and lush, red-toned lighting in the bar recall the building's past as a gentleman's club—which not so long ago excluded both women and Māori. Now it's been thoroughly reclaimed: In an animated projection of a famous painting on the wall, chieftainess Ena te Papatahi puffs away on a pipe. There's one arthouse or classic movie shown each night from Wednesday to Sunday, and occasional Tuesday live music. The bar serves pizza, fries, and drinks.

If you're interested in old Kiwi rural ways, check out the **East Coast Museum of Technology (ECMoT)** ♥, 67 Main Rd., just west of the city in Makaraka (ecmot.org.nz; ✆ **027/600-4152**). It has a pretty impressive collection of old-time fire appliances, farm and military vehicles, and home technology from yesteryear. It's open Friday to Sunday from 10am to 4pm. Admission is NZ$10 adults, NZ$2 children 13 to 18.

At the arty Dome Cinema, filmgoers lounge on comfy beanbags.

Gisborne wouldn't be the obvious place to find NZ's national tree collection, but the internationally recognized **Eastwoodhill Arboretum** ♥♥, 2392 Wharekopae Rd., Ngatapa (eastwoodhill.org.nz; ✆ **06/863-9003**), is located just out of town, some 35km (22 miles) west of Gisborne. Eastwoodhill was the singular passion of a "tree nut," Douglas Cook, who took on the mammoth task of planting the bare-earth site in 1910. Today, the 135-hectare (333-acre) garden boasts some 15,000 exotic and native trees, shrubs, and climbers, including rare species. It's the largest collection of Northern Hemisphere trees in the Southern Hemisphere, so try to come in spring or autumn, when the deciduous specimens are at their showiest. Not surprisingly, Eastwoodhill is a New Zealand Garden of National Significance, with more than 25km (15 miles) of marked tracks to explore. It's open daily 8:30am to 4:30pm. Admission is NZ$18 adults and NZ$5 children 5 to 16. Forty-minute guided walking and jeep tours (NZ$40) are also available between 10am and 3pm, but must be booked at least 2 days in advance.

Farther down Wharekopae Road is **Rere Falls and the Rere Rock Slide Waterwall,** the latter having achieved social media fame for being a natural 60m (197-ft.) waterslide. There are toilets and picnic sites nearby, so you can just sit and admire, or you can slide down on a piece of cardboard or boogie board. (See below for organized tours to this natural phenomenon.)

Organized Tours

Gisborne is one of New Zealand's largest grape-growing regions, and if you like chardonnay, you're in luck: Half of Gisborne's 2,000 hectares (nearly

Māori Culture as a Way of Life

If you've been to Rotorua, you might conclude that many of the cultural performances there are laid on for the tourists—and you'd be right. But here on the East Coast, tradition and speaking te reo Māori are part of everyday life. The East Coast has more than 150 *marae,* and they are a central part of life for many Māori communities, used for celebrations, meetings, and funerals. You can visit many by appointment, including **Te Poho-o-Rawiri Marae,** one of the largest Māori *whare rūnanga* (meeting houses) in NZ. (Call Tasha Irwin at ✆ **027/458-0337** to inquire; it's customary to leave a *koha* [tip] in exchange for an informal tour.) In general, to avoid seriously offending the *tangata whenua* (local people), there are a few rules you must adhere to: You must be invited into a *marae* (which includes the open area in front of the *wharenui,* or meeting house). You can't smoke, drink, or eat in the area, and you must take off your shoes before entering a building.

There are remnants of ancient *pa* sites (Māori fortresses) around the region, but don't expect to find stone ruins as you would in Europe. These settlements were generally built using wood, so very little remains. You might see elaborate trenches (Māori pioneered trench warfare) and indentations that indicated *kūmara* (sweet potato) pits, but very little else. The sites generally occupy spectacular outlooks, ideal locations for spotting the enemy before they arrived. The remains of a formidable fortress can be seen at **Ngātapa** (a half-hour drive northwest of Gisborne), which was the scene of a siege between the famed warrior chief Te Kooti and colonial settlers during the New Zealand Wars in the 1860s.

Apps and interpretative panels will only go so far into explaining the complex relationship between the East Coast's Māori people and *pākehā* (White people, or non-Māori). One way to dig deeper is with an in-depth cultural tour, like those up sacred **Maunga Hikurangi,** a site of profound spiritual and cultural significance to the Ngāti Porou people (see "Sacred Sunrise," p. 273). Check with the isite for more cultural tours that were still in development as we went to press.

5,000 acres) of vineyards are devoted to chardonnay grapes. Gewürztraminer, viognier, pinot gris, merlot, and malbec are also produced here. However, there are only a handful of tasting rooms open to visitors, some only by appointment, and some only in the summer. Visitable standouts include **Matawhero Wines** (matawhero.co.nz; ✆ **06/867-6140**) and **Bushmere Estate** (bushmere.com; ✆ **06/868-9317**). For guided wine tours by bus or bike, contact **Experience Gisborne Tours** (experiencegisborne.co.nz; ✆ **06/927-7021**). The same company also runs **Cycle Gisborne** (cyclegisborne.com), which offers day and multi-day tours, also with bicycle rental. Other tours include visits to the Rere Rock Slide, Eastwoodhill Arboretum, and Tolaga Bay/Ūawa. Tours can be customized; inquire for timing and pricing.

Exploring the East Cape

Over on the north coast, the gateway to the East Cape is the seaside town of **Ōpōtiki,** at the eastern end of the Bay of Plenty. From here you can cut through to Gisborne via the winding Waioeka Gorge (SH2), but you'd miss the East Cape—the isolated heartland that gives the region its character. If you choose to explore the Cape instead, you'll be driving SH35, the last stretch of the scenic Pacific Coast Highway from Auckland. SH35 between Ōpōtiki and Gisborne is a revered coastal section of road ("highway" wouldn't be the appropriate word) with white-sand beaches lined with pōhutukawa trees. Quiet little communities, mostly with their own marae, boast various treasures, such as the numerous historic old churches that dot the coast. The best way to visit is to travel by RV or stay at campgrounds and self-cater, as accommodation and eating options are limited. There's also a solid chance your journey will be delayed by stray livestock in the middle of the road.

Heading east along the coast from Ōpōtiki, you'll first come to **Te Kaha,** where you must ask permission to see the magnificent meeting house with its beautifully carved beams. There's a good swimming beach farther on at **Whangaparāoa,** which was ideal for hauling up the great migration canoe *Tainui* that landed here. Almost halfway along SH35 is **Hicks Bay** and the splendid **Tuwhakairiora meetinghouse** ♥♥, one of the best examples of carving on the East Cape. The carving was done in 1872 and is dedicated to local members of Ngāti Porou who died in overseas wars. There's another great swimming beach here.

Soon, the road descends to sea level and you'll find yourself in **Te Araroa,** where NZ's largest and oldest pōhutukawa tree (around 600 years old) can be found. It's a beaut, especially around Christmas when it's flowering. You should take a 20-minute side trip from here to the very lovely and historic 1906 **East Cape Lighthouse** ♥♥, but bring your A-game, fitness-wise. The views and the lighthouse are worth the 700-step slog up the hill. Better still, bring picnic food and linger in paradise.

Next is **Tikitiki** and the justifiably famous **St. Mary's Church** ♥♥♥. As with many of these structures, it was built in remembrance of Ngāti Porou soldiers who died during World War I. If you're even slightly interested in

Sacred to the Ngāti Porou people, the mountain Te Ara ki Hikurangi is the first place in New Zealand to see sunrise every morning. See "Sacred Sunrise" (p. 273) for details on how to experience it.

Māori culture, you need to see the craftsmanship of this ornate church, built in 1924. The interior is a masterpiece of intricate carvings by local Ngāti Porou.

Ruatōria is Ngāti Porou Central, where the tribe has its headquarters. Although scattered around the country, they are the second-largest Māori group.

Beautiful **Tokomaru Bay** has a lovely beach and some interesting historic buildings. Next you'll reach **Tolaga Bay/Ūawa ♥♥**. Also easily accessible from Gisborne as a day trip, it has New Zealand's longest freestanding wharf at 660m (2,165 ft.) long. It's a summer favorite for local kids; you'll see them dive-bombing off its end. It's also right next to **Cook's Cove Walkway,** an easy 6km (3.7-mile) return hike at the site of Cook's first peaceful interaction with Māori. The walk includes a natural "hole-in-the-wall," a swimming cove safe for kids. However, note that from the start of August until late October each year, it's closed for lambing season. If you're on a tight schedule, the **Ernest Reeve Walkway ♥** at the northern end of Tolaga Bay will take you to a lookout on the cliffs overlooking the bay.

Dive Tatapouri introduces humans to the local sting rays of Tatapouri Bay.

Just before Gisborne is **Tatapouri Bay,** where you'll find high-end glamping (see "Where to Stay,"

SACRED sunrise

At 1,754m (5,754 ft.), Mount Hikurangi/Te Ara ki Hikurangi is sacred to the Ngāti Porou people. Situated 130km (81 miles) north of Gisborne, it's the first place on mainland New Zealand to greet the sun each day and is believed to be the first part of Aotearoa that emerged from the sea when Māui fished up the North Island. Māui's *waka* (canoe) is also said to rest on the summit of the mountain.

Run by **Ngāti Porou Tourism** (1 Barry Ave., Ruatōria; maungahikurangi.com; ✆ **06/864-9004**), **sunrise and guided day tours ♥♥♥** of the site are available. Guides will take you to the nine Māui Whakairo sculptures two-thirds of the way up the mountain, which were created to mark the new millennium. The small group 4WD tours take 4 hours and include a light breakfast or lunch and start from NZ$269.

If you wish to go unguided, there's a Department of Conservation–maintained track to the summit, but it's a challenging 7-hour climb and you must get permission from the *iwi* (tribe) first. A hut with eight bunks also exists below the summit, making it possible to spend the night and get up early to hike the remaining distance for sunrise. The track is occasionally closed for farming or cultural reasons, so check with Ngāti Porou Tourism before you go.

p. 274) and the family-owned **Dive Tatapouri ♥♥♥**, SH35, Tatapouri (divetatapouri.com; ✆ **06/868-5153**). It's the only place in NZ that you can get up-close and personal with sting rays and eagle rays, including Tara, a 250-kg (500 lb.) specimen. And I mean *very* personal; you'll have a chance to pet and feed the wild rays in a natural and relaxed environment. You won't get wet thanks to boots and waders, but the rocky reef isn't great for people with mobility issues—or for those with a fear of fish. Tours operate only at low tide, so they're not on every day; check the website for times/dates. In summer there are more rays in the area, but you're guaranteed to see the resident eagle rays year-round. It's a great bang for your buck; it only costs NZ$65 for adults and NZ$20 for kids (who will love it).

Outdoor Pursuits

BEACHES Gisborne has three major swimming beaches, **Midway, Waikanae,** and **Wainui.** Lifeguards patrol all three in season. **Kaiaua Beach,** 60km (37 miles) north of Gisborne and 6km (3¾ miles) off SH35, is good for fishing, swimming, and picnicking. **Anaura Bay,** 77km (48 miles) north of Gisborne and 6km (3¾ miles) off SH35, has a beautiful beach of unspoiled golden sand, offering safe swimming and good fishing. A 3.5km (2-mile) walk gives lovely scenic views; allow 2½ hours. You can make *marae* visits here; there is also a motor camp.

FISHING Tairāwhiti Gisborne offers everything from freshwater trout fishing to game fishing and surf-casting in the Pacific Ocean, which doesn't require a license—but to avoid a fine or overharvesting, make sure you familiarize yourself with local size and bag limits. (Download the NZ Fishing Rules app or text the name of the fish to 9889.) If you're coming from the Ōpōtiki end, ask at the visitor center about local fishing clubs or guides along SH35 for both sorts of fishing. The best rivers for trout fishing are the Motu, Waioeka, Hangaroa, and Ruakituri, but you will need a license.

GOLF **Poverty Bay Golf Club,** Lytton Road, Gisborne (gisbornegolf.co.nz; ✆ **06/867-4402**), is one of the country's oldest (dating back to 1893). Greens fees are NZ$55 for 18 holes, NZ$35 for 9 holes. The club has a pro shop on-site.

RAILBIKING Just when you thought that Kiwis were running out of absurd ideas for adventure sports, along came Geoff Main and his idea to put a tandem bicycle on unused railway tracks. After 10 years of planning, his dream was realized and the **Gisborne Railbike Adventure ♥♥** (railbikes.nz; ✆ **021/525-700**) was born. I'm a firm believer that tandem activities are often more work than fun (hello, paddleboats), but the bikes Geoff has constructed are nearly effortless to ride (e-bikes are even available), with no real steering or balance needed. His most popular 3-hour tours involve cycling through tunnels and across bridges, but a 1-hour version is also available. Tours start from NZ$52 per person. Participants must be ages 13 and up.

SAUNA After all that activity, what better way to ease your aching muscles than with a beachside sauna under the stars? **The Sauna Project ♥♥♥** (thesaunaproject.co.nz) offers NZ$20 hour-long sessions somewhere stunning three times a week—they move around from time to time but can often be found at gorgeous Tatapouri Bay. Check the website for times and locations (there's one in Napier, too).

SURFING Considered the birthplace of New Zealand surfing, this area is a surfing mecca, with beaches such as **Wainui ♥♥** boasting 250 surfable days per year. There are six different breaks for a range of skill levels, including the world-renowned **Makorori ♥♥♥**, **Sponge Bay ♥♥**, and **Okitu (Pines) ♥♥** beaches. **Midway Beach ♥** is home to the famous Gizzy Pipe, known for its deep barrel rides, while **Waikanae** (Roberts Rd.) is built for beginners. If you want to learn how to surf, **Salt Shack Surf School** (www.saltshacksurfschool.com) or **Surfing with Sarah** (surfingwithsarah.co.nz; ✆ **022/073-9383**) both offer group (NZ$60–NZ$75) and private (NZ$100–NZ$125) lessons, as well as board and wetsuit hire.

WALKING The definitive walk in this area is the **Lake Waikaremoana Track,** one of the country's 10 Great Walks through the forested wilderness of Te Urewera. Read the guides on the DOC website and book your hut beds in advance for this 3- to 4-day backcountry adventure. The **Te Kuri Farm Walkway** on the edge of Gisborne is a shorter, tamer option, winding 5.6km (3.5 miles) through a private farm with panoramic views. The signposted walk can be found at the end of Shelley Road, where there's a parking lot and picnic area.

Where to Stay in Gisborne

As well as holiday homes and campgrounds, you'll find plenty of motels (of varying quality) in Gisborne. **Whispering Sands Beachfront Motel ♥♥**, 22

Among the many different overnight options at Tatapouri Bay Oceanside are these sleek Zen Cabins overlooking the bay.

Salisbury Rd. (whisperingsands.co.nz; ✆ **06/867-1319**), is probably the pick of the bunch—located on vast Midway Beach, with a surf break right out front, it has 14 simple, bright, sea-view apartments. Those on the ground floor have their own picnic tables out on the grass, but in the upstairs ones you can check the surf from your balcony. Rooms start from NZ$250 in winter and NZ$305 in summer.

Tatapouri Bay Oceanside Accommodation ♥♥♥ Shanti Probst and Nathan Foon have taken your average holiday park and turned it into a destination. Sure, they had the location working to their advantage (the sun rises out of the sea on its doorstep), but since taking it over in 2019, they've added a ton of lush new features. The camp today has a children's playground, a boat ramp, barbecue facilities, and downright chic lodgings. The latter run the gamut from glamping tents and tent or camper spaces for those who bring their own, to "Zen" cabins (with cooking facilities and ocean views), a tiny home, and "podlifes," handsome units crafted from former shipping containers. Nice touches abound, like high-quality linens on the beds, lanterns with USB charging power in the tents, and rain showerheads in the shared bathrooms. The more expensive rooms come with free bookings at the outdoor hot tub and sauna, both of which look out to sea—and the roving Sauna Project (p. 274) sometimes pulls up here, too.

516 Whangara Rd., RD3. tatapouri.co.nz. ✆ **06/868-3269.** 24 powered sites, 32 unpowered sites, 7 cabins, 3 glamping tents (summer only). Campsites NZ$25 per person; cabins NZ$150–NZ$350; glamping tents NZ$275. **Amenities:** Coffee bar; cafe; play area; communal kitchen; hot tub; sauna; laundry; BBQ; boat ramp; free Wi-Fi.

Where to Eat in & Around Gisborne

It's absolutely worth leaving the city center for **Tahu ♥♥♥**, 40 Centennial Marine Dr. (tahu.co.nz; ✆ **06/281-0281;** Mon–Fri noon–late, Sat–Sun 9am–late). Owner Jared Johnstone—who traces his ancestry back through 30 generations of Gisborne-dwellers—has infused this restaurant with Māori values: sharing food, welcoming guests, and celebrating the region's abundance (you won't hear it called Poverty Bay around here). The view is spectacular; the food and drinks feature local flavors and native ingredients, like the leaves of *kawakawa* and *horopito*; and every detail reflects a deep connection to place, people, and culture—even the lightshades take the form of traditional eel-traps. Tahu opened in 2023 and sits at the heart of a vibrant new seaside precinct around the renovated surf club on Midway Beach. Order a seafood, vegan, or charcuterie platter (NZ$46–NZ$56) and a cocktail (NZ$20) and watch the sunset, waves, and distant cliffs from the deck or the comfy indoor seating.

For brunch, sashay through the red door of **Flagship Eatery ♥♥**, 14 Childers Rd. (flagshipeatery.co.nz; ✆ **06/281-0372;** Wed–Fri 7am–2pm, Sat–Sun 8am–2pm). It serves up twists on traditional breakfast items, such as house-made kimchi toasties, Cajun lemon tofu scramble, or eggs benny with cold-smoked salmon. Alternatively, fuel up on a vegan, Bali-style brunch at **Zephyr Wainui ♥♥**, 4 Oneroa Rd. (zephyrwainui.co.nz; Tues–Sun 8am–2pm)—think superfood smoothie bowls, raw slices, bagels, and burritos.

For dinner—especially if you're a wine-lover—I recommend **Crawford Road Kitchen ♥♥**, 3/50 Esplanade (crawfordroadkitchen.co.nz; ✆ **06/867-4085;** Tues–Sat 3–9pm), overlooking the river mouth and marina. Here you can enjoy tasty Mediterranean-inspired sharing plates—featuring bruschetta, cheeses, and cured meats—along with a glass or bottle of Gisborne's wide array of chardonnays, chenin blancs, pinot noirs, and merlots (the owners used to run the Gisborne wine center and are experts).

For a superior vineyard lunch in an eye-candy location, try the **Vines at Bushmere Estate ♥♥♥**, 166 Main Rd., SH2, Matawhero (thevines.co.nz; ✆ **06/868-9317;** Wed–Sun 11am–3pm). The food is as elegant as the setting—surrounded by vines, of course—especially the expertly prepared seafood dishes.

Finally, if you're just after a beer, you might end up with a case of decision fatigue at **Sunshine Brewing,** 49 Awapuni Rd. (sunshinebrewing.co.nz; ✆ **06/867-7777;** Mon–Sat noon–8pm, Sun noon–7pm). The oldest independent brewery in the country, it has up to two dozen legacy and seasonal brews on tap.

Where to Stay & Eat Around the East Cape

For overnight stays, the East Cape best caters to independent RV travelers; there are only a few motels and hotels here. Holiday homes for rental do exist (check Airbnb or Vrbo) but are few and far between.

At Te Kaha, 70km (43 miles) from Ōpōtiki, **Te Kaha Beach Resort ♥**, on SH35 (tekahabeachhotel.co.nz; ✆ **07/325-2830;** NZ$250–NZ$360), offers one- and two-bedroom apartments with panoramic views overlooking the eastern Bay of Plenty. The circular restaurant on-site has sweeping views and pretty good prices (main courses NZ$25–NZ$35).

For a stay in a historic property, try the modest but perfectly situated **Waihau Bay Lodge,** Orete Point Road, Waihau Bay 3199 (thewaihaubaylodge.co.nz; ✆ **07/325-3805**), with hostel-style budget rooms and private guest studios. Studio units are NZ$185, while budget rooms are NZ$120. We also highly recommend the **Rangimarie Beachstay ♥♥♥**, 930 Anaura Rd., Anaura Bay (anaura-stay.com; ✆ **021/633-372**), due to its sweet location, above one of the Cape's most picturesque beaches and surrounded by native bush. It has 2-story self-contained cottages sleeping up to four, costing NZ$200 to NZ$240. The bay area has no restaurants, but host Judy Newell will be happy to arrange lunch or dinner with advance notice; the property also has outdoor cooking facilities.

En Route to Napier

The 216km (134-mile) drive to Napier grazes the coast and then heads inland past rugged high-country sheep stations and spectacular gorges. A great place to soak your bones between Gisborne and Hawke's Bay is lovely **Mōrere Hot Springs ♥** (facebook.com/MorereHotSprings; ✆ **06/837-8856**), located in 364 hectares (899 acres) of native rainforest 57km (35 miles) south of Gisborne. You can have a soak in the saltwater springs and go for a walk. Admission is NZ$20 adults and NZ$12 children. It's open Thursday to Monday from 11am to 6pm.

HAWKE'S BAY

216km (134 miles) SW of Gisborne; 423km (262 miles) SE of Auckland; 228km (141 miles) SE of Rotorua

Despite its relative geographic isolation, Hawke's Bay/Te Matau-a-Māui is a favorite weekend destination for Wellingtonians and others wanting to enjoy its lush pastoral charms and opportunities to indulge. If you only have time to visit one wine region in New Zealand, this is arguably the place; 25 different micro-climates have resulted in more varietals than you'll find anywhere else in the country, and in 2023 the region was crowned the country's only Great Wine Capital by an international Bordeaux-based network (it's one of just 12 areas worldwide to earn that honor). The region also produces more apples and pears than any other in NZ, has the most olive trees, and grows 80% of the country's nectarines, peaches, and plums. Add in some of the best restaurants in the country—many featuring this local bounty—plus a growing brewing and distilling scene, and it becomes the ultimate foodie vacation.

Napier/Ahuriri (pop. 67,500), is a favorite of architecture buffs, but the reasons behind its appealingly unified look are tragic. In 1931, a magnitude 7.8 earthquake razed the city and severely damaged nearby Hastings and other centers. The quake and subsequent fires killed some 256 people, but Napier rose again, its 140 new buildings constructed in the Art Deco and Spanish

MĀUI'S great fish

It's said that legendary hero Māui is responsible for the North Island, which he fished up from the sea. As a result, the North Island is known as Te Ika-roa-a-Māui or "the great fish of Māui." In many traditions, the "fish" is a string ray. To see it, flip a map of NZ upside down. You'll find its head in present-day Wellington, its tail in Northland, its fins in Taranaki and the East Coast, its backbone in the mountain ranges that run between Taupō and Rotorua—and the point of Māui's hook, familiar from Disney's *Moana,* is lodged in Hawke's Bay's side at Cape Kidnappers.

Mission styles in vogue at the time. Today, Napier is considered one of the best-preserved Art Deco cities in the world.

Hastings/Heretaunga is the region's commercial center and fastest-growing municipality, with a population of 50,000. As housing prices have increased in recent years, the young and entrepreneurial have made the lower-priced Hastings their home, flocking here to open distilleries and breweries. It lacks Napier's retro cool, but still has plenty of architectural gems of its own.

The "village" of **Havelock North** is more accurately a bougie small town with about 15,000 people. It has dozens of cafes, art galleries, and boutiques running down the spokes of its wagon-wheel core.

Essentials

ARRIVING

Air New Zealand (airnewzealand.co.nz; ✆ **0800/737-000** in NZ) provides daily service between Napier/Hastings and Auckland, Wellington, and Christchurch. The airport is a 5-minute drive from the city and a 20-minute drive from Hastings. **Super Shuttle** (supershuttle.co.nz; ✆ **0800/748-885** in NZ, or 06/835-0055) charges NZ$23 per person to Napier, NZ$50 to Hastings.

Napier is a 5-hour drive from Auckland, 4 hours from Wellington, 2½ hours from Rotorua, 3 hours from Gisborne, and 1½ hours from Taupō. **InterCity** (intercity.co.nz; ✆ **09/623-1503**) operates a daily coach service between Napier/Hastings and Auckland, Gisborne, Rotorua, Taupō, Tauranga, and Wellington. Buses depart from 12 Carlyle St., Napier (next to Clive Sq.).

GETTING AROUND

The Hawke's Bay region is quite spread out, with much of the action taking place in the vineyards, rather than in the cities; it's possible to explore the greater region by organized tour (see p. 284), but to get the most out of a visit, you'll want to drive. The major car rental companies all have desks within the Napier airport. **Hawke's Bay Combined Taxis** (hawkesbaytaxis.nz; ✆ **06/835-7777**) is the biggest local company. Uber has recently arrived in the region, and you can get one from Hastings to Napier for around NZ$50.

VISITOR INFORMATION

The official tourism website for **Hawke's Bay Tourism** is **hawkesbaynz.com**.

The **Napier isite Visitor Centre,** 100 Marine Parade (napiernz.com; ✆ **06/834-1911**), is open daily 9am to 5pm, with extended summer hours. The **Hastings isite Visitor Centre,** 319 Heretaunga St. E (visithastings.co.nz; ✆ **06/873-0080**), is open Monday to Friday 9am to 5pm, Saturday 9am to 3pm, and Sunday 10am to 2pm. The **Havelock North isite Visitor Centre,** at the corner of Te Aute and Middle Roads (✆ **06/877-9600**), is open Monday to Saturday from 10am to 3pm, Sunday from 10am to 2pm.

SPECIAL EVENTS

The height of summer is when Art Deco madness reaches its annual peak: The **Art Deco Festival ♥♥♥** (artdecofestival.co.nz; ✆ **06/835-0022**) is held on the third weekend in February, when up to 40,000 people converge on Napier in their fancy '20s and '30s duds to wine, dine, dance, and drive around in vintage cars. A smaller, more intimate 'Winter Deco' version takes place in July.

The cheekily named **FAWC! Food and Wine Classic** (fawc.co.nz; ✆ **06/834-1918**) is an opportunity for foodies to get friendly with chefs, food producers, and winemakers. It's held twice annually, usually in November and June. In May, the scenic **Hawke's Bay Marathon** (hawkesbaymarathon.co.nz; ✆ **09/601-9590**) attracts thousands of runners to the region.

Exploring Hawke's Bay

NAPIER

The thing you're going to want to do most in Napier is just wander around, possibly pretending you're a 1930s femme fatale or a gangster in spats. Pick up a self-guided walking tour map from the visitor center; it'll take you about 2 hours to do the downtown area properly. Lined with Norfolk pines, **Marine Parade** is Napier's waterfront. **Tennyson Street** is the main thoroughfare in and out.

An Art Deco walking tour in Napier.

You can also get the walking tour map from the **Art Deco Centre ♥♥**, 5 Clive Square East, Memorial Square (✆ **06/835-0022**, daily 9:30am–5pm), which has a selection of retro gifts from the era—everything from jewelry and feather boas to Bakelite telephones and moustache wax. It's run by the **Art Deco Trust** (artdeconapier.com), a group of passionate locals dedicated to preserving and promoting the city's unique architectural heritage. The Art Deco Trust also conducts very interesting **guided Art Deco tours ♥♥** in which a friendly local will walk you around the city center explaining the history and significance of different buildings. Book ahead in summer, because they often sell out. Tours run at 10am and 2pm, run for 90 minutes, and cost NZ$33 adults, or NZ$5 for children ages 12 and under. During the summer, afternoon tours are 2 hours for NZ$36; sometimes evening tours starting at 4:30pm are also on offer. Or, to really get into the swing of things, you can take a **vintage car tour** ♥♥ through Napier and out to Port Ahuriri, where more delightful Deco awaits. The tours start from NZ$270 per car.

Finally, if you're driving to Havelock North, budget time for a quick stop at **Ātea a Rangi** ♥♥ in Waitangi Regional Park, just off SH52. Colloquially known as the Māori Star Compass, this site celebrates and explains the navigational tools used by ancient Polynesians to find New Zealand.

MTG Hawke's Bay ♥♥♥ MUSEUM Like most regional museums, MTG hosts touring exhibitions from around NZ. But the major permanent show that sets this one apart is the **1931 Earthquake Exhibition.** Start your visit with the 20-minute film about the tragedy, then head into the exhibit, which takes visitors right through that terrible day, from the day's weather forecast ("Tuesday 3 February: slight northwest breeze, 24°C, blue sky") to the quake, the fires, and the appalling aftermath, using photographs, artifacts, sound, and a new "shakehouse," a vibrating structure you can step inside to feel the sensation of being in an earthquake. It's moving to hear the quiet, insistent beeping of Morse code messages sent between the HMS *Veronica,* which was in port at the time, and other ships nearby. The museum also focuses on the stories, heritage, and art of the region, and features a good *taonga* Māori (Māori treasures) section. If you're wondering why it's known as MTG, that stands for "Museum, Theater, Gallery," which is appropriate. 1 Tennyson St. mtghawkesbay.com. ✆ **06/835-7781.** Free. Daily 9:30am–5pm.

Changing exhibits at MTG Hawke's Bay dive into local history and art.

National Aquarium of New Zealand ♥♥ AQUARIUM You might think that a small provincial city is a funny place to house the country's national aquarium, and you'd be right, but this local gem has a waterfront location where seawater less than 100m (328 ft.) away is pumped directly into the huge tanks. Fish enthusiasts opened this, the country's first public aquarium, in 1956, and today the vaguely stingray-shaped building has more than 100 species from New Zealand and around the world. An enormous oceanarium spotlights five species of shark and other reef fish from the local area, as well as exotic reef and deep-sea fish. There are also turtles, penguins, and some distinctly non-water-dwelling natives: kiwi and tuatara. You can also have close encounters with little blue penguins for NZ$140, which includes hand-feeding them.

Marine Parade. nationalaquarium.co.nz. ✆ **06/834-1404.** NZ$29 adults, NZ$15 children 3–14; family admission NZ$79. Discounts for seniors and students. Daily 9am–5pm.

HASTINGS & HAVELOCK NORTH

Hastings has its own fair share of Art Deco buildings, but it's the Spanish Mission style for which this town is better known. Architectural gems include the **Methodist Church, Westerman's Building,** and, most notably, the **Municipal Building,** 325 Heretaunga St. E, which underwent a NZ$40-million restoration project recently. The iconic heritage-listed building is now home to the **Toitoi Hawke's Bay Arts and Events Centre,** which includes the **Opera House,** along with new eateries, art galleries, wine bars, and boutiques. The newly revamped Hastings isite can also be found here.

The **Hastings City Art Gallery,** 201 Eastbourne St. E (hastingscityartgallery.co.nz; ✆ **06/871-5095**), is a modern art space for contemporary exhibitions and events that really puts a spotlight on what's happening on the New Zealand art scene. It's also home to **Te Toa ♥**, a shop that sells work by some of the best local contemporary artists and craftspeople. Entry to the gallery is free: It's open Tuesday to Saturday 10am to 4pm. Ask at the info center for maps to the public sculptures installed through Hastings and Havelock North as part of an award-winning revitalization program. For more art, stop at the award-winning **Birdwoods ♥♥**, 298 Middle Rd., Havelock North (birdwoods.co.nz; ✆ **06/877-1395**), which has large-format stone and metal sculptures carved by internationally acclaimed Zimbabwean and NZ artists. There are also a cafe and sweet shop on site. It's open daily from 10am to 4pm (closed public holidays).

The drive to the **Te Mata Peak ♥♥♥**, about 11km (7 miles) southeast of Hastings, is one of the region's top adventures. The 399m (1,309-ft.) limestone ridge rises dramatically from the Heretaunga Plains, and on a clear day, you'll have 360-degree views out to sea and across to the Ruahine, Kaweka, and Maungaharuru ranges with Mount Ruapehu visible in the distance. If you want to stretch your legs on the way up or down, there are loads of walking tracks. The road is long, steep, narrow, and can be crowded on weekends at sunset, so drive with care.

TASTE YOUR WAY around the bay

Hawke's Bay is the birthplace of New Zealand's wine industry. French Marist missionaries planted the first vines in 1851, and today the region has more than 100 vineyards and 80 wineries, with around 35 tasting rooms. Soil and climate conditions are perfect for late-maturing varieties like cabernet sauvignon, riesling, and chardonnay, although syrah from this area is also highly prized. Most wineries open every day for sales, and an increasing number have their own restaurants. The best time to visit is between March and early May, when wine is in production and the vines are turning golden.

If you want to sample some of the region's vineyards but are tight on time, swing by **Smith & Sheth ♥♥**, 4 Te Aute Rd., right behind Porters Boutique Hotel in Havelock North (smithandsheth.com; ✆ **06/650-5550**). Owner Steve Smith founded the Craggy Range vineyard (see below) and is one of NZ's few qualified Master of Wines. Needless to say, he and his colleagues are true authorities on wine, and share their knowledge about all the top producers with NZ$15 flights (waived with a NZ$50 bottle purchase) at this wine bar. Their **Heretaunga Wine Studio experience ♥♥♥** ($150 per person) is a multi-sensory journey (igniting more than just your smell and taste) delivered in three acts over 21⁄2 hours. As per Smith & Sheth's request, I can't spoil the surprise element, but I can say you'll be introduced to a who's-who of NZ wine and the science behind wine production. You don't have to be a wine snob to enjoy it—but be prepared to leave as one. Reserve at least 48 hours in advance.

Pick up a free map from the visitor center for all the tasting rooms. Here are just a handful worth stopping at:

- **Taradale:** In this southwest Napier suburb, **Church Road ♥♥♥**, 150 Church Rd. (church-road.com; ✆ **06/833-8224**), is one of the country's oldest wineries (est. 1897) and has won countless awards, including best tasting room in the country and winemaker of the year. It does daily behind-the-scenes tours, including its new "Versatility of the Grape Experience," which offers insight into its experiments in wine, liquor, and balsamic vinegar. Nearby **Mission Estate Winery ♥♥**, 198 Church Rd. (missionestate.co.nz; ✆ **06/845-9350**), is considered the birthplace of NZ wine, as the oldest winery in the country, founded by French priests in 1851. Here you can dine in the beautifully restored seminary. The wines are pretty amazing, too!
- **West of Hastings: Alpha Domus ♥♥**, 1829 Maraekakaho Rd. (alphadomus.co.nz; ✆ **06/879-6752**), is a boutique winery in the Bridge Pā sub-region. The winery's flagship wine, "The Aviator," is one of this country's best Bordeaux-style reds (and their dessert wine is great, too). **Sileni Estates Winery ♥♥♥**, 2016 Maraekakaho Rd. (sileni.co.nz; ✆ **06/879-8768**), has the advantage of being a top winery (making world-class Bordeaux and burgundy varieties) that also has a gourmet food store, restaurant, and wine discovery center on-site.

There has been an **Australasian gannet colony** at the craggy peninsula of **Cape Kidnappers ♥♥** since the 1870s, and its healthy population now numbers about 6,500 pairs. A half-hour drive from Napier or Hastings, it's the

Trinity Hill Winery ♥♥, 2396 SH50 (trinityhill.com; ✆ **06/879-7778**), is another top producer in the celebrated Gimblett Gravels area. Its Homage wine label is considered a collector's item in NZ. Known for its syrah, **Ash Ridge** ♥♥, 2543 SH50 (ashridgewines.com; ✆ **06/650-4324**), also has a small range of alternative experimental wines made by Lauren Swift, winner of NZ's Young Winemaker of the Year.

- **Te Awanga:** Right on the Te Awanga coast east of Hastings, **Elephant Hill Estate** ♥♥♥, 86 Clifton Hill (elephanthill.co.nz; ✆ **06/873-0400**), is one of the country's newer wineries, with stunning ocean-colored copper buildings. It produces premium single-estate wines.
- **Havelock North & Surrounds:** The best way to visit the wineries in this compact region is by hiring a bike or an e-bike for the day (see "Outdoor Pursuits," p. 285), riding along the gorgeous raised off-road cycle paths, and stopping at the vineyards you fancy. For a more low-key (and cheaper) lunch, roll up to **Askerne Estate Winery** ♥♥, 267 Te Mata Mangateretere Rd. (askernewines.co.nz; ✆ **06/877-2089**), where you can create your own picnic from a selection of meats, cheeses, local fruit preserves, and ice cream. Guided and unguided tasting flights are available—all Askerne's many wines are grown and made right here. **Te Mata Estate** ♥♥, 349 Te Mata Rd. (temata.co.nz; ✆ **06/877-4399**), dates back to 1896 and is one of New Zealand's most prestigious wineries, comprising five vineyards that produce some 40,000 cases a year. Look out for the fluffy highland cattle, whose manure nourishes the grapevines. **Black Barn Vineyards** ♥♥♥, Black Barn Rd. (blackbarn.com; ✆ **06/879-7603**), produces premium Bordeaux-style varieties but also makes award-winning whites (chardonnay, viognier, and sauvignon blanc). It's a beautifully sited boutique operation, with an award-winning bistro (see p. 291), a kitchen shop, accommodation options, and an amphitheater for open-air cinema screenings and live summer concerts. On the other side of Te Mata Peak, **Craggy Range Winery** ♥♥♥, 253 Waimarama Rd. (craggyrange.com; ✆ **06/873-7126**), sits below the imposing escarpment (which is indeed spectacularly craggy). It has a top restaurant (see p. 292) and lovely self-contained cottages, with everything you need for a relaxing retreat. Its Giants Estate Experience (NZ$150) is a 2-hour education in wine appreciation (for novices) or a chance to nerd out on the region's terroir (for experts). It includes a tour of the atmospheric (if chilly) cellars, and samples of aged and premium wines (the 1-hr. NZ$50 version features recent vintages). Budget extra time for a stroll among the sculptures in its extensive gardens—former Prime Minister Jacinda Ardern got married here in 2024.

largest mainland gannet colony in the world. The best time to visit is from early November to late February; it's closed to the public between July and October during the early nesting phase. The best way to visit is on a minibus tour over the farmland (see "Organized Tours," below); it is possible to walk around the coast, but it's a 5-hour return trip that must be precisely timed around low tide to avoid being cut off, and the unstable cliffs occasionally collapse—in 2019 two walkers were hospitalized after being buried in a massive landslide.

Gannets nest in huge swarms at Cape Kidnappers.

Organized Tours

If you want to discover the region's up-and-coming vintners, contact **Prinsy's Tours** ♥♥ (prinsystours.co.nz; ✆ **0800/004-237**), which specializes in the region's younger winemakers, some of which can only be visited on this tour. That's the case with **Element Wines** ♥♥ (boutiqueconnection.co.nz), which is so local that tastings take place in the owners' backyard. Afternoon wine tours (11am–4pm) start at NZ$170 per person. (***Tip:*** If you have a group of four, it costs the same to book an exclusive tour.)

ALL THE DRINKS THAT aren't WINE

If you've had just about enough wine, then it's time to tap into the rest of what Hawke's Bay has to offer: distilleries, cideries, and breweries! First stop is **Hastings Distillers** ♥♥, 231 Heretaunga St. E, Hastings (hastingsdistillers.com; ✆ **06/870-3991**), the newest kid on the block. Its Masonic-inspired space makes for an evocative tasting room for its gin and L'Opera bitter orange aperitif, all created from organic and biodynamic botanicals. Tasting flights are available, as are snacks.

Brave Brewing Co. ♥♥, 205 Queen St. E, Hastings (bravebrewing.co.nz; ✆ **027/460-8414**), has graduated from its garage origins to the brand-new Tribune Precinct. Next door you'll find **Real World NZ** ♥, 211 Queen St. E, Hastings (realworldnz.com), which manufactures natural body products using native ingredients, such as pōhutukawa flowers and kiwi seeds. (You can't drink anything here, but it smells so good you might want to.)

GodsOwn Brewery ♥♥, 3672 SH50 (facebook.com/godsownbrewery; ✆ **027/931-1042**), is far enough out in the country that you'll need a designated driver. It's the first place on the North Island to attempt to grow hops, including varieties not found elsewhere in the country. Wood-fired pizza and beer—which you can enjoy at tables amid the hops—can be ordered from a 1973 caravan. It's also a great place to let the kids run loose, with a massive playground made of recycled tires. (It's closed July–Aug.)

Meanwhile, **Roosters Brewery** ♥, 1470 Omahu Rd., Hastings (roosters.co.nz; ✆ **06/879-5158**), is where the vineyard workers head for lunch and a brewski.

Juliet Harbutt wrote the book on cheese—literally. A London cheese shop owner for 30 years, she authored the *World Cheese Book,* which has sold more than 90,000 copies. Now settled back in the Hawke's Bay region, she shares her expertise with visitors—including her own system of tasting and categorizing cheese—on her **Hunter Gatherer Tours ♥♥♥**, 79 Black Barn Rd. (huntergatherertours.co.nz; ✆ **021/0747-856**). Despite the name, her tours have very little to do with foraging—unless you count Juliet escorting you to orchards with the ripest fruit and wineries with the best wine. The private customized tours always end at her house, where you'll have guided cheese tasting that might just change your worldview. Her tours aren't cheap at upwards of NZ$950 for two people, but they're an experience you can't replicate elsewhere. She also offers a 3-hour private wine and cheese experience at her house: NZ$395 for two.

A perfect complement to Hawke's Bay wines, cheese is the focus of Juliet Harbutt's Hunter Gatherer Tours.

The experts at **Gannet Safaris Overland ♥♥**, 396 Clifton Rd., Te Awanga (gannetsafaris.co.nz; ✆ **06/875-0888**), take visitors out to the gannet colony in an air-conditioned 4WD minibus from September to April, no walking required. In addition to the trill, clatter, and stench of hundreds of large seabirds in close proximity, expect storytelling and larrikin Kiwi humor from your guide—and lots of spectacular views. Three-hour tours depart daily from the company base at Clifton at 9:30am or 1:30pm and cost NZ$99 adults and NZ$50 children ages 5 to 17. Private and sunrise tours also available.

Outdoor Pursuits

CYCLING One of the best ways to see Hawke's Bay is on a bike. There are 200km (124 miles) of mostly off-road, mostly flat scenic trails for all abilities and ages. They meander along the coast, past wineries, and along the top of levees built to prevent flooding, giving gorgeous views over vineyards and apple orchards to the mountains beyond. For trails and more information, visit **Hawke's Bay Trails** at hbtrails.nz. **Tākaro Trails ♥♥♥**, 9 Nelson Quay, Ahuriri, Napier (takarotrails.co.nz; ✆ **06/835-9030**), is one of several companies that will drop you off in one spot, supply you with maps and advice, then pick you up hours or days later somewhere else. If you choose a (pricier) electric bike, you'll barely break a sweat—but you'll still finish the day with a sense of achievement. Tākaro Trails offers various self-guided day trips starting from NZ$75 (NZ$105 for e-bikes), and 2- to 4-day overnight itineraries around the region.

Alternatively, **Coastal Wine Cycles** in the cute seaside town of Haumoana (winecycles.co.nz) rents colorful California cruisers for NZ$50 per day.

A cycling tour of Hawke Bay's wineries.

GOLF Established in 1896, the **Napier Golf Club,** Waiohiki, 1215 Korokipo Rd. SH50, Napier (napiergolf.co.nz; ✆ **06/844-7913**), is an 18-hole championship course close to the city. Greens fees are NZ$80 for 18 holes and NZ$50 for 9. **Cape Kidnappers Golf Course ♥♥♥**, 446 Clifton Rd., Te Awanga (capekidnappers.com; ✆ **06/873-1018**), is one of the finest—and most scenic—courses in the world, designed by legendary architect Tom Doak. The green fees reflect its prestige: It's NZ$700 for 18 holes.

Where to Stay in Hawke's Bay

NAPIER

Scenic Hotel Te Pania ♥♥, 45 Marine Parade (scenichotels.co.nz; ✆ **06/833-7733;** pricing is dynamic, but rates start at NZ$215 for rooms, NZ$400 for suites), curves elegantly around the Parade; has bright, modern rooms; and is close to the action. For old-style charm, try the **County Hotel ♥♥**, 12 Browning St. (countyhotel.co.nz; ✆ **06/835-7800**), an iconic Edwardian building (built in 1909) that's one of only two significant structures to survive the 1931 Napier earthquake. Rates range from NZ$225 for a luxury king room to NZ$325 for the Regal Suite.

Art Deco Masonic Hotel ♥♥ This is, quite simply, a beautiful hotel inside and out. Completely renovated, it oozes Art Deco charm but has all the modern conveniences. The superior rooms are stylish if small, which is somewhat made up for by their back doors leading to a common balcony overlooking Marine Parade. If you want to splash out, the Royal Suite is named as such because Queen Elizabeth II and Prince Philip stayed here during her Coronation Tour of 1953.

Corner Tennyson St. & Marine Parade. masonic.co.nz. ✆ **06/835-8689.** 42 units. NZ$279–NZ$629 double, suites, or apartment. Long-stay and off-peak rates. **Amenities:** 2 restaurants, 2 bars; room service; balcony access; free Wi-Fi.

The Crown Hotel ♥ Set in the cool seaside village of Ahuriri just out of the CBD (Central Business District), the beautiful Spanish Mission–style Crown Hotel was built in 1932. Sadly, the property suffers from issues many older hotels do: noise problems, tiny bathrooms, and room decor that, in some cases, has seen better days. Still, the location is unbeatable, and many rooms have stunning sea views. The hotel also hosts the Globe Theatrette, a 45-seater

Across the street from Napier Beach, 415 Marine Parade does bed-and-breakfast with a bit of extra luxury.

boutique cinema that screens movies from Tuesday to Sunday. Hotel guests get a 20% discount on movie tickets.

Corner Bridge St. & Harding Rd. thecrownnapier.co.nz. ✆ **06/833-8330.** 42 units. NZ$259–NZ$460. Free parking. **Amenities:** Restaurant; bar; room service; free bike storage; laundry service; free Wi-Fi.

415 Marine Parade ♥♥♥ When an old villa came up for sale during the pandemic, locals Esther and Tom Seymour jumped on the opportunity. They didn't just fully refurbish the property—they reconfigured it, creating five generously sized guest rooms. Yes, it's technically a bed-and-breakfast (expect freshly baked bread every morning and port brought to your room with turn-down service in the evenings), but it feels more like a boutique hotel, where it's entirely possible to be as social or as secluded as you like. The little details—like in-room snacks, Zealong teas, and underfloor heating in the bathrooms—make this a luxurious getaway. Located waterfront at the edge of Napier's downtown area, it's walking distance from everything you might need.

415 Marine Parade. 415marineparade.co.nz. ✆ **027/486-9859.** 5 units. NZ$498–NZ$528. Rates include breakfast. **Amenities:** Bicycles; free Wi-Fi.

IN & AROUND HASTINGS & HAVELOCK NORTH

Wonderful and generally upmarket accommodation choices abound here, with the emphasis on rentable holiday homes and B&Bs. We particularly like **Cottages on St. Andrews ♥♥♥**, 14 St. Andrews Rd., Havelock (cottagesonstandrews.nz; ✆ **06/877-1644**), which is just 1km (½ mile) from Havelock North village and has smart, modern studio units, three- and four-bedroom cottages, and more accommodation in the main house. Biggest lure, especially for families? The sheep, alpacas, and donkey roaming the 2-hectare (5-acre) property, which also has a heated outdoor pool. Rates are NZ$180 to NZ$540.

A newer offering of the glamping variety is **Villas & Vines ♥**, 342 Lawn Rd., Clive (villasandvines.co.nz; ✆ **02/766-82839**). Its two luxury safari tents (one sleeps four, the other six) are located close to Havelock, Hastings, and the coast, and sit right on the cycle trail. The feel is completely rural, with ducks waddling about and a million stars glistening above on clear nights. The tents are set right among the grapevines, with lovely luxurious touches inside and on their ample decks—like fairy lights, fluffy pillows, and carpeted wooden floors. But they do get a bit cold inside in winter, and you'll have to walk around the back of the tent to access the bathroom. Rates start at NZ$295.

For those who like to be in the center of things, the new **Quest Hastings ♥♥**, 304 Eastbourne St. E, Hastings (questapartments.co.nz; ✆ **06/280-622**), has a great location smack bang in the middle of town. It has 34 apartments, a mix of studio and one-bedroom—fairly generic, as you'd expect from a chain, but sleek and modern—with variable pricing starting at around NZ$280.

If you'd prefer to linger (and avoid driving) after your wine tasting, many vineyards also boast accommodation options. **Craggy Range** (craggyrange.com/accommodation) has four self-contained cottages with lovely views that each sleep four (from NZ$700) and a couple of lodges that can sleep up to six (NZ$1,450). They all have extremely well-equipped kitchens in case you're inspired to whip up your own masterpieces from all that abundant local produce.

Rosewood Cape Kidnappers ♥♥♥ Probably best known for its acclaimed Tom Doak–designed golf course, which is consistently ranked among the best in the world, this expansive property is part of a 2,500-hectare (6,000-acre) working sheep and cattle farm, where rolling green pastures and verdant bush lead down to the dramatic cliffs and the sea beyond. It's also home to the **Cape Sanctuary,** NZ's largest privately run wildlife restoration project, with 10.6km (6½ miles) of fencing that keeps predators out and protects the nature species within, including kiwi, takahē, and the world's largest gannet nesting colony. Guests can visit the colony on an e-bike tour; they're also welcome to help staff conduct routine health checks on kiwi chicks or tuatara, or help the shepherds tend flocks of sheep (a particular favorite of guests ages 11 and under). If "doing nothing" is more your speed, there's a pampering spa and heated pool; the exquisite suites have fireplaces, soaking tubs, gazillion-thread-count sheets, and other luxuries. But the highlight here is the food: The included meals are inventive and fresh, with much of the produce harvested on site.

446–448 Clifton Rd., Te Awanga. capekidnappers.com. ✆ **06/875-1900.** 23 units (22 suites, 1 cottage). NZ$3,000–NZ$7,000. Rates include breakfast, pre-dinner drinks, and dinner. **Amenities:** Restaurant; bar; babysitting; mountain bikes; concierge; 18-hole golf course; gym and health spa; clay pigeon shooting; outdoor pool; Jacuzzi; room service; free Wi-Fi.

CENTRAL HAWKE'S BAY

Central Hawke's Bay is home to a number of historic homesteads, most of which offer accommodations, like **Oruawharo** in Takapau (oruawharo.com),

Guests gather for a feast on the lawn at Wallingford Homestead.

Gwavas in Waipawa (gwavasgarden.co.nz), and **Ashcott** (ashcotthomestead.com) along SH50.

Wallingford Homestead ♥♥♥ Frommer's insists that I only give a max of three stars, but if I could give four to this property, I would. When I checked in, the manager (or "hello person," as she likes to be known) Jeanette Woerner summed up the Homestead's appeal in a single sentence: "If you don't want to eat, this isn't the place to stay." If you *do* want to eat, Woerner's husband, Chris Stockdale, an award-winning chef, will treat you to true feasts, many of which are crafted by food produced on, or near, the homestead. The dinner and breakfast—both included in the package—were among the best and biggest I've had in New Zealand. The historic homestead, while gorgeous, is almost secondary to the experience (it was undergoing needed cosmetic improvements to its three wings as we went to press). It's almost certainly haunted, and I'm all for it. There's also no cellphone reception out here. Can't stay the night? Wallingford's dining room is open to non-guests for bookings on Friday and Saturday nights. Most of the year, rooms are only available for overnight stays Thursday through Saturday. ***Tip:*** Plan your visit for a winter weekend when the harvest of the property's 1,700 truffle trees is underway.

2914 Porangahau Rd., Wallingford. wallingford.co.nz. ✆ **06/855-4701.** 10 units. NZ$887–NZ$1,400 double. Rates include breakfast and dinner. **Amenities:** Swimming pool; lawn games; guest laundry; free Wi-Fi.

Where to Eat in Hawke's Bay

Many of the best places to eat are at the wineries around Hastings and Havelock North, but good restaurants and cafes can be found everywhere—even in obvious tourist strips. However, be aware that many bars and restaurants (especially in Havelock North and Hastings) may be closed on Mondays and Tuesdays. Beyond those listed below, we highly recommend a meal at **Wallingford Homestead** (see above).

NAPIER

Hapī Ora ♥♥, 45 Hastings St. (hapi.nz; ✆ **064/6561-0142;** Mon–Sat 7am–4pm, Sun 8am–2pm), is the place to stock up on picnic supplies. This deli caters to gluten-free, dairy-free, cane-sugar-free, paleo, and vegan diets (hello, cashew cheese!), as well as supplying excellent coffee and turmeric chai. If you're in the mood for fish and chips, sided by a well-pulled tankard of beer, check out

In a smartly revamped firehouse from the 1920s, Central Fire Station serves up local ingredients with a fine-dining flair.

Paddy's Irish Pub ♥♥♥, 60 West Quay (paddysbar.co.nz; ✆ **064/834-0189**), one of the friendliest joints in the seaside village of Ahuriri (which is just around the water from Napier's city center). It's right near the docks, and the fish tastes like it jumped into the fryer right before you arrived. And for a tasty, cheap pizza in a hopping spot with a fridge full of cold beer, head for **Vinci's Pizza** ♥♥♥, 29A Hastings St. (vincispizza.co.nz; ✆ **06/650-7779;** open daily 11am–8:30pm, slightly later on weekends). You can get your fix by the slice (from NZ$6) or grab a whole pizza (from NZ$30)—easily enough for two, and if you can't agree on the topping you can split it half and half.

Central Fire Station ♥♥♥ MODERN NEW ZEALAND When chef Sam Clark and his pastry chef partner Florencia Menehem decided to open a restaurant in the 1926 fire hall, it would have been easy for them to lean into the industrial theme. Instead, they created the ultimate date night venue, with soft lighting, Art Deco furnishings, and quiet music that's easy to have a conversation over. The only remains of the building's former life are the massive picture windows (once the giant archways through which fire trucks rushed off to emergencies) and a brass fire pole. The regularly changing French- and Italian-inspired menu highlights the region's best suppliers and seasonal produce. Think roast lamb rumps with salsa verde, market fish with scampi butter sauce, and gnocchi with roasted cauliflower and gorgonzola. This is Napier's fine dining at its finest.

163 Tennyson St. centralfirestation.co.nz. ✆ **06/650-1115.** Main courses NZ$44–NZ$48. Daily 5:30pm–late.

Mister D Dining ♥♥ MODERN NEW ZEALAND Situated on the main road, this eatery hums with activity and good vibes. They make all their own bread, pasta, and pastries daily, and everything is fresh and approached in original fashion. The lamb croquettes, for example, are served with date and preserved lemon chutney and yogurt (they're a standout). Plan to save room for the white chocolate mousse with candied apples and green apple salad, which is cool and delicious, just like this place.

47 Tennyson St. misterd.co.nz. ✆ **06/835-5022.** Main courses NZ$38–NZ$45. Dinner reservations recommended. Thurs–Mon 7:30–11am, Thurs–Mon 11:15am–3pm, Wed–Sat 5:30pm–late.

HASTINGS & HAVELOCK NORTH

It's a bit of a no-brainer that you'll want to head for the excellent winery restaurants in this area. For the best of those, see "Taste Your Way Around the Bay" (p. 282) or consider **Black Barn Bistro ♥♥♥**, Black Barn Road, Havelock North (blackbarnbistro.com; ✆ **06/877-7985**). It's one of the few that's located higher in the hills, making it the place to sit with a drink in hand and

FOOD, GLORIOUS hawke's bay FOOD

Most people head to Hawke's Bay for the wine, but the "tastings" here aren't exclusive to alcoholic beverages. Depending on what's in-season, you'll also pass apple and cherry orchards in your travels, many open to the public. A good starting place is the **Hawke's Bay Farmer's Market ♥♥♥**, held at the Tōmoana Showgrounds, Kenilworth Road, Hastings (hawkesbayfarmers market.co.nz; ✆ **027/697-3737**), every Sunday from 8:30am to 12:30pm. The location is fabulous—if you come in spring, the mature trees drop their blossoms all over the stallholders—and the produce is among the very best this country has to offer. There's live music and kids running around happily—it really is a joyful place on a fine day. There's also the **Napier Urban Food Market,** Clive Square East, Napier, held on Saturdays from 8:30am to 12:30pm. The atmosphere is a little less laid-back here, but the food is equally good.

A picturesque **Growers' Market ♥♥♥** is also held at the Sun Dial in the heart of the Black Barn Vineyards, off Te Mata Road, Havelock North (blackbarn.com; ✆ **06/877-7985**), every summer Saturday from 9am to noon. It showcases the new season's fruit and veggies, baked goods, locally roasted coffee, preserves, lavender products, olive oil, and more. If you haven't eaten too many of your purchases, you could then go for lunch at the **Black Barn Bistro** (see above).

With 5,000 trees, **Te Mata Figs ♥**, 205 Napier Rd., Havelock North (temata figs.co.nz; ✆ **027/476-4777**), produces 30 different types of organically certified figs of varying sizes and colors. Its on-site cafe (which is entirely gluten-free) is open year-round and features a small gift shop selling everything from figgy pudding to a fig powder. ***Fun fact:*** All of its trees are "common" or female hermaphrodites, meaning that they're not pollinated by wasps.

Award-winning ice cream maker **Rush Munro's,** 201 Heretaunga St., Hastings (rushmunro.co.nz; ✆ **06/873-9050**), is an institution in these parts. The Hawke's Bay company has been around since 1926 (it's New Zealand's oldest) and is still delighting its fans with 100% natural flavors like passionfruit, mānuka honey, strawberries and cream, blackcurrant, maple and walnut, and hokey pokey (a Kiwi favorite made from vanilla ice cream with bits of honeycomb toffee in it). The Ice Cream Garden is open daily 10:30am to 6:30pm.

gaze down at the plains below. Like nearly every other worthwhile restaurant in the region, Black Barn focuses on local and seasonal ingredients, but you'll encounter plenty of seafood (like line-caught white fish), a handful of vegetarian options (ricotta agnolotti with courgetti and saffron), and mains that range from NZ$22 to NZ$85. After you've eaten and drunk your fill, you can take home goodies from the on-site kitchen shop. Hours vary seasonally, but usually it's open for lunch and dinner starting from 10am (closed Mon–Tues during the winter).

On Hastings' main street, **Fun Buns** ♥ (funbuns.co.nz; ✆ **06/650-0185;** Tues–Sat 4:30–8:30pm, later on weekends) serves up Asian street food, including a wide variety of bao buns—classic pork belly, spicy Thai fried chicken—in a colorful, funky, and cozy space. Tasty cocktails or mocktails—optionally served in vintage teapots—feature syrups homemade from local foraged or donated fruit like plums or cherries. There's a full celiac menu and a vegan one too.

Popular enough to have its own cookbook and food truck, the **Pipi Café** ♥♥, 16 Joll Rd., Havelock North (cafe.pipi.co.nz; ✆ **06/877-8993;** Tues–Sun 4–10pm), was rosy-hued even before "millennial pink" was a thing. The main event here is the traditional homemade pizza, although there are some more inventive plant-based specials on offer, like the tahini and turmeric pizza.

Malo ♥♥, 4 Te Aute Rd., Havelock North (malo.co.nz; ✆ **06/877-2009;** daily 9am–late), is the highlight of the otherwise forgettable Porters Boutique Hotel. Head Chef Bert van de Steeg joined the restaurant after years of cooking at Michelin-starred restaurants, and the menu features Turkish and Asian-inspired dishes with local ingredients.

Craggy Range ♥♥♥ MODERN NEW ZEALAND Craggy Range may be Hawke's Bay's most talked-about restaurant, and it's got the awards to show for it—including the nation's Best Winery Restaurant in 2024, the same year it hosted former PM Jacinda Ardern's wedding. Much of its produce is grown on-site in extensive biodynamic gardens, or comes from local producers. The service is excellent, the setting stunning, the menu changes seasonally to reflect the restaurant's paddock-to-plate ethos—and while you can order a la carte, I highly recommend the five-course tasting menu (NZ$99), with optional wine pairings for an additional NZ$95. (The mashed potato focaccia with camembert-infused butter alone is worth the trip.) As of 2025, there are two dining rooms to choose from; the main restaurant downstairs, or the intimate loft mezzanine. Tucked away upstairs, it offers "familiar, dinner-party style dining"—chef Casey McDonald serves you what he'd cook in his home for his friends: a three-course banquet set menu for NZ$129 (Thurs–Sat from 5pm only).

253 Waimarama Rd., Havelock North. craggyrange.com. ✆ **06/873-0143.** 2-course a la carte NZ$79, tasting menu NZ$99 (wine pairing extra). Reservations recommended. Daily noon–2:30pm and 6pm–late.

St. Georges Restaurant ♥♥ MODERN NEW ZEALAND Award-winning head chef Francky Godinho is so passionate about the farm-to-table

Food at the Craggy Range Restaurant is mostly grown in the massive organic gardens that surround this lodge.

ethos, he grows his own veggies in an on-site organic garden and raises his own cattle. Around 90% of the produce comes from the restaurant's gardens, including the edible flowers that garnish the beautifully presented plates. Dishes change seasonally based on what's in season, with a "chef's choice" menu available in addition to a la carte. Dietary restrictions are also well catered for.

452 St. Georges Rd., Havelock North. stgeorgesrestaurant.co.nz. ✆ **06/877-5356.** Main courses NZ$34–NZ$40. Wed–Sun 11am–10:30pm.

En Route to the Wairarapa: Central Hawke's Bay

The drive to the Wairarapa (and onward to Wellington) via SH2 takes roughly 3 to 4 hours, but budget time for stops. SH2 runs through **Central Hawke's Bay,** including the historic towns of Waipukurau and Waipawa, where you'll find boutique shopping, art galleries, and even more wineries. For a free guided tour of the places of cultural importance to the local *iwi* (tribes), visit **Ngā Ara Tipuna** (tour.ngaaratipuna.co.nz). Developed for mobile phones, the website interprets the Pukekaihau Pā site using audio and videos. Once a thriving Māori settlement dating back to the 1600s, it can be found at Hunter Memorial Park in Waipukurau, where there are also recently updated interpretative panels. A driving tour of the greater region is also available.

En Route to Taupō

A drive along the Napier–Taupō Highway (SH5) will take you about 2½ hours. The road is winding in places and climbs to 708m (2,322 ft.) over the Titiokura Saddle and may be closed by snow in the winter.

TARANAKI & WHANGANUI

9

Halfway between Auckland and Wellington and pointing into the Tasman Sea, Taranaki is truly out there. It boasts a vibrant small city—New Plymouth—in the north, but its heart is the beautiful, sacred, and almost-symmetrical Taranaki Maunga (Mt. Taranaki), which rises up out on the flat countryside like Mt. Fuji (without the concession booths). In 2025, the mountain was formally recognized as an ancestor of Taranaki Māori, and granted legal personhood—it now owns itself.

Taranaki's lush plains make it a leading dairying region, but it's also an energy center with reserves of natural gas and oil both on- and offshore. If "white gold" is milk and "black gold" is oil, this is a rich region indeed. It's considerably less touristy than its counterparts on the North Island's east coast, but that doesn't mean it's lacking in attractions: It boasts a string of surf beaches, hiking trails, art galleries, and some of the country's best botanical gardens. Welcome to "Taradise"!

South of Taranaki, Whanganui is built around its major waterway, literally and figuratively. The mystical Whanganui River—which was already recognized as a legal person in 2017—may look tame, but the longest navigable river in New Zealand is rich in history and the biggest drawcard for visitors to the region. A journey down the river—one of the Great Walks of New Zealand (go figure!)—is something you will always remember.

NEW PLYMOUTH & THE TARANAKI REGION

New Plymouth: 412km (255 miles) W of Napier; 164km (102 miles) NW of Wanganui; 369km (229 miles) SW of Auckland

The Taranaki region is home to roughly 130,000 resourceful souls who love their world-class surf breaks, beautiful parks and gardens, and arts events the rest of the country envies. At the end of 2021, New Plymouth/Ngāmotu (which is often referred to as "Taranaki," although that's actually the name for the entire region) was named the World's Most Liveable City of its size for its public spaces, arts and culture projects, and environmental initiatives. Young families

Taranaki to Wellington

9

TARANAKI & WHANGANUI | New Plymouth & the Taranaki Region

are making their home here, with new projects and creative enterprises making it an invigorating place to be, even if it lacks the package tourism products found elsewhere on the North Island. Most will find that a couple of nights is enough time to explore the major sites, including Taranaki Maunga, an art gallery or museum, and one of its many gardens or beaches.

Essentials

ARRIVING **Air New Zealand** (www.airnewzealand.co.nz; ✆ **0800/737-000** in NZ) provides daily flights into New Plymouth from Auckland, Wellington, and Christchurch. New Plymouth Airport is 8km (5 miles) from the city. **Scott's Airport Shuttle** (www.npairportshuttle.co.nz; ✆ **06/769-5974**) will get you there and back cheaper than a taxi.

Driving, however, is probably your best option. New Plymouth, on SH3, is a 5-hour drive from Auckland, 4 from Taupō, 3 from Hamilton, and a 2-hour drive from Whanganui. You could also arrive via the **Forgotten World Highway (SH43),** a remote, winding, adventure-filled way that runs from Taumarunui in the Ruapehu region to Stratford in Taranaki (p. 256). There is regular coach service from all over the North Island, provided by **InterCity** (intercity.co.nz; ✆ **09/623-1503**).

GETTING AROUND **Citylink** and **Southlink** (trc.govt.nz/bus-routes; ✆ **06/765-7127**) operate local city buses in New Plymouth. If you need a local taxi, try **New Plymouth Taxis** (✆ **06/757-3000**) or **Energy City Cabs** (✆ **0800/181-525** in NZ). For shuttle services around the region, including to the mountain and national park, contact **Taranaki Driven** (taranakidriven.nz;

The Te Rewa Rewa Bridge, designed by Peter Mulqueen, is not just a pedestrian and cycling bridge—it's also a memorial, as this was the site of a major battle during the Musket Wars. In the background is Taranaki Maunga/Mt. Taranaki.

✆ **027/270-2932**). You may also have some luck with Uber, which operates in the city (although there aren't many drivers working for the service).

VISITOR INFORMATION The region's official tourism website is **taranaki.co.nz**. The **New Plymouth isite Visitor Centre,** Puke Ariki, 1 Ariki St. (✆ **06/759-0897**), is open daily from 10am to 5pm. The **South Taranaki isite Visitor Centre,** 121 High St., Hāwera (✆ **06/278-8599**), is open weekdays from 8:30am to 5pm and weekends from 10am to 3pm. **Stratford's isite Visitor Centre,** at the corner of Prospero Place and Miranda St., Stratford (✆ **06/765-6708**), is open weekdays from 8:30 to 5pm and Saturday from 9am to 1pm.

SPECIAL EVENTS

One of Taranaki's biggest events is its **Garden Festival** (gardenfestnz.co.nz), typically held around the region at the end of October and start of November. Events include VIP garden tours, flower arranging workshops, and foodie tours. From late December to late January, New Plymouth's lush Pukekura Park hosts the **Festival of Lights**, offering free entertainment and spectacular artistic lighting displays each night. In February, hundreds of classic American car owners make their way to Taranaki for **Americarna** (americarna.com), when they cruise up and down the streets of towns throughout the region.

Finally, mid-March is when **WOMAD** (womad.co.nz) takes place in New Plymouth, a huge, glorious 3-day festival of world music, dance, and food. In 2026 the organizers took a "year of purposeful rest," but the calendar-highlight looks set to return in 2027 and beyond. (If it does, and you're in town, don't miss it—it's an extremely wholesome party for young and old, held at the best time of year to visit New Zealand, in my view: early autumn.)

Exploring the Towns

NEW PLYMOUTH

Devon Street (East and West) is the main road. Running parallel and to the north are the one-way streets **Powderham** and **Courtenay,** and to the west, **Vivian** and **Leach streets.** The main thoroughfare into the city from the south is **Eliot Street.** Once you've got the hang of the one-way pattern, you'll find it easy to find your way around.

The **Govett-Brewster Art Gallery/Len Lye Centre ♥♥♥**, corner of Queen Street and Devon Street West (govettbrewster.com; ✆ **06/759-6060**), has always been a mainstay for contemporary New Zealand art, with great permanent and temporary exhibitions. The striking Len Lye Centre is hard to miss; it's designed to look like one of the eponymous sculptor's works, with a state-of-the-art cinema and bespoke gallery spaces within. Born in Christchurch, Lye (1901–1980) was an internationally recognized artist and experimental filmmaker who specialized in dynamic moving sculptures. His enormous **Wind Wand** installation on the waterfront has become a city landmark. The galleries are open daily from 10am to 5pm and cost NZ$17 (free for kids under 16).

With a striking exterior of rippling stainless-steel panels, the Len Lye Centre (p. 297) is devoted to the work of Len Lye, renowned for his dynamic kinetic sculptures.

Puke Ariki ♥♥♥, 1 Ariki St. (pukeariki.com; ✆ **06/759-6060**), is Taranaki's regional museum, a strikingly modern structure in the city center that also houses the public library and visitor center. It tells the story of Taranaki past and present, its Māori and Pākehā worlds and how they have interacted—sometimes violently, as was the case during the Land Wars of the 19th century. There is a terrific display of Māori *taonga* (treasures), and although the museum focuses on major themes, it also zeroes in on small stories, like that of Tamanui, the last Taranaki kōkako (a rare native bird). He passed on to the big nest in the sky and is now stuffed and on display—but his progeny are thriving on pest-free islands, and a few have been successfully reintroduced to the region. You can watch a lovely short film about Tamanui and his legacy. Kids will love the prehistoric megalodon (an enormous shark) suspended from the ceiling, and the massive sperm whale flipper—who knew whales had great big hands with finger bones? The museum is open daily from 10am to 5pm; admission is free.

The design of Te Whare Hononga, based on traditional Māori tukutuku latticed paneling, expresses the work of reconciling settlers and local Māori.

Or wander into **Te Whare Hononga** (The House that Binds), 37 Vivian St. (taranakicathedral.nz; ✆ **06/758-3111**), a beautiful, award-winning building housing exhibits that tell the story of reconciliation between the Church of St Mary's and Ngāti Te Whiti *hapū* (subtribe). Guided tours give an overview of the history of land wars, including the settlers' gravesite, Waikato Warriors' Memorial, and how these sites of significance connect to the Taranaki Cathedral. There's also a short animated video addressing St. Mary's conflicted relationship with Māori, paying special attention to the voices that have long called for peace. It's open Monday to Friday 9am to 3pm; entrance is free, but a *koha*—a gift or tip—is welcomed.

If you're driving south, take SH45—known around here as **Surf Highway 45**—rather than the more direct but less interesting SH3. You'll pass some of the best surfing breaks in the country, as well as some nice little towns and access points to Taranaki Maunga.

And if you're interested in the arty folk who live and produce work in the area, you can follow the self-guided **Coastal Arts Trail** ♥ (coastalartstrail.nz), an easy self-drive itinerary of the art galleries, museums, and open studios from Taranaki to the Manuwatū.

HĀWERA

An hour's drive south of New Plymouth, the town of Hāwera is home to what is regarded by many as the best private museum in the country, Nigel and Teresa Ogle's award-winning **Tawhiti Museum** ♥♥♥, 401 Ohangai Rd. (tawhitimuseum.co.nz; ✆ **06/278-6837**). Nigel, a former art teacher, has created life-size exhibits and scale models that encapsulate the history of Taranaki, casting, pasting, and dressing thousands of tiny figurines for the museum's dioramas. In the Traders & Whalers section, you ride in a boat propelled by water through the dark and dingy early 19th century, where wild pigs and warriors brandishing muskets leap out at you, and fast-talking salesmen do deals with the local Māori. The **Tawhiti Bush Railway** takes passengers on a little logging train around the museum environs. Its hours change seasonally, so check its site for details. Museum admission costs NZ$20 adults, NZ$7 for children ages 5 to 15; you'll pay the same amount again for the Traders & Whalers. The railway is NZ$10 adults and NZ$5 children.

Gardens Galore

With its warm climate, high rainfall, and volcanic soil, plants love Taranaki, and you'll love its gardens. There are dozens of public and private gardens to be found, but some of the best are owned and operated by the regional council and have free admission. Here are some favorites, starting in New Plymouth and heading south from there:

- **Pukekura Park and Brooklands** ♥♥♥, Fillis Street, 10 New Plymouth 4310 (✆ **06/759-6060**), is one of the best city parks in New Zealand. There's the beautiful park itself; the **Brooklands Zoo** (daily 9am–5pm); the **TSB Bowl of Brooklands,** a top open-air entertainment venue; playgrounds, a fernery, lakes, fountains, waterfalls, gigantic trees and specialist gardens—and it's all free to visit. Try to visit between Christmas and

February; that's when the **TSB Bank Festival of Lights** ♥♥ takes place and the park is lit by millions of colored lights.

- **Te Kainga Marire** ♥, 15 Spencer Place, New Plymouth (tekaingamarire.co.nz; ✆ **06/758-8693**) is Māori for "peaceful encampment," and you'll understand why when you visit this private inner-city Garden of International Significance, where the focus is on native plants. It's open daily September through April from 9am to 5pm (admission NZ$10 per person).
- **Tūpare** ♥♥, 487 Mangorei Rd., New Plymouth (tupare.info; ✆ **0800/736-222** in NZ), is a gorgeous garden built on a hillside around a 1932 Arts & Crafts homestead sitting by the Waiwhakaiho River. It's open daily all day, every day, but you'll have to ask about guided house tours.
- **Pukeiti** ♥♥, 2290 Carrington Rd. (pukeiti.com), has one of the world's biggest collections of rhododendrons (around 300 varieties) along with camellias, magnolias, and other showy plants, set in native forest with miles of walking tracks. It's best to visit in October and November, when the rhodos are in bloom. Open daily, it's a 30-minute drive southwest from New Plymouth. If you want to fully immerse, a view-rich family hut (sleeping up to 12) is available for rental. ***Note:*** The gardens provide tours via tiny touring bus for those with mobility issues (Fri–Sun, Oct–Mar).
- **Hollard Gardens** ♥ 1686 Upper Manaia Rd., Kaponga (hollardgardens.info; ✆ **0800/736-222** in NZ), is a horticultural oasis out in cow country, with a mix of native forest and colorful flowering plants, productive vegetable garden and food forest. It also has a children's playground. It's open daily.

At family-friendly Hollard Gardens, a scarecrow protects an educational vegetable garden.

The Joy of Gin

If you're a gin-lover, pop in to boutique distillery **Juno Gin,** 16 Sunley St. (juno gin.com; ✆ **020/434-7845**), in the heart of New Plymouth. Its gorgeously designed bottles make great gifts, and what's inside is exceptional too, featuring water from the slopes of Taranaki Maunga and locally sourced botanicals. The cellar door is open Monday to Thursday 10am to 5pm and Friday to Saturday 10am to 7pm, and for NZ$15 you can do a casual tasting (no bookings required). A more involved 1-hour tour costs NZ$35, or for the full 90-minute shebang—including a cocktail, canapes, tastings in the bespoke tasting room, a look inside the distillery, and a gin quiz, if you're game—it's NZ$69. Book in advance for the longer tours.

If you'd like someone to shuttle you from garden-to-garden—and to point out the highlights—**Discover Taranaki** ♥ (discovertaranaki.nz; ✆ **0272/410-458**) organizes a customized gardens tour starting from NZ$125. They offer a foodie tour as well.

Exploring Te Papa-Kura-o-Taranaki (National Park)

This visit-worthy national park dates back to 1900. Formerly known as Egmont National Park—for a time the European name for the mountain was Mt. Egmont, the name bestowed on it by Captain Cook in honor of a British earl who never set foot in Aotearoa—in 2025 a much older name was reinstated, Te Papa-kura-o-Taranaki, meaning the highly regarded and treasured lands of Taranaki. The park and mountain together were also granted legal personhood, meaning it now essentially owns itself, but it is managed by representatives of the national government and the eight Taranaki *iwi* (tribes) for whom the mountain holds deep cultural and spiritual significance.

The park's 33,534 hectares (82,829 acres) are mainly made up of the volcanic peak and forested flanks of Taranaki Maunga. A spectacularly beautiful mountain 2,518m (8,261 ft.) high, it encompasses multiple different habitats (subalpine forest, volcanic scoria, mountain streams and waterfalls, lichen-draped rainforest dubbed "goblin forest," and alpine herb fields). Walking trails range from a 15-minute stroll to multi-day hikes.

For a short, spectacular walk, visit the stunning new-in-2024 suspension bridge on the **Manganui Gorge Track** ♥♥. Soaring almost 50m (164 ft) above the valley floor, it's 100m (328 ft) long and incorporates stainless-steel Māori sculptures by Taranaki artist Wharehoka Smith. It's a walk of 20 minutes to reach the bridge from the Plateau carpark at the end of Pembroke Road (25 minutes' drive from Stratford on the eastern side of the mountain). On a clear day you'll be rewarded with views all the way to the sea.

The area's most popular day walk is the **Pouākai Tarns track** ♥♥, which rewards hikers with an Instagram-worthy shot of the reflection of Taranaki Maunga in a small crystal-clear lake. It's about an 11km return trip, which is

A hiker poses between Lake Pouākai and Taranaki Maunga.

mainly uphill (about 500m/1,640 ft. in elevation gain). The trailhead is located at the end of Mangorei Road. It is moderately difficult, and should take about 3 to 5 hours, depending on how often you stop for photos! If you've got more energy, extend this trip into the highly recommended 19km (11.8 miles) **Pouākai Crossing ♥♥♥** (doc.govt.nz/pouakai-crossing), which continues along a boardwalk across a stunning alpine wetland and around the lower flanks of Taranaki Maunga to the visitor center, with an optional waterfall side-quest. (It takes between 7½ and 9½ hours.) Most people do it in reverse, but I like walking west to east so you can look up at this awe-inspiring volcano the whole time. Note, though, that this is a backcountry hike—trail conditions are considerably less groomed than on Great Walks like the Tongariro Alpine Crossing (see p. 252). Expect the track to be rough, muddy, wet, or icy in places, and be prepared for fast-changing mountain weather. The hike can be further extended into a 3-day circuit.

Another hiking option, though it can be a dangerous one, is to the **summit of Taranaki Maunga,** which takes about 8 hours. It should only be attempted by those who know what they're doing and have the right gear, as the weather can be extremely changeable. Many people have lost their lives on Taranaki; it's New Zealand's second-deadliest mountain. Although ice remains in the crater year-round, it's best to attempt the summit from February to mid-April, when the usually snowy slopes are bare. If you do reach the top, remember that this is a site of great cultural and spiritual significance: It is *tapu*/taboo to stand on the highest point or to eat in the summit area. Have your celebratory beer elsewhere.

Always check conditions first with the **North Taranaki Visitor Centre,** 2679 Egmont Rd. (doc.govt.nz; ✆ **06/756-0990**). A 25-minute drive from New Plymouth on the north side of the mountain, the visitor center is currently operating out of a temporary building (open daily 8am–3:30pm) while a new visitor center is being constructed, scheduled to open in 2027.

Outdoor Pursuits

GOLF Taranaki is home to around 18 courses, including the top-ranked **Stratford Golf Club ♥♥** (stratfordgolfclub.org; ✆ **06/765-6514**), with its views of Taranaki Maunga. Green fees are NZ$40 for 18 holes.

KAYAKING **Canoe & Kayak Taranaki,** 631 Devon Rd., New Plymouth (canoeandkayak.co.nz; ✆ **06/769-5506**), will take you out on the Waitara River for NZ$145 per person. It also does kayak and stand-up paddleboard rentals.

SURFING At the **Beach Street Surf Shop,** 39 Beach St., Fitzroy, New Plymouth (facebook.com/BeachstreetNZ; ✆ **06/758-0400**), you can rent a board and a wetsuit (or buy a secondhand board) and get the latest surf conditions. Or, in Ōakura, hit up **Vertigo Surf,** 2 Tasman Parade (vertigosurf.com; ✆ **027/694-1069**). Private surf lessons (1–2 people) are NZ$80, while group lessons (3–6 people) are NZ$100. You can also rent surfboards, bodyboards, and SUPs.

WALKING There's plenty of that around here, even if you don't venture up the mountain. Walking all or some of the multi-award-winning **Coastal Walkway ♥♥♥** is a must—and it passes right through the city, so you've got no excuses. It's 13km (8 miles) long and runs from Bell Block in the north to Port Taranaki in the south. In places, the ocean crashes against rocks right beside you—or underneath you if you're on the lookout that juts out into the sea, right by Len Lye's *Wind Wand* sculpture. Even on a bad day, you'll find people walking, jogging, and cycling the walkway's length.

Where to Stay in the Taranaki Region

Taranaki has become a destination for entrepreneurial types and young families, so boutique seaside lodges and holiday home rentals aren't far away. There are also plenty of nondescript but affordable motels and hotels.

NEW PLYMOUTH

Directly in the city, the **Millennium Hotel New Plymouth Waterfront ♥** (millenniumhotels.com; ✆ **06/769-5301;** rooms NZ$220–NZ$319) is a very standard looking hotel, with unremarkable rooms and service, but its waterfront location makes it eminently recommendable. **The Devon Hotel ♥♥,**

awesome DAWSON

The 18m (59-ft.) **Te Rere-o-Noke/Dawson Falls,** on the southeastern slopes of Mt. Taranaki, are an impressive sight and easy to reach, just a 20-minute walk from the parking lot. You can learn all about them at the **Dawson Falls Visitor Centre,** 1980 Manaia Rd., Kaponga (✆ **027/443-0248**), open Thursday to Sunday 9am to 4pm. There are lots of walks and hikes you can do from this side of the mountain, too. If you're driving, it's about an hour's drive south of New Plymouth on SH3 towards Stratford and is well signposted.

The owners of Hosking House have turned a lovely Queen Anne–style villa into a stylish B&B.

390 Devon St. E (devonhotel.co.nz; ✆ **0800/843-338** in NZ), feels a hair more luxurious, but its rooms are generally more affordable (NZ$105–NZ$169). It's tops for families thanks to its game room, pool, spa, and free use of bicycles. ***Warning:*** The rooms overlooking the dining area get loud.

Hosking House ♥♥♥ This lovely B&B close to beautiful Pukekura Park is the labor of love of Kiwi Rodney and New Yorker Rachel, who have turned a beautiful old wooden villa into an oasis of tranquility and comfort. And they're really nice, too! Along with the luxurious and historic touches you'd expect (clawfoot tubs!), there are also fresh homemade cakes in tins and a garden in which to savor them.

1 Victoria St. hoskinghouse.com. ✆ **06/758-1681.** 3 suites. NZ$270–NZ$325. Rates include breakfast. **Amenities:** Free Wi-Fi.

King and Queen Hotel Suites ♥♥♥ This chic addition to New Plymouth's high-end accommodation sector makes much of the fact that the hotel is on the intersection of two royal roads. The decor, however, ditches Louis IV for a more modern European/Moroccan look (love the comfy leather sofas). The suites are very urban sophisticated without being pretentious; some have enormous balconies so you can keep an eye on the city action below.

Corner of King and Queen sts. kingandqueen.co.nz. ✆ **06/757-2999.** 17 suites NZ$218–NZ$535. Free parking. **Amenities:** Bikes; gym access; free Wi-Fi.

Nice Hotel ♥♥♥ And very nice it is, too. This used to be New Plymouth's only small luxury hotel, and new competition has made it even better. Rooms are stylish and modern with all the right luxuries, and it has a popular restaurant downstairs (see p. 305). The main hotel building is actually New Plymouth's oldest wooden structure, built in 1870; long-stay suites are in another building next door. The hotel offers little extras like a tropical garden deck, an art collection, and a library where you'll be offered a complimentary drink while you read.

71 Brougham St. nicehotel.co.nz. ✆ **06/758-6423.** NZ$225–NZ$420 double; inquire about package deals. **Amenities:** Restaurant; private dining rooms; bar; bikes; free Wi-Fi.

ŌAKURA

Ahu Ahu Beach Villas ♥♥♥ Fifteen minutes south of New Plymouth, David and Nuala Marshall's lovely beach compound was created by sourcing, recycling, and upcycling all manner of bits and pieces—100-year-old French clay tiles from Stratford Hospital, timbers from ports here and in Nelson, cross-arms from power poles, curtain rails made of rake handles and driftwood—all used to fashion four units and three family villas. They look amazing, and their location is fantastic, in a prime position overlooking the always-animated Tasman Sea. It's luxurious and private and simply sensational, plus you'll feel good that the materials are living their lives all over again with these delightful people.

Upcycled materials have been transformed into charming beach cottages at Ahu Ahu Beach Villas.

321 Ahu Ahu Rd. www.ahu.co.nz. ✆ **06/752-7370.** 7 units. NZ$345 for two people. Breakfast available on request. **Amenities:** Bikes for rent; outdoor firepit; free Wi-Fi.

Where to Eat in New Plymouth

The award-winning **Table at Nice Hotel ♥♥** (nicehotel.co.nz; ✆ **06/758-6423;** daily lunch and dinner) offers a Kiwi take on international flavors, served primarily in small and large share plates, like tiger prawns with romesco pesto, or the crispy pork belly with kūmara puree. It's considered one of New Plymouth's finest restaurants. Also vying for that distinction is **Arborio ♥♥** (arborio.co.nz; ✆ **06/759-1241**), a restaurant, cafe, and bar located at Puke Ariki (65 St. Aubyn St.) serving Italian cuisine daily from 9am until late. (Consider this fair warning: The servings are substantial.)

For coffee, baked goods, full meals, and scintillating cocktails, the **West End Precinct ♥♥**, at the corner of Devon Street West and Queen Street, is a modern and high-end take on the food court. This handsome, fairy-lit courtyard is home to **Public Catering** (publiccatering.co.nz), a new bakery/sandwich spot from the catering company that fed Charles and Camilla when they visited; **Ms. White** (mswhite.co.nz), a purveyor of wood-fired pizzas and craft beers; and the Japanese-inspired cocktail lounge **Snug Lounge** (snuglounge.co.nz).

At the Govett-Brewster Art Gallery, **Monica's Eatery ♥♥**, 42 Queen St. (monicaseatery.co.nz; ✆ **06/759-2038**), is named after Monica Brewster, the gallery's founding patron and women's rights advocate. It's an airy, light-filled space with comfortable street-view booths and a welcoming blond-wood interior. The smashed pea and avocado has a great spicy chile kick, and even the decaf is full-bodied. An array of tasty brunch options ranges from house-made crumpets to pappardelle pasta with ragu.

The Table at Nice Hotel (p. 305).

Elixir ♥♥, 117 Devon St. E (elixircafe.co.nz; ✆ **06/769-9020;** Mon–Sat 7am–4pm, Sun 8am–4pm), is the town's token alternative diner, famous for its mince on toast (kind of like an open-faced sloppy joe). It even sells t-shirts devoted to the dish. There are plenty of other options here too, from smoothies to buddha bowls.

Ozone Coffee Roasters ♥♥, 47 King St. (ozonecoffee.co.nz; ✆ **06/757-5404**), really cares about coffee, to the point where it offers domestic barista workshops to make you better at it, too, which doesn't seem to kill business. It also serves very basic breakfast options (granola or toast). It's open weekdays from 7am to 3pm, Saturday 7am to 2pm, and Sunday 8am to 2pm.

For an excellent craft beer with a side of lunch or dinner, pop into **Shining Peak Brewing**, 59 Gill St. (shiningpeakbrewing.com; ✆ **06/927-3133**). Open daily from late morning until late evening, this brew pub serves up a wide range of tasty, innovative share plates—tuna ceviche with kūmara, Parmesan and goat-cheese cookies, house-made beer ice cream(!)—alongside the award-winning brewery's signature IPAs, sours, lagers, and stouts.

The Social Kitchen ♥♥ CONTEMPORARY In a high-ceilinged old Salvation Army citadel, big dangly lamps have been hung from vintage firemen's ladders, and mounted stags' heads adorn the walls. There's a weird art installation of meat cuts and salami (fake) hung on butcher's hooks and the repeated motif of a bull smoking a pipe and wearing a suit. (Upmarket slaughterhouse meets gentlemen's club?) Whatever it is, the food is great. Cooked over a Mibrasa charcoal oven, the menu has a slight South American lean (think chimichurri with steak, white fish crudo with lime, empanadas stuffed with cheese and jalapeños, and pisco sours to drink). And, as the name implies, it's served in the most social way possible: large and small share plates.

40 Powderham St. social-kitchen.co.nz. ✆ **06/757-2711.** Share plates NZ$9–NZ$64. Daily 5pm–late.

En Route to Whanganui

Heading south, it's a 2½-hour drive from New Plymouth to Whanganui through rolling verdant farmland where cows are queen. Take **Surf Highway 45,** the slightly longer route, if you've got time.

WHANGANUI

164km (102 miles) SE of New Plymouth; 141km (87 miles) SW of Tongariro National Park; 193km (120 miles) N of Wellington; 252km (156 miles) SW of Napier

The Whanganui River begins its 290km (180-mile) journey as snow melt in the upper reaches of Tongariro National Park (see chapter 7), continues on through parts of beautiful Whanganui National Park, and ends in the city of Whanganui (what else would it be called?), where it flows into the Tasman Sea. For Māori, the Whanganui is sacred—one of their traditional proverbs includes the line: *Mai i te Kāhui maunga ki Tangaroa. Kō au te Āwa, kō te Āwa kō au.* "The great river flows from the mountains to the sea. I am the river, the river is me." For most, the city of Whanganui is merely the place to begin or end an incredible outdoor experience in the nearby national park, but it's a town that quietly reveals itself to those with time. A modest population of around 50,000 punches above its weight in creative terms: There are 33 art galleries and hundreds of resident visual artists. Its architecture is equally befitting of a much larger center—there's even a Victorian-era opera house—while its main street, Victoria Avenue, has mature trees lit by fairy lights. (Ghost stories abound; just ask the locals.) Add to this a strong street-art culture—some of the best graffiti in the country can be found here. In 2021, Whanganui was named a UNESCO City of Design.

Essentially, Whanganui offers an authentic Kiwi experience, without the bells and whistles (or the crowds).

Essentials

ARRIVING **Whanganui Airport,** 10 minutes from the city, is serviced by **Air Chathams** (www.airchathams.co.nz; ✆ **0800/580-127** in NZ). Flights to Auckland are offered daily. The city is a 2½-hour drive from New Plymouth or Wellington, 3 hours from Taupō, and 4 hours from Rotorua. **InterCity** (✆ **09/623-1503**) offers coach service between Whanganui and Auckland, New Plymouth, and Wellington.

GETTING AROUND The best way to explore the Whanganui area is by car or bike—it's mostly flat. For information on urban buses, go to **www.horizons.govt.nz**. To get a taxi, try **River City Cabs** (✆ **06/345-3333**). Uber has recently arrived in the city.

VISITOR INFORMATION Go to the **Discover Whanganui** website at discoverwhanganui.nz/visit. The **isite Visitor Information Centre,** 31 Taupō Quay (✆ **06/349-0508**), is open weekdays from 9am to 5pm and until 4pm on weekends.

SPECIAL EVENTS In January is the highly regarded **Whanganui Opera Week** (operaschool.org.nz/opera-week-in-whanganui) for recitals, master-classes, and a gala concert at the Royal Whanganui Opera House. Also in January, the **Whanganui Vintage Weekend** (whanganuivintageweekend.nz) presents arts workshops and exhibitions, vintage fashion contests, classic cars, steam train rides, and river cruises. Over 2 weekends in late March, more than

WHAT THE "h"?

Just when you think you're starting to master teo reo Māori and how to pronounce Aotearoa's place names, Whanganui throws a wrench into the mix. It's pronounced "Wanganui" thanks to a regional dialect. While elsewhere in the country "wh" would indicate a "ph" sound, here the "h" is (almost) silent—it's slightly aspirated, kind of like a posh British person saying "what." You'll also occasionally see it spelled "Wanganui," as the name was only officially changed to the correct spelling in 2017. This dialectal difference affects how locals pronounce all Māori words that have "wh" in them, e.g., the place name Whakahoro, *whānau* (family), or *kōwhai* (yellow, or the flowering tree).

80 studios display their glass, ceramics, printmaking, jewelry, and painting during the **Artists Open Studios Whanganui** (openstudios.co.nz).

Exploring Whanganui

IN & AROUND THE CITY

Founded in 1892, the **Whanganui Regional Museum** ♥♥, Watt Street (wrm.org.nz; ✆ **06/349-1110**), is a compelling introduction to Whanganui's cultural and natural heritage. The museum has a close partnership with local mana *whenua*—Māori who have historic rights over this land—and its collections reflect both Māori and European stories of the region. The highlights are many: an outstanding collection of *taonga Māori* (Māori treasures), the Gottfried Lindauer Gallery of 19th-century portraits, one of the world's most important moa-bone collections, and beautifully preserved examples of historic fashion and textiles. The He Awa Ora—Living River exhibition uses both ancient and contemporary taonga to tell the story of Te Awa Tupua, the Whanganui River, including the background behind the legislation that gave the river the legal rights of a person. The museum is open daily from 10am to 4:30pm and admission is free. Guided tours can be arranged via phone or email (NZ$20 for 1 hour, NZ$60 for a 2-hour behind-the-scenes experience, which includes light refreshments).

If you're looking for a place to picnic, head to **Kowhai Park** ♥, set on the eastern edges of the riverbank across from the main city area. Named by Kiwi news site *The Spinoff* as the best playground in the country, it's trapped in 1959, the year it was built, but is delightful in its peculiarities. You can cook your meal on one of the community barbecues inside a giant pumpkin, swing from an octopus's giant tentacles, or see-saw aboard giant snakes.

St. Paul's Memorial Church ♥ in Pūtiki across the bridge from town (20 Anaua St.) looks like any small Anglican church from the outside. But go in and you'll be overwhelmed by the surprise within: The whole interior is covered with Māori carvings and *tukutuku* (wall panels). If you go on a Sunday, you can attend the local service conducted in te reo Māori. Otherwise, guided tours can be booked through the isite for a *koha* (donation).

A half-hour drive west of town, **Paloma Gardens ♥**, Pōhutukawa Lane, Fordell (paloma.co.nz; ✆ **06/342-7857**), is a private garden with several distinct zones, including the palm garden, the desert house, and the rather forbidding-sounding "garden of death" (featuring poisonous plants). The entry fee is NZ$10, and it's open daily year-round. It's a Garden of National Significance, as is **Bason Botanic Gardens ♥♥**, 552 Rapanui Rd. (basonbotanicgardens.com), 11km (7 miles) northeast of town. It has loads of rare orchids, native and exotic trees, and places to picnic. Entry is free, and it's open daily during daylight hours.

ART STUDIOS & GALLERIES

Dozens of studios and galleries are scattered around the town and its vicinity. For a full list, check out the **Coastal Arts Trail** (coastalartstrail.nz), but there are a few don't-miss experiences and exhibits.

New Zealand Glassworks ♥♥♥, 2 Rutland St. (www.nzglassworks.com; ✆ **06/927-6803**), is an open access glass studio with a gallery and retail space showcasing limited edition collector's pieces, housewares, and jewelry from across Aotearoa. You can even create your own piece—make a paperweight in a 30-minute workshop (NZ$160) or glass tumbler in a 40-minute workshop (NZ$200). All-day group workshops are also available. They're a true baptism by fire, except with safety gear and careful tutelage. It'll give you a whole new respect for Chihuly—and a souvenir to take home.

Housed in a 1960s brutalist office building, **Quartz Museum of Studio Ceramics ♥♥**, 8 Bates St. (quartzmuseum.org.nz; ✆ **06/348-5555**), is not the most glamorous of contemporary museums, but it has one big lure: curator Rick Rudd, a potter whose work has been purchased by Te Papa (p. 321). His personal history and passion for the medium makes the exhibits come alive—and he can almost always be seen at work in the foyer. Showcasing ceramics and pottery from the early 20th century to the present, this is NZ's only museum of ceramic history. A highlight is Rudd's large collection of unusual and abstract teapots.

Moving on Up

Built in 1919, the **Durie Hill Elevator and Tower,** Victoria Avenue (duriehill elevator.co.nz), is New Zealand's only public underground lift and one of only two in the world. A pedestrian tunnel burrows 215m (699 ft.) into the hillside, and then the elevator swoops you 66m (216 ft.) to the summit. Run by a well-known NZ indie musician and a band of Whanganui creatives, the elevator has recently been upgraded, with cool lighting in the tunnel and projections of old photographs on the tunnel walls. From the top, you can tackle the remaining 176 steps up the Memorial Tower, where you can get sweeping views of the Tasman Sea and mountains Ruapehu and Taranaki. It's open daily Monday to Friday 7:30am to 6pm and weekends and public holidays 9:30am to 5pm. Entry to the tunnel is free, and a trip in the elevator costs NZ$2.50 one-way for adults and NZ$1 for children 5 to 18. (Ring the bell and the operator will come down to pick you up.) You can take a 45-minute guided tour for NZ$21 adults and NZ$14 children 4 to 18, family passes NZ$57—online bookings essential.

Whanganui's lively visual arts scene is anchored by the wide-ranging collection displayed at Te Whare o Rehua Sarjeant Gallery.

Te Whare o Rehua Sarjeant Gallery ♥♥, 4 Pukenamu Dr. (sarjeant.org.nz; ✆ **06/349-0506**), holds a collection of more than 8,000 items of national and international significance, spanning 4 centuries of European and New Zealand art history. There's an ever-rotating program of exhibitions and events. It's open daily 10am to 5pm.

Of course, you don't need to enter an art gallery to see the work of local creators. Large-scale outdoor murals and artwork created by local and international artists during the (occasional) **Whanganui Walls Street Art Festival** can be found through the city's downtown core. Stop by the visitor center for a brochure on their locations and the artist statements.

EXPLORING THE WHANGANUI RIVER & WHANGANUI NATIONAL PARK

In 2017, the Whanganui River—known by Māori as Te Awa Tupua—gained legal personhood, the first body of water in the world to do so. Māori advocated for the legislation for years, in order to uphold the *mauri* (life force) of the river.

There are a number of ways to explore the Whanganui River and the road that winds alongside it. Both dip in and out of the southern part of beautiful Whanganui National Park, which was established in 1986, protecting one of the largest tracts of lowland forest remaining in the North Island. Confusingly, however, much of the national park and river are within the Ruapehu region (see chapter 7), and many people access the river from there. Listed below are activities that are based in the Whanganui region.

You can drive the 64km (40-mile) Whanganui River Road from Whanganui to the little settlement of **Pipiriki,** which is just over the Ruapehu border, and the famous Bridge to Nowhere. The road is isolated and winding but very scenic, and you'll pass numerous points of historical interest along the way, including the beautifully restored Kawana Mill, Ātene/Athens, Koroniti/Corinth, and Rānana/London. Just before Pipiriki you'll go through Hiruhārama/Jerusalem, where the redoubtable Sister Mary Joseph founded a Catholic Māori Mission in 1892; in the 1970s, the tiny settlement was also home to Kiwi poet James K. Baxter during his hippie dropout phase, and he established a similarly inclined community there, which vanished after he died.

A 45-minute drive up the river from Whanganui, **The Flying Fox** ♥♥ (theflyingfox.co.nz; ✆ **06/342-8160**) is a delightful slice of hospitality in the middle of nowhere, offering lunch or overnight accommodations (see p. 312), reachable only by aerial cable car (or "flying fox," although a true Kiwi flying fox is actually a zipline) from the opposite bank. You can also get here with a jetboat tour from Whanganui city.

You can also take a nostalgic cruise up the river on the *Waimarie,* New Zealand's only coal-fired paddle steamer, which was built in 1890, sank in 1952, and relaunched in 2000. It was lovingly rebuilt at the **Whanganui Riverboat Centre,** 1A Taupō Quay (waimarie.co.nz; ✆ **06/347-1863**), a museum chronicling the history of riverboats in the area. From October to May, 2-hour narrated cruises travel from the center's wharf up the Whanganui River at 11am and 1pm (check the website for an updated cruise calendar) for NZ$55 adults, NZ$25 children 5 to 19. The center is open on sailing days; admission is free.

The **MV *Wairua*** ♥ (motorvesselwairua.co.nz; ✆ **0800/924-782**), a retrofitted 1904 steamship, also sails up the river; these 3-hour cruises are light on commentary, but include a stop for lunch at Ūpokongaro and a guided tour of St. Mary's Church (p. 271). There's an option to cycle the 8km (5 miles) back to Whanganui on e-bikes along the region's brand-new cycle trail. Cruises depart Moutoa Gardens on Tuesday and Thursday at 11am; tickets can be purchased on-site (NZ$55 adults, NZ$25 children 5–15).

Another fun way to explore the river is with the popular **Whanganui River Road Mail Tour** ♥♥ (whanganuitours.co.nz; ✆ **0211/304-617**), a guided van tour retracing the historic mail runs of old. They travel on weekdays (NZ$88 per person). The same company also runs a full-day trip for NZ$400 called **Discover Te Awa Tupua** that starts with the mail run, then leads on to a 2-hour bike ride along the historic route from Hiruhārama/Jerusalem, then a 2-hour river kayak. It's a great way to experience a fairly remote part of the river by canoe without committing to a 2- to 3-day trip.

Outdoor Pursuits

BEACHES **Castlecliff Beach** ♥♥, 9km (5½ miles) from town, is a Wild West coastal beach with black iron sand—good for swimming and surfing and patrolled by lifeguards in summer. Near the airport, **South Beach** is fun for surfing and fishing, and **Kai Iwi Beach** ♥, 14km (8½ miles) west of Whanganui, has very photogenic cliffs and is safe for kids.

BIKING About 25 minutes north of Whanganui, you'll find **That Place Mountain Bike Park** (that-place.co.nz). Located on privately owned land—with various rustic to luxe glamping accommodation options, too (see below).

New Zealand's longest navigable river, the Whanganui is so significant to this region that it was granted legal personhood in 2017.

Day passes are NZ$28, but you'll need to bring your own bike. **eBikes Whanganui,** 73 Putiki Dr. (ebikeswanganui.co.nz; ✆ **06/348-8008**), offers rentals starting from NZ$30, which you can use at the bike park, or along the cycle path that connects Whanganui to Ūpokongaro, where you can stop for a mid-ride coffee or beer.

GOLF One of oldest courses in NZ and rated as one of its best is the **Wanganui Golf Club,** 14 Clarkson Ave., Westmere (www.wanganuigolfclub.co.nz; ✆ **06/349-0559**). Greens fees are NZ$50 for 18 holes and NZ$30 for 9 holes.

WALKING The 12.5km (7.8-mile) **Atene Skyline Walk** takes 6 to 8 hours, but rewards hikers with views of Mt. Ruapehu and Mt. Taranaki. Best suited to experienced hikers, this track is almost circular but isn't quite a full loop, so add on another 2km to make it back to your car on Whanganui River Road at the end. The entrance to the trail is about a 40-minute drive from the city.

Where to Stay in Whanganui

It's fair to say that Whanganui isn't teeming with upmarket hotels. There are lots of motels, B&Bs, and Airbnbs, though.

The **Flying Fox ♥♥**, 45 minutes out of town (theflyingfox.co.nz; ✆ **06/342-8160**), is one of the region's most unusual accommodations because guests arrive via an aerial cableway (see above). It has three two-bedroom cottages hand-built out of recycled native timbers, and a tiny cabin on wheels, the "Glory Cart." They'll do breakfast or just hang out with you under the huge walnut trees. ***Note:*** There's no cellphone coverage here, though they do have Wi-Fi. Prices are by package only; inquire for rates.

Another glamping option, **Takahuri Glamping ♥♥** 1021 Kaiwhaiki Rd. (takahuriglamping.co.nz; ✆ **06/281-3544**), is located at That Place Mountain Bike Park (see above). It has three gorgeous geodesic domes—max two people—for NZ$295 per night, and a more rustic tiny house for NZ$180, set above the Whanganui River in a bush block that's home to glowworms and kiwi. The domes are insulated and have a log fire, so you should be relatively cozy even in the winter months.

The apartment motel **Aotea Motor Lodge,** 390 Victoria Ave. (aoteamotorlodge.co.nz; ✆ **06/345-0303**), is close to the action. You won't get stunning views and some rooms get street noise, but everything is immaculate and it's got giant two-person spa baths for companionable soaking. Rates run NZ$185 to NZ$245 per night.

Iona Tiny House ♥♥ When local architect Elinor McDouall saw the hull of Iona, a 1924 kauri boat for sale on TradeMe (New Zealand's answer to Craigslist), she knew she had to have it. Now, the 40-foot boat forms the shell of this one-of-a-kind tiny house located on the shores of the Whanganui River. The surprisingly spacious living area, kitchen, and bed are all cradled in the boat's curves. Although the tiny house is designed for two adults to while away the hours, there is a secondary twin-sized bed tucked away in the cutest of cubby holes. The riverside location and proximity to town are unbeatable, but it comes at a cost; Iona is on a busy road, which detracts from the world that McDouall has carefully constructed. Book via Canopy Camping Escapes.
52 Pūtiki Dr., Whanganui. ionatinyhouse.nz. ✆ **021/468-425.** 1 unit. NZ$285. **Amenities:** Kitchen; fireplace; outside bathtub; outside firepit; free Wi-Fi.

Where to Eat in Whanganui

The **Yellow House Cafe ♥♥**, 17 Pitt St. (yellowhousecafe.co.nz; ✆ **06/345-0083;** weekdays 8am–3pm, weekends 8:30am–4pm), welcomes visitors in, you guessed it, a yellow house, serving healthy homemade lunches, all-day breakfast, and fresh donuts from its location near the river.

Guests at the funky Flying Fox can stay in this rustic home or in a variety of other accommodations.

The River Traders & Whanganui Farmers' Market

Farmers' markets are everywhere these days, but this one combines fresh local produce with choice wares from some of the region's artists at great wholesale prices. It's held every Saturday from 9am to 1pm beside the river behind the Whanganui Riverboat Centre. While you're there, you'll see the **Tram Shed** (facebook.com/whanganuitramways; ✆ **06/345-7034**), which houses the lovingly restored Number 12 tram also known as "Mabel." If she's out on display, you can jump in and even go for a ride every Sunday between 1 and 3pm (NZ$5 per person). The tram's hours change seasonally, so check on its Facebook page prior to arrival to confirm.

If you're just after a caffeine fix, swing by **Article** ♥♥, 21 Drews Ave. (facebook.com/Articlewhanganui; ✆ **027/752-2472**), but don't be surprised if you come out carrying far more than just a coffee. This cafe-cum-gallery-cum-vintage shop also carries local artwork.

High-Kut Bistro ♥♥, 21 Victoria Ave. (highkutbistro.co.nz; ✆ **06/345-0147**), is a small, chic space that's date-night worthy. Mains cost close to NZ$30, but you're paying for quality local produce and ingredients, like seared scallops and lamb racks. It serves both lunch and dinner.

Whanganui After Dark

Frank Bar & Eatery ♥, 60 Ridgeway St. (mintasfrank.co.nz; ✆ **06/348-4808**), is a restaurant, nightclub, and even concert venue. (In a place like Whanganui, it pays to be everything to everyone.) The cavernous space, outfitted with industrial furniture, isn't the coziest, but's it's a safe bet for cocktails, alongside food designed to soak up booze (pizza and burgers). It's open Tuesday to Thursday from 4pm to late and Friday to Saturday from 3pm to late.

Just off the main street, you'll find **Porridge Watson** ♥, 30 Drews Ave. (facebook.com/porridgewatson), which isn't a breakfast joint, but rather a bar with regular live music. Hours and upcoming events (including gigs and taco nights) are regularly pasted on its Facebook page.

En Route to Wellington

You can get to Wellington on SH1 via Levin, Waikanae, and Paraparaumu (the better road) or via Palmerston North and the Wairarapa (see chapter 10). Both trips take about 2½ hours. The **Palmerston North isite,** The Square Palmerston North 4410 (manawatunz.co.nz; ✆ **06/350-1922**), is open weekdays 9am to 5pm and Saturdays 9am to 2pm.

WELLINGTON & THE WAIRARAPA

Wellington might be the seat of government—you'll see more suited civil servants here than anywhere else—but Wellingtonians sure know how to party when the ties come off. This is New Zealand's coolest city, a population of a little more than 200,000 shoehorned between a mercurial harbor and the hills, with the South Island on its doorstep and the rest of the North Island at its back. Wellingtonians live with its bracing winds and love it just the same: As the saying here goes, "You can't beat Wellington on a good day!" It's also the country's culinary capital, and the coffee culture is the nation's geekiest. Explore innovative museums, hop on the cable car, see rare native animals at the Zealandia Wildlife Sanctuary, take a craft brewery tour, or get in touch with your funky self while shopping on Cuba Street.

Over the hill to the east lies the Wairarapa, where Wellingtonians come for weekend rebalancing: to sip wine from some of the country's best small vineyards, to shop in boutiques in heritage villages, and to experience the splendid isolation of its wild, unspoiled coast. Directly north of Wellington is the Kāpiti Coast, a long stretch of beaches, estuaries, and islands known for walking and birdwatching, including one of NZ's best opportunities to see a kiwi in the wild.

WELLINGTON

Essentials

ARRIVING

BY PLANE **Wellington International Airport** (wellington airport.co.nz) is 8km (5 miles) southeast of the central city, via the Mount Victoria tunnel or, more scenically, Oriental Parade. It's generally a 15- to 20-minute drive but can take longer during rush hour. **Air New Zealand** (airnewzealand.co.nz; ✆ **0800/737-000** in NZ), **Qantas** (qantas.com; ✆ **0800/808-767** in NZ), **Jetstar** (jetstar.com/nz; ✆ **0800/800-995** in NZ), and **Fiji Airways** (fijiairways.com; ✆ **0800/800-178** in NZ) are the major international carriers. The main domestic airlines serving Wellington are **Air New Zealand, Jetstar,** and **Sounds Air** (soundsair.com; ✆ **0800/505-505** in NZ). The Wellington airport terminal has a large food court, car

Wellington City

RESTAURANTS

- 1154 Pastaria **24**
- Apachè **39**
- Aunty Mena Vegetarian **29**
- Backbencher Gastropub **4**
- Best Ugly Bagels **28**
- Boulcott Street Bistro **10**
- Capitol **44**
- Charley Noble Eatery & Bar **14**
- Chow **40**
- Fratelli **43**
- Graze Wine Bar **16**
- Kisa **31**
- Little Penang **21**

ATTRACTIONS

- City Gallery Wellington **19**
- Katherine Mansfield House & Garden **1**
- Museum of New Zealand Te Papa Tongarewa **41**
- National Library of New Zealand **3**
- Old St. Paul's **2**
- Parliament Buildings **5**
- Te Ara Whānui ki te Rangi/ Space Place **9**
- Wellington Botanic Gardens **8**
- Wellington Cable Car **11**
- Wellington Museum/ Te Waka Huia o Ngā Taonga Tuku Iho **15**
- Wellington Zoo **51**
- Wētā Cave **49**
- Zealandia Te Māra a Tāne **17**

HOTELS

- The Bay Plaza Hotel **47**
- Bolton Hotel **6**
- Booklovers Bed & Breakfast **50**
- The Cobbler **26**
- InterContinental Wellington **12**
- The Intrepid Hotel **23**
- The Marion Street Hostel **38**
- Mövenpick Hotel Wellington **18**
- Naumi Hotel Wellington **36**
- Ohtel **48**
- QT Wellington **42**

Victoria University of Wellington
Kelburn Parade
TUNNEL
The Terrace
Willis St.
Bond St.
Wakefield St.
Manners St.
Dixon St.
Victoria St.
Ghuznee St.
Buller St.
Cuba St.
Marion St.
Egmont St.
Taranaki St.
Courtenay Pl.
Cable St.
Waitangi Park
Oriental Parade
Allen St.
Blair St.
Roxburgh St.
Hawker St.
Kent Terr.
Majoribanks St.
Levy St.
Tennyson St.
Tory St.
Jessie St.
Lorne St.
Vivian St.
TE ARO
MOUNT VICTORIA
College St.
Frederick St.
Haining St.
Wigan St.
Abel Smith St.
Aro St.
Karo Dr.
Arthur St.
Webb St.
Buckle St.
Hopper St.
Cambridge Terr.
Home St.
Elizabeth St.
Queen St.
Pirie St.
Austin St.
Hania St.
Brougham St.
Basin Reserve
Logan Brown 33
Loretta 30
Midnight Espresso 32
Mt. Vic Chippery 46
Nolita 35
The Oatery 22
The Old Quarter 25
Ombra 37
Ortega Fish Shack and Bar 45
Picnic Cafe 7
Pizza Pomodoro 27
Rasa 34
Shed 5 13
WBC 20
NORTH ISLAND
Auckland
Wellington
SOUTH ISLAND
Christchurch
Dunedin

rental desks, currency exchange services, free Wi-Fi, ATMs, and self-service lockers on Level 1 on the parking lot (payment by card only).

Run by Metlink (the city's public transport service), the fully electric **Airport Express Bus** (metlink.org.nz), also called the AX, runs from the airport to the central city and Wellington Railway Station daily at times that coincide with flight schedules. It takes 25 to 35 minutes to reach the city and costs NZ$11 if paying by cash or card (NZ$8.76 if you pay by Snapper Card, the city's metro pass). Kids pay half price. The bus departs from outside the Airport Terminal, or at Stop A at the Railway Station. In addition to free Wi-Fi and luggage racks, it has USB charging ports for phones.

Super Shuttle (supershuttle.co.nz; ✆ **0800/748-885** in NZ) runs between the airport, the city, and the railway station starting at NZ$20 per person.

A **taxi** from the CBD to the airport costs around NZ$40 to NZ$50. Taxi stands are located directly outside the main terminal by Door G.

App-based rideshare companies **Uber** (uber.com), **Ola** (olacabs.com), and NZ-based **Zoomy** (zoomy.co.nz) all operate in Wellington. Due to surge pricing, fares to the city may be more or less affordable than those offered by taxis. There is a designated rideshare pickup area at the airport, right in front of the main ground floor exit, near the taxi rank.

BY CAR SH1 and SH2 lead into Wellington: It's 195km (121 miles) from Whanganui (about 2 hr.), 460km (285 miles) from Rotorua (about 5 hr.), and 655km (406 miles) from Auckland (about 8 hr.). The highway ends right in the city.

BY FERRY Two operators run ferries across the Cook Strait from Picton to Wellington: the **Interislander** (interislander.co.nz; ✆ **0800/802-802** in NZ) and **Bluebridge** (bluebridge.co.nz; ✆ **0800/844-844** in NZ). One way, both charge about NZ$70 per adult foot passenger and from NZ$275 for a small car with two adults. The ferry must be booked well in advance (as a walk-on passenger you may not be able to get a spot on the day of), particularly if you have a specific sailing time in mind during the busy summer months. The crossing takes about 3 hours. Cook Strait is beautiful but can be vile in bad weather, so if you're prone to seasickness, take precautions. ***Tip:*** Book the sunset sailing for great views as you leave the harbor.

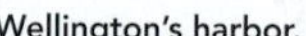

Wellington's harbor.

BY TRAIN & COACH (BUS) **Wellington Railway Station** is on Waterloo Quay. **InterCity** (intercity.co.nz; ✆ **09/623-1503**) runs regular services to all major NZ centers. **Metlink**

(metlink.org.nz; ✆ **0800/801-700** in NZ) operates commuter trains around the Wairarapa and Kāpiti Coast region. **Great Journeys of New Zealand's Northern Explorer Train** (greatjourneysnz.com; ✆ **04/495-0775**) is a scenic route from Auckland (stopping in Hamilton, Ohakune, Palmerstone North, and a handful of other spots along the way) that starts from NZ$239. Most major hostels and hotels are within a short taxi ride of the station.

VISITOR INFORMATION

The official visitor website is **wellingtonnz.com**. The **Wellington isite Visitor Centre** (50 Cable St., Te Aro, on the ground floor of Tākina Wellington Exhibition and Convention Centre; ✆ **04/802-4860**), is open 9am to 5pm Monday to Saturday and 9am to 4pm on Sunday (during winter they may close a little earlier Sun–Tues).

SPECIAL EVENTS

Wellington loves a good party, so there's always an event or festival going on, but here are some of the best. Held biennially (the next one will be in February 2028), the **Aotearoa New Zealand Festival of the Arts** (festival.nz) celebrates the very best in local and international creativity—music, dance, theater, comedy—from all corners of the globe. Its oddball offsider, the **Wellington Fringe Festival** (fringe.co.nz; ✆ **04/212-4725**) is held annually around the same time (Feb–Mar). In August, **Visa Wellington on a Plate** (visawoap.com) honors the best in food, wine, and hospitality, with culinary events all over the region, including the popular Burger Wellington Competition. People come from all over the country in late September and early October to attend the **World of WearableArt Show** (worldofwearableart.com; ✆ **03/547-0864**), known as "WOW." It's Aotearoa's largest arena spectacle, centered around elaborate and one-of-a-kind wearable art. It began life in a tent in Nelson in 1987 and now attracts audiences of more than 60,000 during its 3-week run.

CITY LAYOUT

From the railway station end of town, the major thoroughfare **Lambton Quay** runs roughly parallel to the harbor, and many shops, offices, and government buildings can be found here. **The Terrace,** where some of the larger hotels and apartment complexes are found, is on a hill up above this flat area. **Willis Street, Manners Street,** and **Courtenay Place** (the last having a large concentration of restaurants and bars, along with Hannah's Laneway, Dixon Street, and Tory Street) are other key roads that follow the line of the harbor, leading towards **Oriental Bay. Cuba Street** (home to even more restaurants, vintage shops, and the city's indie scene) runs perpendicular to these.

Neighborhoods in Brief

Te Aro A rare flat spot, Te Aro forms the main part of the CBD and is the social, shopping, and foodie heart of the city. It's colorful and scruffy (in a good way), with a wide range of hotels and restaurants from the very cheap to the top end. Parking is tricky but it's extremely walkable, bordered by the harborfront in the north, Kent Terrace in the east, and The Terrace and the university in the west.

Thorndon Just north of the Parliament Buildings, New Zealand's oldest suburb is full of cute Victorian houses and high-ranking government folks; many politicians have their capital-city crash pads here. It's super close to the central city or the delightful Botanic Garden, with great views and some lovely B&Bs. Parts of it are close to the motorway, however, and parking can be a problem.

Kelburn Full of university students and academics, Kelburn is an up-and-down suburb with gorgeous houses, narrow streets, and million-dollar views. It's west of the CBD and easily accessed via the Cable Car from Lambton Quay.

Mount Victoria At the Courtenay Place end of town, Mount Vic is great for eating out and partying the night away. Most of the parking is residents-only during business hours, but it's a free-for-all after 6pm.

Oriental Bay A little farther around, this is blue-ribbon Wellington, a stone's throw from the CBD so you won't need a car. The area has a number of hotels and some very good cafes and restaurants.

GETTING AROUND

BY BUS & TRAIN To see the main city sights, you shouldn't need a car. Wellington's central city is easy to explore on foot, and it has one of the country's best public transport systems, operated by **Metlink** (metlink.org.nz; (✆ **0800/801-700** in NZ), including buses and commuter trains. Single trip fares are charged according to zones, starting from N$3 (children half price). For better value, buy and pre-load the city's transit card, called **Snapper** (snapper.co.nz)—there's a self-service vending machine at Wellington Airport, or check the website for other locations. It costs NZ$10 and will save you more than 25% off fares with automatic discounts for off-peak travel and starting fares of around NZ$1.50 during off-peak times. Day passes are also available with Snapper; a **Metlink Explorer Day Pass** for most of Wellington city costs NZ$13 and gives you and a child (age 5–15) unlimited travel on

Wellington is anything but a flat city. On the steep slopes of Mount Victoria, homes appear to be stacked atop each other.

public transit (all day on weekends and public holidays, and after 9am on weekdays). To use the card, simply tap on and off. A corresponding Snapper app allows users to top up their cards and check their balances, but cannot yet be used to pay for transit without the physical Snapper card.

Metlink's buses operate daily from 5am to 11pm on most routes; there's a full schedule and trip planner available on its website. The main city bus station is **Wellington Station Bus Interchange** at Lambton Quay. It's adjacent to the main railway station on Bunny Street. Metlink also operates daily commuter trains between Wellington and the Wairarapa and Kāpiti Coast regions, which may also be accessed with a Snapper card.

BY CABLE CAR The historic **Cable Car** (wellingtoncablecar.co.nz; ✆ **04/472-2199**) runs between Lambton Quay and Kelburn every 10 minutes, with a couple of stops along the way. It operates Monday to Thursday from 7:30am to 8pm, Friday 7:30am to 9pm, Saturday 8:30am to 9pm, and Sunday 8:30am to 7pm. A round-trip ticket costs NZ$12 adults, NZ$6 children 5 to 15, and NZ$28 for a family. You can use your Snapper card (see above), but only if your journey includes the Lambton Quay Terminal. For more, see p. 324.

BY CAR Don't rent a car in the city if you don't have to, since street parking is difficult to find, and parking lots are at a premium within the downtown area, costing NZ$20 to NZ$30 for 24 hours. Most hotels only offer paid valet parking, which runs NZ$20 to NZ$50. If you do have to park, download the free app **ParkMate** (parkmate.co.nz), which will save you 25% on the machine rate. If you're flying into Wellington, it's best to wait until you're ready to leave the city to pick up a rental car. Most places you will want to go within Wellington itself are accessible by foot or public transit.

BY FERRY The **East by West Ferry** (eastbywest.co.nz) runs daily 6:15am to 7:30pm between Queen's Wharf, Matiu/Somes Island, and Eastbourne/Days Bay wharf, taking around half an hour. Round-trip tickets are NZ$32 for adults and NZ$16 for ages 5 to 15.

BY SCOOTER Scooting is a super-fun and easy way to navigate the central city's relatively flat streets. Scooter share company **Flamingo** (flamingoscooters.com) offers an app users can download to unlock and pay for their rides. You can expect to pay NZ$1 to unlock, then about NZ$0.65 per minute. Helmets aren't a requirement, but they are recommended.

BY TAXI You'll find taxi stands throughout the CBD. To phone one, try **Wellington Combined Taxis** (taxis.co.nz; ✆ **04/384-4444**). Rideshare services **Zoomy** (zoomy.co.nz) and **Uber** (uber.com) also operate in the city.

Exploring Wellington

TOP ATTRACTIONS

Museum of New Zealand Te Papa Tongarewa ♥♥♥ MUSEUM
Opened in 1996, New Zealand's national museum—Te Papa, as it's generally known—aims to bring the fun into the museum experience without dumbing it down. Interactive technology and world-class exhibitions eloquently tell the story of Aotearoa—its art, culture, history, and environment—over six levels.

The giant squid is a favorite specimen for regular visitors to Te Papa's absorbing Te Taiao nature gallery.

It would take days to properly digest all of the permanent and short-term exhibits, but first-time visitors should start with the stupendous **Gallipoli: The Scale of Our War.** Created with the special effects wizards at Wētā Workshop, it first opened in 2015 for a limited run that keeps getting extended (the latest update is that it will be here until at least 2032). The exhibit commemorates the first battle involving New Zealand troops in World War I, 93% of whom were killed or wounded. It really must be seen to be believed—the eight individuals on which much of the exhibition is based were real-life soldiers, and they've been brought back much larger than life (seriously—they are actually 2½ times larger than life, with every freckle and hair recreated). The exhibit does an excellent job of showing what life in the trenches was really like for Kiwi troops.

Permanent exhibitions include the incredibly kid-friendly **Te Taiao nature gallery,** which examines NZ's biodiversity and the effects of climate change. It features now-extinct animals like the moa and Haast's eagle, alongside a colossal squid—the only one on display in the world, and one of the most complete specimens ever found. There are plenty of interactive features, including a shaking earthquake house and a tsunami tank.

Other permanent exhibits worth seeing include **Blood Earth Fire/Whangai Ahi Ka,** revealing the changing landscape of this country; **Te Marae,** an authentic carved Māori communal meeting place and a compelling introduction to Indigenous culture; and **Slice of Heaven 20th Century Aotearoa,** an introduction to what has united and divided Kiwis since colonization, with stories of how Māori, women, and gay people stood up for their rights through protest and art. My personal favorite, which I head straight to every time I visit, is the **Te Toi Art Gallery**'s portrait room, featuring paintings by Gottfried Lindauer. An interactive tool explains the paintings' historical relevance,

WELLYWOOD'S wētā wonders

New Zealand's movie industry was long a low-key enterprise, but all that changed when director Peter Jackson and Wētā Workshop founder Richard Taylor created the special effects for the blockbuster *Lord of the Rings* trilogy. Since then, the multiple-award-winning Wētā operation has sprinkled high-tech magic on numerous films such as *King Kong*, *Avatar*, and *Rise of the Planet of the Apes*—and of course the three *Hobbit* movies. At Wētā's headquarters, on the corner of Camperdown Road and Weka Street in the southeast suburb of Miramar, you can visit the **Wētā Cave ♥♥♥** and get up close and personal with characters, props, and displays from the *Lord of the Rings* films and many others. Take something special home from the **Wētā Cave Shop,** which has a huge range of collectibles, miniatures, jewelry, books, posters, clothing, and sculptures. Book your 90-minute behind-the-scenes tour (tours.wetaworkshop.com; ✆ **04/909-4000;** NZ$50 adults, NZ$26 children 5–14; book online to save money; some prices include shuttle transfers). It's open daily from 9am to 5:30pm. Take bus route 2 toward Miramar.

In 2021, Wētā Workshop opened up a new outpost in Auckland (p. 81). If you're trying to decide which one to visit, know that the Wellington location is where movies are actually made, and where you'll get more LOTR content. But if you've got a young family, I'd recommend visiting in Auckland instead, because its Universal Studios–style attraction (complete with animatronic monsters) is more interactive. Then again, you could visit both and get two totally different experiences.

A model of Gollum from *The Lord of the Rings*, at Wētā Cave.

highlights key details in each, and even reveals what they look like under infrared light. Each time I find and learn something new.

Visitors can opt for the **Introducing Te Papa Tour,** which costs NZ$60 and includes entry. Guides provide welcome additional context and (often) point out objects that visitors rarely notice. You can also pick up a self-guided tour booklet, and audio guides are available in several languages. The gift shop, **Te Papa Store,** is full of covetable arts, crafts, and Kiwiana books and toys.

Te Papa's two cafes—on Level 1 and Level 4—are reasonable if you don't want to leave the building, with some fun specials tying in with exhibitions or events like Matariki, but you'll likely find better food and coffee elsewhere.

55 Cable St. tepapa.govt.nz. ✆ **04/381-7000.** Free for NZ residents, NZ$35 for others 16 and older. Fees for some activities, tours, and short-term exhibitions. Daily 10am–6pm.

National Library of New Zealand ♥♥♥ LIBRARY There are just three original documents in the National Library's permanent exhibition **He Tohu,** but they are all crucial to Aotearoa's story: 1835's He Whakaputanga or Declaration of Independence; 1840's Treaty of Waitangi; and the 1893 Women's Suffrage Petition, which resulted in New Zealand becoming the first country in the world to give women the vote. You'll hear the human stories of some of the people behind the signatures and learn how these documents have shaped modern NZ. Audio tours are available, and there are free hour-long guided tours on Tuesday, Wednesday, and Thursday at noon—just show up 5 minutes before.

70 Molesworth St. natlib.govt.nz/he-tohu. ✆ **04/474-3000.** Free. Mon–Fri 9am–5pm, Sat 9am–1pm.

Wellington Cable Car ♥♥♥ ATTRACTION Five minutes of seemingly vertical climbing through native bush and over quaint wooden houses with one of the best views of the city and its magnificent harbor—that's the experience you'll be getting for a handful of bucks. (For more details, see "Getting Around," above.) It's also the easiest way to get to the **Wellington Botanic Gardens** (p. 326). Learn all about the history of this service (which has been running since 1902) at the **Cable Car Museum** (museumswellington.org.nz; ✆ **04/475-3578;** free admission; daily 10am–5pm), located in the original winding house at the top.

Cable car runs btw. Lambton Quay and Kelburn. Round-trip ticket NZ$12 adults, NZ$6 children 5–15; NZ$28 families; or pay with a Snapper card. Mon–Thurs 7:30am–8pm, Fri 7:30am–9pm, Sat 8:30am–9pm, Sun 8:30am–7pm.

OTHER THINGS TO SEE & DO

City Gallery Wellington ♥♥ ART MUSEUM As of 2025, City Gallery Wellington is temporarily housed in the National Library of New Zealand in Molesworth St. (see above), while its permanent home—in the gorgeous old Art Deco Wellington Public Library building—undergoes earthquake strengthening. It should return to Te Ngākau Civic Square mid-2026, but check the website for the latest. Regardless of location, the gallery will definitely challenge you with its thought-provoking and sometimes avant-garde collections (painting, sculpture, film, video, industrial and graphic design, and architecture). It can be a bit pointy-headed; you'll notice this more if you've come

TRAFFIC stopping

When you're walking around Wellington, particularly in the Waitangi Park vicinity, near Parliament, and along Cuba Street, keep a close eye on the pedestrian crossing lights. If you look carefully, you'll see they resemble a suffragette, a kapa haka warrior, and a drag queen. Installed in 2019, each is a colorful dedication to someone who played a significant role in Wellington's history.

Old St. Paul's is a charming 19th-century relic.

straight from the more populist Te Papa nearby, but a visit will get you bang up to speed with what's happening in contemporary art in this country.

Civic Square, 101 Wakefield St. citygallery.org.nz. ✆ **04/801-3021.** Free; some international exhibitions may have entry fee. Mon–Fri 10am–5pm, Sat 9am–1pm.

Katherine Mansfield House & Garden ♥ HISTORIC HOME Today she's probably NZ's best-known author, though in her own time Katherine Mansfield was little known in her home country. Mansfield was born in 1888, grew up in this house, and left New Zealand at age 19 for the U.K., where she lived a spirited life in the company of such literary greats as Virginia Woolf, D.H. Lawrence, and T.S. Eliot. She was best known for her modernist short stories, most notably "The Garden Party" and "The Doll's House." Even if you've never heard of her, a visit to this charmingly restored two-story house is a pleasant diversion. Events such as art exhibitions and garden parties (appropriately enough) are held here from time to time; check the website for details.

25 Tinakori Rd., Thorndon. katherinemansfield.com. ✆ **04/473-7268.** NZ$10 adults, NZ$8 seniors, under 18 free. Guided tours (must be booked at least 48 hr. in advance) NZ$10–NZ$20 depending on group size. Tues–Sun 10am–4pm.

Old St. Paul's ♥♥ CHURCH While you're in the area, have a look at Old St. Paul's—a stunningly beautiful Anglican church built in 1866 entirely from native wood and one of the best examples of timber Gothic Revival architecture in the world. Inside, the church positively glows with all that polished wood and stained glass—and perhaps a bit of divine spirit.

34 Mulgrave St. visitheritage.co.nz. ✆ **04/473-6722.** Entry by *koha* (donation). Daily 10am–4pm.

Nicknamed the Beehive, Parliament's modern Executive Office Building was designed to bring lawmakers together, with all offices radiating off a central core.

Parliament Buildings ♥♥ LANDMARK/ARCHITECTURE The country's seat of government on Molesworth Street is just moments from Lambton Quay. The 1970s architectural wonder known as the **Beehive** sits by the Edwardian neoclassical **Parliament House.** The Māori Affairs Select Committee Room, at the front of Parliament House, has specially commissioned carvings and weavings that are worth seeing, too. There are a host of guided tours available, covering the political process, artworks, Māori and women in Parliament, and one for kids—most are free, but must still be booked in advance on the Parliament website. Across the road, the magnificent **Old Government Building,** built in 1876, is the largest wooden office building in the Southern Hemisphere and now houses Victoria University of Wellington's law faculty.

Molesworth St. parliament.nz. ✆ **04/817-9503.** Free admission. Parliament House by guided tour only. Old Government Building open to public daily 9am–5pm.

Te Ara Whānui ki te Rangi/Space Place ♥♥ MUSEUM What sets the upgraded-in-2025 Space Place apart from other astronomy museums is its thorough, seamless weaving of Mātauranga Māori (Indigenous knowledge) with Western science. So while there are interactive displays on the origins of the universe, black holes, rocket launches, astronaut life, and New Zealand's own space industry, you'll also learn about Māori star lore and navigation, the Maramataka or moon calendar, and Matariki, the public holiday now nationally celebrated in midwinter when the star cluster Matariki (Pleiades) rises in the dawn sky. There are planetarium shows on the hour; try to catch the home-grown **Ngā Tohunga Whakatere/The Navigators** (most of the others are Northern Hemisphere imports). If you visit late enough on a clear evening, you'll see the observatory's 150+-year-old telescope in action. Built in 1867 and shipped to NZ for viewings of Halley's Comet, it's still in perfect working order.

40 Salamanca Rd., Kelburn. museumswellington.org.nz. ✆ **04/910-3140.** NZ$16 adults, NZ$10 ages 4–16, NZ$49 families. Daily 10am–5pm (until 11pm Tues & Fri–Sat).

Wellington Botanic Gardens ♥♥ GARDENS Wellington's Botanic Gardens are so close to the downtown core, they're more a part of the city's daily life than most botanical gardens tend to be. The reserve contains a range of flat and wonderfully hilly areas, paths heading off in all directions, and spectacular views of the city. A brochure and map are available from the Wellington visitor center or the Treehouse Visitor Centre inside the garden. A Garden of National Significance, it was established in 1868 and is now 25 hectares (62 acres) in all, with a nice mix of native forest, old exotic trees, and plant collections with seasonal floral displays. The Lady Norwood Rose Garden, with 110 beds, is one of the more formal parts of the garden and is at its best from November to May. The lovely old Begonia House is full of tropical and temperate plants, including orchids and waterlilies, with a gift shop and the Picnic Café next door. There are numerous other little places of interest, like a Peace Garden, a World War I commemorative poppy field, and some naturally occurring glowworms.

Entrance on Glenmore St., Thorndon. wellingtongardens.nz. ✆ **04/499-1400** for Treehouse Visitor Centre. Free. Daily dawn–dusk. Cafe 8:30am–4pm; visitor center weekdays 9am–4pm, weekends 10am–3pm; Begonia House Gift Shop and Cafe 9am–4pm.

Wellington Museum/Te Waka Huia o Ngā Taonga Tuku Iho ♥♥ MUSEUM Once rated one of the 50 best museums in the world by *The Times* in the U.K, this museum aims "to take you back 1,000 years and lead you to a vibrant, present-day Wellington." It doesn't hurt that the museum is located in the historic 1892 Bond Store. Exhibits present the capital's social, cultural, and nautical history in interesting ways, using technology to enhance but not overpower the precious artifacts here. Kids will love the holograms and interactive displays. Permanent exhibits include a film about the 1968 **Wahine** ferry disaster that claimed 51 lives in Cook Strait; the maritime paraphernalia of **Jack's Boathouse;** a reproduction of the historic Bond Store—complete with virtual vermin; and significant *taonga* (Māori treasures).

3 Jervois Quay, Queens Wharf. museumswellington.org.nz. ✆ **04/472-8904.** Free. Inquire for guided tours. Daily 10am–5pm.

The beloved Wellington Cable Car is the best way to scale the heights to reach the Wellington Botanical Gardens.

Zealandia Te Māra a Tāne ♥♥ NATURE RESERVE Visit Zealandia for a powerful introduction to Aotearoa's conservation history, present and future. In 1999, the research reserve invented the predator-proof fence, which is now used throughout New Zealand to keep native animals safe from introduced mammals, and is the reason the capital now throngs with the screeches of kākā parrots, rarely seen in most other parts of the country. Walking Zealandia's tracks during the day, you'll see (and hear) dozens of rare birds; if you take a night tour, you might encounter the resident kiwi, tuatara, glowworms, or frogs. I highly recommend the interactive exhibition in the visitor center for familiarizing yourself with the various birds and their calls; it also features an excellent dramatized film that vividly shows how the country's bird populations were decimated, and the need for sanctuaries like this one. The on-site Rātā Café serves all-day brunch with views over the reserve. A free shuttle leaves hourly from Wakefield Street downtown and the top of the Wellington Cable Car—check the website for times.

31 Waiapu Rd., Karori. visitzealandia.com. ✆ **04/920-9200.** NZ$26 adults, NZ$10 ages 5–17, under 5s free. Tours (include entry for the following day as well) NZ$64 adults, NZ$32 kids; night tours NZ$100 adults, NZ$50 kids (who must be over 12). Daily 9am–4:30pm.

A boardwalk leads a young Zealandia visitor through this wildlife-rich nature sanctuary.

ORGANIZED TOURS & CRUISES

Capital Personalised Tours (captours.co.nz; ✆ **021/280-2406**) offers trips in a sole-use SUV for customized golf, food and wine, craft beer, sightseeing, or *Lord of the Rings* themed trips. Tours start from NZ$220 for adults and NZ$110 for children for a half day. **Kaewa Tours** (kaewatours.co.nz; ✆ **021/280-0075**) will take you on scenic foodie-oriented day trips (including fancy lunch) to the Kāpiti Coast or the Wairarapa, from NZ$427. Another recommended food-tour option is **The Big Foody** (thebigfoody.com; ✆ **021/481-177**), which offers 3-hour walking tours of some of the hippest, tastiest downtown spots for NZ$220.

Wanderlust Tourism Group (wtgl.nz) operates three different brands: a 3-hour city tour (NZ$89); a well-regarded *Lord of the Rings* tour (NZ$175 half day, NZ$325 full day); and **Seal Coast Safaris** (sealcoastsafari.nz; ✆ **021/459-521**), which will take you from the temperate rainforest of Otari-Wilson's Bush across farmland to the city's rugged southern coast to watch fur seals at play—come in spring to see the baby pups (NZ$195 half day).

KID magnets

Wellington Zoo ♥♥, 200 Daniell St. (wellingtonzoo.com; ✆ **04/381-6755**), is your standard small city zoo with one exception: Its Close Encounters experiences allow you to get up-close and personal with the animals. You can feed a giraffe (NZ$129), help look after a snow leopard (NZ$199), or get clambered on by a red panda (NZ$159), among others. A portion of the proceeds go to the Wellington Zoo Conservation Fund. Encounters happen at a set time daily. **Zealandia** (see p. 328) is a better place to see native creatures in the wild, but the Zoo is also doing sterling work—and a section of its animal hospital, The Nest, helps injured native wildlife brought in from outside. General admission is NZ$26 adults and NZ$14 ages 3 to 14, NZ$49 for a family of four; it's open daily 9:30am to 5pm.

If you're in the city during a weekend or on a public holiday, have fun exploring the waterfront on a two- or four-seater covered bike rented from **The Enormous Crocodile Company** ♥, 1 Herd St., Clyde Quay (crocbikes.co.nz; ✆ **027/276-2269**). Even the name will make you smile. Two-seaters are NZ$29 and four-seaters are NZ$44 for 30 minutes.

For a Māori perspective on the nation's capital, **Te Wharewaka o Pōneke Tours** ♥♥ (wharewakatours.maori.nz; ✆ **04/801-7227**) is most well-known for its immersive 2-hour tours of the harbor in a traditionally carved *waka*/ canoe (NZ$115; departs at 9am, 11:30am, 2pm), but it also offers a 2-hour walking tour of the city (from NZ$55) twice daily.

And if you like the idea of enjoying the city from a great height, one of the best ways to do it is with **Wellington Helicopters** ♥, centrally located at Shed 1, 19 Jervois Quay (helicopters.net.nz; ✆ **04/472-1550**). Choose from a variety of flights starting from the short (9 min.) but perfectly scenic city tours for NZ$165 per person.

Outdoor Pursuits

CYCLING **Switched on Bikes** (switchedonbikes.co.nz; ✆ **04/473-1080**) operates from Shed One on Queens Wharf, and offers both rentals and guided bike tours. Rentals start from NZ$35 for a standard bike and NZ$45 for an electric version.

GOLF You'll find top courses within an hour of Wellington's downtown. The **Royal Wellington Golf Club** ♥, 28 Golf Rd., Heretaunga, Upper Hutt (rwgc.co.nz; ✆ **04/528-4590**), was once ranked the best members' club in New Zealand by this country's PGA and still continues to earn top marks. Call the pro shop to schedule a time as a non-member and to learn more about green fees. **Paraparaumu Beach Golf Club** ♥♥♥, 376 Kāpiti Rd., Paraparaumu Beach (paraparaumubeachgolfclub.co.nz; ✆ **04/902-8200**), is considered one of the best links courses in the Southern Hemisphere and has hosted the New Zealand Open 12 times. Green fees are NZ$225 for non-residents; book well in advance.

KAYAKING Owned by New Zealand's Olympic gold medal–winning paddler Ian Ferguson, **Fergs Kayaks,** Shed 6, Queen's Wharf (fergswellington.co.nz; ✆ **04/499-8898**), rents out everything from a giant SUP board to in-line skates, but its bread and butter is kayak rental starting from NZ$28 for an hour. Guided tours—including to Somes Island—are also available from NZ$100. Be prepared, though: Wellington's high winds mean the harbor can get pretty rough.

MOUNTAIN BIKING You'll need pretty good legs for this one—Wellington is not the world's flattest capital city! Based near challenging Makara Peak, about 30 minutes' drive from the CBD, **Mud Cycles,** 421 Karori Rd., Karori (mudcycles.co.nz; ✆ **04/476-4961**), rents bikes for NZ$30 to NZ$100 for 2 hours, depending on the bike; half day and weekly rentals are also available.

WALKING This is a great city for walking, from flat city strolls to more adventurous excursions. The 10.6km (6.6-mile) **Southern Walkway** ♥ runs along the Town Belt from Oriental Bay and Island Bay—all you need to do is follow the pink bollards. Suitable for those of average fitness with some steep portions, it takes about half a day to complete, with great views of the harbor and central city. The climb up **Mount Kaukau** ♥♥, Wellington's highest visible point, will only take you an hour but requires a moderate level of fitness. Tracks to the top begin at Woodmancote Road and Simla Crescent in Khandallah, Sirsi Terrace in Broadmeadows, and Truscott Avenue in Johnsonville. The **Escarpment Track** on the Kāpiti Coast (see p. 344) makes a great out-of-town day trip, or try the **Skyline Walkway** from the Old Coach Road in Johnsonville to Makara Saddle in Karori, a 13.4km (8⅓-mile) 6-hour ridgetop adventure offering spectacular views.

Where to Stay in Wellington

Despite its charms as a tourist destination, Wellington's accommodations still tend to look toward the corporate market, so rates are high even on weekdays. They can vary enormously with dynamic pricing, however, so you might score a bargain—or get unlucky if there's a big event on. Either way, it's best to book well in advance, including for private rentals found on Airbnb.com or Vrbo.com. If you're driving (not recommended), you'll also need to incorporate the cost of parking: Most hotels in Wellington's downtown area charge between NZ$20 and NZ$30 for parking, while public parking lots charge about the same—download the ParkMate app to save 25%.

DOWNTOWN

Expensive

Bolton Hotel ♥♥ This multistory, apartment-style hotel has an elegance and style that exceeds some of its bigger capital-city cousins. The owners have paid meticulous attention to guest preferences, and rooms abound with luscious textural fabrics and unexpected extra touches—a comprehensive minibar, for instance, that includes an umbrella and disposable raincoat, the importance of which can't be overestimated in Wellington. It's colorful, crisp, modern, and close to the heart of the city, and you can often luck into less expensive rates (book direct for best prices). Ask about the classy Bolton suite if you want to indulge; it's very reasonably priced and ideal for families or couples traveling together.

Corner of Bolton and Mowbray sts. boltonhotel.co.nz. ✆ **0800/996-622** in NZ, or 04/472-9966. 139 units. NZ$279–NZ$599 double. Valet parking NZ$40. **Amenities:** Restaurant, cafe, bar; concierge; gym; Jacuzzi; indoor lap pool; sauna; free Wi-Fi.

InterContinental Wellington ♥♥ You'll feel like a rock star as you sweep into the lobby of this plush palace in the heart of the Central Business District (CBD). Perhaps less so if you've just dropped off a tiny Mazda and not a Bentley, but whatever—they'll still park it for you, and do it with a big smile, because the service here is superlative. As for the rooms, they're tremendously comfortable, with top-quality beds and bedding, albeit with big chain hotel looks. Still, many have terrific harbor views, and everything you need is on-site, from a state-of-the-art gym to room service to a top spa.

2 Grey St. wellington.intercontinental.com. ✆ **0800/500-619** in NZ, or 04/472-2722. 239 units. NZ$322–NZ$599 double. Valet parking NZ$50. **Amenities:** 2 restaurants, 2 bars; airport transfers; babysitting; business center; concierge; gym; Jacuzzi; indoor pool; sauna, room service; day spa; free Wi-Fi.

The Intrepid Hotel ♥♥ It's hard to beat this boutique hotel's location just off pedestrian Cuba Street, a stone's throw from great shopping, eateries, and bars, and easy walking distance from many of Wellington's key attractions. Its uncluttered, high-ceilinged rooms are a respite from the city buzz, with cool mauve-grey distressed cotton robes, and free snacks, juices, sodas, morning filter coffee, and use of the nearby Les Mills gym. Downstairs, right by the lift, you'll find the beautifully lit, women-owned Puffin Bar, which has intimate booths and a carefully curated selection of New Zealand wines.

60 Ghuznee St. theintrepidhotel.com. ✆ **04/910-8536.** NZ$240–NZ$400 double. **Amenities:** Bar; gym access; free Wi-Fi.

Every room at the Intrepid Hotel has its own cozy boho chic look.

Expensive/Moderate

Naumi Hotel Wellington ♥♥ There are so many things to love about this artsy hotel. Housed in an Edwardian building, its interior is an explosion of color and creativity: Bold floral wallpapers, neon signs, and giant flowers will make you feel like you've entered an *Alice in Wonderland* dreamscape. Naumi is really two hotels side by side—the newer **Naumi Hotel** has lush larger rooms, while some of those in **Naumi Studio Hotel** (formerly a Salvation Army Hotel) are a bit peculiar in shape or surprisingly tiny. But you can't beat the location: directly on hip Cuba Street. The hotels share a lobby and facilities—a gym, indoor heated pool, and hot tub.

213 Cuba St. naumihotels.com. ✆ **04/913-1800.** 116 units. NZ$170–NZ$600. **Amenities:** Restaurant, cafe, bar; gym; pool; hot tub; free Wi-Fi.

Moderate

Situated above the city at 345 The Terrace, the rooms at the **Mövenpick Hotel Wellington ♥** (movenpick.com; ✆ **04/385-9829**) have fab views of the city below, but they're strangely dark, and it's a steep uphill walk to get home. (Using the VIP elevator at the back of the building helps.) Still, the daily chocolate bar is a nice perk, staff are helpful, and the hotel is pretty affordable for its central location, with rooms starting at NZ$190.

The Cobbler ♥ If you're an introvert, you'll love this extremely central boutique hotel—I didn't see another human the whole time I was there. There's no lobby, and a key code provides entry from the street. Rooms feature nice linens, dark wood, a small kitchenette, and an excellent angled full-length mirror for planning your evening outfit. The hotel's location is both blessing and curse. Eva Street is one of the city's coolest laneways, home to quirky cocktail bars, coffee spots, and the **Wellington Chocolate Factory,** but the Cobbler's walls and windows fail to block out the bass of nearby clubs on weekends or Wednesdays (student night)—you'll need the earplugs provided.

3 Eva St. thecobblerhotel.co.nz. ✆ **04/830-0996.** NZ$175–NZ$350 double. **Amenities:** Free Wi-Fi.

QT Wellington ♥♥ Formerly the Museum Art Hotel, this property—which sits directly across from Te Papa (p. 321)—might be part of a chain, but there's absolutely nothing formulaic about it. It's home to one of the Southern Hemisphere's largest private art collections, displaying memorable works like Michel Tuffery's life-size bull made out of corned-beef cans. (Honestly, the hotel is worth popping into even if you're not staying the night; ask at the lobby bar for a paper guide to the artwork currently on display.) A couple of years ago, QT took its art theme one step further by commissioning local and international street artists to paint massive murals on the walls in its QT Gallery rooms, to stunning results. We had to deduct one star for service, which can be hit or miss, but for art lovers: This is a stylish stay you won't soon forget. If you prefer an apartment stay, QT also owns the next-door **Museum**

Apartment Hotel, with full access to all QT's amenities (museumapartment hotel.com).

90 Cable St. qthotels.com/wellington. ✆ **04/802-8900.** 165 units. NZ$249–NZ$359. Valet parking NZ$30. **Amenities:** Restaurant, cafe, bar; concierge; gym; Jacuzzi; indoor lap pool; room service; sauna; free Wi-Fi.

Inexpensive

The Marion Street Hostel ♥♥♥, 13 Marion St. (themarionhostel.com; ✆ **027/284-3887**), is one of the country's most beautiful backpacker hostels, with loads of natural light and heritage features like exposed bricks, leaving you wondering why you've ever bothered with el cheapo motels. Suitable for all ages, its private rooms with shared bathrooms start at NZ$125; bunk rooms from NZ$42.

MOUNT VICTORIA/ORIENTAL PARADE

The Bay Plaza Hotel ♥ This hotel has recently undergone a light refurbishment, but walk into its tiny bathrooms and you'll discover it's still very much a hotel trapped in the past. (Fair enough; the building dates back to 1906.) But the rooms are very clean, it's well located with nice views of the harbor, and it's got the rare self-service parking lot around the back.

40 Oriental Parade. bayplaza.co.nz. ✆ **04/385-7799.** 76 units. NZ$150–NZ$250 double. Parking NZ$20. **Amenities:** Restaurant, bar; free Wi-Fi.

Booklovers Bed & Breakfast ♥♥ Journalist and book author Jane Tolerton offers four large rooms in her two-story Victorian home, and she's a terrific and knowledgeable hostess who knows just when to leave you alone. All the rooms are named for authors; all are homey and kept spotlessly clean. The whole place heaves with books—if you dabble in the bookshelves you may never want to leave! It's just a short walk from Courtenay Place, or hop on one of the buses that stop right outside the gate.

123 Pirie St. booklovers.co.nz. ✆ **04/384-2714.** 3 units. NZ$290 double. Rates include breakfast. **Amenities:** Free Wi-Fi.

Ohtel ♥♥♥ You may never want to check out of this small, chic boutique hotel with its great location, striking individuality, and total commitment to sustainability. Stylishly furnished throughout, with the owner's collection of mid-century modern furniture and German ceramics (no two rooms are the same), it is perfectly placed, overlooking Te Papa and Oriental Parade. All rooms are large, but the six front-facing ones are the best for views. Then there are the wonderfully indulgent bathrooms, which clever design makes part of the total space (but a strategically positioned curtain guarantees privacy). Staying here is indeed a full sensory experience.

66 Oriental Parade. ohtel.com. ✆ **04/803-0600.** 10 units. NZ$200–NZ$600 double. **Amenities:** Lobby cafe (breakfast & cabinet food); bar; concierge; free Wi-Fi.

NEAR THE AIRPORT

Opened in 2019, **Rydges Wellington Airport ♥**, 28 Stewart Duff Dr. (rydges.com; ✆ **04/896-9150**), is the first and only hotel to be fully integrated with the

Quick Caffeine Fixes

Coffee is exceptional in NZ, and no destination exemplifies this better than the cafes of Wellington. A quick note for North Americans who usually drink drip coffee or Americanos and are confused about how to order: Ask for a long black with a side of milk or extra water, so you can adjust the intensity to your preference. For the best brews, try **Prefab** ♥♥, 14 Jessie St. (pre-fab.co.nz; ✆ **04/385-2263;** weekdays only); **Customs Coffee** ♥♥, 39 Ghuznee St. (coffeesupreme.com); or **Sketchbook Coffee,** 40 Taranaki St. (instagram.com/sketchbookcoffee), whose baristas compete nationally. But my top pick to get to grips with the capital's coffee culture is **Flight Coffee Hangar** ♥♥♥, 119 Dixon St. (hangarcafe.co.nz; ✆ **027/535-0084;** open daily 7am–2pm). Here you can caffeinate for a day of sightseeing with a tasting flight of one blend or single origin made as espresso, cold drip, and flat white; or sample three different flat whites or filter drops, complete with tasting notes. They serve brunch, too.

Wellington airport. Located right above the international terminal, it's a solution to unreasonably early flights, with rooms that start at NZ$175.

Where to Eat in Wellington

Wellington is crammed with restaurants of every stripe from many different cultures. You can generally walk to where you want to go downtown, or catch a cab if it's a bit farther out. The Cuba Precinct is the best place to find everything from the cheap-and-cheerful to the much-lauded. The more traditional (as well as the most touristy) places tend to be closer to the waterfront. Wellington's Central Business District (CBD)—which is where many of the hotels are located—has its fair share of reputable restaurants and cafes, but be aware that they may not be open on weekends because they tend to cater to the office crowd.

CENTRAL CITY

Expensive

Boulcott Street Bistro ♥♥ INTERNATIONAL This long-established, well-regarded restaurant has been pleasing lovers of classic cuisine—grilled meats and fish, French onion soup, crème brulee—for many years now. First-time visitors will be especially delighted by the setting in a heritage Victorian cottage right in the heart of the city. Lunch is a great time to go—you can get a 300g (10½-oz.) T-bone steak with watercress and a "dirty martini salsa" for just NZ$25.

99 Boulcott St. boulcottstbistro.co.nz. ✆ **04/499-4199.** Main courses NZ$25–NZ$49. Reservations only for lunch and dinner before 6pm. Mon–Fri noon–2pm and 5:30pm–late, Sat 5:30pm–late.

Capitol ♥♥ ITALIAN Another stalwart on the local scene, Capitol puts an emphasis on casual quality dining. It's quite an intimate setting: It only seats 44 and has the tiniest kitchen you can imagine, from which comes, among other good things, delicious light and fluffy gnocchi, Parmesan-crumbed lambs' liver, and seared scallops. You'll need to book for lunch, but walk-in diners are welcome in the evening.

10 Kent Terrace. capitolrestaurant.co.nz. ✆ **04/384-2855.** Main courses NZ$34–NZ$40. Wed–Sun 5–9:30pm.

Charley Noble Eatery & Bar ♥♥ INTERNATIONAL Don't worry if you haven't heard of him—Charley Noble isn't the name of the chef at this upmarket establishment, but rather a nautical nickname for the galley chimney aboard ships. It's an apt reference: The seafood bar (with fresh-shucked oysters) is top-notch here, as is the other bar—the cocktail one. Still, this eatery, set in the historic Huddart Parker Building, is primarily a steakhouse with a handful of vegetarian options plus homemade pastas, pot pies, market fish, and an array of intriguing sides (sesame slaw, fire-roasted portobellos).

1 Post Office Sq. charleynoble.co.nz. ✆ **0508/242-753** in NZ. Main courses NZ$38–NZ$49. Reservations only for lunch or Sun dinner. Mon–Fri 11:30am–late, Sat–Sun 5pm–late.

Fratelli ♥♥ ITALIAN This is the place to come for reliably fresh, 100% homemade pasta, gnocchi, risotto, and pizza. Chefs here blend traditional Italian cooking styles with new ideas to create great-value meals like risotto with slow-cooked rabbit, button mushrooms, mascarpone, and preserved lemon. Traditional Italian desserts like tiramisu, *panforte,* and gelato round off a very fulfilling evening. On Monday and Tuesday, enjoy a three-course set menu for NZ$55.

15 Blair St. fratelli.net.nz. ✆ **04/801-6615.** Main courses NZ$26–NZ$42. Reservations recommended. Mon–Sat 5:30–10pm.

Classics like beef filet are expertly delivered at Logan Brown.

Logan Brown ♥♥♥ INTERNATIONAL Very much a Wellington culinary icon, this is probably the city's best-known restaurant. And although it has retained its reputation for truly excellent food, the ambience is not as formal as it once was, despite the leather-upholstered booths, white-clothed tables, Corinthian pillars, and chandeliers big enough to swing on (quite ironic when you consider its location on the inner city's funkiest street). The food, billed as "honest and simple," focuses on seafood and game, like sumptuous *pāua* (abalone) ravioli, and duck breast roasted in *pōhutukawa* (a native tree) honey.

Cuba and Vivian sts. loganbrown.co.nz. ✆ **04/801-5114.** Set menu NZ$110. Reservations recommended. Wed–Sun from 5pm; also Fri noon–2pm.

Shed 5 ♥♥♥ CONTEMPORARY SEAFOOD First erected in 1887 as a wharf store on the Wellington harborfront, later used as both a wool shed and a bustling fish market, today this wooden building is home to one of the city's best seafood restaurants. It has plenty of seats, but thanks to its perennial popularity and award-winning status (including in the country's highest culinary accolades, the Cuisine Good Food Awards), there's a decent crowd even on weeknights. Menu creations are based on the daily catch, delivered straight to the restaurant from the sea, including the finest fish and chips, and king prawn and market fish risotto. The menu also includes lamb, beef, and pork, but vegetarians and vegans will want to head elsewhere.

Shed 5, Queen's Wharf. shed5.co.nz. ✆ **04/499-9069.** Main courses NZ$42–NZ$48. Reservations recommended. Tues–Sat noon–3pm and 5:30–9:30pm.

WBC ♥♥ MODERN NEW ZEALAND It can be a major effort to find this upstairs spot, which is barely signposted, but it's worth the hunt. Plenty of other people think so too—WBC is usually packed. FYI, the initials stand for the Wholesale Boot Company, which once occupied the premises. But let's concentrate on the food, which is mostly about sharing platters (both large and small), raw oysters and clams, and interesting toasts (asparagus and romesco, spicy beef tartare). Standout dishes include the spicy chicken wings with lemon labneh and Thai grilled eggplant salad. Yum.

107 Victoria St. wbcrestaurant.co.nz. ✆ **04/499-9379.** Sharing platters NZ$22–NZ$66. Reservations essential. Tues 5pm–late, Wed–Fri 11am–3pm and 5pm–late, Sat 5pm–late.

Moderate

Apachè ♥♥ VIETNAMESE Named after an alias of a female Communist sniper, Apachè takes a modern approach to North Vietnamese street food—with fresh, flavorful results. Think bang bang grilled lemongrass chicken salad, melt-in-your-mouth "shaking beef," and fruity duck a l'orange curry, There are a handful of vegetarian options, much of the menu is gluten free, and the chicken and pork is all free-range. The Tory Street location is quirky and cozy, with lots of nooks in which to while away a chilly Wellington evening.

66 Tory St. apache.kiwi. ✆ **04/499-2999.** Sharing plates NZ$13–NZ$40. Tues–Sat 5-10pm.

Dumplings, rice rolls, and other Vietnamese delectables fill the menu at Apachè.

Chow ♥ SOUTHEAST ASIAN With its casual, modern interior and its extensive range of noodles, grills, steamed dishes, and salads, this place is a winner with busy professionals and those with dietary restrictions. Dishes

Cool Quarter: Hannah's Laneway

Hidden at the end of an alley at the center of town (behind Dixon St.), **Hannah's Laneway** is a former shoe factory that today houses some of the city's finest artisan food purveyors and bars. These include **Wellington Chocolate Factory ♥♥♥**, 5 Eva St. (wcf.co.nz), which crafts souvenir-worthy chocolate (including varieties made with coconut milk and oat milk for the lactic phobic). Their treats are made with a commitment to ethical trade, with wrappers designed by local artists. Another star of the Laneway, **Pizza Pomodoro ♥♥♥** (13 Leeds St.; pizzapomodoro.co.nz) turns out the city's best Neapolitan-style pizzas—it's mostly a takeout joint, but you can eat your slices and other treats in a nearby park. Afterwards, check out one of the alley's idiosyncratic bars, like **Golding's Free Dive ♥♥** (14 Leeds St.; goldingsfreedive.co.nz)—"It's definitely not minimalism," said the bartender when I asked her to describe the vibe here; there are skis, Star Wars memorabilia, lampshades made from upturned buckets, even a taxidermy marmot. But though the decor is loud, the music isn't, so this comfortably disheveled one-room bar is a lovely spot for conversations, or a quiet drink to end the night. So is neighboring **Hanging Ditch ♥♥** (14 Leeds St.; hangingditch.co.nz), which is a bit more refined and Victorian—leather lounges, low light, and signature bottles of spirits suspended on bungy cords over the bar. The Ditch specializes in cocktails—strong inventive ones and house "ditches," simple spirits with homemade syrup, citrus, and soda. Or skip the alcohol and try the chocolate tea, made from steeped cacao husks, a byproduct from the chocolate factory next door.

(like bao buns, curries, dumplings, and skewers) are meant to be shared, so it's best to go with a friend and order two or three dishes. They also serve a wide array of wine, sake, cocktails, and teas.

45 Tory St. and 11 Woodward St. chow.co.nz. ✆ **04/382-8585.** Main courses NZ$12–NZ$21. Daily noon–midnight.

Inexpensive

1154 Pastaria, 132 Cuba St. (1154.co.nz; ✆ **04/213-9981**), serves—you guessed it—fresh pasta, for around NZ$25 for a plate of conchiglie, pappardelle, or rigatoni. Also in the carb department is **Best Ugly Bagels ♥♥** at 5 Swan Lane (bestugly.co.nz). Are they worth the NZ$9 to NZ$21 price tag? Debatable. But you're paying for a product (bagels) that's rarer than hen's teeth in this hemisphere—and all the ingredients are super fresh. Note for bagel enthusiasts: They hand-roll Montréal rather than New York–style bagels here, meaning they're crispy, airy, and slightly sweet.

For fantastic and cheap Malaysian and South Indian food, go to **Rasa ♥♥♥**, 200 Cuba St. (rasa.co.nz; ✆ **04/384-7088**). You'll stuff yourself for NZ$20 or NZ$25. It's open daily noon to 11pm. We also recommend **Little Penang ♥♥**, 175 Victoria St. (facebook.com/LittlePenang; ✆ **04/382-9818**), for authentic and delicious Malaysian street food. **The Old Quarter ♥♥**, 39b Dixon St. (theoldquarter.co.nz; ✆ **04/385-3916**), does great Vietnamese lunch deals—chargrilled chicken, pho, and various curries—for NZ$21.

SEE YOU IN cuba

Bohemian, hipster, scruffy, exuberant—the people who frequent the Cuba Precinct are a sharp contrast to the suited folks who haunt the business end of town. Go and hang out at **Midnight Espresso** ♥, 178 Cuba St. (✆ **04/384-7014**), for an hour or so and you'll see what we mean. This Cuba Street institution serves well into the wee hours.

After a late night out, it will be time for brunch, not breakfast, and **Loretta** ♥♥, 181 Cuba St. (loretta.nz; ✆ **04/384-2213**), excels at that boozy meal on weekends from 9am. It has Scandinavian vibes and a wood-burning fireplace that's hard to beat in the winter months. Another sweet winter breakfast option is **The Oatery** ♥♥, 14 Left Bank, Cuba St. (theoatery.nz). As the name suggests, it's an ode to oats—you can have hot porridge with seasonal ingredients, granola, overnight oats, chia pudding, a selection of sweet and savory toast, and reasonable coffee. Afterwards, lose yourself in the mazelike secondhand stacks of Pegasus Books next door.

Other convivial and cool eateries include **Ombra** ♥♥, 199 Cuba St. (ombra.co.nz; ✆ **04/385-3229**), which was once home of an adult supplies store (aka sex shop), but now is a picture-perfect Venetian *enoteca,* meaning it takes its wines seriously, but also offers food. **Nolita** ♥ 203 Cuba St. (nolita.co.nz; ✆ **04/213-7874**), is another casual Italian restaurant, but one that's completely plant-based. Nolita makes its own cashew cheeses to top its pizzas and pastas, and they're so good it's hard to believe they're not the real thing. With its enormous corner window, **Kisa** ♥♥, 195 Cuba St. (kisarestaurant.co.nz; ✆ **021/449-820**), is a great place to watch the color of Cuba Street go by while you sample a delicious range of Turkish dips and mezze—dishes like charcoal leeks, spiced wild goat, wild tahr kebabs, and mozzarella böreks. Vegans and coeliacs are well catered to here, and the food arrives quickly even on busy evenings. Half the tables are saved for walk-ins. Save room for the desserts, featuring Middle Eastern delights like dates, labneh, rosewater, sour cherries, and pomegranate.

If you're non-carnivorous or just crave good, healthy food, try **Aunty Mena Vegetarian** ♥♥, 167 Cuba St. (✆ **04/382-8288**). It doesn't look very enticing from the street, but it's always packed, and this Malaysian food joint is even cheaper than Rasa's.

THORNDON/KELBURN

The **Backbencher Gastropub** ♥, 34 Molesworth St. (opposite Parliament; backbencher.co.nz; ✆ **04/472-3065**), once counted former prime minister Jacinda Ardern among its patrons. It's a great place to visit for a beer alongside a light meal and a chuckle at the way the place lightheartedly mocks the local parliamentarians. Up the road and on the way to Kelburn, combine the obvious pleasures of the Wellington Botanic Garden with lunch at the **Picnic Cafe** ♥♥ (picniccafe.co.nz; ✆ **04/472-6002;** daily 8:30am–4pm). Wellingtonians are obsessed with cheese scones (you'll find them at bakeries around the city), and the ones served here are legendary.

In the Kelburn shops you'll find tiny **Graze Wine Bar** ♥♥, 95 Upland Rd. (grazewinebar.co.nz; open Wed–Sun), where you feel like you're right in the kitchen—all the better for watching the chefs at work. In addition to wine and aperitivi there's a wide selection of grazing plates, featuring pierogis, pretzels, and lots of locally sourced sustainable fish (the menu changes every day.) Graze strives to be as low-waste as possible: its fridges, oven, and tiles were sourced secondhand, and the upholstery was sewn from recycled jeans. There are only seven tables, so book ahead or come early.

MOUNT VICTORIA/ORIENTAL PARADE

Is it a gorgeous evening and do you want a complete change? In that case, I suggest you indulge in what Kiwis call a "takeaway" meal (as opposed to "take-out") from **Mt. Vic Chippery ♥♥**, 5 Marjoribanks St. (thechippery.co.nz; ✆ **04/382-8713**), where really good and very fresh fish and chips can be had for a modest sum. With Oriental Bay just around the corner, you will easily find a spot where you can enjoy the view and your fragrant package of goodies.

Ortega Fish Shack and Bar ♥♥ SEAFOOD This is a long-time Wellington favorite, and for good reason: The food is fresh, elegant, and imaginative, without being fussy. Menus change with the season, but you can always find such standout dishes as *gurnard* (a type of white fish) with black risotto, clams, and chorizo; and crepes with orange caramel sauce. Unsurprisingly, fish is the focus, but you can also get a good steak. Decor is eccentric and nautically themed (the original Ortega was a Caribbean fisherman and cook who is said to have inspired Hemingway's *The Old Man and the Sea*).

16 Marjoribank St. ortega.co.nz. ✆ **04/382-9559.** Main courses NZ$39–NZ$45. Tues–Sat 5pm–late.

NEAR THE AIRPORT

Vegans and vegetarians should head straight to **The Botanist ♥♥**, 219 Onepu Rd., Lyall Bay (thebotanistlyallbay.co.nz; ✆ **04/891-0198**), which serves up plant-based treats of the fake-meat variety—banana blossom "fish," sweet and sour "pork"—every day from 9am or 10pm. You can see the sea, there's a sheltered sunny courtyard and an array of craft beer, and the house bubbles cost just NZ$8 a glass. Carnivores might prefer **Puku Pies ♥♥**, Unit 56/70 Kingsford Smith St., Rongotai (pukupies.co.nz; ✆ **04/384-6652**; Mon–Fri 7am–4pm, Sat–Sun 8am–4pm) where you can get hearty pies featuring truly unusual fillings: duck and potato, nachos, fried chicken mash and gravy, steak-and-blue-cheese, *pāua* (abalone), or *palusami* (Samoan corned beef, coconut cream, and taro). **Maranui Cafe ♥♥**

Ortega Fish Shack and Bar.

PICNIC supply CENTRAL

Wellington is a city of sophisticated eaters who expect (and get!) top-quality artisanal food products at their specialty food markets. On Sundays (7:30am–2pm, to 1pm in winter), the **Harbourside Market ♥♥** next to Te Papa on the waterfront is a premier grazing ground, with around 50 vendors (harbourside-market.co.nz). Locals buy the freshest fish straight out of Nino's fish boat, which is moored alongside the action. You can also find ready-to-eat foods such as Hungarian chimney cakes, Stewart Island smoked salmon, organic honey, and much more.

For top-quality food shopping the rest of the week, **Moore Wilson's Fresh ♥♥**, 93 Tory St. (moorewilsons.co.nz), is the place to go. This fourth-generation business (founded in 1918) sold mainly to restaurateurs until it opened its doors to the public in 1998. Today its grocery store/deli offers a dazzling array of fresh produce—including its famous fresh orange juice that's made in front of you (and is indeed delicious)—and has its own demonstration kitchen. It's open Monday to Sat 7:30am to 6pm, and Sunday 8:30am to 6pm, with additional locations in Porirua, Lower Hutt, and Masterton.

(maranuicafe.co.nz; ✆ **04/387-2829;** Mon–Thurs 7am–4pm, Fri–Sun 8am–4pm), on the Parade, Lyall Bay, is a quirky joint located in the distinctive Maranui Surf Life Saving Club building on the windy waterfront, right in front of the city's main surf break. It's a terrific place for coffee, big cakes, and light lunches—with gulls soaring just outside the upstairs windows at table level, you'll soon forget all about the rush of the city. One of the newer cafes in the airport area is the **Spruce Goose ♥**, 30 Cochrane St. and Moa Point Rd., Lyall Bay (sprucegoose.net.nz; ✆ **04/387-2277;** daily 8am–5pm), which offers fantastic views of Wellington's occasionally inhospitable coast—plus lots of live music and no neighbors to complain. Oh, and the food is pretty good, too.

Wellington Shopping

Wellington is known for excellent shopping, from big-name chain shops to high-end boutiques, to some of the best op shopping (that's Kiwi for thrift stores). Start on **Lambton Quay**—known as "the Golden Mile"—for department stores and designer shops. This is lunchtime shopping country for civil servants, so it's crammed with shoe shops, boutiques, and great bookstores. The historic Bank of New Zealand building is now the **Old Bank Arcade ♥** (oldbank.co.nz; ✆ **04/922-0600**), a posh retail arcade featuring top local and international stores with cafes, restaurants, and designer clothing shops. Be sure to visit on the hour to watch the clock within become animated, revealing secrets of the building's history. Along **Ghuznee Street,** you'll find high-end boutiques carrying creations from location designers, including Wellington-made menswear at **Mandatory ♥♥**, 21 Ghuznee St. (mandatory.co.nz; ✆ **04/384-6107**), and ethically made women's wear at **Twenty-Seven Names ♥♥**, 27 Ghuznee St. (twentysevennames.co.nz; ✆ **04/801-6427**). Tiny, adorable **Underlena ♥♥♥**, 56a Ghuznee St. (underlena.com; open Fri–Sat only), has a curated selection of ultra-soft and sexy lingerie, including independent European and New Zealand brands, as well as owner Maxine Kelly's own range of black G-strings and briefs. You'll get a fun, personalized fitting experience here.

Turn onto **Cuba Street,** with its wonderful mix of the strange, the quaint, and the shops that have been there for decades. **Cuba Mall** has beloved Bucket Fountain, a landmark '70s-era tipping-bucket installation that has been fascinating kids of all ages for many a year. The funkiest cafes are here, as are tattoo and piercing joints and members of the city's bohemian set—many of them wearing cool vintage gear from shops like **Hunters & Collectors ♥♥**, 134 Cuba St. (huntersandcollectors.net.nz; ✆ **04/384-8948**); **Ziggurat ♥♥**, 144 Cuba St. (zigguratshop.co.nz; ✆ **04/385-1077**); or one of the two **Recycled Boutiques** on Ghuznee Street and Vivian Street. Viral sensation **Preloved Charlies ♥♥**, 120 Victoria St. (prelovedcharlies.com; ✆ **029/777-9929**), is worth a look in just for the did-we-ever-really-wear-that factor—just be warned that you'll pay as much (if not more) for these curated secondhand early-2000s originals as you would for brand-new threads. For locally handmade gifts—funky earrings, handcrafts, candles, *pounamu* (greenstone)—head to **Welly Collective,** 103a Cuba St. (see wellycollective.co.nz for other locations). One of my top picks is the **Wellington Apothecary ♥♥♥**, 110 Cuba St. (wellingtonapothecary.co.nz; ✆ **04/801-8777**), for locally-made-by-herbalists soaps, bath salts, hand cream, and potions of all sorts—walk in off rowdy Cuba Street and breathe deeply, because this place smells divine. The shop offers frequent seasonal workshops where you'll learn about color, or tea, or medicinal mushrooms, or make candles or perfume.

All the upmarket suburbs have lovely shops to browse, but **Tinakori Road Village** is particularly good. **Tinakori Antiques ♥♥**, 291 Tinakori Rd. (✆ **04/472-7043**), will be dangerous for lovers of fine, old things. **Secondo ♥♥**, 289 Tinakori Rd. (secondo.co.nz; ✆ **04/472-1400**), is a designer consignment shop

ART PIECES TO treasure

If you're looking for really high-quality souvenirs, you can't beat the **Te Papa Store ♥♥♥** at the Museum of New Zealand Te Papa Tongarewa, on 55 Cable St. (tepapastore.co.nz; ✆ **04/381-7013**). It has simply beautiful things—nature and history books, artwork, homewares, greenstone jewelry—and you won't have to pay the local tax (GST) if you're sending gifts overseas.

Also in the CBD, the following shops are worth seeking out. **Kura ♥♥**, 19 Allen St. (kuragallery.co.nz; ✆ **04/802-4934**), is an art and design gallery that showcases work by New Zealand artists, especially Māori, and has a nice range of Māori carving and *pounamu* (greenstone), including smaller souvenir-style items. Also on Allen Street, **Ora Gallery ♥** (23 Allen St.; oragallery.co.nz; ✆ **04/384-4157**) stocks a fine collection of local art and design. It has a cafe onsite, so you can sip a coffee while you're considering what to buy. **Vessel ♥♥**, 87 Victoria St. (vessel.co.nz; ✆ **04/499-2321**), has a great selection of ceramic domestic ware from some of New Zealand's best artists.

that features some very expensive items worn once or twice at swanky dos and passed on. (While you're here, pop into **Goods** ♥♥♥, 342a Tinakori Rd., for coffee and pastries worth crossing town for.)

At the other end of the city in Miramar, **Sheepskin Warehouse** ♥, 32 Tauhinu Rd. (sheepskinwarehouse.co.nz; ✆ **04/386-3376**), has the biggest range of woolen products around, including sheepskin rugs and throws, and will post overseas. GST (the 15% Goods and Services Tax) is deductible.

Wellington After Dark

Wellington is such a fun, creative city by day, it should come as no surprise that it parties hard at night. Whether you want cool bars, hot dance clubs, or something a bit more refined, there'll be something on that should appeal to you.

THE PERFORMING ARTS

Wellington stages the country's biggest performing arts festival, the **Aotearoa New Zealand Festival of the Arts** (see p. 319) every other February (the next one is in 2028). It's also home to the **New Zealand Symphony Orchestra,** the **Royal New Zealand Ballet,** the **New Zealand School of Dance,** and the **New Zealand Drama School.**

The lovely Edwardian **St James Theatre** ♥♥, 77–87 Courtenay Place (venueswellington.com/venues/st-james-theatre; ✆ **04/801-4231**), boasts both a preserved heritage theater and state-of-the-art technology. You can see musicals and professional opera here, and it's also the permanent home of the Royal New Zealand Ballet Company. The rather stylish 1920s **Embassy Theatre** ♥, 10 Kent Terrace (eventcinemas.co.nz/cinema/the-embassy; ✆ **04/384-7657**), now a cinema, was done up for the big, star-studded world premieres of *The Lord of the Rings: The Return of the King* and *The Hobbit: There and Back Again*. It's got a huge screen and flash digital sound system, plus a cafe and bar. **Circa Theatre** ♥, 1 Taranaki St. (circa.co.nz; ✆ **04/801-7992**), has a swell waterfront location next to Te Papa and presents high-quality, interesting productions, some homegrown. Dine on a preshow meal at its ChouChou Restaurant. Tickets range from NZ$20 to NZ$51. **Bats Theatre** ♥♥, 1 Kent Terrace (bats.co.nz; ✆ **04/801-4175**), is New Zealand's top developmental theater, putting on new and experimental plays and dance at great prices (NZ$14–NZ$20).

CLUBS & BARS

Wellington has an abundance of these, the most raucous being around the **Courtenay Place** area. If you wish to avoid heavily imbibing young people, go somewhere else if it's a Wednesday, Friday, or Saturday night.

The bar scene, of course, is in constant motion, and what's hot today might be a ghost town in 6 months' time. Ask around for the happening (or, alternatively, the quiet but atmospheric) places. Closing times vary and depend on whether it's summer or winter and what kind of liquor license the establishment holds. Most Wellington bars stay open until midnight to 2am during the summer months.

Hip Hops

Wellington is considered the craft beer capital of NZ, and Wellingtonians are crazy for these lovingly made creations, as individual and nuanced as good wine. Visit craftbeercapital.com for a full list of breweries (there are around 15) and a self-guided trail map. Want someone else to do the driving? Call Mike from **Craft Beer Tours NZ** ♥ (craftbeertoursnz.co.nz; ✆ **027/535-0008**), and he'll take you to all his favorite spots.

With its Astroturf, bean bags, and picnic tables dominating the parking lot out front, the colorful **Heyday Beer Co.** ♥♥♥, 264 Cuba St. (heydaybeer.com; ✆ **023/439-329**), is always a good time. Inside, there are 14 beers on tap, although you'll never know quite what to expect. (When I was last there, they were pouring a Summer Jam New England IPA, with notes of berry ice cream, and a chocolate stout inspired by birthday cake.) Make a difficult decision easier by ordering the tasting tray (NZ$18). It's open daily from 11am to late and also has a full food menu.

Garage Project ♥♥♥ (garageproject.co.nz) was so small when it started out, it was more nanobrewery than microbrewery. Not any more. Their experimental ethos hasn't changed, but this bunch of beardie guys now pumps out some seriously good beer from two separate breweries, with multiple fun places to try it—the original cellar door at 68 Aro St., a lively pub-style taproom just up the road at 91 Aro St., and closer to town, the **Wild Workshop** taproom and cellar door (7 Furness Lane), where they use wild yeast to make sour beers (among other types). Here you can do a highly recommended and affordable tour—1 hour, six beers, lots of interesting tidbits and matching snacks for just NZ$45 (Fri–Sun only).

One mainstay is the speakeasy-style **Hawthorne Lounge** ♥♥, on the second floor at 82 Tory St. (hawthornlounge.co.nz; ✆ **04/890-3724**). An intimate space harkening back to the 1920s, it serves a curated list of cocktails. For entertainment, you can watch all the couples there on first dates.

Another fave is **The Library** ♥♥♥, 53 Courtenay Place (thelibrary.co.nz; ✆ **04/382-8593**), a lounge bar and reading room (yes, there are plenty of books) with live music, food (fabulous desserts!), and a cool, slightly distressed vibe.

A converted historic cottage down an alley, **Havana** ♥♥, 32a–34 Wigan St. (havanabar.co.nz; ✆ **04/382-8593**), is lots of fun with a lovely staff and terrific Cuban-themed everything. Or try **Dee's Place** ♥♥, 126 Cuba St. (instagram.com/deesplace.nz), a hidden underground whiskey bar. For the most comprehensive selection of wines—1,000 bottles!—hit up **Noble Rot Wine Bar** (noblerot.co.nz; ✆ **04/385-6671**), which also serves canapes, dinner, and a full degustation menu with matching wines.

LGBTQI+ NIGHTCLUBS

Much like the rest of NZ—and maybe even more so than the rest of NZ—Wellington is a welcoming and liberal city. Virtually every venue is LGBTQI+ friendly these days, but there are some excellent long-standing spots worth checking out. **S&M's (Scotty & Mal's)** ♥♥, 176 Cuba St. (scottyandmals.co.nz; ✆ **04/802-5335**), is a classy cocktail and lounge bar with a B&D

EXPLORING THE kāpiti coast

Situated just 40 minutes' drive from Wellington, the **Kāpiti Coast** is a blend of stunning scenery and characterful individuality. Its beaches range from endless expanses of sand to rugged, rocky bays; cute villages are jammed full of creative endeavors; there's a great network of mostly flat cycling and walking tracks; and the jewel in its crown is **Kāpiti Island** ♥♥♥, an oasis for wildlife. (The question of whether the Māori word "Kāpiti" requires a macron is a matter of debate; currently the region has one while the island does not.)

The official visitor site for the region is kapiticoastnz.com. You can drive or take the train, which stops at Paekākāriki, Paraparaumu (the jumping-off point for Kāpiti Island), or Waikanae.

If you're driving, a good stop-off is 15 minutes north of Wellington (take the Porirua motorway exit), where the always-interesting **Pātaka Art + Museum** ♥♥ (pataka.org.nz; ✆ **04/237-1511**) celebrates Porirua's multicultural mélange, showcasing Māori, Pacific Island, and Pākehā (NZ European) arts with fascinating exhibitions. Admission is free and it's open daily, 10am to 5pm.

The delightful village of **Paekākāriki,** a little farther north, is a community of creative people who don't care much for city life. It has a gentle stretch of beach and a nifty collection of offbeat shops. Have an excellent coffee and a Florentine at **Beach Road Deli** ♥, 5 Beach Rd. (beachroaddeli.co.nz; ✆ **04/902-9029**), then climb the stairs to the **Alan Wehipeihana Studio and Gallery** ♥, 1 Beach Rd. (✆ **04/905-9250**), where this local artist has a very informal studio that was previously an auto shop (Fri–Sun 10am–4pm). He creates thought-provoking paintings, sculpture, and carvings and shares his space with other artists—mostly offbeat ones who like to upcycle and create new works with recycled bits and bobs.

For the active, the 4-hour hike from Paekākāriki south to Pukerua Bay (or vice versa) on the **Escarpment Track** is a spectacular half-day adventure, offering sweeping views of Kāpiti Island, swing bridges, narrow rocky pathways, and 1,200 steps. (It might not be ideal for those with a fear of heights.) Or head north to **Queen Elizabeth Park,** Mackays Crossing (✆ **04/292-8625**), between Paekākāriki and Paraparaumu, which offers 650 hectares (1,606 acres) of native bush, walking tracks, and the last area of natural dunes on the Kāpiti Coast. During World War II, 20,000 U.S. Marines were camped here.

Just north of Paekākāriki village, **Steam Incorporated** (steaminc.org.nz; ✆ **0800/783-264** in NZ) keeps alive the romance of steam trains and diesel locomotives, running monthly excursions on the main trunk line to destinations that

(basement and dance) space downstairs that's open on Friday and Saturday nights and has a resident DJ. The **Ivy Bar and Cabaret** ♥, 49 Cuba St. (ivybar.co.nz; ✆ **027/325-8306**), hosts such events as karaoke, drag battles, and Mr. Gay Wellington. Both are best visited on Thursday through Sunday.

THE WAIRARAPA

Just a couple of decades ago, this rural region was a collection of quiet towns where little was happening except the Golden Shears sheep-shearing competitions. Now, it's a weekend playground (and popular wedding venue) for Wellingtonians. The heritage village of **Martinborough** is a prime magnet for its include the Wairarapa, Hawke's Bay, and Wellington. It's open to visitors Monday to Saturday, when workers and volunteers are busy restoring and maintaining its rolling stock, but will mostly be of interest to other steam nerds. (Most activity happens on Thursdays and Saturdays.)

In New Zealand, "wildlife" basically means birds—and a trip to **Kāpiti Island ♥♥♥** is your best opportunity to see a large range of them. A predator-free oasis, it first became a bird sanctuary in 1897 thanks to forward-thinking conservationists. Today, the 1,965-hectare (4,854-acre) island is thriving with species that are rare or extinct on the mainland, such as kākā, saddlebacks, and takahē. It's estimated that as many as 1,400 spotted kiwi breed here. Pack a lunch and follow the signed trails: You're guaranteed to see bird life, no guide or binoculars necessary.

Kapiti Island Nature Tours ♥♥, 29 Marine Parade, Paraparaumu Beach (kapitiisland.com; ✆ **0800/527-484** in NZ), offers tours, year-round transport, and overnight accommodations. For eight generations, the Māori *whanau* (family) who run this company has lived on Kāpiti and now share their knowledge at a relaxed pace on day and nighttime tours. Their glamping tents and cabins are basic, but the food is plentiful—and really, the accommodation is secondary to the main attraction. Prices range from NZ$159 for ferry transport, DOC permit, and a guide's introduction to the island, to NZ$1,189 per couple for transport, DOC permit, guided night walk, and all-inclusive accommodation. During the summer, ferries depart from the corner of Marine Parade and Kāpiti Road at Paraparaumu Beach daily between 8am and 9:30am (check specific departure times) and return between 2pm and 3pm. (For wintertime visits, confirm sailing times directly with Kapiti Island Nature Tours.)

The mainland has a couple of lovely lodging options as well. **Greenmantle Estate Lodge ♥**, 214 SH1, Paraparaumu (greenmantle.co.nz; ✆ **04/298-5555**), is the only luxury lodge on the west coast of the lower North Island, boasting six beautiful suites, a heated swimming pool and Jacuzzi, and a fine-dining restaurant. Tiger Woods once stayed here, if that's a recommendation. Rates are from NZ$750 for two people.

Near Waikanae, at **Ngā Manu Nature Reserve** (ngamanu.org.nz) you can feed eels and ducks, see kiwi and tuatara in a nocturnal enclosure, and walk the forest paths. Entry costs NZ$17 adults, NZ$8 kids, NZ$40 families. They also offer small-group activities and tours, like seeing kiwi in a dusk encounter (NZ$60 adults, NZ$30 kids 7–17) or helping the rangers care for wildlife (NZ$75).

wine. Historic **Greytown** is also popular, its main strip thronged on the weekend with visitors checking out the Victorian buildings and boutique shops. **Masterton** (pop. 26,000) is the region's largest town, the most commercial of the lot and also the most family-friendly. (The city has one of the best playgrounds in the country.) **Featherston** keeps coming up with ways to reinvent itself—it's now New Zealand's only Booktown.

Essentials

ARRIVING If you're driving from the south, take SH2 from Wellington. If you're coming from the north, it's about a 3-hour drive from Napier to Masterton and 1 hour from Palmerston North. For a day trip from Wellington, your best bet may be the regular **Metlink** commuter train, which allows you to avoid the windy roads (and take in your fill of the region's wine safely). Go to **metlink.org.nz** for more information.

VISITOR INFORMATION The website for the region's official tourism arm, **Destination Wairarapa,** is wairarapanz.com. The **Martinborough isite Visitor Centre,** 18 Kitchener St. (✆ **06/306-5010**), is open weekdays 9am to 4pm and weekends 9:30am to 3:30pm.

SPECIAL EVENTS The annual **Martinborough Fair** ♥♥ (martinborough fair.org.nz; ✆ **06/304-9933**), held on the first Saturday in February and the first Saturday in March, is widely thought to be one of the best crafts events in the country, a chance to buy quality New Zealand–made goods in a delightful setting. For a really authentic NZ event, get yourself to Masterton's **Golden Shears** (goldenshears.co.nz; ✆ **06/378-8008**), the world's biggest shearing and wool-handling competition. It's 3 days of bleating, baahing hard *yakka* (that's Kiwi for "hard work"), held late in February or early in March each year. A new, very popular event is Greytown's **Festival of Christmas** (greytownvillage.com/festival-of-christmas), held in July to ensure appropriately wintery vibes. Free outdoor events include live music and circus performances, night markets, light shows, and fake snow.

Exploring the Wairarapa

EN ROUTE FROM WELLINGTON

The Wairarapa is separated from Wellington by the Remutakas, a range of hills that can experience all of the capital's breeziest conditions plus a scattering of snow in the winter. Always take care on this extremely windy road, which is a mix of two and three lanes. It's 62km (39 miles) from Wellington to Featherston, about an hour's drive in normal conditions.

Before you reach "the hill," you'll pass through the **Hutt Valley,** which is made up of two cities, Upper Hutt and Lower Hutt. A bit of a detour east takes you to the seaside suburbs of **Eastbourne** and **Days Bay,** both very pretty for a stroll, a coffee, and something nice to nibble on—and there are a few fun attractions worth a visit. The **Dowse Art Museum** ♥♥, 45 Laings Rd., Lower Hutt (dowse.org.nz; ✆ **04/570-6500**), is an innovative gallery that holds one of New Zealand's largest and most significant public art collections and the best collection of craft art. Exhibitions feature contemporary ceramics, jewelry, glass, textiles, wood, sculpture, and photography. Entry is free, and it's open daily from 10am to 5pm.

FEATHERSTON, MARTINBOROUGH & THE WINERIES

Featherston is the first settlement you reach on SH2 if you're coming from Wellington. Bookended by bookshops, this little town almost tucked into the base of the Remutakas was made an official Booktown in 2018, turning around decades of decline. Now, its annual readers and writers festival in May brings in authors from around the country and the world, and there are other literary events through the year. At any time you can browse its eight bookshops, which all have different specialties, from military history to children's

The Kāpiti Coast & the Wairarapa

books. Train lovers will enjoy the **Fell Locomotive Museum ♥**, SH2 (fellmuseum.org.nz; ✆ **06/308-9379**), home to H1999, the last remaining locomotive of its type in the world and one of six engines designed for use on the Remutaka Incline. (You can climb up and look at the levers, knobs, valves, and switches.) These grunty little characters are an important part of the area's history—they had to climb gradients as steep as 1 in 13 to grind up over the ranges. The museum is open weekends from 10am to 4pm; admission is NZ$7 adults, NZ$2 children over 5, and NZ$15 a family.

From Featherston, you could head south for the rugged coast and **Cape Palliser ♥♥**. This very scenic drive takes you past the spectacular **Putangirua Pinnacles,** fluted columns of rock formed by the "badlands erosion" of an ancient gravel deposit—it's a 30-minute walk to get to them. Back in your car, carry on past the rough-and-ready fishing village of **Ngawi** to the **Cape Palliser Lighthouse** (built in 1897) and the very accessible—but rather pungent—**fur seal colony.**

Most visitors, however, head southeast from Featherston on Highway 53 to **Martinborough ♥♥**, best known as a top winemaking region, with more

Fur seal colony, Cape Palliser (see p. 347).

than 20 tasting rooms in one small area. Lots of sunshine and low autumn rainfall contribute to the rather impressive success of this area's 30-plus small boutique wineries. (In fact, some Hawke's Bay wineries choose to grow their grapes here.) It's part of the **Classic New Zealand Wine Trail,** which comprises Hawke's Bay, Wairarapa, and Marlborough—but unlike Marlborough and Hawke's Bay wines, which are generally available internationally, many Wairarapa vineyards only sell through their cellar doors. As a result, the very best vintages sell out within a few weeks of release.

Visit from late October to early March, when new wine stocks have been released. If you're short on time, drop in to **Martinborough Wine Merchants** ♥, 6 Kitchener St. (martinboroughwinemerchants.com; ✆ **06/306-9040**), which has a comprehensive range of wines in stock, and lots of yummy snacks that go particularly well with wine. They're also known for renting bikes to wobble around the vineyards (weekdays NZ$30, weekends NZ$40, 10am–5:30pm). Otherwise, pick up a wine map from one of the isite visitor centers; your only problem will be deciding which wineries to visit. *Favorite* is a subjective term, but the following all have excellent reputations and are open daily:

- **Ata Rangi** ♥♥ (Puruatanga Rd.; atarangi.co.nz; ✆ **06/306-9570**): One of the region's original vineyards, Ata Rangi sells its outstanding pinot noir in more than 25 overseas markets. You can buy (and taste) it here, along with chardonnay, riesling, rosé, and a cabernet/merlot/syrah blend. Bookings are essential.
- **Poppies Martinborough** ♥♥ (Puruatanga Rd.; poppiesmartinborough.co.nz; ✆ **06/306-8473**): Poppy makes the wine and Shayne does the outdoor stuff. This young couple is passionate about their chosen life, and this is the only place you can buy what they make (pinot gris, sauvignon blanc, riesling, gewürztraminer, chardonnay, rosé, pinot noir). Enjoy it with an absolutely delicious platter of local seasonal foods such as dolmades,

tapenade, artichokes, stuffed peppers, India relish, and local meats. It's open daily from 11am to 4pm.

- **The Runholder ♥♥♥** (89 Martins Road; therunholder.co.nz): This cellar door and restaurant showcase three distinct brands owned by the same company: Tikoranga winery, Martinborough Vineyard, and Lighthouse Gin (a beloved 20-year-old brand started by NZ's first female gin distiller). The winery barrel hall is underground, with the restaurant on top—the building's award-winning glass-heavy design emulates the roof pitch of an old barn that has long been on the property. The cellar door offers wine and gin tastings and snacks, while the light-filled restaurant serves hearty, upmarket New Zealand fare—wagyu beef with duck-egg bearnaise, wood-fired lamb ribs with sheep-milk labneh—with wine to match. It's open for lunch daily in summer with reduced hours in winter.
- **Palliser Estate ♥♥** (Kitchener St.; palliser.co.nz; ✆ **06/306-9019**): At this "boutique Martinborough vineyard with an international outlook," chief winemaker Guy McMaster makes award-winning chardonnay, pinot noir, sauvignon blanc, and pinot gris, plus a nice bubbly. He produces wines

AN art gem IN THE WAIRARAPA

Halfway between Featherston and Martinborough you'll find **Rototāwai ♥♥♥**, 808 Kahutara Rd. (rototawai.co.nz; ✆ **021/473-394**). Opened in 2024, this hidden gem for art, history, and garden lovers is kind of like an antipodean version of Boston's Isabella Stewart Gardner Museum—both feature the eclectic artistic collections of a rich lady in an elegant old house. In this case, the historic colonial homestead is the childhood home of Anna Bidwill, who grew up here in the 1960s, and recently repurchased the property to house—and share—her personal art collection. Spread over the lower floor, the gallery is an insightful introduction to the work of some of Aotearoa's most distinguished contemporary artists (like Dick Frizzell, Bill Hammond, Don Binney, and Graham Sydney) in a peaceful rural setting—and you can walk in the beautifully landscaped grounds, as well. (The Bidwill family have been farming in the Wairarapa since the 1840s, with one ancestor famous for introducing sheep to the region, and another the first European to climb Mt. Ngauruhoe.) It's open daily by appointment only, between 10am to 4pm, and costs NZ$30 for adults, NZ$15 for children 2 to 15. But note there's a minimum charge of NZ$120, since someone has to come and open up the place for you.

Contemporary art at Rototāwai.

under the Palliser Estate and Pencarrow labels. The tasting room is a bit glossier than some of the others in the area; this isn't a bad thing.

- **Gladstone Vineyard ♥♥** (340 Gladstone Rd., Carterton; gladstonevineyard.co.nz; ✆ **06/379-8563**): This vineyard is delightful to look at; the award-winning sauvignon blanc, pinot gris, rosé, pinot noir, and viognier vintages (including the Jealous Sisters range!) are lovely to drink; there's a cafe on-site (open weekends only), and if you really can't face leaving, it also has boutique apartment-style accommodations. If you're here in April, you can do a behind-the-scenes tour. It's generally open on Friday through Sunday from 11am to 4pm, but call ahead to confirm—they close for winter.

GREYTOWN & MASTERTON

From Featherston, head north on SH2 to **Greytown ♥♥**. It has the most complete street of wooden Victorian buildings in the country, most of which are now home to cafes, boutiques, and candy shops, making it a weekend hotspot for Wellingtonians. Alongside all this retail therapy, you'll find a bit of history at the **Cobblestones Museum ♥**, 169 Main St. (cobblestonesmuseum.org.nz; ✆ **06/304-9687**), a collection of pioneer buildings and memorabilia on the original site of the stables operated by Cobb & Co, which shifted mail and passengers to Wellington from 1866. It's open daily 10am to 4pm (until 3pm in winter) and entry is NZ$10, NZ$3 kids.

Masterton is the "big smoke" around here. It's not that fascinating as a regional center, but it does have a few good restaurants and caters well to young families. **Queen Elizabeth Park ♥♥** at its center offers everything from a miniature railway to rowboats to fallow deer. You can learn more about the farming backbone of this region at **The Wool Shed—National Museum of Sheep and Shearing ♥**, 12 Dixon St. (thewoolshednz.com; ✆ **06/378-8008**), built around two historic woolsheds, one dating back to the 1880s. If you can possibly think of any sheep-related question this place doesn't answer, you can ask one of the friendly volunteers. Admission is NZ$10 adults, NZ$3 children, and NZ$20 per family. It's open weekdays from 10am to 4pm and until 3pm on weekends.

Masterton's main cultural draw is **Aratoi: Wairarapa Museum of Art and History ♥♥**, at the corner of Bruce and Dixon streets (aratoi.org.nz; ✆ **06/370-0001**). It's the caliber of art gallery that you'd expect to find in a much larger urban center—yet much of its displayed artwork is created by local artists. You'll see contemporary takes on Māori culture, such as colorful *poi* (balls on cords used in kapa haka performances) woven from jute or *tōtara pou* (columnal or post-shaped sculptures) lit up with LED lights. Its collection of 4,000 objects includes Māori and European *taonga* (treasures), and significant artwork by international artists. It's open Tuesday to Sunday from 10am to 4pm; admission is by *koha* (donation). It's small, so it won't take long to walk through, but budget extra time for **ConArt ♥**, Corner of Queen and Bruce streets (conartnz.com; ✆ **0210/329-560**), a series of open studios housed in shipping containers out back.

From Masterton, you can take an hour-long drive out to **Castlepoint,** a wild environment with one of our most famous lighthouses and a couple of no-nonsense cafes. Plus, if you visit on a late-summer Saturday, you'll come across the iconic **Castlepoint Beach Races,** which have been, er, running since 1872.

Some 30km (18½ miles) north of Masterton on SH2 is the **Pūkaha National Wildlife Centre** ♥ (pukaha.org.nz; ✆ **06/375-8004**). In 2020, Pūkaha's 942 acres were handed back to the Rangitāne (the traditional landowners), who are celebrated in the **Te Hīkoi o Pūkaha** 2-hour guided tour, which connects modern conservation with the Māori worldview (NZ$90 adults, NZ$50 children, NZ$260 for families). It's just one of the facility's many tour options, but if you want to go it alone, entry is NZ$26 adults, NZ$10 children 5 to 15, and NZ$65 for a family pass. Pūkaha is open daily in summer from 9am to 6pm and in winter until 5pm.

Organized Tours

While we're on the subject of wine—and this does start a lot of conversations in the region—you might want to enjoy the grape without even driving over the hill. If so, hop aboard a **Martinborough Wine Tour** ♥ (martinboroughwinetours.co.nz; ✆ **022/307-9480**). You can catch a train in Wellington for a scenic journey to the Wairarapa, where this friendly crowd will pick you up from Featherston train station, visit two wineries in the morning and two after, and provide a three-course lunch (NZ$235; the tour starts at 11am). Guided walking tours of the region's vineyards are also available, this time with **Martinborough Wine Walks** (martinboroughwinewalks.com; ✆ **06/306-9040;** tours take 4–5 hr. and cost NZ$280 per person, with a minimum group size of four).

A Star Attraction

In 2023, the Wairarapa received its Dark Sky Reserve accreditation—the first step in its path to becoming the largest such designated area in the world (wairarapadarksky.nz). Here you'll find personalized stargazing experiences without having to line up for a telescope. Hari and Sam, an astrobiologist and an astrophysicist, will share the wonders of the universe with you in their 90-minute **Star Safari** ♥♥ (1169 Ponatahi Rd., Carterton; star-safari.nz; ✆ **021/66-3808;** NZ$100, children under 15 free with an adult). Bookings are essential. Alternatively, local Chris Murphy will bring his equipment to you with his nomadic **Under the Stars** ♥♥ (underthestars.co.nz; ✆ **06/242-5194**) astronomy tours. Winter is the best time for night skies.

In the countryside east of Carterton and Greytown, **Stonehenge Aotearoa** ♥, 51 Ahiaruhe Rd. (stonehenge-aotearoa.co.nz; ✆ **06/377-1600**), an impressive full-scale adaptation of Stonehenge that incorporates Māori myths, is not really worth visiting in the daytime, unless you don't mind paying the NZ$15 entry fee for what is basically a photo op. Instead, turn up on a Friday or Saturday at 8pm to gaze through the telescope and learn how the structure works. ***Tip:*** Clap or sing as you walk to the center to hear how the structure alters sound. If you can, time your visit to coincide with a significant astrological event, such as a solstice or equinox.

You'll be exercising different muscles, but the **Remutaka Cycle Trail ♥♥♥** (wellingtonnz.com/visit/trails/remutaka-cycle-trail) is hugely popular among two-wheel fans and has opened up areas that were previously only accessible by car. You can do all or part of the 115km (71-mile) Wellington to Wairarapa trail, classed as one of New Zealand's "Great Rides," making it one of the top 23 cycle trails in the country. The trail starts on the Petone Foreshore in Lower Hutt, passes alongside the Hutt River, through tunnels under the Remutaka Range, peaceful farmland, and native forest, and out to the rugged Wairarapa south coast. **Green Jersey Explorer Tours** (greenjersey.co.nz; ✆ **021/0746-640**) offers a 1-day version for NZ$160. It also offers cycle hire for touring the Martinborough wineries, starting from NZ$40.

Where to Stay in the Wairarapa

Opposite the Palliser vineyards, the **Parehua Resort ♥♥**, 52 New York St. W, Martinborough (parehuaresort.co.nz; ✆ **0800/448-891** in NZ, or 06/306-8405), has large, modern cottages and villas that are perfect for a luxurious country stay. You can hole up here and eat at the restaurant; swim; play tennis, pétanque, or croquet; or venture out on a bike and cycle around the vineyards. Rates start from NZ$310.

Located in the heart of Greytown at 109 Main St., the **White Swan ♥** (thewhiteswanhotel.co.nz; ✆ **021/539-528**) is a historic country pub, catering to an urban market, with rooms fairly affordably priced at NZ$210 and up.

If you want to stay in Masterton, the **Copthorne Hotel & Resort Solway Park ♥**, High Street (solway.co.nz; ✆ **0800/808-228** in NZ, or 06/370-0507), can't fully escape its 1970s roots (although the newly renovated bathrooms

The restored Victorian-era Martinborough Hotel.

Bold colors and eclectic furnishings add character to rooms at the Royal Hotel in Featherston (p. 354).

help), but it's a fun place to bring the kids. It's set on 10 hectares (24 acres) and has a gym, heated indoor pool, Jacuzzi, indoor squash court, tennis and volleyball courts, and a playground. Rooms range from NZ$138 to NZ$198.

Brackenridge Country Retreat & Spa ♥♥ It's easy to see why this little village of studios and cottages gets booked-out with weddings nearly every summer weekend. A picturesque getaway that's walking distance from Martinborough, its country farmhouse chic studios have underfloor heating, private patios, and kitchenettes, while the self-contained cottages have all that and then some. The on-site day spa is also a welcome treat after a hard day of wine tasting.

White Rock Rd. brackenridge.co.nz. ✆ **06/306-8115.** 18 units. Studios NZ$169–NZ$340. Rates include continental breakfast. Long-stay rates available. **Amenities:** Indoor pool; day spa; gym; free Wi-Fi.

The Martinborough Hotel ♥♥ From this fine old building's wide covered verandas, you can watch the comings and goings in and around the village's central square. The 1882 hotel has been beautifully restored—they must have bought every clawfoot bathtub in the Wairarapa, except those snapped up by the Royal—and the rooms are sophisticated and elegant. Some are in the old hotel, and others are new rooms in the garden courtyard. Have a meal in the very nice restaurant or chuck down a beer in the public bar.

The Square, Martinborough. martinboroughhotel.co.nz. ✆ **06/306-9350.** 20 units. NZ$199–NZ$399 double. **Amenities:** Restaurant; bar; free Wi-Fi.

The Royal Hotel ♥♥♥ You'll feel like (19th-century) royalty when you stay at the Royal Hotel in Featherston, and for a very reasonable price, too. This old dame was first built in 1868 (complete with horse-stabling facilities) and has recently been restored to its former glory—possibly even more glorious now. Its rooms are sumptuously decorated in earth and jewel tones with a touch of steampunk—heavy velvet curtains, chandeliers, ostrich-feathers in brass vases, antique furniture, clawfoot baths, lots of clocks, and the original wooden flooring. The welcome is warm, just like the fireplace that roars in winter in the downstairs restaurant **Brac & Bow**—which serves hearty local fare and wines, and an exceptional breakfast (for an additional NZ$30). Note this isn't an accessible choice—rooms are on the second floor, up an ancient wooden staircase.

22 Revans St., Featherston. theroyalhotel.co.nz. ✆ **06/308-8567.** 11 units. NZ$180–NZ$350 double. **Amenities**: Restaurant, bar; garden; free Wi-Fi.

Wharekauhau Country Estate ♥♥♥ Would William and Kate, the Duke and Duchess of Cambridge, have stayed here if it wasn't pretty damned exceptional? No doubt the royals were blown away at their first sight of this beautiful accommodation on a 2,000-hectare (5,000-acre) working sheep station. The views out over rugged Palliser Bay hit you like a keening southerly, but in the nicest possible way. For a memory to treasure, go horseback riding and take a gallop along the cliffs.

Western Lake Rd., Palliser Bay, RD3, Featherston. www.wharekauhau.co.nz. ✆ **06/307-7581.** 13 cottages. NZ$2700–NZ$5850. Rates include breakfast, predinner drinks, and 4-course dinner. **Amenities:** Bar; babysitting; bikes; concierge; farm tours; gym; horseback riding; indoor pool; day spa; tennis court; free Wi-Fi.

Where to Eat in the Wairarapa

You'll probably find that you spend as much time eating in winery restaurants and grazing in specialty food shops as going to dedicated eateries, but this abundant region has plenty of good places to get a feed.

MARTINBOROUGH

A Martinborough institution, **Cafe Medici ♥♥**, 9 Kitchener St. (facebook.com/cafemedici; ✆ **06/306-9965**), serves terrific local, seasonal food, and great The People's Coffee Wednesday to Sunday from 8:30am to 4pm. For something a bit different, mosey on over to **Neighbourhood ♥**, 4 Memorial Square (intheneighbourhood.co.nz; ✆ **06/306-6378**), a micro-roastery that's experimenting with roasting beans in wine barrels. Just off the main square, the tiny wine bar **Mesita ♥♥♥**, 14C Ohio St. (mesita.net), serves scrumptious Latin American tapas from 5pm on Wednesday through Saturday and occasional Sundays. Reserve a table because there are only a few, and they get booked. **Union Square Bistro & Bar ♥**, in the Martinborough Hotel (unionsquare.co.nz; ✆ **06/306-8350**), is an upmarket pub with an extensive wine list; you'll want to make a reservation to sit on the streetside patio. Across the road, **Cool Change Bar & Eatery ♥♥** (coolchange.co.nz; Tues–Sun 3pm–late) is where

GOURMET grazing

The Wairarapa is known for its fabulous artisanal food products—you'll be tripping over them everywhere you go these days. Here are a few foodie highlights, starting with the best deli products and the best name:

- **C'est Cheese** ♥♥ For a primo selection of cheeses (mainly New Zealand, but some imported), olive oils, cured meats, chutneys, and other delights, C'est Cheese is open daily (19 Fitzherbert St., Featherston; cestcheese.co.nz; ✆ **06/308-6000**).
- **Schoc Chocolates** ♥ Schoc produces more than 85 different flavors of deliciousness, under the watchful eye of chocologist Murray Langham. A few to ponder: lavender salted caramel, lemon thyme, smoked tea, and carrot and coriander. It's open daily from 10am to 4pm (177 Main St., Greytown; schoc.co.nz; ✆ **06/304-8960**).
- **Greytown Honey** ♥♥♥ Karly Polaschek, a fifth-generation beekeeper, and her husband, a former aircraft engineer, have innovated new ways to keep bees, and in their 1-hour-plus **Beekeeping Experience** tours (NZ$70), you'll also learn loads about New Zealand's famed mānuka honey. Kids (and adults) will love donning a protective suit to meet the bees, prepping and pouring their own jar of honey, and tasting all the different honeys at the end. Tours run all year round, but the best time to visit is in summer when the couple's dahlia farm is in bloom and the bees are more active. The shop's open Friday to Tuesday 10:30am to 2:30pm; tours run on Wednesday, Saturday, and Sunday (58 Moroa Rd., Tauwherenīkau; greytownhoney.co.nz; ✆ **027/577-8478** or 027/460-5329).
- **Aurora Gin** ♥♥ OK, it's not food exactly, but during Aurora Gin Distilleries' 2½-hour gin-making classes (NZ$169; book online) you'll forage for and select from a wide range of edible botanicals, including juniper, angelica root, citrus peels, sarsaparilla, and cassia bark to distill in gorgeous copper presses and flavor your very own gin (76 Hikunui Rd.; auroradistillery.co.nz; ✆ **06/9272125**).

all the locals go for drinks and tapas-style dining—it's got cozy booths, retro decor, good tunes, and outdoor tables that catch the afternoon sun all year. Finally, in the old bank building, you'll find a pair of co-owned, interconnected joints—upmarket **Karahui Restaurant and Wine Bar** for Thai food, and **Tōhi Gin Room and Eatery** ♥♥ (karahui.co.nz; ✆ **06/216-8276**), where you can taste upwards of 40 New Zealand gins, including three of Tōhi's own, titled Home, Land, and Sea (the latter features seaweed as one of the botanicals).

GREYTOWN

In Greytown, the long-established **Main Street Deli Café** ♥, 88 Main St. (mainstdeli.co.nz; ✆ **06/304-9022**), sells deli items (perfect for picnics!) and also has full-service menus. It's open daily from 8am to 4pm. **The Offering** ♥, 65 Main St. (theoffering.co.nz; ✆ **06/304-9645**), is a family-friendly joint (they even have toys for the littles) that caters well to dietary requirements. It's known for classics like eggs benedict and French toast; it's open daily from 7am.

For more substantial meals, two venerable favorites serve hearty country food: **The White Swan ♥**, 109 Main St. (thewhiteswanhotel.co.nz; ✆ **021/539-528**), and the **Greytown Hotel ♥**, 83 Main St. (greytownhotel.co.nz; ✆ **06/304-9138**). Both are open daily.

CARTERTON

A little farther up the road, Mike and Rose Kloeg create delectable treats in an old Brethren church, now the **Clareville Bakery ♥♥**, 3340 SH2, Carterton (theclarevillebakery.co.nz; ✆ **06/379-5333**), is home to one of NZ's best pies: a rather startling lamb cutlet and kūmara mash treat that I guarantee is unlike anything you have ever tasted. They also run a European-style cafe here, open Monday to Saturday 7:30am to 2pm. Mike's citron tart is easily the best I've ever wolfed down, and he's also very passionate about his award-winning breads. Then there's **Aunt Ginger's Kitchen ♥♥**, 52 High St. North, Carterton (facebook.com/AuntGingersKitchen; ✆ **06/216-1481;** Tues–Sun 8am–2:30pm weekdays, 8:30am–2:30pm weekends). The deep teal walls are adorned with florals and ceramics, and the lunch is classic, comfy cabinet food—toasties, lasagna, frittata, arancini, with lots of vegetarian options—served with greens and relish. Their cheese scone was recently crowned the best in the Wellington region, and the coffee's good too.

MASTERTON

In Masterton, **Don Luciano ♥♥**, corner of King and Chapel streets (donluciano.co.nz; daily 7am–2:30pm), is a colorful Central American–themed coffee roastery and cafe. Many people end up at **Entice Café ♥**, corner of Bruce and Dixon streets (entice.co.nz; ✆ **06/377-3166;** daily 8am–4pm), after they've visited the Aratoi museum, which is in the same building. But its food and coffee stand on their own merits (the omelets are first rate). **The Farriers Bar & Eatery ♥**, 4 Queen St. (thefarriers.co.nz; ✆ **06/377-1102;** daily 9am–9pm), is an upmarket, all-occasion pub with friendly service and good-value meals.

MARLBOROUGH & NELSON

11

Marlborough is the unofficial gateway to the South Island, a diverse land mass that stretches for 522 miles (840km). The South Island's Māori name is Te Waipounamu, meaning "the waters of greenstone," but you may also hear locals referring to it as the country's "mainland." This is both due to its size and because oral history holds that it existed first, as the canoe of Māui (which is where yet another name—Te Waka a Māui—comes from). It isn't, however, considered the mainland for its population, which numbers just 1.2 million compared to the North Island's 4 million. The result? Here, you'll have miles of untapped wilderness to explore.

The long distances between the South Island's settlements means that flying is a popular travel option, but when it comes to leaving the North Island and traveling south, we recommend arriving by sea.

Cook Strait is a narrow but stormy piece of water, with crossing made by large car ferries. From the deck, you'll have views that would be impossible to see from the air. Once you enter the long, bush-lined haven of Queen Charlotte Sound, you'll sail through serene waters to **Picton.** A port town, it's the gateway to the wider Marlborough Sounds, as well as to the wineries surrounding nearby **Blenheim.** From here, you can also travel west to the regions of **Nelson, Tasman,** and **Golden Bay,** with their sunny days, stretches of golden sand, and thriving communities of artists.

PICTON

107km (67 miles) E of Nelson and 28km (17 miles) N of Blenheim

Picton and Blenheim are the two main towns of Marlborough province, an area best known as New Zealand's largest wine region. Both are easygoing communities with plenty of amenities, although the smaller Picton/Waitohi, with its seaside charm, may appeal more to visitors. Located at the head of Queen Charlotte Sound, it has a population of 4,800, with its main claim to fame being that it's the arrival point for ferries from Wellington. Unfortunately, many travelers think that's the end of its attributes, when in truth it's also the jumping-off point for the tranquil charms of the Marlborough

Sounds. With over 1,500km (930 miles) of shoreline, the sounds—Queen Charlotte, Kenepuru, Mahau, and Pelorus—are ideal for boating, paddling, hiking, swimming, and disconnecting.

If you don't have an entire week to while away, my recommendation is to budget 1 day to explore the waters of the Sounds (either by foot, kayak, boat, bike, or a combination of the above), and 1 day to explore the wineries of Blenheim and Renwick. Or choose one or the other; squeezing it all into a single day is technically possible, but logistically difficult.

Essentials

ARRIVING

BY PLANE Air service between Picton and Wellington is provided by **Sounds Air** (soundsair.com; ✆ **0800/505-005** in NZ). Contact **Picton Shuttles** (pictonshuttles.nz; ✆ **0800/252-520** in NZ) or **Marlborough Shuttles** (marlboroughshuttles.co.nz; ✆ **0800/203-027**) for transfers between Picton and Blenheim airports. **Picton Airport** (also known as **Koromiko Airport**) is about a 10-minute drive from the port.

BY FERRY This is the most popular and recommended way to arrive into the Marlborough Sounds if traveling from the North Island. Both **Interislander** (interislander.co.nz; ✆ **0800/802-802** in NZ) and **Bluebridge** (bluebridge.co.nz; ✆ **0800/844-844** in NZ) offer multiple daily departures across Cook Strait between Wellington (North Island) and Picton (South Island). It's a 3-hour, 102km (64-mile), highly scenic ride. Prices vary depending on the size of your vehicle and the number of passengers, but you can expect to pay around NZ$300 for two adults with a compact car one-way. Ferries do frequently sell out, so you need to book in advance. For night or late sailings, book a private cabin; it's worth the relaxation, shower, and extra chance for shut-eye (starting at NZ$80 on the Interislander, NZ$50 on Bluebridge).

GETTING AROUND

BY CAR Picton itself is walkable, and tour operators run buses from Picton to Blenheim's wineries. However, if you want to head farther afield to Nelson or Golden Bay, you'll need wheels. Picton is 20 minutes' drive time to Blenheim. For Nelson, allow 2 hours. If heading south to Christchurch via Kaikōura, allow 2½ hours to Kaikōura and another 2½ hours to Christchurch.

BY COACH (BUS) **InterCity** (intercity.co.nz; ✆ **09/583-5780**) connects Picton with Blenheim and Christchurch, Nelson, and the West Coast.

BY TRAIN **Great Journeys of New Zealand's Coastal Pacific Train** (greatjourneysnz.com; ✆ **0800/872-467** in NZ) is a scenic train service running between Christchurch and Picton, stopping in Kaikōura and Blenheim. It takes about 6 hours and starts from NZ$147 to Kaikōura.

BY WATER TAXI To reach boat-in-only accommodation within the sounds or to access the Queen Charlotte Track, contact **Cougar Line** (cougarline.co.nz; ✆ **0800/504-090** in NZ), **Picton Water Taxis** (pictonwatertaxis.co.nz; ✆ **03/573-7853**), and **Arrow Water Taxis** (arrowwatertaxis.co.nz; ✆ **03/573-8229**).

VISITOR INFORMATION

The region's tourism website is **marlboroughnz.com**. The **Picton isite Visitor Centre,** The Foreshore (✆ **03/520-3113**), is open Monday to Friday from 9am to 5pm and Sunday from 9am to 4pm, with extended hours in summer.

Exploring Picton

Picton's foreshore, London Quay, is an attractive, freshly redeveloped scoop of bay looking out to blue waters, and great for swimming. The ferry terminal is at one end and the town wharf at the other. The small shopping area is centered on High Street.

The world's oldest surviving merchant ship is housed at the **Edwin Fox Maritime Museum** ♥ (1 Auckland St., Dunbar Wharf; edwinfoxship.nz; ✆ **03/573-6868**). After sailing around the world a reported 34 times—carrying convicts to Australia, emigrants to New Zealand, and opium to San Francisco—the Edwin Fox was towed to her final resting place in Picton. She's been preserved, not restored, and the museum that opened in her honor in 1990 remains very much rooted in that same era, but it's a rare chance to encounter an artifact of this magnitude. It's open daily from 9am to 5pm and costs NZ$15 adults, NZ$5 children.

If you're traveling with kids, it's good to know about the playground and mini-golf course on the foreshore near the compact yet attractively organized **Picton Heritage and Whaling Museum** ♥, 9 London Quay (pictonmuseum-newzealand.com; ✆ **03/573-8283**). Tire them out first, and then stun them with the museum's exhibits of shark and whale jaws, a whaling gun, carved whale teeth, and even a blue whale embryo. It's a little gruesome, but a diverting way to spend a half hour if you can stomach it.

At the Picton Heritage and Whaling Museum, relics depict Picton's 19th-century past as a whaling port.

Cruising remote inlets of the Marlborough Sounds on the Pelorus Mail Boat.

Boat Tours Around the Sounds

If you want to experience the rural isolation of the Marlborough Sounds, there's no better way to do it than to explore Pelorus Sound from Havelock, aboard **The Mail Run Cruise** ♥♥♥ on the Pelorus Mail Boat (themailboat.co.nz; ✆ **03/574-1088**). Similar tours depart from Picton and travel through Queen Charlotte Sound, such as the **Mail Boat Cruise** ♥ (beachcombercruises.co.nz; ✆ **03/573-6175**). (Beware the similar cruise names for mail runs in different Sounds.) However, Pelorus Sound offers unparalleled serenity, with absolutely no ferries or cruise ships sharing the waters as you deliver mail and supplies to local residents (and their friendly dogs). It operates Mondays, Wednesdays, and Fridays and costs NZ$145 adults; NZ$70 for ages 5 to 15; under 5 free; and families NZ$350. On Mondays and Wednesdays between October and April, lunch is possible at Te Rawa Lodge. Otherwise pack your own and activities for young kids, as it's a long day of sightseeing. You can even have a wine or beer onboard.

If you don't have enough time for the full mailboat cruise, but want a similar experience, Beachcomber Cruises' **Motuara Island Bird Sanctuary Cruise** ♥ (beachcombercruises.co.nz; ✆ **03/573-6175**) is a good half-day option that will enable you to get up close to NZ's threatened birdlife on the predator-free sanctuary. Operating from Picton daily October to April, it costs NZ$120 adults and NZ$80 for ages 5 to 15.

The Marlborough Tour Company's **Seafood Odyssea Cruise** ♥ (marlboroughtourcompany.co.nz; ✆ **03/577-9997**) serves up generous tastings of seafood paired with local wine on a half-day boat tour of Queen Charlotte Sound, departing from Picton. There are brief visits to mussel and salmon farms as well. Cruises run year-round (NZ$180 adults, NZ $90 children 5–15).

Passengers on any vessels may see dolphins, but **E-Ko Tours** ♥, 1 Wellington St. (e-ko.nz; ✆ **03/573-8040** in NZ), makes these marine creatures the

Getting Arty in Havelock

If you're in Havelock, the jumping-off point for several boat tours of the Sounds, be sure to pop into **The Gallery ♥** (60 Main Rd.; thegalleryhavelock.com; ✆ **03/574-2821**), a volunteer-run space exhibiting work by local artists, such as self-taught portrait painter Rebekah Codlin, who grew up on the boat-access-only shores of Marlborough Sounds. There are plenty of investment pieces, but you can also find affordable souvenirs, including pendants by local Māori carver Clem Mellish. Opt for one of Mellish's *pākohe* (argillite stone) pieces; unlike greenstone, it's indigenous to the region and was an important trade item for local Māori.

focus of its tours. You can watch the dolphins from onboard on a Motuara Island Sanctuary and Dolphin Watching Tour (NZ$159 adults, NZ$80 children 5–15, NZ$40 children up to 5), or get into the water alongside wild dolphins on a Dolphin Swimming Tour (NZ$199 adults, NZ$175 children 12–15).

Although **Wilderness Guides ♥♥** (wildernessguidesnz.com; ✆ **03/573-5432**) is perhaps best known for facilitating treks along the Queen Charlotte Track (see below), the operator also excels in double sea kayak excursions. On the half-day tour (NZ$120), from the less-frequented west end of the sound, visitors see eagle rays and seals and learn about the medicinal plants in the bush. Tours are often in sheltered bays, but it's best to book a morning tour to avoid afternoon winds.

The Queen Charlotte Track ♥♥♥

If you love walking but hate carrying things, the Queen Charlotte Track (qctrack.co.nz) is for you. It's a 1- to 5-day experience with stunning views and not a pack in sight. That's because kind people in boats do all the transferring of your baggage for you. Even better, you don't have to stay in cramped huts or tents (unless you want to) as there is lodging along the way. The 73.5km (45-mile) walking track passes through lush bush, around coves and inlets, and along ridges with breathtaking views of Queen Charlotte and Kenepuru Sounds. Although it's considered one of the easier multi-day walks in the country, it requires a reasonable level of fitness. Cyclists will be glad to hear that the track is also one of NZ's Great Rides, and kayaking along the trail is also an option.

A number of outfitters and guides work along this trail, including **Wilderness Guides ♥♥** (wildernessguidesnz.com; ✆ **03/573-5432**), which offers kayak/walk/bike combos. Prices range from independent walks for NZ$945, up to NZ$3,100 for a guided gourmet 5-day experience. **Marlborough Sounds Adventure Company,** London Quay (marlboroughsounds.co.nz; ✆ **03/573-6078**), offers 1-day kayak/hike/bike tours on the QCT from NZ$245, and 4- to 5-day guided tours from NZ$2,690, which includes transport, gear, and accommodations.

Where to Stay in Picton

The Gables ♥♥, 20 Waikawa Rd. (thegables.co.nz; ✆ **03/573-6772**), has three handsome rooms plus two cottage suites (NZ$225–NZ$325). Fully booked? The same couple behind the Gables also run **Escape to Picton,** 33 Wellington St. (escapetopicton.com; ✆ **03/573-5573**), a centrally located boutique hotel that has won "best hotel" at the Hospitality NZ Awards for Excellence. The three suites run from NZ$350 to NZ$495. Meanwhile, **Picton Waterfront Apartments** (pictonwaterfrontapartments.co.nz; ✆ **027/513-8661**) offer just that: self-contained apartments in a variety of spots in the heart of downtown, all with soaring, sunny aspects facing the sea (NZ$413–NZ$920 per night).

For great-value backpacker accommodations, **The Villa,** 34 Auckland St. (thevilla.co.nz; ✆ **03/573-6598**), is hard to beat. It has dorm beds from NZ$28 and double rooms for NZ$87 to NZ$97.

Where to Eat in Picton

As a ferry port and tourist town, Picton's fare consists mainly of midrange cafe meals and pub grub. You won't have trouble finding fresh seafood or takeaway meals. **Gusto** ♥, 33 High St. (gustocafe.co.nz; ✆ **03/573-7171;** Sun–Fri 7am–2pm), one of Picton's top-rated cafes, serves up breakfast basics (eggs, porridge) and lunchtime staples (seafood chowder, steak sandwiches). It's a reliable spot for a good flat white and a filling breakfast.

The waterfront **Sisu** ♥♥, 12 London Quay (sisupicton.co.nz; no phone), offers upmarket shared plates with a Nordic twist thanks to its winemaker/chef owners Stefan and Inkeri. More than 40 wines are available by the glass, and the staff are exceptionally friendly. It's open Thursday to Tuesday, noon to 8:30pm. **Toastie Lords** ♥♥♥, 10 London Quay (toastielords.co.nz; ✆ **021/112-1944;** daily 6:30am–4pm), lives up to the hype, serving creative takes on the classic grilled cheese, such as the award-winning "Pete from

The Mariner Room at The Gables is all done up in soothing shades of blue and tan.

Picton" sandwich, with salmon, cream cheese, pickles and capers. Sandwiches, all with four cheeses, range from NZ$10 to NZ$16, and the filled doughnuts, coffee, milkshakes, and homemade sodas are just as phenomenal. Enjoy your lunch at the park across the way while looking out at the ocean.

The "Pete from Picton" sandwich at Toastie Lords.

At **Oxley's ♥**, 1 Wellington St. (oxleys.co.nz; ✆ **03/573-7645;** daily noon–late), you'll find classic, if unremarkable, pub dishes served hot and fresh at moderate prices; the kūmara fries we sampled were remarkably good. What really sets it apart is plenty of gluten-free and vegetarian options and a bright, nautical interior absent the smell of stale beer.

Only Scoop ♥, 5 Auckland St. (scoopnz.com; ✆ **027/237-5674**), is Marlborough's sole handcrafted ice-creamery. It's fresh and dairy-forward with quite subtle flavors; more unusual options include black licorice, passionfruit lemon custard, and banoffee. Hidden down the side of a Subway, it's open daily from midday, weekends from 10:30am.

Where to Stay & Eat Around the Sounds

Havelock, 33km (20 miles) west of Picton, is known as the Greenshell Mussel Capital of the World. **Mills Bay Mussels ♥♥♥** turns its premium, Sounds-grown mussels into croquettes and pies at its tasting room and eatery at 23a Inglis St. (millsbaymussels.co.nz; ✆ **03/574-2575**). Their mussels are also simply perfect on the half-shell with garlic butter and a side of shoestring fries. It's open Tuesday to Saturday 10:30am to 2:30pm. The giant mussel shells on the roof of **The Mussel Pot ♥♥**, 73 Main Rd. (themusselpot.co.nz; ✆ **03/574-2824;** main courses NZ$27–NZ$42), tip you off as to what's on the menu, whether you like them steamed, marinated, battered, grilled, or served in a chowder. It's open daily in summer, Wednesday to Sunday between September and May; 11am to 3pm and 5pm to 7:30pm (last orders at 2:30pm and 7pm). Reservations are recommended.

A pot of fresh-from-the-bay mussels at Mills Bay Mussels.

Slip into the silent beauty of Queen Charlotte Sound with a night or two at the boat-in-only **Lochmara Lodge ♥**,

Lochmara Bay (lochmara.co.nz; ✆ **03/573-4554**), which has spellbinding views of the bay and bush-covered hills. The lodge has an on-site restaurant, a bathhouse to unkink travel aches, bush walks, an aquarium to observe wild fish underwater, and paddleboards and kayaks. It's not the most luxurious of the lodges in the Sounds, but is one of the more affordable, with rates at NZ$206 to NZ$446 per night. Like much of the Sounds, it closes over winter, typically from mid-May until September. A dedicated water taxi has three scheduled departure times from Picton to Lochmara daily; it costs $90 adults and $45 kids round-trip.

BLENHEIM

115km (73 miles) SE of Nelson and 28km (17 miles) S of Picton

Blenheim/Te Waiharakeke is the commercial center of Marlborough, with a population of over 31,500. It lies at the heart of New Zealand's largest wine region. Even though around 25% of the area continues to be devoted to sheep and beef farming, stand on any high point around Blenheim and you'll see a land peppered with grapevines. In the last 4 decades, Marlborough has established itself as one of the world's premier wine-producing regions, responsible for around three-quarters of New Zealand's total wine production. There are some 150 wineries in the area, with more than 30 tasting rooms or "cellar doors."

Essentials

ARRIVING

BY PLANE **Air New Zealand** has direct flights from Auckland and Wellington (airnewzealand.co.nz; ✆ **0800/737-000** in NZ); **Sounds Air** (soundsair.com; ✆ **0800/505-005** in NZ) flies to Blenheim from Wellington. The **Marlborough Airport** (marlboroughairport.co.nz) is 10km (6 miles) from its town center and has car rental agencies and taxi stands; it's a 15- to 20-minute drive from the airport to central Blenheim. **Marlborough Shuttles** (marlboroughshuttles.co.nz; ✆ **0800/203-027**) provides transfers.

BY TRAIN The scenic **Great Journeys of New Zealand's Coastal Pacific Train** (greatjourneysnz.com; ✆ **0800/872-467** in NZ) between Christchurch and Picton also stops in Blenheim; see p. 360.

BY CAR Take SH1 from Picton (25-min. drive); SH6 from/to Nelson; SH1 from/to Kaikōura and Christchurch.

BY COACH/BUS **InterCity** (intercity.co.nz; ✆ **09/583-5780**) links Blenheim with Picton, Nelson, Kaikōura, Christchurch, and other centers in the South Island.

GETTING AROUND

Plenty of tour operators and shuttles are available in the area, making it possible to explore the region without needing to drive. **Blenheim Shuttles** (blenheimshuttles.co.nz; ✆ **0800/577-527**), **Executive Shuttle** (executiveshuttle.co.nz; ✆ **0800/777-313**), **Marlborough Taxis** (marlboroughtaxis.nz; ✆ **03/577-5511**), and **Wine Country Shuttles** (winecountryshuttles.co.nz;

✆ **021/0818-3272**) all offer door-to-door service. **Blenheim Corporate Cars** (blenheimcorporatecars.co.nz; ✆ **021/0818-3272**) offers a more exclusive, luxury ride with its black Chrysler sedan or Mercedes van and a focus on customer service. In 2025, rideshare app Uber was attempting to establish in Marlborough and may have done so by press time; check its app to see if it succeeded.

VISITOR INFORMATION

The **Blenheim isite,** 8 Sinclair St. (marlboroughnz.com; ✆ **03/577-8080**), is open from 9am to 5pm weekdays and until 4pm on Saturday.

SPECIAL EVENTS

The wineries surrounding Blenheim and nearby Renwick lend themselves to events celebrating the region's freshest fare and best drops. One biggie is the **Marlborough Food & Wine Festival** ♥♥, NZ's longest-running festival. A 1-day event on the second Saturday in February, it amply demonstrates how much this region enjoys a good time. Visit marlboroughwinefestival.com for details.

Exploring Blenheim

Oenophiles might enjoy a visit to the **Marlborough Museum,** 26 Arthur Baker Place (marlboroughmuseum.org.nz; ✆ **03/578-1712**), which has an exhibit on the history of the local wine industry. But it's not just about wine; the first humans in NZ arrived on these shores in A.D. 1250, and some of the early Māori archaeological evidence is here. It's open 11am to 3pm Sunday, Tuesday, and Thursday; admission is NZ$10 for adults, free for kids.

Omaka Aviation Heritage Centre ♥♥♥ MUSEUM No interest in aviation? Not a history buff? It doesn't matter. This museum is guaranteed to capture your imagination. **Knights of the Sky** explores World War I via Sir Peter Jackson's collection of aircraft and memorabilia, plus WingNut Films' expertise. Original and full-scale replica aircraft are displayed in a compelling

At the Omaka Aviation Heritage Centre, a tableau re-creates the death of the notorious Red Baron in World War I.

tableau of wartime scenes, such as ditched aircraft, surrenders, and the crash that killed the Red Baron. The newer **Dangerous Skies** World War II exhibition has the same attention to detail, including an IMAX-like room that immerses viewers in the bombing of Stalingrad. A guided 1½-hour highlights tour costs extra but truly brings the show to life. Every odd year on Easter, Omaka also hosts the **Classic Fighters Air Show** (the next show is in 2027). 79 Aerodrome Rd. omaka.org.nz. ✆ **03/579-1305.** NZ$49 adults, NZ$16 children 5–15, NZ$120 family. Daily 9am–4pm.

Exploring the Wine Country

New Zealand wine buffs still marvel at the juggernaut that is the country's wine industry. In the late 1960s, a smattering of two or three quite ordinary wines were produced from vines only a year or two old. Today, wine is among New Zealand's top exports. Marlborough was an early starter, thanks to wineries such as Brancott Estate, and after Marlborough sauvignon blanc came to the attention of international winemakers, the region became widely known as a producer of wines with notable flavors and aromas. For routes, grab a copy of the latest Marlborough Wine Trail from Blenheim's isite or online at marlboroughwinenz.com.

There are around 30 tasting rooms (called "cellar doors") in the Blenheim area that can be visited by self-driving, tours (see below for details), or bicycle. The latter option is the best one in our opinion, with the terrain flat and the climate good. Here are some of our favorite spots; most are northwest of Blenheim in the towns of Renwick and Raparua.

- **Cloudy Bay** ♥ (230 Jacksons Rd.; cloudybay.co.nz) is part of the Moët Hennessy family. The tasting room has a gorgeous outdoor area with gently swinging chairs hanging from eucalyptus trees. It's (unsurprisingly) known for its widely exported sauvignon blanc, but the easy-to-drink chardonnay is also worth a try.
- **Framingham** ♥♥♥ (19 Conders Bend Rd.; framingham.co.nz) is for when you're sick of sauvignons and stuffy service. With a rock 'n' roll sensibility (there's even an in-house band and an annual Harvest Concert in March), Framingham features rieslings that are better than good.
- The owners of **Hans Herzog Estate** ♥♥ (81 Jeffries Rd.; herzog.co.nz) came to New Zealand from Switzerland, searching for the world's best terroir for the vines they wanted to plant and the wines they wanted to make. The result is one of NZ's most renowned wineries.
- While not technically a winery, **Moa Brewing Company** ♥♥ (258 Jacksons Rd.; moabeer.com) has a family connection—it was started by Josh Scott (of nearby **Scott Family Estate**). Moa beers, ciders, and ginger beer can be found in bottle shops across the country, and the tasting room offers samples of it all. An on-site food truck makes this a perfect inexpensive lunch stop. Open October to May.
- Looking for more beer? Farther down the road, you'll find the beer garden of **Boom Town Brewing Co.** ♥♥ (19 Blicks Rd.; boomtown.nz). The beers here tend to be on the more traditional side of the craft beer spectrum,

A group enjoys charcuterie and wine in the middle of the vineyards at Saint Clair.

including refreshing IPAs and APAs. It's located at **Forrest Wines** (forrest.co.nz), which recently picked up a champion trophy for its Chenin Blanc 2023 at NZ's 2024 National Wine Awards.

- **Nautilus** ♥ (12 Rapaura Rd.; nautilusestate.com) is the younger sister of famed Australian wine label Yalumba. Like many other wineries in the region, sauvignon blanc is its bread and butter, but its claim to fame is that it's the official wine partner of the Royal New Zealand Ballet, launching the partnership with its Vintage Rosé in 2011.
- **Saint Clair** ♥♥♥ (13 Selmes Rd.; saintclair.co.nz) is one of the most-awarded vineyards in NZ, with whites that "tend to evaporate quite quickly in the summer" (or so joke the staff). Drop by for a tasting or call ahead to book one of the restaurant's tables set directly in the vineyard.
- Home to the cellar door of **Whitehaven Wines, The Vines Village** ♥♥ (thevinesvillage.co.nz) isn't a winery per se—it's actually so much more. The 4-acre property includes the **Roots Dry Gin** distillery (rootsdrygin.com), which was awarded the world's best London dry gin in 2023. There's also a deli (complete with a fill-your-own honey jar dispensary), cafe, ice-cream shop, bicycle hire business, and quilt shop among its tenants. There's even a cozy on-site Airbnb (**Distillers Cottage**) with outdoor bath, and a playground for kids to romp on while you relax with a glass of wine.
- A half-hour drive southeast of Blenheim, **Yealands Wines** ♥♥ (corner of Seaview and Reserve rds., Seddon; yealands.co.nz) is an international winner in sustainable wine tourism; the owner has built an impressive winery and an equally impressive tasting room.

ORGANIZED WINE TOURS

Bike Hire Marlborough provides cycles, helmets, and maps (bikehiremarlborough.co.nz; ✆ **021/846-607**). It costs NZ$60 for a gentle full-day self-guided tour among the country's cellar doors, including a map, lock, and transport to/from your hotel in Blenheim or Renwick. If you'd prefer a guided cycle tour, book with **Explore Marlborough** (exploremarlborough.co.nz;

A half-day cycle tour with Explore Marlborough pedals through wine country.

✆ **021/846-607**). A half-day tour visiting three wineries starts at NZ$155, and it's $220 for an e-bike.

Highlight Wine Tours (highlightwinetours.co.nz; ✆ **03/577-9046;** half-day tours 11:30am–5pm; NZ$115 per person in summer, NZ$105 in winter) takes small groups to four or five wineries in the Blenheim/Renwick area, with a lunch at one of the wineries and a sweet little stop at **Makana Boutique Chocolate Factory** (corner of Rapaura and O'Dwyers rds.). Or level up by booking a private tour, where the van is swapped out for a sparkling classic car, such as a 1976 Mustang convertible, a 1957 Chevy Bel Air, or a VW Kombi van.

A wine tour with the **Sounds Connection** ♥♥, 94 Wellington St. (soundsconnection.co.nz; ✆ **03/573-8843**), consists of half- and full-day excursions to Marlborough vineyards from NZ$185 to NZ$250. Groups are small, the choice of vineyards is varied, and the guides are knowledgeable locals.

Where to Stay in Blenheim

14th Lane Urban Hotel ♥♥♥ This building in downtown Blenheim has lived many lives since it was built in the 1940s—a wood and coal merchant, a pub—but its latest incarnation as a boutique urban hotel is its best one yet. The eight spacious rooms (including one that's fully accessible) are light, bright, and airy, with some featuring kitchens.

1A Kinross St. 14thlane.nz. ✆ **03/972-2727.** 8 units. NZ$332–NZ$536 double. **Amenities:** Access to nearby pool and gym; free Wi-Fi.

Hotel d'Urville ♥♥ Housed downtown in one of the few heritage buildings left in Blenheim, this boutique hotel has been lightly refurbished but still offers what one could describe as faded grandeur. Up a sweeping staircase, the spacious rooms are decorated in an eclectic fashion that leans towards the heavy and antique, from the furniture to the exotic fabrics to the lighting. What's to love are its historic details, like the old vault door from its days as the Public Trust office—and the decanter of self-serve complimentary port

Guest rooms at the 14th Lane Urban Hotel (p. 369) are spacious and light-filled.

that can be found in the sitting room behind it. ***Note:*** There's no elevator in this building, so it's not accessibility friendly.

52 Queen St. hoteldurville.com. ✆ **03/577-9945.** 11 units. NZ$285–NZ$306 double. **Amenities:** Guest lounge; free Wi-Fi.

Scenic Hotel Marlborough ♥♥ Pay no attention to the somewhat dated exterior. A multimillion-dollar renovation gave this hotel a fully refreshed interior with just enough technology (automated blinds) and personalized touches (a pillow menu) to make you feel like you're paying far more than you actually are. Two EV charging stations in the parking lot are indicative of the chain's commitment to the environment, but its central location is the top reason to stay here.

65 Alfred St. scenichotelgroup.co.nz. ✆ **03/520-6187.** 54 units. NZ$211–NZ$320 double. **Amenities:** Restaurant, bar; solar-heated outdoor pool; spa and sauna; free Wi-Fi.

Vintners Retreat ♥♥ Situated at the edge of a vineyard with views of the Richmond Ranges, this boutique accommodation complex has 14 self-contained villas ranging from three-bedroom lodges to two-story "manors" with their own private garages. Each has laundry facilities and a fully equipped kitchen, designed for travelers who plan on staying a while. The herb garden, solar-heated pool, Netflix-equipped TVs, and children's playground make this a great base for families.

55 Rapaura Rd. vintnersretreat.co.nz. ✆ **03/572-7420.** 14 units. NZ$300–NZ$750 double. 2-night min. in high season. **Amenities:** Spa baths; outdoor pool; tennis court; pétanque and croquet; playground; free Wi-Fi.

Where to Eat in Blenheim

If you're looking for hearty snacks or picnic food, swing by **The Burleigh Gourmet Pies ♥♥**, 72 New Renwick Rd. (instagram.com/the_burleigh; ✆ **03/579-2531**), a pickup-and-go stop that has a legion of obsessive fans. Be prepared for long lunchtime line-ups.

Arbour ♥♥♥ MODERN NEW ZEALAND *New Zealand Herald* restaurant critic Jesse Mulligan rated Arbour a rare 20/20 in late 2025, saying it "might be the best restaurant in New Zealand." See for yourself. It's tasting menu only, but you can definitely trust co-owner/chef Bradley Hornby. "The Many" is a perfectly curated nine-course degustation menu produced with seasonal, regional ingredients: lamb with thyme jus, black truffle sabayon, or mandarin sorbet with Earl Grey tea crème. Arbour is fully deserving of the "hats" it has won in the Cuisine Good Food Awards, and its title as the 2022 NZ Regional Restaurant of the Year. If you, like me, enjoy an early meal, there are also discounts for eating during "foodie hour" at 5:30pm.

36 Godfrey Rd. arbour.co.nz. ✆ **03/572-7989.** Tasting menu NZ$139, wine pairings NZ$85–NZ$139 extra. Bookings strongly recommended. Thurs–Sat from 5:30pm (Jan–Apr Wed–Sat). Children 10+ only.

Cloudy Bay clams at Arbour.

Frank's Oyster Bar & Eatery ♥♥ MODERN NEW ZEALAND The name of this joint is misleading on so many levels. First off, the man behind the ship is local chef Sam Webb. Second, although it looks like a classic New York bar with its subway tiles and industrial light fixtures, it has a full dinner menu with drinks to match. Which brings us to the third point: There's so much more than oysters. Featuring share plates (including some that can safely be eaten as mains, for those less interested in sharing), the emphasis here is on local. Seafood is from the Sound; bread comes served with locally grown black garlic butter; even the wild game has been hunted and harvested ethically. Vegetarians won't go hungry. Everyone will be happy. Even Frank—whoever he is.

28 Scott St. eatatfranks.co.nz. ✆ **03/579-1778.** Main courses NZ$35–NZ$100. Tues–Sat 4–10pm.

Scotch Wine Bar ♥♥ MODERN NEW ZEALAND The menu in this minimal, busy space changes seasonally; when we visited it included bruschetta with mashed green olives, roasted pancetta, and fresh mozzarella; escargot adorned with garlic butter, parsley, and shallots; and a meltingly tender 4-hour pork belly. Many of the wines are for sale in the walk-in wine cellar next door. Bookings recommended.

24–26 Maxwell Rd. scotchbar.co.nz. ✆ **03/579-1176.** Share plates NZ$12–NZ$50. Mon–Fri 4pm–late.

NELSON & TASMAN

107km (67 miles) W of Picton; 222km (140 miles) NE of Westport; 415km (258 miles) N of Christchurch

New Zealanders often use the name "Nelson" or "Nelson/Tasman" to refer to both the bustling small city of Nelson, on the shore of Tasman Bay, and the adjacent Tasman district, which encompasses the coastal towns of Richmond, Motueka, and Tākaka, as well as Golden Bay and three national parks (see p. 383). Taken together, this is the sunniest playground in New Zealand, boasting 2,500 hours of annual sunshine, tranquil waters, gold-sand beaches, breweries, and vineyards. It's one of the country's most popular destinations, in winter as well as summer—while the rest of the country is lashed with foul winter chills, Nelson Tasman sits in a sheltered haven, blissfully unaware of everyone else's discomfort.

Essentials

ARRIVING

BY PLANE NZ's busiest regional airport, the recently renovated **Nelson Airport** (nelsonairport.co.nz) has direct service to and from Auckland, Wellington, Christchurch, and major provincial centers. It's served by **Air New Zealand** (airnewzealand.co.nz; ✆ **0800/737-000** in NZ) and several regional airlines including **Sounds Air** (soundsair.com; ✆ **0800/505-005** in NZ) and **Originair** (originair.co.nz; ✆ **0800/380-380** in NZ).

The airport is about 8km (5 miles) from the Nelson city center. Several rental car companies have branches just outside the terminal entrance. Taxis are also located at the terminal front, or call **Nelson Taxis** (✆ **03/548-8225**). Nelson's bus service, **eBus** (ebus.nz; ✆ **03/546-0200**) covers the 30-minute ride between the airport and the city, departing on the half-hour daily (last service 6:22pm). Fares are NZ$3 cash, or NZ$2.16 with a bright yellow Bee Card, which will also serve you in nine different regions of NZ. (You can't buy the card at the airport; they're available from Nelson City Council, 110 Trafalgar St. (nelson.govt.nz; ✆ **03/546-0200**) and Tasman District Council, 189 Queen St., Richmond (tasman.govt.nz; ✆ **03/543-8400**).

BY CAR As an alternative route to the more direct SH6 from Picton to Nelson (which takes about 2 hr.), Queen Charlotte Drive offers lovely views of the Marlborough Sounds (not to mention the unusual mailboxes along the way). However, it's a narrow, winding road that needs to be driven with care. The road meets up with SH6 at Havelock to continue to Nelson. The whole trip should take about 2½ hours. If you're coming from the West Coast, the drive from Westport takes 3½ hours; from Christchurch via Lewis Pass, about 5 hours, or Christchurch via Kaikōura-Blenheim, 6 hours.

BY COACH (BUS) **InterCity** (intercity.co.nz; ✆ **03/548-1539**) connects Nelson with numerous towns and cities.

GETTING AROUND

Driving from Nelson to Māpua will take you 40 minutes; from Nelson to Motueka is 50 minutes; and from Nelson to Tākaka at least 2 hours, depending on traffic on Tākaka Hill.

VISITOR INFORMATION

The official tourism website for the region is **nelsontasman.nz**.

Exploring Nelson

The downtown core of Nelson isn't large and is on a grid, which makes navigation easy. If you do lose your bearings, Christ Church Cathedral sits on Church Hill at the south end above Trafalgar Street, while the ocean is to the city's north.

In central Nelson, the cute little street known as **South Street Heritage Precinct** ♥♥ captures the feel of a past era. Just off Nile Street West behind the Rutherford Hotel, it is lined by 16 working-class cottages built between 1863 and 1867, all of which remain intact and are still inhabited. It's a narrow cul-de-sac, so it's best to park nearby and walk. Nearby, atop Church Hill, **Nelson Christ Church Cathedral,** Trafalgar Square (nelsoncathedral.nz; ✆ **03/548-1008**), is open daily free of charge to visitors from 8:30am to 7pm. Built partially of local Tākaka marble, the cathedral features striking stained glass windows and a unique freestanding organ.

Across town, **Founder's Heritage Park** ♥, 87 Atawhai Dr. (founderspark.co.nz; ✆ **03/548-2649**), is a replica historic village containing many of the old buildings and artifacts of Nelson. The complex is a great place to let children run free, with a working small train, a non-working Bristol Freighter plane you can climb inside, and a popular cafe with playground. It's open daily from 9am to 4:30pm; admission is NZ$12.10 for adults, NZ$5.20 for children 5 to 16, and NZ$30 per family. For train rides, check with the **Nelson Railway Society** (nelsonrailwaysociety.co.nz; ✆ **027/341-9787**) for the next running day. Tickets cost NZ$6 for over-14s and NZ$4 for ages 3 to 13.

Just 6km (3¾ miles) outside of town, the **Brook Waimārama Sanctuary** ♥♥, 651 Brook St. (brooksanctuary.org.nz; ✆ **03/539-4920**), is the largest fenced predator-free sanctuary on the South Island. Current residents include kiwi, tuatara, *tīeke* (South Island saddleback), *kākāriki karaka* (orange-fronted parakeet), and *powelliphanta* (large endemic carnivorous snails). Opening times change frequently, so check the site for the latest hours. It costs NZ$27 adults and NZ$12 ages 5 to 15, with family passes for NZ$53; all proceeds support the sanctuary's conservation work. Guided tours are available for NZ$37 adults and NZ$17 ages 5 to 15, or NZ$79 for a family of four. For another NZ$6 to $NZ10 or so, choose a night tour to see ethereal blue-white glowworms and hopefully hear the call of a kiwi.

At the **Nelson Classic Car Museum** ♥♥, 1 Cadillac Way, off Quarantine Road (nelsonclassiccarmuseum.nz; ✆ **03/547-4570**), there are 150 cars on display from over 100 years of motoring, including seriously sought-after models, from a huge pink-and-white Cadillac to a curious Messerschmitt

Classic cars on display at the Nelson Classic Car Museum.

two-seater. Open daily from 10am to 4pm, it costs NZ$19 adults/NZ$8 ages 5 to 15, with family discounts available.

In Stoke, a suburb of Nelson, the **Broadgreen Historic House** ♥, 276 Nayland Rd. (broadgreenhouse.nz; ✆ **03/547-0403**), is a New Zealand Tourism Award winner. A restored two-story cob house built in the mid-1850s, it has 11 rooms furnished to faithfully represent a family home of the period. There's even a dress-up box for children. It's open Monday to Saturday 11:30am to 3pm, Sunday 10:30am to 4pm. Admission is NZ$8 (free for kids under 16). The adjacent **Samuels Rose Gardens,** with more than 560 named varieties, is a beautiful place to stop and smell—well, the roses.

Nelson Provincial Museum (Pupuri Taonga o Te Tai Ao) ♥♥

MUSEUM This well-curated museum is not large, but you could easily spend hours among its permanent collections and changing exhibitions. The first section of the permanent gallery is devoted to the region's exceptionally varied geological features, such as Boulder Bank (see p. 377) and Farewell Spit (p. 388). The next section features local family stories about how life was once lived in this area.

270 Trafalgar St. nelsonmuseum.co.nz. ✆ **03/548-9588.** NZ$7 adults, NZ$3 school children, free for preschoolers. Weekdays 10am–5pm; weekends 10am–4:30pm.

Exploring the Moutere Hills Wineries

Most of Nelson's roughly 20 tasting rooms/cellar doors are scattered along the rolling Moutere Hills and the alluvial Waimea Plains. The wines (riesling, chardonnay, sauvignon blanc, gewürztraminer, cabernet franc, merlot, cabernet sauvignon, and pinot noir) have intense fruit flavors, good acidic balance, and weight. For more on Nelson wineries and updated seasonal hours, visit the **Wine Nelson** website at tastenelsonwines.nz.

One of the best-known producers is **Neudorf Vineyards** ♥♥♥, 138 Neudorf Rd., Upper Moutere (neudorf.co.nz; ✆ **03/543-2643**). Set in a picturesque vineyard, the winery offers tastings of its prize-winning chardonnay, riesling, pinot noir, and sauvignon blanc. It's open daily from 11am to 4pm and has a popular picnic basket menu with a lovely, leafy wine garden to eat it in (from NZ$35 for two). **Seifried Estate Vineyard and Restaurant,** 184 Redwood Rd., Appleby (seifried.co.nz; ✆ **03/544-1600**), has a tasting room, open daily from 11am to 4pm. It's biggest bragging rights are for its luxurious "Sweet Agnes" riesling, the country's most-awarded dessert wine.

Moutere Hills Restaurant & Cellar Door ♥♥, 42 Eggers Rd., Upper Moutere (mouterehills.co.nz; ✆ **03/543-2288**), serves beautifully presented meals in its restaurant along with riesling, sauvignon blanc, and chardonnay. Check its website for seasonal hours.

Wine, Art & Wilderness (wineartandwilderness.co.nz) offers just that; an excellent range of luxury, fully catered outings that include nature, walking in Nelson's three national parks or alpine areas, vineyards, cruises, and art stops, as well as city tours. Want to bike from vineyard to vineyard? See **Cycle Nelson** (cyclenelson.co.nz; ✆ **0800/932-453** in NZ) for tours.

Art Galleries & Studios

This area of New Zealand is known for attracting creatives, craftspeople, and artists; between Nelson and Golden Bay, there are an estimated 300 practicing professional artists, and roughly 40 galleries and studios.

Jens Hansen Gold & Silversmith ♥♥♥, 320 Trafalgar Square (jenshansen.com; ✆ **03/548-0640**), is a name associated with quality New Zealand–made gold and silver jewelry—and *the* handmade ring used in the *Lord of the Rings* trilogy.

Royce McGlashen Pottery ♥♥♥, 128 Ellis St., Brightwater (roycemcglashen.co.nz; ✆ **03/542-3585**), is another high point. A renowned ceramic artist, Royce uses color with artistic abandon, but anyone seeking a hand-thrown matte-black dinner set will also find it in this studio. Other potters include **Peter Gibbs ♥♥** (gibbspottery.com; ✆ **027/240-6933;** by appointment only), who was a professional potter in Nelson's ceramics heyday between 1975 and 1993 and recently switched on his wheel again; and **Steve Fullmer ♥♥♥**, 3 Baldwin Rd., Tasman (stevefullmer.com; ✆ **03/526-6765**), who is one of the country's best. His gallery is open 10am until 4pm most days in the summer.

Master potter Peter Gibbs.

Flame Daisy, 324 Trafalgar Square (flamedaisy.co.nz; ✆ **03/548-4475**), is a glass art gallery with a wide variety of well-priced items. Or drive 20 minutes out of Nelson to **Höglund Art Glass ♥♥♥**, 52 Lansdowne Rd., Appleby (hoglundartglass.com; ✆ **03/544-6500**). Ola Höglund and Marie

KID magnets

- **Nelson Fun Park** Adjacent to Tāhuna Beach and just a 5-minute drive from central Nelson, the fun here includes a waterslide, miniature golf course, and bumper boats (40 Hounsell Circle; nelson funpark.co.nz; ✆ **03/548-6267**).
- **Natureland** ♥♥ Also at Tāhuna Beach, this zoo lets kids get up close with meerkats, primates, and native birds (Hounsell Circle 7011; natureland.nz; ✆ **03/548-6166**).
- **Jester House Cafe** ♥♥♥ There's plenty for kids to do while you enjoy your meal in the outdoor garden, from feeding tame eels to wandering through a woodland filled with handcrafted creatures. It's only open on Fridays from 10am to 5pm, when savvy locals flock there (320 Aporo Rd., Tasman; jester house.co.nz; ✆ **03/526-6742**).
- **Cable Bay Adventure Park** ♥♥ Hit the heights on the 4km (2½-mile) Skywire, a sort of cable-car meets zipline. Cost is NZ$110 (194 Cable Bay Rd.; cablebay adventurepark.com; ✆ **03/545-0304**). Quadding, horse tours, and paintball are also on offer.
- **Pic's Peanut Butter World** ♥ Learn how peanuts are grown, get a birds-eye view of the flavor lab, and make your own peanut butter. One-hour tours and tastings are free, but bookings are essential (49 Saxton Rd.; picspeanut butter.com; ✆ **03/544-8402**).
- **Penguino Ice Cream Cafe** ♥♥ This much-awarded gelateria at 85 Montgomery Square offers a tasting platter of its inventive flavors—like the gold award-winning Biscoff and cream or eucalyptus and mānuka honey—for the ambitious (93 Montgomery Sq., Nelson; facebook.com/PenguinoIce CreamCafe; ✆ **03/545-6450**).

Simberg-Höglund trained at Orrefors and Kosta Boda before emigrating from their native Sweden. They produce stunning, colorful handblown glassware; part of the fun is watching the action in the studio. Their Vase Eclipse range is particularly gorgeous. Admission is free and it's open daily 10am to 5pm.

Rare Creations ♥♥, 150 Māpua Dr., Māpua (rarecreations.co.nz; ✆ **03/540-2225**), calls itself (aptly) an "interactive wooden art gallery." Furniture is made on-site of sustainably grown pine, and they also make fun kinetic toy sets (lots of buttons to press). Check its website for hours, and do stop by, even if you're not in a spending mood.

Outdoor Pursuits

BEACHES Nelson Tasman has dozens of postcard-perfect beaches. Close to the city, the best is **Tāhuna Beach** (also known as Tāhunanui), which offers smooth waters for swimming. Farther afield is the hugely popular **Kaiteriteri Beach** ♥♥, known for its golden sands and turquoise water. From here you can take a water taxi to **Abel Tasman National Park** (see p. 383), where there are more beaches and bays than you can poke a driftwood stick at.

CANYONING **Canyoning Aotearoa** ♥ (canyoningaotearoa.com; ✆ **027/259-2117**) runs half-day canyoning adventures near Lake Rotoiti at St. Arnaud.

With a focus on teaching people canyoning skills while encouraging mindfulness, they won't hold your hand as you rappel down a series of six waterfalls, but will equip you with skills in a safe environment. Compared to the canyoning adventures in Abel Tasman National Park, this tour is shorter with less walking (you only have to walk for about 20 min. to start your adventure, instead of 90 min.), but it's no less epic. Operating during summer, it costs NZ$189.

CYCLING Starting at Nelson's cafes and ending at the Maitai Dam, the 43km (27-mile) **Coppermine Trail** ♥♥♥ is one of the most accessible alpine mountain bike rides in the country, with variations for those with less experience. Visit heartofbiking.org.nz/coppermine-trail for the trail map and info. There are also plenty of cycling trails for a more leisurely day out, including exploring the nearby wineries. **Cycle Nelson** (cyclenelson.co.nz; ✆ **0800/932-453** in NZ) will gladly assist from one of its three bases: Tāhuna Beach, Nelson Airport, and Kaiteriteri Beach. If you have just one day and want to self-guide, we like the coastal 28km (17-mile) ride from Nelson along the **Great Taste Trail** ♥♥ (heartofbiking.org.nz) to Māpua seaside cafes and restaurants (NZ$160 per person). E-bikes are also available for an extra cost.

FISHING The Buller River and its tributaries are popular fly-fishing destinations for trout, especially in nearby **Murchison** (see chapter 12). If you want to catch the big one, the **Stonefly Lodge,** 3256 Motueka Valley Hwy. (stoneflylodge.co.nz; ✆ **03/522-4479**), is just one operator. For heli-fishing, enquire with **Helicopters Nelson** (helicoptersnelson.co.nz; ✆ **03/541-9530**).

GOLF **Nelson Links,** 38 Bolt Rd. (nelsongolf.co.nz; ✆ **03/548-5029**), is an 18-hole course open daily. Greens fees are NZ$75 for nonaffiliated players. **Greenacres Golf Club,** 4 Barnett Ave., Best Island (greenacresgolfclub.co.nz; ✆ **021/198-7611**), also has 18 holes and is open daily; non-members pay NZ$50.

WALKING **Abel Tasman, Kahurangi,** and **Nelson Lakes National Parks** are the big hiking drawcards here (see p. 384). Closer to the city, maps of all the area's walks can be found by searching the city and regional council websites, nelson.govt.nz and tasman.govt.nz.

For a charming city walk, find the Maitai River off Nile Street and follow the signposted walkway to the locals' favorite swimming spot: **Girlies Hole** (named as such because the local girls' school once used this spot for school swimming sports). Or, spend an hour climbing to the **Centre of New Zealand.** The 142m (466-ft.) trek up Botanical Hill does not literally lead you to the center of New Zealand—it was actually the origin point for trigonometrical surveys in the 1870s—but rewards with sweeping views.

Up in Motueka, the **Motueka Sandpit & Estuary** ♥, accessed via Staples Street, is an internationally important seabird habitat, home to many varieties that come here to breed. It's along the Motueka Quay, which also features the wreck of Janie Seddon, a World War II ship.

On the bayshore northeast of Nelson, the **Boulder Bank/Te Pokohiwi** ♥ is a natural 13km (8-mile) spit reaching into Tasman Bay. An 8km (5-mile)

walkway ♥ along the bank is like walking on a naturally formed wharf far into the ocean. You'll need strong ankles. Check tide times before you depart and take sturdy shoes, all-weather clothing, and water; it can be hot and windy. If driving to the start of the walk is not an option, tour company **The Ferry** (nelsonferry.co.nz; ✆ **027/302-9385;** from NZ$25) can oblige, along with offering other tours of Nelson harbor.

Whispering Falls ♥♥♥, about 20 minutes from Nelson, is the kind of local secret that I almost want to keep for myself. A relatively easy 3-hour bushwalk (although there is one river crossing to be avoided after heavy rain), it heads into **Mount Richmond Forest Park** to reach thousands of trickling water droplets, hence the evocative name. You'll feel like you've arrived when you reach the first set of falls just beyond the bridge, but follow the trail markers beyond to the larger upper falls. It's steep, but there's a sunny picnic spot for lunch with valley views. The walk starts from the **Hacket Track** carpark in Aniseed Valley.

WATERSPORTS **Moana SUP,** 7/623 Rocks Rd., near Tāhuna Beach (moananzsup.co.nz; ✆ **027/272-7259**), is the region's only accredited paddleboard school, and also offers SUP (stand-up paddleboard) hire. It's the ideal way to experience Nelson's calm Haven harbor, where you'll have a front-row view of the waterfront mansions arrayed along the Tāhuna hills. Also based near the beach, **Kitesurf Nelson,** 623 Rocks Rd. (kitescool.co.nz; ✆ **021/354-837**), offers lessons and kiteboard hire for those seeking a bit more adrenaline.

Where to Stay Around Nelson

Although there are plenty of nondescript motels to choose from, you won't have much selection if you're after a chain hotel where you can use loyalty points. This region specializes in boutique hotels, holiday home rentals, and B&Bs, most of which are privately owned.

Rutherford Hotel Nelson ♥, T27 Nile St. W (rutherfordhotel.nz; ✆ **03/548-2299**), is a decent, central spot. It has an outdoor pool, two restaurants, a bar, and a cafe. Expect to pay NZ$239 to NZ$300.

Tāhuna Beach Holiday Park ♥♥, 70 Beach Rd., Tāhunanui (tahuna.nz; ✆ **03/548-5159**), is one of the largest motor camps in NZ. Accommodation ranges from motel units (from NZ$192) to cabins (from NZ$98) to tent sites (from NZ$18 non-powered). It has barbecues, playgrounds, and mini golf.

Grand Arden Monaco Nelson ♥

In this bayshore suburb of Nelson, rows of cute brick cottages seem plucked from an English storybook. More apartments than motel units, with ivy clambering around the casement windows, they have comfy paneled sitting rooms with soft leather chairs, French doors opening to a village green, and bedrooms with big, plush beds. Add an on-site restaurant and you're sorted.

6 Point Rd., Monaco. monacoresort.co.nz. ✆ **03/547-8233.** 84 units. NZ$165–NZ$299 double. **Amenities:** Restaurant; gym; jewelry shop; solar-heated outdoor pool; health and beauty spa; courtesy coach; free Wi-Fi.

Wraparound windows in the living area maximize the stunning views at Peak View Retreat.

Maitai Whare Iti ♥♥ Just a 10-minute drive outside of Nelson's city center in the lush Maitai Valley, you'll find this small collection of "adventure cabins" on a hill. (*Whare iti* translates to "small house.") It's a step above glamping; each basic, private tiny house has electricity, running water, and a full bathroom. (They're not accessible, but there is a fully accessible two-bedroom house rental). Beds are in cute loft areas with low ceilings and are accessed via a ladder. There's little cellphone reception, but honestly, in such an idyllic spot you just want to watch the clouds drift past.

571 Maitai Valley Rd. whareiti.co.nz. ✆ **021/497-827.** 4 cabins, 1 house. Cabins NZ$175–NZ$205; house NZ$313. **Amenities:** Communal kitchen; free Wi-Fi.

Peak View Retreat ♥♥♥ Situated on a rugged mountaintop, Peak View surely has the most extraordinary view in Nelson. This luxurious two-bedroom sanctuary feels like an alpine cabin or hiking lookout; a 360-degree vista stretches from native forest to ocean, islands, mountain ranges, and national parks. There are lots of native timbers, a woodburner, a hammock, big decks, sauna, full coffee machine, board games, books, and a wood-fired outdoor hot tub. It's about a 45-minute drive from Nelson city and you'll need a car; an SUV or all-wheel drive is recommended for the gravel road. Stock up on food in town and forget the rest of the world exists. Rifle shooting, a wine tour, a private chef, chakra dance, sound bath healing, and a yoga teacher/masseur are available for an extra cost.

158B Lower Flowers Rd., Whangamoa. peakviewretreat.com. ✆ **022/631-2749.** NZ$850 (winter)–NZ$1,550 (summer). Children 10+ welcome. Min. 2-night stay. **Amenities:** Hot tub; sauna; BBQ; free Wi-Fi.

Pihopa Retreat ♥♥ Surrounded by farmland, forest, and native bush, yet only minutes from the city center, this retreat was once home to the Nelson Diocese estate and originally purchased in 1862. Now it's a luxury getaway with six one-bedroom private villas on 5½ acres. The units, each named for a bishop, are pleasant without being overly ornate (or, conversely, austere). Beds are plush; there's a pillow menu; and complimentary whiskey, port, and chocolate are available. The on-site church (built in 1877), features one of NZ's last remaining full submersion baptismal baths, along with a baptismal font carved by the grandson of the first Māori bishop. A new wellness center is set to open in mid-2026, with a massage studio and Pilates machine.

225 Waimea Rd., Bishopdale. pihoparetreat.nz. ✆ **022/390-4463.** 6 units. NZ$1,750–NZ$1,950 villa. Rates include breakfast. **Amenities:** Gym; spa; outdoor pool; hot tub; courtesy shuttle; free Wi-Fi.

The Wheelhouse Inn ♥♥ Each of the Wheelhouse's five holiday homes comes with a set of binoculars, a marine chart, and a stunning view of the harbor below. From the ceramic seagulls in the trees, to the daybeds fashioned after boat berths, the nautical theme here is hard to miss. Owners Sally and Ralph Hetzel sailed from California to New Zealand over 4 decades ago, but still maintain their laid-back surfer approach to hosting. Self-contained, each house on the hillside is private, with everything you might need for a longer stay.

41 Whitby Rd. wheelhouse.co.nz. ✆ **03/546-8391.** NZ$295–NZ$435 double. 5 units. **Amenities:** Free Wi-Fi.

IN MOTUEKA, TASMAN & MĀPUA

Motueka is mainly known for its motels and backpackers, such as the flash-packer-friendly **Eden's Edge Lodge ♥♥**, 137 Lodder Lane (edensedge.co.nz; ✆ **03/528-4242;** NZ$150–$220), in nearby Riwaka. But the surrounding areas of Māpua, Ruby Bay, Tasman, and Upper Moutere have rich pickings of boutique accommodations for those looking for a peaceful country stay.

The Boot B&B ♥♥ Hidden in a hazelnut grove, this whimsical cottage is actually shaped like Mother Hubbard's shoe. Despite its nursery-rhyme

A one-of-a-kind lodging, The Boot is all cozy charm inside.

The Māpua Wharf

The Māpua Wharf (mapuawharf.co.nz) precinct is a lovely example of businesses working collaboratively to build a unique and thriving community outside the city. A 25-minute drive from Nelson, it's the perfect place to while away an afternoon. Highlights include lunch at the **Apple Shed** (theappleshed.nz; ✆ **03/540-3381**), a sunshine-soaked cafe next to the water serving green-lipped mussels and beer-battered fish and chips; followed by a tipple at the **Rimu Wine Bar** (rimugrove.co.nz/the-wine-bar; ✆ **03/540-2580**). Once you're sufficiently stuffed, wander through one of the many on-site art galleries and gift shops, and satiate your sweet tooth with a real fruit ice cream at **Hamish's** (hamishturner.co.nz; ✆ **03/540-3861**).

origins, it's a getaway for adults only, created by owners Judy and Steve Richards; The Boot's guestbook is full of delightful oversharing about anniversaries and honeymoons celebrated here. The two-level structure is classy rather than kitschy, with a wood-burning fireplace, shower built for two, and a throne of a composting toilet that will make you feel like royalty. The **Jester House Cafe ♥♥♥** (Fridays only; see p. 376) is also on the property.

320 Aporo Rd., Tasman. jesterhouse.co.nz. ✆ **03/526-6742.** 1 unit. NZ$330. Rates include breakfast. **Amenities:** Outdoor fire; BBQ; free Wi-Fi.

Rabbit Island Huts ♥♥ Glamping experiences are a dime-a-dozen in New Zealand, but the owners of these glamping tents and stand-alone huts at the edge of Rabbit Island have perfected the formula. The huts are comfortable, but the common areas make the real difference. The shared kitchen is one you'll actually want to cook in. The firepit is a great place to meet your neighbors, while the shared sauna or secluded outdoor bathtub are possibly the best spots to avoid them. All lodgings are stocked with local Rabbit Island coffee, bread, and milk.

305 Redwood Rd., Appleby. applebyhouse.co.nz. ✆ **027/6632-639.** 6 huts, 2 tents. Huts and tents NZ$220–NZ$265. **Amenities:** Shared kitchen; outdoor fire; BBQ; outdoor bathtub; outdoor shower; free Wi-Fi.

Where to Eat in & Around Nelson

Nelson's restaurants excel in fresh fish and shellfish dishes. Many can be found along the waterfront and in Trafalgar Square.

For some of the best coffee, cakes, and breakfasts in town (we like the breakfast tacos), head for **DeVille ♥♥**, 22 New St. (devillecafe.nz; ✆ **03/545-6911;** Tues–Fri 8am–3pm, Sat 9am–3pm). The Suter Art Gallery's **Suter Café ♥♥**, 208 Bridge St. (thesuter.org.nz/cafe; ✆ **03/548-4699;** daily 9:30am–4:30pm), looks out into the leafy environs of Queens Gardens. It has delicious counter food, with lots of vegetarian, gluten-free, and dairy-free options.

For a quick fix that won't break the bank, **Culture ♥**, 279 Trafalgar St. (culturenelson.nz; ✆ **03/546-9020;** daily noon–9pm), will fill your empty belly. Don't miss the fried pickles and fried Mars Bar bites.

Breweries for Beer Lovers

With a strong hop-growing industry, Nelson really delivers on the beer front, claiming to be the "craft brewing capital of New Zealand." To try more than a few brands, **The Free House ♥♥♥**, 95 Collingwood St. (thefreehouse.co.nz; ✆ **03/548-9391**), is a local favorite, an excellent craft brew pub located in a former church. It's open weekdays from 3pm to late, Saturday from noon, and Sunday from 2pm. **McCashin's ♥♥**, 660 Main Rd., Stoke (mccashins.co.nz; ✆ **03/547-5357**), offers tours by arrangement (bookings essential) and has an on-site kitchen and bar. It's open 11am to late Tuesday to Saturdays. Up the coast, **Golden Bear Brewing ♥** at the Māpua Wharf (goldenbearbrewing.com; ✆ **03/540-3210**) has a friendly vibe with lots of live music, though it is closed July to September.

Boat Shed Cafe ♥♥ SEAFOOD The over-the-water setting is the prime reason for the waiting lists at this busy Nelson landmark. But the Boat Shed is also famous for its fish dishes, its excellent wine list, and its raft of locally brewed beers. It can be noisy and crowded, but those are the signs of a popular place the world over. "Over the water" means what it says—so snag a seat on the (enclosed) veranda, and kick back to the swish-swash of water lapping.

350 Wakefield Quay. boatshedcafe.co.nz. ✆ **03/546-9783.** Main courses NZ$38–NZ$42. Dinner reservations recommended. Mon–Fri 11:30am–late, Sat–Sun 9am–late.

Harry's Hawker House ♥♥♥ SOUTHEAST ASIAN Sited in old legal chambers, the Hawker House is owned by Nelson hospitality legends Tania and Matt Bouterey and serves consistently excellent meals influenced by street food. Sweet-and-sour pork dumplings and massaman spiced lamb shoulder are highlights. It's lively, especially in the early evening when locals gather for pre-dinner drinks.

296 Trafalgar St. hawkerhouse.co.nz. ✆ **03/539-0905.** Main courses NZ$24–NZ$32. Mon–Wed 4pm–late, Thurs–Sat 11am–late.

Hopgood's & Co. ♥♥ MODERN NEW ZEALAND Kevin Hopgood worked with the Roux brothers and Gordon Ramsay in London, and since 2005 he's brought a welcome style and professionalism to Nelson with this calm, contemporary addition to the main street. Expect a showcase of local produce at great prices and a hoard of returning locals. A five-course tasting menu is also available for NZ$110.

284 Trafalgar St. hopgoods.co.nz. ✆ **03/545-7191.** Main courses NZ$42–NZ$47. Reservations recommended. Tues–Sat 5:30pm–late.

Ikko Sushi ♥ CASUAL JAPANESE Sushi fans will love this popular lunch spot tucked away in an alley. The interior is small and forgettable, but the food is spot-on, the service fast and friendly. The salmon teriyaki don is a local favorite, and the delicate tempura don and teriyaki tofu will melt in your mouth. Prices are ridiculously reasonable, though some dishes quickly sell out once the office workers hit at lunchtime.

Marble Arch Arcade, 167 Hardy St. ✆ **03/548-1591.** Main courses NZ$15–NZ$18. Mon–Fri 10:30am–3pm.

River Kitchen ♥♥ CAFE The outdoor riverbank beanbags are the best spot to nab here. Open for breakfast and lunch, this is a lovely place to sit and sip (a nice assortment of beer and wine) or dig into chicken with waffles, creamy seafood chowder, and Philly cheesesteak loaded fries. For a snack, the buttermilk chicken bites and sweet-and-savory scones are great, and the coffee is excellent, as is the service—and it's nice to see walkers with dogs welcomed.

81 Trafalgar St. (entrance on pathway beside the Maitai River). riverkitchennelson.co.nz. ✆ **03/548-1180.** Main courses NZ$25–NZ$29. Tues–Fri 7:30am–4pm, Sat 8am–4pm, Sun 8:30am–4pm.

IN MOTUEKA, TASMAN & MĀPUA

If you're after burgers, visit **The Smoking Barrel** ♥♥ (105 High St., Motueka; facebook.com/thesmokingbarrelnz; ✆ **03/528-0693**). Along with burgers and brisket, there are donuts of unholy persuasions; there's even a bacon and eggs benedict version. Arrive early for the best selection and don't forget your antacids. It's open Wednesday to Saturday 9am to 10pm, and Sunday until 4pm.

Jellyfish Restaurant & Bar ♥♥ SEAFOOD This is a lovely, casual place on the Māpua Wharf, with good beer and wine lists and an eclectic menu prominently featuring the best of the adjacent ocean. Think Fijian citrus cured fish; squid salad; and prawn fettucine, for a start. It's open daily for breakfast, brunch, and lunch.

1 Māpua Wharf, Māpua. thejellyfish.nz. ✆ **03/540-2028.** NZ$24–NZ$39. Daily 9am–3pm.

ABEL TASMAN NATIONAL PARK & GOLDEN BAY

Mārahau: 67km (42 miles) NW of Nelson; Tākaka: 109km (68 miles) NW of Nelson

Abel Tasman may be New Zealand's smallest national park, but it is arguably one of its most beautiful. It protects 22,530 hectares (about 56,000 acres) of coastline, offering limestone and sandstone cliffs and coves, golden-sand beaches, and forested headlands. The village of **Mārahau** is directly at the park's southern entrance, but nearby **Kaiteriteri** offers more accommodation and services. Both are just over an hour's drive from Nelson.

Farther north, Golden Bay sits peacefully beyond the tight twists and turns of Tākaka "Hill," which is a misnomer at best. After tackling the 791m (2,595-ft.) mountain pass, you'll be rewarded with forested parks, golden beaches, and endless beauty. (The northern entrance to Abel Tasman National Park is also here.) The population—which explodes during the summer months with "van-lifers" and tourists—is an interesting mix of dairy farmers, amateur and professional artists, and those wanting a back-to-nature lifestyle.

Essentials

ARRIVING & GETTING AROUND

You'll have no trouble reaching Kaiteriteri from Nelson without a car, either by tour operator or regular bus service. But going "over the hill" to Golden Bay is one trip you'll want to make by car; bus service can be limited or non-existent, and flights are expensive and weather dependent.

BY PLANE **Golden Bay Air** has direct scheduled flights to Tākaka from both Karamea and Wellington (goldenbayair.co.nz; ✆ **03/525-8725**). They also hire cars.

BY CAR To reach Kaiteriteri or Maharau from Nelson, turn right just after Riwaka (don't go over Tākaka Hill). The trip takes just over an hour. The trip from Nelson to Tākaka in Golden Bay via SH60 takes about 2 hours and includes the long, steep, winding Tākaka Hill.

BY COACH (BUS) **ScenicNZ Abel Tasman** (scenicnzabeltasman.co.nz; ✆ **03/548-0285**) operates year-round service from Nelson to Kaiteriteri and Mārahau. **Golden Bay Coachlines** (goldenbaycoachlines.co.nz; ✆ **03/525-8352**) operates a service to Motueka, Tākaka, Collingwood, and the Heaphy Track. **The Better Bus** (betterbus.co.nz; ✆ **027/577-6975**) runs from Nelson or Motueka to Kaiteriteri and Mārahau for NZ$20/$40; its schedules align with water taxi services. Some bus routes—particularly those beyond the Tākaka Hill—only operate in the summer.

Abel Tasman National Park

Abel Tasman is the jewel among New Zealand's most popular national parks. It's a walker's and sea kayaker's paradise and has world-class swimming beaches.

The 60km (37-mile) **Abel Tasman Coast Track** ♥♥♥, one of DOC's 13 Great Walks, takes 3 to 5 days to complete. Those short on time can do a portion of the track in a half or full day by using a pre-booked water taxi service to return to their starting point. **Wilsons Abel Tasman** (abeltasman.co.nz; ✆ **03/528-20270**) offers exceptional 3- or 5-day guided walk options from NZ$1,650. Nights are spent in the family's beachfront homesteads, a unique experience in NZ national parks. The family has lived in the area for eight generations, and the company has a fine array of other walking, kayaking, and cruise options. Ask them to recommend you an itinerary to suit.

Abel Tasman Kayaks ♥, 273 Sandy Bay, Mārahau (abeltasmankayaks.co.nz; ✆ **03/527-8022**), pioneered sea kayaking in this region. Full- and multi-day guided excursions may include walks or seal spotting, or both. Prices range from NZ$150 for a half-day guided tour to approximately NZ$1,800 for a 5-day, fully catered kayak-camping tour. Round-trip bus transport from Motueka or Nelson is available for an extra fee.

Abel Tasman Aqua Taxi, 275 Sandy Bay Rd., Mārahau (aquataxi.co.nz; ✆ **03/527-8083**), offers half and full-day excursions starting from Tōtaranui, Mārahau, and Kaiteriteri, which explore various portions of the park, including a self-guided visit to Awaroa Lodge (see below) for lunch. If you're short

Paddling a double-hulled canoe, a tour group with Waka Abel Tasman learns about Māori customs while exploring the national park's coastal waters.

on time, do the 3-hour scenic cruise (NZ$124) so you don't miss seeing this spectacular unspoiled coast. Be sure to sit up front next to the driver, who will fill you in on the local history.

With **Waka Abel Tasman ♥♥♥** (wakaabeltasman.nz; ✆ **027/527-8160**), your immersion into Māori culture starts before you even board the *waka* (double-hulled canoe) with a traditional *hongi* (nose touch) greeting. Lee-Anne and Todd Jago's tours of the Abel Tasman shoreline—including half-day trips to Split Apple Rock—are more of a cultural-experience-on-water than a conventional paddling trip. You'll learn the *tikanga* (etiquette) associated with *waka,* have a chance to blow the *pūtātara* (shell trumpet), and practice *waka* (salutes)—which are similar to a *haka* on water. Tours start at NZ$110 adults, NZ$70 for kids ages 2 to 14, and NZ$310 for a family of four.

WHERE TO STAY AROUND THE NATIONAL PARK

Abel Tasman Lodge ♥♥ Decorated with the blues and golds of the park's sea, beach, and sky, this lodge is just 400m from the southern park entrance. There's little that owners Tina and Glen haven't thought of: Weber grills are available for use, as are outdoor games, a shoe-wash station for dirty hiking boots, and a gorgeous massage studio for all your post-adventure aches. The highlight, though, is the secluded hot tub, which offers views of the national park. Rooms range in size, with studios, family chalets, and one honeymoon suite available.

295 Sandy Bay Rd., Mārahau. abeltasmanlodge.co.nz. ✆ **03/527-8250.** 15 units. NZ$235–NZ$340 double. Min. 2-night stay. **Amenities:** Hot tub; kitchen w/BBQs; laundry; free Wi-Fi.

Awaroa Lodge ♥♥♥ This is quite possibly the perfect leave-it-all-behind place. The buildings are set in bush, but the wilderness stops at the door. Inside all is warm and spacious, with a fireside lounge, a library, and a restaurant. A summertime garden pizza bar has a convivial atmosphere with keen track walkers hunting down a slice. There is no road access; you arrive/depart by foot, kayak, water taxi, or aircraft. Kayaking, a wellness spa, and guided bushwalks are all here for the doing, and glowworms, fur seals, penguins, and dolphins are all here for viewing. Room sizes vary from standard up to cabin-like family units, which are decorated in bush tones.

Abel Tasman National Park. awaroalodge.co.nz. ✆ **03/528-8758.** 26 units. NZ$263–NZ$699 double. Open Oct–Apr. **Amenities:** Restaurant; pizza bar; spa; free Wi-Fi.

WHERE TO EAT AROUND THE NATIONAL PARK

The Park Café ♥♥ CAFE Since 1986, this casual cafe right at the entrance to the national park has been satisfying locals and delighting visitors with its rustic seaside charm; the third generation of Ritschnys is now getting involved. A cold beer and slices of wood-fired pizza in the shady, attractive garden bar will definitely hit the spot after your walk. The cafe is scattered with art by local carvers, who've also made some of the tables and chairs. Owners Jane and Yirka grow much of the cafe's produce in their own gardens nearby, and diners' food waste is put back to work as compost. There's regular live music with packed dance floors, and if you're lucky you'll catch one of the Park's popular Thursday Open Mic Nights, where locals come out to shine on stage.

350 Sandy Bay Rd., Mārahau. parkcafe.co.nz. ✆ **03/527-8270.** Main courses NZ$29–NZ$32. Thurs–Tues 8:30am–8pm, pizza from 4pm.

Waterfront by Toad Hall ♥ CAFE Order food from the beach?! The team at Motueka icon **Toad Hall** ♥♥, 502 High St. South (toadhallmotueka.co.nz; ✆ **03/528-6456**), has taken their busy family whole-food garden-to-table success and applied it to this new beachside brunch (+ dinner in summer) venture, with a fresh wood-and-white interior and a good-size outdoor patio overlooking the ocean. It offers the classics: eggs, fish, burgers, and tostadas. Reservations aren't required. Even better, while you're sunning yourself on the sand, you can head to the website and click to order food to collect.

1 Kaiteriteri-Sandy Bay Rd., Kaiteriteri. waterfrontbytoadhall.co.nz. ✆ **03/527-8507.** Main courses NZ$20–NZ$32. Daily 8am–4pm (check website for evening hours in summer).

Golden Bay

With a resident population of only 1,430, Golden Bay's main town, **Tākaka,** is known for attracting long-term barefoot visitors who are interested in organic farming, intentional communities, sustainable and natural living, and alternative medicine. **Collingwood,** 28km (17 miles) north, is even smaller and features lovely buildings from the turn of the century, though it has fewer visitor amenities. Part of the area's draw is the weather; it's incredibly mild here. Nevertheless, tourism all but shuts down in July and August; conversely, from December until February, line-ups are long and vacancies rare. Plan your visit accordingly.

GOLDEN BAY'S caves of wonder

Cave formations are common in the Golden Bay area. One of the most famous, **Harwood's Hole,** plummets 176m (577 ft.) from the top of the Tākaka Hill. While you can access its perimeter via a slow drive followed by a long hike, it's not possible to peer down the "hole" without abseiling. Go to nearby **Ngārua Caves** ♥ (ngaruacaves.co.nz; ✆ **03/528-8093**) instead, which offers tours that reveal stalactites and moa bones. It's open from 10am to 4pm (NZ$30 adults, NZ$15 ages 5–15) October to May, by appointment only June to September.

There are two other (free) cave systems worth investigating, both managed by DOC. The massive cave mouth and impressive, rare phytokarst stalagmites of **Rawhiti Caves** ♥ (meaning "sunrise" in Māori) will take you an hour's hike from the carpark. You need to be agile for this outing, and it's not recommended for small children. It's signposted near the end of Packard Road between Tākaka and Pōhara Beach.

The 3-hour **Aorere Goldfields Track** ♥ loop outside Collingwood will take you past **Stafford's Cave** and the **Ballroom Cave,** the latter of which was allegedly used as a venue for dances in the 1880s. For the full experience, come armed with a headlamp and shoes with good tractions.

The surrounding area, starting at Abel Tasman National Park's northern entrance, is rich in natural attractions, notably **Te Waikoropupū Springs** ♥♥ (Pūpū Springs, if you want to sound like a local). The water is said to be among the clearest in the world, though swimming is prohibited; it's *tāpū* (sacred). Its walkway is signposted just north of Tākaka township, with the loop taking about 45 minutes to complete.

New Zealand's first free, non-commercial, publicly accessible **Via Ferrata** (viaferrata.org.nz) opened on Tākaka Hill in November 2024 and has proven extremely popular. You don't need climbing experience for this fixed-rope climbing route, and it's suitable for kids, too. You can hire gear at Ngarua Caves Shop (ngaruacaves.co.nz; ✆ **03/528-8093;** 3 hr. for NZ$8, under-18s free), but demand is high and there are only 23 sets, so it's best to either reserve it by phoning ahead, or renting it for NZ$25 from the **Gearshop** outlets near Nelson (gearshop.co.nz; ✆ **03/547–7081;** in Richmond at 213 Queen St. or in Tāhunanui at 53 Bolt Rd.).

One of the most popular family bushwalks in the region is the easy 90-minute round-trip walk to **Wainui Falls** ♥♥, with lots of swimming holes along the way. The parking lot is signposted 20km (12 miles) northeast of Tākaka. Kids also love **Labyrinth Rocks** ♥♥, at the end of Scott Road, where locals have hidden toys and figurines among the maze-like limestone formations, making for the ultimate game of "I Spy."

Tōtaranui Beach ♥♥♥ in Abel Tasman National Park, about an hour east of Tākaka, is a barely believable stretch of soft golden sand. It's one of Golden Bay's most beautiful swimming beaches, and the drive to get there is among the most scenic—but the road is narrow and winding, so take care.

Via Ferrata's fixed-rope course allows non-climbers to scale Tākaka Hill for expansive views of the Golden Bay area. See p. 387 for details.

If **Wharariki Beach ♥♥** looks familiar to you, that's because it's one of the Microsoft Windows screensavers, notable for its immense carved limestone cliffs and caves. It faces west, where the Tasman Sea can be a roar of hammering surf or (occasionally) as flat as a millpond, but be warned: This is a beach for walkers, *not* swimmers. The carpark is a 20-minute drive from Collingwood; the beach is a 20-minute walk from there. Visit at low tide and on a calm (read: not windy) day to take in the whole beach.

Neighboring **Farewell Spit ♥♥** is a unique sandbank reaching in a gentle 26km (16-mile) curve out into Golden Bay. Its dunes are huge but fragile, and full of migratory birds. **Farewell Spit Eco Tours,** 6 Tasman St., Collingwood (farewellspit.com; ✆ **03/524-8257**), is the only operator with a permit to visit the gannet colony and inter-tidal plain. Tours are 2- to 6½-hour tours and cost from NZ$210 adults, NZ$65 kids.

WHERE TO STAY AROUND GOLDEN BAY

The Golden Bay area is well provided with backpacker hostels and Airbnb options. **Anatoki Lodge Motel,** 87 Commercial St. (the main drag), Tākaka (anatokimotels.co.nz; ✆ **03/525-8047;** NZ$160–NZ$220 nightly), may have dated furnishings, but it's centrally located, clean, and all the rooms have kitchen facilities. The newer **Collingwood Park Motel,** 1 Tasman St.,

Collingwood (collingwoodpark.co.nz; ✆ **03/524-8499;** NZ$185–NZ$285), offers double, studio, and family units with kitchen facilities. The motel is a short drive to Farewell Spit and Wharariki Beach.

For something a little higher-end, the light, bright, beachy **Ratanui Lodge ♥♥**, 818 Abel Tasman Dr., Pōhara (ratanuilodge.com; ✆ **03/525-7998**), is located right off Pōhara Beach, where you have a chance to see *kororā,* little blue penguins. There's a swimming pool and hot tub, and a good restaurant with cocktails (including tasting paddles of locally produced gin), but its biggest selling feature is its accommodating staff. Rooms are NZ$445 to NZ$860, including an a la carte breakfast.

WHERE TO EAT AROUND GOLDEN BAY

The place to eat in Tākaka is **The Wholemeal Café ♥♥**, 60 Commercial St. (wholemealcafe.co.nz; ✆ **03/525-9426**), which has operated inside a former movie theater since 1977, essentially the birth of modern Tākaka's alternative culture. (We recommend also buying their cookbooks, if only for the Green Salad Dressing recipe; it's a cult favorite.) Not far away, **The Dangerous Kitchen ♥♥**, 46 Commercial St. (dangerouskitchen.info; ✆ **03/525-8686**), has excellent pizzas—we like their Popeye, packed with spinach, mushrooms, feta cheese, and kalamata olives.

Nearly everyone in town frequents the alternative **Roots Bar ♥♥♥**, 1 Commercial St. (rootsbar.co.nz; ✆ **03/525-9592;** daily 11am–late), which is known for its consistently delicious burgers. It's typically open daily year-round, with live music.

It's a mission to get to **Toto's Café & Pizzeria ♥**, 400 Tōtaranui Rd. (facebook.com/totoscafepizzeria; ✆ **03/970-7934**), east of Tākaka near Wainui Bay, with a long drive up a gravel road. Most of the year it's open on Sundays only, weather permitting (from Dec–Feb it's open daily except Fri, again weather permitting). But it's a quintessentially Golden Bay experience, where the wood-fired pizzas are prepared in an off-grid, eco-friendly cob building. Soak it all in while gazing at Wainui Inlet as bellbirds and tūī swoop through the surrounding gardens.

The Mussel Inn ♥♥, 1259 SH60, Onekaka (musselinn.co.nz; ✆ **03/525-9241;** daily 11am–late), has been well-loved by locals since 1992, with a "take us as you find us" motto. It brews its own beer, cider, and soft drinks (try a pint of the Captain Cooker mānuka beer, originally brewed by Cook to prevent scurvy), and has communal seating, inexpensive food, live poetry nights and thumping good live music too, often original singer-songwriters. It's halfway between Tākaka and Collingwood. The old cellphones crucified on a post in the garden bar are exactly what Golden Bay is all about.

WEST COAST & THE GLACIERS

12

There's no disputing that the West Coast/Te Tai Poutini is a region unlike anywhere else in the country. It's more length than breadth, with its natural resources and beauty locked between the Tasman Sea on one side and the long chain of the Southern Alps on the other. It's a place where mighty rivers rush out to sea, glaciers creep toward the coast, and waves pound on long sweeps of empty beach. Between its rich history and the colorful characters who make their home here, you'd be hard-pressed to find anything slick or superficial on the West Coast.

Greenstone/pounamu was the first treasure found along the West Coast's wild shores, and it's still the best place in the country to buy contemporary jade carvings. Gold, coal, and timber have also shaped the region's history and continue to figure prominently in what you'll experience here—as will "Coasters," the self-reliant locals.

More than anything, though, the dramatic landscape is what attracts visitors. More than 80% of the land is protected, with 5 of the country's 13 national parks, a World Heritage Area, and rare wildlife sanctuaries located wholly or partially in the region. The West Coast's rainforests contain more native bush than you'll see anywhere else in the country, and are well sustained by the notoriously high rainfall. For this reason, if you've got a helicopter flight, hike, or distance bike ride on the agenda, prepare for plans to change if visiting in the wetter spring months of September to December. (The driest months are Feb, Mar, and Aug.) Regardless of when you visit, bring a raincoat, lots of insect repellent, and a sense of humor; you'll need all three. The tiny biting sandfly insects are brutal, especially if it's about to rain—which is usually not far away on the West Coast.

Essentials

ARRIVING

BY PLANE **OriginAir** (originair.co.nz; ✆ **0800/380-380** in NZ) has direct service to Westport from Wellington, flying four times per week. **Air New Zealand** (airnewzealand.co.nz; ✆ **0800/737-000** in NZ) has air service between Hokitika and Christchurch; to get to Greymouth from there, book a shuttle (NZ$50) with **Greymouth Taxis** (greymouthtaxis.co.nz/airport-shuttle; ✆ **03/768-7078**). **Golden Bay Air** (goldenbayair.co.nz; ✆ **03/525-8725**) serves

West Coast

0
50 mi
0
50 km
Auckland
NORTH ISLAND
Area of detail
Wellington
Christchurch
SOUTH ISLAND
Dunedin
Karamea
Kahurangi National Park
Little Wanganui
Kawatiri
St. Arnaud
Mōkihinui
Seddonville
Murchison
Nelson Lakes N.P.
Granity
Waimangaroa
Inangahua
Westport
Cape Foulwind
Reefton
Charleston
Springs Jct.
Paparoa N.P.
Ikamatua
Punakaiki
Barrytown
Lake Sumner F.P.
Blackball
Nelson Creek
Runanga
Moana
Taramakau R.
Greymouth
Arthur's Pass N.P.
L. Brunner
Kumara
Otira
Arthur's Pass
Hokitika
L. Kaniere
Craigieburn F.P.
Ross
Hokitika Gorge
TASMAN SEA
L. Coleridge
Harihari
Aoraki/Mt. Cook National Park
Abut Head
Whataroa
Ōkārito
Westland/Tai Poutini National Park
Franz Josef/Waiau
Fox Glacier Village
Malte Brun
Gillespies Beach
Aoraki/Mt. Cook
L. Tekapō
Fairlie
Aoraki/Mt. Cook Village
Lake Tekapō
Heretaniwha Pt.
L. Pukaki
Twizel
Lake Ōhau Alpine Village
L. Benmore
Haast
L. Ōhau
Ōmarama
Jackson Bay
Okuru
Haast Pass
Makarora
Mt. Aspiring National Park
Jackson Bay
L. Hāwea
Cascade Pt.
L. Wānaka
Mt. Aspiring
Wānaka
Tarras
Awarua Pt.
Big Bay
Cromwell
Arrowtown
Clyde
Alexandra
Yates Pt.
Fiordland National Park
Queenstown
SOUTHERN ALPS
6
63
65
7
73
8
83
85

passengers walking the Heaphy Track, with its flights between Karamea and Tākaka. Flights only operate with a minimum of two passengers.

BY TRAIN Greymouth is perhaps most well-known as the end (or start) point for the **TranzAlpine** ♥♥ (greatjourneysnz.com; ✆ **0800/872-467** in NZ) railway. The famous 4½-hour journey runs between Christchurch and Greymouth, carrying passengers through the Southern Alps' high-alpine passes, including past braided rivers and waterfalls. The most popular direction is to travel from Christchurch to Greymouth, although you can travel either way or round-trip. One-way fares start at NZ$249 per person. If you're weighing up this option against renting a car or taking a bus, be aware that the train only stops briefly at Arthur's Pass. Both the road and train follow roughly the same route and similar views, but it's easier to admire them from the train's viewing carriages. It's also possible to connect to bus routes throughout the region.

BY COACH (BUS) **InterCity** (intercity.co.nz; ✆ **03/365-1113**) offers routes to/from all main South Island centers including Nelson, Queenstown, Westport, Greymouth, Hokitika, the Glaciers, Haast, and Wānaka. **East West Coaches** (eastwestcoaches.co.nz; ✆ **027201-8825**) has a daily shuttle service to/from Christchurch, Westport, Reefton, Punakaiki, and Greymouth.

En Route to the West Coast: Murchison

Technically in the Nelson/Tasman region, the inland town of Murchison is conveniently halfway between Nelson and Westport. If your prime objective in the area is to fish, kayak, or raft, it's well worth a stop, as it straddles the Upper Buller Gorge. While much smaller than Westport, Murchison (pop. 490) does have a little grocery store, cafes, and accommodation.

It's also where you can find a sight unique in the world: a pocket of fire burning perpetually in the forest at the **Natural Flames Experience** ♥♥, 47 Waller St. (naturalflames.co.nz; ✆ **027/698-7244**). After being picked up in Murchison, you'll travel by 4WD and then walk a forest path wreathing through ancient beech forests. Once you reach the flames—fueled by natural gas seeping from the ground—you'll use them to prepare tea and pancakes with beechdew honey. The daily tour, which runs from early October through April, takes 4 hours and costs NZ$125 for adults and NZ$85 for children, with a maximum group size of seven.

Murchison is also only a 30-minute drive from the area's top attraction: **Lake Rotoroa** in **Nelson Lakes National Park** ♥♥, an area known for its tramping and mountain biking. Visit doc.govt.nz for detailed walking maps and an updated list of outfitters operating within the park.

OUTDOOR PURSUITS

JETBOATING & SWINGBRIDGE **The Buller Canyon Jet** ♥, SH6, Murchison (bullercanyonjet.co.nz; ✆ **03/523-9883**), offers the best-priced jetboat ride in NZ, at only NZ$125 (NZ$75 kids 14 and under, NZ$370 two adults and three children). On a 40-minute trip, you'll travel at speeds of up to 85km per hour (53mph) and do plenty of V8-powered spins. Jetboats depart

The Murchison area is known for its superb trout fishing, with top lodges like the Eleven Owen River Lodge (p. 394) catering to anglers.

from the **Buller Gorge Swingbridge Adventure & Heritage Park** (bullergorge.co.nz; ✆ **03/523-9809**), home to NZ's longest swingbridge and a "Comet Line" zipline ride. That's NZ$40 for adults and NZ$20 for children, and the swingbridge is NZ$12.50 and NZ$5 respectively. It's affordable, but remember that you're in a country loaded with swingbridges that are completely free to walk across.

MOUNTAIN BIKING Following a once-forgotten miners' trail from the 1870s, the **Old Ghost Road ♥♥♥** is one of the area's premiere mountain bike tracks. An 84km (52-mile), grade 4 trail, it starts in Lyell (about 30 min. west of Murchison on SH6) and ends near Seddonville on the coast. In its entirety, the journey takes 2 to 5 days. Bookings for the track's huts and campsites must be made in advance through oldghostroad.org.nz. For guided experiences and bike rentals, the site also lists reputable outfitters and tour operators.

WHITEWATER RAFTING & KAYAKING Murchison is one of the country's few whitewater destinations, known for its Earthquake Rapids, which are a grade 3 or 4, dependent on the water level. There are two operators of note: **Wild Rivers Rafting ♥♥** (wildriversrafting.co.nz; ✆ **022/698-1245**) and **Ultimate Descents ♥♥**, 38 Waller St., Murchison (rivers.co.nz; ✆ **03/523-9899**). Both offer 4-hour tours for NZ$180 for adults, though Wild Rafting also offers discounts for groups of three or more. Ultimate Descents's family tour is a little more kid-friendly, as it only goes down Class 2 rapids and is suitable for children as young as 5. (Kids cost NZ$160.) Unfortunately, there aren't any kayak or canoe operators that offer guided tours, but if you're a skilled paddler, the **New Zealand Kayak School ♥♥**, 111 Waller St., Murchison (nzkayakschool.com; ✆ **03/352-5786**), offers gear rental. (Inquire for rates.) The school is also renowned country-wide for multi-day instruction, including its 4-day intro to whitewater kayaking course, which starts at NZ$1,195.

WHERE TO STAY & EAT IN MURCHISON

Head to the **Cow Shed Restaurant ♥**, 37 Waller St. (lazycow.co.nz/eating; ✆ **03/523-9523;** daily 4pm–9pm, closed July–Aug), for your most reliable fill of food, namely pizza. The newest accommodation in town, **Grand Suites Murchison ♥♥** (grandsuitesmurchison.co.nz; ✆ **03/663-2030**), offers modern and well-equipped suites with views of the surrounding ranges. It has king studios and multi-bedroom suites with kitchenettes starting from NZ$175. The **Murchison Motorhome Park ♥**, just north of town on SH6 (murchisonmotorhomepark.co.nz; ✆ **027/482-6199**), has clean and updated facilities to accompany its small $75 cabins—but be forewarned that its gates close promptly at 8pm.

The **Eleven Owen River Lodge** ♥♥, 173 Owen Valley Rd. E (eleven experience.com; ✆ **03/523-9075**), is one of the best fishing lodges in New Zealand, a multi-award-winning luxury country retreat, with customizable fly-fishing packages, including cottage accommodation decorated with natural textures, such as wool blankets and rattan armchairs, three-course meals, and guided fishing excursions. You'll enjoy happy hour and then eat with the other guests over dinner, a convivial way to discuss the day's catch (or the ones that got away).

Maruia River Retreat ♥♥♥ Not to be confused with Maruia Hot Springs (which are nearly an hour farther south, but also along the Maruia River; see chapter 13), this all-inclusive luxury wellness retreat has become its own destination, with morning yoga sessions, organic food, therapeutic spa and massage treatments, and guided forest walks. Its strong environmental credentials include battery-powered everything, charged from its own micro-hydro system. Run by two yoga teachers, the seven private villas are set within a 500-acre "state of nature" estate, the perfect setting for forest bathing. We mean that literally: Their hot tub and sauna are surrounded by moss and native rainforest. Its location along the main road is both a blessing and a curse—it's not a massive trek to get here, but there is some noise from traffic. Luckily, you'll probably be too blissed out to notice it.

SH65, 35km (22 miles) S of Murchison. maruia.co.nz. ✆ **03/523-9323.** 7 units. NZ$1,250–NZ$1,850. Rates typically include breakfast, dinner, and yoga. Inquire for special packages. **Amenities:** Kitchenettes; hot tub; Finnish sauna; infrared sauna; spa; walking tracks; Wi-Fi (free in main areas only).

Even the hot tub at Maruia River Retreat is designed to immerse guests in nature.

WESTPORT

Westport: 101km (63 miles) N of Greymouth; 226km (140 miles) SW of Nelson

If you're traveling from Nelson south on SH6, Westport will likely make its way onto your itinerary as your first stopping point on the West Coast. It's the region's second-largest town, and for those with ample time to explore, it holds a few surprises, including a rich history of mining, a chance to meet some unforgettable West Coast personalities, and a rafting tour deep through underground caves. It's also the only gateway to remote and beautiful natural treasures 90 minutes farther north, near the village of Karamea. But if you're keen to get straight to the glaciers or have limited time, drive south to Greymouth or Hokitika instead.

Essentials

By car, the drive from Nelson to Westport via Buller Gorge (SH6) takes approximately 3½ hours; it takes about 2 hours to drive to/from Greymouth via SH6 (also signposted as the Great Coast Rd.). The drive from Christchurch via Lewis Pass and the Buller Gorge takes 4 hours.

VISITOR INFORMATION

The **Westport isite Information Centre,** 123 Palmerston St. (westport.nz; ✆ **03/789-6658**), is open in summer daily from 9am to 5pm. In winter, it's open 9am to 4:30pm weekdays and 10am to 4pm weekends.

Exploring Westport

Westport is built around the mouth of the Buller River, a stretch of water that draws adventure-seekers. But back in the 1860s, Westport first attracted prospectors searching for gold, and later for "black gold" (coal). To learn more about the region's mining history, you can visit the small but well-presented **Museum of Kawatiri ♥**, 123 Palmerston St. (pounamupathway.com/kawatiri; ✆ **03/789-6658**). Open daily from 9am to 5pm (NZ$25 adults, NZ$5 children 5–15), it's in the town's isite, just beside the **Clock Tower Chambers,** a striking early-20th-century building on the main strip that's impossible to miss.

But if there's anything to know about the West Coast's history, it's that brewing and mining go hand-in-hand. Started in 1950 as a miners' brewery, **Shortjaw Brewing ♥**, 10 Lyndhurst St. (shortjaw.co.nz; ✆ **03/789-4079**), is the last privately owned brewery in the region. The name refers to the adult whitebait fish. One of its co-owners is a beer writer, who has helped craft a new range of beers made entirely from South Island–grown malt and hops. Its taproom is open Wednesday through Saturday from noon until 7pm.

Westport is also home to a seal colony at **Tauranga Bay,** about 15 minutes south of town, where there are a number of short walking tracks.

Westport's beaches attract surfers, and Bazil's Hostel & Surf School (p. 396) gets them ready to ride the waves.

Another one of the town's more popular activities is surfing. Murals and paintings cover nearly every surface at the homey **Bazil's Hostel & Surf School ♥♥**, 54–56 Russell St. (bazils.com; ✆ **03/789-6410**). One of the owners is a surfing champion, and the hostel is an eclectic enclave of adventure enthusiasm that offers surf and yoga, SUP tours, bikes for hire, and more (see below for lodging info). The accredited surf school has daily lessons (from NZ$90) or board and wetsuit hire (NZ$45). For lessons at the area's beaches, contact surf coach Mark Perana at **Westcoast Surf ♥**, 299 Tauranga Bay Rd. (wcsurf.co.nz; ✆ **027/255-2651**). He offers gear hire (you're going to want a wetsuit) as well as 2-hour group lessons for NZ$90 per person.

In Denniston, on a subalpine plateau 25km (15 miles) northeast of Westport, coal was discovered in 1861. By 1879, it was being delivered to a rail terminus at the base of the plateau, down grades as steep as 80%, by a feat of engineering: the **Denniston Incline,** where full coal trucks going down simultaneously pulled a line that hauled wagons uphill. Apart from a rough path, these wagons were the only way residents could reach the settlement until the mine shut in the late 1960s. The Denniston Experience is no longer in operation (though you may still see signs for it), but several walking trails with interpretative panels—ranging from 30 minutes to 4 hours in length—will guide you past the site's many relics. For a guided experience that will shuttle you to the top of the plateau, contact **Outwest Tours ♥♥** (outwest.co.nz; ✆ **0800/688-937**), which offers a 5-hour small group tour departing at 9:30am from the Westport isite. It costs NZ$150.

Where to Stay in & Around Westport

Your best bet in Westport is one of the many motels along Palmerston St. or the Esplanade. Otherwise, the **TripInn Hostel,** 72 McQueen St. (tripinn.co.nz; ✆ **03/789-7367**), offers dorm beds (NZ$35) and private rooms (from NZ$90) in an 1860s building, now protected under the NZ Historic Places Trust. The homey **Bazil's Hostel & Surf School**, 54-56 Russell St. (bazils.com; ✆ **03/789-6410**), has a chill vibe. Kitchen, barbecue, and lounge facilities are shared. In addition to dorm beds (NZ$45), there are self-contained doubles (NZ$100), a self-contained apartment (NZ$130), and campervan and tent sites. See above for Bazil's adventure-oriented offerings.

Near Seddonville, there's **Gentle Annie Seaside Accommodation and Campground ♥♥**, 298 De Malmanches Rd., Mokihinui (gentleannie.co.nz; ✆ **027/418-8587**). It isn't close to much, really, but sometimes that's the point. In addition to the campground (unpowered sites NZ$16, powered sites NZ$21), there are well-equipped and homey cottages (NZ$125–NZ$200) and micro-cabins (NZ$45) nestled in the native bush, and just a short walk to the beach. There's also an on-site coffee shop in a former milk shed, with fresh goods baked daily, and private wood-fired hot tubs.

At **Carters Beach**, near Cape Foulwind, there are also a selection of Airbnbs and baches to rent; try **Carters by the Sea Beachside Studio Apartments ♥♥**, 27 Marine Parade (cartersbythesea.nz; ✆ **021/119-2573**). The apartments are spacious and quiet, and handy to the family-friendly **Donaldos**

Cafe and Beach Bar, 23 Marine Parade (donaldoscafe.co.nz; ✆ **03/7897409**), next door. While out this way, dine nearby at the **Star Tavern,** 6 Lighthouse Rd. (startavern.co.nz; ✆ **03/789-6923**), which offers the likes of chicken or beef burgers for NZ$26 or pork schnitzel (NZ$35).

Where to Eat in Westport

This is the land of cold beers and hot pies, so it's only fitting that the most popular joint in Westport is the **West Coast Pie Company** ♥♥, 285 Palmerstone St. (westcoastpies.co.nz; Tues–Sat 7am–3pm), which specializes in homemade wild game pies, like honey and mānuka smoked wild pork, spiced wild nanny goat, or venison steak and cheese. It puts just as much love into its inventive daily salads, like spiced carrot with lentils served with a tahini sumac dressing. For dinner, **Denniston Dog** ♥, 18 Wakefield St. (denniston dog.co.nz; ✆ **03/789-5030;** weekdays 10am–3am, weekends 9am–3am), is known for its fish and chips, but it's also got veggie and gluten-free options

KARAMEA

96km (60 miles) NE of Westport

The coastal road north from Westport ends at the settlement of Karamea (pop. 567). Many tourists don't venture farther north than Westport, lending this little town its off-the-beaten-track vibe—even though it's actually at the start (or end) point for the **Heaphy Track,** a literal beaten path. Some might call it sleepy; others will call it secluded. If you think you'll fall into the second category, Karamea's relative isolation will pay off in dividends, with ample opportunities to surf, cycle, or kayak; explore its limestone cave systems in **Kahurangi National Park;** or just relax and walk along the beach.

Essentials

Self-driving is the best way to explore this area of the West Coast. Karamea is 96km (60 miles) north of Westport, but you should budget 1½ to 2 hours for the drive; at least 25km (15 miles) of roadway is steep and winding, especially over the Karamea Bluff. **Karamea Express** buses (karameaexpress.co.nz; ✆ **03/782-6757**) travel regularly from Westport. Drop-offs can be made in town or at the start of the Heaphy Track. Bookings are essential.

VISITOR INFORMATION

The township has a handful of stores (including a small Four Square supermarket), gas station, and cafes. The **Karamea Information Centre,** 106 Bridge St. (karameainfo.co.nz; ✆ **03/782-6652**), is open Monday to Friday from 9am to 4pm, and on Saturdays from 9am to 1pm.

Exploring Karamea

Most travelers spend just a night in Karamea before hiking the **Heaphy Track** (see below), but if you've got a few spare days, it's well worth exploring Kahurangi National Park's **Oparara Basin,** about a 35-minute drive from town. Once there, a visit to the **Oparara Arch** ♥, should be at the top of your

Grasslands along the Heaphy Track.

list. One of the biggest limestone arches in the southern hemisphere, it's an easy 20-minute walk—but be prepared for a geological wonder that resembles more of a tunnel than an arch. Just over a mile farther down the road is the 5-minute path to **Crazy Paving Cave** (so named for the unusual floor pattern) and **Box Canyon** ♥. Budget at least 20 to 30 minutes to explore both, and bring a good flashlight; you'll have no problem spotting cave wētā and ancient seashells embedded in the walls. Also in the park is **Honeycomb Hill Specially Protected Area** ♥♥♥. Discovered by local cavers in 1976, it's in pristine condition, complete with *moa* (extinct ostrich-like birds) skeletons. That's why you can only gain access to this restricted area on a guided tour, such as with **Oparara Guided Tours** (oparara.co.nz; ✆ **03/782-6652**). A 2½-hour tour costs NZ$95 for adults, NZ$45 for children under 12. Longer options, with pickup in Karamea, are also available. Dress warmly and be aware that no walking sticks are allowed in the caves.

Outdoor Pursuits

FISHING The Karamea River offers good trout fishing, while surfcasters can try their luck between Flagstaff and North Beach, or from Fisherman's Rock at the southern end of Scott's Beach. Visitors between September 1 and November 14 have the opportunity to try a uniquely Kiwi foraging hobby: netting whitebait on a tidal river. Contact **Fish & Game NZ** (fishandgame.org.nz; ✆ **04/499-4767**) to purchase an appropriate license and for regulations.

MOUNTAIN BIKING Karamea's Heaphy Track is one of only two Great Walks in the country that allows mountain bikers. Needless to say, it's a popular sport in the area with many designated paths. Inquire at the info center for bicycle hire, tours, and suggested routes.

RAFTING The Karamea River is one of the best rivers in the country for whitewater paddling, with Class 3, 4 and 5 rapids—although some of the best portions can only be accessed by helicopter. For experienced paddlers, **Ultimate Descents ♥♥**, 38 Waller St., Murchison (rivers.co.nz; ✆ **03/523-9899**), has a 1-day heli-rafting experience on the technical lower gorge's Class 5 rapids deep in Kahurangi National Park (NZ$650, ages 15 and up).

WALKING & TRAMPING There are two major hikes in this area: the famous **Heaphy Track ♥♥♥** and the more difficult-to-access **Wangapeka Track,** which is for expert trampers only. Both tracks take about 4 days. Like all other Great Walks, Heaphy Track has huts and campsites along the route, but they must be booked and paid for in advance. Huts on the Wangapeka Track are available on a first-come, first-served basis and require hut tickets, which are available from DOC info centers and some outdoor outfitters. (Visit doc.govt.nz for a full list of backcountry hut ticket retailers.) For something a little less time-consuming, there's the 40-minute **Nīkau Walk.** Drive to the Kōhaihai River mouth at the start of the Heaphy Track. It's a loop walk that's suitable for all ages.

Where to Stay & Eat in Karamea

Eating options are limited in Karamea, yet the food that you will find isn't lacking, owing to hikers coming off the trails who want good tucker and a cold beer. The **Karamea Village Hotel's restaurant ♥**, corner of Waverley Street and Wharf Road (karameahotel.co.nz; ✆ **03/782-6800**), is an archetypal NZ country pub (est. 1876) with a menu and daily blackboard specials to match. Expect NZ home-cooked classics such as roast meats, whitebait, and lamb.

With studio, one-bedroom, and two-bedroom units, **Karamea River Motels ♥**, 31 Bridge St. (karameamotels.co.nz; ✆ **03/782-6955**), is suited to families or travelers aiming to spend a few days in the area (NZ$129–NZ$149 double).

The wryly named the **Last Resort ♥**, 71 Waverley St. (lastresort.co.nz; ✆ **03/782-6617**), is anything but. It has eco-friendly accommodations to suit

The eco-friendly Last Resort in Karamea welcomes diners and overnight guests.

all budgets, including backpacker dorm rooms (NZ$37), lodge rooms with shared bathrooms (NZ$74) or private baths (NZ$107), studios with kitchenettes (NZ$130), and self-contained cottages (NZ$155–NZ$170). Facilities include laundry, a guest kitchen, and a full-service restaurant. It's also one of the best places in town to eat. In the morning, you can find fresh baked goods, while in the evening daily specials include dishes such as lemon pepper crusted snapper fillet with chorizo potatoes and hollandaise, or pasta with homemade coriander pesto. (If you have an allergy to cats, be forewarned that some friendly felines like to frequent the dining area.)

PUNAKAIKI

The drive south from Westport has some of the best coastal views in the country, reminiscent of Australia's Great Ocean Road. It's filled with dramatic limestone cliffs, towering bluffs, and dense subtropical forest, and it's hard not to stop constantly for photos. (There are only a few viewpoints, so if you see one approaching, be sure to safely pull over.)

Midway between Westport and Greymouth, **Punakaiki** is less of a town and more of a collection of hotels, alongside an info center and a solitary cafe. There's no gas station, grocery store, or even reliable cell phone service, so arrive prepared.

The reason most travel here is to see the **Pancake Rocks and Blowholes ♥♥**. Rare limestone layers formed by sea and seismic action eons ago, the natural landmark is best viewed at high tide when there is a westerly swell running; the sea surges into deep caverns before spouting high in the air. The walkway to the rocks is wide, well-maintained, and easily negotiable, although it can be busy on summer days. You only need to make a quick roadside stop to see the rocks, but Punakaiki's location at the entrance to the **Paparoa National Park ♥♥** may be reason to extend your stay. When it fully opened in 2020, the purpose-built **Paparoa Track** became the first new Great Walk in 25

Punakaiki's famed Pancake Rocks, with a small blowhole.

years—giving mountain bikers and novice hikers access across the Paparoa Ranges for the first time.

THE PAPAROA TRACK ♥♥♥

The only Great Walk purpose-built to accommodate both hikers and mountain bikers, the Paparoa Track serves as a memorial to 29 miners who died in 2010's Pike River Mine disaster. The 55km (34-mile) journey takes 3 days to hike or 2 days to cycle, passing through lush rainforest and alpine tussocks. Users stay in DOC huts, which must be booked and paid for in advance at bookings.doc.govt.nz. Although the path can be traveled in either direction, it's recommended to start from the Smoke-ho parking lot north of **Blackball,** a small former mining village. There's not much there—apart from the legendary Blackball Salami Company and **Formerly the Blackball Hilton,** 26 Hart St. (blackballhilton.co.nz; ✆ **03/732-4705**). The inn has seen better days, to put it mildly, though staying here is considered a rite of passage among Coasters. Fortunately, there are now also a handful of Airbnbs in the village.

You can also stay in Greymouth or Punakaiki and book a shuttle to the start of the track. **Paparoa Great Walk** ♥ (paparoagreatwalk.co.nz), a family-owned business, offers reliable daily transportation, gear transfers, and car relocation services. Lacking gear or know-how? **Paparoa Guided Walks** (paparoaguidedwalks.com; ✆ **027/727-2762**) has all-inclusive multi-day excursions from NZ$1,599, which includes the use of a backpack, sleeping bag, and hiking poles. If wheels are your preferred mode of transport, **Cycle Journeys** (cyclejourneys.co.nz; ✆ **03/377-2060**) will kit you out with everything you need for a self-guided 2-night excursion.

OTHER WALKS IN THE AREA

Both the **Truman Track** ♥ and the **Punakaiki Cavern Walk** ♥ (both signposted off SH6, just south of Punakaiki) take under an hour to walk and are suitable for families. Wear good shoes and bring a flashlight. The **Pororari River Track** ♥♥ starts at the bridge over the Pororari River, 1km (just over half a mile) north of the national park's visitor center. It passes through dense bush and dramatic limestone cliffs with a popular swimming hole about 15 minutes down the track. Allow 2 hours to return. For more details and other walks, visit the **Paparoa National Park Visitor Centre,** SH6 (doc.govt.nz; ✆ **03/731-1895**).

Where to Stay & Eat in Punakaiki

A number of *baches* (holiday homes) and Airbnbs are available for rental north of Punakaiki on SH6. Although some are beachfront or only a short walk from the beach, they're farther from the Pancake Rocks and best for travelers with cars. There are few places in the village that serve food, so stock up on groceries in Greymouth or Westport.

If you don't have a car or are camping, you'll find **Punakaiki Beach Camp** ♥, 5 Owen St. (punakaikibeachcamp.co.nz; ✆ **03/731-1894**), directly in the village. It offers very basic beachside accommodation, but the showers are hot, it's an easy walk to Pancake Rocks, and there's a morning coffee cart on-site.

Paparoa's Glow-in-the-Dark Caves

Underneath Paparoa National Park lies an extensive subterranean world of limestone caves. Based in Charleston, which is about halfway between Westport and Punakaiki, **UnderWorld Adventures,** SH6 (caverafting.com; ✆ **0800/116-686** in NZ, or 03/788-8168), is the only DOC-approved tour operator that can take you there. On the **Underworld Rafting ♥♥** tour, you'll be outfitted in wetsuits and float down an underground river through a maze of glowworm caves and multi-level chambers. It's a magical experience, like travelling through the night sky. Water confidence, swimwear, and a towel are required. NZ$245 adults; NZ$175 for children 16 and under; families of two adults and two children NZ$745. Other tours are available for those who want to stay dry.

Rafting through glowworm caves with UnderWorld Adventures.

Its relatively new riverfront cabins (NZ$105) are a step up: small but comfortable, with front-row views of the Paparoas. Campsites (NZ$20–NZ$24) and luxury self-contained houses (NZ$350) are also available.

Just around the corner is the village's main social hub, the **Punakaiki Tavern ♥**, at the corner of SH6 and Owen Street (punakaikitavern.co.nz; ✆ **03/731-1188**). The rooms (starting at NZ$165) are clean, but the main selling point is the cellphone reception (it's hard to come by in these parts) and the fire in the pub.

It's all about the view at the **Scenic Hotel Punakaiki ♥♥**, 4237 SH6 (scenichotelgroup.co.nz/punakaiki/scenic-hotel-punakaiki; ✆ **03/731-1168**), which is just a stone's throw from the Tasman Sea. It offers 63 rooms with ocean or garden views, a restaurant, and a bar. Rates are NZ$390 to NZ$818. Its **Ocean View Restaurant & Bar ♥** (daily 7am–late) serves a full cooked breakfast for NZ$35; the lunch menu ranges from soup (NZ$15) to beef salad (NZ$35); for dinner, expect the beef filet with blue cheese and *kūmara* (sweet potato) fries to set you back NZ$50.

As the name suggests, **Pancake Rocks Cafe Punakaiki,** 4300 Coast Rd., SH6 (pancakerockscafe.com; ✆ **03/731-1122;** Sat–Thurs 8am–10pm, Fri until 11pm), is all about pancakes, with an all-day menu featuring sweet and savory options. They're overpriced (NZ$28–NZ$33) due to their location, though this hungry writer could barely finish half her stack of bacon and banana. Pizzas, which are on the greasy side, are also available in the evenings. For just another roadside stop, it's actually a comfy place to eat in; there's even a family area in the back with couches and a piano.

En Route to Greymouth via Reefton

If you're heading down SH7 to Greymouth, schedule a rest stop in Reefton. The historic town's claim to fame is that it was the first place in the Southern Hemisphere to get electricity. More recently, the **Reefton Distilling Co. ♥♥**, 10 Smith St. (reeftondistillingco.com; ✆ **03/732-7083**), has put the community back on the map. Known nationwide for its line of Little Biddy gins, it also produces blueberry liqueur, vodka, and whisky. The distillery has a range of tours, tastings, and guest experiences starting from NZ$39 for ages 18 and over; NZ$10 ages 5 to 17; under 5 free. It's open from 10am to 4pm daily.

GREYMOUTH

101km (63 miles) SW of Westport; 45km (28 miles) N of Hokitika; 290km (180 miles) SW of Nelson

The landing place for Māori canoes traveling to the southern region seeking greenstone (jade), aka pounamu, Greymouth is embraced by the Grey River. It's the largest town in the region but not really designed for tourists, even though it's the stopping point for the **TranzAlpine** railway. Most visitors will find that a night is more than enough to hit up the town's main attraction, **Monteith's Brewery** (see "Where to Eat in Greymouth," p. 406), or to stock up on supplies before heading up or down the coast. It's advisable to fuel up your car here or in Hokitika, because gas prices will increase as you drive to more remote locations elsewhere in the region.

Essentials

Like the rest of the West Coast, Greymouth is best accessed by driving. It can be reached via SH6 from Hokitika and Westport. From Christchurch via Lewis Pass and Reefton take SH7, or SH73 via Arthur's Pass; allow approximately 3½ hours. For a short but worthwhile scenic detour, drive Lake Brunner Road through Moana and past Lake Brunner.

VISITOR INFORMATION

The **Greymouth isite Information Centre,** 164 Mackay St. (westcoasttravel.co.nz; ✆ **0800/473-966** in NZ, or 03/768-7080), is open daily from 9am to 5pm.

Exploring Greymouth

A replica West Coast gold mining town, **Shantytown Heritage Park ♥**, 316 Rutherglen Rd. (shantytown.co.nz; ✆ **03/762-6634**), features gold-panning and a steam train running on a track through the bush. Otherwise, interactive experiences are limited and displays feel worn. Consider this a rainy-day activity, particularly if you have kids. Shantytown's hours are 9am to 4pm daily, with the train running at 11am, 12:30pm, and 2pm. Admission is NZ$39.50 adults, NZ$19.50 kids aged 5–17, NZ$31.04 seniors and students, NZ$95 family pass for 2 adults and 2 children. Gold panning costs NZ$10 extra per pan.

Located in the former Bank of NZ building (ca. 1924), **Left Bank Art Gallery ♥**, 1 Tainui St. (leftbankartgallery.nz; ✆ **03/768-0038**), exhibits paintings, woodware, and textiles by local artists and craftspeople. A collection of pounamu is on permanent display, showcasing work by leading jade carvers from across NZ.

Spend an hour or so immersed in Māori culture and history at **Māwhera Pā** ♥♥, 45 Tainui St. (pounamupathway.com/mawhera; ✆ **03/789-6658**), which still has that new-museum smell. Run entirely by the Ngāi Tahu tribe and on the site of the former Māori village, it has an excellent range of audio-visual exhibitions exploring Māori myths and history. It's open daily 9am to 5pm; adults NZ$45, children NZ$15, family NZ$99. Online bookings recommended.

Outdoor Pursuits

CYCLING Starting from Greymouth, the **West Coast Wilderness Trail** ♥♥ runs inland towards Kumara before heading south to Hokitika and ending in Ross. The 133km (83-mile) trail is grade 2 and 3 and takes around 4 days to complete; e-biking is a popular option. Visit westcoastwildernesstrail.co.nz for maps, bicycle hire, suggested accommodation, gear shuttles, and tour operators.

SURFING Best for intermediate to expert surfers, the main breaks are on **Cobden** and **Blaketown** beaches, both signposted about 5 minutes north of central Greymouth, and just north of Rapahoe at **Nine-Mile Beach.**

WALKING The **Point Elizabeth Walkway** ♥♥ starts at Rapahoe and follows the coast south around the headland through the bush to the Cobden

GHOSTS OF THE goldmining past: WAIUTA

The West Coast is littered with specters of its prosperous mining past. One of the best-known is **Waiuta** ♥♥, the company town for the South Island's largest gold mine from 1906 to 1951. It produced nearly 750,000 ounces of gold (today worth about NZ$1.6 billion), until a ventilation shaft collapsed in 1951, forcing its residents to abandon their homes. Today, the ghost town—which once had a population of 600—is managed by DOC (doc.govt.nz). Simultaneously eerie and captivating, Waiuta does not have rangers on-site but does have interpretative panels and signed walkways throughout, leading visitors through the town's ruins, including an Olympic-size pool, the barber shop, and even some homes with their furnishings still within. You'll need to use your imagination to conjure up what Waiuta once looked like, as fireplaces are all that remains of most of the homes.

If you want to up the spook factor, book an overnight stay in the bunks at the historic **Waiuta Lodge** ♥ (doc.govt.nz; ✆ **03/731-1895**). One of the few drive-up DOC huts, it's fully equipped with crockery and even has electricity (NZ$17 adults, NZ$8.50 children 5–18). Free camping for RVs is also available.

Waiuta is a 1-hour drive inland from Greymouth on SH7 into Victoria Forest Park. Budget half a day to explore its entirety, longer if you'd like to do the 3-hour hike to Big River. The turnoff (just past Ikamatua) is clearly marked, but the final 20 minutes of the drive past Blackwater is on a historic coach road that's narrow and winding. It can be accessed in a 2WD car or motorhome, but it's best to take it slow.

Beach road end. The 5.5km (3.4-mile) track takes about 2 hours one way. If the tide is low, return along the beach.

Where to Stay Around Greymouth

GREYMOUTH

Part of an NZ chain that can vary in terms of accommodation and amenities, the **Greymouth Seaside Top 10 Holiday Park** ♥, 2 Chesterfield St. (top10greymouth.co.nz; ✆ **03/768-6618**), doesn't disappoint. It's not just for those in motorhomes; there are cabins (NZ$89–NZ$169), and motel and apartment units (NZ$189–NZ$550).

Coleraine ♥, 61 High St. (colerainegreymouth.nz; ✆ **03/768-0077**), caters to both leisure travelers and the corporate market with its bright, airy, and spacious suites and apartments (with full kitchens) for NZ$199 to NZ$311. Centrally located, it offers free pickup from the TranzAlpine train upon request and depending on availability.

Walking distance from the railway station, the **Copthorne Hotel Greymouth** ♥, 32 Mawhera Quay (millenniumhotels.com; ✆ **03/768-5085**), was refurbished in 2022, though the outside is still rather tatty. Rooms, starting at NZ$225, are clean and comfortable, with views of the river.

Global Village Backpackers ♥♥ This hostel's colorful themed decor—involving totems, masks, and flags from around the world—is straight out of the 1990s and may not appeal to everyone. But it's the cleanest hostel you'll ever encounter, with a well-equipped kitchen, big library, comfortable common areas (including a cozy nook of a TV room), and even an outdoor hot tub and sauna. Light and airy, it's filled with birdsong coming from Sawyer Creek, which backs the property. Quiet and comfortable with large private double rooms and solid bunks, it will make you fall in love with hostels again. Borrow a bike to cruise along the West Coast Wilderness cycle trail and grab a hostel voucher for NZ$11 movies at the nearby **Regent Theatre.**

42–54 Cowper St. globalvillagebackpackers.co.nz. ✆ **03/768-7272.** 9 private rooms; 2 mixed dorms; 1 women-only dorm. Dorms NZ$40–NZ$42; private rooms NZ$88–NZ$216. **Amenities:** Sauna; hot tub; free use of kayaks and bicycles; free pickup from TranzAlpine; free Wi-Fi.

KUMARA

Theatre Royal Hotel ♥♥♥ When Kerrie and Mark Fitzgibbon purchased this former goldminers' hotel and dance theatre (ca. 1876), it was derelict. Now restored to its Victorian-era glory, it manages to hit the right historic notes without erring too much on the side of grandma's B&B, and it won Best Country Hotel in NZ's 2023 Hospitality Awards. There are framed photos of the rooms' namesakes (such as Richard John Seddon, Kumara's first mayor and NZ's longest-serving premier), but minimal florals and no creepy porcelain dolls. The renovation also means the hotel isn't the least bit drafty. Popular with cyclists on the West Coast Wilderness Trail, it offers bicycle storage and e-bike power stations. There are also cottages both new and historic behind the hotel, and across the road, the heritage Bank of New Zealand building has been refurbished into two luxurious suites; the golden Seddon Suite bathroom, with its clawfoot bathtub, was once the original gold-weighing office. There's a continental breakfast available, and meals at the on-site bar and restaurant are worth traveling for.

81 Seddon St. theatreroyalhotel.co.nz. ✆ **03/736-9277.** 6 rooms; 10 cottages; 2 suites. NZ$180–NZ$360 rooms, NZ$190–NZ$210 cottages; NZ$234–NZ$300 suites. Discounts for booking direct; packages available. **Amenities:** Restaurant, bar; bike storage; free Wi-Fi.

Where to Eat in Greymouth

Monteith's Brewery ♥♥ BREWPUB Locals love Monteith's coast fried chicken, made from marinated free-range Waitoa chicken, served with ranch dipping sauce. The beer is now brewed off-site, but 45-minute brewery tours and tastings are offered daily at 4pm. (Grab one of five daily early-bird tickets for NZ$30, otherwise it's NZ$40, both including a six-pack.)

Corner of Turumaha St. and Herbert St. thebrewery.co.nz. ✆ **027-444-9985.** Main courses NZ$22–NZ$54. Daily 11am–9pm.

Sevenpenny ♥♥ CAFE & RESTAURANT With its vivid wallpaper, green wall, and glass light fixtures, Sevenpenny is possibly the most cosmopolitan place in Greymouth. It's also where you'll find the poshest porridge, a weekly creation that varies but frequently involves chocolate. Breakfast is standard (eggs benny and smashed avo), though lunch offers a great crispy chicken, cream cheese, and cranberry burger. Dinner involves the likes of lamb shoulder and pork belly. The food is tasty and service is prompt.

9 Tainui St. sevenpenny.co.nz. ✆ **03/762-6879.** Breakfast and lunch main courses NZ$17–NZ$26; dinner mains NZ$25–NZ$46. Sun–Tues 7am–2:30pm, Wed–Sat 7am–2:30pm and 5:30pm–8pm.

A flight of craft beers at Monteith's Brewery.

HOKITIKA

45km (28 miles) S of Greymouth; 147km (91 miles) N of Franz Josef Glacier

Hokitika is a buzzy destination, albeit not as buzzy as it was in the gold rush years, when some 102 pubs were scattered about the town. Today, the focus is on greenstone, the beach, the surrounding lakes, and the many artists that ply their craft here. The town is well set up for tourists, with plenty of activities, attractions, accommodation, and places to buy or carve your own *pounamu* (greenstone or jade carving).

Essentials

Like the rest of the West Coast, Hokitika is best reached by car, with road access from both the north and south via SH6.

VISITOR INFORMATION

The **Hokitika isite Visitor Centre,** 41 Weld St. (✆ **03/755-6166**), is open weekdays from 8:30am to 5pm, and on weekends from 10am to 4pm; in summer (Dec–Feb) it stays open weekdays until 6pm and weekends from 9am to 5pm. Hokitika's visitor information website is hokitika.org.

SPECIAL EVENTS

The annual **Wild Foods Festival** (wildfoods.co.nz) is a celebration of all things wild and foraged, including some that are truly weird: Think huhu grubs, seagull eggs, horse semen, wasp larvae ice cream, or lamb testicles. The 1-day event is usually held in mid-March, with tickets sold online.

Exploring Hokitika

Photographers won't want to miss **Hokitika Gorge Scenic Reserve ♥♥**, with its startling blue-green water. A 2km (1.2-mile) loop takes you through rainforest, over waterfalls, and across two swing bridges. It's an easy walk that takes about 45 minutes with plenty of time for pictures. The reserve is located 33km (about a 30-min. drive) east of Hokitika. Meanwhile, the lush half-hour **Blue Spur Bush Walk ♥** just outside Hokitika is a beautiful way to blow off the cobwebs; kids will love the long rock squeeze, like a forest secret passage. The track is slippery, dotted with hidden mine shafts off-trail, and has a few missing markers, so keep a close watch.

For more virgin West Coast bush, there's also the **West Coast Treetop Walk,** 1128 Woodstock-Rimu Rd. (treetopsnz.com; ✆ **0508/8733-8677;** NZ$32 adults, NZ$16 children, NZ$77 family; book online for 10% off). One of Hokitika's newest attractions, its zipline and walkways tower high in the ancient rimu and kamahi tree canopy. But given the number of free bushwalks on the West Coast, it may not be the best investment of your time or money. It's open from 9am to 5pm in the summer and 9am to 3pm in winter; last entry is 45 minutes before closing.

Just 10 minutes south of Hokitika, **Lake Mahinapua** was originally a coastal lagoon, its access to the sea cut off by a gradual build-up of sand dunes. **West Coast Scenic Waterways ♥**, 389 Ruatapu Rd. (westcoastscenicwaterways.co.nz;

Panning at Ross Historic Gold Town

New Zealand's largest gold nugget ever unearthed was found in Ross, a village about 25km (15 miles) south of Hokitika. If you're after your own pot of gold, alluvial gold can still be found in the area. Stop at the **Ross Goldfields Information & Heritage Centre** (✆ **03/755-4077**) to pick up a gold pan ($20 online/$22 walk-ins) and get a quick tutorial before walking 10 minutes up the road to the nearby Jones Creek. It's been designated as a recreational fossicking (prospecting) area, which means no permits are needed—and yes, finders keepers! Just be warned: The experience might invoke your inner Gollum. Legend has it that one diligent couple recently found enough gold flakes to make wedding bands.

✆ **027/4301-777**), rents kayaks (NZ$70 for a half-day hire) as well as offering a 90-minute sunset cruise (NZ$60 adults, NZ$30 kids 5–13, NZ$5 kids under 5).

The Hokitika Museum ♥♥ MUSEUM This small but carefully curated museum is in the restored Carnegie Public Library building, circa 1908. The collections include artifacts from the 1860s gold-mining era and an exhibition of the people and places of the early district by photographer Charles Robert Kirk (1876–1954). The photographs of Māori leaders are compelling, as is the audiovisual section on greenstone and gold. For visitors curious about the strange appeal of whitebait, the museum has answers to frequently asked questions.

17 Hamilton St. hokitikamuseum.nz. ✆ **03/755-6898.** NZ$6 adults, under 16s free. Daily 10am–4pm.

The National Kiwi Centre ♥ NATURE CENTER Housed in a nocturnal setting, kiwi can be viewed at close quarters through glass, scratching around in their habitat. The other main attraction is eels, so tame that they are hand-fed by visitors at 10am, noon, and 3pm daily. It's a good rainy-day activity, but if you're on an extended trip through NZ, this will be far from your first—or last—chance to see kiwis and eels. If you're short on time or cash, give this one a miss.

64 Tancred St. thenationalkiwicentre.co.nz. ✆ **03/755-5251.** NZ$38 adults, NZ$20 kids 5–16, NZ$99 family pass. Daily 9:30am–4:30pm.

Where to Stay in Hokitika

Fitzherbert Court Motel ♥ The Fitzherbert isn't particularly memorable—even the bedspread is the same print you'll see in rooms across NZ. But the rooms are exceptionally clean, don't look dated, and have self-contained kitchens, three simple qualities that make them feel homey. The motel is also easy walking distance to the Glow Worm Dell just down the road. Its only downfall is that same road; you may hear noise from the large trucks that pass by at night.

191 Fitzherbert St. fitzherbertcourt.co.nz. ✆ **03/755-5342.** 12 units. NZ$135–NZ$180. **Amenities:** Jacuzzis; guest laundry; locked bike storage; free Wi-Fi.

HUNTING greenstone ON THE WEST COAST

From the beginning, the West Coast's history has been defined by "fossicking" (the act of searching for gemstones)—first for *pounamu* (known as greenstone or jade) and later for gold. Prized by Māori both for its decorative beauty and suitability for weaponry, pounamu is found exclusively on the South Island and primarily on the West Coast. If you look closely, you might be able to spot some on shores south of Punakaiki and north of Milford Sound, including at **Hokitika Beach.** Look for a stone that's grey to milky in color and feels soapy; rub it with water and you'll reveal the green beneath. (Don't get fooled by serpentine, which looks similar, but crumbles when dropped.) If you can physically carry it in your backpack, you can keep it.

Hokitika is considered "the" place to buy greenstone, with more than half a dozen pounamu shops within easy walking distance of one another. But before you invest in your own *taonga* (treasure), there are a few things to consider. First, pounamu is of great cultural and spiritual importance to Māori; it's considered *tapu* (sacred). Its legal guardian is Ngāi Tahu, the local *iwi* (tribe), who ensure it's collected in a sustainable manner. Unfortunately, the market has been flooded with black market jade, including greenstone that's been harvested illegally or imported from China or Canada. When buying pounamu, ask about its origins and look for Ngāi Tahu certification; this is the only guarantee that it's been harvested and carved legally within NZ. Finally, it's tradition for pounamu to be a gift—that isn't to say you can't purchase a piece for yourself, but it is a good excuse to convince your traveling companions to buy it for you.

You can watch carvers at work at **Westland Greenstone ♥**, 34 Tancred St. (✆ **03/755-8713**), which offers a large selection of jade at factory prices. If mass-produced isn't your thing, head over to **Wilderness Gallery ♥♥♥**, 29 Tancred St. (wildernessgallery.co.nz; ✆ **03/755-7575**). Along with photography and other giftware, this shop carries contemporary and traditional pounamu pieces made from *tahutahi pounamu* (one of the rarest types of greenstone) by Makaawhio carvers. The copper-plated feathers are also gorgeous, as are the fossilized rock pendants. At **Heritage Jade ♥♥**, 86 Revell St. (heritagejade.co.nz; ✆ **027/844-8881**), you'll find Ngāi Tahu carver Colin Davidson's work, including pendants made from unusual types of jade, such as white speckled kokopu pounamu. If green isn't your color, **Hokitika Craft Gallery ♥♥**, 25 Tancred St. (hokitikacraftgallery.co.nz; ✆ **03/755-8802**), sells similar designs carved from *aotea* (a light blue stone that's also unique to the West Coast) or fossilized shells from Waimate.

Bonz 'n' Stonz ♥♥, 16 Hamilton St. (bonznstonz.co.nz; ✆ **03/755-6504**), wouldn't be my top pick for buying pounamu, but it is the best place to carve your own. Solomon Island–born master carver Steve Gwaliasi will lead you through the process of turning a piece of jade, bone, or *pāua* (abalone shell) into a keepsake (starting from NZ$120). Even with no experience, the results are surprisingly professional, but be forewarned that Gwaliasi's approach is that of a mentor—if you're looking for a super structured experience, this isn't it; it helps to arrive with a clear idea of what you'd like to create. Children 8 and up are welcome, but spots are limited; bookings are a must.

Hokitika Fire Station ♥♥♥ There are plenty of high-end abodes on the outskirts of Hokitika, but this boutique hotel is the most luxurious place to stay directly in town. Housed in a historic fire house, the hotel has five self-contained apartments, each named after a former fire chief. Other nods to the building's history include light fixtures made from fire ladders and fire police helmets. Each tranquil, uniquely decorated unit features either a kitchenette with a Nespresso coffee machine or a full kitchen. Currently, this spot is on fire as the hottest place to stay, so book well in advance.

9 Hamilton St. hokitikafirestation.co.nz. ✆ **021/180-5882.** 5 units. NZ$320–NZ$420. **Amenities:** Laundry facilities; bike storage; free Wi-Fi.

Lobby of the Hokitika Fire Station Apartments.

Teichelmann's Bed & Breakfast ♥♥♥ Teichelmann's has built a big reputation for its hospitality. Situated opposite the Hokitika Museum, the elegant heritage home was built for a Dr. Teichelmann in 1910 and has been lovingly restored. Guest rooms exude comfort with large beds, down blankets, and central heating. The hospitality extends to complimentary port and sherry in the lounge and very good breakfasts. It's a busy B&B, so book ahead.

20 Hamilton St. teichelmanns.co.nz. ✆ **03/755-8232.** 6 units. NZ$320–NZ$350. Rates include breakfast. **Amenities:** Free Wi-Fi.

Where to Eat in Hokitika

Fat Pipi Pizzas ♥♥, 89 Revell St. (fatpipipizza.co.nz; ✆ **03/755-6373**), serves the world's first whitebait pizza! It also offers standard pizzas with plenty of gluten-free and vegetarian options, alongside more creative fare, like the Chicken Lick'in pizza, topped with smoked chicken, apricot sauce, and cream cheese. A large will run you NZ$35. It's open Thursday to Monday from 5pm to 8pm.

A winner of the country's best toastie competition, **The Hokitika Sandwich Company ♥♥♥** (hokitikasandwichcompany.com; ✆ **03/429-2019**) is so popular it recently expanded to Christchurch. The magic formula here is fresh everything: freshly baked bread (once they run out, they stop making sandwiches for the day); local meats, cheeses, and greens; and condiments made in-house daily. Seating is limited, so grab yours to-go (or order it online for pickup) and eat it on the beach. Made-to-order sandwiches are from NZ$12

A fresh Italian sub from the Hokitika Sandwich Company.

for a half or NZ$23 for a whole. It's open Tuesday to Saturday from 10am to 2pm (but it sometimes runs out of ingredients earlier).

FRANZ JOSEF & FOX GLACIERS

Franz Josef: 188km (117 miles) SW of Greymouth; 24km (15 miles) N of Fox Glacier; 134km (85 miles) SW of Hokitika

It seems improbable that you could find a glacier on a South Pacific island or ice in a temperate rainforest, but that's New Zealand for you: full of surprises. Nowhere else in the world will you find glaciers 300m (1,000 ft.) above sea level and just 12km (7½ miles) from the sea. The Franz Josef and Fox glaciers and their respective villages are a small part of the 115,000-hectare (284,000-acre) **Westland Tai Poutini National Park,** an area popular for heli-hiking, tramping, mountain climbing, ski touring, and hunting. Catering to tourists, this is by far the most popular and visited spot on the West Coast. But be prepared for the best-laid plans to change; the West Coast's weather is notoriously fickle. Especially during the wet spring months, the most popular walks may close and helicopters may not fly.

So, what are the differences between Franz Josef and Fox glaciers and their respective townships? **Fox Glacier** is bigger, longer, with better helicopter and walking options, and is typically less crowded. **Franz Josef Glacier** is steeper, resulting in striking blue crevasses and ice caves that you can see on a guided walk. Franz Josef's township has a better visitor center and is busier overall, with more food and accommodation options. Short walks will take you to both glaciers. They're just a half-hour drive apart, but the road between the two is narrow, winding, and often full of tourist traffic, so it should be undertaken with care.

Ice-trekkers on Franz Josef Glacier.

Essentials

SH6 follows the coast from Hokitika to Franz Josef Glacier and Fox Glacier, one of the country's great drives. It pays to be aware that this is the only road in or out of the area. In adverse weather, check the NZTA website (nzta.govt.nz) for road closures and travel advice. Fuel up in Fox if you're headed farther south to Haast; it's the last gas stop for 120km (75 miles). The villages of Fox Glacier and Franz Josef are small; either can be walked end-to-end in under 15 minutes. **InterCity** (intercity.co.nz; ✆ **03/365-1113**) coach service connects the two towns with daily bus services.

VISITOR INFORMATION

The **Westland Tai Poutini National Park DOC Visitor Centre & isite,** 69 Cron St., Franz Josef (doc.govt.nz and glaciercountry.co.nz; ✆ **03/752-0360**), is open 8:30am–5pm daily.

Exploring the Glaciers

Although you'll see the Franz Josef glacier signposted just south of town (turn onto Glacier Access Rd. just after the Waiho River bridge), you're going to have to walk to get decent views. The most popular is the **Franz Josef Glacier/Kā Roimata o Hine Hukatere Walk ♥♥♥**. An easy 1.6km round-trip, it follows a well-graded path to an excellent view of the glacier. Be aware that the walk sometimes closes in this dynamic environment. Check the sign in the parking lot for the latest conditions and advisories. Barriers must never be crossed; if you want to walk on the glacier, book a heli-hike.

To see Fox Glacier, drive towards Lake Matheson on Cook Flat Road, walk the 6.4km (4-mile) **Fox Glacier South Side Walkway,** or book a scenic flight or a heli-hike. In total, there are dozens of walking tracks in Glacier Country, so consult with staff at the isite to find your best option.

Safety tip: The weather can change rapidly in this region. Always have warm and waterproof clothing and insect repellent; sandflies here are huge.

HELICOPTER TOURS

Heli-biking, heli-hiking, heli-rafting—you name it, you can fly to it. This is definitely the way to see a glacier up close.

The most popular heli-hike option is a scenic flight with a guided glacier walk (from NZ$699), which takes roughly 4 hours and requires a moderate level of fitness. For scenic flights, the classic is a 30-minute tour covering both glaciers (from NZ$350), although you can also do trips like see the face of Aoraki/Mt. Cook, NZ's highest peak, combined with a glacier landing (from NZ$445).

Since weather and glacier conditions can worsen during the day and shut down flights, book well in advance and choose the day's first flight. The good news is that there are a plethora of experiences and about a dozen operators, their offices peppering the main streets of Fox and Franz Josef. All offer similar products at similar price points, so it pays to stop at the isite for advice about the next departure time.

For guided heli-hikes, contact **Fox Glacier Guiding ♥♥♥**, 44 Main Rd., Fox Glacier (foxguides.co.nz; ✆ **0800/111-600** in NZ, or 03/751-0825), or

BIRDING CRUISE TO white heron sanctuary

If you're driving from Hokitika to the glaciers in the summer, be sure to stop at **Whataroa,** 35km (22 miles) north of Franz Josef, adjacent to the Ōkārito lagoon, home to more than 70 bird species. To see the nesting grounds of the rare *kōtuku* (white heron), you can visit the nearby Waitangiroto Nature Reserve with **White Heron Sanctuary Tours ♥♥♥** (whiteherontours.co.nz; ✆ **0800/523-456** in NZ, or 03/753-4120). After a scenic jetboat ride from Whataroa to the reserve, you'll walk roughly half a mile over a forest boardwalk to a hide, where you should be able to view white herons and spoonbills. The 2½-hour tours depart at 9am, noon, and 3pm and costs NZ$150 adults, NZ$75 children 12 and under. Tours operate rain or shine and run from September to February.

A rare white heron with chicks.

Franz Josef Glacier Guides ♥♥♥, 6 Main Rd. (franzjosefglacier.com; ✆ **0800/484-337** in NZ, or 03/752-0763). Both offer ice-climbing tours for the more intrepid. **The Helicopter Line ♥♥♥** (helicopter.co.nz; ✆ **0800/807-767** in NZ, 03/752-0767 in Franz Josef, 03/751-0767 in Fox Glacier) is a reliable choice for scenic heli flights.

Beyond the Glaciers: What to See & Do

The **seal colony at Gillespies Beach ♥** is a resting spot for seals during winter months and a scenic hiking spot. Half of the 21km (13-mile) journey is on a narrow unpaved road; take Cook Flat Rd. from Fox and turn onto Gillespies Beach Rd. Of the five walking tracks, the shortest (the **Miners Cemetery Walk**) is a poignant history lesson. The area once had a considerable population, as the headstones reveal. The longest walk, the **Galway Beach Tramping Track,** is a 3½-hour roundtrip from the Gillespies Beach carpark. Follow the signposts through native rimu trees to the remote beach. Stay clear of the seals, however, never putting yourself between them and the sea (their escape route).

On the coast north of Franz Josef, tiny **Ōkārito** is nestled between wild bush and beach, with pleasing buildings and striking mountain-view walks. Kayak gently through rainforest and lagoon and bird-watch with **Ōkārito Kayaks ♥♥**, 1 The Strand, Ōkārito (okarito.co.nz; ✆ **03/753-4014**). A 2-hour guided paddle starts at $150 per person, and freedom rentals start at $80 each.

The **West Coast Wildlife Centre ♥**, Cron Street, Franz Josef (wildkiwi.co.nz; ✆ **03/752-0600**), is a hatchery for NZ's rarest kiwi, the rowi. If you're visiting in spring or summer, ask if any kiwis have hatched recently; if so, the

An Ōkārito Kayaks tour of the Ōkārito Lagoon.

VIP Backstage Pass ticket may be worth considering (NZ$95 adults, NZ$55 kids, NZ$249 family pass, $93 senior/student). It includes penguin viewing and a fully guided tour through the incubation and rearing facility, though be aware viewing chicks isn't guaranteed depending on Department of Conservation needs. It's open daily from 8:30am until 5:30pm. All-day passes cost NZ$65 for adults, NZ$42 for kids, NZ$199 for families, and $63 for seniors/students. Both pass options are actually worth 2 days (48 hr.).

After a day of exploring, **Waiho Hot Tubs** ♥, 64B Cron St., Franz Josef (waihohottubs.co.nz; ✆ **03/752-0009**), offers the ideal way to warm up. Its wood-fired hot tubs filled with fresh mountain stream water are sequestered in the rainforest, with hourly soaks starting from NZ$98 for one; adding relaxing Epsom salts costs another NZ$10. It's open from 11:30am in summer and 2:30pm in winter, and visitors are welcome to bring their own drinks and nibbles.

Where to Stay Around the Glaciers

FRANZ JOSEF

The 20 units in the **Punga Grove Motel & Suites** ♥, 400 Cron St. (pungagrove.co.nz; ✆ **0800/437-269** in NZ, or 03/752-0001), are surrounded by huge, lush tree ferns and rainforest (book direct to save on its units, which are NZ$190–NZ$320). Each unit comes with fully equipped kitchenettes. Executive studios have gas fires and ensuite spa baths.

It doesn't matter if you're a family, a flashpacker, or a couple, **Rainforest Retreat** ♥♥, 46 Cron St. (rainforest.nz; ✆ **03/752-0220**), has accommodation to suit. Its varied accommodations range from powered campsites (NZ$46–NZ$66), to motel rooms (NZ$140–NZ$295), to deluxe tree huts (NZ$345–NZ$465).

FOX GLACIER

Bella Vista Fox ♥, SH6 (bellavista.co.nz; ✆ **03/751-0129**), is your standard midrange motel on the main strip, but its staff go above and beyond to ensure your visit goes off without a hitch. (The front desk feels like a mini-info center, and there's strong Wi-Fi.) Studios and one-bedroom units are NZ$119 to NZ$206.

The rooms are stylish and spacious at **Te Weheka Hotel Fox Glacier ♥♥**, 15 Main Rd., SH6 (teweheka.co.nz; ✆ **0800/313-414** in NZ, or 03/751-0730), with king or twin beds, big bathrooms with tubs, and balconies. It also has an on-site restaurant, a guest lounge, and a library (from NZ$280 double).

Where to Eat Around the Glaciers

FRANZ JOSEF

Locals love **SnakeBite Brewery ♥**, 28 Main Rd. (snakebite.co.nz; ✆ **03/752-0234**). Despite its name, the specialty isn't beer but rather Kiwi cafe fare and Southeast Asian food, including hawker rolls, steamed bao buns, and curries. There's also middling coffee and a bakery case full of homemade cakes, meat

PHOTOGRAPHING lake matheson

Lake Matheson, 5km (3 miles) from Fox Glacier township, shows up on all the postcards, but what the pictures don't show is the **Lake Matheson Walk ♥**, an easy track around the lake that takes about 1½ hours. On clear days, you'll enjoy great views of Aoraki/Mt. Cook and Mt. Tasman. But it's only when the lake is perfectly still and the sky is clear that you'll be able to capture an image of the mountains reflected in the water. This usually happens at dusk or dawn. **Café Lake Matheson** (see "Where to Eat") is at the parking area where the walk starts.

Photogenic Lake Matheson.

pies, even Bavarian donuts. Brave the love ballads playing obnoxiously from 7:30am on, and pick up an excellent chicken satay wrap to take with you on your hike. Much better coffee and cozier vibes can be found at **Full of Beans Café ♥♥** (fullofbeanscafe.co.nz; ✆ **03/752-0139**) with its couches, dim lighting, and pleasant music—though do be aware you are now in the home of the NZ$7.50 flat white coffee.

Over at 30 Cron St, **Alice May ♥♥** (alicemay.co.nz; ✆ **03/752-0130;** daily 4–8:30pm) is named for one of NZ's most famed manslayers (whose perceived unfair sentencing provoked protests in 1915), and sits somewhere between a familiar pub and the classiest restaurant in town. It serves New Zealand favorites: roast pork with apple sauce, braised lamb shanks, and Akaroa salmon, ranging from NZ$21 to NZ$47. Best of all, it runs a courtesy vehicle on request.

Akaroa Salmon at Alice May.

FOX GLACIER

Named for the faithful dog that accompanied 19th-century surveyor Charles Edward Douglas on his journeys mapping the West Coast, **Betsey Jane ♥♥**, 27 Cook Flat Rd. (✆ **03/751-0780;** daily 4pm–late), offers NZ$20 takeaway fish 'n' chips on Thursdays and Fridays, as well as stylish in-house dining: the alpine venison with black truffle oil and mushroom risotto is very popular. Once a two-bedroom cottage, it overlooks mountains and farmland.

If you're after breakfast or lunch, head to the **Matheson Cafe ♥♥** on Lake Matheson Road (lakematheson.com; ✆ **03/751-0878;** daily 8:30am–3pm). It's a stone's throw from the magnificent mirror lake—walk around it first to whet your appetite for waffles with raspberry mousse, pork belly poke bowl, or Korean fried chicken burger.

Other options include **Café Neve,** Main Road (✆ **03/751-0110;** daily 8am–3pm in winter; until 7pm in summer), which acts as everything to everyone with its extensive takeaway, pizza, and cafe menu. Prices reflect its remoteness (NZ$28 for a veggie wrap with fries), but the service is good and food comes fast.

En Route to Queenstown: Haast

This UNESCO World Heritage Area is a treasure for those who love hunting, hiking, and fishing. The main settlements are **Haast** and **Haast Junction** on

SH6, and **Haast Beach** on Jackson Bay Road. There are a couple of places to eat, sleep, and fuel up, but to avoid high prices and low selection, this area is best for those who are prepared to self-cater and, as the Kiwis say, "Get amongst it."

Haast is a 90-minute drive south of Fox on SH6. This is the only road through the area, so in bad weather, check the NZTA website (nzta.govt.nz) for road closures and travel advice.

Past Haast, the dramatic highway to **Wānaka** (see p. 476)—a route that took 40 years to build—is magnificent, moss-covered, and often misty, following the course of the Haast River for much of the way, winding through high, jagged peaks. Frequent stops are advised, which shouldn't be a problem given the countless waterfalls and photo opportunities. Traveling nonstop to Wānaka on SH6 takes about 2 hours; add one more to get to Queenstown, but do stop before Wānaka to enjoy a tranquil 1-hour round-trip tramp on the **Blue Pools Track ♥♥**, north of Makarora in Mt. Aspiring National Park, which takes you to icy, Listerine-clear waters.

VISITOR INFORMATION

The **DOC Awarua/Haast Visitor Centre,** on the corner of SH6 and Jackson Bay Rd. (✆ **027/303-4890**), is open daily from 9am to 4:30pm except for Christmas Day.

WHERE TO STAY & EAT IN HAAST

In the 1970s, Haast was an isolated settlement where daring young men in their helicopters captured live wild deer to establish deer farms and begin the production of farmed venison. The past lives on in the decor of the **Hard Antler Bar & Restaurant ♥**, Marks Road, in Haast Township (facebook.com/HardAntlerBarHaast; ✆ **03/750-0034**), where a forest of antlers adorn pretty much everything. Lunchers should try the local delicacy, whitebait sandwiches, or the snapper and chips, and diners keen on a good steak will find it here. It's open daily from 7:30am to late (main courses NZ$19–NZ$52).

Asure Aspiring Court Motel Haast ♥, Marks Road, Haast Township (aspiringcourtmotel.com; ✆ **0800/500-703** in NZ or 03/750-0703), is close to the handful of shops and eateries. It has 13 one- or two-bedroom units (from NZ$230).

The Wilderness Lodge Lake Moeraki ♥♥, SH6, 30km (19 miles) north of Haast (wildernesslodge.co.nz; ✆ **03/750-0881**), is a secluded, riverside luxury ecotourism destination. Rooms are spacious and decorated in soft natural tones, echoing the rainforest outside. Rates (NZ$635–NZ$1,010 per person, with a 2-night min. Nov–Mar) include accommodation, breakfast, dinner, and a daily guided activity in the river and rainforest. There's also a restaurant, kayaks, walking trails, and a wine cellar on-site. See if you can spot the resident rare, white New Zealand *kōtuku* (heron).

13

CHRISTCHURCH & ENVIRONS

For 150 years, pretty Christchurch/Ōtautahi was known as the Garden City, thanks to its beautiful botanic gardens and its Old English and French Gothic architecture. All that changed in February 2011, following the second destructive earthquake in 5 months. Today, in its post-earthquake garb, Christchurch is a city on the rise—literally—as architects, designers, artists, and resilient citizens combine skills to reshape the city. On the rise, too, is a sense of excitement for Christchurch's future as new housing, cafes, bars, and hotels open and find their footing.

Most visitors make the mistake of only staying for a night or two. But given its proximity to the snowcapped mountains, hot springs, family-owned vineyards, and seaside communities with long sandy beaches, Christchurch is the ideal base for day trips to adventures farther afield.

ESSENTIALS

Arriving

BY PLANE **Christchurch International Airport** (christchurch airport.co.nz) welcomes over seven million passengers a year; of all the South Island airports, it's the most reliable (compared to Queenstown's tiny airport, flights into Christchurch are less likely to be cancelled due to weather). **Air New Zealand** (airnewzealand.co.nz; ✆ **0800/132-476**) operates daily domestic and international flights from/to the city. Economy airline **JetStar** (jetstar.com) connects the city with Wellington, Auckland, Queenstown, Melbourne, Sydney, and Brisbane. The airport is only 10km (6 miles) from Cathedral Square. Transfers from/to the airport include **Super Shuttle** (supershuttle.co.nz; ✆ **0800/748-885** in NZ) with a 24-hour daily service. A pre-booked shared ride costs NZ$25 from the airport to the central city. All taxi companies work the airport; taxi fares run around NZ$50 to the city. You can catch an Uber for about the same; the airport has a dedicated ride-share pickup area. The airport is also on multiple bus routes into the city (metroinfo.co.nz).

BY CAR The drive time from Picton is 4½ hours; from Kaikōura it's 2½ hours. From Dunedin it's 5 hours, and from Oamaru 3 hours.

BY COACH (BUS) **InterCity** (intercity.co.nz; © **03/365-1113**) has scheduled services to/from Christchurch, linking the city to nearly all main centers and tourist attractions in the South Island.

BY TRAIN **Great Journeys of New Zealand** (greatjourneysnz.com; © **04/495-0775**) connects Christchurch to Greymouth and Arthur's Pass via its **TranzAlpine** route (from NZ$289), and to Kaikōura, Blenheim, and Picton via its **Coastal Pacific** route (from NZ$147 btw. Picton and Kaikōura; from NZ$259 for the whole route). These itineraries are primarily intended as scenic journeys, but they get the job done. No passenger trains operate south of Christchurch. The **Christchurch Railway Station** is on Clarence Street, Addington.

Getting Around

BY CAR Christchurch is a city of suburbs, and driving will provide easier access to nearby destinations such as Akaroa (1½ hr. away) and Hanmer Springs (1¾ hr. away). Compared to other major cities in NZ, free or affordable parking is fairly easy to find here, even close to the city center. (Even valet parking at downtown hotels tends to be more affordable.) As you drive and exit your vehicle after parking, keep a careful eye out for cyclists, who dominate the streets here more than any other place in NZ.

BY PUBLIC BUS **Metro** (metroinfo.co.nz; © **03/366-8855**) operates bus services in the Christchurch area. Check the website for comprehensive information on fares, timetables, and routes; its mobile app is **MetroGo.** The **Bus Interchange** near the corner of Lichfield and Colombo streets has a staffed MetroInfo kiosk, waiting rooms, cafes, restrooms, and a real-time bus tracking system that tells you how many minutes until your bus arrives. You can use your credit/debit card or digital payments such as ApplePay to tap and pay on the bus, or the Interchange sells pre-loaded **Metrocards.** If you plan on taking more than one trip, this is the most affordable option.

Many Metro routes are often (but not always) identified by color, repeated in timetables, bus colors, and stops. For example, if traveling to the airport from the Interchange, you hop on the Purple Line traveling on a (usually) purple bus.

BY SCOOTER & E-BIKE Christchurch's straight, flat, and easy-to-navigate streets lend themselves well to zipping around by shared scooter or e-bike. **Lime** (li.me) operates within the city and can be used by downloading its free app.

BY TAXI & RIDE SHARE Taxi stands are scattered around the inner city and at all transport terminals. Taxis are unlikely (but not unknown) to respond to being hailed within a quarter-mile of a stand, but can be booked via NZ taxi app **YourRide** (yourride.nz). **Uber** is also available.

Visitor Information

The official tourism website for the region is **www.christchurchnz.com**. At press time, Christchurch's city center isite is closed. The closest official information center is a 20-minute drive north of the city in Kaiapoi, at 143 Williams St. (© **03/327-3134**). It's open weekdays only from 9am to 3:30pm.

City Layout

Cathedral Square (aka **the Square**) is the centerpoint of the city, with the main streets laid out in a grid system, surrounded by four main avenues—**Bealey, Moorhouse, Deans,** and **Fitzgerald.** *Note:* The 19th-century cathedral is still in the process of being rebuilt following the 2011 earthquake. The **Avon River** curves through Hagley Park and the central city. The **Port Hills,** which rise above the horizon south of the city, are a useful landmark when you need to get your bearings.

The Chalice sculpture in Cathedral Square, erected in 2001, survived the 2010 and 2011 earthquakes and stands as a symbol of Christchurch's rebirth.

NEIGHBORHOODS IN BRIEF

A strange anomaly in Christchurch is the upside-down-ness of what makes a neighborhood desirable. While the leafy suburb **Fendalton,** with its expensive homes, sits close to the airport, the eastern beachside suburb of **New Brighton** struggles (in part due to the chilly winds that whip off the sea).

Southeast of the center city, **Woolston,** once an industrial area, has been reinvented as a shopping destination, with its hub the high-end Edwardian-influenced shopping complex the Tannery. **Sumner,** a sheltered bayside village and a popular destination for recreational cyclists, has busy cafes and a beach favored by walkers. **Lyttelton** has been a port town since the first settlers arrived in the 1880s. It was damaged in the 2011 quake, but its quirky streets and heritage houses have a timelessness that embraces the new and retains the old. It is a hot spot for coffee aficionados and those who like to dine well.

South of the city center, the suburb of **Sydenham** has more commercial offerings, but also boasts some of the city's best restaurants.

Papanui Road in the northwest of the city and **Riccarton Road** in the northeastern segment are lively dining areas lined with accommodation options—motels mostly, but also B&Bs and apartments.

Special Events

Christchurch is the festival capital of NZ—no matter when you visit, it's bound to coincide with a festival of some sort. The **World Buskers' Festival** (worldbuskersfestival.co.nz), has brought color and culture to Christchurch's central city streets for generations, with both busking and ticketed shows. It runs for 2 weeks at the end of January, with free public acts of contortion and juggling, along with comedy, jazz, and circus shows.

The **Canterbury A&P Show** (theshow.co.nz), held over a weekend in mid-November, is an agricultural show, but it's not just for farming folk; shows range from dressage and show jumping to wood chopping and sheep shearing competitions. Plenty of food trucks and beer gardens help to round out its celebratory vibe.

Every year on the last Saturday of February, Hagley Park becomes a city within a city, holding New Zealand's largest music festival across multiple stages for 2 days: **Electric Avenue** (electricavenue.co.nz). Its diverse offerings include electronic dance acts, alternative rock, reggae dub, and Kiwi favorites. The leafy green setting, 5 minutes' walk from the city, offers chill vibes and makes it popular for both the young and young at heart.

EXPLORING CHRISTCHURCH

Central City & Cathedral Square

Arts Centre ♥♥♥ LANDMARK An important cluster of 135-year-old Victorian Gothic-style buildings, this postcard-worthy destination captures the essence of Christchurch as it once was—walking into the historic courtyard will make you feel like you've hopped on the train to Harry Potter's Hogwarts. More than just a photo stop, it has been extensively restored post-earthquakes. Here you'll find the **Observatory Hotel** (p. 431), wine bar **Cellar Door** (p. 435), art galleries, boutiques (including **Frances Nation Home ♥♥**, which specializes in NZ-made homewares and gifts), and the vintage-feel **Lumière Cinemas.**

Bounded by Worcester Blvd., Rolleston Ave., Hereford St., & Montreal St. artscentre.org.nz. ✆ **03/366-0989.**

Canterbury Museum ♥ MUSEUM In 2023, the historic Canterbury Museum (first established in 1867) closed for earthquake strengthening and redevelopment. It's anticipated to reopen in 2029 with new exhibits and programming. Check its website for information about the pop-up exhibits and venues that are open in the interim, covering the city's history, including its

The Arts Centre: a gorgeous collection of Victorian Gothic buildings in the heart of Christchurch.

Opened in 2003, the modernistic new building for the Christchurch Art Gallery Te Puna o Waiwhetū weathered the earthquakes with only minor damage, thanks to seismic-resistant design.

relationship with Antarctica. You can also visit its outposts, including **Quake City** (below) and the **Ravenscar Museum** (p. 424).

11 Rolleston Ave. canterburymuseum.com. ✆ **03/366-5000.**

Christchurch Art Gallery Te Puna o Waiwhetū ♥♥ ART GALLERY One of the largest permanent collections in NZ, the museum houses more than 5,500 paintings, sculptures, prints, drawings, and crafts emphasizing work from the Canterbury region, as well as hosting regular touring international and national shows. However, it's not large; you can easily explore the full gallery in an hour. Once you're done, pop into the museum shop, which carries Kiwiana gifts and souvenirs that you'll actually want to take home and use, including storybooks and toys for kids.

Worcester Blvd. & Montreal St. christchurchartgallery.org.nz. ✆ **03/941-7300.** Free (fees may be charged for special exhibitions). Daily 10am–5pm (until 9pm Wed).

Quake City ♥♥ MUSEUM A special exhibition owned by the Canterbury Museum (p. 421), Quake City is devoted to examining the cause and effects of the devastating 2010 and 2011 earthquakes, which killed 185 people. With firsthand accounts from survivors and live video footage of the event, it's categorically "dark tourism," but it's also a moving testament to the resilience of Cantabrians. There are a few fun interactive features (a sand table simulates liquefaction, and there's a spot where you can jump to generate your own "earthquake") and items on display (the Christchurch Cathedral's massive spire and a 1907 time capsule found during the city's clean-up). Quake City sometimes falls short in providing context for international visitors unfamiliar with the region's geography and what Christchurch was like "before," but it will likely appeal to geology, architecture, and urban planning nerds, who should budget an hour for their visit.

299 Durham St. N. quakecity.co.nz. ✆ **03/365-8375.** NZ$20 adults, free for kids under 15 accompanied by an adult (NZ$8 without an adult). Daily 10am–5pm. Discount combination ticket with Ravenscar House Museum (below).

Christchurch

ATTRACTIONS
Air Force Museum of New Zealand **35**
Arts Centre **11**
Canterbury Museum **8**
Christchurch Art Gallery Te Puna o Waiwhetū **13**
Christchurch Botanic Gardens **7**
Christchurch Gondola **30**
He Puna Taimoana **1**
International Antarctic Centre **2**
Orana Wildlife Park **2**
Quake City **15**
Ravenscar **9**
Transitional Cathedral **22**
Tūranga (Central Library) **18**
Willowbank Wildlife Reserve **2**

HOTELS
The Adina Heritage Hotel Christchurch **17**
The Classic Villa **10**
Commodore Airport Hotel **3**
Crowne Plaza Christchurch **19**
Drifter **24**
Hotel Montreal **6**
Jailhouse Accommodation **36**
The Mayfair **5**
The Muse Art Hotel **23**
Observatory Hotel **12**
Otahuna Lodge **38**
Studios at Bealey Quarter **4**

RESTAURANTS
5th Street **34**
C1 Espresso **25**
Cassels & Sons Brewery Bar **29**
Child Sister **20**
Grizzly Baked Goods **32**
Hello Sunday **33**
King of Snake **16**
The Little High Eatery **27**
Manu **14**
Portershed **37**
Tussock Hill Vineyard **31**
Twenty Seven Steps **21**
Utopia Ice **28**
The Welder **26**

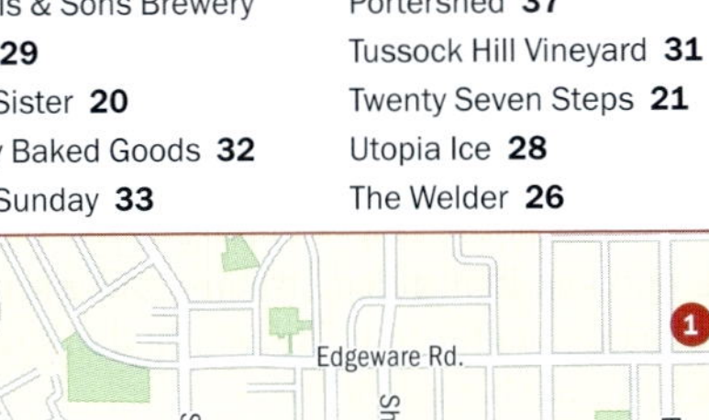

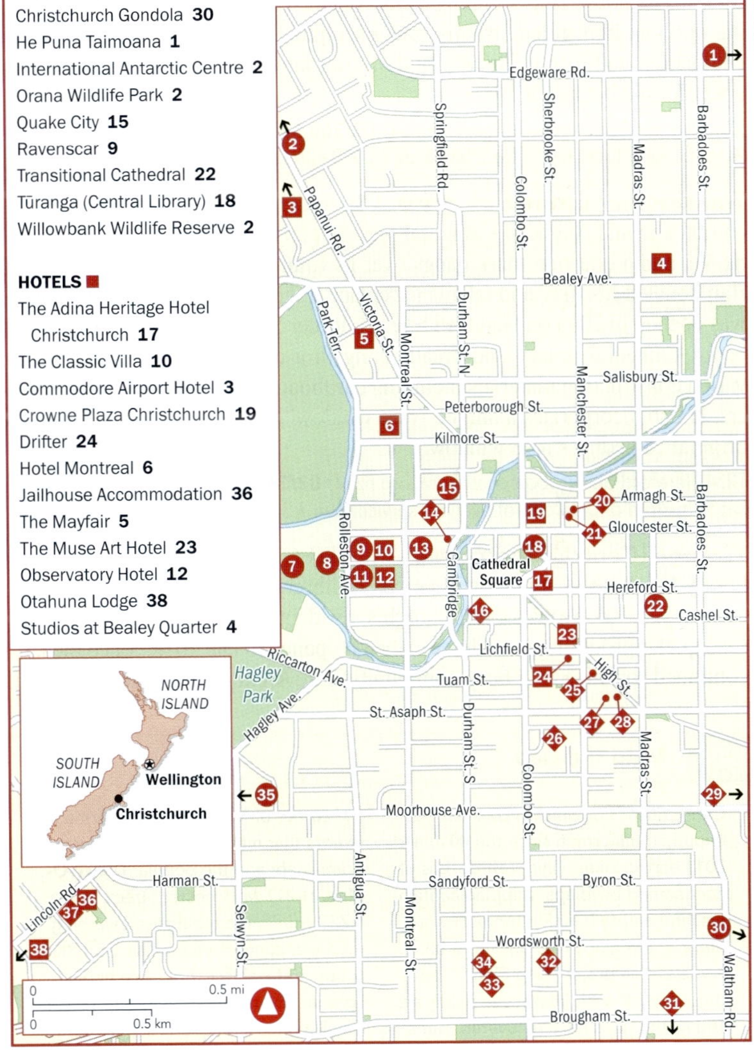

Ravenscar ♥♥ ART MUSEUM Operated by the Canterbury Museum (p. 421), this art gallery houses the belongings of private collectors Jim and Susan Wakefield. When their home was destroyed by the earthquakes, the pair decided to use the insurance payments to fund an architecturally significant "house museum" to showcase their belongings. In each of the house's rooms—including a bedroom, living room, dining room and library—you'll find their furniture (including pieces designed by David Linley, King Charles's cousin), artwork (historic and contemporary pieces by Gottfried Lindauer, Bill Sutton, Frances Hodgkins, and others), jewelry, trophies, and books. The house is as stunning as its contents, with vaulted ceilings, reflecting pools in light-filled atriums, and a sculpture garden. Art and architecture enthusiasts will love it. But if you don't fall into one of those two categories, give this small space a miss.

52 Rolleston Ave. ravenscarhouse.com. ✆ **03/366-5052.** NZ$25 adults, NZ$5 children 2–15. Guided tours (2pm Wed, Sat, Sun) NZ$10 extra. Daily 10am–5pm.

Transitional Cathedral ♥♥♥ CHURCH/ARCHITECTURE Christchurch's iconic Anglican Cathedral was severely damaged in the 2011 earthquake, and a question mark hangs over its future. Japanese architect Shigeru Ban donated his time and talents to replace it, and this Transitional Cathedral was opened in 2013 on Hereford Street/Latimer Square. Ban's so-called Cardboard Cathedral is airy and breathtaking in a different way, making use of varied construction materials including cardboard tubes and shipping containers. It also incorporates a unique "rose window" that features images from the original cathedral's rose window.

T234 Hereford St. cardboardcathedral.org.nz. ✆ **03/366-0046.** Admission free. Mon–Sat 9am–4pm or until end of evening service; Sun 7:30am–end of 5pm service.

Tūranga (Central Library) ♥♥ ARCHITECTURE/LANDMARK Can a library be a tourist attraction? Legions of library tourists (it's a thing) would argue "yes," as would Christchurch's residents, who flocked to the new earthquake-proof library in droves when it opened in late 2018. Since then, it's continued to thrive as a busy community hub. Architecturally stunning, with

Mind the Gap

Christchurch's downtown core has been entirely transformed since the 2010 and 2011 earthquakes, which left dozens of condemned buildings, shipping containers, and empty lots. For more than a decade, the globally acclaimed urban revitalization project **Gap Filler** filled these "gaps" with interactive public art. Today, the gaps have recovered, but a couple of mainstays remain: **#chchswing**, an adult-sized architectural swing set on the corner of Manchester and Armagh streets that makes for a perfect Instagram snap; and the popular **Dance-O-Mat,** at 211 Manchester Street. Pop a NZ$2 coin in the repurposed washing machine, connect your music with Bluetooth, and wait for the dance floor to light up. Even King Charles and Queen Camilla once indulged in some swing dancing here on the last day of their 2012 Royal Jubilee Tour.

A look at the interior of the innovative Transitional Cathedral.

references to local geology and Māori culture throughout, the five-story building deserves a walkthrough at the very least, and its marigold-tiled bathrooms have a cult following for enabling flawless, golden-hued selfies. On the ground level, you'll find an interactive discovery wall where you can learn about Christchurch's history; a community space for completing puzzles; and the very good **Foundation Café ♥♥**, which has excellent coffee and cheese scones. The second level is a kids' paradise, with a large playhouse, LEGO, plenty of cushions, and a massive video gaming screen. As with most public libraries in New Zealand, Wi-Fi is free, as is computer use, even for non-members.

60 Cathedral Sq., Christchurch. ccc.govt.nz. Admission free. Mon–Fri 9am–8pm, Sat–Sun 10am–5pm.

Outlying Attractions

Air Force Museum of New Zealand ♥♥ MUSEUM For fans of all things fast, furious, and capable of flight, this is the national museum for the Royal New Zealand Air Force, located on the former air base at Wigram, 15 minutes' drive from the city and airport. Two hours is about the time most guests need to experience this museum, which includes an interactive flight game, history hall, and historic planes on display—everything from Spitfires and Skyhawks to Tiger Moths. There's a cafe, and an excellent guided tour that takes visitors behind the scenes to see the workshop, where more historic aircraft, vehicles, engines and other elements of military history are conserved.

45 Harvard Ave., Wigram. airforcemuseum.co.nz. ✆ **03/343-9532.** Free for NZ residents & intl. military personnel; NZ$15 other adults, under 18 free. Guided tours NZ$5 (under 12s free) at 11am, 1:30pm & 3pm. Daily 9:30am–4:30pm.

He Puna Taimoana ♥ BATHS Fully wheelchair-accessible and family-friendly, He Puna Taimoana has a steam room, sauna, cold-plunge pool, and a much-raved-about cafe, **Saturdays.** Locals love the complex, but visitors may be less impressed, as it doesn't really have the advertised "stunning ocean views." The ocean is obscured by a fence, and can only been seen from the sauna and the top pool (the smallest of five and the most likely to be crowded). During fall, winter, and spring (Apr–Sept), hustle to the pools before sunrise on Tuesdays, Thursdays, and Saturdays and you can bathe while watching the first golden rays of the sun color the eastern sky. It'll set you back NZ$99, but you get a 2-hour soak, a robe to wear, a free mocktail, and an optional guided meditation.

195 Marine Parade, New Brighton. hepunataimoana.co.nz. ✆ **03/941-7818.** Peak/off-peak pricing NZ$20–NZ$25 adults, NZ$15–NZ$20 ages 4–15, free for kids under 4, NZ$51–NZ$56 family pass. 4 daily sessions between 10am–7:30pm, plus Fri 8pm–9:45pm (adults only). Bookings essential.

Kids love the penguins at the International Antarctic Centre.

International Antarctic Centre ♥♥ ATTRACTION The Antarctic Centre might seem like a strange tourist attraction for Christchurch, but the city is one of five gateways worldwide to the icy continent. Every year, more than 2,600 scientists and staff depart from Christchurch's Airport bound for Antarctica. Their work is celebrated here, where visitors can ride on a Hägglund (an all-terrain vehicle used on the continent), brave a "winter storm" (a laughable experience for those from northern climates—the temperature only lowers to 18°F), and learn about the research taking place at the South Pole. The highlight is probably its rescued little blue penguins and white flippered penguins—two species that don't actually live in Antarctica, but are very cute. (Learn more about them from their handlers on a "backstage" tour.) There are lots of hands-on activities, especially for kids, and you can easily spend 2 to 3 hours here. It's also a great place to kill time while waiting for a flight out, as it's only a 5-minute walk from the airport terminal.

Orchard Rd., adjacent to Christchurch Intl. Airport. iceberg.co.nz. ✆ **03/357-0519.** All-day pass with unlimited Hägglund rides and entry to 4D theater NZ$74 adults, NZ$49 children 6–15, NZ$199 families. Daily 9am–4:30pm.

Parks & Gardens

Christchurch Botanic Gardens ♥ GARDENS The turquoise-and-yellow Peacock Fountain by the main entrance on Rolleston Avenue makes a colorful splash, heralding the beauty of the 23 hectares (57 acres) of gardens, with one of the country's finest collections of exotic and local plants, including heritage roses, a tropical conservatory, and an herb garden. Guided 40-minute tours in an all-weather EV are offered by **Christchurch**

Hagley Park: An Urban Oasis

In 1855, the Canterbury Provincial government set aside 165 hectares within the planned city for a public park. **Hagley Park** ♥♥♥ extends from the inner city (Rolleston and Park aves.) to Riccarton, Merivale, and Addington; it is not gated and can be entered at any accessible place. Within its boundaries are a golf course, polo grounds, winter and summer sports fields, tennis courts, a cricket oval, botanic gardens, urban art installations, walking and running tracks, and boatsheds renting out canoes and kayaks. It also has a restaurant (the **Curator's House**), cafe (**Ilex**), and children's playground. The **Canterbury Museum, Arts Centre,** and **Christchurch Art Gallery** are nearby.

Attractions (christchurchattractions.nz/botanic-gardens-tour; pickup by peacock fountain; NZ$30 adult, NZ$15 children). A map with suggested walking tracks is available from the garden's visitor center.

6 Rolleston Ave. ccc.govt.nz. ✆ **03/941-8999.** Free. Conservatories daily 10am–4pm. Ilex cafe daily 9am–5pm (closes 4pm June–Aug).

Orana Wildlife Park ♥♥ ANIMAL PARK Set on 80 attractively laid-out hectares (198 acres), this park is New Zealand's largest wildlife reserve, with the emphasis on a natural environment (so it's "open range," with few fences or cages). The park hosts cheetahs, lions, lemurs, rhinos, giraffes, monkeys, and meercats. The most popular activity for visitors? Helping feed the giraffes!

A giraffe gets a leafy snack from a visitor at Orana Wildlife Park.

743 McLeans Island Rd. oranawildlifepark.co.nz. ✆ **03/359-7109.** NZ$40 adults, NZ$13 ages 5–14, NZ$92 family of 5. Daily 10am–5pm.

Willowbank Wildlife Reserve ♥ ANIMAL PARK The attractive waterways, islands, and trees here are home to wallabies, otters, deer, an alpine aviary with kea, and a number of heritage farm animals including kunekune pigs (a breed unique to NZ). Kiwis can be seen in the always-nighttime nocturnal house. Capybaras, the world's largest rodent, are a recent addition, and you can feed them; bookings are essential for the daily 2pm tour, which costs NZ$45 for adults and NZ$20 for children (must be 8 or older), plus the cost of Reserve entry. Just a 20-minute drive north of the city center, it's a good way to kill a few hours—but far from your only opportunity to see a kiwi in the South Island.

It is, however, the only place in the South Island you can feed a stick of celery to a capybara.

60 Hussey Rd. willowbank.co.nz. ✆ **03/359-6226.** NZ$37 adults, NZ$13 children 5–15, under-4s free; family pass (2 adults and 2 children) NZ$93. Daily 9:30am–5pm.

Organized Tours

With its attractively walkable downtown core, Christchurch lends itself to walking tours, which are a must-do before you explore the city on your own. **Walk Christchurch** ♥ (walkchristchurch.nz; ✆ **03/366-0989**) offers pretty standard 2-hour tours covering key heritage buildings and the earthquake's aftermath for a very affordable NZ$25 adults and NZ$10 ages 12 to 16. Tours leave from in front of The Arts Centre's clock tower at 2 Worcester Boulevard.

Then there's the hop-on, hop-off **Christchurch Tram** ♥ (christchurch attractions.nz; ✆ **03/366-7830**), which has 18 stops throughout the city; the full circuit takes about 50 minutes to complete. It's decently priced at NZ$40 adults, NZ$10 for ages 5 to 15; a family pass of 2 adults and up to 3 children is NZ$95. (When booking on **Christchurch Attractions,** look for package deals such as The Christchurch Pass, which combines a tram pass, **Christchurch Gondola** trip, and **Punting on the Avon** for NZ$114; see p. 430 for descriptions of these individual activities.)

But if I were to choose any tour, it would be with **Watch This Space** ♥♥♥. These captivating walking tours examine the evolving legacy of street art in the city, in relation to its heritage buildings and the rebuild after the earthquake. Typically lasting for 2 hours at a relaxed pace, tours cost NZ$120 for one to two people and NZ$60 per person thereafter (discounts for children and larger groups). Email tours@watchthisspace.org.nz to book; proceeds go back to the charitable trust. Watch This Space also offers an interactive map of current murals and street art throughout the city at watchthisspace.org.nz, if you prefer to go the self-guided route.

Outdoor Pursuits

BEACHES The Christchurch region has dozens of beaches.

- **Best for families:** Originally a holiday suburb, **Sumner** ♥♥ is favored by city dwellers on weekends. Its attractive beach—said to be the city's warmest—is a magnet for swimmers, surfers, and volleyball players. There are plenty of good cafes and ice cream shops nearby. Or, if you have access to a car, drive through the tunnel to Lyttelton and hit up **Corsair Bay** ♥. Compared to Sumner, the small stretch of sand barely qualifies as a beach, but the sheltered shallow water, changing facilities, and diving dock make it an ideal spot for young families.
- **Best for surfing: Taylor's Mistake** ♥♥ is a surfer hangout with holiday homes tucked into the cliffs. There is no public transit to the beach, so you'll need a car. **New Brighton** ♥ is also popular for catching waves, but the neighborhood was hit hard by the earthquake and is gritty around the edges.

- **Best for paddling:** If you're looking for calm waters and want to avoid the crowds, drive west down Governor's Bay Road past Lyttelton until you reach the stunning and calm **Rapaki Bay ♥♥**. Follow the track east of the wharf and you'll find a sandy stretch that's perfect for launching stand-up paddleboards and kayaks.
- **Best for long walks:** The interconnected **Woodend, Pegasus,** and **Waikuku Beaches ♥♥♥** are roughly a 30-minute drive north of the city on SH1. Each beach has plenty of parking, lots of surf, and miles of sand stretching in either direction, yet you may not even pass a single other soul on your journey.

BIKING Christchurch is a cyclists' paradise thanks to its overall flat city terrain and renowned Port Hills mountain biking trails.

Bike lanes have been marked off in several parts of the city, and parking lots provide bike racks. The International Airport even has a bike reassembly station. For rentals and guided tours, contact **Chill ♥**, 287 Durham St. S (chillout.co.nz; ✆ **03/365-6530**). Bike rentals start from NZ$45, with a range of models that include e-bikes, mountain bikes, and gravel bikes. Bike racks, kids' bikes, baby seats, and trailers are also available.

For a jolt of adrenaline, the Christchurch Adventure Park has a zipline soaring above the Cashmere Hills.

For mountain biking, the **Christchurch Adventure Park ♥** (christchurchadventurepark.com; ✆ **0508/247-478** in NZ) is where you can learn or refine skills on beginner to advanced trails, with lessons and rentals available. A chairlift takes riders to the top. For those wanting to go a little faster, there's a zipline and The Rush, the world's first motorized uphill cable ride, which will zoom you backward and then rocket you back down. No jetpack required.

BLOKARTING & DRIFTKARTING Christchurch is a windy city, and therefore a prime place for blokarting. A sport unique to NZ, it's essentially land sailing in a three-wheeled vehicle. Regardless of whether you're 8 or 80, the staff at **Velocity Karts ♥♥** (Bexley Reserve on Pages Rd.; velocitykarts.nz; ✆ **03/3888-222**) will show you the literal ropes. The activity is best combined with a spin on the motorized Drift Karts (yet another NZ invention), where you learn to "drift" through the course's corners. Bookings are essential. Velocity is open most Thursdays through Sundays, with activities starting at NZ$30 per person.

Ain't No Mountain High Enough

There's no argument—the **Christchurch Gondola** ♥, 10 Bridle Path Rd. (christchurchattractions.nz/christchurch-gondola; ✆ **03/366-7830**), offers one of the best views in the city. After riding 862 horizontal meters (2,828 ft.) up from the Heathcote Valley, you'll arrive at the terminal atop Mount Cavendish, where you'll have 360-degree views of turquoise harbors and the peaks of the Southern Alps. It runs daily from 10am to 5pm.

Want to know a secret, though? If you've got a car and a bit of energy, you can save the NZ$42 (NZ$22 kids 5–15) by walking or driving to the top for free. The most popular hike is the easy but steep **Bridle Path,** which starts from the gondola parking lot. The less-trafficked **Major Hornbrook** track from Lyttelton will get you there as well. Budget 45 to 60 minutes for both walks. Or drive along Summit Road until you reach the roadside pullout underneath the terminal, where the road widens. It's unmarked, but from there it's just a 5-minute walk up a well-trodden path to the gondola's cafe, where you can buy a cold drink and act like you did the entire slog to the top.

BOATING **Punting** is an idyllic way to spend an afternoon, especially since someone else is doing all the work. You'll spot the well-dressed young men and women from **Punting on the Avon** ♥ (christchurchattractions.nz/punting; ✆ **03/366-7830**), sporting straw hats as they pole their way up the Avon River, round the Oxford Terrace and Worcester Boulevard. You can reserve a ride at the Antigua Boatsheds at 2 Cambridge Terrace for NZ$42 adults and NZ$30 for ages 5 to 15. It's an exceedingly pleasant 30-minute ride, which is ample time to enjoy the lush riverbank and lapping water. If self-guided is more your flavor, you can rent your own canoe, kayak, rowboat, or paddleboat from the same location, starting from NZ$23 for an hour.

GOLF The Canterbury region boasts over 60 courses. **Harewood Twin Courses** ♥♥, 371 McLeans Island Rd. (harewoodgolf.co.nz; ✆ **03/359-8843**), is the largest golf club in the South Island, with two 18-hole courses. Green fees are NZ$90 for 18 holes. Billing itself as "the thinking person's course," **Clearwater Resort** ♥♥♥, 40A Clearwater Ave. (clearwatergolf.co.nz; ✆ **03/360-2146**), was developed by golfing legend Sir Bob Charles and course designer John Darby, who dreamed of an "immaculately challenging course." It's NZ$195 for 18 holes. A fine on-site restaurant and lounge will help you recover afterward.

Farther afield, you'll find **Fable Terrace Downs** ♥♥♥ in Rakaia (terracedowns.co.nz; ✆ **03/318-6943**), a 50-minute drive from Christchurch. The high-end, high-country course has spectacular views of Mount Hutt, 70 bunkers, eight lakes, rolling fairways, on-site accommodations, and a beautiful clubhouse. Green fees start at NZ$95 for 18 holes.

HIKING Ancient volcanic hills close to the city paired with ocean vistas make Christchurch a great walking city. Popular day hikes include the **Crater Rim Walkway** ♥, which takes 9 to 10 hours in its entirety, but can be walked in sections; and **Godley's Head** ♥♥ a 3-hour oceanside walk starting at

Taylor's Mistake. Find an excellent interactive track map for all city and hinterland walks at ccc.govt.nz/parks-and-gardens/explore-parks/walking-track-map.

JET-BOATING Several operators offer exhilarating spins up the stunning blue Waimakariri River. The most established is **Alpine Jet Thrills** ♥♥ (alpinejetthrills.com; ✆ **03/263-6263**), which offers 1-hour trips through the Waimakariri Gorge from NZ$155 adults, NZ$125 children.

WHITEWATER RAFTING **Hanmer Springs Attractions** ♥ (hanmerspringsattractions.nz; ✆ **0800/661-538** in NZ) offers 2-hour rafting trips along the Waiau River. This is a scenic adventure for families, rather than thrill seekers—even though cliff jumping is part of the fun, the rapids themselves only reach a grade 2 level. It costs NZ$169 for adults, NZ$99 for ages 6 to 13, and NZ$379 for families of five.

Where to Stay in Christchurch

EXPENSIVE

Hotel Montreal ♥♥♥ The theme of this stylish boutique all-suite hotel is polo, reflecting the owning family's involvement in the sport. But don't come expecting saddle chairs and paintings of horses: The decor is more for the "horsey set," with lots of leather, velvets, and tony neutral colors (the contemporary art and comfy furniture throughout is so outstanding that guests often inquire about purchasing). The hotel has a swank bar and restaurant (cocktails and tapas, anyone?), courtyard with pizza oven, and a croquet green. All is possible for this crack staff, and inquiries are welcomed by the front desk.

363 Montreal St. hotelmontreal.co.nz. ✆ **03/943-8547.** 26 units. NZ$499–NZ$1,659 suite. **Amenities:** Restaurant, bar; croquet green; in-room iPads; fitness center; free Wi-Fi.

The Mayfair ♥♥ Situated on the edge of the central city, the chic and sleek Mayfair hotel opened in 2022. Its plushly carpeted contemporary rooms are decorated in neutral tones and filled with natural light from floor-to-ceiling windows. Oversize TVs, blazing fast internet, and Dyson hair dryers in each bathroom are just some of the welcome high-tech touches here. Downstairs, the **Majestic at Mayfair** cafe is popular with locals and hotel guests alike. In the evening, it transforms into a buzzy cocktail bar and restaurant, serving slow-cooked meats and fresh, zesty salads.

155 Victoria St. mayfairluxuryhotels.com. ✆ **03/595-6335.** 67 units. NZ$314–NZ$669 double. **Amenities:** Restaurant, bar; access to nearby gym; free Wi-Fi.

Observatory Hotel ♥♥♥ Is this the most iconically "Christchurch" hotel in Christchurch? It's only been open since 2022, but I can already say with certainty: "Yes." Much of that has to do with its setting, right in the heart of the famed **Arts Centre** ♥♥♥ (p. 421), a mixture of Old English and French gothic buildings that were once the campus for the University of Canterbury. Today the Arts Centre houses galleries, boutique retailers, a mini-cinema and wine bars—and this hotel. But while its castle-like exterior pulls guests back in time, its sumptuous interior has all the modern conveniences,

Sink into a couch in the Observatory Hotel's elegant lounge.

and is filled with bright, colorful contemporary artwork by local painters and illustrators. Each room is individually decorated and equipped with fine furniture made in Canterbury. A quiet enclave that's walking distance from everywhere you might want to go, it has everything you need for a city stay.

9 Hereford St. observatoryhotel.co.nz. ✆ **03/666-0670.** 33 units. NZ$349–NZ$1,299 double. Rates include continental breakfast. Parking NZ$30. **Amenities:** Lounge; gym; free Wi-Fi.

Otahuna Lodge ♥♥♥ An 1895 Victorian mansion snuggled into gentle green hills, Otahuna Lodge is New Zealand's largest private historic residence. It has a kitchen garden and orchard, and all the fittings and furbelows that might befit the lifestyle of Canterbury's landed gentry. Owned and hosted by Hall Cannon and Miles Refo, this Relais & Chateaux property successfully combines the style of the Edwardian era with the amenities of today. It's swathed in comfort and luxuries. Yes, it's pricey, but you'd expect that for one of *National Geographic*'s 100 Hotels of a Lifetime, a distinction it achieved in 2024. Rates include breakfast and a five-course seasonal degustation dinner. The hotel is expert in arranging fly-fishing, golfing, horseback riding, heli-touring excursions, and more.

Rhodes Rd., Tai Tapu. otahuna.co.nz. ✆ **03/329-6333.** 7 units. NZ$2,600–NZ$6,800. Rates include breakfast and dinner. **Amenities:** Restaurant, bar; bikes; concierge; gym; outdoor pool; tennis court; walking and biking trails; wine cellar; free Wi-Fi.

EXPENSIVE/MODERATE

The Classic Villa ♥♥ This 1897 central city home is steeped in history. It's been a chaplain's house, student flats, and an old folk's home; now it's a stylish boutique hotel right in the heart of the action, opposite the Arts Centre. Upstairs accommodations were added in 2006. These rooms are modern, lighter, and sunnier than the original downstairs rooms, but the downstairs rooms have much more architectural character. Large downstairs dining and sitting rooms open onto a small private garden where you can enjoy a quiet drink after a day's sightseeing. Despite its size, it has a strong feeling of home and is a little more personable than nearby Orari (another former heritage home that's now a hotel).

17 Worcester Blvd. theclassicvilla.co.nz. ✆ **03/377-7905.** 12 units. NZ$299–NZ$599 double. Rates include breakfast. **Amenities:** Bar; bike rentals; free Wi-Fi.

Crowne Plaza Christchurch ♥♥ What was once a 17-story earthquake-damaged office building is now Christchurch's biggest executive-style hotel, boasting responsive customer service, a restaurant that offers a filling feed, and rooms with luxurious touches like window seats and sound systems in the bathrooms. The decor is modern with an Art Deco flair. What really sets this hotel apart is its exceptional location and views of the Avon River. It's walking distance to everything, and its height puts it literally one above the rest.

764 Colombo St. christchurch.crowneplaza.com. ✆ **03/741-2800.** 204 units. NZ$209–NZ$474 double. Parking NZ$25. **Amenities:** Restaurants, bar; fitness center; concierge; 24-hr. room service; free Wi-Fi.

MODERATE

The Adina Heritage Hotel Christchurch ♥♥ Offering charm and character in what was originally the Old Government Building (ca. 1913), the Heritage has huge spaces and scads of elegant details (tessellated entry tiles, brass railings, French doors, Scarlett O'Hara–worthy staircase), adorning its central-city site. The accommodations comprise good-size, fully self-contained one-, two-, and three-bedroom suites, each with kitchen (including dishwasher) and living area.

28–30 Cathedral Square. heritagehotels.co.nz. ✆ **03/983-4800.** 35 units. NZ$234–NZ$619 suites. **Amenities:** Restaurant; gym; indoor pool; tour desk; free Wi-Fi.

Commodore Airport Hotel ♥♥ A sizable property with 156 rooms, the Commodore has been owned and run by the Patterson family since 1971. The quality service, staff, and ambience are far removed from the standard airport hotel experience. For starters, the property is not "at" the airport, but on Memorial Avenue, a route from central Christchurch to the airport via the leafy suburb of Fendalton, which also explains the lush sprawl of the hotel's 7-acre grounds. It's a winning combo of charm, outstanding staff (no request is too difficult for this competent team), and full-service facilities.

449 Memorial Ave., Burnside. commodorehotel.co.nz. ✆ **03/358-8129.** 156 units. NZ$295–NZ$669 double. Free parking. **Amenities:** Restaurant, bar; bike rental; business center; fitness center; indoor pool; complimentary shuttle transfer to/from airport; free Wi-Fi.

Drifter ♥♥♥ The design-led Drifter is the most stylish hostel we've ever seen. It offers a range of brand-new hotel and dorm rooms outfitted with quality fixtures and natural textures in soothing blush, sand, greens, caramel, and chocolate. Different bed and bunk configurations make it great for groups and families. The shared working, cooking, dining, and lounging spaces include a library, movie room, a bespoke vending machine filled with gourmet New Zealand foods, and even a self-guided yoga studio; just select a workout and

A restful guest room at the Drifter, which is part hotel, part hostel, with a host of amenities.

namaste away. There are countless thoughtful touches; the premium suite even has a record player and a selection of vinyl. Occupying the ground floor, **The Rambler ♥♥♥** (therambler.co.nz; ✆ **022/182-4296**), an excellent restaurant and bar, hosts Drifter's community events: there are DJ sets every Friday and Saturday from 6pm, arts and crafts nights, daily happy hour from 4pm, and more.

96 Lichfield Street. thedrifter.com/christchurch. ✆ **03/659-0066.** NZ$52 (single bed in 8-person dorm)–NZ$413 (premium double). **Amenities:** Bar/restaurant; library; movie room; yoga/fitness room; free Wi-Fi.

The Muse Art Hotel ♥ The hallways of the Muse Art Hotel—a former office building—are brightened by murals painted by local Christchurch street artists. Otherwise, the hotel is surprisingly short on "art." Its decor is formulaic: Art Deco–esque velvet furnishings offset by metallic and marble finishes. But the Muse's saving grace is that it's exactly what you'd expect for its price range: clean, comfortable, and central. There's no parking lot, but you should have no trouble finding a free spot on the street overnight.

159 Manchester St. themusehotel.co.nz. ✆ **03/365-0319.** 40 units. NZ$319–NZ$345 double. **Amenities:** Free Wi-Fi.

INEXPENSIVE

There are numerous reasonably priced and good motels along Riccarton Road, Bealey Avenue, and Papanui Road. It's a competitive market, so don't forget to ask about special deals.

Jailhouse Accommodation ♥♥ What's in a name? Well, from 1874 to 1999, this hostel was the site of the Addington Prison. Evidence of its history can be found in one of the cells, which has been preserved with some of the artwork from its inmates. The rest of the cells have been converted into 6- and 10-bed backpacker dorms, and private twin, single, double, and family rooms. While it wins major marks for its unusual setting, its downfall is that the rooms are as small as a prison cell (because, well, you know). All the hard white surfaces also mean noise in the corridor is amplified, but since it's not known as a party hostel, you're guaranteed a night's sleep so good that it almost feels criminal.

338 Lincoln Rd., Addington. jail.co.nz. ✆ **03/982-7777.** Shared dorms NZ$44–NZ$55; private rooms NZ$110–NZ$132. **Amenities:** Kitchen; cinema lounge; guest laundry; bike hire; pool table; espresso bar; free Wi-Fi.

The Studios at Bealey Quarter ♥ A newer property, this is an affordable, clean, straightforward motel within walking distance of the city center. Its sister property, the **Lodge at Bealey Quarter**—which caters to the backpacker crowd—is directly next door, as is the Bealey pub. The latter can get busy on weekends, which is great for those looking to make friends. Those who want shut-eye earlier than 11pm (which is when the pub closes) might want to give both properties a pass, particularly on weekends.

247 Bealey Ave. bealeyquarter.co.nz. ✆ **03/667-6610.** 39 units. Motel NZ$110–NZ$225; dorms from NZ$41. **Amenities:** Laundry; BBQ area; free Wi-Fi.

Where to Eat in Christchurch

Contemporary restaurants and tiny cocktail bars line the Spanish Mission–style, car-free laneway **New Regent Street** ♥♥ (soulofthecity.co.nz). It's a top neighborhood for dinner, and for dessert, stroll along to see Frank, the giant gorilla statue outside **Rollickin' Gelato Bar** ♥♥♥ at number 35 (rollickin.co.nz; ✆ **03/365-4811**). Their homemade gelato, dairy-free sorbets, and boxed make-at-home (or your hotel) desserts are the lure here, in an array of changing flavors. It's open daily from 11am to 10pm (until 11pm on Friday and Saturday nights). There's also a second outlet at 98 Cashel St., near the Riverside Markets, with the same nightlife-friendly hours.

Want to sample the region's best wines without leaving town? Make a reservation at **Cellar Door** ♥♥ (cellardoor.nz; ✆ **03/925-8497**), nestled in the iconic Arts Centre building at 1 Hereford St. This romantic little restaurant offers curated wine tasting flights, celebrating the region's finest bottles with fresh seasonal food to match. It's open daily from noon until late.

EXPENSIVE

5th Street ♥♥ NEW ZEALAND MODERN From the street, you probably wouldn't think much of this unassuming spot. But the warehouse exterior opens to an atrium filled with hanging plants, natural light, and Art Deco detailing. The top-rated food is just as memorable—share plates heavy on vegetables and bright, punchy flavors, such as buttered carrots with romesco and goat's cheese, or slow-roasted lamb shoulder with pickled onion and cucumber labneh.

5 Elgin St., Sydenham. www.5thstreet.co.nz. ✆ **03/365-9667.** Share plates NZ$15–NZ$80. Reservations essential. Daily 4:30pm–late.

Hello Sunday ♥♥♥ CAFE From its sunny name to its even sunnier, plant-filled location in a refurbished 19th-century post office, Hello Sunday delivers fine-dining brunch any day of the week. It's reputed to have the best

Eggs Benny in Christchurch, the old breakfast standard deliciously jazzed up with leek and preserved-lemon potato hash, and offers hearty mains such as shakshuka and buffalo chicken hotcakes, too. They even suggest cocktails with brunch, so you can pair a salted caramel espresso martini with that eggs Benedict. If you want a table on the weekend, book in advance.

6 Elgin St., Sydenham. hellosunday.co.nz. ✆ **03/260-1566.** NZ$25–NZ$38. Weekdays 7:30am–3pm, weekends 8am–3pm.

Exquisite cocktails and entrees at Hello Sunday.

Manu ♥♥♥ ASIAN-PACIFIC FUSION A striking, luxe interior with velvet booths, Manu is staffed with wonderful souls born to the hospitality profession. Manu's flavors are surprising and the dishes visually striking, with an emphasis on seafood, such as tuna poke, crispy prawn balls, and *pāua* (abalone) spring rolls; there are also inventive goat, beef, lamb, and pork dishes. I have never seen duck nachos with whipped feta and pineapple salsa on a menu before, but it works. You'll need reservations for this popular dining experience.

151 Cambridge Terrace. manu.co.nz. ✆ **03/421-3887.** Main courses NZ$17–NZ$48. Reservations essential. Daily 5pm–late.

Tussock Hill Vineyard ♥♥♥ WINERY You don't have to drive to Akaroa or the Waipara Valley to experience one of Canterbury's best winery experiences. Hidden at the end of a residential street high in the Port Hills,

Reservtions are essential for stylish, convivial Manu, with its inventive Asian-Pacific fusion menu.

FOOD for the indecisive

Can't get everyone to agree on a place to eat? Christchurch's food halls might just prevent a family feud. **The Little High Eatery ♥**, 255 St. Asaph St. (littlehigh.co.nz), was the first, and it has nine restaurants today, which include a sushi shop, the highly rated **Bacon Brothers' ♥** burger bar, a fried chicken and gin bar, and Thai street food. Just check in with the host, grab a table, and wait for your buzzer to light up. For someplace a bit quieter, head to **The Welder ♥♥**, 20 Welles St. (thewelder.nz). A complex dedicated to health and wellness, it features a tapas and wine bar, a modern Italian eatery, two plant-based cafes, a saki and yakitori restaurant, and a couple of bakeries. Its small, plant-filled atrium is a calmer and more upscale spot to enjoy a meal.

Another newcomer to the Central City is the **Riverside Market ♥♥** (riverside.nz), at the corner of Lichfield Street and Oxford Terrace. In addition to the cheesemongers, fishmongers, and bakeries you'd expect from any indoor market, it's home to eateries serving up everything from gelato and tea to fried chicken, roti, and ramen. You can grab your meal to go, choose from one of the many sit-down restaurants, or go across the street to **King of Snake ♥♥**, 79 Cashel St. (kingofsnake.co.nz; ✆ **03/365-7363**), which serves modern Asian share plates.

The Welder, Little High Eatery, and Riverside Market are all open daily, from morning 'til night, with trading hours for individual outlets varying.

you'll find this small, family-owned winery and restaurant overlooking the city, its vineyard below, and the Southern Alps beyond. Surrounded by greenery, it's got the most idyllic location, and the menu boasts the likes of oysters, lamb shoulder with roasted nectarine mustard, and sake vanilla rice pudding—all with wine matching, of course. Request a table near the windows, although there isn't really a bad seat in the house.

210 Huntsbury Ave., Cashmere. tussockhill.co.nz. Share plates NZ$23–NZ$89. Wed–Thurs 10am–4pm; Fri–Sun 10am–5pm. Bookings recommended.

Twenty Seven Steps ♥♥ RUSTIC EUROPEAN New Regent Street's architecture makes an elegant backdrop for this streamlined space, featuring handsome arched windows. Look for generous dishes such as aged Canterbury beef fillet with Yorkshire pudding and duck fat potato fondant, or the Kiwi dessert classic of sticky toffee pudding with salted caramel and vanilla ice cream.

16 New Regent St. twentysevensteps.co.nz. ✆ **03/366-2727.** Main courses NZ$39–NZ$60. Mon–Sat 5–10pm.

MODERATE/INEXPENSIVE

C1 Espresso ♥ CAFE Here's the thing: Coffee snobs will probably tell you that C1 doesn't have the best flat white, and food critics will say that the service can be hit-or-miss at best. (C1 even publishes the worst of its TripAdvisor reviews on its highly entertaining menu.) But this cafe, housed in the former High Street Post Office building, is a helluva lot of fun anyway. Food—nachos, burgers, hot dogs—is delivered to your table at high speed through pneumatic tubes. The bathrooms are behind a secret doorway, where

Harry Potter audiobooks play while you do your business. Water comes from a Singer sewing machine. You can even get your face printed on a hot chocolate. Verdict? Visit for the novelty factor alone.

185 High St. c1espresso.co.nz. No phone. NZ$6.90–NZ$27. Mon–Fri 7am–9pm, Sat–Sun 7am–5pm.

Cassels & Sons Brewery Bar ♥ BREWPUB You can't go wrong with beer and a pizza. That's the classic combination that this brewpub—one of the only wood-fired breweries in the world—relies on. Naturally, the pizza is also wood-fired, although Cassels & Sons' lamb shanks, mac & cheese, and pub snacks go with a cold brew just as nicely. There's plenty of indoor and outdoor seating, and frequently there's live music. All the makings of a relaxing afternoon out.

3 Garlands Rd., Woolston. cassels.nz. ✆ **03/389-5359.** Breakfast NZ$9–NZ$28; all-day main courses NZ$24–NZ$35. Daily 8am–late.

Child Sister ♥♥ CAFE This cafe, located right across from the wonderful, whimsical Margaret Mahy playground, is one of the best places to fill you up for the day. The light, bright, and airy space serves up classic staples and inventive brunch and lunch, some with a Korean twist—like kimchi rice, honey butter waffle fries, or potato leek chili cheese scones.

277 Manchester St. facebook.com/childsistercafe. ✆ **03/222-2117.** Main courses NZ$20–NZ$27. Daily 8am–4pm (kitchen closes 2:30pm).

Grizzly Baked Goods ♥♥♥ BAKERY It wasn't long after Sam Ellis started baking bagels to sell at the farmers' market that his hobby grew into a full-blown business. Now you can pick up his filled donuts, pastries (including melt-in-your-mouth almond bearclaws) and bagel sandwiches from five locations around Canterbury. The goods sell out early, but this is one stop worth waking up for.

33 Buchan St., Sydenham. grizzlybakedgoods.com. ✆ **03/964-0650.** Pastries and sandwiches from NZ$5.50. Also at 56 Cashel St.; inside The Welder at 20–26 Welles St.; at Ohoka Farmers Market (Fri only); and at Christchurch Farmers' Market, Riccarton Bush (Sat only). Hours vary but usually 8–9am to mid-afternoon.

Portershed ♥♥ VEGAN Stock up on a wide variety of vegan sweets, treats, and groceries at this popular cafe, locally beloved for its twist on Kiwi favorites. Cabinet food includes "sausage" rolls, sandwiches, satay chickpea wraps, and savory pies, whereas the full menu offers plant-based burgers, Mexican-inspired dishes, and a particularly hearty Buddha bowl heaving with crisp greens, toasted seeds, grains, and fresh vegetables. Do indulge in one or two of their nut-based cakes and slices; the Pinkalicious, a chocolate-caramel-raspberry marshmallow confection, is delicious fun indeed. There's also a range of interesting coffee and milk alternatives; try a Blue Dream, a bright blue butterfly-pea latte.

322 Lincoln Rd., Addington. portershed.co.nz. Message via facebook.com/portershed cafe. NZ$17–NZ$27. Tues–Sat 8am–5pm.

Utopia Ice ♥♥ GELATO Another success story of the Christchurch Farmers' Market, this small-batch ice creamery moved into the sweetest little shopfront in the beachside village of Sumner, where it serves up homemade gelato, vegan ice cream, and freshly baked waffles. Flavors are local and ever-changing; as well as the classics, consider bay leaf lemon curd honeycomb or Aperol blood orange.

15 Wakefield Ave., Sumner. facebook.com/utopiaice. ✆ **03/326-6768.** Hours change seasonally; generally open until 9pm in warmer months.

Nightlife & Entertainment

PERFORMING ARTS

The brand-new home of the **Court Theatre,** on the corner of Colombo and Gloucester streets (courttheatre.org.nz), is one of only seven theaters globally that was built by its own theater troupe; the Court is New Zealand's largest theater company. As well as its high-quality theater, we recommend the excellent late-night improv laugh-fest Scared Scriptless, Australasia's longest-running comedy show. It's on most Fridays at 9pm; tickets are NZ$25.

Just off New Regent Street, the **Isaac Theatre Royal,** 145 Gloucester St. (isaactheatreroyal.co.nz), is the spiritual heart of Christchurch's arts scene, hosting live theater, concerts, and musical performances. The iconic building has stood in this place since 1906. Civic and performance venue **Christchurch Town Hall,** 86 Kilmore St. (facebook.com/ChristchurchTownHall), offers intimate concerts and public speaking events. A number of small theaters also exist, most notably **Little Andromeda** (littleandromeda.co.nz), tucked away at 134 Oxford Terrace in the River Market complex. Settle into the intimate 100-seat theater to enjoy more improv, comedy, and indie plays.

The brand-new **One New Zealand Stadium** (onenewzealandstadium.co.nz) aka **Te Kaha,** will host crowds of tens of thousands for major sporting and cultural events; it's due to open in April 2026.

BARS

Those looking for a raucous night out will find it at one of the bars located in the River Market, with **Fat Eddie's** ♥, Level 1/76 Hereford St. (fateddiesbar.co.nz), being a local fave. It's open Tuesday to Saturday until the wee morning hours, with live music line-ups nearly every night.

For date night vibes, New Regent Street is the place to go. That's where you'll find the **Last Word** ♥♥, 31 New Regent St. (lastword.co.nz; ✆ **022/094-7445**), a cozy whiskey and cocktail lounge. It's charismatic and

Organ pipes above the bar testify to the Church Brew Pub's previous life as a Gothic Revival church. See p. 440.

DAY TRIPS TO THE wineries

Home to more than 80 wineries, the Canterbury region is now NZ's fourth-largest winemaking area. The combination of long hours of sunshine; stony, free-draining soils; low rainfall; extended autumns; and cool winters produces grapes with complex and developed flavors. The region is well suited to producing red wines such as cabernet, merlot, and pinot noir.

The main area to explore is the **Waipara Valley** (about 45 min. north of the city), although a small handful of wineries can be found near **Akaroa** on the Banks Peninsula (90 min. south). Both areas are substantially less commercial than those you'll find in the famed wine regions of Hawke's Bay and Marlborough. It's best to double-check winery hours and food options prior to arrival, because they frequently change. The **North Canterbury Wine Region** website (northcanterburywines.co.nz) has an interactive map listing tasting rooms (called "cellar doors"), producers, and restaurants throughout the region.

Driving north of Amberley, the first winery you'll likely see is the **Waipara Hills Winery,** a woefully grandiose building on the corner of the highway. Skip it and head around the corner to the much more beautiful **Pegasus Bay Winery & Restaurant ♥♥♥**, 263 Stockgrove Rd. (pegasusbay.com; ✆ **03/314-6869;** open Thurs–Mon 10am–5pm), run by the

Visiting the vineyards at Greystone Wines.

cute, and it has an outstanding list of whiskeys and a sprinkling of top-drawer wines.

The Church Brew Pub, 124 Worcester St. (churchpub.co.nz; ✆ **03/595-1533**), is both a cornerstone of Christchurch's live music scene and worth a visit just to appreciate its thoughtful restoration. The former 1875 Gothic church was earthquake damaged but has been renovated with an eye to its heritage features, such as pews for seating, and its bar, nestled in front of the soaring pipe organ.

SIDE TRIPS FROM CHRISTCHURCH

If you are traveling without a car, **Leisure Tours ♥** (leisuretours.co.nz; ✆ **03/384-0999**) and **Hassle-free Tours ♥** (hasslefreetours.co.nz; ✆ **03/385-5775**) can both get you to the Christchurch and Canterbury region's top sites. Prices vary by itinerary. **Canterbury Trails ♥♥** (canterburytrails.co.nz;

Donaldson family, who have been seriously involved with wine for over 30 years. They make high-quality sauvignon/semillon, chardonnay, merlot cabernet, pinot noir, and riesling. If you only have time for a glass, sample yours while wandering through the pristine gardens.

Just across the highway, several other wineries are clustered along the easily bikeable Georges Road. The organic **Greystone Wines,** 8 Vineyard Lane, Waipara (greystonewines.co.nz; ✆ **03/314-6100;** open Thurs–Mon 11am–4:30pm), offers a four-course Trust the Chef lunch with wine pairings for NZ$149 per person (excluding wine, it's NZ$105 per person); book for this via the website. Greystone also has a spectacular glass-walled, glass-ceilinged, two-person eco-cabin, the **Greystone PurePod,** ideal for stargazing in these inky black night skies. The pod-only rate is NZ$649; pod plus a food hamper is NZ$848. Book the cabin via purepods.com.

Another organic winery, **Terrace Edge** ♥♥, 328 Georges Rd. (terraceedge.co.nz; ✆ **021/0843-5268**), is one of only two local producers of Albariño (a zippy white wine) and also makes its own olive oil. In is tasting room (open Thurs–Mon 11am–4pm) you can sample five organic wines, olive oil, and table olives for NZ$20. Bookings are recommended.

At the end of the road, **The Boneline** ♥♥♥, 376 Ram Paddock Rd. (theboneline.co.nz; ✆ **027/434-2683;** open daily 11am–4pm), doesn't have as glossy a tasting room as some of the others, but there's something to be said for its stunning rows of iconic cabbage trees backed by mountains. There's also plenty to be said for the wines: There's a sauvignon blanc that tastes like pie crust and a rosé that's as refreshing as a cold beer on a hot day. Tastings are typically free, there's a simple sharing menu, and you can walk around the property on weekends. (Ask for a map.) They also have an Airbnb, **Waipara Vineyard Retreat** ♥, for around NZ$350 a night.

Leisure Tours (leisuretours.co.nz; ✆ **03/384-0996**) offers full-day excursions to the Waipara Valley starting at NZ$145.

✆ **03/384-6148**) does guided day trips to Akaroa and Arthur's Pass, and specializes in small group or private tours.

Rated as one of the world's most spectacular train journeys, the **TranzAlpine** ♥♥♥ train travels from the east coast, over the Canterbury Plains and through the heart of the Southern Alps to the West Coast. It's a super-easy way to see a lot in a day, although there is only a 1-hour stop in Greymouth before the return trip departs. It's worth noting, however, that the train follows the exact same route you can drive in a car, so if you have a rental, it may not be worth the extra investment. For reservations (starting from NZ$289), contact **Great Journeys of New Zealand** (greatjourneysnz.com; ✆ **04/495-0775**).

Akaroa

After French whaler Jean-François Langlois took back to France word of New Zealand's rich land and forests, a handful of Gallic settlers set sail in 1840 to colonize Akaroa Harbor. They were too late, however—the British had beaten them to it with the signing of the Treaty of Waitangi. The colonization plan was abandoned, but the settlers stayed on. Today they are remembered in small settlements around Akaroa: Le Bons Bay, Duvauchelle, and French Farm. Other than its street names, Akaroa is not particularly French in style, but it is a pretty town and makes a fun day or overnight trip from Christchurch, with its dolphin tours, vineyards, cheeseries, gardens, and old-world charm.

ESSENTIALS

ARRIVING Akaroa isn't far from Christchurch in distance (it's only 75km [46½] miles away), but you'll still need to budget 90 minutes to drive there on SH75. Past Little River, the road becomes hilly and windy. If time allows, follow the signs for the scenic route, which takes about an extra 20 minutes. It will give you absolutely epic views down to the turquoise bays of the water below. **Akaroa French Connection** (akaroabus.co.nz; ✆ **0800/800-575** in NZ) offers regular coach departures from Christchurch city center with brief scenic stop-offs for NZ$70 round-trip.

VISITOR INFORMATION The official visitor site for the region is akaroa.com. Ignore conflicting information online; there is no longer an Akaroa isite Visitor Centre.

EXPLORING AKAROA

Akaroa's attractive waterfront is very walkable, with homes, cafes, and shops sprinkled along pretty scoops of bay. Leave some time to stroll out to the lighthouse along Beach Road.

Painter, sculptor, and horticulturist Josie Martin has combined her talents to astonishing effect at **The Giant's House** ♥♥♥, 68 Rue Balguerie (thegiantshouse.co.nz; ✆ **03/304-7501**). Martin has surrounded her historic home with landscaped gardens and massive, surreal mosaic sculptures. Budget at least 45 minutes to explore the space and aim to arrive early to beat the crowds. The garden and on-site cafe are open daily from 11am to 4pm (they close at 3pm May–Sept); entry costs NZ$35 adults, NZ$20 ages 2 to 15.

The boat-filled harbor in Akaroa.

A mosaic sculpture in the garden of The Giant's House.

Explore Akaroa Harbor or swim with rare Hector's dolphins on one of several scenic cruise options with **Black Cat Cruises** ♥ (blackcat.co.nz; ✆ **03/304-7641**). Trips depart morning and afternoon from Main Wharf and cost from NZ$125 for adults and NZ$60 for children (ages 5–15). Black Cat's Dolphin Promise means that if you don't see dolphins, a future cruise is free.

Across the harbor, a 20-minute drive from town, another top attraction is **Shamarra Alpacas** ♥♥ (shamarra-alpacas.co.nz; ✆ **03/304-5141**). During a 1-hour tour (NZ$60 adult, NZ$35 child 3–15) you'll have the chance to cuddle the fluffiest, cutest alpacas against a panoramic backdrop of the harbor, and purchase beautiful cashmere-like alpaca garments and blankets, too. Bus pickups are available from town, but bookings are essential.

Departing from Akaroa village, **Pōhatu Penguins** ♥♥ (pohatu.co.nz; ✆ **03/304-8542**) offers a wide range of walks, kayaks, farmstays, and self-drive tours in and around the Flea Bay Marine Reserve (tours from NZ$115 adults, NZ$75 ages 5–15), down on the coast near Akaroa Head. The knowledgeable tour guides are also volunteers working on penguin conservation.

NZ's night sky is spectacular, and family-run **Akaroa Stargazing** (akaroa stargazing.com; ✆ **021/024-30328**) offers nighttime astronomy tours outside of town in the hills of the Banks Peninsula. Comfy outdoor chairs, blankets, and a hot drink will have you contemplating your place in the universe in no time (NZ$109 for adults, NZ$69 children, for 90 min. of outdoor stargazing). If it's raining, there's an indoor option. For daylight hours, a half-hour sun viewing from Akaroa's lighthouse (NZ$39 adult, NZ$19 child) will give you a new view of our home star. A wonderful way to spend a sunset is the Astronomy Bites tour (NZ$379/NZ$199), which takes you from sungazing to stargazing with a grazing platter of local snacks.

HIKING THE BANKS TRACK

Consider this: Miles of coastal farmland scenery; undisturbed colonies of fur seals, penguins, and dolphins; sheltered turquoise bays; the rustic comforts of trampers' huts; and enough moderate exertion to keep you honest. This is what you get walking **Banks Track** ♥♥ (bankstrack.co.nz; ✆ **03/304-7612**). The track twice climbs to 600m (1,970 ft.) and features rugged, exposed headlands, so a reasonable level of fitness is required. The season runs from October through April. There are both 2- and 3-night options starting from NZ$220, which includes transport from Akaroa to the first hut and accommodations. The 3-day option includes having your pack transported.

A TALE OF TWO hot springs: HANMER SPRINGS & METHVEN

Hanmer Springs, located about 1½ hours north of Christchurch, has attracted visitors for over 125 years, thanks to its natural hot springs and adventure activities. But it's now got serious competition: The alpine village of **Methven,** just an hour west of the city, has recently unveiled its own hot springs complex.

Here's how the two destinations stack up:

HANMER: BEST FOR FAMILIES

With 22 thermal pools filled with water from a nearby natural thermal bore, the **Thermal Pools & Spa ♥♥**, 42 Amuri Ave. (hanmersprings.co.nz; ✆ **03/315-0000;** from NZ$40), are Hanmer's main drawcard. Super kid-friendly, they even have waterslides here! That's cool if you're a kid, less so if you're an adult looking for a serene getaway. We'd say this family-friendly vibe extends throughout the entirety of the resort town. After a soak in the springs, it's easy to wander up the main street, get an ice cream cone, play a game of mini-golf, or pop into some of the boutiques. Since this *is* New Zealand, bungy jumping or jetboating with Hanmer Springs Attractions (hanmerspringsattractions.nz) is also available, and there are extensive hiking and cycling trails through pine and native forest. The 2-hour hike to the 41m (135-ft.) **Dog Stream Waterfall ♥♥** is one of the area's best.

Accommodations are easy to find in Hanmer; simply check Airbnb or Bookabach.com for one of the area's many holiday home rentals.

METHVEN: BEST FOR ROMANTIC GETAWAYS

Methven was once considered a wintertime destination (it's the village for the

WHERE TO STAY IN AKAROA

French Bay House ♥♥ These bright and modern rooms don't distract from this beautiful 1874 villa's building's storied history. Although ample in size and big enough to accommodate the plushest of king-size beds, the sloping ceilings in some rooms might pose a problem for taller folks. You likely won't spend much time in your room, though; guests frequently share tales of their day with one another over a glass of wine in the common living area, or spend their downtime in the peaceful garden. An impressive spread is set out for breakfast, including hand-rolled croissants and eggs from the Richardsons' own hens.

113 Rue Jolie. frenchbayhouse.co.nz. ✆ **027/473-9562.** 4 rooms. NZ$295–NZ$360 double. Rates include breakfast. **Amenities:** Complimentary bikes; free Wi-Fi.

SiloStay ♥♥ Located midway between Christchurch and Akaroa in Little River, SiloStay has turned grain silos into award-winning two-story guest accommodations. Downstairs, each custom-designed unit has its own kitchenette and living area; upstairs there's a balcony, a queen-size bed, and a skylight for stargazing. If serenity is what you seek, request a silo placed farther back from the road. An accessible silo is also available.

SH75, Little River. silostay.kiwi.nz. ✆ **03/325-1977.** 9 units. NZ$225–NZ$275 double. **Amenities:** Kitchenette; cycle hire; bicycle storage; free Wi-Fi.

excellent **Mount Hutt Ski Area;** mthutt.co.nz), but that all changed when the architecturally stunning **Ōpuke Thermal Pools and Spa ♥♥♥**, 35 Mount Hutt Station Rd., Methven (opuke.nz; ✆ **03/261-6800;** from NZ$33 adults, NZ$22 children), opened its doors in late 2021. Although it doesn't use geothermally heated water (it's warmed by one of the largest solar farms in the country), Ōpuke is a much more peaceful experience than Hanmer' thermal pools, thanks to capped visitor numbers. There's also an adults-only area, with starlit grottos and a swim-up bar. Kids still have plenty of room to go wild in in their own area, which comes equipped with water cannons, a lazy river, and lifeguards.

After a soak, mount a UTV to zoom around the banks of the icy blue Rakaia River with **Dirt Bandits ♥♥**, 2597 Rakaia Barrhill Methven Rd. (dirtbandits.co.nz; ✆ **027/302-6157;** from NZ$79). Or try knife throwing, archery, or skeet shooting at **NewZengland ♥♥** (newzengland.co.nz; ✆ **021/158-4259;** from NZ$50).

One of the best 1- to 2-hour hikes near Christchurch will take you across private farmland to **Washpen Falls ♥♥**, 590 Washpen Rd., Windwhistle (washpenfalls.co.nz; ✆ **027/208-6998**). The cash-only NZ$10 fee (NZ$5 per child), is a small price for access to the well-maintained trail. In addition to the eponymous waterfall, you'll be rewarded with views across the Canterbury Plains to the sea. If you want to stay the night, there are luxurious accommodations with an outdoor wood-fired hot tub.

For accommodations directly in Methven, you won't have trouble finding a room; plenty of ski lodges offer apartment-style rooms all year-round. Then again, it's so close to Christchurch that it makes for an easy day trip from the city.

WHERE TO EAT IN AKAROA

Akaroa is a cruise-ship port, so you'll have no problem finding somewhere to dine here—waterfront restaurants line the main promenade along Beach Road. Dine with lapping harbor views at **Ma Maison ♥♥**, 6 Rue Balguerie (mamaison.co.nz; ✆ **03/304-7668;** Mon–Thurs noon–9:30pm; Fri–Sat 11:30am–10:30pm; Sun 11:30am–9:30pm). It has some of the best seafood in town—reservations are recommended. For a gourmet picnic, **Akaroa Butchery & Deli ♥♥**, 67 Rue Lavaud (akaroabutchery.nz; ✆ **03/304-7038**), has a beautiful range of goods championing Canterbury and NZ producers, alongside its meats; it's closed Sundays and Mondays.

Arthur's Pass ♥♥

Nestled in the Southern Alps on SH73, the pass between Canterbury and Westland has become a destination in its own right, and Arthur's Pass village (pop. minuscule) has a limited supply of modest accommodations. The area has several ski fields and many short walks; Arthur's Pass National Park is a favorite of hikers. If you like a dramatic landscape and weather conditions to match, this is the place for you.

ESSENTIALS

ARRIVING From Christchurch, take State Highway 73 to Arthur's Pass National Park. The alpine village of Arthur's Pass is 2 hours from Christchurch and your halfway mark to the West Coast. Budget enough time to stop and walk among the spectacular limestone formations at the **Castle Hill Conservation Area/Kura Tawhiti ♥♥♥**, which can be found midway between Christchurch and Arthur's Pass.

You can also get to Arthur's Pass on the **TranzAlpine train** (see p. 441), which stops here on its journey from Christchurch to Greymouth.

If traveling by car beyond Arthur's Pass to the West Coast, make sure to pull over at the **Otira Viaduct Lookout ♥♥**, 8 minutes north of the village. Not only does it have one of the best views of the area, you have a good chance of seeing *kea,* the world's only alpine parrots, gathered here. Don't leave your gear or car unattended; keas are fearsomely destructive.

VISITOR INFORMATION The **Arthur's Pass Department of Conservation (DOC) Visitor Info Centre** is at 104 W. Coast Rd. (✆ **03/318-9211;** daily 8:30am–4:30pm, some days open until 5pm in Dec–Feb). Check in here before heading out on any hikes; the weather in this area is extremely changeable, and weather warnings should be heeded.

HIKING AROUND ARTHUR'S PASS

Snow, avalanches, and over 4,000mm (160 in.) of rain a year pummel the walking tracks here. There are many 2- to 3-day tramps and shorter walks that deliver you to thundering waterfalls, wild rivers, dripping beech forests, and a wealth of bird life. ***Be warned:*** A lot of them are tough going and require a degree of skill in navigation with map, compass, or GPS. Be aware of your ability, and *always* bring extra food and plenty of warm clothing.

Two short walks worth doing are **Devil's Punchbowl Waterfall ♥** and **Bridal Veil.** Each takes about 1 hour. The **historic village walk ♥** is a pretty wander that can be accomplished easily if you've stopped off at Arthur's Pass on the return TranzAlpine journey. For those with more time and ambition, the 6km (3¾-mile) **Bealey Spur Track ♥♥** offers stunning views of the surrounding area and takes about 2½ hours to complete. Ask at the visitor center for maps.

WHERE TO STAY IN ARTHUR'S PASS

There aren't many places to stay directly within Arthur's Pass Village, a tiny village of privately owned *baches* (holiday homes). Your best bet is to check Airbnb listings for here or for Castle Hill, a small alpine village about 45 minutes away. However, note that Castle Hill also is mostly baches—you'll need to arrive with groceries and fully fueled up.

Otira Stagecoach Hotel ♥♥♥ This century-old hotel has the overflowing packrat vibe of an eccentric great-grandparent's rambling old mansion. It's stocked with antiques, collectibles, and creative taxidermy; you could certainly set a murder mystery here. Nine miles north of Arthur's Pass,

At the Wilderness Lodge in Arthur's Pass, every window seems to have a jaw-dropping mountain view, and guided activities take guests outdoors to hike, climb, birdwatch, and stargaze.

it's right by the railway, so it can be noisy, and bathrooms are shared. But it offers basic, satisfying meals and diverting pioneer history, and something about the place makes you fall into pleasant conversation with your fellow guests. It's certainly one of the most interesting hotels in NZ.

St. Hwy. 73, Otira. otirahotel.co.nz. ✆ **03/738-2890.** 8 rooms w/shared baths. NZ$145–NZ$220 double. **Amenities:** Restaurant; bar; free Wi-Fi.

Wilderness Lodge ♥♥♥ This 4,000-acre sheep farm and hotel includes extraordinary outdoor experiences in its nightly rates. Guests can hike through a moa forest; birdwatch and stargaze with local experts; and learn about sheep shearing and sheepdog training. For an additional fee they can go kayaking, take a waterfall photo safari, or go mountain climbing. Back at the lodge, they relax in colorful, well-maintained rooms with eye-popping views over Waimakariri valley and mountain peaks. The on-site restaurant is quite good, too. A true adventure!

St. Hwy. 73, Arthur's Pass. wildernesslodge.co.nz. ✆ **03/318-9246.** 24 units. NZ$610–NZ$970 double. Rates include breakfast, dinner, and guided activities. **Amenities:** Restaurant; bar; canoe trips; free Wi-Fi.

Kaikōura

The Kaikōura coast, 2 hours north of Christchurch, is wild and ruggedly beautiful. The snow-capped Seaward Kaikōura Range crouches almost to the sea in places, and the kilometer-deep offshore canyon results in an abundance of marine life—several species of whales, dolphins, and seals make this vibrant coastline their home, which is what most people come here for (*kaikōura* means "to eat crayfish"). The town became a Dark Sky Reserve in 2024, and the controls on artificial light have made this a stunning spot for stargazing; see kaikouradarksky.nz for more.

ESSENTIALS

ARRIVING The drive from Christchurch via SH1 to Kaikōura takes 2½ hours. **InterCity** (intercity.co.nz; ✆ **03/365-1113**) runs regular coach service between Christchurch and Kaikōura; fares vary, but expect to pay around NZ$28 to NZ$44. Kaikōura is also a stop on the **Great Journeys of New Zealand's Coastal Pacific** (greatjourneysnz.com; ✆ **04/495-0775**) train, on the way north from Christchurch or south from Picton (Christchurch to Kaikōura is NZ$147; the whole journey starts at NZ$259).

VISITOR INFORMATION The official visitor website is kaikoura.co.nz.

WHERE TO STAY IN KAIKŌURA

If you're traveling by RV, **KiwiCamp** (kiwicamp.nz), offers a basic, secure lot with powered sites for NZ$25 per site. Hot showers, Wi-Fi, laundry, and kitchen facilities are available for small additional payments via a Penny card, which you buy for NZ$5; visit help.kiwicash.nz/hc/en-nz for the full list of retailers and where you can use it.

There are tons of motel and backpacker options in Kaikōura, but **The White Morph** ♥, 92/94 Esplanade (heritagehotels.co.nz/the-white-morph; ✆ **0800/368-888** in NZ), is as well located as they come, and offers rooms with kitchenettes and sea views starting at NZ$225.

My top mid-range pick for couples and singles is **Clifftop Cabins** ♥♥♥, 277 Scarborough St. (clifftopcabins.co.nz; ✆ **021/664-052**) These cozy, beautifully appointed cabins hug the northern edge of the Kaikōura Peninsula, with vast views from the outdoor bath. Cabins cost NZ$350–NZ$400 per night.

For true luxury, go to the stunning **Hapuku Lodge & Treehouses** ♥♥♥, 1 Station Rd. off SH1 (hapukulodge.com; ✆ **03/319-6559**). Handcrafted furniture, big, well-designed bathrooms, and generous beds all add up to a fantastic stay at this country lodge. It has a price tag to match the experience, however, with rooms starting at NZ$1,649.

WHERE TO EAT IN KAIKŌURA

The seafood here is as fresh as it gets, and you obviously can't leave without ordering up some *koura* (crayfish), for which the region is renowned. Twenty minutes north of town you'll find the fuss-free **Nins Bin** ♥♥ (ninsbin.co.nz; ✆ **020/486-3474**), a little roadside trailer that has been selling just that since 1977. In addition to whole, fresh crayfish (from NZ$95), you can feast on whitebait patties, live mussels, and fish 'n' chips. It's open daily from 10am to 4pm.

Back in town, the tiny **Tipsy Foodies** ♥♥, 14 West End (tipsyfoodies.foodship.co.nz; ✆ **03/319-5637**), serves quick bites: great hamburgers, *kūmara* (sweet potato) fries, kebabs, and pizza with local Emporium Brewing beer on tap (I liked the hazy ale). For something more upmarket, the local favorite is the nautical style of **Pier Hotel** ♥, 1 Avoca St. (thepierhotel.co.nz; ✆ **03/319-5037**). It has an excellent view and offers a seafood-heavy menu

wildlife experiences IN KAIKŌURA

Whales and other marine mammals are a big draw in Kaikōura. They're not all that hard to spot: The **Ōhau seal colony** is roadside, about 22 minutes north of Kaikōura on SH1 (the road between Christchurch and Blenheim). There's a well-signed carpark and a boardwalk alongside the highway, where you can watch them at play. Seals also bask in the sun along the **Kaikōura Peninsula Walkway,** a rocky headland loop about 3km (2 miles) south of town. The area is also globally renowned as a seabird hotspot.

Beyond these free ways to spot critters, there are a number of top-notch guided encounters with experts. Here are some of the best:

- **Whale Watch Kaikōura ♥♥♥** (whalewatch.co.nz; ✆ **03/319-6767**) is an awe-inspiring outing that gives passengers a good chance of having close encounters with giant sperm whales, dolphins, and seals. An award-winning, locally owned tourism company, Whale Watch is the only operator permitted in this protected marine area. Sperm whales cruise and snack about 7 miles offshore, and seeing one has a 95% success rate. (A guaranteed 80% refund covers the disappointment of a no-show.) Two-hour tours start from NZ$175 for adults and NZ$60 for ages 3 to 15.
- **Seal Swim Kaikōura ♥♥♥** (sealswimkaikoura.co.nz; ✆ **0800/732-579** in NZ, or 03/319-6182) will take you to swim and snorkel with New Zealand fur seals. Though completely wild, they're also curious, so you have a good chance of a close, face-to-face encounter. The 2½-hour tours have been run by the same local Kaikōura family since 1987. Tours cost NZ$179 adults, NZ$129 kids 12 to 15. Check the website for tour dates, which are tide- and weather-dependent.
- **Wings Over Whales ♥♥** (whales.co.nz; ✆ **0800/226-629** in NZ, or 03/319-6580) offers an airborne perspective on whale-watching via a 30-minute flight (from NZ$250). Success rate is around 90%, and although it lacks the drama of sharing the sea with a whale, seeing the full length of these ocean giants from above has its own wonder. If you're short on time, this is probably the best choice.
- **Albatross Encounter ♥♥** (albatrossencounter.co.nz; ✆ **0800/733-365** in NZ, or 03/319-6777) is a birdwatching cruise focusing on seabirds, including albatross, mollymawks, gannets, and petrels. They put on quite a circus wheeling and skimming the waves, resulting in great pictures. The cost is NZ$185 adults and NZ$85 children 3 to 14.

including succulent crayfish. It's open for lunch and dinner, but often closes early on winter evenings.

The **Craypot Kitchen & Bar ♥**, 70 West End (thecraypotkaikoura.co.nz; ✆ **03/319-6027**), is open daily and is well placed on the main street opposite the carpark. It's a good, relaxed place for lunch. The Sicilian seafood soup (NZ$30) hits just the right spot.

QUEENSTOWN, WĀNAKA & FIORDLAND

14

Queenstown and the southwestern section of the South Island hold some of Aotearoa's greatest natural beauty. At its heart is the iconic Fiordland National Park, with its dramatic glacier-covered peaks and hundreds of waterfalls (some of which drop directly into the sea). A protected area that's bigger than Yosemite and Yellowstone National Parks combined, it's just a part of the wider Te Wāhipounamu UNESCO World Heritage site—2.6 million hectares (6.4 million acres), about 10% of New Zealand's total landmass. It's an area that gives a whole new meaning to the word "wilderness."

Fiordland/Ata Whenua and its most famous attraction, **Milford Sound/Piopiotahi,** are best accessed from the gateway town of **Te Anau.** But most visitors use the hip and hedonistic alpine resort of **Queenstown** as an initial gateway to this region—and as a destination unto itself for skiing, jetboating, partying, and more. Its more laid-back sister town, **Wānaka,** just an hour away, is another popular visitor hub.

QUEENSTOWN

404km (250 miles) SW of Franz Josef; 263km (163 miles) SW of Mount Cook; 117km (73 miles) S of Wānaka; 172km (107 miles) NE of Te Anau

Queenstown/Tāhuna welcomes nearly four million visitors a year, many drawn by its reputation as "the adventure capital of the world." There are certainly enough crazy and/or heart-pumping activities here to give adrenaline addicts the rush they're craving. But Queenstown also attracts more sedate travelers, drawn by the prospect of long leisurely days spent in the vineyards in **Gibbston,** in the perfectly preserved historic towns of **Cromwell** or **Arrowtown,** or beautiful and outdoorsy **Glenorchy,** plus alpine walks and boat trips across Lake Whakatipu.

Famed for its international winter ski profile, Queenstown is a year-round destination—although locals will tell you the best time to visit is fall, when there's less chance of rain, visitor numbers are

Central Queenstown

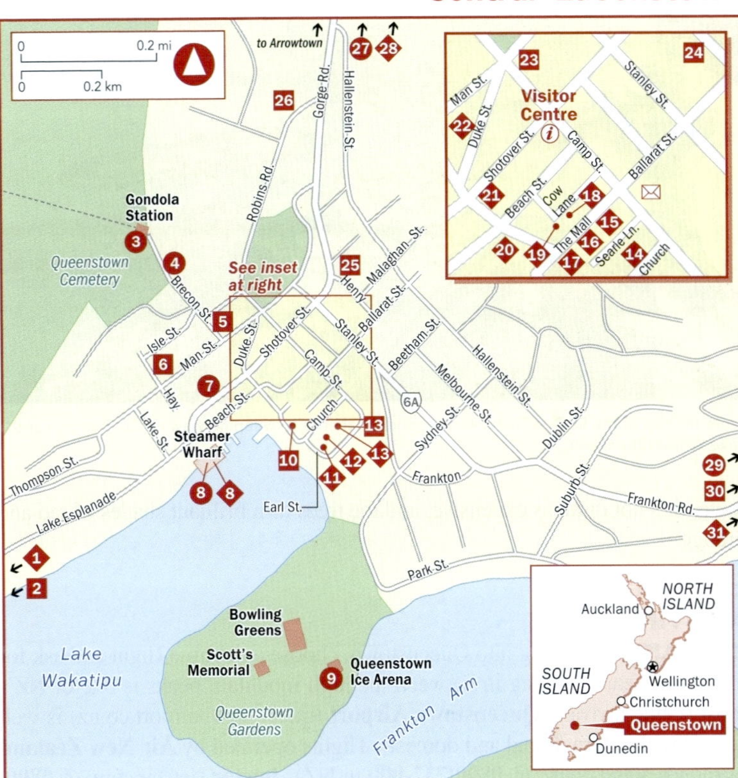

ATTRACTIONS

Kiwi Park **4**
Goldfields Mining Centre **29**
Kingpin Queenstown **4**
Onsen Hot Pools **27**
Queenstown Ice Arena **9**
Skyline Gondola **3**
Steamer Wharf & TSS *Earnslaw* **8**
Thrill Zone **7**

HOTELS

Browns Boutique Hotel **6**
The Dairy Hotel **5**
Driftaway Holiday Park **30**
Eichardt's Private Hotel **10**
Kāmana Lakehouse **2**
LyLo **23**
mi-pad **24**
QT Queenstown **2**
Queenstown Holiday Park Creeksyde **26**
The Rees Hotel & Luxury Apartments **30**
Sherwood **30**
The Spire Hotel **13**
Sudima Five Mile **30**
Tahuna Pod Hostel **25**

RESTAURANTS & BARS

Bardeaux **16**
The Boat Shed **31**
Botswana Butchery **11**
The Bunker **18**
Canyon Brewing **28**
The Cow **19**
Devil Burger **14**
Fergburger **21**
Left Bank Bistro **22**
Madam Woo **17**
Minus 5° Ice Bar **8**
Nest Kitchen & Bar **1**
No5 Church Lane **13**
Sunfire **7**
Vudu Cafe & Larder **20**
The Winery **15**
Yonder **12**

From the top of the Skyline Queenstown gondola, there's a sweeping view of Queenstown and Lake Whakatipu below.

lower, it's not quite as expensive, and the trees turn brilliant shades of red and orange.

Essentials

ARRIVING

BY PLANE If flying into Queenstown, choose a daytime flight and ask for a window seat—landing in between the high mountain peaks is one of NZ's most scenic arrivals. **Queenstown Airport** (queenstownairport.co.nz) is well served with international and domestic flights operated by **Air New Zealand** (airnewzealand.co.nz; ✆ **0800/737-000** in NZ), **Jetstar** (jetstar.com; ✆ **0800/800-995** in NZ), **Virgin Australia Airlines** (virginaustralia.com; ✆ **0800/670-000** in NZ), and **Qantas** (qantas.com.au; ✆ **0800/808-767** in NZ). The city is a roughly 15-minute drive from the airport. **Super Shuttle** (supershuttle.co.nz; ✆ **0800/748-885** in NZ) offers door-to-door airport/downtown transport for NZ$20 per person, minimum 2 people. **Taxis** and rideshare service Uber are also available; you can expect to spend about NZ$33 to get downtown. Via the **Orbus** public bus network (see below), it's just NZ$2.50. By bus, the journey takes about 30 minutes. Most major **rental car agencies** are located in the airport, including **Avis** (✆ **03/442-3808**) and **Hertz** (✆ **0800/654-321** in NZ).

BY CAR Drive times are approximately 6 hours from Christchurch, 4 hours from Dunedin (but allow time for stops in Central Otago's historic towns), 6 hours from Franz Josef (with extra time for stops at waterfalls), 2 hours from Te Anau, 5 hours from Milford Sound, and 3 hours from Invercargill. Roads affected by weather always have warnings or closures signposted well in advance.

BY COACH (BUS) **InterCity** (intercity.co.nz; ✆ **03/365-1113**) has regular services connecting Queenstown to other major centers, including Christchurch, Wānaka, and Dunedin.

GETTING AROUND

BY CAR Having a car will allow you to easily explore Queenstown's surrounds or make a day trip to Wānaka, but it also comes at a cost. Parking in the downtown area is difficult to find, and parking costs are high, including at hotels. Be prepared to spend a while circling the block, even for a paid parking spot. Wilson Parking has parking lots in Church Street, Stanley Street, and Man Street, but even these fill early. Council carparks are generally cheaper than private, and they are free at night from 6pm to 8am. Visit qldc.govt.nz/parking for info and a map. Most car parking is now cashless.

Luckily, most activities offer a pickup or shuttle bus from downtown Queenstown or directly from your accommodations. As such, it's possible to arrive car-free, or to leave your wheels parked on the outskirts of town (you'll find large parking areas at the Remarkables Park Town Centre and the new Five Mile shopping complex near the airport).

BY PUBLIC TRANSIT Queenstown's **Orbus** public bus and ferry network (orc.govt.nz/orbus) costs flat-rate fares of just NZ$2.50; to plan your route, download the Transit app. For automatic discounts and easy tap-on-and-off access, pre-load a **BeeCard** (beecard.co.nz), which can be used in many regions around NZ. They may be purchased from Queenstown Ferries skippers, with cash from bus drivers, or from the Queenstown isite (see below). Bus fares can be paid for with cash, but it's twice the price (NZ$4).

BY TAXI In addition to rideshare app **Uber,** a number of cab companies operate in Queenstown. **Queenstown Taxis** (queenstowntaxis.com; ✆ **0800/788-294** in NZ) has a 24-hour manned call center. Fares from the town center to most accommodations are between NZ$15 and NZ$30; you can expect to pay roughly the same, more, or a little less for rideshares, which operate on surge pricing. You can also hire an EV by the hour with **Ryd** (ryd.co.nz).

VISITOR INFORMATION

To plan your trip, visit queenstownnz.co.nz, Destination Queenstown's official website. The **Queenstown isite Visitor Centre,** corner of Shotover and Camp sts. in the Clocktower building (queenstownisite.co.nz; ✆ **03/442-4100**), is open daily from 9am to 5pm (8:30am–8:30pm in summer). It offers impartial tour and activity booking and doubles as a convenient pickup point for many group tours. For information and advice on outdoor activities such as tramping or cycling, the **Department of Conservation's (DOC's) Whakatipu-wai-Māori/Queenstown Visitor Centre** is at 50 Stanley St. (doc.govt.nz; ✆ **03/442-7935**). It's generally open Monday to Saturday from 8:30am to 4:30pm.

SPECIAL EVENTS

The best Queenstown events are related to sports, like the competitive **Queenstown Marathon** (queenstown-marathon.co.nz) in November. Mountain festival **Snow Machine** (snow-machine.com) celebrates the end of the ski season in September, and the **Queenstown Pride Festival** (winterpride.co.nz)—one of the Southern Hemisphere's most popular Pride events—takes place at the end of August and start of September.

Three drag queens take the stage for Queenstown's over-the-top Pride celebration.

Exploring Queenstown

Queenstown's lakefront downtown area is compact, with most shops, restaurants, and amenities within easy walking distance. The central shopping area is bordered by Marine Parade on the lakefront, Camp Street to the north of that, and Shotover Street, which runs into Lake Esplanade. You can have a picnic on the little beach along Lake Whakatipu, then wander along the path to the adjacent grounds of the **Queenstown Gardens ♥**.

To get a full measure of the town, take the short but sweet ride up the **Skyline Queenstown gondola ♥** (skyline.co.nz; ✆ **03/441-0101**). It offers impressive views over the city and lake, with activities at the top, including luging, paragliding, mountain biking, and ziplining (see "Top Eight Adrenaline Activities," p. 462), as well as guided walks to the summit or saddle of Ben Lomond (see "Walking," p. 464). There's also a cafe and restaurant at the top. However, the gondola is pricey (NZ$66 adults, NZ$46 ages 6–14, NZ$179 for a family of four), considering you can get similarly epic views for free from many of the area's roadside pullout views or hiking trails.

The 1912 vintage steamship **TSS *Earnslaw* ♥♥** (realnz.com; ✆ **03/249-6000**) cruises Lake Whakatipu in style, departing from downtown's Steamer Wharf. Affectionately known as the "Lady of the Lake," the *Earnslaw* was built to serve remote farming communities around Lake Whakatipu; she could once carry 1,500 sheep and 30 cattle on her decks. Today, she is the only hand-fired, commercial passenger-carrying steamship operating in the Southern Hemisphere, ferrying up to 350 passengers a day on scheduled excursions across the lake. Ninety-minute cruises to Walter Peak depart multiple times daily for NZ$115 adults and NZ$58 ages 5 to 15. If you haven't done a farm tour elsewhere, it's worth the extra cost for a **Walter Peak Farm Tour ♥♥**, which includes the cruise, plus farming demonstrations, a guided walking tour of the station, and tea with freshly baked scones. This lengthens the cruise to

Book well ahead for a lake cruise to Walter Peak on the historic coal-fired steamship TSS *Earnslaw.*

3½ hours but will be one of your most memorable experiences in Queenstown. It costs NZ$155 adults and NZ$78 ages 5 to 15. Other options include guided horse treks and barbecue dining across the lake. The TSS *Earnslaw* is one of Queenstown's most popular activities, so book in advance to guarantee your preferred sailing time. RealNZ also offers a slightly cheaper 90-minute lake cruise on the **Spirit of Queenstown,** a modern catamaran, also departing from Steamer Wharf, for NZ$69 adults, NZ$35 children.

An antidote to all the high-octane pursuits in Queenstown, the **Onsen Hot Pools** ♥♥ are a short drive north of the city center at 160 Arthurs Point Rd. (onsen.co.nz; ✆ **03/442-5707**). Getting your own private hot tub overlooking the Shotover River is nice—but when you're offered bubbly, potato chips, and ice cream to enjoy while you're soaking, you're living the dream. Retractable roofs make stargazing possible on a clear night and offer shelter on a rainy day. The newer "outdoor" pools are essentially the same experience, minus the retractable roof. The Instagram-ready pools often book out days (sometimes weeks) in advance, so book ahead, though last-minute reservations are sometimes available. Pools fit up to four people and start at NZ$117 per person. Each session lasts an hour and includes your choice of drink and snack, and a complimentary shuttle service. They're open daily 9am to 11pm.

Whether you choose to bathe indoors or out, the Onsen Hot Pools are a wonderfully relaxing change from the usual tourist activities.

KID magnets

Many Queenstown adventures have high minimum-age requirements, but these fun, family-friendly activities don't.

- **Family Adventures** ♥♥♥ Suitable for ages 3 and up, Family Adventures specializes in "soft adventures." Its scenic 4WD excursion into Skipper's Canyon allow visitors to see old mining relics and jetboats in action, before embarking on a 90-minute gentle rafting tour down the safest section of the Shotover River (familyadventures.co.nz; ✆ **03/442-8836;** from NZ$299 adults and NZ$185 children 3–17).
- **Kiwi Park** ♥ Operating rain or shine, this 5-acre park (51 Brecon St., kiwibird.co.nz; ✆ **03/442-8059**) is home to indigenous birds and lizards, including tuatara, kea, and, of course, kiwi. There's a conservation show and eight set kiwi encounter times daily. Buy tickets online in advance (NZ$64 adults, NZ$32 ages 6–15, family of 5 NZ$150; daily 9am–6:30pm). Park at the Skyline Gondola carpark a 2-minute walk away (20% discount when validated).
- Nextdoor to Kiwi Park at 35 Brecon St., **Kingpin Queenstown** ♥♥ (kingpinplay.com; ✆ **03/668-0687**) has an arcade, VR games, bowling lanes, escape rooms, private karaoke rooms, and restaurants. It's open Monday to Thursday 11am to 10pm, Friday 11am to midnight, Saturday 10am to midnight, and Sunday 10am to 10pm.
- **Thrill Zone** ♥, 53 Shotover St. (thrillzone.co.nz; ✆ **03/441-1159**), also offers VR experiences (from NZ$65); indoor, outdoor, and VR escape rooms (from NZ$118 for two); and glow-in-the-dark mini-golf (from NZ$30).
- In addition to skating, kids will love the bumper cars on ice at the **Queenstown Ice Arena** ♥, in Queenstown Gardens (29 Park St.; queenstownicearena.co.nz; ✆ **03/441-8000**). Open year-round, it costs NZ$43 for a bump and skate combo; family passes are NZ$160.

Queenstown's history is intertwined with that of the early-19th-century gold rush, with the gold fields in the region being among the richest in the world. To see a gold mining demonstration, head 40 minutes west of Queenstown on SH6 to the **Goldfields Mining Centre** ♥ in Kawarau Gorge (goldfieldsmining.co.nz; ✆ **03/445-1038**), accessed via a narrow but stable bridge crossing over the river. Admission—which includes a guided tour and the chance to pan for gold—is NZ$45 adults, NZ$25 children, and NZ$120 for families of four. It's open daily 9am to 5pm (10am–4pm May–Aug). ***Note:*** Many organized tours departing from Queenstown include gold panning, so don't take this one if that's your main interest. On all you're almost guaranteed to find (miniscule specks of) gold.

Exploring Arrowtown

For an enjoyable outing at a less hectic pace, visit Arrowtown, 20km (12 miles) northeast of Queenstown on the banks of the Arrow River. Gold was discovered here in 1862, and the township still has several heritage sites and buildings along its main strip, Buckingham Street. Most visitors do it as a day trip, but if you're looking for a quieter place to spend the night or want to eat at one of Arrowtown's acclaimed restaurants, it's a great location for exploring the greater Queenstown area.

The shops lining **Buckingham Street** and its adjoining alleyways are exactly what you'd expect in any tour bus stop, selling made-in-China trinkets, souvenirs, and outdoor gear. There are some exceptions, though. **Off the Wall ♥**, 18 Buckingham St. (offthewallgallery.co.nz), specializes in NZ-made goods, including Kiwiana-themed children's books, wall hangings, and homewares. Owned by a local family of gold prospectors, **The Gold Shop ♥♥**, 29 Buckingham St. (thegoldshop.co.nz), is worth a stop just to gawk at some of the largest gold nuggets in existence. (Some are displayed by the front door, but ask to hold the largest one ever found, which is hidden behind the counter.) Its natural gold flake lockets are a popular souvenir, starting from NZ$390.

The **Lakes District Museum,** 49 Buckingham St. (museumqueenstown.com; ✆ **03/442-1824;** daily 9am–4pm), is not particularly well-curated and the packed exhibits feel a bit worn. If you're not in the mood to read museum signage, save yourself the NZ$14 (NZ$6 children) entry fee. You can, however, rent a gold pan and trowel here and take them down to the Arrow River to try your luck yourself. It's just NZ$5.

The partially restored **Chinese Settlement ♥♥** along Bush Creek is a sharp contrast to the historic European storefronts of Buckingham Street, only a 5-minute walk away. Some 3,564 Chinese migrants flocked to Otago in the late 1800s to try their luck in the goldfields. In Arrowtown, they were segregated from the rest of the community, living in humble shacks that can be explored today, including the tiny rooms of Ah Lum's general store and huts tucked away under rocky outcrops. To find it, walk north on Buckingham

The nearby goldrush town of Arrowtown is included on Best of Queenstown day trips with Altitude Tours.

SEEING skippers canyon BY 4WD

Skippers Canyon ♥♥, 22km (13 miles) north of Queenstown, at the head of the Shotover River, is another area that opened up with the discovery of gold in 1862. Within 4 months of that first find, more than 10,000 miners were in the canyon, living in "hellish hard conditions." The hills and gullies are treeless, and even campfire cooking is near-impossible without fuel. Yet the miners still came, and eventually the rough camps became settlements with grog shops, schools, and stores. Over time, the settlements have disappeared, but a few isolated dwellings have survived, despite the harsh climate.

The road to Skippers is frequently described as "narrow and winding," but in truth it is more akin to driving along a shelf built of rock. I highly recommend taking a tour with someone else at the wheel. Tour companies offering 4WD tours include **Queenstown Heritage Tours** ♥♥ (queenstown-heritage.co.nz; ✆ **03/409-0949;** from NZ$240 adults, NZ$150 ages 16 and under). **Nomad Safaris** ♥♥♥ (nomadsafaris.co.nz; ✆ **0800/688-222** in NZ) offers a 4-hour 4WD safari into the canyon for NZ$299 adults and NZ$155 children, with a maximum group size of six (or four to make sure everyone has a window seat). Tours include tea and the opportunity to pan for gold.

Street, then head downhill through the picnic area. The entrance is near the junction of Bush Creek and the Arrow River.

Guided Tours

Here, almost more than anywhere else in the country, I recommend taking at least a half-day guided tour at the beginning of your stay. It will give you a good sense of the lay of the land, add some historical context, and suggest ways to spend the rest of your time. (Plus, they usually hit up *Lord of the Rings* filming locations, if that's your thing.)

There are countless tour companies to choose from; here are some of the best. **Altitude Tours** ♥ (altitudetours.co.nz; ✆ **03/441-4788**) offers daily guided tours of Queenstown, Glenorchy, and Milford Sound. Its half-day Best of Queenstown Scenic Tour (NZ$229 adults, NZ$129 children up to age 15) is a great sampler for those short on time, with knowledgeable guides and pre-recorded videos that are legitimately funny. It visits the Shotover River, Arrowtown, and Gibbston, but stops are often rushed, and the 30-minute boat ride on Lake Whakatipu at the end feels tacked-on.

Nomad Safaris' Lord of the Rings Glenorchy tours play up the region's connections to the hit movie franchise.

Nomad Safaris ♥♥♥ (nomadsafaris.co.nz; ✆ **0800/688-222** in NZ) has around a dozen tour options—truly something for everyone. Many are geared towards *Lord of the Rings* fans, who will love the vehicle fleet's vanity plates, named for movie characters, and drivers who were extras in the films. But Nomad can also take you on guided walks, an e-biking wine tour, or quad biking. If you're a Tolkien fan, opt for the half-day Glenorchy *LOTR* tour, which has the most locations, including Isengard and the Forest of Lothlórien. Tours start from NZ$255.

Recently voted Best Luxury Tours in NZ for 3 years running, **Alpine Luxury Tours** ♥♥ (alpineluxurytours.co.nz; ✆ **027/319-4494**) offers private guided tours in a luxury Land Rover, which hit up all the top sites. Local founder Lee Saunders's relationships with landowners also gives him exclusive access to a number of areas, including trips into private oases of scenery that recall the Routeburn Track—think waterfalls, thick forests, bellbirds, and moss—without the crowds. Alpine's most popular tour (also exclusive access) is a heli-hike to the surreal Middle-earth waterfalls of Rivendell on the Earnslaw Burn. All tours are customizable; inquire for rates.

Exploring the Wine Country

Central Otago's rugged hillsides and sunny valleys are clad in vineyards that produce some of the country's most distinctive wines. Sitting at 45 degrees—the same latitude as Bordeaux in the Northern Hemisphere—it's known for its pinot noir (roughly 70% of the plantings), chardonnay, sauvignon blanc, pinot

QUEENSTOWN TOURS TO MILFORD SOUND: yea or nay?

Many tour operators in Queenstown market some variation of a day trip to Milford Sound, but before you buy, be aware that you're signing up for one heck of a long day—boiled down, it's a 10-hour drive to take a 2-hour boat ride. Plus, all the tour buses depart from Queenstown at roughly the same time, meaning they also arrive at en-route scenic stops at the same time. You'll be in paradise…but pushing through crowds to see it.

The truth is that **Te Anau** (see p. 484) is the best (and generally more affordable) base for exploring Fiordland. But if you are fixed on the idea of taking a tour from Queenstown, reliable tour operators include **GreatSights** (greatsights.co.nz; ✆ **0800/744-487** in NZ), **RealNZ** (realnz.com; ✆ **0800/656-501** in NZ), and **Southern Discoveries** (southerndiscoveries.co.nz; ✆ **0800/264-536** in NZ). Tours start from NZ$175, including your scenic boat cruise on Milford Sound.

Another option is flying to Milford Sound on a **scenic flight.** It's not the most environmentally friendly option, but it is the best for saving time. These scenic flights typically include flights to/from Milford Sound (with views over its glaciers and lakes) plus a 2-hour boat cruise or a hike; a slightly cheaper option lets you return by coach, which also affords a closer view of the remarkably beautiful landscape between Queenstown and Fiordland. All options can be booked at the isite, with prices starting at NZ$520. Of course, these flights are dependent on weather, as bus tours are not.

gris, and riesling. Many companies offer tours of the region. Most small group half-day tours include a stop at three to four wineries (usually including the wine cave at Gibbston winery) with a small lunch or shared platter. All are priced similarly, with discounts for direct bookings. (Look on the companies' websites for promo codes.)

On **Alpine Wine Tours** ♥ (alpinewinetours.co.nz; ✆ **021/0293-7491**), a professional (but not too professional; this is a wine tour, after all) guide will take you to three wineries in a small passenger van. The half-day tours depart in the morning (NZ$289) or afternoon (NZ$269), with a generous shared food platter at one of the stops. If food is what you're after, though, try the evening Progressive Dinner & Wine Tour (NZ$479). The only one of its kind in the region, it includes a dish and wine pairing at each stop.

Appellation Central Wine Tours ♥ (appellationwinetours.nz; ✆ **03/442-6920**) offers a half-day Boutique Wine Tour for NZ$279, contrasting three different sub-regions over four vineyards, including a platter lunch. Their full-day Gourmet Food & Wine Tour (NZ$329) tastes 20+ wines, covering four vineyards in Gibbstown, Bannockburn, and Cromwell, plus a wine cave tour, cheese tasting, and a five-dish cooked lunch. Vineyards can vary, so if there's one you'd especially like to visit, mention it when you book.

A more affordable option is the NZ$199 5-hour Original Wine Tour with tastings at three wineries with **Queenstown Wine Trail** ♥♥ (queenstown winetrail.co.nz; ✆ **03/441-3990**). The tour includes time for an optional winery lunch at your own expense—which honestly, you're going to want to soak up the wine, so this tour works out to the same cost.

INDIVIDUAL WINERIES TO VISIT

- **Amisfield Winery** ♥♥♥, 10 Lake Hayes Rd. (amisfield.co.nz; ✆ **03/442-0556**): Producing award-winning pinot noir, aromatic whites, and sparkling wines, this winery has one of the best restaurants in the region, if not the world; it was named third-best international restaurant by U.S. *Food & Wine* magazine in 2025. It's 10 minutes from Queenstown.
- **Carrick** ♥♥, 247 Cairnmuir Rd., Bannockburn (carrick.co.nz; ✆ **03/445-3480**): This certified organic vineyard offers lovely pinot noir, chardonnay, and a rich pinot gris. As well as a cellar door, the winery has a good restaurant with a wonderful view of the "burn" (creek) and hills that were riddled by sluice-mining guns in gold rush days.
- **Chard Farm** ♥♥, SH 6, 20 minutes west from Queenstown (chardfarm.co.nz; ✆ **03/442-6110**): Just past the Kawarau bungy bridge is one of New Zealand's most spectacularly situated vineyards, straddling a narrow ledge between rugged mountains and the river gorge (it's reached via the narrow Chard Road above the Kawarau River). Sample its pinot noir, riesling, pinot gris, and gewürztraminer.
- **Gibbston Valley Wines** ♥♥, SH 6, Gibbston Valley (gibbstonvalley.com; ✆ **03/442-6910**): This is where it all started; Gibbston released Central Otago's first commercial vintage in 1987. Now producing award-winning single vineyard organic wines, Gibbston also has a wine cave, a tasting

Strolling in the vineyards on a Queenstown Wine Trail day trip.

room, cheeseries, a gift shop, and its own luxury **accommodations ♥♥♥**: 24 private villas on the edge of the vineyard, with superb beds, top-notch service, and, of course, access to wine. Villas start at NZ$830 per night, including breakfast and an evening wine-tasting session. In 2025, Gibbston's spa retreat claimed the World Spa Awards' NZ Best Resort Spa title—for the sixth consecutive year.

- **Kinross ♥**, 2300 SH 6 (kinross.nz; ✆ **03/746-7269**): This winery serves wines under its own name, but it is also the tasting room for five other boutique local wineries, making it a one-stop shop if you're short on time.
- **Mt. Difficulty Wines ♥♥**, 319 Felton Rd., Bannockburn (mtdifficulty.co.nz; ✆ **03/445-3445**): This winery is a leading producer of pinot noir, as well as riesling, chardonnay, pinot gris, and merlot. It also has a pleasant lunch cafe with a heavenly view.
- **Mt. Rosa ♥♥♥**, 91 Gibbston Back Rd. (mtrosa.co.nz; ✆ **03/441-2493**): This is the antidote to large commercial vineyards; don't be surprised to see dogs in the tasting room or to have the owner pour you a glass of wine. The wines are terrific, but ask for the "special water"—a grappa made from riesling grapes. Mt Rosa also sells mulled wine kits, perfect for crafting après-ski treats (NZ$120).
- **Peregrine ♥♥**, SH6, Gibbston Valley (peregrinewines.co.nz; ✆ **03/442-4000**): Named after the falcon now found only in the Central Otago region, Peregrine produces excellent pinot noir, pinot gris, riesling, and rosé.

Outdoor Pursuits

CYCLING Whether you're after mountain biking or calm recreational cycling, you'll find something to suit you in Queenstown. For guided tours of the Queenstown Lakes region—including out to the vineyards—contact **Ride to the Sky ♥** (ridetothesky.co.nz; ✆ **021/295-4626**), which offers e-biking

TOP EIGHT adrenaline activities

Queenstown offers so many tours and adventure activities that covering them all would make this book too heavy to lift. Here are my top choices of activities likely to get your blood pumping—some of which you can only experience in Queenstown.

1. **Experience extreme G-forces in a jet sprint boat.** Jetboating, an NZ invention, can now be done on braided rivers across the country, but the Shotover River is where commercial jetboating was created in 1958. The **Shotover Jet ♥♥** (shotoverjet.com; ✆ **03/442-8570**) offers incredible sightseeing on the Shotover River's unreal blue waters, though if you've already been on a jetboat, you might find its spins a bit sedate. One level up, thrill-wise: the jet sprint boat. The custom-built four-seat boats at the **Oxbow Adventure Co. ♥♥♥**, 2696 Gibbston Hwy. (oxbow.co.nz; ✆ **09/307-6353**), can accelerate from 0 to 100kmph (60 mph) in just 2½ seconds, and they do spins that put the same amount of pressure on your body as you'd experience in a stunt jet plane. Rides are short, but guaranteed to get your blood pumping. Oxbow's boats operate on a pond—which makes it a good option for when river levels are too high for jet boats.
2. **Take the ultimate leap of faith.** Queenstown has three bungy-jumping sites: Kawarau Bridge, at 43m (140 ft.) high, was the world's first commercial bungy operation, and the only spot where you can touch the water at the peak of your dive. The Nevis Bungy is the highest bungy site in NZ at 134m (440 ft.). The Ledge Bungy, reached from the Skyline Gondola, has awe-inspiring views. **A.J. Hackett Bungy ♥♥♥** (bungy.co.nz; ✆ **0800/286-4958** in NZ) operates them all, with jumps from NZ$240 to NZ$320.
3. **Fly through trees.** At the top of the Skyline gondola, **Ziptrek Ecotours ♥** (ziptrek.co.nz; ✆ **0800/947-873** in NZ) runs a series of six ziplines that zoom high over the forest, including the world's steepest zipline, which reaches speeds of 70kmph (43mph). Staff (very reasonably) don't let you go that fast, but it's still pretty fun—and a real rush for those who are afraid of heights. Rides start at NZ$119.
4. **Make like a shark.** This is probably one of the stranger Queenstown activities: **Hydro Attack ♥♥** (hydroattack.co.nz; ✆ **027/477-9074**)

tours starting from NZ$225. For independent bike touring, **Better by Bike ♥♥**, in Arrowtown (betterbybike.co.nz; ✆ **027/7245-378**), offers rentals ranging from mountain bikes to e-bikes, starting at NZ$85 per adult and NZ$65 per child's bike, plus family-friendly add-ons like tow-behind kids' seats. Visit Queenstown Trails Trust (queenstowntrails.org.nz) for a full map of local trails. My pick is the 55km (34-mile) **Lake Dunstan Trail ♥♥♥** between Cromwell and Clyde, skirting the lake. One of NZ's Great Rides, it has incredible views of Lake Dunstan's blue waters, but will also challenge your technical skills, as it's grade 3 in spots. (I wouldn't recommend it to those with a fear of heights.) My other top bit of advice? Rent an e-bike and you'll enjoy it so much more. **Trail Journeys ♥♥♥** in Clyde (trailjourneys.co.nz; ✆ **03/449-2150**) will kit you out with e-bikes from NZ$139 (NZ$89 standard is the world's only commercial operator of semi-submersible boats (painted like sharks) that can dive under the water at speeds of 40kmph (25mph), before diving out again and racing across the lake at 80kmph (50mph). A 15-minute ride in this torpedo-esque watercraft is NZ$179.

5. **Zoom downhill on a luge.** Yet another invented-in-NZ activity, the luge carts at **Skyline ♥♥** (skyline.co.nz; ✆ **03/441-0101**) let you zoom down the hill, around bends and through tunnels, controlling your speed by pumping the handles. Once isn't enough; you'll want to purchase the gondola-plus-3-ride combo pass: NZ$89 adults, NZ$62 ages 6 to 14, and NZ$239 for a family of four.
6. **Careen down waterfalls.** Canyoning is popular throughout NZ, with participants rappelling, walking, climbing, jumping, and swimming through river gorges. In summer, **Canyoning New Zealand ♥♥** (canyoningnewzealand.co.nz; ✆ **03/428-0071**) and **Canyon Explorers ♥♥** (canyonexplorers.nz; ✆ **03/441-3003**) both operate half-day trips from Queenstown that are suitable for beginners, starting from about NZ$249. Be prepared to get wet.
7. **Swim through whitewater rapids.** The grade 3 to 5 rapids of the Shotover River are a mecca for whitewater rafters, and **Challenge Rafting ♥♥** (raft.co.nz; ✆ **03/442-7318**) offers a half-day rafting tour from NZ$299. For wetter thrills, though, try river surfing or river sledging, which fully submerge you in the rapids (in a wet suit, of course), with a bodyboard to keep you afloat. **Serious Fun Riverboarding ♥♥♥** (riverboarding.co.nz; ✆ **03/442-5262**) operates a popular 4½-hour excursion on the Kawarau River, for NZ$275 adults, NZ$255 kids ages 8 to 17, and NZ$1020 for a family of four.
8. **Become a human catapult.** Brought to you by the team at AJ Hackett Bungy, the **Nevis Catapult ♥♥♥** (bungy.co.nz; ✆ **0800/286-4958** in NZ) propels daredevils 150 meters (almost 500 ft.) out across the Nevis Valley, reaching speeds that exert up to 3Gs of force on the body. It costs NZ$295. If you'd prefer to drag a friend into your bad ideas, may we suggest the **Nevis Swing ♥♥**? This tandem swing is kind of like a seated bungy jump. In total, you'll complete a 300m arch over the valley. It costs NZ$325 per person.

bike). If you're on an e-bike, the Lake Dunstan ride should take you about 4 hours.

FISHING The visitor center can advise you on several recognized trout-fishing guides offering everything from hourly rates to a bespoke full-day excursion. Father-son duo Trevor and Simon of **Queenstown Fishing ♥♥** (queenstownfishing.co.nz; ✆ **021/904-462**) offer shared charters starting from NZ$285 for 2 hours.

FUNYAKING Sitting in an inflatable canoe and floating downstream at 8kmph (5mph), enjoying the scenery, is my idea of a sensible adventure. With **Funyaks ♥♥♥** (dartriver.co.nz; ✆ **03/442-9992**), you'll jet-boat up the Dart River for 75 minutes, then paddle back to Glenorchy in stable inflatable

Outings with Funyaks combine a jetboat ride with a leisurely scenic paddle back down the river to Glenorchy.

canoes. No need for daredevil confidence—it's a family trip guaranteed to please everyone. The price—from NZ$429 off-peak for adults, NZ$329 for children aged 5 to 15—includes transport, guides, and a picnic lunch.

GOLF The ultimate in Queenstown golf is **Millbrook Resort ♥♥♥**, Arrowtown (millbrook.co.nz; ✆ **0800/800-604** in NZ), where greens fees start at NZ$245 for 18 holes on one of two championship Bob Charles–designed courses. Carts, equipment, instruction, and a free shuttle from Queenstown are available. Set on a peninsula with its own private wharf, the 18-hole **Queenstown Golf Club ♥**, Kelvin Heights (queenstowngolf.co.nz; ✆ **03/442-9169**), is a full-service course with 18 holes costing NZ$110 to NZ$200 depending on the season.

SKIING From late June to September, international skiers and boarders flock to Queenstown to enjoy the accessible slopes of **Coronet Peak,** the closest ski hill to Queenstown (coronetpeak.co.nz), and its sister site, the **Remarkables** (theremarkables.co.nz); the wide open cruisy slopes at **Cardrona,** with its 360-degree views at the top (cardrona.com); and the challenging downhills at **Treble Cone,** near Wānaka (treblecone.com).

Heli-skiing is hot in these mountain regions with plenty of thrills (and fresh powder). **Harris Mountains Heliski** (heliski.co.nz; ✆ **03/442-6722**) and **Glacier Southern Lakes Heliski** (glaciersouthernlakes.co.nz; ✆ **03/442-3016**) are two recommended tour operators.

WALKING A reasonably testing walk is the 2- to 3-hour uphill **Queenstown Hill Track ♥**, which starts and finishes on Belfast Terrace. There are also several excellent walks around Lake Whakatipu, including the easy **Bob's Cove Track and Nature Trail ♥♥**, which starts 14km (9 miles) from Queenstown on the road to Glenorchy. Towards Arrowtown, circuit beautiful **Lake Hayes ♥♥**. Head up the **Skyline Gondola ♥** (skyline.co.nz) to take guided walks in the Ben Lomond area, starting at NZ$149 adults, NZ$99 children (or walk to the mountain's summit on a NZ$229/NZ$159 day trip).

Shopping

Queenstown sells a range of top-quality New Zealand–made goods, from sheepskin products, leather, and outdoor wear to fine crafts, pure wool hand-knits, and jewelry. **Goldfields Jewellers** ♥, 26 Ballarat St. (goldfields jewellers.co.nz; ✆ **03/442-9356**), has a fine collection of *pounamu* (jade) and particularly specializes in investment opal jewelry. It also stocks a selection of famed NZ designer **Karen Walker**'s jewelry range (karenwalker.com), and a collection of official *Lord of the Rings* and *The Hobbit* designs straight from Middle-earth; the One Ring or Arwen's Evenstar pendant can be yours at last. **Te Huia** ♥♥♥, The Mall, 38 Buckingham St. (✆ **03/442-4992;** tehuianz.com), stocks gorgeous **Untouched World** (untouchedworld.co.nz) designer merino, as well as Merinomink garments that combine 100% merino wool with possum fur for pure luxury (possum is considered an invasive species, so harvesting its fur helps the overall environment, plus it is wonderfully warm and soft stuff). **Miller Road Fragrance Studio** ♥, 45 Beach St. (millerroad.co.nz; ✆ **03/428-2080**), is an inviting half-retail (candles, hand cream, perfumes) half-workshop space, where you can create your own signature scent.

For honey from all corners of NZ (including affordably priced mānuka), head to **BuzzStop** ♥♥, 26 Hansen Rd., Frankton (buzzstop.co.nz; ✆ **021/942-808**), housed in a 60-year-old woolshed in the artisan Country Lane retail village, and run by a fifth-generation beekeeper. Visitors can sample the honey before buying, including ginger and chile-infused options. In addition to a small cafe and play area, there are beehives on-site., and visitors can try their hand at honey spinning, with hour-long workshops daily at 10:30am and 3pm in winter, and 9:30am in summer (adults NZ$79, children 5–15 NZ$59, family packages also available). Walk away with a personalised jar of fresh honey each.

Where to Stay in Queenstown

Queenstown has more than 20,000 guest beds, ranging from backpacker hostels to holiday apartments (book with Airbnb or Vrbo/Bookabach), international-class hotels to family lodges, and they keep coming. Even with multiple new additions, it still pays to book well in advance to secure a room and the best prices.

EXPENSIVE

The Dairy Hotel ♥♥ Once a 1920s general store and, yes, dairy, the Dairy has grown beyond a simple B&B and is now a small boutique hotel run by the art-forward Naumi chain. The bedrooms aren't massive, but are boldly decorated with colorful floral wallpapers, tartan carpets, and jewel-toned textiles. The common spaces are just as joyously colorful, and include a reading room and a lounge, where happy hour (5–6pm) drinks and charcuterie are served nightly beside a roaring fire. ***Note:*** It's a 150m (490-ft.) uphill walk from the town center.

10 Isle St. naumihotels.com. ✆ **03/442-5164.** 13 units. NZ$369–NZ$700 double. Parking NZ$20. Children 12+ only (except in 4-bdrm. apt.). **Amenities:** Bar; bike rentals; outdoor Jacuzzi & firepit; free Wi-Fi.

Eichardt's Private Hotel ♥♥♥ The property claims to have New Zealand's most prominent lakeside address. No argument there: Lake Whakatipu's little waves wash gently on the narrow beach just across the street. The original hotel was a Victorian hostelry, but clever design (including a classy glass-walled addition) has transformed the 19th-century structure into a small, luxurious boutique hotel with eight suites, a penthouse, and one 2-bedroom residence—all with fireplaces (the residence comes with a fully equipped kitchen). A bar/restaurant at the hotel's entrance offers a la carte breakfasts and tapas-style evening menus. A splendid old-school upstairs room titled The Parlour offers hotel guests a whisky nightcap.

Marine Parade. eichardts.com. ✆ **03/441-0450.** 10 units. NZ$1,925–NZ$4,290. Rates include breakfast & evening drink. **Amenities:** Restaurant, bar; babysitting; library; free Wi-Fi.

Kāmana Lakehouse ♥♥ A contemporary take on a ski lodge, this high-altitude hotel (in fact, the highest in town) has marble finishes, metal accents, and hanging fireplaces, offset by organic wooden elements. It's consciously designed to get guests out of their rooms, which—while sleek and comfortable—pale in comparison to the common areas. The on-site restaurant is outstanding, but what you're really paying for is the stunning view (which not all rooms have). Being located at the top of a steep hill means it's easy to walk the 3km (less than 2 miles) into town, but you may need a taxi to get back. It's a luxurious stay, but if it's too rich for your budget, a reservation at the hotel's restaurant **Nest** (see "Where to Eat," below) to take in the panoramic scenery might be enough.

139 Fernhill Rd. kamana.co.nz. ✆ **03/441-0097.** 73 units. NZ$235–NZ$751 double. Free parking. **Amenities:** Restaurant; hot tubs; ski storage; free Wi-Fi.

QT Queenstown ♥♥ If Kāmana Lakehouse (see above) prioritizes common spaces above rooms, then QT is its inverse. The rooms start at a generous 400 square feet, with standalone soaker tubs, QT's trademark king-size gel beds, and Dyson hairdryers. As an art-forward hotel, each room comes equipped with glossy coffee table books, plus cocktail shakers and a minibar of local artisan snacks and brews. Town is only a 5-minute walk away, but you might find your room difficult to leave—especially if you have a lakeview room with a Juliet balcony.

30 Brunswick St. qthotels.com/queenstown. ✆ **03/450-3450.** 67 units. NZ$432–NZ$1,039 double. Parking NZ$35. **Amenities:** 2 restaurants, bar; rooftop pool; 24-hr. room service; sauna; free Wi-Fi.

The Rees Hotel & Luxury Apartments ♥♥♥ This modern, eco-friendly combination of hotel-style rooms and fabulous one- to four-bedroom apartments is terraced down the banks of Lake Whakatipu midway between the airport and the town. Its out-of-town location is actually an advantage, because the rooms have a wonderful sense of privacy and staggering views. (Plus, the regular shuttle into town eliminates the need to drive anywhere.) You'll love the extra touches that lend a sense of history, including a library

The guest lounge at the lakeside Rees Hotel & Luxury Apartments.

of rare books, a wine cellar featuring New Zealand's best collection of Bordeaux wines, the excellent on-site restaurant, a gallery of original paintings, and an overall sense of being safely in the capable hands of pros who really know how to look after guests.

377 Frankton Rd. therees.co.nz. ✆ **03/450-1100.** 150 units. NZ$436–NZ$764 double. **Amenities:** Restaurant, bar; airport transfers; babysitting; bike rentals; concierge; gym; room service; free Wi-Fi.

The Spire Hotel ♥♥ A true boutique hotel with updated mid-century modern furnishings (love the Eames-style lounge chairs) and lots of burnished woods and leather, the Spire has 10 suites, each comprising a large bedroom, a bathroom, and a generous balcony with comfortable outdoor furniture. Church Lane links the lakefront to the town's main throughfares and business center, and a number of good cafes and restaurants are close by, including on-site restaurant and bar **No5 Tamarind** (for which you receive a NZ$50 dining credit when you book direct). We had to knock off one star, however, for the noise in rooms that face the nightclub across the street (ask for a quiet room when you book).

3–5 Church Lane. thespirehotel.com. ✆ **03/441-0004.** 10 units. NZ$1,100–NZ$1,564 suite. Rates include breakfast, evening drink. Parking NZ$40. **Amenities:** Restaurant, bar; concierge; 24-hr. room service; free Wi-Fi.

MODERATE

Browns Boutique Hotel ♥♥ You'll feel right at home at Browns, a good-value lodging with character and friendly, knowledgeable local hosts. The hillside Tuscan-style property (great views!) offers spacious rooms with big bathrooms and luxurious beds. Size-wise, it's on a par with The Dairy and Queenstown House, although being purpose-built, it has a more distinct small-hotel character. The guest rooms are on two levels, with generous living areas and patios on the ground floor. Town is just a 4-minute walk downhill.

26 Isle St. brownshotel.co.nz. ✆ **03/441-2050.** 10 units. NZ$405–NZ$685 double. Rates include breakfast. **Amenities:** Library; DVDs; ski storage; drying room; free Wi-Fi.

mi-pad ♥ At this self-styled "next generation" smart hotel, you use an app to do everything from checking in to changing the lighting in your room. (Don't worry; if you don't want to download the app, there are still in-room controls and a front desk.) Everything is designed to be eco-friendly, but the overall effect is that of an upscale hostel. Rooms are small and most don't have balconies; the furniture is modular, coffee and tea facilities are in the corridor, and the en-suite toilet and shower are right next to the bed. Centrally located with some free street parking nearby, it's best for travelers on a budget who want a quiet place to call their own and don't plan on spending much time in their room.

4 Henry St. mipadhotels.com. ✆ **022/506-6523.** 55 units. NZ$167–NZ$296 double. **Amenities:** Rooftop patio; ski lockers; lounge; free hot drinks and soups; guest laundry; free Wi-Fi.

Sherwood ♥♥ Sherwood has serious eco-cred. Striving to be zero-waste, it's solar-powered, and 100% of its organic scraps are composted and returned to the kitchen garden. Guests are as well taken care of as the environment: A sauna is available for private bookings, and the hotel offers daily yoga classes (from NZ$25). Room rates are at the higher end of the mid-range spectrum, but the rooms have a few issues. Yes, they have cool boho furnishings (cork walls, thick wool blankets, and crystals as decor), but they can't escape the narrow, darkish "1980s motor lodge" look. Plus, no one likes a plastic shower curtain, or being able to hear their neighbors through the walls. Location-wise, Sherwood is a short drive from the center, which means you don't have to worry about a place to park—but you will have to drive to get anywhere.

554 Frankton Rd. sherwoodqueenstown.nz. ✆ **03/450-1090.** 78 units. NZ$246–NZ$346 double. Free parking. **Amenities:** Restaurant; drying room; sauna; bikes for rent; yoga classes, free Wi-Fi.

Sudima Five Mile ♥ With its striking facade designed to imitate the surrounding peaks, this hotel is part of the Five Mile shopping complex, about 10 minutes outside of town. Being surrounded by lots of chain stores takes away from the Queenstown experience, but it has legitimate pluses: You won't have trouble finding parking, you can easily stock up on groceries or supplies for an outdoor adventure or picnic, and you won't have to deal with noise from all the bachelor and bachelorette parties that congregate downtown. The rooms, decorated in neutral tones, are clean and comfortable, and some have views of the Remarkables mountain range.

20 Grant Rd., Frankton. sudimahotels.com. ✆ **03/242-8222.** 120 units. NZ$242–NZ$469 double. Free parking. **Amenities:** Restaurant; babysitting; spa; free Wi-Fi.

INEXPENSIVE

Driftaway Holiday Park ♥♥, 11 Lake Ave., Frankton (driftawayqueenstown.co.nz; ✆ **03/409-1142**), and **Queenstown Holiday Park Creeksyde ♥♥**, 54 Robins Rd. (camp.co.nz; ✆ **03/442-9447**), both offer tent and campervan sites from NZ$75 depending on season; and a large range of cabins, villas, and self-contained units from NZ$169 to NZ$475 per night. Driftaway is brand-new, architecturally designed, and lakeside with groovy hot tubs, but is based on Queenstown's outskirts in Frankton; Creeksyde is a quirkier, colorful collection of buildings in a garden setting, a 5-minute walk from Queenstown proper. Meanwhile, both **Lylo ♥**, 47 Camp St. (lylo.com/queenstown; ✆ **03/927-4204**), and **Tahuna Pod Hostel ♥**, 11 Henry St. (tahunapodhostel.co.nz; ✆ **03/442-7052**), offer "pods" (you climb inside your own little unit with a blind or curtain you can close), making them popular with backpackers. From NZ$67 a night for a pod in a shared room.

Where to Stay in Arrowtown

There are a number of vacation rental listings in Arrowtown (look at Airbnb or Vrbo/Bookabach); for a hosted experience, **Arrowtown Lodge ♥**, 7 Anglesea St. (arrowtownlodge.co.nz; ✆ **03/442-1101;** NZ$260–NZ$520), has individual semi-detached cottages that replicate something of Arrowtown's gold-rush heritage. It's a 2-minute walk to cafes and shops.

Millbrook Resort ♥♥♥ This luxury resort is so generously sized it's essentially a village. Three minutes from Arrowtown and twenty minutes from Queenstown, the hotel offers a range of lodging options, from studio, one-, and two-bedroom suites to good-value two-, three-, and four-bedroom self-contained cottages (ideal for families or friends traveling together), to luxurious fairway homes with sweeping views of the surrounding fairways and mountains and a babbling stream nearby. Numerous on-site dining options mean you never have to leave the property to eat out. The resort also has good walks around and alongside the extensive grounds, not to mention one of the country's best championship golf courses. Even non-golfers are wowed by the handsome, imaginative landscaping.

Malaghans Rd., Arrowtown. millbrook.co.nz. ✆ **0800/800-604** in NZ. 160 units. NZ$670–NZ$1,170. **Amenities:** 4 restaurants, bar; babysitting; bike rentals; children's programs; 27-hole golf course; driving range and putting greens; fitness center; outdoor hot pools; lap pool; room service; spa; tennis courts; free Wi-Fi.

Where to Stay in Glenorchy

Headwaters Glenorchy Eco Lodge ♥♥♥ In 2019, *TIME Magazine* named this rustic-luxe slice of paradise—Camp Glenorchy, as it was branded then—one of the World's 100 Greatest Places. As soon as you step inside, it's easy to see why. NZ's only net-positive energy accommodations, the complex has been built for sustainability with odorless composting toilets, recycled wastewater, and a large solar garden—but its vibe is a beautiful take on the classic summer camp, though undoubtedly upmarket. And like any good summer camp, it has plenty of activities on offer, such as yoga sessions or 2- to 5-night guided tours into the surrounding mountain paradise for an extra cost. As for food, the on-site restaurant makes the most of the extensive kitchen garden, orchard, and glasshouse; the associated **Mrs Woolly's General Store ♥♥**, 64 Oban St. (mrswoollysgeneralstore.nz; ✆ **03/409-0051**), has very good coffee, a high-quality gift shop, and a cabinet groaning with hearty pastries and baked goods. There's also a tidy, scenic campground. In fact, the whole complex is feel-good; it's run by a trust, with profits returned to the community.

42 Oban St., Glenorchy. theheadwatersecolodge.com. ✆ **03/409-0401.** 14 chalets, 3 quad bunkrooms, 1 cottage. Bunk rooms NZ$525; cabins NZ$1,050–NZ$2,350; cottage NZ$3,200. **Amenities:** Kitchen; guest laundry; BBQ area; storage lockers; free Wi-Fi.

Where to Eat in Queenstown

Queenstown has so many cafes and bars, cocktail joints, and fine-dining restaurants that the various establishments jostle for space and attention. During high-season months (Nov–Mar), dinner reservations are highly recommended. For snacks, food carts line the lakefront, with offerings as eclectic as oysters and churros.

EXPENSIVE

Botswana Butchery ♥♥♥ GRILL From the butcher-knife handle on the historic cottage door to the menu full of aged beef and lamb cuts, game, and fish (farmed salmon, Pacific tuna), this garden-lakefront institution prides itself on premium local meat and seasonal ingredients. The food is outstanding, especially dishes that highlight unique South Island ingredients like West Coast whitebait, Canterbury duck leg cassoulet, or the venison tartare (wild Fiordland red deer). The restaurant has a lively atmosphere, divided into a main downstairs restaurant and Garden Room, with private dining rooms and a lounge bar upstairs. On evenings when the mountain air is nippy, log fires warm the cottage. Fixed-price Banquet menus are available in addition to the extensive main menu.

17 Marine Parade (garden end). botswanabutchery.nz. ✆ **03/442-6994.** Main courses NZ$41–NZ$61. Reservations recommended. Mon–Sun 11am–11pm.

The Bunker ♥♥♥ INTERNATIONAL Don't judge a book by its cover—or The Bunker by its outward appearance. Hidden behind a rustic wooden door, inside is all soft lights, sparkling glassware, delicious food fragrances, and, if it's a chilly night, a log fire. Luxury! The menu is resplendent with flavorful tastes: seared scallops, Bluff blue cod, a fermented mushroom risotto, and local wagyu. A "taste of the south" five- or eight-course degustation menu offers a comprehensive rollout of specialty (and often local) ingredients: kingfish, pāua tortellini, lamb rump, pumpkin and goat cheese, popcorn ice-cream, and cheeses. The bar upstairs offers smooth single malts and a dizzying cocktail list.

14 Cow Lane. thebunker.co.nz. ✆ **03/441-8030.** Main courses NZ$49–NZ$95 Reservations essential. Daily 5–10pm (bar until 4am).

Flavorful meals at The Bunker often feature local ingredients.

Nest Kitchen & Bar ♥♥ MODERN MEDITERRANEAN Located inside the Kāmana Lakehouse (see p. 466), Nest makes the most of its status as the "highest alfresco dining" in Queenstown. The dramatic roofline and Art Deco furnishings complement a stunning view of the lake below, but it's not the only reason to trek up the hill. An extensive breakfast menu offers an elevated take on the usual favorites (pancakes with orange marmalade and chocolate-hazelnut crémeux, or spicy Turkish eggs with garlic-cumin labneh). The dinner menu is a three-course set for NZ$115, or a degustation for NZ$149, with wine pairing options for an additional NZ$50/NZ$90. There are four inventive options you can choose for each course, such as a braised wagyu short-rib donut; miso-glazed eggplant; and burnt honey pannacotta. Even if you don't have the time or budget for a full meal, Nest is worth stopping into for a Queenstown-themed cocktail in the cozy lounge, complete with hanging fireplaces.

139 Fernhill Rd. nestqt.co.nz. ✆ **03/901-0284.** Set menus NZ$115–NZ$149. Reservations recommended. Daily 7–11am and 5–9pm.

MODERATE

The Boat Shed ♥♥ CAFE Located at the Frankton Marina, the Boat Shed is just far enough out that it doesn't get packed with tourists—but it still gets line-ups of locals hungry for breakfast and lunchtime. With ample natural light, it has views of the water and a seasonal menu. A few classics you can always expect include its eggs benedict (served over a house-baked English muffin with perfect herb hollandaise), avocado toast, wild mushrooms on sourdough, and a selection of muffins available to-go.

9300/847 Frankton Rd. boatshedqueenstown.co.nz. ✆ **03/441-4146.** Main courses NZ$20–NZ$32. Daily 8am–4pm. (Kitchen closes 3pm.)

Canyon Brewing ♥ BREWPUB What's better than going on the Shotover jet? Watching it zip by while you're warm and dry and enjoying a cold pint of beer. Located right next to the Shotover River, this microbrewery—one of the newest in Queenstown—serves its own range of beers and share plates (such as fried chicken and prawn toast), as well as woodfired skewers (including pork belly, spiced lamb) and pizzas. Owned by the same folks who run the Boat Shed, it's a popular spot with locals for "Sunday sessions" (as Kiwis call leisurely Sunday drinks with friends), likely owing to its picturesque location and the fact that it's on the number two bus route (so no one has to drive).

1 Arthurs Pt. Rd. canyonbrewingqt.co.nz. ✆ **03/442-8692.** Share plates NZ$18–NZ$25, pizzas NZ$32. Daily 11am–8pm (Fri–Sat to 9pm).

Left Bank Bistro ♥♥ PARISIAN-STYLE CAFE Enjoy a Parisian breakfast without ever leaving Queenstown! Named after that hallowed French haunt of artists, writers, and philosophers, it's part open French kitchen and part Parisian tea room with a menu that skips from modern New Zealand cuisine, such as smashed avo, to traditional French fare like daily baked pastries, crepes, and brioche French toast. The space is adorned with art posters from the 1930s through 1950s and mosaic floor tiles that were shipped in from France.

8 Duke St. sofitel-queenstown.com. ✆ **03/450-0045.** Main courses NZ$16–NZ$25. Reservations recommended. Daily 6:30–11am.

Madam Woo ♥♥ CHINESE/MALAY For some 125 years, 5 Ballarat Street has housed food businesses, including a long-time grocery store, a vegetable and candy shop, and, since 1972, a number of restaurants now relegated to history. When Madam Woo opened in 2014, it (she?) introduced a new style of eating to Queenstown: Asian street food in a comfortable restaurant. The decor captures the faded grandeur of colonial Malaysia and Singapore—charming if ever so slightly kitsch. A large bar takes center stage, the longest wall has bench and cushion seating for small tables, and The Parlour Bar upstairs was likely the parlor of the family who lived above the shop. The menu is based on the street food of Malaysia, such as hawker rolls: sturdy *roti* (flat breads) acting as edible plates for mains (fish, curry, shellfish, pork, chicken), crisp greens, chiles, herbs, and sauces. Chef Esteban Pozzi's menu also offers larger dishes such as sesame chile tofu stir fry; laksa; beef rendang, and crispy pork belly salad.

5 The Mall, waterfront end of Lower Ballarat St. madamwoo.co.nz. ✆ **03/442-9200.** Main courses NZ$20–NZ$78. Daily noon–late.

No5 Church Lane ITALIAN Tucked down a side street in the heart of Queenstown is this brand-new Italian restaurant from the successful Eichardt's group, which runs the neighboring Eichardt's Private Hotel (p. 466). Pasta is handmade, of course, and although the chefs don't promise traditional Italian cuisine, they do promise "dishes people actually want to eat on a night out." That means a comforting menu with deep, slow-cooked flavor: focaccia soaked with olive oil and served with truffle mascarpone; classic spaghetti cacio e pepe; pappardelle ragu; eggplant parmesan; and of course tiramisu for dessert (with Bailey's Irish Cream–infused mascarpone). Italian wines and natural oysters are classy extras. It's also open for breakfast, serving Tuscan ricotta and zucchini omelets, bacon and egg butties (sandwiches)—and, if you missed dessert the night before, tiramisu waffles.

3–5 Church St. no5churchlane.com. ✆ **03/450-2166.** Main courses NZ$32–NZ$55. Reservations recommended. Mon–Fri 7:30–10:30am, Tues–Sat 4–9pm.

Sunfire ♥♥ MODERN NEW ZEALAND New in 2024, Sunfire's menu is heavy on the smoked and seared; the imported Josper charcoal oven can cook a doorstop steak in 4 minutes. There's also beautiful grilled haloumi or snapper, and they blister the most common vegetable to sweet, savory perfection: charred cabbage with walnuts, tahini, and raisins is very delicious indeed. The restaurant site on Steamer Wharf has an outdoor area that makes the most of its lakeside position with huge views and the scent of fresh water all around, giving a casual dining vibe—just with really good food.

Ground floor, Steamer Wharf, 88 Beach St. sunfire.co.nz. ✆ **027/786-3473.** Dinner share plates NZ$8–NZ$35; dinner main courses NZ$32–NZ$48. Daily 8:30am–late.

Fresh-off-the-grill steak at Sunfire.

Yonder ♥ KIWI A casual spot for sunny streetside outdoor eating, live music in the evenings, and nearly all-day dining, Yonder has quickly become a go-to brunch spot for the young and in-the-know. A handy online menu allows you to easily filter all meals by dietary options or allergies (why doesn't everywhere do this?). The menu "heroes" include Moroccan tagine and beef brisket, share plates offer the likes of crispy miso tofu and crumbed halloumi "fries," while the loaded focaccia stars toppings such as smashed lamb kofta and braised mushrooms. At night, Yonder transforms into a live music and comedy venue, though it's plenty loud enough in the daytime, too. 14 Church St. yonderqt.co.nz. ✆ **03/409-0994.** Share plates NZ$21–NZ$26, main courses NZ$31–NZ$39. Daily 8am–late.

INEXPENSIVE

The Cow ♥♥, Cow Lane, off Beach Street (thecowpizza.co.nz; ✆ **03/442-8588;** Tues–Sat 5–10pm), is a woody, moody, and very popular pizzeria. If your budget has taken a beating on your trip, console yourself with the pepperoni pizza, pasta bolognese with fresh green salad, or one of the homemade soups. All are excellent value (and quite tasty).

Vudu Cafe & Larder ♥♥ CAFE Breakfast and lunch are a workout at this extremely popular cafe; it offers meals packed with toothsome layers of hearty ingredients. The Rhubarb Explosion French toast includes rhubarb compote, coulis and cream; lunch may be a tofu-kale-chili scramble on hearty rye bread, or lamb, potato, apple and chickpea stew piled on labneh with flatbread. The cabinet is groaning with sweet and savory baked goods and packed sandwiches, too. Lines are long, so turn up when they open. You'll be amazed at the large, fabulous 1950s aerial image of old Queenstown covering one wall; how times have changed. 16 Rees St. vuducafe.co.nz. ✆ **03/409-0625.** Main courses NZ$12–NZ$25. Daily 7:30am–3:30pm.

Fergburger: Is It Worth the Wait?

If you're not already in the know, you're probably wondering, "What's the deal with the line-up at **Fergburger**?" (42 Shotover St.; fergburger.com; ✆ **03/441-1232**). It's a fair question, given that the queue stretches down the street every day from 7am to 2:30am, closing only for cleaning. Allegedly, Fergburger makes some of the best burgers not just in NZ, but *in the world.* Locals, however, will tell you that **Devil Burger** (5/11 Church St.; devilburger.com; ✆ **03/442-4666**) is better. Ultimately, we think that Fergburger's appeal relies partially on being another adventure activity; only the most stubborn will survive the long wait. But if you have your heart set on it, you can also cheat by calling your order in ahead of time. Both Fergburger and Devil Burger are similarly priced, with burgers running from NZ$17 to NZ$29.

Lines out front are an everyday occurrence at Fergburger.

Where to Eat in Arrowtown

The boutique holiday village of Arrowtown has a renowned foodie scene, with some of the cutest and most picturesque cafes in NZ, as well as gourmet and fine-dining options.

Amisfield Winery & Bistro ♥♥♥ MODERN NEW ZEALAND One of NZ's best restaurants, this much-awarded scenic beauty by Lake Hayes serves up a world-class set menu. It changes regularly depending on what's in season, but it hardly matters; the food is so inventive, with each ingredient treated so artfully, that it hardly resembles a regular meal but rather culinary theater. You simply arrive to partake in the degustation that executive chef Vaughan Mabee and his team have designed for you, as befitting Mabee's ranking in the international 2024 Best Chef Awards. The wine list is magnificent, and the sommelier's advice is trustworthy. You'll need 2½ hours for lunch and 4 for dinner.

10 Lake Hayes Rd. amisfield.co.nz. ✆ **03/442-0556.** Lunch NZ$395, dinner NZ$595, optional wine pairing NZ$195/NZ$395. Reservations essential. Wed 7–11pm, Thurs–Sun noon–3pm and 7–11pm (hours change seasonally; check website). Not appropriate for young children.

Aosta ♥♥♥ MODERN ITALIAN Named for the northern Italian valley, this contemporary and light eatery blends Italian cooking techniques with

A contemporary Italian take on local seafood at Aosta.

Otago produce. That doesn't mean heavy pastas and pizzas: Aosta is about wonderfully attentive service and perfectly plated seasonal meals, like bluefin tuna ragu with tomato tagliatelle, or barbecue octopus with kūmara and *bagna càuda* (garlic-anchovy dipping sauce). Ordering the famed tiramisu—which is theatrically assembled right at your table—is a dramatic and delish finale for the meal.

18 Buckingham St. aosta.nz. ✆ **029/0200-0019.** Main courses NZ$44–NZ$48. Reservations recommended. Daily 5–8pm.

Arrowtown Bakery ♥ BAKERY This cute corner takeaway serves up great coffee and smash-hit savory meat pies, such as lamb and mint, venison, or spicy chicken, all encased in flaky pastry. Other goodies include bacon and egg butties, rolls, sandwiches, and a range of chocolatey, creamy baked treats. There's regularly a queue out the door, but it moves quickly; the busiest time is lunch, between noon and 2pm. There's an adjoining cafe, but it's the pies that have a cult following.

14 Buckingham St. ✆ **03/442-1587.** Pies NZ$7. Daily 7am–3pm.

The Fork and Tap ♥ GASTROPUB Most visitors to Arrowtown will be drawn to the Fork and Tap for its large, sunny garden patio, complete with a playground and sand pit for kids. But inside the historic pub is where it's at, with red leather banquettes and antiques throughout. The wait time for food can be long during the lunch and dinner rush, but if you're after a mid-afternoon snack, you can't beat this spot for a craft beer (there are 19 on tap) and a share cheese board, pizza, or meat platter.

51 Buckingham St. theforkandtap.co.nz. ✆ **03/442-1860.** Lunch mains NZ$28–NZ$32; dinner mains NZ$27–NZ$45. Daily noon–late.

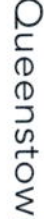

Postmasters Kitchen + Bar ♥♥ NEW ZEALAND/INTERNATIONAL As the name implies, this pretty garden cafe and restaurant occupies Arrowtown's venerable postmasters' home. Indoors the tables extend to include what was a many-windowed sunporch, and outdoors the gardens have been paved to create a large courtyard opening off the street. It's open for breakfast, lunch, and dinner, with a kids' menu; coffee and cakes are available all day. The seasonal dinner menu is a showcase of New Zealand ingredients: green-lipped mussels, beef brisket, lamb, and seasonal fruit.

54 Buckingham St. www.postmasters.co.nz. ✆ **03/442-0991.** Main courses NZ$22–NZ$48. Mon and Wed–Fri 11am–9pm; Sat–Sun 10am– 9am.

Queenstown Nightlife

This is a party town, so if you enjoy after dark socializing, you've come to the right place. An ivy-draped hideaway tucked into 14 Cow Lane, **The Bunker** ♥♥♥ (thebunker.co.nz; ✆ **03/441-8030**) has a first-rate restaurant downstairs and a *very* popular cocktail lounge above. **Bardeaux** ♥♥, Eureka Arcade, 11 The Mall (remarkablehospo.co.nz/bardeaux; ✆ **03/442-8284**), is a classy wine bar with attentive staff, a large cocktail selection, and nearly 500 whiskies and wines, many of the latter from Central Otago. **The Winery** ♥, 29 Ballarat St. (thewinery.co.nz; ✆ **03/409-2226**), is the resort's in-town cellar door (wine-tasting room), where you can sample wines from a selection of more than 60 varietals and buy at cellar door prices. It also has whisky (mostly the Scottish variety) and honey tastings.

Minus 5° Ice Bar, Steamer Wharf (minus5icebar.com; ✆ **021/1193-7966**), lets you spend the night on ice—literally—in its 80-ton ice bar. It's all about hand-sculpted ice furnishings, fur-lined ice seats, and vodka cocktails. It's more of a tourist attraction than a cocktail bar; even kids are welcome to indulge in mocktails. Big coats and woolly gloves are provided, and you get to joyfully smash your ice cups at the end. Icy sessions are from 2pm every hour until 10pm.

WĀNAKA

145km (90 miles) S of Haast; 117km (73 miles) N of Queenstown

The perfect place to spend a couple of days recharging, the lakeside town of Wānaka has seen huge growth in the past 10 years, with stylish homes and holiday houses perched hillside and lakeside, and a buzzing cosmopolitan center with good shops, restaurants, cafes, and bars. The town of Wānaka has Lake Wānaka as its focus point, with the mountain backdrop always in view. The gateway to Mount Aspiring National Park, it is under the jurisdiction of the Department of Conservation (DOC), which translates to maintained walking tracks, excellent maps, and weather guidance for those going into wilderness areas.

Essentials

ARRIVING & GETTING AROUND

Wānaka is a 5-hour drive from Christchurch, 3½ hours from both Dunedin and Te Anau, and 1⅕ hours from Queenstown on SH6. The shorter 1-hour route to/from Queenstown on SH89 (also known as the Crown Range Rd.) is considerably more scenic, as it's the highest altitude main road in NZ, reaching altitudes of 816m (2,678 ft.). However, in winter you will need chains on your tires. It is also sometimes closed due to snow and ice. **InterCity** (intercity.co.nz; ✆ **03/365-1113**) provides regular coach service linking Wānaka to other major centers, including Queenstown and the West Coast. **Ritchies** (ritchies.co.nz/queenstown) also operates a daily shuttle service to/from Queenstown, with stops at Cardrona and Cromwell. It costs NZ$40. Contact **Yello!** (yello.co.nz; ✆ **0800/443-5555** in NZ) for charter transport and getting around

Cycling along the lakefront bike path in Wānaka.

places other transport doesn't go (you can't miss this transport operator—it's all yellow!).

VISITOR INFORMATION

The official website for **Lake Wānaka Tourism** is **wanaka.co.nz**. The **Lake Wānaka isite Visitor Centre,** 103 Ardmore St. (© **03/443-1233**), is open daily from 9am to 5pm. The **Department of Conservation (DOC),** at Ardmore St. and Ballantyne Rd. (© **03/443-7660**), provides information on Mount Aspiring National Park and all DOC tracks in the area. Also worth picking up is the **Neat Places' foldable map** of Wānaka (neatplaces.co.nz), available for free from local retailers; it highlights the city's best restaurants and shopping.

SPECIAL EVENTS

The **Warbirds Over Wānaka International Air Show** (warbirdsover wanaka.com) combines classic vintage and veteran aircraft, machinery, fire engines, and tractors with dynamic Air Force displays and aerobatic teams in the natural amphitheater of the Upper Clutha Basin. It's held every second Easter in even-numbered years, with events scheduled for 2026 and 2028. In odd-numbered years, you can catch the sister show in Blenheim, **Classic Fighters** (classicfighters.co.nz).

Exploring Wānaka

Wānaka is a destination that best caters to outdoor adventurers, who are keen to get out on its waters or trails (see "Outdoor Pursuits," p. 478). But there are a handful of other attractions, particularly for families.

Since 1973, Stuart Landsborough, aka Professor Puzzle, has drawn thousands (now hundreds of thousands) of visitors annually to the confusing passageways of his elaborate Great Maze at **Puzzling World** ♥♥, SH89, 2km (1¼ miles) from Wānaka (puzzlingworld.co.nz; © **03/443-7489**). The crazy

Soaring Above It All

On a flightseeing tour with **Southern Alps Air ♥♥**, 48 Helwick St. (southern alpsair.co.nz; ✆ **0800/345-666** in NZ), all passengers get a window seat for superb views over glaciers, snowcapped mountains, rivers, forests, and the two national parks. An excellent range of options runs from short flights (NZ$450) to a Milford Sound flight-and-cruise for NZ$749 adults, NZ$560 kids 5 to 15. Former CEO and pilot Paul Cooper, who flew the route for 30+ years and has now handed the business over to his son Ryan, says it's not unusual for people to have tears of awe in their eyes as they fly above the mountains.

Tilted House, Leaning Clock Tower, and a Hologram Hall will test your perceptions. It's always interesting and a great place for kids. The most fun is a combo ticket including the illusion rooms and maze; NZ$33 adults, NZ$24 children 5 to 15. It's open daily from 9am, with last admission at 4:30pm (5pm in winter). Allow a good 2 hours for your visit. Landsborough himself is now retired, but is a character; ask about the NZ$100,000 Psychic Challenge he established, which lasted 30 years without a winner.

A stone's throw away, the **National Transport & Toy Museum ♥** (nttmuseumwanaka.co.nz; ✆ **03/443-8765**) has a huge collection of every toy you've ever heard of—from teddy bears to Barbie dolls, LEGO to Meccano sets. A massive collection of cars and trucks and tractors and tanks sprawls through hangars and Quonset huts. The collections and exhibitions are well done. It's open daily 8:30am to 5pm, and admission is NZ$23 adults and NZ$6 children 5 to 15.

Organized Tours

Eco Adventures Wānaka ♥♥♥ (ecowanaka.co.nz; ✆ **027/923-1420**) offers a unique tour involving a boat cruise on Lake Wānaka, landing on the island of Mou Waho (an eco-sanctuary), with an hour's guided walk to the summit of the hill, to a lake upon a mountain upon a lake. It's pure magic and costs NZ$295.

With sunset and sunrise departure times available, **Ridgeline's ♥♥** (ridgelinenz.com; ✆ **027/390-2152**) 4-hour photo safari travels to some of the most photogenic spots in Wānaka. No instruction is provided, but it will take you to photography locations you wouldn't be able to access in a 2WD vehicle. It's NZ$1,210 for one to two people; extra people NZ$440 each.

WanaHaka (wanahaka.co.nz; ✆ **021/519-730**) offers you a traditional Māori welcome and tour of wineries in Wānaka and the wider Central Otago region. The 3-hour Express Wine Tour starts at NZ$149 per adult, including not just tasting a dozen wines but hearing *kōrero* (stories) of the extensive Māori history of the region. It's the only wine tour in Central Otago to do so.

Outdoor Pursuits

CANYONING For a tobogganing, rappelling, and swimming adventure guaranteed to thrill, contact **Deep Canyon ♥♥** (deepcanyon.co.nz;

✆ **03/443-7922**), pioneers of the sport in New Zealand. Their 7½-hour Beginner Canyon adventure visits one of two local streams depending on conditions and costs NZ$410, including lunch. Deep Canyon operates October through April and offers a range of day trips, including those for experienced canyoners.

CLIMBING There's a lot of excellent, stable climbing in the area. **Wānaka Rock Climbing ♥** (wanakarock.co.nz; ✆ **022/015-4458**) can introduce you to all the best places. You'll pay NZ$219 for a half-day intro to the sport and the area.

GOLF **Wānaka Golf Club ♥♥**, 12 Ballantyne Rd. (wanakagolf.co.nz; ✆ **03/443-7888**), is a challenging 18-hole course with astounding views. There's a well-stocked pro shop and driving range; it costs NZ$120 for 18 holes or NZ$70 for 9 holes.

KAYAKING & SUPING Lake Wānaka empties into the Clutha, the second-longest river in the country, where it forms a series of rapids and whirlpools. The result? It's one of only two places in the South Island where you can paddle whitewater. Kayak tours with **Paddle Wānaka ♥♥♥** (paddlewanaka.co.nz; ✆ **021/926-949** in NZ) are ideal for beginners (ages 12 and up). Tours range from leisurely excursions on the lake to more challenging Clutha River travel and start at NZ$229 adults and NZ$189 children. Even at depths of 20 meters (65 ft.), you'll see trout clearly swimming at the bottom of the lake. Paddle Wānaka also offers hourly kayak and SUP hire from NZ$23.

JETBOATING The top jetboating in the region is with **Wilkin River Jets ♥♥♥**, SH6, Makarora 9382 (wilkinriverjets.co.nz; ✆ **03/443-8351**), between Fox Glacier and Wānaka. Locals say it's better than the much-lauded Dart River experience at Glenorchy, near Queenstown. With an hour's ride for NZ$160 adults and NZ$110 children 3 to 14, it's also cheaper, and offers a mix of thrill riding and the softer approach, so you get a good feel for this

Hike up to an alpine lake with Eco Adventures Wānaka.

remote region. They also offer combo packages that include a helicopter flight, bushwalk, and river jet from NZ$695 per person. **Wānaka River Journeys ♥♥** (wanakariverjourneys.co.nz; ✆ **03/443-4416**) explores the braided Matukituki River and includes a wilderness walk into native beech forest to a waterfall. You have the option of being met at the top of the river by helicopter for a flight into Mount Aspiring's magnificent glacial areas. The river journey with a wilderness walk is NZ$339 for adults, NZ$209 for kids 15 and under; a jet/heli/walk combo is NZ$1,049 for adults and NZ$649 for ages 4 to 14.

Take a Walk, then Unwind in a Sauna

Among the many exceptional walks in the area (choose one from wanaka.co.nz/walking-and-hiking), we recommend **Isthmus Peak ♥♥♥**, between Wānaka and nearby Hāwea. It's of similar elevation, length, and views to the better-known (and over-trafficked) Roy's Peak, but best of all, it'll enable you to visit **The Secret Sauna ♥♥** (thesecretsauna.nz) in Hāwea afterward, where you can book shared or private sessions in a beautiful barrel sauna, alternating the steamy heat with cold Lake Hāwea plunges. Book your sauna session online; it's magical at night.

MOUNTAIN BIKING DOC's brochure on bike trails in the Wānaka area is available from its office at Ardmore Street and Ballantyne Road. Mountain bikes can be rented from **Racer's Edge/Mountain Bikes Unlimited,** 99 Ardmore St. (racersedge.co.nz; ✆ **03/443-7882**). The **Wānaka Tracks** app is downloadable for iPhones and Androids.

PACKRAFTING From October to April, **Wanaka River Journeys ♥♥** (wanakariverjourneys.co.nz; ✆ **03/443-4416**) takes adventurers out on the Matukituki River, where you can paddle a sturdy inflatable canoe in turquoise waters amid spectacular scenery. It costs NZ$429 for adults and NZ$329 for ages 10 to 14, with families of four NZ$1349.

Shopping

Downtown Wānaka's shopping area is full of NZ designers and makers. Wānaka-based **Wilson & Dorset ♥♥**, 53 Helwick St. (wilsondorset.com; ✆ **027/226-3776**), specializes in luxury sheepskin throws, pillows, and rugs in a range of colors. Its concept store also carries products from local artisans, including Simon King utensils made of native rimu and framed originals by Nelson-based artist Georgina Hoby Scutt. Candles from the Remarkable Candle Co. come in recycled bottles are named for the area, with smells like "gold rush," "Arrowtown snowberry," and "pinot noir." Just down the street, **Gifted Design ♥**, 19 Helwick St. (gifteddesign.co.nz; ✆ **03/443-2035**), carries Australian-brand Elk and made-in-Wānaka George & Edi candles, alongside oodles of adorable children's wear. **Corner Store ♥**, on the corner of Helwick and Dunmore streets (cornerstoresupplies.co.nz; ✆ **03/443-6699**), carries men's and women's streetwear from across NZ, including designs by Mons Royale, a line of technical merino clothing based in Wānaka. If Kiwiana is what you're after, **Wonder Room ♥♥**, 80 Ardmore St. (wonderroom.co.nz;

✆ **03/443-5071**), is your best bet. The gift and clothing store carries everything from laser-cut wood prints of Wānaka's lakefront to doormats that read "Kia Ora."

Where to Stay Around Wānaka

During the pandemic, many of the area's best lodges shifted from renting out individual rooms to becoming exclusive holiday rentals, where you have to rent out the whole lodge to stay. The good news? This means there are more holiday homes to choose from. It's best to check Airbnb and bookabach.co.nz for places to spend the night.

Edgewater Resort ♥♥ Situated right on the shores of the lake, a 20-minute stroll from the town center, this resort-style property is for those who want more than just a room. Its extensive list of facilities includes tennis courts, a 9-hole putting green, a children's playground, a pool, and in-room spa treatments. Although it's now more than 30 years old, the building has aged well, thanks to frequent upgrades and refurbishments, with the most recent in 2025. Each of its one- and two-bedroom suites has an outdoor balcony or terrace. If you're after space and value, go for the one-bedroom suites, which have bigger bathrooms with double tubs.

Sargood Dr. edgewater.co.nz. ✆ **03/443-0011.** 104 units. NZ$263–NZ$525 double. **Amenities:** 2 restaurants, bar; free transfers from Wānaka Airport (ask when booking); babysitting; bike rentals; kids' playground; concierge; putting green; 2 Jacuzzis; limited room service; spa; sauna; 2 tennis courts; bikes and kayaks for hire; free Wi-Fi.

Hampshire Holiday Park ♥ Close enough to town to be walkably convenient, but far enough away to be reasonably quiet, Hampshire is the most central Wānaka holiday park, with the usual tent, campervan, and cabin offerings, with or without ensuites. Without ensuites, but still very nice, are a set of brand-new two-person "Tiny Cabins" that are modern and extremely comfortable. They're absolutely sun-drenched, with air-conditioning, kitchenette, decks, and cozy beds. The whole facility is large, clean, and well-run, with friendly staff. With its range of accommodation and proximity to the lake and a supermarket across a pleasant public park, it's a good budget self-catering option.

212 Brownston St. hampshireholidayparks.co.nz. ✆ **03/443-7883.** Unpowered sites from NZ$52, cabins NZ$256–NZ$375 (min. 2-night stay). **Amenities:** Kitchen; laundry; kids' playground; BBQ; free Wi-Fi.

Limetree Lodge ♥♥♥ True luxury boils down to a few elements: genuinely warm hospitality, beauty (in the natural surroundings and in the guest rooms), and good food. Limetree Lodge scores on all those points. Visitors stay either in one of four large ensuite guest rooms, each with French doors leading to a veranda; or in one of two suites (the most fabulous is the Black Peak Suite, with two bedrooms, a private lounge with fireplace, and a kitchenette). All are outfitted with special comforts—heated floors, fresh flowers, high-quality mattresses, special teas, and chocolate. The lodge has a saltwater

Rustic comfort meets modern luxury in the guest lounge at Waiorau Homestead.

pool for hot days and a lounge with log fires for wet days. Breakfasts are true feasts, running the gamut from house preserves and granola to hot meals incorporating eggs from the resident hens. For those wanting to dine in, hosts Pauline and John will arrange for a guest chef or food delivered from a restaurant—or prepare an in-house gourmet evening meal themselves (extra charge). A truly special place.

Ballantyne Rd., RD2. limetreelodge.co.nz. ✆ **03/443-7305.** 6 units. NZ$349–NZ$499. Rates include breakfast, pre-dinner drink, and free shuttle service to/from local restaurants. **Amenities:** Croquet lawn; helipad; Jacuzzi; pétanque; pitch-and-putt golf; saltwater pool; spa pool; free Wi-Fi.

Waiorau Homestead ♥♥♥ This gorgeous old homestead is tucked into an idyllic rural setting near Cardrona Alpine Resort. The rooms are homey and inviting, decorated with Otago artwork and shades of blue, turquoise, grey, cream, and warm natural tones to reflect the varying colors of the surrounding mountains and lakes. Hosts Blyth Adams (a chef) and Anne Lockhart offer three large, beautifully appointed guest rooms with ensuites and a separate self-contained, self-catering studio pool house with an outdoor fire. The property is 20 minutes from Wānaka, but once you get here you won't want to leave anyway—especially once you sit down to one of Blyth's meals.

2127B Cardona Valley Rd. waiorauhomestead.co.nz. ✆ **027/443-2225.** 4 units. NZ$250–NZ$390 double. Dinner by arrangement. **Amenities:** Airport transfers (fee); free use of bikes; outdoor Jacuzzi; outdoor pool; free Wi-Fi.

Where to Eat in Wānaka

The popular, casual **Kai Whakapai Cafe & Bar ♥**, lakefront at the corner of Ardmore and Helwick streets (kaiwhakapai.co.nz; ✆ **03/443-7795**), is good for pizzas and well-stuffed sandwiches and coffee; the toasted salmon bagel is excellent. It's also a favorite spot for those seeking local brews on tap (good wine list, too). There's a busy bar in the evening and great people-watching all day (daily 7am–10:30pm).

Big Fig ♥♥♥ NEW ZEALAND Usually packed with happy eaters, Big Fig offers slow-cooked food served fast, dishing you a heaping bowl from a hot cabinet full of delicious roasted meats, vegetables, and flavorful crunchy salads. Menus change daily but could include slow-cooked beef cheeks, meatballs, harissa butterbean stew, and carrot and apple slaw, all with sauces and dressings. This place is where everyone will tell you to go to eat—meals are hearty and nourishing, and the cafe is low on fuss but big on taste. No bookings; just turn up. There's also a separate breakfast menu, and takeaway is available too. 105 Ardmore St. bigfig.co.nz. ✆ **03/443-5023.** Bowls NZ$17/NZ$24/NZ$30. Daily 8am–8:30pm.

Bistro Gentil ♥♥♥ FRENCH Bringing Gallic gastronomy to Wānaka, this modern-rustic bistro relies on its extensive kitchen garden and orchard for some of the freshest meals you'll find in the region. Of course, some ingredients have to be sourced elsewhere, but local is key. Service is attentive and friendly, and the dinner menu is a triumphant rollout of South Island–grown and caught products such as salt-baked beetroot with whipped ricotta; Angus beef with red-onion relish and potato dauphines; and venison strip loin with celeriac puree. The wine list is available by the glass or half-glass, and thanks to the bistro's Enomatic wine system, opened wine stays fresh. 76A Golf Course Rd. bistrogentil.co.nz. ✆ **03/443-2299.** Main courses NZ$42–NZ$65. Mon–Sat 6pm–late; Sun 6:30pm–late.

Burrito Craft ♥♥♥ BURRITOS Here's the thing: Ordering Mexican food in NZ is like ordering seafood in a landlocked country—it's just a bad idea. There are rare exceptions to this rule though, and this food truck is one of them. While far from authentic, the burritos are a saucy delicious mess of guacamole, refried beans, and other fillings that are excellent value for money. If you like your food spicy, order one level up on the spice-o-meter from what you normally would. Gluten-free, dairy-free, and vegan options are available upon request. It's part of an eclectic and thriving food-truck scene in this area, and for a taste of under-the-radar local favorites, you could choose a different meal each night. 51 Brownston St. burritocraft.co.nz. ✆ **020/443-4430.** Burritos NZ$17–NZ$19. Daily noon–8:30pm.

Beanbags & Cookies: A Night at the Movies

See a flick and soak up some local flavor at **Cinema Paradiso ♥♥♥**, 72 Brownston St. (paradiso.nz; ✆ **03/443-1505**), a true Wānaka icon, if not a national treasure. This unique movie theater with three screens has been adored since it opened in 1994 for its quirky take on a night at the movies. It's like watching a film at someone's house (if the house had a Morris Minor parked in the theater) with vintage sofas, big soft chairs, cushions, and beanbags that say sit down, sprawl out, and have a good time. The homemade cookies at intermission have become legendary; the scent of them baking through the first half of the movie is hard to resist. Secret-recipe real fruit ice cream is served, and wine, beer, and light meals can be ordered as well.

The pizzas at Francesca are justly famous.

Francesca ♥♥♥ ITALIAN "Best pizza ever." Ask a local about Francesca, and that's the response you'll likely get. Somehow the traditional Italian dishes here seem more flavorful than those of other Italian joints in town. Francesca won a *Denizen* magazine Best Restaurant gong in 2025 and recently had a decor refresh, with a new enclosed outdoor patio and interiors full of luxe-earthy details: dripping candlewax, wood, stone, and greenery, blending the same modern-traditional vibes as the food. As for the menu, the handmade gnocchi with beef cheek is a bestseller, and the spring risotto is resplendent with peas, kale, and broccolini. Those famed pizzas include a lamb sausage pie with pomegranate and goat cheese; prawn, crème fraîche, and pesto; and more.

93 Ardmore St. francescawanaka.co.nz. ✆ **03/443-5599.** Main courses NZ$36–NZ$95, pizzas NZ$28–NZ$35. Daily noon–3pm and 5pm–late.

Kika ♥♥♥ NEW ZEALAND Holding strong as one of the hottest restaurants in Wānaka, Kika is owned by award-winning English-trained chef James Stapley. It bills itself as "modern sharing," with global inspirations drawn from Stapley's extensive experience; plates are ample in size and inspired by seasonal produce. Expect complex dishes such as whole fish with roasted fennel and scampi bouillabaisse, lamb shoulder with ras el hanout and date chermoula, or asparagus with egg yolk puree, tarragon mayo, and truffle vinaigrette.

2 Dunmore St. kika.nz. ✆ **03/443-6536.** Plates NZ$26–NZ$89. Daily 5:30pm–late.

Relishes Café ♥♥ INTERNATIONAL Lakefront Relishes has been a top spot for years and I've had some of my most satisfying fish meals here. I'm not the only one who has had that experience, and they don't take reservations, so people are often turned away for lack of space. You'll just have to try your luck. Relishes has a simple, country-style interior, nothing flashy, but the food it serves, especially the baked blue cod served with hazelnut and lemon butter, is memorable. The countertop cookies are pretty good, too.

1/99 Ardmore St. relishescafe.co.nz. ✆ **03/443-9018.** Main courses NZ$18–NZ$29. Daily 7am–3pm.

TE ANAU & FIORDLAND

172km (107 miles) SW of Queenstown; 116km (72 miles) S of Milford Sound; 157km (97 miles) NW of Invercargill

The gateway to Fiordland National Park, a 1.2-million-hectare (3-million-acre) World Heritage Site, **Te Anau** is a resort town, with a permanent population of about 4,000 that swells to over 10,000 in summer. It's set on the eastern

Te Anau & Fiordland

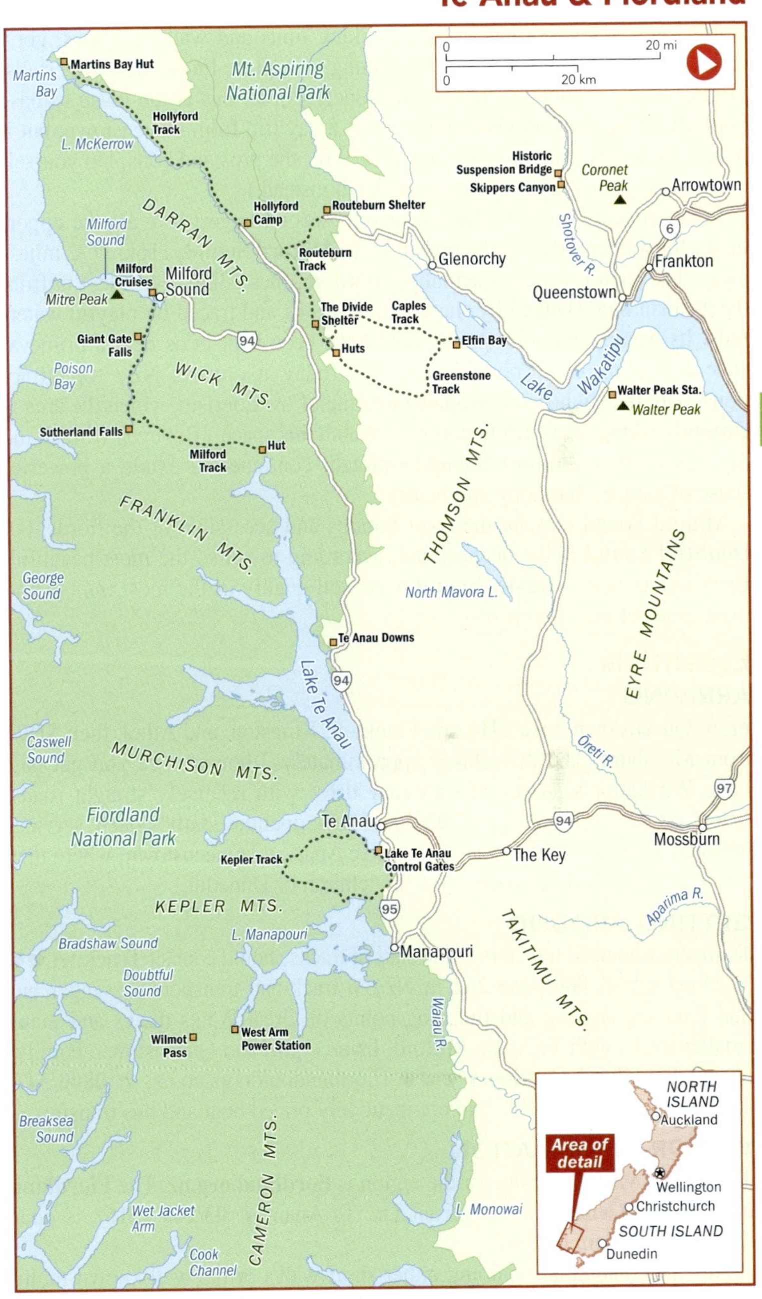

14
QUEENSTOWN, WĀNAKA & FIORDLAND
Te Anau & Fiordland

shore of Lake Te Anau, the largest of the South Island lakes; curiously, the eastern shoreline is virtually treeless, while its western banks are covered in dense forest. The area has excellent hiking trails and walking tracks, good cafes, and places to stay. If you're coming to explore Fiordland's waterfalls, virgin forests, mountains, rivers, and lonely fiords, this is the place to base yourself. (Yes, you can visit Fiordland as a day trip from Queenstown, but it makes for a very long day; see box p. 459 for the pros and cons. Do yourself a favor and plan a night or two in Te Anau instead.)

What attracts visitors to New Zealand's second-largest lake are the opportunity for watersports and the proximity to **Milford Sound,** 116km (72 miles) away. The sound, which is actually a fiord, reaches 23km (14 miles) in from the Tasman Sea, flanked by sheer granite peaks and traced by playful waterfalls. Its waters and surrounding land have been kept in as near a primeval state as humans could possibly manage. Today, it's one of NZ's top attractions, with the slightly unfortunate outcome of overtourism, which the area is currently taking measures to combat. (Watch this space.) But even with all the big bus tourists, Milford Sound/Piopiotahi continues to exude a powerful sense of nature's harmony and beauty.

Milford Sound may be the most famous and accessible of the fiords, but **Doubtful Sound** is the deepest and, according to some, the most beautiful. Even farther south, **Dusky Sound** may well qualify as the most remote and mysterious of the famous trio.

Essentials

ARRIVING

From Queenstown, take SH6, via Frankton, Kingston, and Athol, then SH94 from Mossburn. The drive takes approximately 2 hours; once you get past Lake Whakatipu's shores, it's an easy drive with relatively straight roads. **InterCity** (intercity.co.nz; ✆ **03/365-1113**) operates daily coach services between Te Anau and Invercargill, and Te Anau and Queenstown, where they connect with scheduled routes to Christchurch or Dunedin.

GETTING AROUND

Trampers who need transfers to the start of tracks should contact **Tracknet** ♥♥ (tracknet.net; ✆ **0800/483-262** in NZ), a track-and-transport passenger bus that links the starting and finishing points of Great Walks tracks and many smaller tracks with Te Anau, Milford, Invercargill, and Queenstown. Family-owned **Fiordland Outdoors** ♥♥♥ (fiordlandoutdoors.co.nz; ✆ **0800/347-453**) also provides reliable and competitively priced boat and bus transfers.

VISITOR INFORMATION

The official visitor website for the region is **fiordland.org.nz**. The **Fiordland isite Visitor Centre,** 80 Lakefront Dr., Te Anau (✆ **03/249-7516**), is open daily from 8:30am to 6pm.

Anyone contemplating doing either short walks or the well-known multi-day tramps (hikes), should stop at **DOC's Fiordland National Park Visitor**

Centre, Lakefront Drive, Te Anau (doc.govt.nz; ✆ **03/249-7924**), for maps and a talk with the rangers about that day's conditions. If you're doing one of the Great Walks, you're required to pick up your hut permit here (even if you've already booked and paid online) and register your itinerary for safety reasons. This is also where you'll catch shuttles to the start of the tracks, and there's a small on-site museum.

Exploring Te Anau & the Lake

You're not going to get lost in little Te Anau, which is on a grid system, with the lake to its west. The main street, fittingly called Town Centre, is where you'll find restaurants, two grocery stores, shops, and outdoor outfitters.

Your first stop in Te Anau should be at **Fiordland Cinema ♥♥♥**, 7 The Lane, Te Anau (fiordlandcinema.co.nz; ✆ **03/249-8844**), a cool boutique movie house that was custom built to screen a 30-minute narrated film **Ata Whenua ♥♥**. Based on 2 years of footage filmed by helicopter pilots in Fiordland National Park, it's absolutely stunning (it brought tears to my eyes) and gives you a sense of the park's scale and what makes it truly unique. It's just a bonus that the cinema is also home to the **Black Dog Bar,** a restaurant and cocktail bar with evening dining from 5pm. You can even take your wine or drinks in while you watch the movie. The movie screens daily at 5pm and 6pm for NZ$12.

Next up is the **Punanga Manu o Te Anau/Te Anau Bird Sanctuary ♥**, which can be found beside the DOC visitor center. It's home to rare and endemic bird species, including takahē and kākā. If you visit in the spring months, you may even be lucky enough to see their chicks.

For a beautifully relaxed day on Lake Te Anau, **Fiordland Historic Cruises ♥♥** (fiordlandhistoriccruises.co.nz; ✆ **03/249-8174**) will invite you aboard *Faith*, a historic sailing ship. Besides their 3-hour daytime cruises (NZ$165 adults, NZ$80 ages 5–17), for the same price they offer a 90-minute evening champagne cruise that includes drinks and gourmet canapés and the opportunity to drive the boat or help hoist the sails (sailors' and captains' hats provided!). For something a little speedier, **Cruise Te Anau ♥♥** (cruiseteanau.co.nz; ✆ **021/178-4481**) will jet you to the awe-inspiring South Fiord of the lake in a former America's Cup chase boat on its 3-hour Waterfall Adventure (NZ$270 adults; NZ$220 children). After marveling at the views, you can take short walks to lakes and waterfalls, with a light snack onboard afterward. Chris is an informative skipper,

The *Faith* sets sail for a day out on Lake Te Anau with Fiordland Historic Cruises.

and it's definitely the quickest way to get a taste of the mountains and fiords without a long drive or hike.

If those sound a bit too sedate for your tastes, **Fiordland Jet** ♥ (fjet.nz; ✆ **0800/253-826** in NZ) operates a fun jetboat ride down the Upper Waiau River to Lake Manapouri, with lots of 360° spins, stops at *Lord of the Rings* filming locations, and a short guided walk on the Kepler Track. Afterwards, you can opt to cycle back to Te Anau on the newly formed **Lake2Lake Cycle Trail** ♥. While the hour bike ride back to town is a great way to see the area with lots of photo stops along the way, it's best for those who are super-confident cyclists, because the trail is very loose gravel. Standard bikes can be rented for NZ$240 adults, NZ$145 ages 5 to 15; e-bikes cost NZ$40 more.

Exploring Milford Sound/Piopiotahi

No matter what the weather is like, Milford Sound is memorable. Its 14 nautical miles offer scene after scene of misty peaks and sheer rocky mountains, reaching heights of 1,800m (5,900 ft.). New Zealand fur seals laze on rocky shelves, and dolphins play in water that reaches depths of 600m (2,000 ft.). Striking **Mitre Peak,** which soars 1,692m (1,551 ft.) straight up from the sea, is New Zealand's most recognizable sight, having adorned artworks, chocolate boxes, and calendars since the 19th century.

Yes, it rains a lot around here, and the weather is extremely changeable, even in summer; come prepared. You may not glimpse the mountaintops through the rain, but you'll see and hear hundreds of waterfalls. As NZ's number one tourist attraction, the phrase "wetter is better" holds true.

In summer, coaches pour in one after the other for cruises, which means hundreds or thousands of people may be joining you for a look at this special place. But if you can overlook these numbers, you'll be rewarded with unforgettable landscapes.

THE MILFORD ROAD

The road to Milford Sound is world-famous. Although it can be completed in 2 hours, allow at least 3 so you can stop to look at the many natural attractions along the way. SH94 from Te Anau leads north along the lake, with islands and wooded distant shores on your left. Since many visitors plan their visit to coincide with boat cruise departure times, the major scenic stops can get congested. The majority of tour buses (including those coming from Queenstown) depart from Te Anau between 9am and 10am and arrive at **Mirror Lakes** (a fantastic photo stop) around 10:30am, **Knobs Flat** (the last flush toilets before you reach Milford) at 11am, **The Chasm** (a beautiful rocky valley) at 12:30pm, and the village of **Milford Sound** at 1pm. Long story short? It pays to leave an hour earlier, even if it means you'll be waiting around for your cruise to start once you arrive in Milford.

The drive is often a slow one, especially in wet conditions, as you make your way through steep gorges and between walls of solid rock and moss-covered inclines. I would discourage anyone from taking a motor home on this road because it is narrow, steep, and winding with a lot of bus traffic—and if

For the classic Milford Sound experience, marvel in its spectacular vistas from the deck of a lake cruiser, like this Southern Discoveries tour boat.

that doesn't put you off, the dark, narrow Homer Tunnel will. The road is usually very busy in summer and there can be delays, especially at the tunnel. ***Remember:*** There is nowhere to fuel up in Milford or after leaving Te Anau, so make sure your tank is full. This is *not* a road you want to be "marooned" on—in any season. During the winter months, all drivers on Milford Road are required to carry chains for their vehicles. Road conditions can be checked with the NZTA on milfordroad.co.nz.

If you're not keen to self-drive after reading that, but also don't want to be a sardine packed on a big tour bus, local operator **Trips & Tramps** ♥♥♥ (tripsandtramps.com; ✆ **03/249-7081**) organizes small group day trips to Milford Sound, which include the classic boat cruise, stops at all the best photo points en route, and guided hikes on trails along the Milford Road. Tours cost NZ$299 adults and NZ$235 children.

Homer Tunnel, about 100km (65 miles) into the journey, is a major engineering marvel: a 1.2km (¾-mile) passageway first proposed in 1889, begun in 1935, and finally opened in 1940. It wasn't until 1954 that a connecting road was completed and the first private automobile drove through. There's no lighting in the tunnel and it's very narrow. Drive with extreme care! Also keep an eye out for kea, who like to frequent this area (and peck at the rubber on cars).

About 6km (3¾ miles) past the tunnel, stop and walk to the **Chasm.** The pleasant 15-minute round-trip goes through mossy undergrowth and beech forest to see a rather wonderful feat of natural erosion on the **Cleddau River.**

AROUND THE SOUND

Cruising

To be fully appreciated, Milford Sound must be seen from the deck of a cruise vessel. Don't get too hung up on trying to figure out which tour operator to cruise with—their itineraries are nearly identical. (You'll see all the boats doing exactly the same 2- to 3-hour circuit.) My only real advice is that if you're self-driving, arrive early to nab a good seat on the boats, as they can get packed. As you cruise, keep an eye out for Hector's dolphins and Fiordland crested penguins.

Prices differ depending on whether you join the cruise vessel in Queenstown, Te Anau, or at Milford Sound, and whether you arrive at the docks via coach, fixed-wing plane, or helicopter. Fares and inclusions vary from operator to operator, and seasonal rates may apply, but expect to pay around NZ$199 adult, NZ$170 child for a coach/cruise/coach tour from Te Anau, and NZ$240 adult, NZ$216 child from Queenstown. Fly/cruise/fly tours from Queenstown will cost around NZ$730 for an adult, NZ$490 for a child.

One of the best Milford experiences is waking up in the watery light of a new day on the sound itself after an overnight stay. **RealNZ** ♥ (realnz.com; ✆ **0800/656-501** in NZ) offers overnight cruises with private cabins and kayaking excursions, from NZ$669 adults and NZ$399 children. Meals are included, but transport to Milford is extra.

Southern Discoveries ♥ (southerndiscoveries.co.nz; ✆ **0800/264-536** in NZ) offers Milford Sound cruises including the good-value "Discover More Cruise" comprising a 2-hour cruise on the Sound, a picnic lunch, and **Milford Underwater Observatory** ♥♥, where visitors descend 10m (33 ft.) beneath the fiord surface to observe underwater life (NZ$199 adults, NZ$109 children; book direct online for 10% off).

Kayaking & Hiking

It is quite something to be gliding over the dark green water in your own kayak. Run by the "mayor of Milford," **Rosco's Milford Kayaks** ♥♥ (roscos milfordkayaks.com; ✆ **03/249-8500**) offers several Milford Sound kayaking adventures, including a "Milford Track Paddle and Walk," with a scenic paddle around the sound's Deepwater Basin and a walk along the final section of the Milford Track (NZ$180 per adult, ages 12+).

Exploring the Sound with Rosco's Milford Kayaks gives you an entirely different perspective on the scale of the fiord's landscapes.

New Zealand's most famous hike, the 4-day Milford Track, has a number of vistas that stop trampers in their, yes, tracks.

The biggest adventure in this area is the 4-day **Milford Track ♥♥♥**, NZ's premier Great Walk hiking trail. Once dubbed "the finest walk in the world," it has become somewhat a victim of its own success, with the mandatory hut bookings selling out in seconds every year. Booking a guided walk will help you get around this. **Ultimate Hikes** (ultimatehikes.co.nz; ✆ **03/450-1940**) gives you the luxury of relaxing in a private lodge each night after hiking that day's section; 4-night packages run from NZ$2,829 for a shared bunkroom to NZ$3,649 to NZ$5,899 for a private ensuite room. You can also just get a taste of this iconic hike on a day tour with **Trips & Tramps ♥♥♥** (tripsandtramps.com). They run a guided walk to the **Giant Gate Falls ♥♥** near the end of the track, an easy 11km (7-mile) round-trip journey from Sandfly Point, plus an afternoon boat cruise for NZ$360 adults and NZ$240 children. Want to go it your own? **Fiordland Outdoors** (fiordlandoutdoors.co.nz) offers transfers to Sandfly Point for NZ$75 adults and NZ$25 children.

A Sky-High View of the Sound

I'm not a huge fan of scenic flightseeing because of the environmental costs, but one of my most memorable NZ travel experiences has to be a short scenic helicopter flight over Milford Sound. These flights are only about a half-hour, but landing on the Tutoko Glacier and flying so close to the park's highest mountain peaks gives you a true sense of the scale of this incredible place. Contact **Milford Sound Helicopters ♥♥♥** (milfordsoundhelicopters.com; ✆ **03/249-8384**); the 25-minute flight is NZ$595.

Exploring Doubtful Sound ♥♥

Doubtful Sound makes an idyllic day excursion from Lake Manapouri. At 21m (69 ft.), it's the deepest of the fiords. Filled with ancient rainforest, cascading waterfalls, towering peaks, and abundant wildlife, it's an unforgettable experience. An air of complete silence, broken only by birdcall, adds to the mystery. Doubtful Sound is five times bigger than Milford, and although it can't boast Mitre Peak, its still waters mirror 1,200m (3,900-ft.) **Commander Peak.** Another difference between the two sounds is that you always know Milford is close to civilization because of the buzz of aircraft going to and from the airstrip and the multitude of buses arriving daily. Doubtful is much more remote.

There's no way to get to Doubtful Sound on your own, but **RealNZ** (realnz.com; ✆ **0800/656-501** in NZ) provides excellent daylong cruises to the area, costing NZ$359 adults, NZ$179 children.

Where to Stay in Te Anau & Fiordland

Numerous motel complexes line the Te Anau waterfront, and backpackers are well served. The 25-unit **Te Anau Lakefront Backpackers ♥**, 48–50 Lakefront Dr. (teanaubackpackers.co.nz; ✆ **0800/200-074** in NZ, or 03/249-7713), has dorm beds (NZ$30–NZ$42), glamping tents (NZ$156), and en-suite doubles (NZ$136–NZ$229). There are barbecue grills as well as car and gear storage.

Fiordland Lakeview Motel & Apartments ♥♥, 42 Lakefront Dr. (fiordlandlakeview.co.nz; ✆ **03/249-7546**), has large, new, comfortable rooms and studios that face the lake and have lots of modern touches; the deluxe studio has a flatscreen TV panel mounted above the bath, heated bathroom flooring, a washer/dryer, coffee machines, patio, and automatic blinds. Rates run from NZ$275 to NZ$475.

The staff at **Asure Explorer ♥♥** (explorermotel.co.nz; ✆ **0800/777-800** in NZ) are among the best in the biz and are generous with their time and knowledge, booking tours for guests and dispensing advice. The clean motel rooms (from NZ$15) are also way bigger than average, with plenty of room to spread out, and are only a 5-minute walk from the town center. Book direct to save 15%.

While the main areas at **Shakespeare House Bed and Breakfast ♥♥**, 10 Dusky St. (shakespearehouse.co.nz; ✆ **03/249-7349**), may be dated, the rooms have been freshly refurbished and are incredibly comfortable and clean, as well as well-priced (from NZ$210). The included breakfast is continental, but hot breakfasts are available upon request.

There are a number of DOC-administered campsites (first-in, first-served) along the Milford Road. Unless you're a photographer after a sunrise or sunset shot, or want to be alone in Milford Sound at night, there's little reason to overnight in Milford. There is virtually nothing here, apart from the dock where the boats depart. However, the one real accommodations option happens to be the exquisite **Milford Sound Lodge ♥♥♥**, SH94, Milford Sound (milfordlodge.com; ✆ **03/249-8071**). Newly renovated in 2025, it offers luxury chalets and studios starting at NZ$925, as well as powered campervan parking for NZ$120 a night; it also has the **Pio Pio** cafe and bar on site. Packages with cruises are available.

Chalets at the Milford Sound Lodge offers a surprising bit of luxury right on the threshold of Fiordland National Park.

Te Anau Lodge ♥♥ The old-world charm of Te Anau Lodge could be due to its 1936 origins as a convent in the Southland township of Nightcaps (it was relocated here), but loving attention from its owners/restorers has only enhanced all of that. Large rooms and bathrooms glory in such titles such as Mother Superior's Room (a cozy space decorated with florals), the Music Room (with its sleigh and garden views), and the Belfry (which boasts a super-king bed and views of the Luxmore mountains). Breakfasts are served amid stained-glass windows in the old chapel or outdoors in the courtyard—choose from full or continental.

52 Howden St. teanaulodge.com. ✆ **03/249-7477.** 9 units. NZ$175–NZ$445 double. Rates include breakfast. **Amenities:** BBQ grills; bikes; laundry; library; guest lounge; free Wi-Fi.

Where to Eat in Te Anau

There's no debate: The best lunch stop in town is **Miles Better Pies ♥♥♥**, 17 Town Centre (milesbetterpies.co.nz; ✆ **03/249-9044**). From September to June starting from 6am, it has lines out the door for its perfect pastry, which is both tender and flaky. The savory fillings—mince and cheese, lamb and mint, and vegetarian curry being just some of the options—are great, too.

Sandfly Café ♥, 9 The Lane (✆ **03/249-9529**), is a favorite Te Anau cafe (and not just because it basically has a monopoly in town)—friendly and open 7am to 4:30pm, with excellent, diverse fare: banana and chocolate chip muffins, bacon and Parmesan scones, sushi, and venison pie. Though it's hard to avoid ordering the delicious bacon and egg roll (NZ$16) every morning you're in town.

The Fat Duck Gastropub in Te Anau caters to hungry hikers.

Popular food truck Bao Now! Te Anau (try saying it; it's fun!) has moved into full-time permanent digs and is now known as **Ditto ♥♥♥**, 92 Town Centre (eatatditto.co.nz; ✆ **03/249-4182**). I have been recommending this Kiwi-Asian food joint to anyone who will listen—it has the freshest dumpling and bao buns, the biggest sushi bowls, Vietnamese savory pancakes, and loaded fries. It's open most days from 11:30am to 8:30pm, but check ahead for hours during the winter months. The terms laid-back, casual, and friendly were invented for **The Fat Duck Gastropub ♥♥**, 124 Town Centre (thefat duck.co.nz; ✆ **03/249-8480;** Wed–Thurs 5pm–late, Fri–Sun 11:30am–late). The cooks must have hungry hikers in mind when they prepare their very hearty food, always freshly made with good local produce and generous servings. This popular family restaurant won NZ's Best Gastropub in 2025 and offers an excellent steak (though it's NZ$70) and duck-fat potatoes. Other menu items include pork belly, venison, and seafood linguini, plus smaller plates such as dumplings and popcorn chicken. Service is excellent.

In a converted vintage cottage, **The Redcliff Bar & Restaurant ♥♥**, 12 Mokonui St. (theredcliff.co.nz; ✆ **03/249-7431**), offers good food, a garden bar, and live music daily. The dinner menu includes New Zealand venison and wild hare and Fiordland fish. Menu prices reflect Te Anau's remote location; despite its pub-like exterior, this isn't a cheap meal, with mains priced at NZ$38 to NZ$60.

AORAKI/ MOUNT COOK, MACKENZIE & WAITAKI

15

This may be the region that best captures the essence of New Zealand's South Island: small in size, huge in diversity. The landscape stretches from the massive peaks of World Heritage–listed Aoraki/Mount Cook National Park, across the savannah-like Mackenzie basin with its high-country lakes and rivers, to a seaside town rich with original Victorian architecture. A determined traveler could skim it in a day, but its geological, geographical, and historical points are so different, so outstanding, it would be like sitting down to a banquet and eating only bread and water. Lingering is rewarded.

As you wind inland from the town of Geraldine on SH79, there is a point where the landscape changes abruptly, shedding its Canterbury "Englishness" (hedges and neat green fields) to slip into the vastness of the Mackenzie Country. Jagged mountains appear in the distance, and ahead but unseen lie Lakes Tekapō and Pukaki, Aoraki/ Mount Cook National Park, and the long run of the Waitaki River valley to Ōamaru on the coast. Then, just as you sight Lake Tekapō, suddenly the recognizable tent-like peak of Aoraki (Mount Cook) dwarfs everything. The entire landscape is painted in shades of blue, from the turquoise blue waters to the pale blue of the glaciers. You have arrived in one of New Zealand's most iconic destinations.

LAKE TEKAPŌ

225km (140 miles) or 3 hr. from Christchurch

Lake Tekapō/Takapō is one of three large lakes in the Mackenzie Country, and its townsite is a popular stopover for those making the long journey farther south to Queenstown and Fiordland. One of its biggest attractions is the Church of Good Shepherd, an inherently photographable stone building on the lake's shores. Tekapō is also located in the heart of the Aoraki Mackenzie International Dark Sky

outlaw & FOLK HERO

For over 100 years, the Mackenzie was sheep country, until the construction of canals for hydroelectricity transformed the dry tussock lands into grasslands, making dairy farming a sustainable option. Its heritage of high-country sheep stations hasn't been forgotten, though; its legends continue to be celebrated. The most famous of these is about James Mackenzie (sometimes spelled Mckenzie), a Scottish sheep rustler to whom the area owes its name. He seems to have spent not much more than a few years in NZ, but he left a legacy that lives on.

The tale of Mackenzie is murky, but it goes something like this: In 1855, the Scot was arrested when he was found with 1,000 stolen sheep near Tekapō. He claimed that he was a drover who had been hired to drive the sheep to Otago. After being found guilty of sheep rustling, he managed to escape from his road gang twice, before eventually being pardoned and becoming a folk hero. According to the government website NZ History, "Those who resented the power of wealthy landowners identified with him, and his rebellious spirit inspired many who did not fit easily into genteel Canterbury society."

Today, a memorial alongside Mackenzie Pass Road marks the spot where Mackenzie was captured. His faithful dog Friday—who legend has it was trained not to bark during a sheep stealing raid—is also commemorated in a statue of the pair in Fairlie.

Reserve, one of the best places in the country—and arguably the world—to view the night sky unadulterated. Don't expect to be served up a platter of packaged experiences here, but if you're looking for a place to soak it all in (literally, in the case of the town's pretty hot pools), you couldn't have arrived at a better spot.

Essentials

ARRIVING & GETTING AROUND

The region is served by **InterCity** (intercity.co.nz; ✆ **03/365-1113**) with regular connections to Christchurch, Queenstown, Fiordland, and Mt. Cook Village. **Tekapo Shuttle** (tekaposhuttlenz.com; ✆ **020/4114-8740**) runs transfers between Tekapō and Aoraki/Mt. Cook for NZ$90 one-way, as well as rides to the observatory (NZ$40).

VISITOR INFORMATION

The official tourism website for the wider Mackenzie Country region is **mackenzienz.com**. There is no official isite in the village, but there is an info center inside the **Kiwi Treasures** giftshop in the Lake Tekapō village center (✆ **03/680-6686**).

Exploring Tekapō

The sole place of worship in Tekapō, **Church of the Good Shepherd ♥♥♥**, 23 Pioneer Dr. (churchofthegoodshepherd.org.nz; ✆ **03/685-8389**), has become part of the NZ iconography, appearing on postcards and social media feeds. Built in 1935 in a dramatic setting right on the lake's edge, this

The Mackenzie Country

unassuming stone church is easy to find; just follow anyone carrying a selfie stick. (Aerial photography is limited around this iconic spot, thanks to a ban on the flying of drones in the vicinity.)

Another iconic sight in the area is the masses of multi-colored **Russell lupins** (or lupines). They once grew freely on roadsides and waterways throughout the region, but they're an invasive species, and conservationists fear they may adversely affect Mackenzie's biodiversity, displacing native flora and changing the flow of braided rivers. As a result, they're currently being sprayed—but many locals believe some should be left intact because they're so popular with tourists. In November and December, the remaining flowers should be at their peak around the water's edge.

Tekapō Springs ♥♥, 6 Lakeside Dr., Tekapō (tekaposprings.co.nz; ✆ **0800/235-3823** in NZ), uses a heat reversal technique to heat water *and* make ice, resulting in hot pools that sit side-by-side with an outdoor ice rink and a small snow tube park. Sledding and skating is only available in the winter, but you can access the facility's three hot pools, steam and sauna, day

Fuel Up: Roadside Stops En Route to Tekapō

The 3-hour drive from Christchurch to Tekapō on Highway 8 isn't the most scenic by NZ standards—at least not until the very end—but you may not notice if you make the most of your roadside stops.

In Geraldine, where you turn off SH1 to head west on SH79, you can sample the full range of Barker's jams and chutneys—which can be found in pantries across NZ—or fill up with the full menu at the **Barker's Foodstore & Eatery** ♥, 71 Talbot St., Geraldine (barkersfoodstore.nz; ✆ **03/693-9727**). It's open Monday to Sunday, 8:30am to 4:30pm. If you're after a grab-and-go style meal, drive on to Fairlie, home to the famous-in-NZ **Fairlie Bakehouse** ♥♥, 74 Main St. (fairliebakehouse.co.nz; ✆ **03/685-6063**). Its somewhat unconventional pies—including flavors such as pork belly with apple and crackling, and lamb with mint—are sold as far away as Christchurch.

From Fairlie, continue west on SH8. If time allows, stop off at the tiny historic settlement of Burke's Pass, home to the **Three Creeks Shop** ♥♥, SH8 (threecreeks.co.nz; ✆ **03/685-8544**), a village in itself that sells vintage memorabilia, and collectibles, all housed within a 1950s service station and trading post. It also offers several types of accommodations from NZ$175 per night; call to inquire how to book.

spa, and cafe year-round. The combination of activities is perfect for families, not so perfect for adults who want to soak away stress—if you fit into the latter category, avoid this one during the busy school holidays. Visiting on a winter evening, however, with snow on the hills across the lake, can be magical. It's open weekdays from 11am to 7pm, weekends 10am to 7pm. All-day passes start from NZ$40 for adults, NZ$23 for kids 5 to 15, and NZ$105 for families. Combo deals for other activities are also available.

Basking in a hot pool at Tekapō Springs.

A huge mural of the endangered *kakī*, or black stilt, overlooks the airy kitchen/dining room at Haka House Lake Tekapō.

Where to Stay in Tekapō

Many of the cottages (baches) in Tekapō are available to rent. In addition to airbnb.com and bookabach.co.nz, you can try booking through agencies **Lake Tekapo Holiday Homes** (tekapoholidayhomes.co.nz) or **Discover Tekapo** (discovertekapo.co.nz) if you want to have folks nearby who can help with any issues that may arise.

Lakes Edge Holiday Park ♥♥, 2 Lakeside Dr. (lakesedgeholidaypark.co.nz; ✆ **0800/853-853** in NZ, or 03/680-6825), known locally as "the camping ground," enjoys a prime lakefront location. Options include campsites (from NZ$64) and cabins and motel rooms of varying sizes (NZ$221–NZ$574). Amenities include barbecues and a shared lounge and kitchen.

Grand Suites Tekapo ♥, 14 Greig St. (grandsuitestekapo.co.nz; ✆ **03/663-7049**), offers some of the best rooms for the best value in town, even if they are somewhat devoid of personality. Its 28 rooms all feature kitchenettes (with a small stovetop, so you don't have to rely on a microwaved meal) or kitchens. Rates run NZ$495 to NZ$595.

Haka House Lake Tekapo ♥♥♥, 5 Motuariki Lane (hakahouse.com/lake-tekapo; ✆ **03/7400-426**), offers a new state-of-the-art, two-story hostel located right next to the Dark Sky Project's observatory. You can enjoy its unobstructed lake views from the airy second-floor lounge room or the generous main floor kitchen. Appealing to flashpackers, each cozy, properly curtained bunk (from NZ$60) has its own light and charging port; lockers have charging ports too, so you can easily charge your devices. Sound-proofed private rooms with ensuites are also available, but expensive (NZ$223 and up). Note there's no air-conditioning in the summer.

touch **THE SKY**

Tekapō is a prime place for stargazing, and not only because the University of Canterbury's **Mount John Observatory** is located here. The local council was the first in NZ to put in place lighting ordinances to protect its near-prehistoric night sky, and it's currently part of the gold-certified **Aoraki Mackenzie International Dark Sky Reserve,** the most prominent of a handful of regions in NZ with various certifications from DarkSky International. Tekapō's skies aren't just largely free of light pollution, but thanks to its altitude, geography, and weather, there's also a high number of clear nights.

In 2019, **The Dark Sky Project ♥♥** (formerly known as Earth & Sky) opened the doors to its NZ$11-million facility, which combines Māori astronomy and science in its immersive **Dark Sky Experience ♥♥**, 1 Motuariki Lane (darksky project.co.nz; ✆ **03/680-6960**). The 45-minute daytime experience (NZ$59 adults, NZ$39 children 5–17, NZ$157 families) allows visitors to feel the "heartbeat" of the stars, visualize how Polynesian voyagers found their way to Aotearoa using constellations, and see the Brashear Telescope, a 9m-tall (29½-ft.) telescope built in 1894. It's a good introduction to astronomy, but if you want to fully take advantage of your time there, come prepared with questions.

When a clear night is in the forecast, the **Summit Experience ♥** (NZ$219 adults, NZ$169 ages 5–17) takes visitors up to the working Mt. John Observatory. The guides are exceptionally knowledgeable, you'll have the opportunity to look through telescopes at nebulas and the moon, and there will be an astrophotographer on hand. However, it's a classic case of an excellent tour being turned average by a large group size—you may have to line up to look through the telescope, and the experience may feel rushed.

While that is the only tour company that visits the observatory, others in town offer stargazing at a lower price: **Tekapo Stargazing ♥**, SH8 (tekapostargazing.co.nz; ✆ **03/680-6579**), operating out of Tekapō Springs, combines stargazing with hot pools starting at NZ$139 (NZ$84 kids 10–15). It also offers an indoor virtual reality stargazing option for when cloudy skies hide the view. **Silver River Stargazing ♥**, 48A D'Archiac Dr. (silverriverstargazing.com; ✆ **03/680 6866**), hosts its experiences at locations with minimal light pollution and boasts small group sizes (from NZ$99 adults, NZ$79 children 5 and up, NZ$299 families). All experiences are between 1½ and 2 hours, with warm drinks included.

If you're intent on stargazing, plan ahead: Know that wintertime is best for clear skies, and try to schedule your visit for when the moon is waning, rather than waxing.

Dark Sky Project stargazing session.

Where to Eat in Tekapō

Despite being a tourism hub, Tekapō has relatively limited eating options. If you plan on staying for a while, choose accommodations where you can cook. The town has a large and relatively well-stocked Four Square supermarket.

Located in Haka House (see above), **25 Degrees Lake Tekapo ♥**, 5 Motuariki Lane (25degreeslaketekapo.com; ✆ **03/741-3830;** burgers NZ$21–NZ$23; daily 11am–9pm), is a New Zealand take on a retro American diner, offering juicy burgers dripping in sauce, salads, buffalo wings, hot dogs, loaded fries, cocktails, and shakes with a dramatic amount of whipped cream topping.

The Greedy Cow ♥♥, 16 Rapuwai Lane (greedycowtekapo.com; ✆ **027/434-4445;** daily 7:30am–4pm), serves excellent coffee, house-made pastries, and a solid breakfast and brunch menu of elevated favorites; try the attractive and delicious French toast or pancakes with bacon or berries.

For moderately priced Japanese, there's **Kohan ♥♥**, 6 Rapuwai Lane (kohannz.com; ✆ **03/680-6688;** Mon–Wed and Fri–Sat 11:30am–2pm and 6–8pm). It serves very fresh sushi and sashimi (the salmon comes directly from a nearby salmon farm), tempura, and noodle soups. The NZ$42 bento box is a local favorite, and you can also take away to eat on the lakefront.

En Route to Aoraki/Mt. Cook Village: Lake Pukaki

Less than an hour after heading southwest from Tekapō, your car window will once again be filled with brilliant turquoise waters and cloud-piercing peaks as you skirt the shoreline of Lake Pukaki. There is no township at Lake Pukaki, although there are some accommodations nearby (see "Where to Stay Around Aoraki," p. 505).

For a spectacular photo op, pull off SH8 at the Info Centre building. Formerly an isite, it's now a shopfront where you can pick up a pack of delicious fresh wares from **Mt. Cook Salmon Farm ♥** (alpinesalmon.co.nz; ✆ **03/435-0427**). Or drive 12km (7½ miles) farther, turning up SH80 toward Aoraki/Mount Cook Village, where you'll find another viewpoint with plenty of parking, tables, and toilets, making for an ideal picnic spot.

AORAKI/MT. COOK VILLAGE

105km (65 miles) from Lake Tekapō

A land of rugged peaks capped by icy glaciers, Aoraki/Mount Cook Village is the main access point for Aoraki/Mt. Cook. At 3,724m (12,218 ft.), the peak is NZ's highest; *Aoraki* translates to "cloud piercer." Owing to its height and technical difficulty, it's used by mountaineers to train for Everest, including by Sir Edmund Hillary, who was the first to summit Everest alongside Sherpa Tenzing Norgay.

There are 19 peaks over 3,000m (9,840 ft.) found throughout the 72,000-hectare (178,000-acre) **Aoraki/Mount Cook National Park,** and about a third of the park is permanent snow and ice, including the **Tasman Glacier.**

A statue of Sir Edmund Hillary, who trained here for climbing Mt. Everest, stands outside the Sir Edmund Hillary Alpine Center in the Hermitage Hotel, the starting point for many tours and activities in Aoraki/Mt. Cook National Park.

The village itself is small, even by New Zealand standards, with a population that swells from 100 to a whopping 300 in the summertime. Eating and lodging options are limited, and prices reflect the remote location. While it's definitely worth visiting (the vistas, even on an overcast day, are among the country's most stunning), a day trip or 1 night is more than enough time, unless you plan on doing a longer hike or multiple tours in the park.

Essentials

ARRIVING & GETTING AROUND

BY CAR The peak of Aoraki/Mount Cook is visible from both the West Coast and Mackenzie Country, so if you plug "Mount Cook" into your GPS, you might be directed instead to Fox Glacier, a 5-hour drive away. Solution? Be sure to type in "Mount Cook Village." Aoraki/Mount Cook Village is reached via SH80 (the turnoff is well-signed), off SH8; the drive from Tekapō takes about 90 minutes, from Twizel only 45 minutes. Care should be taken on all area roads during fall/winter when surfaces can become icy and slippery. Note that the only gas station in Aoraki/Mt. Cook Village is a pump that only takes cards, charges a premium price, and may or may not issue a receipt—if possible, fill up before leaving Twizel or Tekapō.

BY COACH/BUS **InterCity** (intercity.co.nz; ✆ **03/365-1113**) runs services from Christchurch and Queenstown to Aoraki/Mount Cook Village. **Tekapo Shuttle** (tekaposhuttlenz.com; ✆ **020/41148740**) runs a 1-day tour from Tekapō to Aoraki/Mt. Cook for NZ$149 and transfers between the two for NZ$90.

VISITOR INFORMATION

The **Aoraki/Mount Cook National Park Visitor Centre** ♥♥, 1 Larch Grove (doc.govt.nz; ✆ **03/435-1186**), is open daily from 8:30am to 4:30pm in winter and until 5pm in summer. Operated by the Department of Conservation (DOC), it offers brochures and all the usual updates on weather, track, and road conditions, but it also has a mini-museum detailing the natural and human history of the park, including original artwork and the heart-tugging audiovisual "The Race to Be First." A small info center also exists inside the **Hermitage Hotel,** 89 Terrace Rd. (hermitage.co.nz; ✆ **03/435-1809**).

ORIENTATION

You'd be hard-pressed to get lost in this tiny and well-signed village. A T-intersection at the end of SH80 marks the entrance to the village. Turn left and you'll wind up at the Aoraki/Mount Cook National Park Visitor Centre; turn right to drive to the Hermitage Hotel.

Other important turnoffs from SH80: Hooker Valley Road leads to the start of the Hooker Valley walk, while Tasman Valley Road ends at the Tasman Glacier.

Exploring the Aoraki/Mount Cook Area

Most tours depart from within the Hermitage Hotel, which is also home to **Sir Edmund Hillary Alpine Centre** ♥ (hermitage.co.nz; ✆ **03/435-1809**). It has a small cinema with multiple documentaries running daily, including *Hillary on Everest,* a 75-minute documentary; and the 20-minute *Mount Cook Magic,*

A tour with Mount Cook Ski Planes & Helicopters (p. 504) lands on Tasman Glacier.

a 3D movie that replicates the thrill of aerial sightseeing. It also has a planetarium and a museum/gallery documenting pioneering days. Admission is NZ$29 adults, NZ$15 children 14 and under.

Aerial sightseeing tours are one of the most popular options. **Mount Cook Ski Planes & Helicopters,** Mount Cook Airport, SH80 (mtcookskiplanes.com; ✆ **03/430-8026**), is licensed to land scenic flights on Tasman Glacier and in Aoraki/Mount Cook National Park (from NZ$379). The **Helicopter Line,** Glentanner Park (helicopter.co.nz; ✆ **03/435-1801**), also has several tours, including a popular 55-minute flight over Aoraki/Mount Cook, the Main Divide, and Tasman Glacier (from NZ$875). A cheaper option is 25 minutes for NZ$385.

Another intriguing option is to view Tasman Glacier from Tasman Lake, cruising among icebergs that have "calved" off of the glacier. **Glacier Explorers** ♥ (glacierexplorers.com; ✆ **0800/686-800** in NZ) offers a 3-hour excursion that includes a 1-hour boat ride, where you may be able to touch the icebergs and even snag some ice for a nightcap back in your hotel room. Be aware that it's a 25-minute walk on uneven ground from the excursion bus to the boat docks. The tour costs NZ$209 adults, NZ$95 children 4 to 14; there are no tours June through August. Tours depart from the Hermitage Hotel.

Also based at the Hermitage Hotel, **Big Sky Stargazing** (hermitage.co.nz; ✆ **0800/686-800** in NZ) offers an opportunity to take advantage of the Aoraki Dark Sky Preserve, although being nestled between mountains means clear sky conditions occur less frequently here than elsewhere in Mackenzie—and on fair nights, you might have to line up to see through the telescope. On cloudy nights, you'll be guided through the night sky from within a 360-degree digital planetarium. Admission is NZ$159 adults, NZ$89 kids.

SHORT WALKS & HIKING

Although the national park is massive, much of it is inaccessible. Winter conditions and adverse weather can quickly close high-alpine paths, including the popular Mueller Hut route. Luckily, the handful of walks accessible to your average traveler are among the country's best and most picturesque. Here are the area's best day hikes:

- **Blue Lakes and Tasman Glacier Lake** ♥♥ (1 hr. minimum): Starting from the parking lot located up Tasman Valley Rd., 7km off SH80, this path takes you past the Blue Lakes and to Tasman Lake, located at the end of NZ's longest glacier. The lake freezes over in the winter, but in the summer its chalky waters are filled with floating icebergs. This is a relatively easy walk, but it's an uphill climb and you'll need sturdy footwear.
- **Hooker Valley Track** ♥♥♥ (3 hr.): Easily the most trafficked hike in the park, this journey will take you across swing bridges, between old moraine ridges, and give you views of Mueller Lake and Mount Sefton's glaciers. It's also a great walk if you hate going uphill—over 10km (6 miles), you only have an elevation change of 124m (406 ft.). It starts at the White Horse Hill campground at the end of Hooker Valley Rd., and ends at the iceberg-speckled Hooker Lake, where you can see Aoraki/Mount Cook. Due to

A Glacier Explorers boat ride on Tasman Lake.

repairs, the last section of the track to the lake is currently closed but is likely to reopen in fall 2026.

- **Sealy Tarns Tracks** ♥ (3–4 hr.): Some call this trail the "Staircase to Heaven," while others (me) call it "the Never-Ending Stairmaster." The 2,200 stairs that make up this track will take you 600m (1,968 ft.) up to the freshwater lakes of the Sealy Tarns—and one of the best views in the area. It starts from the White Horse Hill campground (end of Hooker Valley Rd.) and ends with a picnic table at the top; the perfect place to catch your breath before heading back down. You'll also cover a portion of this track if you do the 4-hour (one-way) hike up to the **Mueller Hut,** which has 360-degree panoramic views of the valleys below. It's best done as an overnight tramp, but the hut fills quickly in summer, so you need to book far in advance through doc.govt.nz.

Note: If you're beginning a walk from the White Horse Hill Campground, be aware that the parking lot is busy. If you're not keen to walk the extra 2km (1.2 miles) from town to the start of the tracks, arrive early.

Where to Stay Around Aoraki

IN AORAKI/MOUNT COOK VILLAGE

The DOC-managed **White Horse Hill Campground**—the starting point for many of the area's walks—has 60 unpowered campsites, and fills up on a first-come, first-serve basis (NZ$20 adults, NZ$10 kids 5–17). The newly renovated **Haka House Aoraki Mt Cook** (hakahouse.com/aoraki-mt-cook; ✆ **03/7400-428**) offers luxurious curtained bunks from NZ$55 and private rooms from NZ$140.

The Hermitage Hotel ♥ Originally built of cob and handmade bricks in 1884, today's Hermitage looks nothing like the one of yesteryear, but the views of Aoraki/Mt. Cook are the best in the village. Of course, it's all for naught if you book a standard room (which also will likely show signs of wear and tear) without a view. The hotel is basically a one-stop-shop for guests: It has three dining options (see "Where to Eat," below) and tours can be booked from the gift shop's attractions desk, many of which leave directly from the lobby. A little too rich for your budget? Come for a drink instead. A divine place to reward yourself after a long walk, the lounge has sweeping views—it's the best place in the village to watch the colors of the mountains change as the sun sets.

Terrace Rd., Aoraki/Mount Cook Village. hermitage.co.nz. ✆ **03/435-1809.** 216 units. NZ$355–NZ$695 double. Seasonal rates available. **Amenities:** 3 restaurants; lounge; free Wi-Fi.

IN LAKE PUKAKI

Lakestone Lodge ♥♥ Every morning, owners Mike and Anna Bacchus wake up to a view that most could only dream of—their inn is located directly at the head of Lake Pukaki's turquoise waters. The adults-only lodge is completely off-grid but doesn't skimp on luxurious features: underfloor heating in the bathrooms, two-person soaker tubs facing Aoraki/Mt. Cook, and facials and massages on offer. A cooked breakfast heavy on local products is included, and guests can sign up for a set evening dinner. Here, it's all about immersing yourself in the environment. There are no TVs in the rooms (although there is a shared media center), but you are directly across from the Alps 2 Ocean cycle trail, and a DOC trail backing the hotel has 360-degree views of the surrounding area. Lakestone also runs a night-sky experience (complete with mulled wine and hammocks) from February to November and has a telescope for guest use.

4589-SH8. lakestonelodge.co.nz. ✆ **03/971-1871.** 6 units. NZ$600–NZ$1,490. **Amenities:** Restaurant; complimentary bikes; outdoor firepit; on-site helipad; free Wi-Fi.

Even the bathrooms at Lakestone Lodge have stupendous views of Lake Pukaki and the mountain peaks beyond.

THE long ride: ALPS TO OCEAN CYCLE TRAIL

The longest continuous cycle ride in the country, the **Alps 2 Ocean Cycle Trail** begins in the alps of Aoraki/Mount Cook National Park and ends at the ocean in Ōamaru 6 days and 315km (195 miles) later. Riders pass through national parks and heritage centers, skirt glacial lakes, and ride past limestone cliffs and vineyards. The beginner to medium-grade bike trail starts 2km (1¼ miles) north of Aoraki/Mount Cook Village. The first section includes a short helicopter flight to Tasman Point, although options are available to access the track at points that don't require a helicopter hop. From there, the trail varies from bike paths to gravel roads to some on-highway riding. Highlights along the way include **Ōmarama,** with its clear skies, glider planes, and elegantly-fluted **Clay Cliffs;** the **Ōtemātātā-to-Aviemore section,** which includes a crossing of the Waitaki river via two huge hydroelectric dams; the **Kurow-Duntroon-Ōamaru leg** with its caves sheltering Māori rock art, fossil sites, and weird rock formations (Elephant Rocks); and finally, the **neoclassical limestone buildings** in the coastal town of Ōamaru. Details about affiliated tour operators, outfitters, accommodations, and eateries can be found on the comprehensive Alps 2 Ocean website (alps2ocean.com) alongside maps.

Where to Eat Around Aoraki

There are no grocery stores in Aoraki/Mt. Cook Village, so if you're self-catering, you'll want to stock up in Twizel or Tekapō before you drive into the national park. As for eating out, options are limited, and although most dietary requirements can be met, it won't be in the most imaginative fashion. If you're vegetarian, for example, get ready to load up on carbs.

The **Panorama Room,** the Hermitage Hotel's fine-dining restaurant (hermitage.co.nz; ✆ **03/435-1809**), has floor-to-ceiling windows that provide wraparound views. Ultimately though, it's an average restaurant with higher-than-average prices. Both service and food can be hit-or-miss, so if you've been saving up for a special night, keep your pennies until the next stop.

Also in the Hermitage, the self-service **Sir Edmund Hillary Café & Bar** (open daily 8am–5pm, 10am–4pm in winter) is more casual in style, offering pizzas, sandwiches, and beverages. Its selling feature isn't the food, but the view; it has an outdoor patio from which you can see Aoraki.

TWIZEL

67km (42 miles) from Aoraki/Mount Cook Village; 57km (35 miles) from Lake Tekapō

Twizel was once a company town, built in 1968 by the Ministry of Works to house all those who worked on the hydroelectric canals, dams, and lake projects. Now, though, it's a vacation spot, thanks to its proximity to rivers, lakes, and Aoraki/Mt. Cook Village; it's probably the best base for day trips to Aoraki. Twizel has a Four Square supermarket, a number of cafes, bars, and takeout joints, and an ATM in the shopping center.

There are only a handful of tour operators in Twizel itself, including **Red Cat Biplane Flights ♥♥♥**, 1 Harry Wigley Dr., Pukaki Airport (redcat.co.nz; ✆ **027/4733-228** in NZ), which offers what's guaranteed to be one of the most over-the-top flights of your life in a Red Cat biplane (an open cockpit plane with two sets of wings, one above the other). You'll be fully dressed for the event in provided leather flying jackets, goggles, and helmets. There are four flight options (from NZ$325), including "Dambuster," a 50-minute thrill ride that features a landing for lunch at the Omarama airstrip. Inquire for availability and seasonal rates.

Where to Stay Around Twizel

Twizel is a town of holiday homes, with plenty of options listed on airbnb.com and bookabach.co.nz, aka Vrbo. **Twizel Holiday Park ♥**, 122 Mackenzie Dr. (twizelholidaypark.co.nz; ✆ **03/435-0507**), a tidy conversion of what was once the township's maternity hospital, offers plenty of roaming space for kids, with cabins, campsites, and cottages (NZ$23–NZ$270). Wi-Fi and bike rental are available.

The epitome of rustic luxury, **High Country Cabin ♥♥♥** (highcountry cabin.co.nz) is an open-concept cabin surrounded by 10 acres on a sheep farm; it was even featured in *Dwell* magazine for its Instagrammable interior, including antler chandeliers, reclaimed wooden furniture, and cowhide chairs. It books out months in advance for NZ$620 per night.

SkyScape ♥♥♥ Made nearly entirely of glass, the architecturally stunning SkyScape cabins are designed to take advantage of their location on a high-country cattle station deep in the Aoraki Mackenzie Dark Sky Reserve. Half-glass, half-grass roofs allow these private eco-units to blend into the hills, and each come with current star charts, binoculars, and astronomy books—but, of course, clear skies are never guaranteed. (No-moon winter

High Country Cabin books out months in advance.

nights Mar–Oct are best for visibility.) If the stars aren't out, you'll at least enjoy trying to stargaze from the luxury two-person outdoor cedar bathtub. SkyScapes are so popular they have to be booked weeks in advance—either directly, or through GlampingHub.com.

47 Ben Ohau Rd. skyscape.co.nz. ✆ **021/111-0218.** 3 units. NZ$750–NZ$990. Rates include breakfast; dinner available on request. Adults only. **Amenities:** Kitchenette; free Wi-Fi.

Where to Eat in Twizel

Make your breakfast or lunch stop at **Logans Floating Café & Restaurant** at **High Country Salmon ♥**, 2602-SH8 (highcountrysalmon.co.nz; ✆ **0800/400-385** in NZ; cafe daily 8am–9pm; mains NZ$28–NZ$42; fish shop & deli 9am–5pm daily), to enjoy the freshest possible Chinook salmon in dishes like salmon chowder, salmon and crab burgers, salmon carpaccio, and sushi. You can also catch a fish here (Thurs–Mon 9am–4pm).

If you're not feeling fish at 9am (fair enough), head over to **Mint Folk & Co. ♥♥**, 4A Market Place (mintfolks.co.nz; ✆ **03/435-3155;** Mon–Tues and Sat 7:30am–3pm, Wed–Fri 7:30am–10pm; mains NZ$18–NZ$31), which has a full breakfast menu catering to a range of dietary requirements (and yes, there's salmon here, too).

Ministry of Works Bar & Eatery ♥♥ REGIONAL Popular MOW has a beer garden, playground, and sometimes live music. Its name comes from the town's one-time main government employer, which built not just the town but the giant hydroelectric dam that reshaped the entire region. In a nod to history, the owners have given over a wall to original street maps of Ōtemātātā and Twizel townships, inviting all those who ever worked and lived there to add their family names on the addresses. Craft beers are on tap, and the menu offers small plates (dumplings, fried chicken, pork belly bao buns) and mains including burgers, lamb rump, and, of course, salmon.

Burgers, sharing plates, and craft beer at Ministry of Works Bar and Eatery.

2 Market Place. mowbar.co.nz. ✆ **03/435-3257.** Main courses NZ$35–NZ$45. Daily 2pm–late.

En Route to Ōmarama: Lake Ōhau

As SH8 leaves Twizel heading for Omarama, large signposts indicate that the turnoff ahead will bring you to a lake, a ski field, and a lodge, **Lake Ōhau Lodge ♥♥**, 2295 Lake Ohau Rd. ohau.co.nz; ✆ **03/438-9885**), which is the main attraction here. Even if you only stop for lunch on the deck, you will treasure the silence, the peace, the forest scents, and the exceedingly down-to-earth staff. The fabulous glimpse of Aoraki/Mt. Cook across the lake is a bonus. Stay if you can; ask about the bed, breakfast, and dinner rate. Dinner is held at shared tables with your delightful fellow guests.

WAITAKI DISTRICT

Ōmarama: 203km (126 miles) from Aoraki/Mount Cook; 30km (18 miles) from Twizel

At **Ōmarama,** instead of continuing on SH8 to the Lindis Pass and into Central Otago, turn onto SH83 to discover one of the South Island's best-kept secrets: the Waitaki Valley. Its glacier-carved landscape and large lakes have all the majesty of the Scottish Highlands, yet its vibe is pleasantly down-to-earth, much more so than other more-touristed parts of the Otago region. The Waitaki Lakes—Benmore, Aviemore, and Waitaki—are manmade, created between 1928 and 1968 when three hydroelectric power stations were built on the Waitaki River.

Ōmarama

In the 1880s, **Ōmarama** was a staging post for the coach from Ōamaru to Wānaka. Today the attractions of this small town include **glider planes** (glidequeenstown.com; ✆ **021/826-336;** 1-hr. Ōmarama flight NZ$750), **sheep-shearing** demonstrations (thewrinklyrams.co.nz; ✆ **03/438-9751**), and **hot tubbing** with mountain views in pure alpine water (hottubsomarama.co.nz; ✆ **03/438-9703**). Roughly a 30-minute drive outside the township (follow SH8 north until you reach a well-marked turnoff onto Quailburn Rd.) are the eerie **Clay Cliffs** ♥♥ (claycliffsnz.com), a geological anomaly of sand pinnacles and ravines. The cliffs are located on private land, accessed only via an unpaved road. But the NZ$10 per-car/$20 per-campervan fee (paid online beforehand or cash in an honesty box at the entrance) is a small price to wander through the hoodoos.

The Waitaki Lakes & Waitaki Valley

From Ōmarama, SH83 skirts **Lake Benmore** briefly, but the size of the lake is better appreciated from the top of Benmore Dam. **Lake Aviemore** was created in the 1960s by what had once been a deep riverbed. The last lake, **Waitaki,** was built by hand for a Depression-era make-work project using only shovels and picks. A cluster of houses built in the 1940s for workers remains.

Set right by a main bridge over the Waitaki River, **Kurow** (more correctly, the Māori placename Te Kohurau) is a typical rural town, with a few shops and cafes lining the highway. The old village post office has been converted to a tasting room for one of the local wineries, and some Victorian-era buildings still stand, including the pretty vicarage and chapel of St. Albans. The **Kurow Information Centre & Museum,** 57 Bledisloe St. (kurow.org.nz; ✆ **03/436-0950**), on the main thoroughfare, is a country museum that puts into perspective the days when big high-country sheep runs were divided and sold

NZ'S SECRET wine region

By now, you're likely familiar with the sauvignon blancs of Marlborough and syrahs of Hawke's Bay. But chances are you haven't heard of NZ's hidden wine region, nestled in the Waitaki Valley. The first grapes were only planted here in 2001. With a cool climate, long dry autumns, and complex geological features (including greywacke, schist, and limestone), the area is making a name for itself by producing distinctive and complex pinot noirs, reislings, and gewürztraminers. Most of the region's wineries are small and privately owned and, as such, only a couple have tasting rooms open to visitors. To taste wines from across the region, visit the family-owned **River-T Wines,** a 5-minute drive south of Kurow at 5292/1 Kurow Duntroon Rd. (rivertestate.co.nz; ✆ **021/292-4081**), which stocks the world's largest range of Waitaki Valley wines, alongside its own label of paddock-to-glass wines. A small food menu is also available in its tasting room (cellar door), which is open September to June, daily 10am to 5pm.

as smaller properties. It's open weekdays 9:30am to 4:30pm, and, if volunteers are available, weekends 10am to 12:30pm.

After leaving Kurow, keep an eye out for a pull-off to see the **Takiroa Māori Rock Art Site** ♥, about 15 minutes south on SH83. Underneath a limestone overhang, you'll find a cave with charcoal and red ochre drawings that date back to 1400.

The Takiroa site is one of many in the **Waitaki Whitestone Geopark** (vanishedworld.co.nz), a 7,200-square-km (2,800-sq.-mile) area of geological significance full of fossils, sinkholes, and limestone formations that's currently awaiting UNESCO certification. Within this geopark, the small town of **Duntroon** is fossil central; the area's limestone contains the richest known marine fossil record from the Oligocene epoch some 20 to 30 million years ago. Fossilized mammals are the focus of the volunteer-run **Vanished World Heritage Centre** ♥, 7 Campbell St., Duntroon (vanishedworld.co.nz; ✆ **027/431-2024**), where kids will love being able to handle and unearth actual fossils. It's open from 10am to 4pm daily (hours may differ; check ahead) and costs NZ$10 adults and NZ$5 for children 5 to 16. Duntroon also has a restored working **blacksmith's forge** (blacksmith.net.nz) and an old jail to explore.

ŌAMARU

112km (70 miles) north of Dunedin; 203km (126 miles) from Aoraki/Mount Cook; 43km (27 miles) from Duntroon

When you first drive in, Ōamaru might appear like another ho-hum, unassuming coastal town. That is until you reach its Victorian Precinct, where massive ornate buildings built of locally hewn white limestone will make you feel like you've traveled back in time to the 1880s. Not only is Ōamaru home to the country's largest collection of Victorian-era heritage buildings, it's also the staging ground for one of the world's largest steampunk communities. (For the uninitiated, steampunk is a retro-futuristic science fiction subgenre rooted in 19th-century steam-powered machinery.) Yup, it's a bit niche, but it's found a firm following among the farmers of Ōamaru, who realized they could turn scraps of metal found on their farms into steampunk-inspired inventions. It doesn't matter if you're a history buff or an adult who still loves to play dress-up; this is the place to jump on a penny-farthing (big-wheeled bicycle) and let your imagination run wild.

Essentials

ARRIVING & GETTING AROUND

BY CAR Dunedin to Ōamaru via SH1 is a 1½-hour drive. Christchurch to Ōamaru via SH1 is a 3-hour drive. Ōamaru can also be accessed via SH83 and the Waitaki Lakes district.

BY COACH (BUS) **InterCity Coaches** (intercity.co.nz; ✆ **03/365-1113**) has regular scheduled services operating from main centers north and south of Ōamaru.

VISITOR INFORMATION

There is no isite, but the **Waitaki & Ōamaru Visitor Centre** can be found inside Whitestone City at 12 Harbour St. It's open daily from 10am to 4pm. The official website for the wider region is **waitakinz.com**.

SPECIAL EVENTS

The annual **Steampunk NZ Festival** (steampunk.org.nz) is held around late May/early June with events including a fashion show, gala ball, and even teapot racing. Costumes are optional, but encouraged. In a similar vein, the **Victorian Fete** (victorianoamaru.co.nz) is hosted every November.

WHITESTONE city

Some 150 years ago, Ōamaru was known as the best-built town in the country, especially its commercial center, which extended from the small harbor and creek. Today, many of the grand neoclassical Victorian-era buildings—public houses and hotels, warehouses, offices, banks, bakeries, and shops selling everything from patent medicines to fancy feathered hats—are still in use. This is thanks, in large part, to the limestone they were constructed from.

When the town was first established, settlers discovered the local limestone hills could be quarried. Ōamaru limestone is soft to cut, easy to carve, reasonably easy to build with, and improves with age. (As it weathers, it hardens.)

The 19th-century streetscapes in Ōamaru were fine examples of space and grace. Then the port began to falter, and the business center moved to Thames Street. Harbour Street and neighboring Tyne and Itchen streets became a backwater. It wasn't until 1985, when a film crew sought permission to use the streets as a backdrop for a Victorian setting, that Ōamaru fully realized its potential. In 1987, the formation of the Ōamaru Whitestone Civic Trust enabled the purchase and restoration of many of the old buildings, and that, combined with support from the New Zealand Historic Places Trust, has seen Ōamaru regain its status as an architectural prize.

ORIENTATION

SH1 from Dunedin becomes Severn Street at the top of the South Hill. SH83 joins SH1 at Pukeuri, which leads to the north end of the town. **Thames Street** is the main thoroughfare, while the parallel **Harbour Street** is where you'll find shopping, attractions, and art galleries.

Exploring Ōamaru

The historic **Victorian Precinct** ♥♥♥, on Harbour and Tyne streets (victorian oamaru.co.nz), is a restoration marvel. Elegant buildings rescued from obscurity now house boutique artists' studios, gift shops, distilleries, cafes, vintage stores, and outlandish art galleries. It will make you wonder if you're still in NZ; your confusion will only increase further when you see a perfectly average resident going about their business while riding a penny-farthing (or a high-wheeler, one of those old-timey bikes with the giant front wheel).

Boutiques and cafes now inhabit the restored buildings of Ōamaru's Victorian Precinct.

Wandering among the cafes and artisans will yield many unexpected delights, but don't let a stair climb put you off Donna Demente's **Grainstore Gallery** ♥♥♥, which moonlights as a musical parlor. It's two flights up and there's a small suggested *koha* (donation) to see the artist at work on her whimsical portraiture and masks.

If you, too, would like to dress in period costume (as they say, "when in Oamaru"), the best place to do it is at **Whitestone City** ♥♥ (whitestonecity.co.nz), an interactive museum housed in an 1882 grain store. While some of the displays are dated (and I don't mean that in a historic way), this is the best place to gain further insight into the area, its architecture, and its history from knowledgeable local guides. You'll also have a chance to dress in an outfit of the era, play period games, and ride the only penny-farthing carousel in NZ. It's open daily from 10am to 4pm.

A brochure from the Ōamaru Info Center lists those buildings of heritage significance that are accessible to visitors. Among them are the **Harbour Board Office** (1876), Harbour Street; the **Criterion Hotel** (1877), Tyne Street; and the **ANZ bank** (1871), **Forrester Gallery** (1884), and **Opera House** ♥♥♥ (1907), all on Thames Street. They're all architectural gems, but the Opera House is a standout, with an interior as beautiful as its exterior, complete with elaborate plastering and gilding galore. Concerts and other live performances are regularly held here; check oamaruoperahouse.co.nz.

The popular sunset penguin parade at Ōamaru Penguins.

Entering **Steampunk HQ ♥♥♥**, 1 Humber St. (steampunkoamaru.co.nz; ✆ **027/778-6547**), feels like walking onto the film set of a dystopian movie, or perhaps a portal to an apocalyptic realm. In fact, going into "the Portal" is just one of this superb attraction's interactive art, light, and sound installations. Entry is NZ$15 (NZ$5 kids under 16, NZ$30 families) but come equipped with a pocketful of NZ$2 gold coins to operate the large-scale science fiction–inspired machines outside. It's open daily 10am to 4pm; expect to browse for an hour or so.

Afterwards, mosey toward the beachfront and see what steampunk style has wrought in the **Friendly Bay Steampunk Playground ♥♥**. This child (and inner child) pleaser is a contender for NZ's most unique playground (although I'm still giving that honor to Whanganui's Kowhai Park). It features a massive penny-farthing that children can swing from, a futuristic slide, and "trees" that look like the War of the Worlds passed this way.

Wildlife enthusiasts won't want to miss a tour of **Ōamaru Penguins ♥**, 17 Waterfront Rd. (penguins.co.nz; ✆ **03/433-1195**). Many of the *kororā* (little penguins) spend the day at sea and waddle back to their colony under the harborside cliffs at night. Book your spot for the evening viewing at sunset (NZ$50 adults, NZ$30 children 5–17; rates NZ$70/NZ$42 for the closest, best seating)—and wear your warmest clothes; it can get cold. Allow a half-hour before your booked slot to browse the brand-new interactive visitor center (play penguin Tinder!).

Tours of the **Whitestone Cheese Factory ♥**, 3 Torridge St. (whitestonecheese.com; ✆ **03/434-0182**), are also available on weekdays at 10am, though you must book in advance. In addition to seeing the factory at work, you'll get to taste the excellent finished product, which is sold across NZ. The 90-minute tour costs NZ$35 for adults and is free for children under 16. Another NZ$10 will get you a wine pairing, too.

Where to Stay in Ōamaru

Mariner Suites ♥, 47 Tyne St. (marinersuites.nz; ✆ **03/434-7788**), provides modern, upscale motel-style rooms at the edges of the Victorian precinct, with water views. Rooms start from NZ$250.

The Old Confectionary ♥♥ This once-derelict building has been rescued and brought back to its 1880s-era grandeur with colorful floral wallpapers, chandeliers, velvet textiles, and **Ōamaru stone columns.** The two apartments here also feature modern conveniences including ensuite bathrooms with underfloor heating, full kitchens, and heaters in each bedroom. Located just steps away from the Victorian precinct, it's the most comfortable spot for a multi-night stay.

26 Tees St. oldconfectionery.co.nz. ✆ **021/022-10093.** 2 units (each sleeps up to 4 people). NZ$360–NZ$385. **Amenities:** Storage; laundry; free Wi-Fi.

Pen-y-bryn Lodge ♥♥♥ *Pen-y-bryn* is Welsh for "top of the hill," an apt description for this Victorian heritage homestead. Listed with the New Zealand Historic Places Trust, this single-story timber home (one of Australasia's largest) has a billiards room, library, and drawing room reflecting the lodge's journey from Victorian times to the 21st century. Antique furniture, paneling, and oak parquet flooring are constants in the public rooms, but huge log fires, flowers, and soft, elegant furnishings remind that this is a home where guests are welcome.

41 Towey St. penybryn.co.nz. ✆ **03/434-7939.** 5 units. NZ$670–NZ$890 double. Rates include breakfast and pre-dinner drinks; dinner can be arranged. Children 13 and older only. **Amenities:** Billiards room; in-house spa services; laundry service; free Wi-Fi.

Poshtel ♥♥ Housed in an 1896 heritage building, each of Poshtel's 16 rooms is individually decorated in a mash of vintage sporting memorabilia

Guests gather in the Victorian parlor at Pen-y-bryn Lodge.

and steampunk. On paper, that might sound horrific, but there's just the right amount of commitment to the steampunk theme (such as steam gauges as toilet paper holders) without going overboard. I stayed in the Farming Suite, which was decorated with metal tractor seats and antler coat hooks. The luxury boutique hotel is walking distance from the Victorian Precinct, and a welcome treat at the end of the Alps 2 Ocean Cycle Trail. (Bike storage is available.)

126 Thames St. poshtelnz.com. ✆ **03/434-8888.** 16 units. NZ$160–NZ$320 double. Rates include breakfast. **Amenities:** Bike storage; free Wi-Fi.

Where to Eat in Ōamaru

A little cafe with big, lush interior vibes, **Tees St. Café** ♥♥, 3 Tees St. (teesstcafe.com; ✆ **03/434-7004**), is on the edge of the Victorian Precinct and the little sister to the famed Cucina (see below). Can't decide? Order the breakfast board, with panna cotta, granola, bruschetta with pumpkin and feta, and a poached egg and fresh orange, carrot, and ginger juice (NZ$25). Need some morning-after grease? The NZ$28 Argentinean-style beef burger with onion jam should do the trick. The coffee is excellent and, perhaps even better, available early; the cafe is open weekdays from 7am to 3pm and weekends 8:30am to 3pm.

The "Pick and Shovel" room at Ōamaru's Poshtel.

With its exposed bricks and bright blue bar seats, **Fat Sally's ♥**, 84 Thames St. (fatsallys.co.nz; ✆ **03/434-8368**), has a relaxed, cheeky atmosphere that is also buzzing with bar patrons. The menu leans toward generously portioned, elevated pub fare: burgers, pork belly, ribs, and fish 'n' chips.

Scotts Brewing Company ♥, 1 Wansbeck St. (scottsbrewing.co.nz; ✆ **03/432-2244**), is a purpose-built craft brewery so close to the historic precinct it qualifies as the neighborhood brew bar, with a patio on which to sample one (or all) of its ever-changing beers. The kitchen turns out stone-baked pizza made with local Whitestone cheeses from NZ$17, as well as small bites including loaded fries, wings, Asian meatballs, and tacos.

Cucina ♥♥♥ ITALIAN A continual winner of the *Cuisine* Good Food Awards (the highest culinary accolade in the country), this restaurant blends the food traditions of South America and Italy. (Its owners, Yanina and Pablo Tacchini, are originally from South America, and both have ancestry in Spain and Italy.) It's an unlikely pairing, but one that creates transcendent meals, especially when NZ ingredients are thrown into the mix. In addition to fresh pasta and starters like empanadas stuffed with 55-day aged dry beef and caramelized onion, there's a selection of very meaty mains and delightful desserts including tiramisu and Argentinean churros. Pace yourself; you'll want to try something from every course. Good thing, too, because a "trust the chef" tasting menu of four courses is available, with wine pairings extra.

1 Tees St. cucinaoamaru.co.nz. ✆ **03/434-5696.** Main courses NZ$40–NZ$50. Reservations recommended. Tues–Sat 5pm–late.

Riverstone Kitchen ♥♥♥ INTERNATIONAL A short drive north of Ōamaru, this classic countryside eatery has many fans. It's the culinary playground of chef/restaurateur Bevan Smith, who's produced several popular NZ cookbooks inspired by Riverstone's kitchen and gardens. The name comes from the local river stones (greywacke) washed to a smooth pale gray by glacial ice and the Waitaki River. Outside, a well-equipped play space delights the kids, and a large kitchen garden and orchard supplies seasonal fruit and vegetables. Locally produced ingredients include early potatoes, stonefruit, berries, pork, lamb, and venison. Bookings are advised. Or order online for a takeaway to pick up from 11:20am—think hot smoked salmon, carrot cake, sandwiches, and chicken salad. This is also where you'll find the **Riverstone Castle,** a modern castle built entirely of local whitestone, which periodically hosts tours of its interior for NZ$30 adults/NZ$20 under-15s; see the latest schedule at facebook.com/riverstonecastlenz.

1431 SH1. riverstonekitchen.co.nz. ✆ **03/431-3505.** Main courses NZ$40–NZ$48. Sun–Thurs 9am–4pm, Fri–Sat 9am–4pm and 6pm–late.

16 DUNEDIN, SOUTHLAND & STEWART ISLAND

Visitors tend to overlook the areas covered in this chapter, which is unfortunate, because Dunedin, Southland, and Stewart Island offer some of the country's most diverse flora and fauna (petrified forests, yellow-eyed penguins, Hector's dolphins, and kiwi); intriguing rural towns; rich Māori history; and probably one of the least harried travel experiences in all of New Zealand.

Split across Southland and Otago, the South Island's southern heel is the country's coolest and rainiest region, a climate that produces lush grasslands for dairy-sheep and dairy farming (and epic waterfalls). This swath also has the longest daylight hours in NZ—summertime adventurers enjoy daylight well past 9 or 10pm, and in winter, its southern latitude means you may be lucky enough to spot Aurora Australis (the Southern Lights) dancing across the skies.

Invercargill/Waihōpai and the nearby country town of Gore are the region's commercial centers, but most visitors prefer to base themselves in the beautiful university town of Dunedin/Ōtepoti. It's the only place in Aotearoa where Scottish heritage has left a distinct mark, most noticeable in the way many residents roll the letter *r*.

Stewart Island/Rakiura, New Zealand's third-largest island, is considered one of the best places in the country to see a kiwi in the wild. It's an area of raucous birdcall, lush native vegetation, and lingering Southern traditions.

The province of Southland also includes the cascading waterfalls and snow-capped mountain peaks of Fiordland and its most famous attraction, Milford Sound. However, we've included these in chapter 14, since they're most often visited as a day trip from Queenstown.

DUNEDIN

283km (175 miles) S of Queenstown; 366km (227 miles) S of Christchurch; 220km (136 miles) N of Invercargill

Originally named New Edinburgh by the 344 Scots who settled here in 1848, Dunedin is filled with grand Victorian architecture befitting its 19th-century status as the top dog in New Zealand's wealthiest region. That status disappeared with the demise of gold

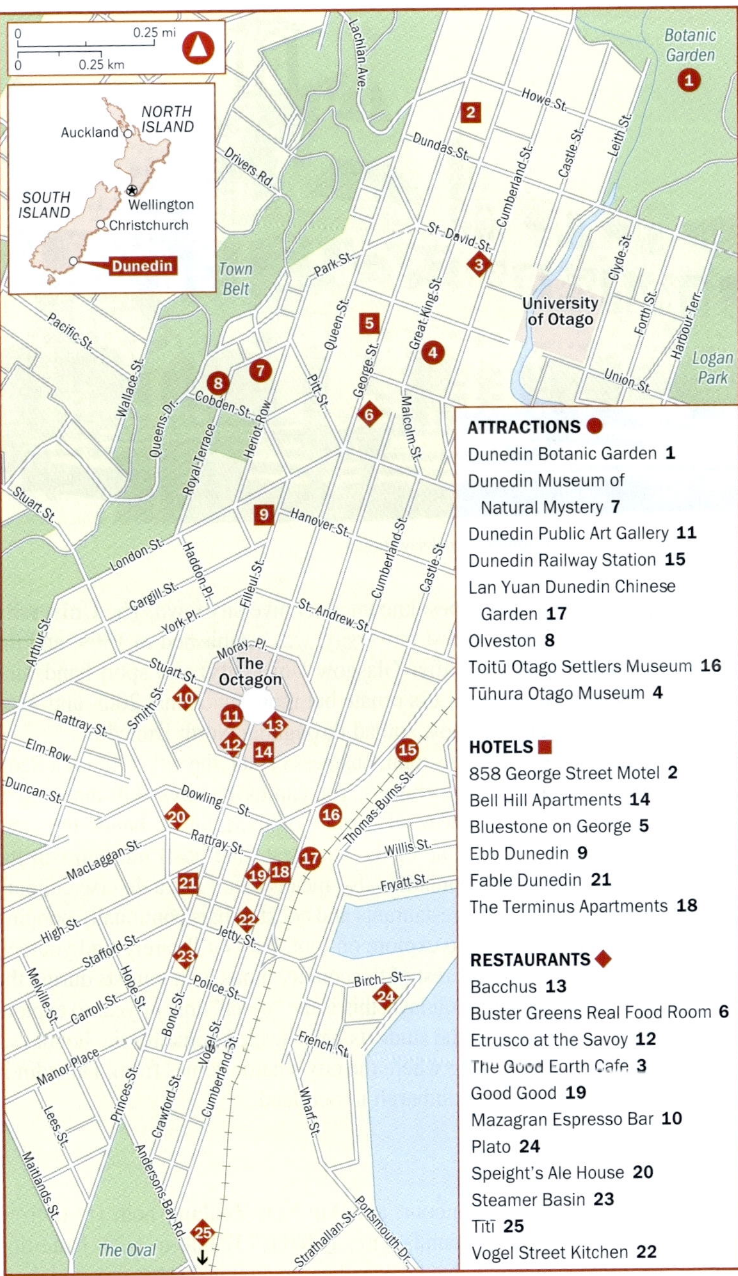
0 0.25 mi
0 0.25 km
NORTH ISLAND
Auckland
Wellington
SOUTH ISLAND
Christchurch
Dunedin
Botanic Garden
Town Belt
University of Otago
Logan Park
The Octagon
The Oval
Lachlan Ave.
Howe St.
Dundas St.
Drivers Rd.
Cumberland St.
Castle St.
Leith St.
St. David St.
Park St.
Clyde St.
Great King St.
Queen St.
Forth St.
Harbour Terr.
Union St.
Pacific St.
Wallace St.
Queens Dr.
Cobden St.
Heriot Row
Pitt St.
George St.
Malcolm St.
Royal Terrace
Stuart St.
Hanover St.
London St.
Haddon Pl.
Filleul St.
Cargill St.
York Pl.
St. Andrew St.
Arthur St.
Moray Pl.
Smith St.
Rattray St.
Elm Row
Duncan St.
Dowling St.
Thomas Burns St.
Willis St.
MacLaggan St.
Fryatt St.
High St.
Jetty St.
Stafford St.
Melville St.
Hope St.
Police St.
Birch St.
Carroll St.
Bond St.
Vogel St.
French St.
Manor Place
Princes St.
Crawford St.
Lees St.
Wharf St.
Maitlands St.
Andersons Bay Rd.
Strathallan St.
Portsmouth Dr.
ATTRACTIONS
Dunedin Botanic Garden 1
Dunedin Museum of Natural Mystery 7
Dunedin Public Art Gallery 11
Dunedin Railway Station 15
Lan Yuan Dunedin Chinese Garden 17
Olveston 8
Toitū Otago Settlers Museum 16
Tūhura Otago Museum 4
HOTELS
858 George Street Motel 2
Bell Hill Apartments 14
Bluestone on George 5
Ebb Dunedin 9
Fable Dunedin 21
The Terminus Apartments 18
RESTAURANTS
Bacchus 13
Buster Greens Real Food Room 6
Etrusco at the Savoy 12
The Good Earth Cafe 3
Good Good 19
Mazagran Espresso Bar 10
Plato 24
Speight's Ale House 20
Steamer Basin 23
Tītī 25
Vogel Street Kitchen 22

The facade of Dunedin's magnificent railway station.

mining, and today the city is best known as a university town. The **University of Otago,** New Zealand's oldest university, was established in 1869, and the original buildings (patterned after Glasgow University) still sport handsome bluestone and slate detailing. Less ornate but more functional 20th- and 21st-century university buildings now spread throughout North Dunedin.

Although Dunedin is Otago's main business center, the city still has a Scottish soul and a penchant for quirkiness. You can have a dress kilt made up in your clan tartan, hear the music of dozens of indie music bands live, and explore what's undoubtably one of the strangest (and best) museums in the country. The large student population also means that it has a diverse culinary and nightlife scene, with new restaurants and cocktail bars continually popping up. A compact city, it's easy to explore on foot, but you'll rarely find yourself lost in a crowd. And while the rest of the country hums with tourists during the busy December and January holidays, this is the "quiet" time of year to explore Dunedin's beaches, since all the students have headed home for the holidays.

In case you were wondering where the city's name comes from: Dunedin is the ancient Gaelic name of Edinburgh in Scotland.

Essentials

ARRIVING

BY PLANE **Jetstar** (jetstar.com) and **Air New Zealand** both fly to/from major NZ centers (airnewzealand.co.nz; ✆ **0800/737-000** in NZ). Note that flights are often cancelled due to weather, including heavy fog and high winds. The **Dunedin Airport** (dunedinairport.co.nz) is 30 minutes south of the city. All the major car rental companies have kiosks at the airport; taxis charge approximately NZ$90 for the trip into town. Uber is also available, which may be slightly more or less pricey depending on surge pricing. Door-to-door shuttle services with **Airport Shuttles Dunedin** (airportshuttlesdunedin.co.nz; ✆ **0800/477-800** in NZ) cost considerably less, with discounted fares for two or more passengers. The cost is roughly NZ$27; book online.

BY CAR SH1 is the main route in and out of the city. Dunedin is approximately a 5-hour drive south of Christchurch; 2 to 3 hours northeast of Invercargill; and 4 hours from Queenstown, if driving inland through Central Otago.

BY COACH (BUS) **InterCity** (intercity.co.nz; ✆ **03/471-71433**) provides regular coach connections throughout the South Island.

GETTING AROUND

BY BUS Run by the Otago Regional Council, the **Orbus** service (orc.govt.nz/orbus; ✆ **0800/672-8736** in NZ) is easy and affordable to use. Most city buses leave from the vicinity of the Octagon. Bus timetables are available online and from the Dunedin isite at 50 The Octagon. Fares can be paid for in cash, but if you plan on exploring via bus, it pays to get a **BeeCard** (retailers can be found at beecard.co.nz), which offers automatic discounts on every trip when you tap-on and tap-off. The cards cost a minimum preload fee of NZ$5. The cards can also be used in many regions in NZ, including Queenstown Ferries and its Orbus bus network.

BY CAR Once you familiarize yourself with the one-way systems and the interrupted street pattern around the Octagon, Dunedin is incredibly easy to negotiate. Most central streets have "pay and display" **metered parking** for 2 to 3 hours at a time, and public parking lots are easy to find throughout the city. Permitted times and payment methods are clearly posted.

VISITOR INFORMATION

Dunedin's official regional visitor website is **dunedinnz.com**. The **Dunedin isite Visitor Centre,** 50 The Octagon (✆ **03/474-3300**), is open daily from 9am to 5pm and weekends until 4:30pm.

Exploring Dunedin

Rather than having the usual square at its heart, Dunedin has the tree-lined **Octagon,** which acts as a central meeting place. This is where you'll find municipal chambers, a cathedral, countless cafes, wine bars and pubs, and a massive statue of the Scottish bard Robbie Burns, who sits in majesty "with his back to the kirk and his face to the pub." The Octagon divides the city's main street into **George Street** to the north and **Princes Street** to the south. A popular shopping area is along George Street, while the newly revitalized **Warehouse Precinct,** including Vogel Street, is just south of the Octagon. The city center is at the head of Otago Harbour, encircled by a 200-hectare (500-acre) strip of greenery, the **Town Belt.**

Originally built in 1906, Dunedin's **Railway Station** ♥ at 20 Anzac Ave. could have fallen from the pages of a fairytale with its turrets, colonnades, and imposing stained-glass windows depicting lit-up steam engines (in the ticket

Baldwin Street.

hall). It was described as Flemish Renaissance by designer George A. Troup, and it's recently undergone an award-winning restoration. While the station is no longer a stopping point for commuter trains, it has a number of scenic journeys catering to tourists (see "Riding the Rails into the Heartland," p. 529).

Another super fun, but brief stop everyone should make is to **Baldwin Street** ♥. According to the *Guinness Book of World Records,* it's the world's steepest residential street, with an equally intense sidewalk gradient. Non-residents are discouraged from driving up it, so you'll need to take the 270 steps up. It's a real slog and will leave you breathless—both from the climb and from the view at the top.

The 28-hectare (69-acre) **Dunedin Botanic Garden** ♥ (dunedinbotanicgarden.co.nz; ✆ **03/477-4000**) was the first to be established in New Zealand in 1869. At the northern end of Castle Street, it features the renowned Rhododendron Dell, which is best in the spring months (generally Oct–Nov), when 3,000 rhododendron plants bloom. Within the garden's grounds, you'll also find an Edwardian conservatory garden (with its own giant corpse plant), rose gardens, an aviary that houses native parrot species kea and kākā, and the historic **Northern Cemetery** (northerncemetery.org.nz). The gardens and the cemetery are open daily, free of charge.

Dunedin Museum of Natural Mystery ♥♥♥ MUSEUM You know that 1929 Disney animation of the Skeleton Dance, the one usually played around Halloween? If it creeps you out, you'll want to steer clear of this small private museum. Curated by artist Bruce Mahalski—who is known for creating intricate and strikingly beautiful sculptures and masks made out of bones—this 1870s Victorian villa houses an extensive skull collection (including, yes, human skulls) alongside plastinated and mummified animals, ethnological art, and other unusual cultural artifacts. But what truly sets this macabre museum apart—other than the obvious—are the stories that Mahalski tells

Salt, Sea & Surf

Dunedin has famously claimed it's "like Bali, but with wetsuits." With a dozen unspoiled white-sand beaches within an easy drive, it's easy to see why. You may not always want to swim in the chilly waters, but from a scenic point of view, they're worth a visit.

The stretch of sand that runs between the suburbs of **St. Kilda** and **St. Clair ♥♥**, is where surfers hone their skills. It's also home to seaside cafes, boutiques, and a retro dinosaur-themed playground that's sure to delight kids. No wetsuit is necessary at the **St. Clair Hot Salt Water Pool ♥**, where you can pretend you're in a tropical paradise as you relax in the warm waters and listen to the crash of waves on the rocks beside you. Tucked between the rocky shore and open sea, pool temperatures are always maintained at a pleasing 82°F (28°C). It costs NZ$9.20 adults; NZ$4.30 for children, and NZ$20 for families and is open weekdays from 6am to 7pm and weekends 7am to 7pm, between October and April.

The many rocky coves and caves around Dunedin's beaches are both beautiful and unique, but tracks and access are sometimes closed due to landslides. **Long Beach ♥** is a beautiful 1.5-mile (2.5km) beach walk to large caverns, about 30 minutes northeast of the city and popular with local rock climbers. Be careful of disturbing lounging seals or scuttling *kororā* (little penguins). More sea caves and arches can be found at **Doctor's Point Reserve ♥**, 30 minutes north of Dunedin near Waitati.

with his placards, carefully and colorfully identifying each object's provenance. Mahalski believes the museum, which is set in his home, is his greatest work of art. He's usually on site and very happy to answer questions. As the sign on his desk reads, he's "actually very friendly," despite his bone-collecting ways.

61 Royal Terrace. royaldunedinmuseum.com. ✆ **021/0329-906.** NZ$10 adults, NZ$5 children, families NZ$20. Fri noon–5pm, Sat–Sun 10am–5pm.

The Dunedin Museum of Natural Mystery is an engaging cabinet of curiosities.

Dunedin Public Art Gallery ♥♥ ART MUSEUM When the Dunedin Public Art Gallery opened in 1996, art lovers throughout the country celebrated. The space is still one of the best in the country and has received acclaim for both its collection and its architecture, with its soaring, glass-ceilinged atrium. There are significant holdings of European art, Japanese prints, and French Impressionist works (including the only Monet in a New Zealand public collection), along with a comprehensive collection of contemporary and early New Zealand art, and a gallery dedicated to the works of Kiwi painter Frances Hodgkins. A foyer shop sells arty things, and the gallery has free Wi-Fi.

30 The Octagon. dunedin.art.museum. ✆ **03/474-3240.** Free admission. Daily 10am–5pm.

Lan Yuan Dunedin Chinese Garden ♥♥ GARDEN Dunedin has a considerable Chinese community, with its roots dating back to the 1860s Otago gold rush, and the Scholar's Garden acknowledges the important part the Chinese played in local history. This gated oasis of water and graceful trees (between the harbor and the business district) was designed and built in Shanghai, dismantled, shipped to Dunedin, reconstructed, and opened in 2008. Despite the unusual provenance, the garden doesn't have an artificial atmosphere; instead, it offers an aura of scholarly calm. The garden also has a good, albeit small, gift shop.

39 Queens Gardens. dunedinchinesegarden.com. ✆ **03/477-3248.** NZ$13 adults, free for children under 13 accompanied by adults. Daily 10am–5pm.

Olveston ♥♥♥ HISTORIC HOME One of New Zealand's best examples of an old-fashioned stately home, this 35-room Jacobean-style mansion was designed by London architect Sir Ernest George and built between 1904 and 1906 for the wealthy Theomin family. It is said that traveling and shopping was a hobby of the family patriarch—and didn't he do well? Inside this delightful residence you'll find a trove of Eastern decorative arts—in bronze, cloisonné, ivory, ceramics, jade—and over 250 paintings. If the room seems dark on a sunny day, it's the protective UV-ray film on the windows. Touring this house is time-travel at its best—it's been meticulously preserved, so it feels like the family popped out for a minute, leaving you to look around everywhere from the dining room to the billiards room. Viewing is by 1-hour guided tour only, but leave

Olveston Historic Home.

another 15 minutes to appreciate the garden, house exterior, the family motor car (a 1921 Fiat 510 Tourer), and to browse the gift shop.

42 Royal Terrace. olveston.co.nz. ✆ **03/477-3320.** NZ$26 adults, NZ$15 school-age children. Tours daily at 9:30am, 10:45am, noon, 1:30pm, 2:45pm, and 4pm; reservations recommended.

Toitū Otago Settlers Museum ♥♥♥ MUSEUM Originally conceived as the Early Settlers Museum, after a major revamp in recent years this institution now draws raves for its brilliantly curated exhibits. It no longer focuses only on the colonizers—its exhibits start from Māori settlement and continue to the present day. These range from a re-creation of a family cabin in a sailing vessel—simulating the voyage that brought settlers from Scotland to this distant land (an evocative display of comforts and hardships)—to a vintage Buick and the country's first coal-fired ovens. Every corner of this vast building holds much of interest.

31 Queens Garden. toituosm.com. ✆ **03/477-5052.** Free admission. Daily 10am–5pm.

Tūhura Otago Museum ♥♥ MUSEUM Established in 1868, this institution near the university campus is New Zealand's fourth-largest museum, with over 1.7 million items; most people are surprised by the depth of its large ethnographic, natural history, and decorative arts collections. These include Southern Land Southern People, an exhibition of southern Māori art and artifacts, their stories and treasures. The three following exhibits are well worth the additional entry fees charged for them. The new **Tūhura Science Centre ♥♥♥**, NZ's largest, claims to be the only bicultural science center in the world, telling the Māori creation story alongside art and science. An absolute don't-miss for families with kids, it has 45 interactive hands-on exhibits, including an infinity room, a tornado machine, an earthquake table, and the always-popular double-helix slide. The warm, humid **Tropical Forest ♥♥** is a butterfly house (complete with a three-story waterfall) that's home to moths and butterflies from Costa Rica and the Philippines; you can see them in various stages of the chrysalis process, and watch newly emerged butterflies be released at 11am daily. The only 3D planetarium in Australasia, the **Perpetual Guardian Planetarium ♥♥** delivers an excellent interactive presentation that explores how the Otago sky will look on the night of your visit. Ask your presenter for advice on the best time and place

A young visitor greets a butterfly in the Tūhura Otago Museum's Tropical Forest.

to try to view the Aurora Australis, or Southern Lights, which can be visible this far south.

419 Great King St. otagomuseum.nz. ✆ **03/474-7474.** Basic admission NZ$20 adults, under age 18 free; general exhibits plus Science Centre & Tropical Forest NZ$30 adults, NZ$13 kids 3–18, family NZ$80; general exhibits plus planetarium NZ$30 adults, NZ$13 kids 3–18, family NZ$80; all-access pass NZ$35 adults, NZ$15 kids 3–18, families NZ$85. Daily 10am–5pm.

Just Outside the City: The Otago Peninsula

The 33km (20-mile) Otago Peninsula is a busy ecotourism corridor, particularly at the headland known as Taiaroa Head. It's home to a number of bird and sea mammal colonies, including those that shelter *kororā* (little penguins), fur seals, and *pakake* (New Zealand sea lions). This is also the only mainland

Rare Birds in the Bush

As soon as you arrive at the **Orokonui Ecosanctuary ♥♥** (orokonui.nz; ✆ **03/482-1755**), you'll hear birdsong—a rarity today in much of NZ's wilderness, due to predation. One of NZ's newest wildlife sanctuaries—and one of the few in the South Island—Orokonui is 307 hectares (759 acres) of regenerated bush in the Orokonui Valley, 20km (12½ miles) northeast of Dunedin.

An opportunity to travel back in time and see Aotearoa as it once was, it's fully fenced and predator-free with a 1,000-year plan for the future. Here, you can see wild *tūī* (a type of honeyeater); kākā parrots; brightly colored *takahē* (flightless birds once thought extinct); eels; Otago skinks; and *tuatara* (an ancient reptile). The two latter species do roam freely in the sanctuary, but since they're difficult to find, some are kept in an enclosure for easy viewing. The blue, chicken-size, red-beaked takahē, however, are often seen and are a delight if you do. Feeders with viewing platforms make finding birdlife a breeze.

NZ's rather recalcitrant native birds and other species make this a good place for a 1-hour guided tour, a mostly gentle walk that will unlock some of the history and wonders of the NZ bush. The 2-hour tour goes deeper in the forest, with steeper sections. All tours start at 10:30am and should be booked online; prices start at NZ$60 for adults and NZ$30 for children, with families NZ$150. However, you can walk the forest paths yourself for NZ$26/NZ$13, or with an NZ$65 family pass. There's also an on-site cafe; don't come for the food, but do come for the view. The reserve is at the top of Blueskin Road (Rapid No. 600), Waitati; hours are Thursday to Monday 9:30am to 4:30pm.

A takahē runs free at the Orokonui Ecosanctuary.

breeding location for *toroa* (massive northern royal albatross), and one of the few places to see *hoiho* (yellow-eyed penguins), incredibly rare penguins endemic to NZ. If the wind is right, you can spot the albatrosses gliding outside the **Royal Albatross Centre** (see below) for free, but to see the endangered yellow-eyed penguins in their natural habitat, you'll need to book a tour. (See The OPERA, below.)

As for the adorable little penguins, these guys can be found on coastlines throughout the South Island—but if you're intent on seeing them here, you can book a tour with a naturalist. The **Blue Penguins Pukekura Experience ♥♥** (bluepenguins.co.nz; ✆ **021/2259962;** NZ$65 adults, NZ$45 children, NZ$185 two adults/two children) offers refunds if you see fewer than five penguins. It takes place at dusk nightly, when the penguins come ashore at Pilots Beach below the cliffs of the headland. Pukekura offers transport from the Dunedin isite for an additional fee, but if you choose to self-drive, note that afterward you'll have to drive back to Dunedin in the dark for 45 minutes on a winding seaside road. You may want to seek out accommodation down the road in Portobello, where there are a handful of motels and B&Bs.

Larnach Castle ♥♥ HISTORIC HOUSE Larnach Castle may be small by European standards, but it's clear William Larnach had more than a simple bungalow in mind when he set about constructing this marvelous edifice in 1871. No doubt keen to impress his French heiress wife, he hired 200 workmen for 3 years just to build the shell; a host of European master craftsmen took another 12 years to complete the interior. The carved foyer ceiling alone took three craftsmen 6½ years to finish. The Georgian hanging staircase is the only one in the Southern Hemisphere. Larnach came to New Zealand from Australia in the late 1860s to set up the first Bank of Otago. He later became a member of Parliament, but with three marriages behind him and a family history dotted with scandal and misfortune, he committed suicide in the Parliament Buildings in Wellington. (His first two wives both died at the age of 38, and his third dealt him a fatal emotional blow by dallying with a son from his first marriage.) After his death, the Crown used the castle as a mental hospital.

145 Camp Rd., off Highcliff Rd. larnachcastle.co.nz. ✆ **03/476-1616.** NZ$51 adults, NZ$18 ages 5–14, families NZ$118. 1-hr. guided tours daily 9:30am and 11:30am (NZ$77 adults, NZ$44 ages 5–14). Summer daily 9am–7pm; winter daily 9am–5pm.

The OPERA ♥♥♥ NATURE RESERVE NZ's yellow-eyed penguins—easily identifiable by the band of yellow around their eyes—are one of the world's rarest, with only 163 breeding pairs left in the wild on the country's mainland. Like most of NZ's endemic bird species, their numbers have been decimated by predators, habitat loss, and disease. The Otago Peninsula Eco Restoration Alliance (aka OPERA) is one of the few places you can observe them in the wild. The 1½-hour tour begins with an informative slide show; you're then driven 5 minutes across farmland to an extensive network of tunnels and hides that took 8 years to build. Here you'll be able to watch the penguins at close quarters without disturbing them. You'll need sensible walking shoes, as there's at least 2km (around 1¼ mile) of walking involved, much of it uphill and steep. But you'll be rewarded with coastal views, the chance to see little penguins in their nests, colonies of fur seals, possibly New Zealand sea lions, and incredible swirling tangles of bull kelp—all fantastic photographic opportunities (note that no flash is allowed near the penguins). Binoculars and rain jackets are provided.

Pakihau Rd. theopera.co.nz. ✆ **03/478-0286.** 90-min. tour NZ$75 adults, NZ$30 ages 5–14, NZ$175 family pass; check website for other options and combos. Tours Oct–Mar at 11:45am, 1:15pm, 2:45pm, and 4:45pm; Apr–Sept at 3:45pm only.

Royal Albatross Centre ♥♥♥ The world's only mainland colony of albatross, this protected rookery offers a unique opportunity to see these magnificent, vulnerable birds at unusually close range, leaving you with a lasting impression of their power and beauty. The Albatross Centre has a small museum that's free, and it's also possible to see the birds gracefully careening around the headland for free. However, a guided tour gives you the best vantage point to see chicks in their nests, especially during the hatching and feeding season, January through August. (Binoculars provided.) The best time to visit is in the late afternoon or early evening, when parent birds are returning to the nest. It's a 2-minute walk up a path to the observatory; mobile carts are available for visitors with accessibility concerns. The 1-hour Albatross Classic tour is fascinating enough, but I recommend spending an additional NZ$10 for the 90-minute Unique Taiaroa tour, which takes you through the fascinating history of the headland, from Māori *pā* (fortified village) to the large underground World War II fort and tunnel system.

One of the residents of the Royal Albatross Centre.

1260 Harrington Point Rd., Taiaroa Head. albatross.org.nz. ✆ **03/478-0499.** Free entry to Albatross Centre. Tours from NZ$65 adults, NZ$15 children, families NZ$140. Reservations essential. Daily 11:15am–9:15pm.

Day Trip from Dunedin: Karitāne & Moeraki

The highway (SH1) between Ōamaru (p. 511) and Dunedin hugs the coast for many miles, providing sea views on one side of the road, with rolling farmland and gentle bush-clad hills on the other. North of Dunedin some 40km (25 miles) is the quiet coastal settlement of **Karitāne,** home to **Karitāne Māori Tours ♥♥** (karitanemaoritours.com; ✆ **027/237-4889**). They'll take you for a refreshing, soul-lifting 2-hour paddle around the estuary and sandspit in a *waka unua* (double-hulled canoe), with personable guides offering traditional storytelling, tree-planting, and a discussion of local history. It's NZ$150 for adults and NZ$95 for children, with a family of four NZ$415.

Another 40 minutes' drive north will bring you to Moeraki, where the **Moeraki Boulders** ♥ (moerakiboulders.co.nz; ✆ **03/439-4827**) have become locally famous. The 60-million-year-old *kaihinaki* are a collection of large, spherical boulders that pop up like giant half-eggs along the shoreline; they're unexpectedly fun to walk among, simply for their amazing sculptural forms. Much like pearls formed inside oysters, the boulders were forged in ancient sea secretions. They're well signposted (indeed, you can literally see them from space via Google Maps) and it's a 10-minute walk from the DOC parking lot to the boulders. The Moeraki Boulders Café (also well-signed) is considerably closer, but you have to buy a coffee at the restaurant or pay NZ$2 to access its private track. It's open daily.

Organized Tours

IN DUNEDIN

Athol Parks has held jobs as a cab driver and a journalist in Dunedin. Now, he shares his expansive knowledge of the history that's shaped the city on his **City Walks** ♥ (citywalks.co.nz; ✆ **02/7356-9132**) tours, starting from NZ$50 for adults and NZ$5 for children. Intimate and interactive, itineraries range from a classic walking tour of Dunedin's historic buildings to his laneways walk through the new Warehouse Precinct.

If you want to go further back in time, I highly recommend a cemetery tour with Gregor Campbell from **Tales from Darkest Dunedin** ♥♥♥ (darkest dunedin.co.nz; ✆ **021/641-110**). Based on his company's name, I thought I was headed out on a hokey ghost tour—but as it turns out, Campbell is a historian, urban explorer, and self-proclaimed "taphophile" or graveyard enthusiast. There is nothing spooky about his 90-minute guided tours of the Northern Cemetery (NZ$60 adults, NZ$35 ages 10–15), which is where some of Dunedin's most famous founders are buried. Instead, Campbell has painstakingly researched the sometimes sad, sometimes scandalous backstories behind the tombstones, which he delivers with humor and tenderness. He also

RIDING THE RAILS INTO THE heartland

Dunedin Railway ♥♥ (dunedinrailways.co.nz; ✆ **03/477-4449**), offers a trio of scenic train trips showcasing NZ's diverse landscape: inland; to Ōamaru; and north along the east coast. Most well-known is the famed 5-hour **Taieri Gorge** trip inland, offering views of golden landscape, towers of schist rock, tussock grasses and wildflowers, and tumbling waterfalls. There are open-air carriages, which give you a chance to marvel at the engineering prowess that allowed the original steam trains to climb from sea level to the high plains of the Maniototo, including through 10 tunnels and across bridges. With all that being said, if you've been driving through the country, you might find the views a bit redundant; the experience is most likely to wow those who have been flying around the country. Trips start at NZ$119 adult one-way, NZ$39 ages 2 to 15; visit the website for the full range of sightseeing options.

CYCLING TOURS THROUGH THE heartland

The Central Otago region is one of my favorite regions, and I think it's best explored in a manner that allows you to wander through the streets and shops of historic towns like Clyde, Ophir, Ranfurly, and Naseby, all of which feature original buildings from the 1800s, high-end boutiques, and cafes serving beautiful food. The opportunity to do so is one of the reasons that the **Otago Central Rail Trail** ♥♥♥ (centralcycletrail.co.nz) has become one of the country's most popular bike rides. Following a former railway line between Middlemarch and Clyde, it can be done as a day trip, although its full length takes about 4 days to cycle. Since it follows the rail line, the gradient is smooth, and you get the bonus of traveling across some very cool viaducts and through long railway tunnels. It presents up-close heartland Otago at its finest, with its tawny landscape of tussock grass, wild herbs, and rocky uplands. More than a dozen tour operators service the trail, with both guided and unguided options available. Clyde's **Trail Journeys** ♥♥ (trailjourneys.co.nz; ✆ **03/449-2150**), for example, will kit you out with everything you need, including well serviced and clean gear. Its highly personalized services also include luggage transfers to your accommodation each day.

offers "true crime tours" of Victorian Dunedin, and tours of Larnach Castle or Dunedin's historic city center; check website for the full list.

ON THE OTAGO PENINSULA

You can't get any more local than Mateo Winter, whose family has called the area home since 1863. He offers half-, full-, and multi-day small group tours introducing visitors to the region's history, conservation, and wildlife with his company, **UntamedNZ** ♥♥ (untamednz.co.nz; ✆ **022/098-9654**). All Winter's tours include pickup from your accommodation and high-res wildlife photography that he takes during your tour. Private charters are also available.

Monarch Wildlife Cruises ♥♥ (wildlife.co.nz; ✆ **0800/666-272** in NZ, or 03/477-4276) offer an excellent way to see a variety of wildlife along the peninsula, including the magic of seeing albatross on the wing. Crews are experienced in conservation and know everything about the albatrosses, New Zealand fur seals, yellow-eyed penguins, and other species you're likely to see. Prices start from NZ$70 for adults and NZ$28 ages 5 to 14 for a 1-hour cruise, running three times an afternoon in summer and at 2:30pm in winter.

Outdoor Pursuits

FISHING Nearby Port Chalmers is known for its stellar salmon and trout fishing from October to April. If you want to try your hand at shark fishing, deep-sea fishing, saltwater, or light-tackle sport fishing, try **Ezifish Charters** ♥ (ezifish.com; ✆ **027/283-3117**).

GOLF Founded in 1896, **The Otago Golf Club** ♥ (125 Balmacewen Rd., Maori Hill; otagogolfclub.co.nz; ✆ **03/467-2096**) is an 18-hole championship course with a fully stocked pro shop. Visitors pay NZ$110 for 18 holes. The gorgeous, seaside **St. Clair Golf Club** ♥ (20 Isadore Rd.; stclairgolf.co.nz; ✆ **03/487-7076**) is also popular; greens fees are NZ$90 per person.

SURFING Dunedin is famous for its surf, from fun beach breaks to advanced waves. **Esplanade Surf School** (espsurfschool.co.nz; ✆ **021/484-141**) offers lessons with qualified International Surfing Association coaches. A beginner group lesson is NZ$70 adults, NZ$50 children; family lessons NZ$250; and bespoke one-on-ones NZ$110, best for the experienced surfer wanting to dip a toe into these cool southern waters. Board and wetsuit rentals are also available.

Where to Stay in Dunedin

Consider this fair warning: Dunedin is notoriously cold and damp during the winter months, both inside and out. Central heating in private homes is non-existent (many are heated by wood fires), although insulation is becoming more common. If you choose to book an Airbnb or a smaller hotel, look for these critical words: "electric blanket," "heat pump," or "double-glazed windows."

Bell Hill Apartments ♥♥ The Bell Hill Apartments look like your favorite university professor handed you the keys to their city apartment for the weekend. Each of the large, two-story apartments have a lived-in feeling in the best possible way; from chess pieces spilling out of their bag, to the dog-eared books, to the whiskey in a decanter ready to pour. Although the interiors are new (the 19th-century building was fully renovated in 2021), they retain attractive heritage details like papier-mâché ceilings resembling pressed tin. With their park-facing balconies, high ceilings, and loft bedrooms, the atrium-like spaces are glorious for a night or two, but designed for much longer stays, with built-in laundry facilities and fully equipped kitchens stocked with breakfast goods.

The Bell Hill Apartments offer plenty of space, with a cozy living room and loft bedroom.

462 Moray Place. bellhillapartments.co.nz. ✆ **021/352-994.** 3 units. NZ$495–NZ$595 double. **Amenities:** Free Wi-Fi.

Bluestone on George ♥♥♥ Free Wi-Fi that's lightning-fast; a washer/dryer and fully stocked kitchen in each unit; bathrooms with heated floors; and comfy beds with a choice of fiber or feather pillows—is there a travel need/wish that isn't addressed by the Bluestone? We can't think of one. Heck, they will even deliver continental breakfast to your room if you request it. Located on a quiet street that's an easy walk from the Octagon and all its action, this motel even has hotel-like decor in soothing, silvery grays and blues, and is more affordable than other places with these amenities. A top pick.

571 George St. bluestonedunedin.co.nz. ✆ **03/477-9201.** 55 units. NZ$248–NZ$271 double. **Amenities:** Business center; gym; free Wi-Fi.

Subtle, sophisticated room decor at Bluestone on George (p. 531).

Ebb Dunedin ♥♥ With its glass-fronted facade, Ebb could easily be mistaken for a new office building—but take one step within the open-air four-story atrium and you'll discover a stunning space filled with art, and a cafe surrounded by lush plant life. Rooms in this boutique hotel, which opened in 2021, feature luxurious details like curated minibars with pre-mixed cocktails and free-standing soaker tubs. There are private lounges with fireplaces on each floor. With its hallways of landscapes and contemporary artwork by local artists that reflect the region's Māori and Scottish ancestry, it's a grown-up and contemporary contrast to the city's heritage properties at the same price point—a welcome addition for travelers looking for something a little different.

82 Filleul St. ebb-dunedin.co.nz. ✆ **03/260-6800.** 27 units. NZ$370–NZ$755 double. **Amenities:** Free Wi-Fi.

858 George Street Motel ♥♥ Is the term *luxury motel* oxymoronic? In this case it's accurate. Within walking distance of the Otago Museum and University of Otago campus, this motel was designed in 1999 by local architect Ian Butcher with thought and consideration; he won a national architect's award for the project. It has been recently refurbished with decor that would put even some luxury hotels to shame. (The contrasting gray and yellow textiles lend a refined elegance to the space, as does all of the burnished wood.) The underfloor heating in the bathrooms is a welcome treat in chilly Dunedin, and the kitchens are well-equipped. One- and two-bedroom studios and suites are available.

858 George St. 858georgestreetmotel.co.nz. ✆ **03/474-0047.** 13 units. NZ$195–NZ$320 double. Free parking. **Amenities:** Laundry; free Wi-Fi.

Fable Dunedin ♥♥ Once known as the Wains Hotel, Dunedin's oldest hotel has taken many forms since it opened in 1862, and its 2020 renovation is no exception. Over NZ$3 million was spent to turn this formerly forgettable hotel into a true luxury property. It now has a very good on-site restaurant, a bar with tenders who remember your likes and dislikes, and top-quality bedding. Like many other new properties in NZ the design notes here are Art Deco, with pops of plaid playing homage to the city's Scottish history. Limited secure valet parking is available for NZ$40 a day; book in advance.

310 Princes St. fablehotelsandresorts.com. ✆ **03/477-1145.** 48 units. NZ$270–NZ$728 double. Valet parking NZ$40 (book in advance). **Amenities:** Restaurant; gym; concierge; room service; free Wi-Fi.

The Terminus Apartments ♥♥ When Antonia Wood and Steve Macknight purchased this 1880s hotel, it had fallen into disrepair. In their renovation of the property, they decided to expose its bare bones, including the original brick (some still painted with early street advertisements) and wooden beams. The rest was upcycled into reclaimed wooden furniture, which is offset perfectly against stainless steel appliances and polished concrete floors. These lofts are best for the self-sufficient: Guests are expected to check themselves in to the lodging (you're sent an access code prior to your arrival), and all units have full kitchens. Don't feel like cooking? There's a bakery, high-end restaurant, and wine bar located in the building at street level. The only drawback to staying here? The apartments are located beside a busy intersection, so there is some traffic noise.

42 Queen Gardens. theterminus.staydirectly.com. ✆ **021/056-2450.** 8 units. NZ$160–NZ$280 double. **Amenities:** Free Wi-Fi.

Where to Stay on the Otago Peninsula

Kaimata Retreat ♥♥ Step onto the decks of this ecolodge complex and you might see a seal diving in the waters of the inlet below. A 30-minute drive from Dunedin on winding country roads, Kaimata's lodge, studios, and cabin are ideal for a night or two of pristine peacefulness, especially if you're exploring the Otago Peninsula. The vibe is soothing—honey-colored

With direct beach access, Kaimata Retreat is well suited to a peaceful getaway.

macrocarpa wood and wrap-around windows with panoramic sea views, and spectacular stars at night. There's direct beach access, and Karen, your friendly host, can arrange local wildlife tours and water activities. Although there's free Wi-Fi, there's no phone reception. The lodge and cabins are self-catering, but Karen's happy to give dining recommendations that are a 12-minute drive away, such as the **Portobello Hotel & Bistro ♥**, 2 Harington Point Rd. (portobellohotelandbistro.com; ✆ **03/4780-759**). She and I can both recommend the latter's lamb burger with a pint of local craft beer.

297 Cape Saunders Rd., Otago Peninsula. kaimataretreat.co.nz. ✆ **027/206-6905.** 3 units. NZ$300–NZ$600 double. 2-night min. stay. **Amenities:** Laundry; kitchenette; free Wi-Fi.

Larnach Lodge & Stable Stay ♥♥ First things first: Lodgings here are not actually *in* the historic Larnach Castle (see p. 527). But they are in structures purpose-built in the estate's spectacular gardens, meaning that guests get the same eye-candy views the castle's founder had (guests also get free tours of the mansion). As for the rooms, they're handsome and contemporary but with touches that recall the castle next door, like four-poster beds, walls painted in richly saturated Victorian-era colors, and overstuffed armchairs (note that the more economical "stable" rooms are less plush than the lodge rooms). Many guests add to their stay an elegant dinner served in the castle. A luxury country house, **Camp Estate** (campestate.co.nz), is also available on castle grounds.

145 Camp Rd., Otago Peninsula. larnachcastle.co.nz. ✆ **03/476-1616.** 19 units. NZ$195 Stable Stay room; NZ$385 Larnach Lodge room; NZ$610 Camp Estate room. Meals and activity packages available. **Amenities:** Guest laundry; free Wi-Fi.

Where to Eat in Dunedin

As a university town, Dunedin has many cafes and bars that cater to the student population, but that doesn't mean only fast-food outlets (although there are plenty of these). In this intellectual hangout, good wine, good food, and good coffee are more important than chicken nuggets and a burger, so you'll find plenty of posh as well as budget options.

EXPENSIVE

Bacchus ♥♥ MODERN NEW ZEALAND Dunedin's longest-established restaurant looks out over the Octagon. Try to get a window seat if you can, as the city life is a pleasant distraction while you wait between courses. It's a sophisticated spot, a favorite with lunching businessmen, and just the place to relax in leather chairs while enjoying lamb rump with sundried-tomato crust, or confit duck with coconut rice and mango salsa.

12 The Octagon, 1st floor. bacchusdunedin.nz. ✆ **03/474-0824.** Main courses NZ$39–NZ$48. Mon–Fri noon–late, Sat 5:30pm–late.

Plato ♥♥♥ SEAFOOD Chef Nigel Broad opened this popular restaurant in 2002, and it has been a star on the Dunedin culinary scene from day one. Situated on the wharves in what was once a "seafarer's rest" (a cheap 19th-century accommodation for merchant seamen), it is a pleasantly eccentric-looking place, decorated with a quirky collection of teapots, kitchen utensils, and other bric-a-brac. But you come here for the seafood, which is super-fresh and often served in creative preparations (you might get a curry with pomegranate, a side of avocado and seaweed salad, or something else interesting). Take a cab; it's easy to get lost in the wharf area.

2 Birch St., Inner Harbour. platocafe.co.nz. ✆ **03/477-4235.** Main courses NZ$43–$47. Tues–Sat 5pm–late.

Tītī ♥♥♥ SEASONAL NEW ZEALAND Named for the muttonbirds that nest in the hills nearby, Tītī is well worth the drive for its award-winning fine dining with front-row views of St. Clair beach. The refined menu, with mains ranging from NZ$38 to NZ$42, features the likes of organic chicken with local mushrooms and soy caramel, fried mozzarella and grilled eggplant, or Otago fish with new potatoes. Alternatively, put your trust in the kitchen and choose the Feed Me option, a five-course degustation featuring the chef's current favorite dishes. The wine list puts Waitaki and Central Otago wines at center stage.

24 The Esplanade, St. Clair. titi.co.nz. ✆ **03/466-3610.** Main courses NZ$38–NZ$42; degustation NZ$55 lunch, NZ$95 dinner. Dinner reservations strongly recommended. Tue 5pm–late, Wed–Sat 11:30am–2pm and 5pm–late (Apr–Sept no lunch Wed–Thurs).

Artfully presented fine dining at Tītī.

MODERATE/INEXPENSIVE

A bright and modern brunch spot close to the university campus, **Buster Greens Real Food Room ♥♥**, 466 George St. (bustergreens.co.nz; ✆ **03/470-1233**), is the perfect place to start your day, with its expertly made barista coffees, smoothie bowls, and spiced Turkish eggs. Superfood-inspired, its cold-pressed juices and smoothies round out the offerings. It's open weekdays from 6:30am to 3:30pm, Saturdays from 7:30am to 3pm, and Sundays from 8:30am to 3pm. Just after a coffee? Try **Mazagran Espresso Bar ♥**, 36 Moray Place (✆ **03/477-9959**), which supplies the coffee beans for most of Dunedin's leading cafes. It's open weekdays from 7am to 3:30pm and on Saturdays from 10am to 2pm.

Etrusco at the Savoy ♥♥ ITALIAN Three generations of Gianones have now waited tables at Etrusco; the family has owned this Dunedin institution since 1995. Located on the first floor of the historic Savoy building, the

Sushi of the South: Cheese Rolls

If you've been in the South Island for any length of time, you've likely seen cheese rolls at a cafe, displayed right alongside the ubiquitous lolly cake (another NZ specialty). They're typically made of sliced white bread that's spread with a cheesy onion paste, rolled into a tube and toasted. But did you know that the Southland is the birthplace of the cheese roll? Recipes for the snack—sometimes called "sushi of the south"—date back to the 1930s. Almost unheard of in the North Island, this cabinet food is so popular throughout Otago and Southland that there have been cheese roll competitions; variations such as deep-fried cheese rolls; and entire academic studies dedicated to the delicacy.

large, wooden-floored pizzeria and spaghetteria is invariably packed with customers enjoying good-value meals. There's a big range of authentic pasta dishes and thin crust pizzas oozing with delicious toppings, and in the unlikely event that you're still hungry, there are Italian breads, antipasti, and wonderful homemade *dolci* (desserts). The restaurant takes delight in getting a bit rowdy, so don't expect intimate conversations.

8A Moray Place. etrusco.co.nz. ✆ **03/477-3737.** Main courses NZ$22–NZ$33. Reservations essential. Daily 5:30pm–10pm.

The Good Earth Cafe ♥♥ CAFE This local favorite is located just 2 blocks away from the Otago Museum on the university campus. As the name implies, it specializes in fresh organic and vegetarian meals (such as vegan seitan scramble or turmeric chickpea fritters), but you can still order a steak filet sandwich or ask for your eggs with bacon. Naturally, gluten-free and vegan baked goods are also available. It's popular and has bad acoustics, so if you arrive at lunchtime expect quite the din. There's plenty of seating available.

Corner of Cumberland and St. David sts. ✆ **03/471-8554.** Main courses NZ$20–NZ$30. Mon–Fri 7am–4pm, Sat–Sun 8am–4pm.

Good Good ♥♥ BURGERS Tucked away in the Warehouse Precinct, this space is everything the kids on 90210 wanted the Peach Pit to be: graffiti walls, neon basketball hoops, and couches set up in living room vignettes. It might sound like a den for university students, but low music

Good Good hits the spot when you need a burger loaded with all the fixings.

volume makes it accessible to all (when I was there, the youngest patron was about 6, while the oldest was about 70). Burgers are prepped from within an on-site caravan, and served super saucy and American-style, with cheddar cheese, plenty of pickles, and the softest of brioche buns. They even sell their own merch.

22 Vogel St. goodgood.co.nz. ✆ **022/490-4767**. Burgers NZ$22–NZ$26. Tues–Sun 11:30am–2pm and 5–8pm.

Vogel Street Kitchen ♥♥ COMFORT FOOD Opened in late 2014, this is the first cafe/bar to settle in what was a street of industrial warehouses. Echoing concrete floors and hissing espresso machines cannot quite smother the sounds of young corporates out for lunch or chasing after-work drinks. The all-day menu includes breakfast favorites and standout wood-fired pizzas along with, more unusually, wood-fired sandwiches, such as lemon, garlic, and thyme chicken with pickled radish and aioli (NZ$24). The well-curated wine list features South Island wines, there's a small selection of cocktails, and the coffee is excellent.

76 Vogel St. vogelstkitchen.nz. ✆ **03/477-3623.** Main courses NZ$16–NZ$30. Mon–Fri 7:30am–2:30pm, Sat–Sun 8:30am–3pm.

Shopping

If you want something with a "bonny wee Scottish" flavor, head for the **Scottish Shop,** 17 George St. (scottishshop.co.nz; ✆ **03/477-9965**). It has a wide range of tartan and heraldic goods, right down to tartan ties.

The award-winning **University Book Shop ♥♥**, 378 Great King St. (unibooks.co.nz; ✆ **03/477-6976**), offers just about anything you're likely to want to read. It's open weekdays from 9am to 5:30pm and weekends 10am to 4pm. Secondhand bookshop lovers will want to inspect every one of the 20,000-plus volumes inside **Dead Souls Bookshop ♥♥♥**, 393 Princes St. (deadsouls.co.nz; ✆ **021/0270-8540**), a glorious emporium filled with collectible, antiquarian, and general secondhand books, plus New Zealand small press and art books. It's open Monday through Saturday 10am to 5pm. **Milford Galleries ♥♥**, 18 Dowling St. (milfordgalleries.co.nz; ✆ **03/477-7727**), is the best dealer showing and selling contemporary New Zealand art; it's open weekdays 9am to 5pm and Saturday 11am to 3pm.

For a truly unique gift to take home, head down the graffiti-filled **No Name Alley** (which can be accessed via Police St.) to find the natural health company **Wild Dispensary ♥♥** (wilddispensary.co.nz; ✆ **021/185-0471**), which offers tastings of its award-winning elixirs and bitters made with locally sourced wild herbs and native botanicals. You can also do a tasting and take home a treat from **Dunedin Craft Distillers ♥♥♥**, 8 Roberts St. (dunedincraftdistillers.nz; ✆ **027/479-7714**), which turns rescued bread into booze, including cacao vodka made with nibs from local **Ocho Chocolate ♥** (ocho.co.nz; ✆ **03/425-7819**). Ocho, too, offers tours and tastings of its local chocolate, including one made with *horopito* and *kawakawa.* Tours are daily at 11am and cost NZ$30 per person.

Dunedin After Dark

Dunedin's nightlife ranges from its legendary university swill holes to smart, upmarket wine bars and a boutique casino. There are also good theaters, a multiscreen movie theater, and several cafes that double as live-music venues. For concerts and musicals, there's the gorgeous **Regent Theatre,** on the Lower Octagon (regenttheatre.co.nz; ✆ **03/477-8597**), host to a range of national and international musicals and concerts. Ticket prices vary.

For a nightcap, the most happening hangouts change on the regular; the bars lining the Octagon are a sure bet for a fun night out. Another fun spot is **Speight's Ale House** ♥, 200 Rattray St. (thealehouse.co.nz; ✆ **03/471-9050**). Now a popular chain of brewpubs with around 15 locations nationally, Speight's got its illustrious start in Dunedin in 1876. Tours and tastings are available for NZ$45 adults, NZ$25 children (with discounts available if combined with lunch or dinner at the brewhouse); book ahead at speights.co.nz/the-brewery. The Alehouse is open daily for lunch and dinner from 11:30am to late.

Craft beer at Steamer Basin.

Craft beer enthusiasts will likely prefer **Steamer Basin** ♥♥ (steamerbasin.co.nz; ✆ **027/922-7817**), tucked away in a historic building on No Name Alley (accessed from Bond St., btw. Jetty and Police St.). It brews highly quaffable IPAs, saisons, stouts, lagers, and ales, made with ingredients sourced from a 100-mile radius. It's all served alongside pizzas, available whole (NZ$22) or by the slice (NZ$7). Summer hours (Oct to early Apr) are Wednesday to Sunday, 2pm to 8pm; if you're visiting in winter, check the website for times.

En Route to Invercargill & Stewart Island

Two main roadways link Dunedin with Invercargill. **SH1** is the more direct route, via Balclutha, Gore, and Edendale, but you can also leave SH1 in central Balclutha and take the well-signposted **Southern Scenic Route** to Invercargill via Owaka and the Catlins. As its name implies, it is considerably prettier.

THE CATLINS

Owaka 113km (70 miles) SW of Dunedin

Situated along the Southern Scenic Route, **the Catlins** contains the most significant area of native forest on the east coast of New Zealand. Rain falls in this area 214 days a year, but don't hesitate to step into the weather. Good walking tracks wind through forests of rimu and totara, and big sweeps of

L. Whakatipu
L. Te Anau
Te Anau
EYRE MTS.
GARVIE MTS.
Athol
The Key
L. Manapouri
Mossburn
Fiordland N.P.
Lumsden
Roxburgh
Sutton
Raes Junction
Lawrence
Allenton
Riversdale
Waiau R.
Nightcaps
Ōreti R.
Winton
Gore
Waipahi
Milton
Cluthа R.
Tuatapere
Mataura
Balclutha
Te Waewae Bay
Pahia Pt.
Riverton
Makarewa
Edendale
Kākā Point
Catlins Conservation Park
Owaka
Nugget Pt.
Invercargill
Papatowai
Fortrose
Tokanui
Bluff
Waikawa
Chaslands Mistake
FOVEAUX STRAIT
Codfish I./ Whenua Hou
Ruapuke I.
Rakiura National Park
Rakiura/ Stewart Island
Oban
Mt. Allen
South Cape
0 30 mi
0 30 km
NORTH ISLAND
Auckland
Wellington
SOUTH ISLAND
Christchurch
Dunedin
Area of detail
Invercargill
Queens Park
Victoria Ave.
Gala St.
Leet St.
Water Tower
Kelvin St.
Victoria Railway Hotel
Yarrow St.
Spey St.
Deveron St.
MacMaster St.
Bond St.
Mersey St.
Dee St.
Don St.
Doon St.
Queens Dr.
Leven St.
Esk St.
Jed St.
Railway Station
The Crescent
Tay St.
To Transport World
Otepuni Creek
Forth St.
Otepuni Gardens
Tyne St.
St. Mary's Basilica
Eye St.
To Airport
Tweed St.
Teviot St.
Ness St.
Annan St.
Liddel St.
Clyde St.
NithSt.
Conon St.
Ettrick St.
Bowmont St.
Ythan St.
Elles Rd.
Crinan St.
Earn St.
Balmoral Dr.
0 0.5 mi
0 0.5 km
Dalrymple St.
Grace St.

empty beach are never far away, making the soggy tramp worth it. While there's no question that it's beautiful, some may feel it lacks the "wow" factor of other regions—and it's for this reason you're more likely to have it all to yourself.

The Catlins is a region that will likely appeal most to the self-catering and the self-contained, because vast areas of wilderness mean that gas stations, restaurants, and cellphone reception are all in short supply. It's also best to time your visit for the spring, summer, or fall—during the frosty winter months, many attractions and restaurants close.

Visitor Information

The official visitor site is **catlins.org.nz**, while **southernscenicroute.co.nz** has a good interactive map of attractions, walks, and photo stops. In Owaka (the largest township), head to the **Catlins Info Centre,** 10 Campbell St. (✆ **03/415-8371**), for maps and travel advice (it's also the site of the Owaka Museum; see below). Cellphone reception is limited through the area, so it will be helpful to grab a paper handout map.

Exploring the Catlins

The following sites can be visited on a day trip driving the 2½ hours from Balclutha to Bluff along the Southern Scenic Route, although it's best if you can budget 2 days or more to truly enjoy them all.

Drive 6.5km (4 miles) south from Balclutha and turn left on Kākā Point Road to the coast. Continue south from Kākā Point to **Nugget Point ♥♥**, so named for its wave-eroded rocks, which resemble massive gold nuggets. A 20-minute roundtrip walk will take you to a viewing platform beside a lighthouse—and along the way, you may see fur seals in the rock pools below. At dusk or dawn, you might also spot penguins at the nearby **Roaring Bay** hide.

As you drive through Owaka, keep an eye out for **Teapot Land ♥** on the right-hand side, which is, as they say, "world famous in New Zealand." Local Graham Renwick has arranged over 1,300 teapots from around the world in his yard. Entry is by donation. Don't worry if you miss it; there are more weird attractions to come. **The Owaka Museum ♥**, 10 Campbell St., Owaka (owakamuseum.org.nz; ✆ **03/415-8371**), is a darn good introduction to the area and its marine history. This rugged coastline is still described as a "shipwreck coast," and the museum houses relics from the wreck of the liner *Manuka,* which sank on a reef in 1929. Admission is NZ$10 adults, children free, and it's open daily 8:30am to 5pm.

In Papatowai, look for the big green house-truck signposted **Lost Gypsy Gallery ♥♥♥**, 2532 Papatowai Hwy. (thelostgypsy.com), where craftsman Blair Somerville produces whimsical automata (mechanical toys) from found objects, including old cans, seashells, and twists of wire. He's labored for 2 decades building works meant to be touched, and there are more than 121 buttons to push, wind, and play. His gallery is free to visit (watch for the literal "train" of thought within), but the NZ$10 it costs to enter the "theatre" will be the best money you spend in NZ. There, you'll find larger-scale kinetic and

Found objects are given new life at the Lost Gypsy Gallery, an eccentric charmer of a museum.

electronic sculptures, including a bicycle-powered television, and a garden full of tentacles. Kids are welcome (only those 13 and up in the theater) but need to be carefully watched; this is an attraction geared to adults as most of the curios on display are delicate. Budget at least 45 minutes for this stop. It's open Thursday to Tuesday from 10am to 5pm, November to April only. If you arrive in the off-season, you can still turn the cranks on the giant metal whale and sheep skeleton riding a bicycle, both located in the parking lot. If you don't leave here with a massive grin on your face, I worry that you're dead inside.

Farther down the road, the 1-hour round-trip walk to/from the **Cathedral Caves** ♥, 18km (11 miles) from Papatōwai (cathedralcaves.co.nz; NZ$15 adults, NZ$2 children 5–14, card only) starts in the signposted carpark 2km/1¼ miles off the Southern Scenic Highway. The track is through coastal bush to Waipati Beach and the 200m-long sea-formed caves. Access to the caves is restricted to 2 hours on either side of low tide from October to May. (Don't even think about trying to access it in the off-season; it's on private land and well-fenced.) Tide timetables are published in regional daily newspapers and on the website, but this is a remote area, so check the notice boards at the entrance for updated information. A flashlight is necessary, insect repellent is advised, and expect to get your feet wet. Do not disturb any penguins or fur seals sheltering in the caves.

McLean Falls ♥♥ is another worthwhile stop, just west of Cathedral Caves. According to the signpost, it will take you 40 minutes round-trip to reach the 22m (72-ft.) falls. It's a short but rewarding uphill climb, with a walk through a goblin forest. **Purakaunui Falls** ♥♥ offers a shorter (and arguably easier) walk through native bush to a similarly spectacular multi-tiered waterfall.

Turn off the highway at Tokanui to reach **Curio Bay,** where you can see penguins, alongside dolphins. However, it may be most well-known for being the site of a fossilized forest, which you can see the remains of at low tide. **Tumu Toka Curioscape ♥**, 590 Waikawa Curio Bay Rd. (curioscape.co.nz; ✆ **03/246-8897**), is a relatively new interpretative center providing context to the site through its small—but heavily interactive—museum. Your ticket (NZ$10 adults, NZ$5 children 15 and under, NZ$30 families) includes features you can unlock on the pathways outside. Skip the "immersive theatre" experience; it is like watching one of those regional tourism videos they show you on airplanes. A cafe, surfing beach, and campground (with cellphone reception!) are also here. It's generally open weekdays from 11am to 6:30pm, and weekdays until 7pm, but as with all businesses in the Catlins, it's best to call ahead to confirm seasonal hours (they rarely update their websites).

A pair of penguins at Curio Bay.

Where to Stay in the Catlins

Don't expect any big hotels in the Catlins; accommodation here is limited mostly to self-contained rentals. In addition to the listings below, check bookabach.com and airbnb.com for additional rentals. (There are plenty in the surf haven of Curio Bay, for example.) Holiday parks, backpackers, and freedom campsites are also easy to come by.

Kaka Point Luxury Spa Accommodation ♥ "Spa" here means something very different from what you may be thinking; it refers to the fact that these two self-contained units have Jacuzzi bathtubs big enough for two (or three, depending on how ambitious you are). Rooms are large and elevated, but the main selling point here is a wraparound wall of windows with views of the ocean. It's also best for independent travelers, as there's no front desk on-site.

26 Esplanade, Kaka Point. kakapointluxuryspaaccommodation.co.nz. ✆ **027/399-7900.** 2 units. NZ$325. 2-night min. stay. **Amenities:** Kitchenette; free Wi-Fi.

Pounawea Motor Camp ♥ This motor camp has an enviable site on a sheltered waterfront with characterful owners. Right by the estuary, with well-fitted and -kitted (if small) cabins, and powered sites for campers and campervans, this property should fit the bill for many travelers—especially those with kids, thanks to the abundant birdlife and good bushwalks. Another plus: Visitors have use of a well-stocked communal kitchen and a large table to share.

Park Lane Pounawea, Owaka. facebook.com/www.pounaweacamping. ✆ **03/415-8483** to book. NZ$80–NZ$90 cabins; NZ$45 RV sites. **Amenities:** Playground; pool; free Wi-Fi.

Where to Eat in the Catlins

Reservations are essential at **The Point Café & Bar ♥**, 58 Esplanade, Kaka Point (facebook.com/thepointcafeandbar; ✆ **03/412-8800;** Tues–Sun noon–late), partially because it's the only restaurant in town. Having a monopoly doesn't lessen the quality of the food, though; the seafood chowder is really delish. It's right across from the beach, but a parking lot blocks the best views. Set in a former one-room schoolhouse. the family-run **Niagara Falls Cafe ♥**, 256 Niagara Waikawa Rd., Niagara (niagarafallscafe.co.nz; ✆ **03/2468-577**), makes everything in-house, from the bread to the dips and sauces. Again, the seafood chowder is the best pick on the menu. There's plenty of seating, including at picnic tables in the garden out back, and it's open daily in the summer (dinner reservations recommended), Thursday to Monday from 11am to 3pm in the winter.

GORE

190km (118 miles) S of Queenstown; 217km (135 miles) SW of Dunedin; 67km (42 miles) NE of Invercargill

Situated inland, well north of the Southern Scenic Route, this pleasant rural Central Southland town has a few worthwhile stops for visitors just passing through. You may want to stay longer if you happen to be a fisherman or a country music fan: The **Mataura River** is one of the best spots to angle for brown trout (see p. 547), and Gore/Maruawai plays host every May to the 10-day **Tussock Country Musical Festival** (tussockcountry.nz).

The big must-see for most, though, is the **John Money Art Collection ♥♥♥** on permanent display at the **Eastern Southland Gallery,** 14 Hokonui Dr. (esgallery.co.nz; ✆ **03/208-9907**). Money was a collector of Indigenous art for

The Eastern Southland Gallery's outstanding Indigenous art collection is a surprising find in a rural town like Gore.

most of his life, and, concerned that his collection of would be broken up after his death, he bequeathed it all to the gallery in Gore. It is astounding that 300 high-quality pieces of art would land in a small country town, in a building that was once a Carnegie public library. Native African, Australian, Māori, and Pacific art, and a collection of New Zealand artists Ralph Hotere and Rita Angus are on exhibit. Admission is free and it's open most days from 10am to 4:30pm.

Pop across the road to the **Old Hokonui Museum & Distillery ♥♥**, 16 Hokonui Dr. (oldhokonui-museum-distillery.nz; ✆ **03/203-9288**). for an immersive stroll through well-curated exhibitions detailing the district's cheeky moonshine history. Very good (legal) local whiskey and gifts are for sale. It's open weekdays 9am to 5pm and Saturdays 10am to 2pm.

Next stop: **The Croydon Aviation Heritage Centre ♥**, on the outskirts of Gore at the old Mandeville Airfield, 1558 Waimea Hwy. (croydonaviation.co.nz; ✆ **03/208-6046**), to see restored vintage aircraft from the 1920s and '30s, including one of the largest collections of de Havilland aircraft. It's open daily in summer 9am to 4pm, in winter 10am to 3pm (NZ$12 ages 13 and up).

Where to Eat & Stay in Gore

If you're vegetarian or gluten-free, you won't necessarily starve in Gore, but you won't have a lot of options at dinnertime—this is a region known for its beef and venison. Gore's best restaurant, **Howl at the Moon ♥**, 2 Main St. (✆ **03/208-3851**), offers unadventurous but well-prepared classics like barbecue pork belly and lemon dill salmon fillet. For breakfast or lunch, **Miss Cocoa Coffee ♥♥**, 1558 Waimea Hwy. (facebook.com/misscocoacoffee; ✆ **03/208-9662**), is worth driving the 10 minutes from the center of town to a former railway station beside the Croydon Aviation Centre. The menu is small but reasonably diverse, including a chicken waffle sandwich, pulled pork bao, and Moroccan lamb salad. The cabinet is full of pastries and baked goods, including prawn-filled croissants, spanakopita, quiches, and desserts.

If you're overnighting, there are a handful of bed-and-breakfasts, motels, and hotels. Our pick would be the friendly **Croydon Lodge ♥**, 100 Waimea St. (croydonlodge.co.nz; ✆ **03/208-9029**), just on the edge of town. It has a busy on-site restaurant (good, if overpriced), plenty of parking, and free Wi-Fi. Rooms start from NZ$185.

INVERCARGILL

190km (118 miles) S of Queenstown; 217km (135 miles) SW of Dunedin

Originally settled by Scottish immigrants in 1853, this southernmost city was surveyed in 1856 by New Zealand's first Surveyor-General, John Thomson, who decided the main streets (named for Scottish rivers) would be 40m (130 ft.) wide, giving the city its extremely spacious look. Unfortunately, outside of business hours these same wide streets can create a "no one lives here" appearance. Don't judge this book by its cover, however; Invercargill's population of roughly 58,000 clearly likes to shop, eat out, and enjoy good beers and wine, and a multimillion-dollar post-pandemic redevelopment of the downtown core has given the city lots of new entertainment, shopping, hotel, and eating options.

Like much of Southland, farming is the backbone of the economy in Invercargill/Waihōpai; just beyond the city boundaries, dairy, venison, and lamb producers earn millions. With its more than 1,000 motel and hotel beds, the city can be used as a jumping-off place for the wilderness areas of Fiordland, the Catlins, and Stewart Island, provided that you're prepared to drive.

Essentials

ARRIVING & GETTING AROUND

Air New Zealand (airnewzealand.co.nz; ✆ **800/737-000** in NZ) has service between Invercargill and Auckland, Wellington, and Christchurch. **Stewart Island Flights** (stewartislandflights.com; ✆ **03/218-9129**) has daily scheduled flights to/from Invercargill/Stewart Island. **InterCity** (intercity.co.nz; ✆ **03/471-71433**) has regular coach services linking Invercargill with all major South Island centers. If you're driving, take SH6 from Queenstown or SH1 from Dunedin.

Exploring Invercargill

Invercargill, it seems, has an affinity for all things fast, furious, and motorized. This is perhaps in part thanks to local Burt Munro, a name familiar to those who saw the 2005 movie *The World's Fastest Indian.* Munro bought and modified motorcycles for some 62 years, achieving a speed record at age 68 with his 47-year-old bike on the Bonneville Salt Flats, USA. In 1977, Munro sold the motorcycle, a 1920 Indian Scout, to the Hayes family, who display it along with other Munro memorabilia at the **E. Hayes Hardware Store,** 168 Dee St. (ehayes.co.nz; ✆ **03/218-2059**).

A quartet of vintage red trucks at Bill Richardson Transport World (p. 546).

Bill Richardson Transport World ♥♥♥ MUSEUM Reportedly the largest collection of Ford vehicles on the planet, Transport World showcases a 1940 Dodge Airflow fuel tanker (built for the Texaco Oil Company in 1939), seemingly every Ford truck made, and seven rare examples of the eight production models made before the Model T Ford, which was released in 1908 (the missing car is the Model B). In addition, the museum displays over 300 carefully restored vehicles of all models and makes, as well as less-transport-oriented collections dedicated to lawnmowers, fuel pumps, jukeboxes, HMV, Cadbury (with a wall that smells like chocolate), and even a LEGO room to keep kids busy. My top two pieces of advice: (1) Bring a sweater (the warehouse-like space is cold), and (2) drink plenty of water. Each of the themed toilets is an attraction of its own, and you'll want an excuse to check out every one.

491 Tay St., Hawthorndale. transportworld.co.nz. ✆ **0800/151-252** in NZ. NZ$40 adults, NZ$20 ages 5–14. Daily 10am–5pm.

Classic Motorcycle Mecca ♥♥ MUSEUM Unlike Transport World's collection—which is so diverse that it can appeal to nearly anyone—Motorcycle Mecca is singular in its purpose. Housed in a heritage building are 300 motorcycles from over 60 manufacturers dating back as far as 1902, including custom-built designs by NZ's John Britten, a large exhibition of Brough Superiors, and the only tandem motorcycle ever made. The new Begg Bunker displays 16 of the 18 cars that NZ racecar builder George Begg designed, while the top floor has an exhibit dedicated to the women of motorbiking and racing. As with Transport World, the bathrooms are a must-see.

25 Tay St. motorcyclemecca.nz. ✆ **0800/151-252** in NZ. NZ$40 adults, NZ$20 ages 5–14, family pass NZ$100. Daily 10am–5pm.

PARKS & GARDENS

Right by the **Te Unua Museum of Southland,** 108 Gala St. (teunua.nz; ✆ **03/211-1777**), currently under construction and expected to open sometime in 2027, you'll find the main entrance to **Queens Park** ♥, a cool, green 80-hectare (200-acre) oasis. It's a perfect place to wander or let the kids run loose. You'll find formal rose gardens, a rhododendron walk, an iris garden, a Japanese garden, a wildlife sanctuary, a walk-through bird aviary, duck ponds, tennis courts, and an 18-hole golf course. The aviary has a good parrot collection and is best visited in early morning or late afternoon when the birds are most active. Rose enthusiasts can get their fill at **Anderson Park** ♥, 91 McIvor Rd., the former estate of prominent Invercargill businessman Sir Robert Anderson. The park sports groomed lawns, native tree groves, Georgian gardens, Anderson's grand house, and a replica Māori *whare whakairo* (carved meeting house).

Outdoor Pursuits

BEACHES **Oreti Beach,** 9.5km (6 miles) west of Invercargill, out past the airport, is safe for swimming. This broad expanse of sand stretches from Omaui at the southern end right around to Riverton. Popular with dog walkers, it can get very windy, and there are surf patrols in attendance during summer.

CYCLING Connecting Invercargill to Bluff, the 25km (15.5-mile) **Te Ara Taurapa** pathway may be walked or cycled. Along the way, six interpretative panels tell the story of the Ngāi Tahu tribe's journey in the region.

FISHING Southland has numerous fishing hotspots, many within 30 minutes of Invercargill. The famous **Mataura River** offers some of the world's best trout fishing. The season in most areas opens October 1 and goes to April 30 (there are exceptions, so check the regulation guide available at fishandgame.org.nz). Local guide Graeme Watson of Southland Fly Fishing (southlandflyfishing.co.nz; ✆ **027/430-1398**) will show you the best spots to cast your line.

WALKING **Sandy Point Domain,** 7km (4⅓ miles) west of the city, has 13.5km (8 miles) of attractive walking tracks through totara forest and sand dunes. An hour's drive northwest, the **Tuatapere Hump Ridge Track** ♥♥, 31 Orawia Rd., Tuatapere (humpridgetrack.co.nz; ✆ **027/390-4520**), was added to the Great Walks network in 2024; it's an excellent 3-day walk for those of moderate to high fitness levels, with visitors staying in huts along the way.

Where to Stay in Invercargill

While Invercargill may seem less geared to tourists than other South Island destinations, during the busy summer months it still has high occupancy rates, so book in advance if possible. Accommodations are mainly motels, but upscale hotels are arriving along with the downtown's revitalization. An excellent option is **The Langlands** ♥♥♥, 59 Dee St. (thelanglands.co.nz; ✆ **03/214-0568;** NZ$248–NZ$391 double). Rooms feature local artwork and plush bedding, which you may need to crash on after a night of partying: The

The sleek rooftop bar at The Langlands.

hotel has three bars, including one on the seven-story building's rooftop, with 360-degree views of the surrounding city (it's glorious at sunset). Honestly, it's so nice that you'll forget you're in the Deep South. Also on site: a collection of smart eateries, including a cute Melbourne-lite laneway bar.

Ascot Park Hotel ♥♥, at the corner of Tay Street and Racecourse Road (ascotparkhotel.co.nz; ✆ **03/219-9076**), may not the prettiest building on the block with its clunky 1980s architecture, but for quiet, comfortable accommodations at a very good price (NZ$197–NZ$299 double) and with darn good amenities (indoor pool, sauna, and restaurant), Ascot Park nails it.

The Tower Lodge Motel ♥ (towerlodgemotel.co.nz; ✆ **03/217-6729**), set opposite the city's water tower landmark at 119 Queens Dr., is a pretty standard motel with studio, one-bedroom, and two-bedroom units. What makes it a stand-out is its exceptionally clean rooms, attentive staff, and good location walking distance from restaurants and shops. Plus, the price is right at NZ$135 to NZ$160.

Where to Eat in Invercargill

The main road, Dee Street, has the usual string of decent, medium-range places for dinner, such as excellent Korean food at **Korean Bob ♥**, 146 Dee St. (koreanbob.nz; ✆ **027/935-3833**); a reasonable Kiwi take on Mexican at **Amigos ♥**, 10 Dee St. (amigos.co.nz; ✆ **03/214-0474**); good pizzas and classic Kiwi mains (lamb shanks; fish and chips; whitebait patties) at **Tuatara Cafe & Bar ♥**, 30–32 Dee St. (tuataralodge.co.nz; ✆ **03/214-0954**); and upscale pub meals at **Speight's Ale House ♥♥**, 38 Dee St. (speightsalehouseinv.co.nz; ✆ **03/214-5333**).

Brew'd ♥♥ CAFE On the ground floor of The Langlands Hotel, Brew'd is open at 6:30am, Invercargill's earliest, so it's the place to go when you need a solid breakfast and excellent coffee before hitting the road. It's no last-resort truck stop, though; the food is hearty and thoughtfully presented, and it's a pleasure eating in the fresh wood-and-green interior. It offers a well-stocked cabinet of lighter options, a good seafood chowder, a large range of breakfast eggs (benedict, Florentine, royale, shakshuka), French toast, and "croffles": croissant waffles filled with delights such as strawberry or pistachio mascarpone cream. The young, happy staff are even smiling this early in the morning.

5 Don St. thelanglands.co.nz/brewd. ✆ **03/928-5851.** Main courses NZ$17–NZ$31. Weekdays 6:30am–4pm, weekends 7am–4pm.

The Grille ♥♥ CAFE Though it's located inside Transport World, this isn't your typical museum cafe. The Grille is a destination for Invercargill locals, with its retro-themed space and huge playroom for kids (with a closed door so you can see but not hear them). Expect typical breakfast and lunchtime fare beautifully prepared, from waffles and pancake stacks to burgers or cauliflower soup. Gluten-free and dairy-free options are also available.

491 Tay St. transportworld.co.nz. ✆ **03/217-1202.** Main courses NZ$15–NZ$31. Daily 8am–4pm.

BLUFF

27km (17 miles) from Invercargill

Bluff is known throughout the country for its namesake shellfish, Bluff oysters. One of the few wild oyster beds still producing a yearly harvest, the bounty lies under Foveaux Strait (the stretch of sea separating the mainland from Rakiura/Stewart Island). The flavor of Bluff oysters is briny, and markedly different from that of farmed oysters. The season's duration is determined by the Bluff Oyster Management Company, but it usually opens in March and closes in July. The annual **Bluff Oyster & Southland Seafood Festival ♥♥♥** is held between late April and May (bluffoysterfest.co.nz).

Apart from oysters, Bluff/Motupōhue is known as the southernmost town in NZ. It's the departure point for ferries to Rakiura/Stewart Island (although if you are sailing from Bluff to Stewart Island, you'll be better off staying overnight in Invercargill, which has a wider range of hotels and restaurants). Bluff is also the end of Te Araroa or "the Long Pathway," a hiking trail that starts in at the top of the North Island in Cape Reinga and takes around 4 to 5 months to complete. If you see a scraggly stranger with a pack arriving at **Stirling Point** (the trail's official end), offer to buy them a beer—they may have hiked 3,000km (1,865 miles) to get there. Shorter walks are also available, such as the **Foveaux Walkway,** a 2-hour hike around Bluff's rugged coastline. The track begins at Ocean Beach Road and ends at Stirling Point, or vice versa. You can also walk over **Bluff Hill** through wind-groomed vegetation for views of Rakiura/Stewart Island. The 30-minute **Glory Track** starts at Stirling Point and finishes at Gunpit Road.

Bluff oysters.

If you find yourself staying longer in Bluff, you might want to try its top attraction: cage diving with Great White Sharks. **Shark Experience ♥** (sharkexperience.co.nz; ✆ **03/212-7112**) operates from late November through June out of Bluff and dives near Edward Island, Foveaux Strait. A reasonable level of fitness is necessary, and a scuba certification is preferable though not essential, since a scuba introduction is provided before the dive. Day trips run from 7am to 5pm, including time needed to get to the dive area (NZ$599); you can also join the tour just to sightsee for NZ$299. A camera with waterproof casing is recommended.

Where to Stay & Eat in Bluff

Lands End Boutique Hotel ♥♥ This is as far as the road goes; SH1 ends (or starts) here. So this small hotel, big on style and comfort, is also wonderfully serene. Spacious en-suite bedrooms (super-comfortable beds) and sea views also recommend it. The Oyster Cove Café is next door (see below), or host Lynda Jackson will happily recommend Bluff eateries if guests want to explore.

SH1, 10 Ward Parade, Stirling Point. landsendhotel.co.nz. ✆ **03/212-7575.** 5 units. NZ$347–NZ$417 double. Rates include breakfast. Free parking. **Amenities:** Free Wi-Fi.

Oyster Cove Café and Bar ♥ SEAFOOD The hospitality and freshness of the seafood makes this a crowd-pleaser. We recommend anything/everything that features blue cod, bluff oysters, or mussels. Be aware that "mutton bird" is not a type of flying sheep but the young of a variety of gull. It's a local delicacy—and an acquired taste. Oyster Cove is open mostly for lunch and has limited evening hours (dinner is served Thurs–Sun until 6pm in winter).

SH1, 8 Ward Parade, Stirling Point. oystercove.co.nz. ✆ **03/212-8855.** Main courses NZ$18–NZ$33. Dinner reservations essential. Mon–Wed 10:30am–3pm, Thurs–Sun 10:30am–7pm (longer in summer; call ahead for hours).

TJ's Kitchen ♥♥♥ SEAFOOD & BURGERS Takeout fare moves up a notch when you get burgers as juicy and overloaded as these; there are more than a dozen options, along with heavily loaded fries. Grab a parcel of steaming, fresh battered oysters in season; you won't get as close to the catch as this, and they can be elusive menu options depending on weather and the catch.

42 Gore St. ✆ **03/212-7391.** Burgers NZ$15–NZ$20; oyster prices (seasonal) at least NZ$3 per oyster. Daily 11am–7pm.

RAKIURA/STEWART ISLAND

30km (19 miles) SW of Bluff, across the Foveaux Strait

Anyone who tries to visit Stewart Island in a day won't be giving this near-perfect place a chance. It is a cliché to call it one of NZ's best-kept secrets, but it probably deserves this label more than any other place in the country.

NZ's third island is far bigger than most people imagine; with an area of 1,680 sq. km (655 sq. miles), it is about the size of Singapore or Fiji. Only 3% of the island is inhabited—the rest is untouched native bush, exquisite white- and golden-sand beaches, bird sanctuaries, and rugged mountains. All this makes it a naturalist's and hiker's paradise, and the perfect place for a remote yet accessible holiday. However, it's perhaps most well known as one of the best places to see a kiwi in the wild; 13,000 of the country's 68,000 kiwi call Stewart Island home. In fact, the "wild" can include spotting one on the streets while out for an evening stroll.

The main village of **Oban** is your landing point, and where the human population (approx. 390) lives. Most permanent residents are involved in

A secluded beach on Rakiura/Stewart Island.

commercial fishing or tourism, while a small number of other Kiwis have invested in holiday homes (or "cribs," as they're called in Southland).

Originally called *Te Punga o Te Waka a Maui* by Māori, which translates as "the Anchorstone of Maui's Canoe," Stewart Island is more commonly known as Rakiura, which means "the great and deep blushing of Te Rakitamau," an early Māori chief. It now refers to the vivid colors of dawn and twilight and the Aurora Australis, which can sometimes be seen from this Dark Sky Sanctuary.

Today, the island community carefully protects its amazing natural heritage. This is Aotearoa the way it used to be—a place where native birds will land within inches of your teacup—and should not be overlooked. If you only have 1 night to spare, Rakiura is certainly possible, but it's best to set aside 2 to 3 nights to fully take it in.

Note: The village is open to tourism during the summer months (from roughly Sept–May), and all but shutters in the winter, when locals seek out warmer shores. If you arrive between June and August, many restaurants, hotels, and tour operators will be on hiatus.

Essentials

ARRIVING

BY PLANE Air transport is provided by **Stewart Island Flights** (stewartislandflights.co.nz; ✆ **0800/737-000** in NZ) from Invercargill Airport/Stewart Island Airport. The round-trip fare is NZ$274 adults, NZ$175 children. **Stewart Island Helicopters** (stewartislandhelicopters.com; ✆ **0800/234-890** in NZ) offers scenic flights, transfers to/from Bluff (NZ$480 per person), and charter flights for hikers and hunters.

BY BOAT The passenger-only ferry, operated by **Real NZ** (realnz.com; ✆ **03/212-7660**), will take you from Bluff to Stewart Island in an hour. Ferry times vary with seasons, but summer sees at least three runs a day, with at

ROUGH sailing

If you're taking the ferry, know that Foveaux Strait is one of the most unpredictable passages in the world, and seas can be extremely rough. If you're prone to seasickness, come prepared. (There's a pharmacy a short walk from the ferry docks in Bluff at 128 Gore St. that sells motion sickness medication. Ask for "Sea Legs"; they work remarkably well.) It may be only a 1-hour trip, and the large catamaran boats are known for their stability in rough seas, but the swells can be huge. Because bookings are heavy for flights, it's not always possible to swap the ferry return trip for a flight, but the "ferry one-way, fly one-way" option can be booked ahead. This gives you two perspectives and eliminates a difficult water crossing if the oceans are up.

least two in winter. The ferry deposits you on the wharf at Oban within a few hundred meters of the center of the small village. One-way fares are NZ$135 adults, NZ$69 children. Secure car and campervan parking (extra cost) is available near the Bluff ferry terminal.

GETTING AROUND

Most things on the island are within walking distance, though reaching some spots will mean an uphill walk. You can rent cars (NZ$125 a day; expect to pay a premium on fuel), electric bikes, and motor scooters from the **Stewart Island Visitor Terminal** (realnz.com), on the wharf. **Stewart Island Electric Bikes,** 4 Main Rd. (stewartisland-electricbike-hire.co.nz; ✆ **020/4023-8155**), also rents e-bikes for $72.50 per half-day. Charter boats and water taxis can be arranged for sightseers, hunters, divers, trampers, and fishermen; you can make reservations for these at the visitor terminal too.

VISITOR INFORMATION

The **Stewart Island Visitor Terminal,** 12 Elgin Terrace (realnz.com; ✆ **03/219-1400**), in the Red Shed, is open daily 9am to 4pm. However, be aware that it's not an isite and is operated by a private tour company with a vested interest in making sales: **Stewart Island Experience.** (More on it below.) You can also visit the **Department of Conservation (DOC) Rakiura National Park Visitor Centre,** 15 Main Rd. (doc.govt.nz; ✆ **03/219-0009**), for hut passes, emergency locator beacons, and information on the best short, half-day, full-day, and multi-day walks. It has knowledgeable staff, a mini-museum, and an area for watching DVDs on rainy days. It's open weekdays 8:30am to 4:30pm and Saturdays 9:30am to 2:30pm.

Exploring Stewart Island/Rakiura

A new heritage center houses the voluminous collection of the **Rakiura Museum Te Puka o Te Waka ♥**, Main Rd. (rakiuramuseum.co.nz; ✆ **03/219-1221**), which has some 5,000 artifacts and items showcasing the island's history, from early Māori settlements through to later endeavors such as whaling, tin mining, timber milling, and commercial fishing. The museum is typically open from 10am to 4pm (to 3pm on weekends and in winter), but check ahead for hours.

Another rainy-day activity is watching the 40-minute *A Local's Tail* film at the **Bunkhouse Theatre ♥**, 10 Main Rd. (bunkhousetheatre.co.nz; ✆ **027/867-9381**). Narrated by Lola the dog, it's a quirky film about Stewart Island's history. Don't expect high production values, but do expect to be entertained. It's NZ$25 per person and shows on request (minimum 2 people) so bookings are essential, either by phone or via bunkhousetheatre@gmail.com. Other films are on offer, too, though the theater is closed in winter.

WALKING & HIKING

Stewart Island offers unparalleled walking and hiking opportunities, with 150 miles (240km) of tracks. Trampers will enjoy undisturbed native vegetation and see hundreds of birds. It is important to remember that rain falls on Stewart Island about 275 days of the year, so bring good waterproof clothing and expect mud. The weather is very changeable, often swinging from rain to warm sun in the space of an hour. Track surfaces are varied and include long sections of boardwalk, which protects the native vegetation. The DOC visitor center in Oban (see "Visitor Information," above) sells hut passes and provides trail maps.

Money Business

There are no banks on the island itself; the nearest bank is in Invercargill. Most Stewart Island businesses have debit and credit card facilities, and there is an ATM at the 4 Square supermarket.

Comfortable huts are conveniently spaced along the tracks (ranging in size from 6 to 24 bunks), but they're packed in summer. There's a 2-night maximum stay in any one hut, and you can use tents as well. You will be fined if you are found using the huts without paying fees.

One of DOC's Great Walks of New Zealand, the 36km (22-mile) **Rakiura Track ♥♥♥** follows the open coast, climbs over a 300m (980-ft.) forested ridge, and traverses the sheltered shores of Paterson Inlet. The track requires a moderate fitness level and can be comfortably hiked in 3 days, year-round. Huts cost NZ$66 per person per night, campsites NZ$28 per person per night during the Great Walks season (Oct–Apr); fees are less the rest of the year.

The **North West Circuit ♥♥** requires a much greater level of fitness and is recommended for experienced trampers, who need to be completely self-sufficient and prepared for 7 hours of tramping a day for 10 days. This track has long stretches of mud and is dangerous once snow falls. It takes in the northern third of the island and the island's highest peak, Mount Anglem (980m/3,200 ft.). Likewise, the **Southern Circuit,** which can be added to the above or done separately, is a wilderness experience that requires 6 to 7 days of tramping.

Stewart Island Day Walks range from 15 minutes to 7 hours and spread out in a number of directions from Oban. They include comfortable walks to Observation Rock, Golden Bay, Lonneckers Bay, Lee Bay, and Ringaringa

Sighting an endearing *tauhou* in the native forest on predator-free Ulva Island, on a tour with Ulva Island Explorer.

Beach (a great spot for shell hounds when the tide is right), and longer walks to Māori Beach (7-hr. round-trip) and Garden Mound (5-hr. round-trip). Another option is to walk one way and then order a water taxi home.

Ulva Island ♥♥♥ is one of the best soft-core walking experiences of all. It's a short boat trip to somewhere close to paradise—a predator-free island home to endangered and vulnerable birds, including titipounamu/rifleman, tīeke/South Island, and kiwi. Take a tour (see "Organized Tours") or catch a water taxi to the island (NZ$30 adults/NZ$20 child round-trip for two or more people from Golden Bay, which is a 20-min. walk over the hill from Oban). There are walks from 20 minutes to 3 hours. You can spend several hours on the island—and if you're a keen photographer or naturalist, you'll want to—and arrange your return pickup with the water taxi when you land.

ORGANIZED TOURS

All the tours mentioned below are run by **Stewart Island Experience** (realnz.com; ✆ **03/212-7660**), which is owned by **RealNZ.** While I encourage visitors to book with local and family-owned operators whenever possible, the service RealNZ offers on the island is exceptional; if you've only got 1 night, all its tours and ferries are timed to allow you to transfer with ease. It's possible to do the Village, Ulva Island, and Wild Kiwi Encounter tour all in 1 day.

SPOTTING the national icon

Rakiura is considered one of the best places in the country to see a kiwi in the wild, which is partially a numbers game—the island is home to an estimated 20,000 of the country's 70,000 kiwi. A subspecies of the southern brown kiwi, the Rakiura tokoeka is unusual in that it's also active in the daytime. However, night is the best time to spot these endangered birds, either deep in the bush, on beaches foraging for insects among the kelp, or even in town on Oban's sports field. To increase your likelihood of seeing one, your best bet is to book a tour with experts who know how to hear (and spot) them. **Stewart Island Wild Kiwi Encounter ♥♥♥** (stewartislandexperience.co.nz; ✆ **03/ 212-7660**) starts at the ferry terminal with a short, but very thorough presentation on their ecology and behavior. Afterwards, you'll board a catamaran headed for a boat access–only reserve, with opportunities to see yellow-eyed penguins en route. Once there, there's no guarantee that you'll see any kiwis—entirely wild, the birds aren't banded or tracked—and it can feel a bit like a game of silent follow-the-leader with flashlights. But the guides are expertly tuned to the sound of kiwis shuffling in the dark, and will do their best to spot one for you. Operating from October to May, it costs NZ$259 for ages 15 and over.

A 90-minute small bus tour of Oban village and the surrounding bays, the **Village & Bays Tour ♥** touches on the area's history, but mainly focuses on the contemporary culture and challenges of living on an isolated island. It is a bit of a quick "tiki" tour, but a great option if you've just arrived or are looking for an activity on a rainy day (NZ$59 adults, NZ$29 children 5–15).

Ulva Island Explorer ♥♥♥ is a 2½-hour taster tour of the predator-free island for those short of time, or who want a guided walk before returning to explore again on their own. Leaving from the ferry wharf at Halfmoon Bay, it includes a ferry cruise that hugs the shore for sightings of old whaling stations, early settlers' huts, and boatbuilding endeavors. On Ulva, a guide takes the group along well-formed tracks at a leisurely pace through native forest and bush with birdlife fluttering ahead, behind, and over (NZ$145 adults, NZ$75 ages 5–14).

Where to Stay on Stewart Island/Rakiura

Holiday rentals are available through bookabach.com/Vrbo.com and airbnb.com, and can be the smart way to go in these parts, especially because dining out options are so limited.

Observation Rock Lodge ♥♥♥ Hoping to spot the Aurora Australis, or Southern Lights, while you're this far south? Here's your top option—the lodge's bedrooms, decks, and lounge face southwest, giving you prime viewing in comfort. Host Annett not only keeps a close eye on the aurora forecast but also serves up delicious meals for guests both morning and evening (she's

Guest rooms are set up to maximize the panoramic views at Observation Rock Lodge.

a trained chef, and it shows). There are friendly local birds, plentiful advice on things to do, and panoramic mountain and water views catching both sunrise and sunset. This may well be the best place you stay in all of New Zealand.

7 Leonard St., Halfmoon Bay. observationrocklodge.co.nz. ✆ **027/444-1802.** 3 units. NZ$495–NZ$1,275, including add-ons (meals, tours). Rates include free ferry/airport transfers. No credit cards. **Amenities:** Outdoor bathtub; sauna; free Wi-Fi.

South Sea Hotel ♥ A Stewart Island icon thanks to its longevity and good looks, this waterfront hotel has been featured on countless postcards for years. Lodging options range from backpacker rooms with shared facilities to self-contained motel units.

Halfmoon Bay, 3-min. walk from ferry wharf. southseahotel.co.nz. ✆ **03/219-1059.** 42 units. NZ$90–NZ$230 double. **Amenities:** Cafe; bar; free Wi-Fi.

Stewart Island Lodge ♥♥ Spot this from the jetty and you will hope that it's where you're staying. Perched high on the hill—with views to match—it oozes comfort with wide verandas and huge windows facing the sea. Promise becomes reality as you and your bags are transported up the (steep) hill. (Be aware that if you're booked on a nighttime kiwi encounter, you'll have to hike uphill back home to bed.) Bedrooms are oversized, with a walk-in dressing room, and open to a shared balcony/veranda. The light-filled guest lounge is the perfect place for stargazing, and there's a shared kitchen for preparing meals.

14 Nicol Rd., Oban. stewartislandlodge.co.nz. ✆ **03/249-6000.** 6 units. NZ$565 double. 2-night min. stay, children 12+ only. Rates include breakfast and free airport/ferry transfers. Closed June–Aug. **Amenities:** Kitchen; BBQ; laundry; free Wi-Fi.

Where to Eat on Stewart Island/Rakiura

Eating options are very limited on Rakiura. If you plan on staying longer than 2 nights, or if your accommodations don't offer food as part of the package, it pays to choose lodging with a kitchen and arrive with groceries bought in Invercargill. (There is a grocery store on the island, but its prices reflect its remote location.)

KaiKart Takeaways ♥ (facebook.com/kaikartSI; ✆ **027/330-4044**) is a mobile caravan on Ayr Street, Oban, beside the museum and school. Its fish and chips are many visitors' favorite takeout, closely followed by venison burgers. KaiKart is generally open for a couple of hours at lunch and dinner during the summer; check its Facebook page for hours. Prices range from NZ$5 to NZ$20.

If you want to eat at the waterfront **South Sea Hotel** ♥, 26 Elgin Terrace (southseahotel.co.nz; ✆ **03/219-1059**), the epicenter of the village, you'll need a dinner reservation. Expect friendly bar service, seafood, and a Sunday-night pub quiz that is louder, funnier, and ruder than most visitors expect (Prince Harry was a keen participant at one point). It's open for breakfast, lunch, and dinner, with dinnertime mains costing between NZ$26 and NZ$46.

The Snuggery, 9 Elgin St. (facebook.com/thesnuggeryrakiura), is a cozy cafe with retro living room vibes. Closed over winter, it does a deservedly roaring trade with locals and visitors in summer (Tues–Sat 8am–3:30pm). The region's famed cheese rolls are a specialty, and there's occasional live music and other events.

17

PLANNING YOUR TRIP TO NEW ZEALAND

A small country overflowing with sights and activities, New Zealand has the welcome mat out at all times. This chapter has been designed to smooth your journey to Aotearoa, providing the lowdown on those practicalities that can occasionally trip up the unprepared, such as road rules, cultural etiquette, currency issues, power voltage, even how to catch a cab. As ever, it is simply a matter of knowing what to expect.

ENTRY REQUIREMENTS

Passports & Visas

A **passport** is required for all entering visitors, and it must be valid for at least 3 months beyond your departure date from New Zealand.

Canada, France, Germany, Ireland, the Netherlands, and the U.S. are a few of the dozens of countries that have **visa-waiver arrangements** with NZ allowing a stay for up to 3 months. Australian citizens do not need visas. U.K. passport holders who can produce evidence of the right to reside permanently in the U.K. can be granted a visitor visa for up to 6 months upon arrival.

While visitors from visa-waiver countries do not require a visa, they must apply for an **NZeTA (New Zealand Electronic Travel Authority)** before they travel. This includes those entering on cruise ships. NZeTA's may be acquired for NZ$17 on the free NZeTA app or NZ$23 if completed online at nzeta.immigration.govt.nz. You'll also need to pay an international visitor levy (IVL), which costs NZ$100. It takes between 10 minutes and 72 hours for applications to be processed.

For further information of visa-waiver countries or general queries on work or study visas, contact a New Zealand embassy or consulate or **New Zealand Immigration** (immigration.govt.nz).

Customs

For information on what you're allowed to take into New Zealand, contact **New Zealand Customs Service,** The Customhouse, 17–21

Whitmore St., Box 2218, Wellington, 6140 (customs.govt.nz; ✆ **04/473-6099** or 0800/428-786). ***Warning:*** As an island nation, NZ is extremely strict about biosecurity. A forgotten apple in your luggage will earn you an immediate NZ$400 fine.

For details on what you're allowed to bring home, contact the following:

U.S. Citizens: U.S. Customs & Border Protection (CBP), 1300 Pennsylvania Ave. NW, Washington, DC 20229 (cbp.gov; ✆ **877/287-8667**).

Canadian Citizens: Canada Border Services Agency, Ottawa, Ontario, K1A 0L8 (cbsa-asfc.gc.ca; ✆ **800/461-9999** in Canada, or 204/983-3500).

U.K. Citizens: HM Customs & Excise, Crownhill Court, Tailyour Road, Plymouth, PL6 5BZ (hmce.gov.uk; ✆ **0845/010-9000;** from outside the U.K., 020/8929-0152).

Australian Citizens: Australian Border Force, Customs House, 5 Constitution Ave., Canberra City, ACT 2601 (abf.gov.au; ✆ **1300/363-263;** from outside Australia, 61/2-6275-6666).

GETTING THERE

The cost of getting to New Zealand is likely to be one of your single biggest cash outlays, so it makes sense to shop around. We've done extensive studies at Frommers.com and have found that the websites SkyScanner.com and Momondo.com uncover the lowest prices most consistently. Timing your purchase can also make a big difference, in terms of the cost. The sweet spot for booking airfares to New Zealand was 6 to 8 weeks before the flight, again, according to our studies. Also check out the travel offers listed for your country of origin on the Tourism New Zealand website, **newzealand.com**.

By Plane

Air New Zealand (airnewzealand.co.nz; ✆ **0800/737-000** in NZ) is the dominant airline on the U.S.–NZ Pacific route. Nonstop flights operate from Los Angeles, San Francisco, Houston, Honolulu, and New York. From Asia, several airlines, including Air New Zealand and **Singapore Airlines** (singaporeair.com), fly direct to New Zealand. From Australia many airlines have connecting services from Europe, India, Asia, and South and North America. From the wider Pacific, **Air Tahiti Nui** (airtahitinui.com), **Fiji Airways** (fijiairways.com), and Air New Zealand have direct flights to New Zealand. From Europe, **Emirates** (emirates.com) generally has the most direct options via Dubai.

Auckland Airport (aucklandairport.co.nz; ✆ **0800/247-767** in NZ or 09/275-0789) is the major hub for most airlines arriving in New Zealand, followed by **Christchurch International Airport** (christchurchairport.co.nz; ✆ **03/353-7777**). If you plan to spend most of your time in the South Island, it makes sense to fly into Christchurch, but depending on your airline, you may have to fly into Auckland and then transfer to domestic flights to other centers. If connecting or flying directly from Australia, you can also find nonstop flights from major Australian cities to **Queenstown Airport** (queenstown airport.co.nz; ✆ **03/450-9031**). Budget carrier **Jetstar** (jetstar.com) offers direct flights to **Hamilton Airport** (hamiltonairport.co.nz) from the Gold Coast and Sydney.

Airline prices vary according to seasonal demand as well as capacity. New Zealand's **peak tourist season** is December through February; **shoulder season** is usually regarded as from March to May, and later in the year September and October. **Low season** runs from April through to August, except for those areas that have ski/snow seasons.

By Boat

New Zealand is a popular **cruise ship destination,** though visits have declined by more than 40% in the last few seasons. (Cunard, for instance, has cancelled most of its NZ cruises in 2026, apparently because of the country's strict biosecurity rules for ship hulls.) Many cruises coming to New Zealand also visit Australia and typically range in length from 5 to 18 days. Cruise ports include **Bay of Islands, Auckland, Tauranga, Napier, Wellington, Christchurch (Lyttelton), Akaroa, Dunedin (Port Chalmers),** and **Milford Sound (Fiordland National Park).** You can fly to Australia or New Zealand to join a cruise (many start from Sydney or Brisbane), or you can take a segment on a world cruise that includes New Zealand.

Cruise lines with New Zealand on their itineraries include but aren't limited to **Carnival** (carnival.com; ✆ 800/764-7419); **Cunard** (cunard.com; ✆ 800/728-6273); **Regent Seven Sea Cruises** (rssc.com; ✆ 877/505-5370), **Royal Caribbean** (royalcaribbean.com; ✆ 305/341-0204) **Princess Cruises** (princess.com; ✆ 800/774-6237); and **Oceania Cruises** (oceaniacruises.com; ✆ 800/531-5619).

GETTING AROUND

By Plane

Air New Zealand (airnewzealand.co.nz; ✆ **0800/737-000** in NZ, or 64/9/357-3000) is the dominant domestic carrier, linking many of the smaller centers (such as Invercargill and Napier) to main hubs. Discount airline **Jetstar** (jetstar.com; ✆ **0800/800-995**) has regular scheduled flights between Auckland, Wellington, Christchurch, and Dunedin. Other smaller regional airlines operate on internal routes; see the "Arriving" sections in individual destination chapters for details.

Air New Zealand regularly offers packages and deals on its site; its **Grabaseat** website (grabaseat.co.nz) is where you'll find the cheapest seats available for domestic flights. Grabaseat is also available as an app, with customized alerts to price drops or real-time sales.

By Car, Motorcycle, or RV

To travel into the heartland and to roam the big spaces, it's necessary to hit the road, either via coach (bus) or by driving a rental car, motorcycle, or motorhome. If the holiday is planned around only three or four destinations, combining air travel with a self-drive rental could be the best choice.

New Zealand's road network encompasses State Highway One (SH1), which runs the length of both islands, and a number of regional highways. Two-lane highways are the norm, with four-lane motorway sections near Auckland, Hamilton, Wellington, Christchurch, and Dunedin. Motorway sections are likely to be paved with smooth asphalt, but other highways/roads have a rough surface of chipped stones sealed with a film of bitumen. Most international drivers find it rougher and noisier than expected. Many roads have unpaved shoulders, so drivers must take care not to drift off the sealed surface. Expect gravel roads in rural/farmland areas.

Unfortunately, Kiwi motorists have a reputation for aggressive driving and tailgating, but strict policing is having its effect.

Petrol (gas) prices fluctuate greatly and vary significantly by location, but tend to sit on the higher side of the spectrum. At press time, gas cost around NZ$2.35 per liter for regular gas (91 octane) and NZ$1.87 per liter for diesel. Service (gas) stations have clear displays of prices. Note that prices are per liter, not per gallon.

Most major town and cities have **metered street parking** accepting payment by coins, credit card, or via mobile phone app. Instructions are marked clearly on each meter. If metered times are exceeded, the fines are heavy.

RENTING A CAR

Having a car is a great way to see the country. Every major city has rental car companies, including local companies (see below) and international brands such as **Avis** (avis.com), **Budget** (budget.com), **Hertz** (hertz.com), and **Thrifty** (thrifty.com). Most accept overseas booking.

Visitors planning to self-drive a rental car or motorhome (RV) should be over 21 years of age, although some firms require a minimum of 23 years and a maximum of 75 years. A valid overseas drivers' license or an international license is required.

Rental car agencies use **dynamic pricing,** so you will see a wide range of costs dependent on how far in advance you book, the demand, and the season. Cars in NZ are required to get a roadworthy certificate or warrant of fitness annually, so even those in the budget range should be in reasonable working order. Inclusions are not a given, but at an average of NZ$25 per day for a high-mileage used compact car, what you see is pretty much what you get. The newer, late-model rental cars from international firms (Hertz, Budget, Avis) average around NZ$100 a day, but discounts are often available depending on seasonal availability and length of rental. Daily rates can range from NZ$55 (e.g., Toyota Yaris) to NZ$107 (Toyota Corolla) a day. During the high-season months of December through March, don't expect too many discounts and always make sure to double-check how many kilometers are included. **Vroom Vroom Vroom** (vroomvroomvroom.co.nz) is a reliable cost-comparison and booking site for all of the country's major car and caravan rental agencies

Recommended local firms include **Jucy** (jucy.co.nz; ✆ **0800/500/079** in NZ), which has a range of vehicles, from el cheapo compacts from NZ$38 a

RULES FOR safer driving

You don't need a special driver's license to drive in NZ—you can typically use a valid overseas permit or an international license. But don't arrive unprepared. You'll hear this many times during your trip, but the **roads here *are* different.** They're often narrow and winding, with mountain ranges to traverse and countless one-way bridges. And that's not even taking into consideration rain, snow, ice, or other weather hazards that may slow down your travel! Drive times are not to be underestimated. (Always budget more time than your mapping app suggests.) Here are some of the road rules—and etiquette tips—that will help keep you safer on NZ roads.

- Drive on the left. Keep left.
- Wearing a **seatbelt** is compulsory.
- Speed limits are in **kilometers per hour.** On highways, the limit will generally be 100kmph or 110kmph, while in built-up areas such as towns or cities, it will be 50kmph, although lower speed limits may be signposted. Watch out for 80kmph areas, as police cameras are often set up in these spots.
- Do **not pass on solid yellow lines** or at any time the driver cannot see a clear road for 100m.
- No turning is allowed on **red traffic lights.**
- It is illegal to use a mobile phone while driving in NZ.
- All **one-way bridges** are clearly signposted as to who should give way. If you have a small red arrow in your direction (vs. a larger black or white arrow) you must yield to oncoming traffic. These bridges exist even on major roads, so pay close attention to signs that indicate you're approaching one.
- At **roundabouts,** always yield to cars coming from the right.
- If it's dark, raining, or foggy, **turn on your headlights.** This is required by law at any time when you can't clearly see a person or vehicle 100 meters away.
- If you are driving **under the speed limit,** it's common courtesy to use passing lanes to allow other drivers to safely pass. If no passing lane exists, use the road pull-outs or laybys accordingly. This is also the safest course of action if you've got a tailgater on your bumper. If someone allows you to pass in this fashion, it's common practice to give them a quick "thank you" wave or beep with your horn.
- **Check NZTA for live road updates** before you depart (nzta.govt.nz/traffic-and-travel-information). Road closures are frequent during the summer construction months and due to inclement weather.
- Road signs, markings, and rules will be slightly different from what you're familiar with. Before you hit the road, take the free **Tourist Driving Test** at driving tests.co.nz/roadcode/tourist.

day to upmarket 4WDs from NZ$95 a day. Prices can be considerably higher in summer. Jucy has airport locations in Auckland, Christchurch, and Queenstown. **GO Rentals** (gorentals.co.nz; ✆ **09/974-1598**) is one of the country's largest independent car rental agencies, with rates that tend to be in the middle of the market. GO has locations in Auckland, Waiheke Island, Wellington, Nelson, Christchurch, Dunedin, and Queenstown.

If your schedule is flexible, you may be able to save big using relocation agent **Transfer Car** (transfercar.co.nz). It advertises deals on one-way car and campervan hire with major rental agencies, often for as little as NZ$1 per day.

A final suggestion: The website **AutoSlash.com** tracks prices once a reservation is made on it, and will rebook you if prices drop at the less expensive rate. The editor of this guide saved several hundred dollars on a New Zealand rental this way.

RENTING A MOTORHOME (RV)

For holidays free of worries about lodging and transportation, consider renting a motorhome or campervan. Recreational vehicles (RVs) range from basic vans with a bed in the back to multi-berth units with toilets and kitchens. Before you make your booking, it's important to determine how much space you need, as well as whether you plan to freedom camp. If so, the unit you rent will need to be certified as self-contained. (See box below for the definitions of *freedom camping* and *self-contained.*)

As with car rentals, it pays to reserve in advance. Post-pandemic, campervan agencies are still rebuilding their fleets and also rely on dynamic pricing, which means that rental costs can range from NZ$75 per day to NZ$500 per day. Renters should also be aware of **road user charge recovery fees** for diesel vehicles, which typically is not included in online quotes. A mandatory government fee, it's usually passed from rental agencies onto renters, and is typically between NZ$0.07 and NZ$0.09 per kilometer. Some rental agencies will incorporate a flat road user charge recovery fee into add-on packages

Freedom Camping

If you're looking to cut costs on your accommodation, look no further than freedom camping! Throughout New Zealand, camping in your vehicle is permitted at no cost in designated areas. There are over 500 free campsites across the country, from spots in a busy parking lot to beautiful beachside sites.

However, freedom camping puts pressure on environments and communities, so there are strict conditions. First, most regions require that your vehicle is "fully self-contained," meaning that you can live in it for 3 days without getting more water or dumping waste. Certified self-contained vehicles will have a sticker on the rear window or bumper verifying its status. (Most motorhome rentals come equipped with these stickers.) Secondly, you may only freedom camp in designated areas for a specified period of time, which varies by each local government council.

It can be difficult to navigate each council's website, so download the **Rankers** (rankers.co.nz) or **Campermate** apps (campermate.com). In addition to listing free and budget campgrounds with user reviews, these apps also map out dump sites, public restrooms, water sources, and fuel stations. (Facilities at freedom campsite are very basic or altogether nonexistent, so it's important to know what's nearby.)

Finally, always have a back-up plan. The most popular sites fill up early in the day (they are free, after all!), meaning you might need to be prepared to drive on to the next one.

(which, in addition to insurance, include extras like picnic chairs), which can add up to cost savings depending on how far you intend on driving.

Major mid-range companies with depots in Auckland, Christchurch, and Queenstown include **Jucy** (jucy.co.nz; ✆ **0800/500-079** in NZ), **Britz** (britz.co.nz; ✆ 0800/081-042), **Maui** (maui-rentals.com; ✆ **0800/688-558**), and **Travellers' Autobarn** (travellers-autobarn.co.nz; ✆ 0**800/348-348;** in Auckland and Christchurch only). **Wilderness** (wilderness.co.nz; ✆ **09/282/3606**) offers slightly higher-end options, with locations in Auckland and Christchurch. You can also hire privately owned vans and motorhomes from **Camplify** (camplify.co.nz), which is like Airbnb for RVs.

Vroom Vroom Vroom (vroomvroomvroom.co.nz) offers cost-comparison and booking services for all of NZ's major campervan and motorhome rental agencies. **Rankers** (rankers.co.nz) is another good place to compare campervan quotes. Relocation agent **Transfer Car** (transfercar.co.nz) advertises one-way campervan hire with major rental agencies, often for as little as NZ$1 per day, which can be a great deal if your schedule is flexible.

By Taxi or Ride Share

Taxi stands featuring a number of different licensed taxi companies are located at all transport terminals and in major shopping and accommodation areas of cities and towns. Driver identification and rates should be clearly displayed. Taxis are unlikely (but not unknown) to respond to being hailed within a quarter-mile of a stand. Drivers don't expect a tip, but if they handle a lot of luggage or perform other special services, a tip will be accepted.

Global ride-sharing services **Uber** (uber.com) and Australian-owned **Ola** (ola.co.nz) are available in major cities across the country, but less likely to be found in small cities and towns. Their local competitor is **Zoomy** (zoomy.co.nz), which has a better track record for paying drivers fairly (and tends to be a bit cheaper). Like all rideshares, these apps charge rates based on dynamic pricing, which means they may be more or less expensive than a taxi, dependent on the time of day and demand.

By Interisland Ferry

Crossing the Cook Strait between the North and South Island by ferry is a classic case of "it's not about the destination, but the journey." Not just a means to an end, it's a scenic and memorable experience. The ferry travels at a slow speed through the Marlborough Sounds, with the potential to sight dolphins and seals. It's a 3-hour, 92km (57-mile) journey.

Two ferry companies operate between Wellington and Picton. The **Interislander** ferry system (interislander.co.nz; ✆ **0800/802-802** in NZ) usually has five or more daily crossings. **Bluebridge Cook Strait Ferry** (bluebridge.co.nz; ✆ **0800/844-844** in NZ) also sails multiple times daily. Ferry facilities include licensed bar, TV lounges, and children's play areas, as well as private cabins if you are willing to pay extra. Both ferries offer a comparable service for roughly the same price, although Bluebridge has slightly smaller ships and

TURNING TO THE internet or apps FOR A HOTEL DISCOUNT

Before going online, it's important that you know what "flavor" of discount you're seeking. Here are several types of discounts, plus advice on booking strategies:

1. **Discounts available via virtual private networks (VPNs).** There's more and more evidence that online consumers get different prices based on what the average income is in the area they live. By disguising your identity and locale with a VPN, and picking a less affluent region to search from, you will likely be shown lower prices on hotel rooms. Note that you will have to get a VPN subscription, but they tend to be quite reasonably priced. ***Tip:*** If you set your VPN to search from Ireland, you will get results in English, and will ensure that ALL fees are listed, because EU law prohibits hidden fees.
2. **Extreme discounts on sites where you bid for lodgings without knowing which hotel you'll get.** You'll find these on such sites as **Priceline.com** ("Express Deals") and **Hotwire.com**, and they can be money-savers, particularly if you're booking within a week of travel (that's when the hotels resort to deep discounts to get beds filled). As these companies use only major chains, you can rest assured that you won't be put up in a dump. For more reassurance, install the Chrome extension **HotelCanary** on that browser. It will identify what hotel is being shown on both Priceline and Hotwire. I think you'll be pleasantly surprised by the quality of many of the hotels that are offering these "secret" discounts.
3. **Discounts on chain hotel websites.** Not long ago, all of the major chains announced they'd be reserving special discounts for travelers who booked directly through the hotels' websites (usually in the portion of the site reserved for loyalty members). They weren't lying: These are the lowest rates at the hotels in question some 80% of the time, though discounts can range widely, from as little as $1 to as much as $50. Our advice: Search for a hotel that's in your price range and ideal location (see below for where to do that) and then, if it is a chain property, book directly through the online loyalty portal.
4. **Savings found by using the right hotel search engine.** They're not all equal, as we at Frommers.com learned after putting the top 20 sites, and 6 AI services, to the test around the globe. We discovered that **Trivago.com** and **Google Travel** both listed the lowest rates most consistently.
5. **Last-minute discounts.** Booking last minute can be a great savings strategy, because prices sometimes drop in the week and days before travel as hoteliers scramble to fill their rooms. But you won't necessarily find the best savings through companies that claim to specialize in last-minute bookings. Instead, use the sites recommended in point 2 of this list.

It's a lot of surfing, I know, but in the hothouse world of hotel pricing, this sort of diligence can pay off.

is perceived as the more "budget" option. Fares depend on the size of your vehicle, your departure time, and the number of passengers. Check both operators' websites for regular specials. Note that high swells and severe winds can affect scheduled departure and arrival times.

During peak season, bookings must be made weeks in advance, particularly if you want to book your car on the ferry. Year-round, it's best to book at least a few days in advance, as all the sailings typically sell out. If you have rented a vehicle, confirm with the rental agency first that ferry crossings are permitted.

By Coach (Bus)

Coach travel is a cost-effective, worry-free way of getting around. Most provide some kind of commentary and stop frequently for refreshments. Smoking is not permitted. **InterCity** (intercity.co.nz; ✆ **09/583-5780** in Auckland, and ✆ **03/377-0951** in Christchurch) operates three-star coaches on New Zealand's most comprehensive coach bus network, visiting some 600 towns and cities, with daily scheduled service. ***Reminder:*** Book coach journeys in advance during peak travel periods (summer and holidays). InterCity's fares are dynamic, meaning the further in advance you book, the cheaper they generally are. Discounts are offered to students, seniors (ages 65 and over), backpackers with valid ID cards, and children.

Shuttles (minivans) offer a transport alternative to/from main centers and to/from tourist hotspots. Fares and schedules vary according to seasonal demand. Check shuttle services at local isite offices.

By Train

Commuter passenger rail networks are incredibly limited in NZ, with long-distance services only offered by **KiwiRail** (kiwirail.co.nz; ✆ **0800/801-070**) between Hamilton and Auckland, and between Palmerston North and Wellington. The good news? The other train journeys that do exist cater primarily to overseas tourists and travel through some of the country's best scenery. KiwiRail operates three major **Great Journeys of New Zealand** (great journeysnz.com; ✆ **0800/872-467;** +64 4 495 0775 overseas) routes: **The Northern Explorer** from/to Auckland and Wellington; **The Coastal Pacific,** to/from Picton and Christchurch; and **The TranzAlpine,** to/from Christchurch and Greymouth. In addition to the day-long scenic adventures, the company also offers guided tours and excursions from the train lines. Journeys start from around NZ$250 for a standard one-way adult fare. The trains including open-air viewing carriages, comfortable seating, and a cafe car.

TIPS ON ACCOMMODATIONS

Throughout New Zealand, you'll see accommodations (and some attractions) boasting about their **Qualmark** (qualmark.co.nz) certification, which is a "mark of quality." This seal means the business has been audited by Tourism New Zealand and offers a professional, trustworthy, or sustainable product or service. Qualmark even comes with its own star rating system. However, Qualmark is voluntary and "pay to play," meaning only those properties that request assessments—and can afford to participate in the certification program—can earn a Qualmark seal of approval. The bottom line: Just because a hotel lacks Qualmark certification doesn't mean it isn't trustworthy or worth visiting!

Pricing: Some bed-and-breakfasts, hostels, and motels have just one or two standard sets of tariffs: Lower rates for the "winter" months (Apr–Sept) and higher rates for the "summer" months (Oct–Mar). Otherwise, **dynamic pricing** is standard practice for accommodations across the country. Also known as surge pricing, this is when prices are adjusted based on demand. For all pricing in the book, I've included the range of what you might expect to pay at the low and high end of dynamic pricing schemes—but rates can become inflated if there is high demand. Finally, **price doesn't guarantee quality:** An NZ$200 hotel could be better than one down the street charging twice its price.

> **A Note on Hotel Prices**
>
> Price ranges for accommodations are based on the following scale:
>
> **Inexpensive** (NZ$40–NZ$150)
> **Moderate** (NZ$150–NZ$350)
> **Expensive** (NZ$350–NZ$2,000 and up)

Note that New Zealand has an across-the-board **legal ban on smoking** in public buildings, including hotels and hotel rooms. It is also a legal requirement that all public buildings have reasonable access for travelers with disabilities, but in the case of B&Bs and backpacker lodgings, it pays to double-check before booking.

HOTELS, MOTELS & B&BS In New Zealand, **a hotel** generally provides a licensed bar and restaurant, and guest rooms do not usually have cooking facilities. When a venue is referred to as a **lodge** it usually means it's a luxury accommodation, often with included meals and/or drinks. **Bed-and-breakfasts** offer rooms and usually access to common areas or gardens. A breakfast (cooked or continental) is included in the rate, and hosts typically live on-site. For options go to bedandbreakfastnz.co.nz. A **pub** is a country hotel that offers more modest accommodations—some rooms may share bathrooms, and meals are often served in the bar. New Zealand also has plenty of independent and franchised **motels** offering affordable and comfortable units with kitchen facilities and parking. You'll almost always get the cheapest rate by booking direct via a provider's website or calling up, rather than on aggregator sites like Booking.com (though that's a good way to compare your options).

HOLIDAY HOMES/BACHES/CRIBS Often called "cribs" or "baches," **holiday homes** are privately owned houses, apartments, or cottages, usually in or near popular tourist destinations. For options check out Bookabach.co.nz (now part of **Vrbo.com**) or Airbnb.com.

HOSTELS & BACKPACKERS Hostels (also called "backpackers") are budget accommodations that can vary from a bunk bed in a dorm room to family rooms and doubles with private bathrooms. Amenities usually include a shared kitchen to prepare meals. The majority of YHA hostels in NZ closed their doors in December 2021; those remaining and operating under the YHA name are all privately owned.

HOLIDAY PARKS & CAMPGROUNDS New Zealand's **holiday parks** are probably the most underrated affordable accommodation option—even if you're not camping or traveling by RV. Many offer glamping, cabins, or other

An Airbnb by Any Other Name

By now, you probably know that **Airbnb** (airbnb.com) and its alternatives, such as **Vrbo** (vrbo.com), are popular the world over. New Zealand is no exception, but if you're after unique accommodation, there are a couple of Kiwi-specific sites that you should familiarize yourself with. Long-standing local holiday-home rental site **Bookabach** (bookabach.co.nz) was recently bought by the same parent company as Vrbo, meaning listings on the two sites overlap, so you can use either. One site that has won many devotees is locally owned **Canopy Camping** (canopycamping.co.nz), a collection of rustic to high-end glamping sites and cabins on private land, usually in stunning wilderness locations or on farms. Generally, the properties (which include geodesic domes, safari tents, and shipping containers) are private and fully self-contained with luxurious details like outdoor bathtubs. They are available exclusively through Canopy Camping's site. Meanwhile, newcomer **Riparide** (riparide.com) is also gaining traction with its curated collection of holiday homes surrounded by nature. As always with holidayhome platforms, check cancellation policy, reviews, amenities, and any extra fees.

self-contained accommodation; some even have their own on-site motels. They also typically include extensive facilities geared to families: playgrounds, swimming pools, barbecue areas, and shared kitchens. Check out **Top 10 Holiday Parks** (top10.co.nz; © **0800/867-836** in NZ) and **Holiday Accommodation Parks New Zealand** (holidayparks.co.nz; © **04/298-3283**).

In contrast, a **"campground"** in NZ tends to be a simple spot where you can pitch your tent or park your RV. There may or may not be staff on-site, and there will likely be basic facilities (an outhouse or flush toilet) but very little else. **DOC** (doc.govt.nz) manages more than 200 campgrounds across the country.

RESPONSIBLE TOURISM

New Zealand has become world-renowned for its innovative sustainable tourism practices. In a response to concerns about overtourism, the NZ government has vowed to shift to a regenerative tourism model. And starting in 2018, New Zealand began asking travelers to commit to **The Tiaki Promise:** a challenge to act as guardians for the country, by caring for its people, environment, and culture. The five core values of The Tiaki Promise are to protect nature, keep NZ clean, be prepared, drive carefully, and show respect. Suggestions for how to meet these values can be found at tiakinewzealand.com.

The following are some of the most critical ways you can help to protect the country.

Protect the Environment

New Zealand's stringent biosecurity laws exist for good reason. One that may seem unusual, however, is that visitors are required to arrive with clean hiking boots and gear. This is, in part, to prevent the spread of **kauri dieback**

disease, which is fatal to the endemic trees. It's spread through soil and there is no cure. You'll find shoe and boot cleaning stations at trailheads across the country. Use them accordingly. More information can be found at kauriprotection.co.nz.

Demonstrate Cultural Respect

If you choose to visit a *marae* or participate in a Māori cultural experience during your visit to NZ, you'll be guided through the correct etiquette—so don't worry about making a mistake! Each *marae* may have slightly different protocol, but generally speaking, you can expect to be met with a pōwhiri or ritual greeting, which may involve a ritual challenge and songs. Do not enter the *marae* grounds until you have been invited in. Once inside, you'll be asked to remove your shoes before entering the *wharenui* (meeting house). Inside, photos may or may not be allowed; ask your hosts first. Finally, do not sit on tables or countertops where food is prepared or served (this includes on outdoor picnic tables), as this is considered offensive.

At some sacred sites, such as Cape Reinga, it's *tapu* (taboo) to consume food or drink (yes, including water). Signs will clearly indicate where eating and drinking is and is not permitted. *Iwi* (tribes) are also increasingly requesting that visitors show respect for sacred mountain peaks by not climbing them, including Mt. Ngāuruhoe (aka "Mt. Doom") in Tongariro National Park. If you're uncertain about what's appropriate, DOC provides site-specific information.

A Word About Drones

The use of drones is heavily regulated through New Zealand due to their impact on wildlife, safety, privacy, and Māori cultural values. You will need permission to fly your drone for recreational or commercial purposes on public land. In some locations, you'll see signs indicating drones aren't allowed. Location-specific permits for flying drones on public lands may be acquired through DOC. In "green" zones, permits cost NZ$207 and are approved immediately online (permits-licences.doc.govt.nz/apply-to-fly-green-zones). In orange and red zones (which include most national parks), permits take longer to process, are more costly, and are rarely approved.

Working Vacations

If you'd like to work during your trip, you'll need to acquire a working holiday permit. There are usually plenty of short-term working opportunities, especially in the summer when orchards, market gardens, and vineyards need part-time workers. Go to **seek.co.nz** or **seasonaljobs.co.nz**. The New Zealand hospitality industry also employs large numbers of working tourists. Details of visa and work permit requirements are available from **New Zealand Immigration** (immigration.govt.nz).

Volunteer Travel, WWOOFing & Housesitting

Committing a day or two of **volunteer work** while you're on vacation is one way to interact with locals and make a positive difference. **DOC,** for example, frequently recruits international volunteers to help with planting native trees and habitat clean-ups. Volunteer opportunities are posted to doc.govt.nz/get-involved/volunteer. (*Note:* You may need to provide a police certificate, and travel insurance is strongly recommended.) If one of these options isn't possible due to your schedule, note that taking a garbage bag to the beach or into the bush and doing a clean-up as you walk is a simple but effective way to give back.

It's important to note that you don't need a special visa to volunteer in NZ, **provided you're not receiving anything in exchange.** So, if you'd like to volunteer in exchange for room and board (an incredibly popular activity across the country), you'll need a valid work visa—like a working holiday visa—in order to do so. If you've got one, you'll find plentiful opportunities on **WWOOF** (World Wide Opportunities on Organic Farms; wwoof.nz), **HelpX.net** (helpx.net), and **Workaway.info** (workaway.info). There are also several Facebook groups connecting volunteers and hosts; one of the biggest is **Volunteer Haven NZ.** Another option is housesitting, which may mean living in other peoples' homes and caring for their pets. Some Facebook groups exist for housesitting in NZ, but **Kiwi House Sitters** (kiwihousesitters.co.nz) is by far the most active housesitting site in the country and the easiest way to find placements, ranging in length from just a couple of nights to months at a time. It costs NZ$89 for an annual membership.

[Fast FACTS] NEW ZEALAND

ATMs ATMs are common and can be found inside and outside banks, in major shopping centers, in supermarkets, and at gas stations. Some smaller towns and remote locations don't have ATMs, but many local retailers will allow you to use a debit card (called EFTPOS) to get cash—though they usually expect you to buy something in exchange.

Business Hours **Banks** are open Monday through Friday 9:30am to 4pm and on weekends in some shopping malls. **Shopping hours** are generally 9am to 5:30pm, with malls and large retail outlets open until 6pm and from 10am on weekends. Many service (gas) stations in larger centers operate 24 hours.

Cellphones Using your own phone on "roam" can be prohibitively expensive. The simplest way to keep in touch is to buy an eSIM (check if your phone is compatible), which are very affordable in NZ. Physical SIM cards are available on arrival at the airport or from a mobile phone provider like **Spark** (spark.co.nz), **Vodaphone** (vodafone.co.nz), or **2degrees** (www.2degrees.nz), The two former providers offer the best coverage. However, the mountainous topography means there are still large areas—even close to cities—where you'll have little to no cellphone reception (so you'll be glad you brought a guidebook!).

Disabled Travelers New Zealand is a relatively good destination for visitors with disabilities. Since 1975, every public building and major renovated structure in the country has been required by law to provide reasonable and adequate access for those with disabilities. In addition, accommodations with five or more units must provide at least one room for guests with disabilities. For general info, see the CCS Disability Action (ccsdisabilityaction.org.nz). For an inclusive directory, visit makingtrax.co.nz.

Drinking Laws The minimum drinking age is 18 in pubs, and proof of age is required if you look under 30. Beer and wine can be purchased from most supermarkets, and spirits, beer, and wine from liquor stores. Wine can also be bought at specialty wine shops and wineries. Police stage random drug and alcohol testing on roads in cities and small towns to check for drinking and driving; you must stop on request and are required to take a breath test.

Electricity The voltage is 230 volts and plugs are of the flat, three-pronged variety (with the top two prongs angled). If you bring a hair dryer, it should be dual-voltage, and you'll need an adapter plug. Most motels and some B&Bs have built-in wall transformers for 110-volt, two-prong razors. Other electrical equipment will require its own transformer.

Emergencies For ambulance, fire, or police, dial 111. (911 will not work.)

Health At the time of publication, **vaccinations** are not required to enter NZ. Make sure your **health insurance** covers you when you're out of the country; if it doesn't, consider buying travel insurance before leaving home. Health insurance is strongly advised because New Zealand's public and private medical/hospital facilities are not free to visitors, except in the event of accidents. New Zealand healthcare includes a no-fault accident scheme that extends to visitors to the country. The Accident Compensation Corporation (ACC) provides coverage in the form of medical expenses and some hospital expenses to visitors who may be injured in an accident.

Visitors arriving with **prescription drugs** should have a doctor's letter or certificate confirming their prescription drug requirements to avoid problems with Customs at point of entry. It is not necessary to pack anti-diarrheal and/or anti-emetic products because these are available over-the-counter in pharmacies—as are most generic prescription drugs for common problems like headaches, coughs, fevers, and flu. Even small towns have a **pharmacy** or chemist shop for OTC remedies, and **medical centers** are available nationwide.

Bugs, Bites & Wildlife Concerns New Zealand has few dangerous animals, but some areas are plagued by wasps in summer, and sandflies all year round. Mosquitos, sandflies, and bush flies (sometimes known as blue-bottles) are best dealt with via personal repellent. Katipo spiders (related to black widows) can inflict painful bites, but these spiders are incredibly rare. Anyone allergic to insect stings/bites should carry antihistamine products. Give marine mammals like sea lions, seals, and orca a wide berth; shark attacks happen but are rare.

Earthquakes & Tsunamis Earthquakes occur daily across NZ, but most are weak and can't be felt. In a more severe earthquake, do not go outside. Drop to the ground (under strong furniture, if possible), and protect your head, neck, and vital organs in a brace position. If you are near the coast and the earthquake is long (more than a minute) and strong (if it's difficult to stand), immediately head inland or to higher ground. More information and advice can be found at getready.govt.nz.

Extreme Weather Extreme weather conditions can spring up out of nowhere. A change in the wind direction can mean gale-force winds, or cold driving southerly storms of hail, even snow in midsummer. Storms in the mountain ranges that divide the North and South Island into West Coast and East Coast regions cause rivers to rise suddenly—hikers planning to be in mountain regions must check in with DOC or track authorities and leave notice of departure/return dates and planned routes. NZ has an excellent Search and Rescue service, but the exercises are expensive and not taken lightly. Go to mountainsafety.org.nz for lots of great resources to help you plan a safe trip. Inclement weather is also known to frequently affect road conditions. Check nzta.govt.nz for road reports.

Sunburn New Zealand's clear air and fierce sun are a dangerous combination, and the country has an extremely high incidence of melanoma. Vacationers should apply a good

WHAT THINGS COST IN NEW ZEALAND

Taxi from the airport to downtown Auckland	NZ$50–NZ$90
Double room, moderate	NZ$150–NZ$350
Double room, inexpensive	NZ$120–NZ$150
Three-course dinner for one without wine	NZ$70–NZ$100
Bottle of beer	NZ$4.50–NZ$10
Cup of coffee	NZ$4.50–NZ$6.50
Admission to most art galleries and museums	NZ$20–NZ$35 for international visitors

sunscreen, wear hats, and keep necks, arms, and backs covered especially between the hours of 11am and 4pm.

Internet & Wi-Fi Many airports, cafes, and stores offer free Wi-Fi access. Most accommodations will offer free Wi-Fi, except in remote areas where access is via satellite. Most **youth hostels** have at least one computer you can use for Internet access. Most **public libraries** offer computers and Internet access for free, as do many **isite visitor centers.**

The dominant telecommunication company, **Spark,** has wireless hot spots throughout the country for Spark users, usually at public phone booths.

LGBTQI+ Travelers Same-sex marriage was legalized in NZ in 2013, and LGBTQI+ travelers should feel at ease across the country, particularly in city centers. Pride events are hosted across the country year-round. The **International Gay and Lesbian Travel Association (IGLTA;** iglta.org) has an online directory of gay- and lesbian-friendly travel businesses and tour operators.

Mail It costs NZ$4.70 to NZ$7.20 (depending on size) to send an airmail letter to the U.S., Canada, U.K., or Europe. Sending parcels is much more expensive, starting from around NZ$40 for a 1-lb. (500g) parcel. Post offices will receive mail and hold it for you for up to 2 months. (Free for the first week.) *Poste Restante* (held mail) service operates in main towns and centers; go to nzpost.co.nz/personal/receiving/manage-my-mail-parcels/poste-restante for details.

Money & Costs Frommer's lists exact prices in the local currency. For daily currency conversions, check at any bank or currency exchange office. ***Tip:*** Use a mix of **cash** and **credit/debit cards** to cover every option on your holiday. Carry enough cash to cover airport incidentals, tipping, and transportation to your hotel, or withdraw money upon arrival at an airport ATM. Ensure that your **ATM card** is compatible with New Zealand systems; the machines generally accept four-digit PINs, but it always pays to check with your bank branch or office before leaving home.

Most businesses take **MasterCard** and **Visa.** American Express and Diners Club are likely to be accepted in resort areas and major cities but not in smaller towns—and sometimes incur extra fees.

THE VALUE OF NZ$ VS. OTHER POPULAR CURRENCIES

NZ$	US$	Can$	UK£	Euro €	Aus$
NZ$1	$.58	C$.79	£.43	€.49	A$.87

Safety New Zealand is one of the world's safest holiday destinations; still, individuals must expect to assume responsibility for personal health and possessions. Street crime—mugging and pickpocketing—is rare, but use common sense and be wary of ill-lit streets or drunken groups. Police do not normally carry guns, but are armed with tasers, sprays, and batons. Policing is by car and in cities by foot patrols. CCTV coverage is widespread. There is concern about the growth of gangs and drug use, particularly on the North Island, so you may see security guards at shops in some areas.

Senior Travel Discounts or "concessions" for those 65 and over are frequently available; inquire when making reservations for lodgings and attractions. Carry photo ID.

Smoking New Zealand has an across-the-board legal ban on smoking in public buildings. It is already widely discouraged in public places (parks, sidewalks, bus shelters) and banned in hospitals, restaurants, trains, planes, buses, and most accommodations. It is not unusual for a smoker to be told to "pick up your butts" if seen smoking in public. Packets of cigarettes currently cost NZ$33, a figure that should only go up. However, a plan to make NZ smoke-free by 2026 now seems unlikely to be met, after the government repealed key legislation.

Student Travel Discounts or "concessions" for students are widely available at attractions and by tour operators. You'll need proof of your student status, such as the **International Student Identity Card** (**ISIC;** isic.org), which qualifies students for substantial savings on rail passes, plane tickets, entrance fees, and more. The ISIC card is accepted by many tourism operators, including hotels, bars, transport providers, theaters, major attractions, and tour companies. Cards issued in the U.S. also provide students with basic insurance.

Taxes A national 15% **Goods and Services Tax (GST)** is a government tax levied on all goods and all services no matter how large or small, including restaurant bills. GST is typically included in advertised prices (rather than added on afterwards).

Time New Zealand is located just west of the International Date Line, and its standard time is 12 hours ahead of Greenwich Mean Time. Thus, when it's noon in New Zealand, it's 7:30am in Singapore, 9am in Tokyo, 10am in Sydney; midnight in London, and 4pm the previous day in San Francisco. In New Zealand, daylight saving time begins in late September and goes to early April.

Tipping Generally speaking, tipping is not customary in New Zealand, with a few caveats: Taxi drivers appreciate a fare being rounded up, as in "Keep the change, driver." Tipping in restaurants is optional, but hospitality staff always appreciate a tip if a meal/drink has been delivered swiftly with care.

Visitor Information The official **Tourism New Zealand** website is **newzealand.com**, where you can get comprehensive details for every aspect of your trip. **I-SITE** is New Zealand's official visitor information network, with more than 60 **isite Visitor Centres** (isite.nz) scattered around the country. These isites provide **free** services and maps, and the staff is friendly and ready to advise and book lodging, activities, travel, tours, and events. **Department of Conservation (DOC)** offices (doc.govt.nz) are staffed by friendly, knowledgeable, and helpful individuals, whose main task is to preserve our conservation areas and national parks. They too are happy to pass on local knowledge and essential visitor information.

Index

See also Accommodations and Restaurant Indexes, below.

General Index

A

Abbey Antiques, 114
Abel Tasman National Park, 383–386
Accommodations, *See also* Accommodations Index
Adrenalin, 140
Adventure Cycles, 89
Air Force Museum of New Zealand, 425
Akaroa, 441–445
Alberton, 85
Alexandra Blossom Festival, 37
Alexandra Park Raceway, 92
All Blacks, 74
Allpress Olive Grove, 124
The Alpine Centre, 250–251
Alps 2 Ocean Cycle Trail, 12, 507
Americarna, 297
Ananda Tours, 122
Anglican Christ Church, 148
Antiques, 114
Aoraki, 501–507
Aotea/Great Barrier Island, 126–131
***The Aotearoa History Show*, 20**
Aotearoa New Zealand International Festival of Arts, 36, 319
Arataki Visitor Centre, 90
Aratiatia Rapids, 232
Architecture, 4–5, 23–24
Arrowtown, 456–458
Arrowtown Autumn Festival, 36
Art, 22–23
Art by the Sea, 84
Art Deco Festival, 36, 279
Arthur's Pass, 445–447
Artists Open Studios Whanganui, 308
Arts Centre, 5, 421
AT Hop card, 72, 120
ATMs, 570
Auckland, 60, 68–119
Abbey Antiques, 114
accommodations, 92–102
Adventure Cycles, 89
air travel, 68–69
Alberton, 85
Alexandra Park Raceway, 92
All Blacks, 74
antiques, 114
Art by the Sea, 84
AT HOP card, 72
attractions, 74–82
Auckland Adventure Jet, 90
Auckland Airport, 68
Auckland Anniversary Day Regatta, 70
Auckland Art Gallery Toi o Tāmaki, 75
Auckland Botanic Gardens, 88
Auckland Bridge Climb, 83
Auckland Domain, 87
Auckland Explorer Bus, 72
Auckland Live, 116
Auckland Marathon, 70
Auckland Sea Kayaks, 82
Auckland Zoo, 75–78
Avondale Market, 115
bars, 117–119
beaches, 85
The Big Foody, 78
Bijoux Gallery, 115
Britomart, 114
bungy jumping, 83
bus travel, 69–70, 72
Butterfly Creek, 86
car travel, 70, 73
casino, 117
Chancery Square, 114
Cheltenham, 85
City Farmers' Market, 115
clubs, 117–119
Commercial Bay, 114
consulates, 73
Cornwall Park, 87
Country Antiques, 114
currency exchange, 73
Customs Street, 71
cycling, 89
dentists, 73
Devonport, 71, 84–85
Devonport Chocolates, 85
Devonport Explorer Tours, 84
Devonport Naval Museum, 85
dining, 103–113
doctors, 73
Dove-Myer Robinson Park, 87
Eden Gardens, 88
Eden Park Tours, 79
Edmund Hillary, 114
embassies, 73
emergencies, 73
Ewelme Cottage, 85
Explore Group. 82
families, 86
fast facts, 73–74
ferries, 72–73
Fingers, 114
food tours, 78
gardens, 87–88
golfing, 90
High Street–Vulcan Lane–O'Connell Street, 114
Highwic, 85
historic houses, 85
horse racing, 92
hospitals, 73–74
jetboating, 90
John Stephens Antiques, 114
Karangahape Road, 71
kayaking, 82, 91
Kelly Tarlton's Sea Life Aquarium, 86
kids, 86
Kura Gallery, 114
LGBTQI+ nightlife, 119
lost property, 74
luggage storage, 74
magazines, 74
markets, 115
Matakana Tours, 78
Matakana Village Farmer's Market, 115
Matariki Festival, 70
Mission Bay/St. Heliers, 71
Mount Eden/Epsom, 71
Museum of Transport and Technology (MOTAT), 79
music, live, 117
Narrow Neck Beach, 85
neighborhoods, 71
New Zealand Maritime Museum, 83–84
Newmarket, 71, 115
newspapers, 74
nightlife, 116–119
Nourishing Nature, 78
Ohen, 115
Otara Market, 115
parks, 87–88
Parnell Rose Garden, 87
Parnell, 71, 115
Pasifika Festival, 70
performing arts, 116–117
Peter Raos Glass Gallery, 85
Piha Surf School, 91
Poi Room, 115
Ponsonby/Herne Bay, 71
post office, 74
Power to the Pedal, 89
public transit, 72
Quay Street, 71
Queen Street, 71, 114
Rainbow's End, 86
Rangitoto Island, 82
rugby, 74, 92
sailing, 91
scooters, 73
shopping, 114–115
Sky Tower, 79–80
SkyCity Auckland Casino, 117
Social Nature Movement, 91
sports, spectator, 92
surfing, 91
swimming, 91
Takapuna, 71
Takarunga/Mount Victoria, 85
Tāmaki Paenga Hira Auckland War Memorial Museum, 80–81
taxis, 73
Te Arai Links, 90
Titirangi, 71
tours, 72, 78, 82, 88–89
train travel, 69–70, 72
Twenty-Seven Names, 114
Unity, 114
Vault, 114
Viaduct Basin, 82–84
visitor information, 70
Waitematā Harbor, 71, 82–84
walking, 92
WE-AR, 115
Wētā Workshop Unleashed, 81–82
wineries, 126–127
Australia–New Zealand Army Corps, 20–21
Authentic experiences, 1–2
Autumn, 34
Avocado Food & Wine Festival, 192
Avondale Market, 115

B

Babich Wines, 126
Balloons Over Waikato, 167
Banks Track, 443
Barbecue, 27–28
Barefoot Sailing Adventures, 151
Barrier Air, 127
Bars, *see* Nightlife
Bats, 30
Bay of Islands, 143–156
- accommodations, 151–154
- Anglican Christ Church, 148
- Barefoot Sailing Adventures, 151
- Bay of Islands Kayaking, 148
- biking, 150
- Cable Bay, 144
- Carino Wildlife Cruises, 145
- Coopers Beach, 144
- dining, 154–156
- Discover the Bay, 146
- Dolphin Eco Cruise, 145
- Doubtless Bay, 144
- Earl Grey Fishing Charters, 150–151
- fishing, 150–151
- golfing, 151
- InterCity, 143
- Jazz and Blues Festival, 37
- Karikari Peninsula, 144
- Kawakawa, 145–147
- Kemp House, 149
- Kerikeri Farmers' Market, 150
- Kerikeri Mission Station, 149
- Kerikeri River Track, 149
- Kerikeri, 143–144, 149–150
- Kororipo Pā, 149
- Mangōnui, 144
- Ngawha Springs, 150
- Ocean Adventure, 146
- Old Packhouse Market, 150
- Otehei Bay, 148
- Paihia, 144–147
- Pompallier Mission, 148
- *R Tucker Thompson*, 151
- Russell Museum, 148
- Russell, 144, 148–149
- sailing, 151
- Taipa, 144
- Te Ahurea, 149
- Te Hononga Hundertwasser Memorial Park, 146
- Tokerau Beach, 144
- Urupukapuka, 148
- Waitangi, 144–147
- Waitangi Day, 144–145
- Waitangi Golf Club, 151
- Waitangi Mountain Bike Park, 150
- Waitangi Treaty Grounds, 146–147
- Wharepuke, 149

Bay of Islands Kayaking, 148
Bay of Plenty, 165, 190–206
- accommodations, 199–204
- Avocado Food & Wine Festival, 192
- dining, 204–206
- dolphin swimming, 198
- fishing, 198
- Flavours of Plenty Festival, 192
- Katikati, 195
- kayaking, 198
- kiwis, 195
- Mount Maunganui, 194–195
- National Jazz Festival, 192
- Ōhiwa Oyster Festival, 192
- One Love Festival, 192
- riverbugging, 199
- SUPing, 198–199
- surfing, 199
- Tauranga, 192–193
- Te Puke, 195
- Te Urewera, 196
- tours, 197–198
- Waihī Beach, 190, 195
- walking, 199
- watersports, 199
- Whakaari/White Island, 197
- Whakatāne Kiwi Trust, 195–196
- Whirinaki Te-Pua-a-Tāne Conservation Park, 196

Beaches
- Auckland, 85
- best, 14–15
- Christchurch, 428–429
- Coromandel, 185
- Dunedin, 523
- Far North, 161
- Gisborne, 273
- Invercargill, 546
- Nelson, 376
- Whanganui, 311

Beehive building, 326
Bennett's of Mangawhai, 136
The Big Foody, 78
Bijoux Gallery, 115
Bikes and Beyond, 121
Biking, 150, 253–254, 311–312, 429
Bill Richardson Transport World, 14, 546
Birds, 30–32
Blenheim, 365–371
Black Water Rafting Company, 11
Blokarting, 1, 429
Blue Duck Station, 2
Bluff, 549–550
Boating, 430
Books, 24
Brick Bay, 126
Brickell, Barry, 23
Bridal Veil, 446
Britomart, 114
Bungy jumping, 83, 235
Busby, James, 19
Butterfly Creek, 86

C

Cable Bay, 24, 144
Cable Bay Vineyards, 124
Calendar of Events, 36–37
Cambridge, 169–171
Campion, Jane, 25
Canopy camping, 6
Canterbury A&P Show, 420
Canterbury Museum, 421–422
Canyon Brewing, 29
Canyoning, 185–186, 376–377, 478–479
Cap Reinga, 157–159
Cape Brett, 161
Cape Rodney-Okakari Point Marine Reserve, 132
Car rental, 561
Carino Wildlife Cruises, 145
Caro, Niki, 25
Casino, 117
The Catlins, 538–543
Catton, Eleanor, 24
Caves, 174–175, 387
Celebrate Pasifika Festival, 36
Central Hawke's Bay, 293
Chancery Square, 114
Chardonnay Affair, 266
Cheltenham, 85
Chidgey, Catherine, 24
Christchurch, 2, 23–24, 418–440
- accommodations, 431–435
- Air Force Museum of New Zealand, 425
- Arts Centre, 421
- bars, 439–440
- beaches, 428–429
- biking, 429
- blokarting, 429
- boating, 430
- Canterbury A&P Show, 420
- Canterbury Museum, 421–422
- Christchurch Art Gallery Te Puna o Waiwhetū, 422
- Christchurch Botanic Gardens, 426–427
- dining, 435–439
- driftkarting, 429
- food halls, 437
- golfing, 430
- Hagley Park, 427
- He Puna Taimoana, 425–426
- hiking, 430–430
- International Antarctic Centre, 426
- jetboating, 431
- neighborhoods, 420
- nightlife, 439–440
- Orana Wildlife Park, 427
- performing arts, 439
- punting, 430
- Quake City, 422
- Ravenscar, 424
- tours, 428
- Transitional Cathedral, 424
- Tūranga (Central Library), 424–425
- whitewater rafting, 431
- Willowbank Wildlife Reserve, 427–428
- wineries, 440–441
- World Buskers' Festival, 420

Christchurch Transitional Cathedral, 4–5
City Farmers' Market, 115
City Gallery Wellington, 324–325
Claris Airfield, 127
Classic Motorcycle Mecca, 546
Classic New Zealand Wine Trail, 28–29
Coast to Coast Race, 36
Coffee, 29–30
Colonization, 18–19
Commercial Bay, 114
Cook, James, 17
Coopers Beach, 144
Cornwall Park, 87
Coromandel Peninsula, 62, 132, 165, 179–190
- accommodations, 187–188
- beaches, 185

Coromandel Peninsula, *(continued)*
- canyoning, 185–186
- Corozip, 182
- dining, 189–190
- Driving Creek Railway, 182
- fishing, 186
- Flaxmill Bay, 183
- Goldmine Experience, 181
- golfing, 186
- Hahei's Mautohe Cathedral Cove, 183
- Hot Water Beach, 184–185
- kayaking, 186–187
- Kiwi Christmas trees, 181
- The Lost Spring, 183
- Mercury Bay Museum, 183
- Paeroa, 184
- The Pinnacles, 186
- pōhutukawas, 181
- Rapaura Watergardens, 182
- scuba diving, 187
- Shakespeare Cliff Lookout, 183
- snorkeling, 187
- surfing, 187
- Thames Historical Museum, 181
- tours, 185
- Waiau Falls, 183
- walking, 187
- The Waterworks, 182–183
- Whangamatā Beach Hop, 181
- Whitianga Ferry, 183
- ziplining, 182

Corozip, 182
Costs, 572
Country Antiques, 114
The Cove Waipu, 136
COVID-19, 21
Craggy Range, 24
Crankworx, 210
Craters of the Moon, 233
Crump, Barry, 24
Cuba Precinct, Wellington, 338
Cultural performances, 218–220
Cultural respect, 569
Currach Irish Pub, 128
Customs, 558–559
Customs Street, 71
Cycling, 12, 89, 285–286, 329, 377, 404, 461–463, 547

D

Dark Sky Project, 11, 351
Dawson Falls, 303
Devil's Punchbowl Waterfall, 446
Devonport, 71, 84–85
Devonport Chocolates, 85
Devonport Explorer Tours, 84
Devonport Naval Museum, 85
Dining, 25–30; *see also* Restaurants Index
Dinosaur House, 254–255
Disabled travelers, 570
Discounts, online, 565
Discover the Bay, 146
Distilleries, 284
Diving, 141
Dolphin Eco Cruise, 145
Dolphin swimming, 198
Doubtful Sound, 491–492
Doubtless Bay, 144
Dove-Myer Robinson Park, 87
Driftkarting, 429
Drink, 28–30
Drinking laws, 570–571
Driving, 560–564
Driving Creek Railway, 23, 182
Duff, Alan, 24–25
Dunedin, 20, 23, 518–538
- accommodations, 531–533
- beaches, 523
- dining, 534–537
- Dunedin Museum of Natural Mystery, 14, 522–523
- Dunedin Public Art Gallery, 524
- Dunedin Railway, 5, 529
- fishing, 530
- golfing, 530
- Karitāne, 528–529
- Lan Yuan Dunedin Chinese Garden, 524
- Larnach Castle, 527
- Moeraki, 528–529
- nightlife, 538
- Olveston, 524–525
- The OPERA, 527–528
- Orokonui Ecosanctuary, 526
- Otago Peninsula, 526–528, 530, 533–534
- Royal Albatross Centre, 528
- shopping, 537
- surfing, 531
- Toitū Otago Settlers Museum, 525
- tours, 529–530
- Tūhura Otago Museum, 525–526

Durie Hill Elevator and Tower, 309

E

Earl Grey Fishing Charters, 150–151
Earle, Augustus, 22
Earthquake, 2
East Cape, 271–273, 276–277
East Coast Museum of Technology (ECMoT), 269
Eastwoodhill Arboretum, 269
EcoZip Adventures, 123
Eden Gardens, 88
Eden Park Tours, 79
Edmond, Lauris, 24
Edmund Hillary, 114
Edwin Fox Maritime Museum, 360
Elephant Gallery, 130
Elephant Hill, 24
ENZed, 37–41
Europeans, 17–18
Events Calendar, 36–37
Ewelme Cottage, 85
Explore Group. 82

F

Families, *see* Kids
Farm tours, 2
Fast facts, 570–572
FAWC! Food and Wine Classic, 279
Featherston, 346–350
Ferries, 72–73, 564–566
Festival of Christmas, 346
Festival of Lights, 297
Fieldays, 167
Fingers, 114
Film, 24–25
Fine Wine Tours, 127
Fiordland, 484–493
- accommodations, 492–493
- Doubtful Sound, 491–492
- flightseeing, 491
- hiking, 490–491
- kayaking, 490–491
- Milford Sound, 488–491

Fish and chips, 27, 108
Fishing, 150–151, 186, 198, 221, 236, 273–274, 377, 398, 463, 530, 547
Flavours of Plenty Festival, 192
Flaxmill Bay, 183
Flightseeting, 235, 491
Food, 26–28; *see also* Dining and Restaurants Index
Footprints Waipoua, 10
Forests, 32
Forgotten World Highway (SH43), 256
Fox Glacier, 411–416
Frame, Janet, 24
Franz Josef Glacier, 411–416
Freedom camping, 563
Fullers Bay of Islands, 158
Fullers Ferries, 120
Fullers' Waiheke Hop-on Hop-off Explorer Tour, 122
Funyaking, 463–464

G

Gannets, 2
Garden Festival, 297
Gee, Maurice, 24
Geothermal pools, 4, 210–211, 217
The Giant's House, 442
Gillespies Beach, 413
Gin, 29
Gisborne, 265–271, 273–276
- accommodations, 274–275
- beaches, 273
- Chardonnay Affair, 266
- cultural experiences, 270
- dining, 276
- East Coast Museum of Technology (ECMoT), 269
- Eastwoodhill Arboretum, 269
- fishing, 273–274
- golfing, 274
- Ngāti Porou Tourism, 273
- Poverty Bay, 269
- railbiking, 274
- Rere Falls, 270
- Rhythm and Vines Music Festival, 266
- sauna, 274
- surfing, 274
- Tairāwhiti Museum and Art Gallery, 268
- tours, 270–271
- walking, 274

Glaciers, 411–416
Glenfern Sactuary, 129
Glowworms, 2–3
Goat Island Marine Discover Centre, 132
Goat Island, 132
Godwits, 2
Gold rush, 20
Golden Bay, 386–389
Golden Shears, 346
Goldmine Experience, 181

Golfing, 90, 151, 186, 221, 235–237, 274, 286, 303, 312, 329, 377, 430, 464, 479, 530
Good Heavens, 130
Gore, 543–544
Grace, Patricia, 24
Great Barrier Island, *see* Aotea/ Great Barrier Island
Greenstone, 409
Greymouth, 403–406
Greytown, 350–351

H

Haast, 416–417
Hagley Park, 427
Hahei's Mautohe Cathedral Cove, 183
Hairy Feet Waitomo, 170
Hallertau, 29
Hamilton, 165–169
Hamilton Gardens, 4, 168–169
Hamilton Zoo, 168
Hāngī, 2, 28
Hanmer Springs, 444
Harbourside Market, 340
Hastings, 281–284
Havelock, 362
Havelock North, 281–284
Hāwera, 299
Hawke's Bay, 277–293
- accommodations, 286–289
- Art Deco Festival, 279
- breweries, 284
- cideries, 284
- cycling, 285–286
- dining, 289–293
- distilleries, 284
- FAWC! Food and Wine Classic, 279
- food markets, 291
- golfing, 286
- Hastings, 281–284
- Havelock North, 281–284
- Hawke's Bay Marathon, 279
- MTG Hawke's Bay, 280
- Napier, 279–281
- National Aquarium of New Zealand, 281
- tours, 284–285
- wine, 282–283

He Puna Taimoana, 425–426
Helicopter tours, 412–413
Hell's Gate Geothermal Park and Mud Spa, 218
High Street–Vulcan Lane–O'Connell Street, 114
Highwic, 85
Hiking, 4, 399, 427, 443, 446, 490–491, 504–505, 553–554
Hillary, Edmund, 21
Historic houses, 85
History, 16–22
Hobbiton Movie Set, 170
Hobson, William, 19
Hokitika, 407–411
Hokitika Wildfoods Festival, 36
Holidays, 35
Hongi, 2
Horse racing, 92
Horseback riding, 221, 236
Hot pools, 4, 215–218, 233–235
Hot Water Beach, 4, 184–185
Hotels, *see also* Accommodations Index
Huka Falls, 231
Hulme, Keri, 24
Hundertwasser Art Centre & Wairau Art Gallery, 4, 138–139
Hundertwasser, Friedensreich, 23

I

Ihimaera, Witi, 24
Independence, 20–21
InterCity, 143
International Antarctic Centre, 426
International Dark Sky Reserves, 4, 130
Invercargill, 544–548
Ironman New Zealand, 230
IronMāori, 230
Island Aviation, 127

J

Jackson, Peter, 24–25
Jade, 409
Jazz and Blues Festival, 37
Jetboating, 90, 236, 392–393, 431, 479–480
John Stephens Antiques, 114
Juno Gin, 301

K

Kaiaua Fisheries, 132
Kaikōura, 447–449
Kaitaia, 157–158
Kaitaia Airport, 156
Kapa haka, 2
Kāpiti Coast, 344–345
Karamea, 397–400
Karangahape Road, 71
Karikari Peninsula, 14, 44
Karitāne, 528–529
Katherine Mansfield House & Garden, 325
Katikati, 195
Katipo spiders, 31
Kauri Coast, 159–164
The Kauri Museum, 137
Kawakawa, 145–147
Kāwhia, 4
Kayak Waiheke, 123
Kayaking, 82, 91, 186–187, 198, 221–222, 236–237, 303, 330, 393, 413, 479, 490–491
Kelburn, 320
Kelly Tarlton's Sea Life Aquarium, 86
Kemp House, 23, 149
Kennedy Point Wines and Olive Oil, 124
Kerikeri, 143–144, 149–150
Kerosene Creek, 215
Kidman, Fiona, 24
Kids, 86
- Nelson, 376
- Queenstown, 456
- Rotorua, 214–215
- Taupō, 234
- Wellington, 329
- Whangārei, 139–140

Kitekite Falls, 90
Kiwi, 2, 195, 555
Kiwi Christmas trees, 181
Kombucha, 29
Kororā (little penguins), 2
Kororāreka, 19
Kororipo Pā, 149
Kura Gallery, 114

L

Lake Dunstan Trail, cycling, 12
Lake Matheson Walk, 415
Lake Ōhau, 509–510
Lake Pukaki, 501
Lake Rotopounamu, 238
Lake Taupō, cruises, 232–233
Lake Tekapō, 495–501
Landmarks, architectural, 4–5
Language, 37–41
Lan Yuan Dunedin Chinese Garden, 524
Larnach Castle, 527
Lava Glass, 231
Learn 2 Surf Waipu's kiosk, 136
Leigh, 132
Lemon & Paeroa, 29
LGBTQI+ 119, 343–344, 572
Lindauer, Gottfried, 22
Lions Rock, 90
Literature, 24
Little penguins, 2
Lord of the Rings, 24–25
The Lost Gypsy, 14
The Lost Spring, 183

M

Mackenzie, James, 496
Makereti, Tina, 24
Manawatu, Becky, 24
Manea Footprints of Kupe, 159–160
Mangōnui, 144
Mansfield, Katherine, 24
Māori, 16–17, 28
Māori marae, 2
Māori rock carvings, 232
Māori village, 214–215
Māpua Wharf, 381
Mārahau to Tōtaranui (beach), 15
Marlborough, 357–371
- accommodations, 363–365, 369–370
- Blenheim, 365–371
- dining, 363–365, 370–371
- Edwin Fox Maritime Museum, 360
- The Gallery, 362
- Havelock, 362
- Marlborough Food & Wine Festival, 366
- Omaka Aviation Heritage Centre, 366–367
- Picton, 357–364
- Picton Heritage and Whaling Museum, 360
- Queen Charlotte Track, 362
- tours, boat, 361–362
- wine, 367–369
- wine tours, 368–369

Marshall, Owen, 24
Martinborough, 346–350
Masterton, 350–351
Matakana, 131–132
Matakana Tours, 78
Matakana Village Farmer's Market, 115
Matariki Festival, 36, Festival, 70

McCashin's, 29
Meat pie, 27
Mercury Bay Museum, 183
Methven, 444–445
Milford, 459
Milford Sound, 488–491
Mission Bay/St. Heliers, 71
Mitai Māori Village, 220
Modern New Zealand, 22
Moeraki, 528–529
Mōrere Hot Springs, 277
Motorhomes, 54–57, 563–564
Mount Cook Village, 501–507
Mount Eden/Epsom, 71
Mount Hobson, 130
Mount John Observatory, 500
Mount Karioi, 172
Mount Maunganui, 194–195
Mount Ruapehu, 249–250
Mount Tarawera, 11
Mount Victoria, 320
Mountain biking, 222, 237, 330, 393, 398, 480
Moutere Hills, 374–375
MTG Hawke's Bay, 280
Mudbrick Vineyard and Restaurant, 124
Murchison, 392–394
Muriwai, 90
Museum of New Zealand Te Papa Tongarewa, 13, 321–323
Museum of Transport and Technology (MOTAT), 79
Museums, best, 13–14
Music, live, 117
Musket Wars, 18–19

N

Napier, 4, 279–281
Napier–Taupō Highway (SH5), 293
Narrow Neck Beach, 85
National Agricultural Fieldays, 37
National Aquarium of New Zealand, 281
National Army Museum, 264
National Jazz Festival, 192
National Kiwi Centre, 408
National Library of New Zealand, 324
National Transport & Toy Museum, 478
Nature experiences, 2–4
Nelson, 372–383
- accommodations, 378–380
- art galleries, 375–376
- beaches, 376
- breweries, 382
- canyoning, 376–377
- cycling, 377
- dining, 381–383
- fishing, 377
- golfing, 377
- kids, 376
- Moutere Hills, 374–375
- Nelson Provincial Museum, 374
- SUPing, 378
- walking, 377–378
- watersports, 378
- wineries, Moutere Hills, 374–375

Nelson Arts Festival, 37
New Plymouth, 294–299
New Zealand Company, 18
New Zealand Maritime Museum, 13, 83–84
Newmarket, 71, 115
Ngarunui Beach, 171
Ngāti Porou Tourism, 273
Ngawha Springs, 150
Ngongotahā, 214–215
Nightlife
- Auckland, 116–119
- Christchurch, 439–440
- Dunedin, 538
- Queenstown, 476
- Wellington, 342–344
- Whanganui, 314

North Island, 60–64, 131–132
Northland, 133–164
- Bay of Islands, 143–156
- diving, 141
- Far North, 156–164
- Kauri Coast, 159–164
- North Island, 60, 131–132
- Northland Ferries, 143
- Poor Knights Islands Marine Reserve, 141
- Tūtūkākā, 141
- Whangārei, 134–143

Northland Ferries, 143
Nourishing Nature, 78
NZ Blues and BBQ Festival, 210
NZ Cider Festival, 37

O

Ōamaru, 5, 23, 511–517
Ocean Adventure, 146
Ohakune Carrot Festival, 249
Ohakune Hot Tubs, 254
Ohen, 115
Ōhinemutu Māori Village, 220
Ōhiwa Oyster Festival, 192
Old Packhouse Market, 150
Old St. Paul's, 325
Olive oil, 124
Olveston, 524–525
Omaka Aviation Heritage Centre, 14, 366–367
Omanawanui Track, 90
Ōmarama, 510
One Love Festival, 192
Onetangi Bay (Waiheke Island), 14, 122–123
The OPERA, 527–528
Ora Garden of Wellbeing, 230
Orakei Korako Geothermal Park and Cave, 217, 228
Orana Wildlife Park, 427
Oreville Stamping Battery, 129
Oriental Bay, 320
Orokonui Ecosanctuary, 2, 526
Ostend Market, 121
Otago Central Rail Trail, cycling, 12
Otago Peninsula, 526–528, 530, 533–534
Otara Market, 115
Otehei Bay, 148
Otumuheke Stream Spa Thermal Park, 234

P

Pacific Coast Highway, North Island, 132
Packrafting, 480
Paeroa, 184
Paihia, 144–147
Palm Beach, 123
Palmerston North isite, 314
Paparoa National Park, 400–402
Parks, Auckland, 87–88
Parliament House, 326
Parnell, 71, 115
Parnell Rose Garden, 87
Pasifika Festival, 70
Passage Rock Wines, 124
Passports, 558
Pelorus Mail Boat Cruise, 11
The Penguin History of New Zealand (Michael King), 20
Performing arts, 116–117, 342, 439
Personhood, 33
Peter Raos Glass Gallery, 85
The Piano, 25
Picton, 357–364
Picton Heritage and Whaling Museum, 360
Piha, 90–91
The Pinnacles, 186
Planning, 33–37, 558–573; *see also* Calendar of Events: Holidays; Weather
Plant life, 32–33
Pōhatu Penguins, 443
Pōhutukawa, 32–33, 181
Poi Room, 115
Polynesian Spa, 216
Pompallier Mission, 148
Ponsonby/Herne Bay, 71
Poor Knights Islands Marine Reserve, 141
Power to the Pedal, 89
Possums, 30–31
Poverty Bay, 269
Puhi Kai Iti Cook Landing Site, 18
Pūkorokoro Miranda Shorebird Centre, 132
Pumula, 173
Punakaiki, 400–402
Punting, 430

Q

Quake City, 422
Quay Street, 71
Queen Charlotte Track, 362
Queen Street, 71, 114
Queenstown, 450–476
- accommodations, 465–470
- adrenaline activities, 462–463
- Arrowtown, 456–458
- cycling, 461–463
- dining, 470–475
- fishing, 463
- funyaking, 463–464
- golfing, 464
- kids, 456
- Milford, 459
- nightlife, 476
- Queenstown Marathon, 453
- Queenstown Pride Festival, 453
- shopping, 465
- skiing, 464
- Skippers Canyon, 458
- Snow Machine, 453
- tours, 458–459
- walking, 464
- wine, 459–461
- wineries, 460–461

R

R Tucker Thompson, 151
Rafting, 398–399
Raglan, 171–173
Railbiking, 274
Rainbow's End, 86
Rainfall, 35
Rakiura, *see* Stewart Island
Rangiputa Beach, 161
Rangitoto Island, 82
Rapaura Watergardens, 182
Rarohara Kūtai & Kai Festival, 129
Ravenscar, 424
Redwoods Treewalk, 211–213
Reefton, 403
Rere Falls, 270
Responsible tourism, 568–570
Restaurants, *see* Restaurants Index
Rhythm and Vines Music Festival, 266
Ring of Fire Festival, 209
Riverbugging, 1, 199
Riverside Adventures, 171
Roadside stalls, 29
Ross, 408
Rotorua, 207–228
- accommodations, 223–226
- Crankworx, 210
- cultural performances, 218–220
- dining, 226–228
- fishing, 221
- geothermal reserves, 210–211, 217
- golfing, 221
- Hell's Gate Geothermal Park and Mud Spa, 218
- horseback riding, 221
- hot pools, 215–218
- kayaking, 221–222
- Kerosene Creek, 215
- kids, 214–215
- Māori village, 214–215
- Mitai Māori Village, 220
- mountain biking, 222
- Ngongotahā, 214–215
- NZ Blues and BBQ Festival, 210
- Ōhinemutu Māori Village, 220
- Orakei Korako Cave and Thermal Park, 217
- Polynesian Spa, 216
- Redwoods Treewalk, 211–213
- Secret Spot Hot Tubs, 218
- shopping, 228
- Te Pā Tū, 219–220
- Te Pō, 220
- Te Puia, 213–214, 220
- Velocity Valley, 220
- Village of Te Wairoa, 211
- Wai Ariki Hot Springs & Spa, 216
- Waikite Valley Hot Pools, 218
- Waimangu Volcanic Valley, 217
- Wai-O-Tapu Thermal Wonderland, 217
- walking, 222–223
- white-water rafting, 221–222
- ziplining, 223
- Zorbing, 221

Rotorua Marathon, 37
Rototāwai, 349
Royal Albatross Centre, 528
Royal A&P Show of New Zealand, 37
Ruapehu Region, 246–264
- accommodations, 258–262
- The Alpine Centre, 250–251
- biking, 253–254
- dining, 263–264
- Dinosaur House, 254–255
- Forgotten World Highway (SH43), 256
- Mount Ruapehu, 249–250
- Ohakune Carrot Festival, 249
- Ohakune Hot Tubs, 254
- Ring of Fire Festival, 209
- snow activities, 249–251
- Taumarunui, 255–256
- Tongariro Alpine Crossing, 252–253
- Tūroa Ski Area, 251
- walking, 251–253
- Whakapapa Ski Area, 250
- Whanganui River, 256–258

Rugby, 74, 92
Russell, 144, 148–149

S

Sailing, 91, 151
Salty Bushman, 130
Sanctuary Mountain Maungatautari, 2, 171
Scooters, 73, 128–129
Scuba diving, 187
Sculptureum, 126
Seabird Coast, 132
SeaLink Travel Group, 120, 128
Seasons, 34–35
Secret Spot Hot Tubs, 218
SH1, 538
Shadbolt, Maurice, 24
Shakespeare Cliff Lookout, 183
Share plates, 27
Sharks, 31
Shopping
- Auckland, 114–115
- Dunedin, 537
- Queenstown, 465
- Rotorua, 228
- Wānaka, 480–481
- Wellington, 340–342

Skiing, 464
Skippers Canyon, 458
SkyCity Auckland Casino, 117
Skydiving, 237
Sky Tower, 79–80
Snorkeling, 187
Snow Machine, 453
Social Nature Movement, 91
Soft drinks, 29
Soljans Estate, 127
Solspring, 173
South Island, 64–67
Spellbound Glowworm and Cave Tour, 175
Sports, spectator, 92
Spring, 34
St. Faith's Church, 23
St. Mary's Church, 4, 23
Steampunk Festival, 36–37, 512
Stewart Island, 550–557
Stone Store, 23
Stonyridge, 123
Summer, 34
SUPing, 198–199, 378, 479
Surf Highway 45, 306
Surfing, 91, 187, 199, 274, 303, 404, 531
Swimming, 91
Swingbridge, 392–393

T

Tāhunanui, 14
Taipa, 144
Tairāwhiti Gisborne, *see* Gisborne
Tairāwhiti Museum and Art Gallery, 268
Takapuna, 71
Takarunga/Mount Victoria, 85
Tales from Darkest Dunedin, 11
Tāmaki Paenga Hira Auckland War Memorial Museum, 13, 80–81
Tāne Mahuta, 156, 160
Taranaki, 294–306
- accommodations, 303–305
- Americarna, 297
- Dawson Falls, 303
- dining, 305–306
- Festival of Lights, 297
- Garden Festival, 297
- gardens, 299–301
- gin, 301
- golfing, 303
- Hāwera, 299
- Juno Gin, 301
- kayaking, 303
- New Plymouth, 294–299
- surfing, 303
- Te Papa-Kura-o-Taranaki (National Park), 301–302
- walking, 303
- WOMAD, 297

Tasman, 372, 380–381, 383; *see also* Nelson
Tasman, Abel, 17
Tasman Glacier, 501
Taumarunui, 255–256
Taupō, 229–246
- accommodations, 238–243
- Aratiatia Rapids, 232
- bungy jumping, 235
- climbing, 235
- Craters of the Moon, 233
- dining, 243–246
- fishing, 236
- flightseeing, 235
- golfing, 235–237
- horseback riding, 236
- hot pools, 233–235
- Huka Falls, 231
- Ironman New Zealand, 230
- IronMāori, 230
- jetboating, 236
- kayaking, 236–237
- kids, 234
- Lake Rotopounamu, 238
- Lake Taupō, cruises, 232–233
- Lava Glass, 231
- Māori rock carvings, 232
- mountain biking, 237
- Ora Garden of Wellbeing, 230
- Otumuheke Stream Spa Thermal Park, 234
- skydiving, 237
- Taupō DeBretts Hot Springs, 233
- Taupō Museum, 230

Taupō, *(continued)*
- Wairakei Terraces and Thermal Health Spa, 234
- walking, 237–238
- white water rafting, 238

Tauranga, 192–193
Tāwharanui Regional Park, 131–132
Tawhiti Museum, 13
Te Ahurea, 149
Te Anau, 484–494
- accommodations, 492–493
- dining, 493–494
- Doubtful Sound, 491–492
- flightseeing, 491
- hiking, 490–491
- kayaking, 490–491
- Milford Sound, 488–491

Te Ara Whānui ki te Rangi/Space Place, 326
Te Arai Links, 90
Te Aro, 319
Te Hononga Hundertwasser Memorial Park, 146
Te Matatini Kapa Haka Aotearoa Festival, 168
Te Oneroa a Tōhe 90-Mile Beach, 156, 158
Te Pā Tū, 219–220
Te Paki Sand Dunes, 156, 158
Te Papa-Kura-o-Taranaki (National Park), 301–302
Te Pō, 220
Te Puia, 213–214, 220
Te Puke, 195
Te reo Māori, 40
Te Rerenga Wairua Cape Reinga, 156
Te Urewera, 196
Te Whara Track, 139
Te Whare Taonga o Waikato Museum and Gallery, 169
Tekapō Springs, 497–498
Temperature, 35
Thames Historical Museum, 181
Thorndon, 319–320
Timber Trail, cycling, 12
Tipping, 26
Titirangi, 71
Toast Martinborough, 37
Toitū Otago Settlers Museum, 14, 525
Tokaanu Thermal Pools, 246
Tokerau Beach, 144, 161
Tongariro Alpine Crossing, 252–253
Tongariro National Trout Centre, 246
Tours
- Auckland, 72, 78, 82, 88–89
- Bay of Plenty, 197–198
- boat, 361–362
- cave tours, 174–175
- Christchurch, 428
- Coromandel, 185
- Dunedin, 529–530
- farm, 2
- Gisborne, 270–271
- Hawke's Bay, 284–285
- helicopter, 412–413
- historical tour, North Island, 57–60
- motorhome tour, South Island, 54–57
- Queenstown, 458–459
- Stewart Island, 554–555
- Waiheke Island, 122, 127
- Wairarapa, 351–352
- walking, 464
- Wānaka, 478
- Wellington, 328–329
- wine tours, 368–369

Tramping, *see* Hiking
Transitional Cathedral, 424
Treaty of Waitangi, 19–20
Tu Tika Tours, 139
Tuatara, 30
Tūhura Otago Museum, 525–526
Tūranga public library, 24, 424–425
Tūroa Ski Area, 251
Tūtūkākā, 141
Twentieth century, 21–22
Twenty-Seven Names, 114
Twilight Glow Worm Kayak, 171
Twizel, 507–509

U

Unity, 114
Urupukapuka, 148

V

Vault, 114
Velocity Valley, 220
Viaduct Basin, 82–84
Victorian Fete, 512
Village of Te Wairoa, 211
Vineyards, 123–124, 126
Visas, 558
Visual arts, 22–23
Volunteer work, 569–570

W

Wai Ariki Hot Springs & Spa, 216
Waiau Falls, 183
Waiheke Island, 119–125
- accommodations, 124–125
- Allpress Olive Grove, 124
- Ananda Tours, 122
- AT Hop card, 120
- Auckland Transport, 120
- Auckland Wine Tours, 127
- Babich Wines, 126
- Bikes and Beyond, 121
- Brick Bay, 126
- Cable Bay Vineyards, 124
- car rentals, 120–121
- dining, 125
- EcoZip Adventures, 123
- Fine Wine Tours, 127
- Fullers Ferries, 120
- Fullers' Waiheke Hop-on Hop-off Explorer Tour, 122
- Kayak Waiheke, 123
- Kennedy Point Wines and Olive Oil, 124
- Mudbrick Vineyard and Restaurant, 124
- olive oil, 124
- Onetangi Bay, 122–123
- Ostend Market, 121
- Palm Beach, 123
- Passage Rock Wines, 124
- Sculptureum, 126
- SeaLink Travel Group, 120
- Soljans Estate, 127
- Stonyridge, 123
- tours, 122, 127
- vineyards, 123–124, 126
- Waiheke Auto Rentals, 120–121
- Waiheke Community Art Gallery, 121
- Waiheke Island Historic Village and Museum, 121
- Waiheke Island Jazz & Blues Festival, 121
- Waiheke Island Wine Tours, 122
- Waiheke Musical Museum, 121
- West Brook Winery, 127
- wineries, 126–127
- ziplining, 123

Waihī Beach, 190, 195
Waiho Hot Tubs, 414
Waikato, 165–179
- accommodations, 175–177
- Balloons Over Waikato, 167
- Cambridge Raceway, 169
- Cambridge, 169–171
- cave tours, 174–175
- dining, 177–179
- Fieldays, 167
- Hairy Feet Waitomo, 170
- Hamilton Gardens, 168–169
- Hamilton Zoo, 168
- Hamilton, 165–169
- Hobbiton Movie Set, 170
- Mount Karioi, 172
- Ngarunui Beach, 171
- Pumula, 173
- Raglan, 171–173
- Riverside Adventures, 171
- Sanctuary Mountain Maungatautari, 171
- Solspring, 173
- Spellbound Glowworm and Cave Tour, 175
- Te Matatini Kapa Haka Aotearoa Festival, 168
- Te Whare Taonga o Waikato Museum and Gallery, 169
- Twilight Glow Worm Kayak, 171
- Wairēinga/Bridal Veil Falls, 171
- Waitomo, 173–175
- Zealong Tea Estate, 168

Waikite Valley Hot Pools, 218
Waimangu Volcanic Valley, 217
Waimarino, 246
Wai-O-Tapu Thermal Wonderland, 217
Waipoua Forest, 160
Waipu Caves Farm Park, 136
Waipu Caves Scenic Reserve, 136
Waipu Cove Beach, 136
Wairakei Geothermal Power Station, 228
Wairakei Terraces and Thermal Health Spa, 234
Wairarapa, 344–356
- accommodations, 352–354
- Dark Sky Reserve, 351
- dining, 354–356
- Featherston, 346–350
- Festival of Christmas, 346
- Golden Shears, 346
- Greytown, 350–351
- Martinborough Fair, 346
- Martinborough, 346–350
- Masterton, 350–351
- Rototāwai, 349
- tours, 351–352
- wineries, 346–350

Wairēinga/Bridal Veil Falls, 171
Waitākere Ranges, 90
Waitaki District, 510–517
Ōamaru, 511–517
Ōmarama, 510
Steampunk NZ Festival, 512
Victorian Fete, 512
Waitaki Lakes, 510–511
Waitaki Valley, 510–511
wine, 511
Waitaki Lakes, 510–511
Waitaki Valley, 510–511
Waitangi, 19–21, 144–147
Waitangi Day, 36, 144–145
Waitangi Golf Club, 151
Waitangi Mountain Bike Park, 150
Waitangi Treaty Grounds, 146–147
Waitematā Harbor, 71, 82–84
Waititi, Taika, 25
Waitomo, 173–175
Waiuta, 404
Waka Abel Tasman, 12
Walking
Aoraki, 504–505
Auckland, 92
Bay of Plenty, 199
Coromandel, 187
Far North, 161
Gisborne, 274
Invercargill, 547
Nelson, 377–378
Rotorua, 222–223
Ruapehu, 251–253
Stewart Island, 553–554
Taranaki, 303
Taupō, 237–238
Wellington, 330
West Coast, 399, 404–405
Whanganui, 312
Wānaka, 476–484
accommodations, 481–482
canyoning, 478–479
climbing, 479
dining, 482–484
golfing, 479
jetboating, 479–480
kayaking, 479
mountain biking, 480
National Transport & Toy Museum, 478
packrafting, 480
shopping, 480–481
SUPing, 479
tours, 478
Warbirds Over Wānaka International Air Show, 36, 477
The Waterworks, 182–183
WE-AR, 115
Weather, 34–35
Wellington, 315– 344
accommodations, 330–334
Aotearoa New Zealand Festival of the Arts, 319
bars, 342–343
Beehive, 326
City Gallery Wellington, 324–325
clubs, 342–343
coffee, 334
Cuba Precinct, 338
cycling, 329
dining, 334–340
golfing, 329
Harbourside Market, 340
Katherine Mansfield House & Garden, 325
kayaking, 330
Kelburn, 320
kids, 329
LGBTQI+ nightlife, 343–344
Mount Victoria, 320
Mountain biking, 330
Museum of New Zealand Te Papa Tongarewa, 321–323
National Library of New Zealand, 324
neighborhoods, 319–320
nightlife, 342–344
Old St. Paul's, 325
Oriental Bay, 320
Parliament House, 326
performing arts, 342
shopping, 340–342
Te Ara Whānui ki te Rangi/ Space Place, 326
Te Aro, 319
Thorndon, 319–320
tours, 328–329
walking, 330
Wellington Botanic Gardens, 326–327
Wellington Cable Car, 324
Wellington Fringe Festival, 319
Wellington Museum, 327
Wētā Cave, 323
World of WearableArt Show, 319
Zealandia Te Māra a Tāne, 328
Wellington Cup Race Meeting, 36
West Brook Winery, 127
West Coast, 390–411
accommodations, 393–394, 396–397, 399–402, 405–406, 408–410
cycling, 404
dining, 393–394, 397, 399–402, 406, 410–411
fishing, 398
greenstone, 409
Greymouth, 403–406
hiking, 399
Hokitika, 407–411
jade, 409
jetboating, 392–393
Karamea, 397–400
kayaking, 393
mountain biking, 393, 398
Murchison, 392–394
National Kiwi Centre, 408
Paparoa National Park, 400–402
Punakaiki, 400–402
rafting, 398–399
Reefton, 403
Ross, 408
surfing, 404
swingbridge, 392–393
Waiuta, 404
walking, 399, 404–405
Westport, 394–397
whitewater rafting, 393
Wild Foods Festival, 407
Westland Tai Poutini National Park, 411
Westport, 394–397
Wētā, 30
Wētā Cave, 323
Wētā Workshop, 25, 81–82
Whakaari/White Island, 197
Whakapapa Ski Area, 250
Whakatāne Kiwi Trust, 195–196
***Whale Rider*, 25**
Whale watching, 449
Whaling, 20
Whangamatā Beach Hop, 181
Whanganui, 307–314
accommodations, 312–313
art studios, 309–310
Artists Open Studios Whanganui, 308
beaches, 311
biking, 311–312
dining, 313–
Durie Hill Elevator and Tower, 309
galleries, 309–310
golfing, 312
nightlife, 314
walking, 312
Whanganui Farmers' Market, 314
Whanganui Opera Week, 307
Whanganui River, 310–311
Whanganui Vintage Weekend, 307–308
Whanganui Farmers' Market, 314
Whanganui Opera Week, 307
Whanganui River, 256–258, 310–311
Whanganui Vintage Weekend, 307–308
Whangapoua Beach, 130
Whangārei, 134–143
accommodations, 140–142
Adrenalin, 140
attractions, 137–139
Bennett's of Mangawhai, 136
The Cove Waipu, 136
dining, 142–143
Hundertwasser Art Centre and Wairau Māori Art Gallery, 138–139
The Kauri Museum, 137
kids, 139–140
Learn 2 Surf Waipu's kiosk, 136
Te Whara Track, 139
Tu Tika Tours, 139
Waipu Caves Farm Park, 136
Waipu Caves Scenic Reserve, 136
Waipu Cove Beach, 136
Wharariki, 15
Wharepuke, 149
Whataroa, 413
Whirinaki Te-Pua-a-Tāne Conservation Park, 196
White Heron Sactuary Tours, 413
White-water rafting, 221–222, 238, 393, 431
Whitianga Ferry, 183
Wild Foods Festival, 407
Wildlife, 2, 30–32, 449
Willowbank Wildlife Reserve, 427–428
Wine, 28–29, 282–283, 367–369, 459–461, 511
Wineries
Christchurch, 440–441
Moutere Hills, 374–375
Waiheke Island, 126–127
Wairarapa, 346–350
Queenstown, 460–461
Winter, 35

WOMAD, 297
Women, voting, 20
Working vacations, 569
World Buskers Festival, 36,
Festival, 420
World of WearableArt Show, 319
World War I, 20–21
WOW (World of Wearable Art), 37

Z

Zealandia Te Māra a Tāne, 2, 328
Zealong Tea Estate, 168
Ziplining, 123, 182, 223
Zorbing, 1, 221

Accommodations

14th Lane Urban Hotel, 7, 369
415 Marine Parade, 287
858 George Street Motel, 532
Abel Tasman Lodge, 385
Abstract Hotel, 95
Acapulco Motor Inn, 241
Adina Heritage Hotel Christchurch, 433
Admirals Landing Bed and Breakfast, 100
Ahu Ahu Beach Villas, 6–7, 305
Anatoki Lodge Motel, 388
Anchor Lodge, 188
Aotea Motor Lodge, 313
Arista of Rotorua, 223
Art Deco Masonic Hotel, 286
Ascot Park Hotel, 548
Asure Aspiring Court Motel Haast, 417
Asure Explorer, 492
Aura, 224
Awa Motel, 203
Awaroa Lodge, 386
Bay Plaza Hotel, 333
Bazil's Hostel & Surf School, 396
Bell Hill Apartments, 531
Bella Vista Fox, 415
Belle vue Boutique Lodge, 238
Bethells Beach Cottages, 101
Black Swan Lakeside Boutique Hotel, 224
Bluestone on George, 531
Boatshed Hotel, 124–125
Bolton Hotel, 330–331
Booklovers Bed & Breakfast, 333
Boot B&B, 380–381
Bow Street Studios, 177
Bowentown Beach Holiday Park, 202
Brackenridge Country Retreat & Spa, 353
Braemar on Parliament Street, 96
Brenton Lodge, 188
Bridge to Nowhere Lodge & Campground, 262
Browns Boutique Hotel, 467
Cable Bay Stays, 161
Carters by the Sea Beachside Studio Apartments, 396
Clarence Hotel, 200
Classic Villa, 432–433
Clements Hotel, 176
Clifftop Cabins, 448
Cobbler, 332
Collingwood Park Motel, 388–389
Commodore Airport Hotel, 433
Convent Hotel, 99
Copthorne Hotel & Resort Solway Park, 352–353
Cottages on St. Andrews, 287
Creel Lodge, 241–242
Crown Hotel, 286–287
Crowne Plaza Christchurch, 433
Croydon Lodge, 544
Dairy Hotel, 465
Devon Hotel, 303–304
Driftaway Holiday Park, 468
Drifter, 433–434
Duke of Marlborough, 152
Dusk and Dawn Domes, 102
Ebb Dunedin, 532
Eden's Edge Lodge, 380
Edgewater Resort, 481
Eichardt's Private Hotel, 466
Eleven Owen River Lodge, 394
Emerald Inn, 100–101
Fable Auckland, 93
Fable Dunedin, 532–533
Finlay Jacks Backpackers, 241
Fiordland Lakeview Motel & Apartments, 492
Fitzherbert Court Motel, 408
Flying Fox, 312
Forgotten World Motel, 261
French Bay House, 444
Gables, 363
Gentle Annie Seaside Accommodation and Campground, 396
Glenfern Sanctuary, 131
Global Village Backpackers, 405
Grand Arden Monaco Nelson, 378
Grand Mercure Puka Park Resort, 188
Grand Suites Murchison, 393
Grand Suites Tekapo, 499
Great Ponsonby Arthotel, 98
Greymouth Seaside Top 10 Holiday Park, 405
Haka House Aoraki Mt Cook, 505
Haka House Lake Tekapo, 499
Haka Lodge Taupō, 241
Hakarimata Hideaway Retreat, 175–176
Hampshire Holiday Park, 481
Hapuku Lodge & Treehouses, 448
Harbour View Motel & Apartments, 200
Headwaters Glenorchy Eco Lodge, 469–470
Hermitage Hotel, 505–506
High Country Cabin, 508
Hilton Auckland, 93
Hilton Lake Taupō, 238
Hokitika Fire Station, 409–410
Hosking House, 304
Hotel Armitage and Conference Centre, 200
Hotel Britomart, 93–94
Hotel d'Urville, 369–370
Hotel DeBrett, 94
Hotel Fitzroy, 98–99
Hotel Indigo Auckland, 96–97
Hotel Montreal, 431
housewithnonails, 176
Huka Lodge, 6, 238–239
ibis Budget, 102
InterContinental Wellington, 331
Intrepid Hotel, 331
Iona Tiny House, 313
Jailhouse Accommodation, 434–435
Kaimata Retreat, 533–534
Kaka Point Luxury Spa Accommodation, 542
Kāmana Lakehouse, 466
Karamea River Motels, 399
Kauri Villas, 140
King and Queen Hotel Suites, 304
KiwiCamp, 448
Lake Taupō Holiday Resort, 7, 240
Lake Tekapo Holiday Homes, 499
Lakes Edge Holiday Park, Tekapō, 499
Lakestone Lodge, 506
Lands End Boutique Hotel, 550
Langlands, 547–548
Larnach Lodge & Stable Stay, 534
Last Resort, 399–400
Le Chalet Suisse, 241
Limetree Lodge, 481–482
Lochmara Lodge, 364–365
Lodge 9, 140–141
Lupton Lodge, 141–142
Maitai Whare Iti, 379
Manuka Lodge, 259
Mariner Suites, 515
Marion Street Hostel, 333
Martinborough Hotel, 353
Maruia River Retreat, 7, 394
Mayfair, Christchurch, 431
Milford Sound Lodge, 492
Millbrook Resort, 469
Millennium Hotel New Plymouth Waterfront, 303
mi-pad, 468
Mount Maunganui Beachside Holiday Park, 202
Mövenpick Hotel Wellington, 332
Murchison Motorhome Park, 393
Muse Art Hotel, 434
Naumi Hotel Auckland Airport, 102
Naumi Hotel Wellington, 332
Nice Hotel, New Plymouth, 304–305
Novotel Auckland Airport, 102
Novotel Hamilton Tainui, 175
Observation Rock Lodge, 555–556
Observatory Hotel, 7, 431–432
Ōhope Beach Top 10 Holiday Park, 203
Ōhope Beachpoint Apartments, 203
Ohtel, 333
Old Confectionary, 515
Old Oak, 161–162
Omaka Lodge, 261
On The Point – Lake Rotorua, 224
Oranleigh Lodge, 261
Otahuna Lodge, 23, 432
Otira Stagecoach Hotel, 446–447
Parehua Resort, 352
Park Hotel Ruapehu, 260
Peak View Retreat, 379
Peaks Motor Inn, 258
Pen-y-bryn Lodge, 515
Pihopa Retreat, 379–380
Plateau Lodge, 260
Poronui, 239
Poshtel, 515–516
Pounawea Motor Camp, 542
Powderhorn Chateau, 258
Punakaiki Beach Camp, 401

Punga Grove Motel & Suites, 414
QT Auckland, 94–95
QT Queenstown, 466
QT Wellington, 332–333
Quarters, 242
Queenstown Holiday Park Creeksyde, 468
Quest Hastings, 288
Quest Newmarket Apartment Hotel, 100
Rabbit Island Huts, 381
Raglan Backpackers, 177
Rainforest Retreat, 414
Rangimarie Beachstay, 277
Ratanui Lodge, 389
Rawene Holiday Park, 162–163
Reef Resort, 241
Rees Hotel & Luxury Apartments, 466–467
Regal Palms, 224–225
Regent of Rotorua, 225
Rendezvous Heritage Auckland, 97
River Birches, 242–243
Riverside Escapes, 162
Rocky Mountain Chalets, 259
Rosewood Cape Kidnappers, 288
Rosewood Kauri Cliffs, 152–153
Royal Hotel, Wairarapa, 354
Ruapehu Country Lodge, 258–259
Russell Orongo Bay Holiday Park, 152
Rutherford Hotel Nelson, 378
Rydges Wellington Airport, 333–334
Sanctuary at the Bay of Islands, 152
Sands Hotel Hokianga, 163
Scenic Hotel Bay of Islands, 151–152
Scenic Hotel Marlborough, 370
Scenic Hotel Punakaiki, 402
Scenic Hotel Te Pania, 286
Shakespeare House Bed and Breakfast, 492
Sherwood, 468
SiloStay, 444
Silver Fern Rotorua, 225
Skotel Alpine Resort, 261
SkyScape, 7, 508–509
Snowman Lodge and Spa, 258
SO/ Auckland, 95
South Sea Hotel, 556–557
Sovereign Pier on the Waterways, 188
Spire Hotel, 467
Staydium Glamping, 99–100
Stewart Island Lodge, 556–557
Studios at Bealey Quarter, 435
Sudima Auckland City, 97
Sudima Five Mile, 468
Suncourt Hotel and Conference Centre, 241
Takahuri Glamping, 312–313
Tarlton's Lodge, 152
Tasman Holiday Park Coromandel Town, 188
Tasman Holiday Parks Pāpāmoa, Mount Maunganui, 202
Tatapouri Bay Oceanside Accommodation, 275
Te Anau Lakefront Backpackers, 492
Te Anau Lodge, 493
Te Kaha Beach Resort, 276–277
Te Weheka Hotel Fox Glacier, 415
Teichelmann's Bed & Breakfast, 410
Telephone Exchange, 240
Terminus Apartments, 533
Theatre Royal Hotel, 7, 405–406
Tiny House Escapes, 177
Tongariro Crossing Lodge, 260–261
Tongariro Suites, 259–260
Top 10 Holiday Park, 152
Tower Lodge Motel, 548
Treetops Lodge and Estate, 6, 225–226
Trinity Wharf Tauranga, 200
TripInn Hostel, 396
Twizel Holiday Park, 508
Underhill Valley, 176
Verandahs Parkside Lodge, 99
Villas & Vines, 287–288
Vintners Retreat, 370
Voco Auckland City Centre, 95
Waihau Bay Lodge, 277
Wainui Seaside Glamping, 203–204
Waiorau Homestead, 482
Waitākere Resort and Spa, 101
Waitomo's Top 10 Holiday Park, 177
Wallingford Homestead, 289
Wanderlust Hostel, 201
Watercliff, 201–202
Whakapapa Holiday Park, 261
Wharekauhau Country Estate, 7, 354
Wharepuke, 153–154
Wheelhouse Inn, 380
Whispering Sands Beachfront Motel, 274–275
White Horse Hill Campground, 505
White Morph, 448
Wilderness Lodge Lake Moeraki, 417
Wilderness Lodge, 447
Woodlyn Park, 177

Restaurants

1154 Pastaria, 337
25 Degrees Lake Tekapo, 501
5th Street, 435
Acropolis, 142
Akaroa Butchery & Deli, 445
Alice May, 416
Alpha Street, 178
Alpino Cucina e Vino, 178
Amano, 103
Amigos, 548
Amisfield Winery & Bistro, 74
Aosta, 474–475
Apache, 336
Arbour, 10, 371
Arrowtown Bakery, 475
Article, 314
Atticus Finch, 226
Auckland Fish Market, 107
Aunt Ginger's Kitchen, 356
Aunty Mena Vegetarian, 338
Awildian Gin, 189
Bacchus, 534
Backbencher Gastropub, 338
Baduzzi, 103
Beehave Craft Meadery, 244
Benny & Brew, 204
Best Ugly Bagels, 337
Bestie Café, 108
Betsey Jane, 416
Big Fig, 483
Big Mountain Mead and Ruapehu Brewing Co., 263
Bistro Gentil, 483
Bistro Saine, 103–104
Bistro, 243–244
Black Barn Bistro, 291–292
Blue Breeze Inn, 109
Blue Duck Station, 8, 262
Blue Rose Catering, 110–111
Boat Shed Café, 382
Boat Shet, 471
Boatshed Cafe, 164
Bobby's Fresh Fish Market, 204
Bodega Deli and Eatery, 109
Botanist, 339
Botswana Butchery, 470
Boulcott Street Bistro, 334
Brantry Restaurant, 244
Brew'd, 548
Bunker, 470
Burger Burger, 109
Burleigh Gourmet Pies, 370
Burrito Craft, 483
Buster Greens Real Food Room, 535
Butter Boom Croissanterie, 178
C1 Espresso, 437–438
Cable Bay Store, 163
Cafe Awa, 206
Café Hanoi, 106
Cafe Medici, 354
Café Melbourne, 189
Café Neve, 416
Camina, 190
Canyon Brewing, 471
Capers Café + Store, 227
Capitol, 334–335
Casito Miro, 125
Cassels & Sons Brewery Bar, 438
Cazador, 111, 113
Central Fire Station, 290
Charley Noble Eatery & Bar, 335
Charlotte's Kitchen, 154
Chez Louis's food truck, 206
Child Sister, 438
Chilli Cove Indian Eatery, 190
Chow, 336–337
Ciabatta Cafe and Baker, 227
Cibo, 112
Cider Factorie, 204
Cigol, 206
Clarence Tauranga Restaurant, 204
Clareville Bakery, 356
Cocoro, 109
Cool Change Bar & Eatery, 354–355
Coromandel Oyster Company, 189
Coromandel Smoking Co., 189
Cow Shed Restaurant, 393
Cow, 473
Cozy Corner, 243
Craggy Range, 8, 292
Crawford Road Kitchen, 276
Craypot Kitchen & Bar, 449
Cucina, 517
Currach Irish Pub, 131
Cyprus Tree, 263
Dangerous Kitchen, 389
Denniston Dog, 397

Depot Eatery, 106
DeVille, 381
Ditto, 494
Dizengoff, 109
Don Luciano, 356
Duck Island Ice Cream, 178
Duke of Marlborough Hotel, 8, 155
Eastwood Café, 227
Eat Streat, 226
Eggsentric, 189–190
Elliott Stables, 107
Embra, 244
Engine Room, 113
Entice Café, 356
Esther, 104
Etrusco at the Savoy, 535–536
Fainting Goat, 226
Farriers Bar & Eatery, 356
Fat Dog Café and Bar, 227
Fat Duck Gastropub, 494
Fat Pipi Pizzas, 410
Fat Sally's 517
Federal Delicatessen, 106
Fergburger, 474
Fisherman's Wharf Café, 206
FishSmith, 108
Flagship Eatery, 276
Forest, 111, 113
Fork and Tap, 475
Francesca, 484
Frank Bar & Eatery, 314
Frank's Eatery & Bar, 263
Frank's Oyster Bar & Eatery, 371
Fratelli, 335
French Café, 8, 111
Fresh and Tasty Takeaways, 163
Full of Beans Café, 416
Fun Buns, 292
Gather Café, 205
Gemmayze Street, 108
Giapo, 107
Glass House Restaurant, 126
Good Earth Café, 536
Good Good, 536–537
Gothenburg, 177
Graze Wine Bar, 338
Greedy Cow, 501
Greenwods Fresh Catch, 108
Grey Roasting Co., 178
Greytown Hotel, 356
Grille, 548
Grizzly Baked Goods, 10, 438
Gumdiggers Café, 137
Gusto, 363
Hallertau Brewery, 113
Hannah's Laneway, 337
Hapī Ora, 289
Harbour Eats, 106–107
Hard Antler Bar & Restaurant, 417
Hare and Copper Eatery, 245–246
Harry's Hawker House, 382
Hello Sunday, 435–436
High-Kut Bistro, 314
Hokitika Sandwich Company, 10, 410–411
Hopgood's & Co., 382
Howl at the Moon, 544
Huhu Café, 179
Huka Honey Hive, 244
Ikko Sushi, 382–383
Indi's, 178
Island Gelato, 125
Izakai, 28, 205–206
Jellyfish Restaurant & Bar, 383
Jimmy Coops, 243
Johnny Nation's Chocolate Éclair Shop, 263
Just Like Martha, 111–112
Kai Whakapai Cafe & Bar, 482
KaiKart Takeaways, 557
KaiZen at Go Vino, 189
Karahui Restaurant and Wine Bar, 355
Karamea Village Hotel's restaurant, 399
Kawau Kitchen, 113
Kika, 484
Kingi, 104
Kohan, 501
Kopi, 177
Korean Bob, 548
La Pizzeria, 263
Lady Janes Ice Cream Parlour, 226
Landing Cafe, 164
Left Bank Bistro, 471–472
Leigh Eats, 132
Lionel's, 244–245
Little Penang, 337
Logan Brown, 8–10, 335
Logans Floating Café & Restaurant, 509
Lukes Kitchen, 189
Ma Maison, 445
Macau, 204
Madam Wood, 472
Made, 178
Māha Restaurant, 153–154, 156
Main Street Deli Café, 355
Malo, 292
Mangōnui Fish Shop, 163
Manu, 436
Maranui Café, 339–340
Marina Woodfired Dining, 143
Marsden Estate Winery, 156
MASU by Nic Watt, 106
Matheson Cafe, 416
Mesita, 354
Metita, 106
Middle Waiheke Restaurant, 125
Miha, 190
Miles Better Pies, 493
Mills Bay Mussels, 364
Ministry of Works Bar & Eatery, 509
Mint Folk & Co., 509
Miss Cocoa Coffee, 544
Mister D Dining, 290–291
Monteith's Brewery, 406
Mount Delice, 205
Mount Made Ice Cream, 205
Mt. Vic Chippery, 339
Mudbrick Vineyard and Restaurant, 124
Mussel Inn, 389
Mussel Pot, 364
My Fat Puku, 131
Neighbourhood, 354
Nest Kitchen & Bar, 471
Niagara Falls Café, 543
Nins Bin, Kaikōura, 448
No5 Church Lane, 472
Non Solo Pizza, 112
North Drift Café, 163
Ocean View Restaurant & Bar, 402
Odettes, 106
Offering, 355–356
Ola's Arepas, 109
Old Quarter, 337
Only Scoop, 364
Onyx, 178
Opus Fresh, 263
Origine, 104–105
Ortega Fish Shack and Bar, 339
Oxley's, 364
Oyster Cove Café and Bar, 550
Paddy's Irish Pub, 290
Pancake Rocks Cafe Punakaiki, 402
Panorama Room, 507
Parc, 226
Park Café, 386
Peekaboo Backyard Eatery, 163
Pepper Tree Restaurant and Bar, 189
Pickles Bar & Eatery, 178
Picnic Café, 338
Pier Hotel, 448
Pipi Café, 292
Plateau Bar + Eatery, 245
Plato, 534–535
Plough and Feather, 155
Poco Tapas and Wine Bar, 227–228
Point Café & Bar, 543
Ponsonby Central, 109
Ponsonby International Foodcourt, 109
Porridge Watson, 314
Portershed Christchurch, 438
Postmasters Kitchen + Bar, 475
Pour House, 189
Powderkeg, 263
Prego, 109
Puku Pies, 339
Punakaiki Tavern, 402
Quay Kitchen, 142
Raglan Roast Coffee, 178
Rasa, 337
Redcliff Bar & Restaurant, 494
Regent Room Restaurant and Wine Bar, 228
Relishes Café, 484
Replete Café and Store, 243
Rita's, 205
River Kitchen, 383
Riverstone Kitchen, 517
Roots Bar, 389
Rotorua Night Markets, 226
Rustica, 205
Sabroso, 228
Sage Restaurant, 155
Sails, 105
San Ray, 110
Sandfly Café, 493
Schnappa Rock, 142–143
Schnapps Bar, 263
Scotch Wine Bar, 371
Scotts Brewing Company, 517
Scratch Bakers, 107–108
Sea People, 205
Sevenpenny, 406
Shack, 179
Shed 5, 336
Sir Edmund Hillary Café & Bar, 507
Sisu, 363
Smoking Barrel, 383
SnakeBite Brewery, 415–416
Snuggery, 557

Social Kitchen, 306
Somerset Cottage, 204–205
Soul Bar and Bistro, 105
Special Mention Café, 205
Sri Pinang, 108
St. Georges Restaurant, 292–293
Star Tavern, 397
Station Cafe, 263
Sugo, 204
Sunfire, 472
Sunshine Brewing, 276
Surf Shack Eatery, 206
Suter Café, 381
Taco Amaiz, 107
Tahu, Gisborne, 276
Tairua Beach Club, 190
Tātahi/The Beach, 264
Tees St. Café, 516
Terra Restaurant, 154
Terrace Restaurant and Bar, 264
Third Wheel Coffee Co., 154
Tio Ōhiwa Oysters & Takeaways, 206
Tipsy Foodies, 448
Tipsy Oyster Tapas and Bar, 154
Tītī, 535
TJ's Kitchen, 550
Toastie Lords, 363
Tōhi Gin Room and Eatery, 355
TopSail, 142
Toto's Café & Pizzeria , 389
Tuatara Café & Bar, 548
Tussock Hill Vineyard, 10, 436–437
Twenty Seven Steps, 437
Two Mile Bay Sailing Club, 243
ULO's Kitchen, 179
Union Square Bistro & Bar, 354
Urbano, 226
Utopia Ice, 439
Vinci's Pizza, 290
Vines at Bushmere Estate, 276
Vino Vino, 125
Vogel Street Kitchen, 537
Vudu Cafe & Larder, 473
Wallingford Homestead, 8
Waterfront by Toad Hall, 386
WBC, 336
West Coast Pie Company, 397
White Swan, 356
Wholemeal Café, 389
Yellow House Café, 313
Yonder, 473
Zephyr Wainui, 276

Photo Credits

p i: Dmitry Pichugin/Shutterstock; p iii: Courtesy of Nomad Safaris; p 2: Courtesy of Nomad Safaris; p 3: Shaun Jeffers/Shutterstock; p 5: Alarico/Shutterstock; p 6: Courtesy of Ahu Ahu Beach Villas; p 7: Courtesy of SkyScape; p 9: Courtesy of Logan Brown; p 10: Courtesy of Tussock Hill Vineyard; p 11: Courtesy of The Pelorus Mail Boat Cruise/Mike Heydon; p 12: Janice Chen/Shutterstock; p 13: Courtesy of Museum of New Zealand Te Papa Tongarewa/Jeff McEwan; p 15: Iam_Anuphone/Shutterstock; p 17: Darrenp/ Shutterstock; p 19: Prachaya Roekdeethaweesab/Shutterstock; p 22: David Steele/Shutterstock; p 25: Sreya Babu/Shutterstock; p 27: Courtesy of Apachè; p 29: Courtesy of Cable Bay Vineyards; p 31: Janusz Pienkowski/Shutterstock; p 32: Ross Gordon Henry/Shutterstock; p 44: Daniela Constantin/Shutterstock; p 46: Courtesy of Tree Walk; p 48: Tupungato/Shutterstock; p 49: Courtesy of Altitude Tours; p 51: Courtesy of Hamilton Gardens; p 53: Courtesy of Waka Abel Tasman/Oliver Weber; p 56: Maridav/ Shutterstock; p 58: Chameleons Eye/Shutterstock; p 59: Courtesy of Kate Evans; p 62: David Eastwell/ Shutterstock; p 63: Courtesy of Cathedral Cove Kayak Tours; p 64: Trabantos/Shutterstock; p 66, top: Courtesy of Wilderness Lodge Arthur's Pass; p 66, bottom: Courtesy of Hermitage; p 67: Shutterstock/ Stanislav Fosenbauer; Ch 4- Auckland:; p 71: HeliHead/Shutterstock; p 74: Fabrizio Andrea Bertani/ Shutterstock; p 75: ChameleonsEye/Shutterstock; p 78: Courtesy of The Hotel Britomart; p 80: Matiascausa/Shutterstock; p 81: Courtesy of Tāmaki Paenga Hira Auckland War Memorial Museum; p 83, top: Courtesy of Explore Group; p 83, bottom: ChameleonsEye/Shutterstock; p 84: DmitrySerbin/ Shutterstock; p 87: Courtesy of Kelly Tarlton's Sea Life Aquarium/Poppy Moss; p 88, top: Courtesy of Cornwall Park; p 88, bottom: Courtesy of Aucky Walky; p 91: Courtesy of Auckland Sea Kayaks; p 94: Courtesy of Hotel DeBrett/Kristian Frires; p 96: Courtesy of Hotel Indigo Auckland/Jonny Valiant; p 98: Courtesy of Great Ponsonby Art Hotel; p 101: Joy Mace; p 102: Courtesy of Naumi Hotel Auckland Airport; p 104: Courtesy of Indigo Hotel/ Jonny Valiant; p 105, top: Courtesy of Origine/TMP CREATIVE; p 105, bottom: Courtesy of SOUL Bar & Bistro Ltd; p 107: Courtesy of Cafe Hanoi; p 109: Nick Reed; p 110, top: Courtesy of San Ray/Matteo Giraudo; p 110, bottom: Courtesy of Kate Evans; p 112: Greta Kenyon; p 116: ChameleonsEye/Shutterstock; p 118: Courtesy of Churchill; p 119: Courtesy Lime Bar/ Kevin Fraser; p 120: Troy Wegman/Shutterstock; p 122: Courtesy of EcoZip Adventures; p 123: Courtesy of Stonyridge; p 125: Courtesy of The Boatshed Hotel; p 129: InProgressImaging/ Shutterstock; p 134: Corners74/Shutterstock; p 139: Barrac Underwood © Hundertwasser Art Centre; p 140: Czech the World/ Shutterstock; p 141: Shutterstock/ Bill Xu; p 142: Courtesy of TopSail; p 144: Courtesy of Fullers; p 145: Courtesy of Carino Wildlife Cruises; p 147: Shaun Jeffers/Shutterstock; p 153: Courtesy of Wharepuke; p 155: Courtesy of Sage Restaurant/Shaun Jeffers; p 157: Courtesy of Explore Group; p 159: Thomas Hagenau/Shutterstock; p 160: Courtesy of Kate Evans; p 162: Courtesy of Cable Bay Stays; p 164: Courtesy of Kate Evans; p 169: Courtesy of Hamilton Gardens; p 170: Nikolay 007/Shutterstock; p 172: Evgeniya Hook Media/Shutterstock; p 174: Courtesy of Waitomo Adventures; p 175: Courtesy of Underhill Valley/Brook Sabin; p 177: Courtesy of Housewithnonails; p 179: Courtesy of Gothenburg; p 181: CB_ travel/Shutterstock; p 182: Courtesy of Driving Creek Railway/Josh Neilson Photography; p 183: Courtesy of The Waterworks; p 185: Stefano Ember/Shutterstock; p 190: Courtesy of Camina; p 191: Courtesy of Tourism Bay of Plenty; p 193: Courtesy of Tourism Bay of Plenty; p 194: Jef Wodniack/Shutterstock; p 196: Hans Wismeijer/Shutterstock; p 200: Courtesy of Tourism Bay of Plenty; p 201: Courtesy of Watercliff; p 203: Courtesy of Wainui Seaside Glamping/Lisa Sun; p 206: Courtesy of Tourism Bay of Plenty; p 208: Rininii/Shutterstock; p 212: Courtesy of Tree Walk; p 213: Stefano Ember/Shutterstock; p 215: Courtesy of National Kiwi Hatchery; p 216: Courtesy of Wai Ariki Hot Springs and Spa; p 217: SoftlyRooted/ Shutterstock; p 219: CarolinDr/Shutterstock; p 222: Rodcoffee/Shutterstock; p 225: Courtesy of Treetops Lodge and Estate; p 230: Courtesy Love Taupo; p 232: Milosz Maslanka/Shutterstock; p 233: Leonard Zhukovsky/Shutterstock; p 235: Courtesy of Taupo DeBretts Spa Resort; p 239: Courtesy of Huka Lodge;

p 240: Courtesy of Lake Taupō Holiday Resort; p 242, top: Courtesy of The Quarters; p 242, bottom: Courtesy of River Birches; p 245, top: Courtesy of Embra; p 245, bottom: Courtesy of Lionel's restaurant in Taupō; p 248: Guaxinim/Shutterstock; p 249: Iv4ngrigoryev/Shutterstock; p 250: NataliaCatalina.com/ Shuuterstock; p 253: Cktravels.com/Shutterstock; p 255: Courtesy of Nevalea Alpacas; p 256: Courtesy of Forgotten World Adventures; p 257: Courtesy of Bridge to Nowhere Lodge; p 259: Courtesy of Tongariro Suites/Trevor Shanahan; p 268: Courtesy of Kate Evans; p 269: Courtesy of Dome Cinema; p 272, top: Courtesy of Courtesy of Nati Growth/Brennan Thomas/Strike Photography; p 272, bottom: Courtesy of Dive Tatapouri; p 275: Courtesy of Tatapouri Motor Camp & Retreat/Jordan Perry; p 279: Courtesy of Art Deco Trust; p 280: Courtesy of MTG Hawke's Bay; p 284: Ed Goodacre/Shutterstock; p 285: Courtesy of Hunter Gatherer Tours and Cheese & Wine Experiences; p 286: Kirsten Simcox; p 287: Courtesy of 415 Marine Parade/Florence Charvin; p 289: Courtesy of Wallingford Homestead; p 290: Courtesy of Central Fire Station; p 293: Courtesy of Craggy Range; p 296: Krug_100/Shutterstock; p 298, top: MiNiProduction/Shutterstock; p 298, bottom: Courtesy of Taranaki Cathedral/Andy Spain Photograpy; p 300: Courtesy of Hollard Gardens; p 302: Gregorioa/Shutterstock; p 304: Courtesy of Hosking House; p 305: Courtesy of Ahu Ahu Beach Villas; p 306: Courtesy of Nice Hotel; p 310: Courtesy of Te Whare o Rehua Sarjeant Gallery-Image supplied; p 312: PK289/Shutterstock; p 313: Courtesy of the Flying Fox; p 318: Celeste Fontein; p 320: Trabantos/Shutterstock; p 322: Courtesy of Te Papa/Jeff McEwan; p 323: Travelanza Media/Shutterstock; p 325: RobNaw/Shutterstock; p 326: Gary Yim/Shutterstock; p 327: Milosz Maslanka/Shutterstock; p 328: Courtesy of Zealandia/Rebecca Chrystal; p 331: Courtesy of The Intrepid Hotel; p 335: Courtesy of Logan Brown; p 336: Courtesy of Apachè; p 339: Brit Harrison; p 348: Wirestock Creators/Shutterstock; p 349: Courtesy of Rototāwai; p 352: Emagnetic/Shutterstock; p 353: Courtesy of The Royal Hotel Featherston; p 360: Courtesy of Picton Heritage & Whaling Museum; p 361: Courtesy of The Pelorus Mail Boat Cruise/Mike Heydon; p 363: Hallie Graham; p 364, top: Courtesy of Toastie Lords; p 364, bottom: Courtesy of Mills Bay Mussels/YoungBuckNz; p 366: Courtesy of Omaka Aviation Heritage Centre/Richard Briggs; p 368: Courtesy of Saint Clair Family Estate; p 369: Courtesy of Explore Marlborough/Sarah Watkins/Lucalia Photography; p 370: Courtesy of 14th Lane Urban Hotel/Adena Teka Photography; p 371: Richard Briggs; p 374: Shutterstock/RuslanKphoto; p 375: Courtesy of Peter Gibbs; p 379: Courtesy of Peak View Retreat; p 380: Courtesy of The Boot B&B; p 385: Courtesy of Waka Abel Tasman; p 388: Courtesy of Via Ferrata; p 393: Courtesy of Eleven Owen River Lodge; p 394: Courtesy of Maruia River Retreat; p 395: Courtesy of Bazil's Hostel & Surf School; p 398: Hot Pixels Photography/ Shutterstock; p 399: Courtesy of Last Resort/John Foster; p 400: Shutterstock/ Nawit; p 402: Courtesy of UnderWorld Adventures; p 406: Courtesy of Monteith's Brewery; p 410, top: Still Vision; p 410, bottom: Courtesy of The Hokitika Sandwich Company; p 411: Jan Mika/Shutterstock; p 413: Courtesy of White Heron Sanctuary Tours; p 414: Courtesy of Okarito Kayaks/Marios Galvalas; p 415: James Whitlock/ Shutterstock; p 416: Courtesy Alice May; p 420: FiledIMAGE/Shutterstock; p 421: Courtesy of The Arts Centre; p 422: BrianScantlebury/Shutterstock; p 425: Boyloso/Shutterstock; p 426: International Antarctic Centre; p 427: Courtesy of Orana Wildlife Park; p 429: Courtesy of Christchurch Adventure Park; p 432: Courtesy of The Observatory Hotel/The Arts Centre/Jane Ussher; p 434: Courtesy of Drifter Hotel; p 435, top: Vantangenz; p 435, bottom: Courtesy of Manu/Charlie Rose Creative; p 439: Courtesy of The Church Brew Pub; p 440: Courtesy of Greystone Wines; p 442: Nicspixels/Shutterstock; p 443: Courtesy of The Giant's House; p 447: Courtesy of Wilderness Lodge; p 452: Naruedom Yaempongsa/Shutterstock; p 454: Courtesy of Queenstown Tourism; p 455, top: Courtesy of RealNZ/Walter Peak; p 455, bottom: Saz00/ Shutterstock; p 457: Courtesy of Altitude Tours/Sophie Piearcey; p 458: Courtesy of Nomad Safaris/ Matthew Hawke/PukuArt Queenstown; p 461: Courtesy of Queenstown Wine Trail; p 464: Courtesy of Funyaks/Chris McLennan; p 467: Courtesy of The Rees Hotel & Luxury Apartments; p 470: Courtesy of The Bunker; p 473: Courtesy of Sunfire/Matt Finlay; p 474: Gracethang2/Shutterstock; p 475: Courtesy of Aosta/Isabella Garland; p 477: Janice Chen/Shutterstock; p 479: Courtesy of Eco Adventures Wānaka; p 482: Courtesy of Waiorau Homestead; p 484: Courtesy of Francesca; p 487: Courtesy of Faith in Fiordland; p 489: Courtesy of Milford Sound Lodge/Southern Discoveries Cruises; p 490: Courtesy of Milford Sound Lodge/Rosco's Milford Kayaks; p 491: THP Creative/Shutterstock; p 493: Courtesy of Milford Sound Lodge; p 494: Courtesy of The Fat Duck Gastropub; p 498: Courtesy of Tekapō Springs; p 499: Courtesy of Haka House Lake Tekapō's; p 500: Courtesy of Dark Sky Project/Miles Holden; p 502: Courtesy of Hermitage; p 503: Courtesy of Mount Cook Ski Planes & Helicopters; p 505: Courtesy of Hermitage; p 506: Courtesy of Lakestone Lodge; p 507: Courtesy of High Country Cabin; p 508: Courtesy of Ministry of Works Bar & Eatery; p 513: Danny Ye/Shutterstock; p 514: Courtesy of Ōamaru Penguins/ Rob Suisted; p 515: Courtesy of Pen-y-bryn Lodge/James Glucksman; p 516: P McNicholl; p 520: Courtesy of DunedinNZ/Tessa Calogaras; p 522: Courtesy of Dunedin NZ Visual Library; p 523: Mark Wallbank; p 524: Courtesy of DunedinNZ; p 525: Courtesy of DunedinNZ/Hayden Parsons; p 526: Courtesy of DunedinNZ; p 528: Don Mammoser/Shutterstock; p 531: Courtesy of Bell Hill Apartments/ Trev Hill; p 532: Courtesy of Bluestone on George; p 533: Courtesy of Kaimata Retreat; p 535: Courtesy of Tītī/Nick Beadle; p 536: Courtesy of Good Good/Alex Hodge; p 538: Courtesy of Steamer Basin/Roady; p 541: Courtesy of Lost Gypsy Gallery/Hayden Campbell/Blacklabel Photography; p 542: KCEmperor/ Shutterstock; p 543: Courtesy of Eastern Southland Gallery; p 545: Courtesy of Bill Richardson Transport World; p 547: Courtesy of The Langlands/Frank J. Visser Photography Ltd; p 549: Queenie LY Wong/ Shutterstock; p 551: R.Vickers/Shutterstock; p 554: RealNZ/Ulva Island Explorer; p 556: Courtesy of Observation Rock Lodge.